CENTRAL AMERICA
BY
CHICKENBUS

Vivien Lougheed

Prince George
1993

Repository Press
R.R. 7, Site 29, Comp. 8
Prince George, B.C.
V2N2J5

This book is dedicated to my two
daughters,
Fay and Shawn

Buses at market in Huehuetenango

Primary editing by Kathi Hughes

Secondary editing by Shawn Lougheed
and Shauna MacRae

Cover by Harvey Chometsky

Maps by Joanne Armstrong

Electronic Lay-out by Arthur Soles

ACKNOWLEDGEMENTS

There are so many people who have helped me write this book that I am not certain where to start. First of all I would like to thank John for the pushes he gave me when I was discouraged. He always insisted that I continue to write. I would like to thank my children for always supporting and helping me when I am writing. I would also like to thank them for becoming travellers that I am proud of. I would like to thank the Prince George <u>Citizen</u> for the encouragement and support they have given me in being a travel writer. I would like to thank my fellow colleagues who always encouraged me to travel and write, and my principal, Kerry Firth for allowing me to take leave from my positition with the School District 57 in order to obtain material to write about. Thank you, Kathi Hughes who never forgets to acknowledge my writing and for all the work she did in editing this book while still remaining my friend. My spelling is called an "educational challenge". I would like to thank the Morales family in Guatemala City for their support and kindness when I am in their wonderful city. Last, I would like to thank everyone who I came in contact with while travelling in Central America. This would include both fellow travellers and local people. Many gave me information without the knowledge that I was collecting material for a book and others went out of their way to collect added information for me. I would like to give a special thanks to Jim Ratzlaff, Abbotsford, B.C. for information on the Darien Gap, Al Weeks from Edmonton, Alberta, Greg Cornell from Vernon, B.C., and Roxalin Penty from MacKenzie, B.C. Without the support and companionship of fellow travellers, no travel book would be possible or necessary.

Thanks to all of you.

INTRODUCTION

Why would anyone want to go to Central America? It is politically hot; all we hear about are the riots, the wars and the human rights violations. The media information in North America should discourage even the bravest of journalists, never mind the stupidest of travellers. Yet, many Canadians, Americans, French, Swiss and Germans are down there. There are also Italians, Austrians, South Americans and Japanese. These travellers are a special breed of people, and if you are looking at this book, you may be one of them. If you want what you have at home, then stay there. If you want a splendid adventure and a cultural experience, then Central America may be the place for you.

I have been to Central America many times and would not hesitate to go again. I find the Spanish language very romantic, easy to learn and the words feel good when coming off the tongue. If you attempt to speak Spanish, the local people will help you. One starts by learning "please" and "thank you" and using them every time possible. Then, even if you develop only one word per day, at the end of the month, you should have thirty words. All languages may be supplemented by sign language which is universal. Often just knowing the town or street you want to go to is sufficient. Sometimes the local people will take you to where you want to go, or they will point in the direction you should be going. In Central America, the people want so much to be helpful that they will give you directions even if they do not know where you want to go. Therefore, it is beneficial to ask two or three people where your place of interest is; if the directions are consistent, then you should be okay.

I find that travelling in Central America is quite cheap. If you get a good fare to Mexico City (ticket prices have gone up somewhat since the first edition of this book) you can chickenbus down to Central America in no time. Because Mexico City is the largest city in America, good fares are available from anywhere. If you wish to avoid Mexico City, you may have to pay a bit more. Panama City may be the next best bet. Because Panama is a large business center, there are many decent plane fares and connections available. Costa Rica could also be a good bet.

Since the last edition, tourism has developed tremendously in Costa Rica, and you can now get excellent excursion fares to that country if going for only a month or less.

You can live in Central America for as little as ten dollars per day. If staying in one place for a month, you can make the trip even cheaper as a small house may rent for as little as $50.00 - $75.00 US per month. If you rent, you may cook your own meals and shop in the market. Beer would be your greatest expense.

The beaches along the Pacific coast are spectacular with good fishing, surfing and sun-bathing. The Caribbean has a visual beauty that cannot be matched anywhere in the world. The villages are pleasant and the food is delicious. I had the best seafood meal in the world in La Libertad in El Salvador. The native Indians are a wonderful, gentle and colorful people. They are one of the best attractions in Guatemala. Their textiles are incomparable and cheap.

You are safe in Central America so long as you use common sense and obey some simple rules. Do not get drunk in public. Do not get mixed up in the dope trade. Do not voice your political opinions in public. Do not criticize the country to the people that live there. You are there by choice; they are there forever. Remember, you are a target. You are obviously not a local person; therefore, you must have money. Every traveller has money. If you are drunk or stoned, or walking alone at night in a secluded area, you may as well wave a "here I am, come and get me" flag. But, this could happen in northern Iceland too. If you are careless, you ask for trouble. Some travellers are quiet, polite, peace-loving and understanding people. These are the ones that have the best and safest time. You will find that most locals want to know about your country and compare it with theirs. However, nobody likes to hear an outsider loudly criticize their country when, in fact, the outsider usually knows very little. Go to learn and do not try to change things. Take your knowledge home and make your own society better.

Lastly, Central America is unspoiled. Except for Costa Rica and parts of Guatemala, it is not crowded with tourists. For example, when visiting places like Tikal, you are left alone to imagine the lives of the Mayans and listen to their ghosts moving with the monkeys in the trees. There is no loudspeaker telling the Texan Jaycees to board the air-conditioned bus in five minutes, and the locals have not been ripped off by hordes of souvenir-grabbing cheapskates or offended by many bare-skinned, overweight sunbathers. However, recently, this is also changing. It is now too late to go to a few places in Central America and, if you wait too long, it will be necessary to find a new paradise for real travellers.

So, go to Central America. Enjoy the people, food, culture, ruins, jungles, volcanoes, animals, parks, beaches and museums and come back richer in ways that our society often does not understand.

People using this book should be aware that political circumstances in Central America can change rapidly. Also, our news on Central America is often not accurate. Always take the advice either of your consulate or the consulate of the country you are entering. Recently, there was a peace negotiated in El Salvador after twelve years of war. However, it is difficult to get a visa to go there. Once the peace has definitely been established, this will improve. In Guatemala, it is easy to get into the country, but because of increased tourism, the military is now starting to rob the gringos. On the other hand, a few years ago, Panama was not the place for gringos; today, it is the most delightful country in Central America for gringos to visit. In North America, there is very little information about Central

America so once you are there, ask other travellers for the latest gossip or get the information from the country's consulate.

Lastly, you may run into trouble. You could be shot. You could land in jail. You could have an accident. You could get sick. However, as I check my local paper today or any other day, I find all these events occurring in my country also. Also remember, Costa Rica has been peaceful and without an army for decades. Panama now is developing a democracy and welcomes the visitor with the courtesy fit for royalty. El Salvador is again ready for tourism and is simply delightful (once you get past all the guns).

Some of the information in this book is limited. I have relied on my own experiences, on information picked up from others and on official information given to me by the tourist bureaus of the various countries. I am most familiar with Guatemala and Costa Rica. I have certainly not checked out all the attractions and hotels by myself. Some things change, and I take no responsibility for these changes. However, the information on El Salvador is the latest first-hand information available, some of it even unknown to the tourist office in that little country. Many of my recommendations are based strictly on personal experience. Some of the really out of the way places are exciting and fun to visit. But, use this only as a guide, not as a bible. Explore beyond what you read. You should start your travels where this books stops.

Do not expect similar information for each country or in each section. Read and prepare ahead for each visit; ask questions and gather as much additional information as possible. Your best travel guide will be your fellow travellers and the local friends you make in the areas you are exploring.

Many things change rapidly, but many things never change. For an example, Costa Rica is building up so rapidly that, within six months, the information gathered for the beach area is outdated. But the beaches and parks remain the same. Though the prices listed in this book may be a bit out of date or the occasional recommended place may be closed, for the most part you will find this guide accurate and useful. Even when the hotels and restaurants become outdated, the ruins, palaces and beaches will remain the same. Have a wonderful time!

HOW TO USE THIS BOOK

This book is a general book. For example, I recommend some hikes and some beaches, some possible river trips and some islands that are interesting to visit but I do not cover every specific hike available in a country. For these you will need specialized books. I do not cover the big resorts or more expensive places because this book is for the ecologically minded chickenbusers who travel with local transportation instead of a car, use local accommodations instead of American chain hotels and eat in local restaurants or markets instead of the large chain restaurants where the money leaves the country.

The guide itself has the countries in alphabetical order and then the cities in each country in alphabetical order. I give a basic introduction to the country, covering visas, civic holidays, transportation schedules, telephone information and so on. I then introduce a city, list some of the places to stay, places to eat and then what can be visited from this city or town. I may suggest a day trip where you in fact would like to spend the night in the village. In that case I have tried to cross list place names. In other words, I will list the village in its alphabetical order but then refer you to another page for more detailed information.

Previous editions of this book have had maps of the cities in them, but I have found these totally useless and difficult to read. Most tourist offices in Central America now offer maps that are much better than what can be reproduced in a book like this.

Transportation schedules are found in the introductions to the countries.

If you find additional or more accurate information anywhere in Central America, please write to the publisher so that any further printings may be updated. This has happened in the past, and I have given credit to the people who have written to me. If you should write, I shall give you credit for in the next edition.

MEDICAL INFORMATION
Vaccinations

An International Vaccination Certificate from your country is required and should be kept with your passport. The problem is not when you enter most other countries, but when you re-enter your own country. If you have not been vaccinated, you may be subjected to a three-week isolation period at your expense. Although I have never been asked for this certificate, I always have it ready.

Recommended shots:

Typhoid fever	Good for 10 years
Paratyphoid	Good for 1 year
Tetanus	Good for 10 years
Polio	Booster every 10 years
Hepatitis	Good for 3 to 6 months
Malaria Tablets	Taken 2 weeks before leaving and for 6 weeks after returning.
Cholera	Good for 6 months
Yellow Fever	Good for 10 years

General Health

Supplement the lack of protein, dairy products and your usual dietary intake with vitamins and minerals in capsule form. Yogurt tablets help the intestines stay in their customary condition.

Salt and water must be taken to prevent dehydration. Mineral water, which has a fair amount of salts, can be purchased almost anywhere and a good idea is to have a bottle once every two hours during the day if it is hot. Beer is not good in the heat of the day but very pleasant, in moderate amounts, in the evenings. Carry your empty bottle of water with you and exchange it whenever you need a refill. This way you won't be charged extra for the bottle nor will it be necessary to drink from the plastic bags that are often offered. This will help decrease the pollution in Central America.

If you want pure water, you can take a water-tight jug and purify your water by using a filter or using heavy metal like iodine tablets or silver tablets. There are some excellent light-weight filters on the market and most large sports stores like REI and Mountain Equipment carry these products.

Drinking directly from rivers or streams is not safe. Many hotels have bottled water for clients and some have safe tap water, but if you are unsure, don't take a chance. Use mineral water, even to brush your teeth. Chlorine tablets can be used as an extra precaution against impurities in the bottled water obtained in the hotels, but these tablets are not strong enough for unpurified water. Belize often uses rain water for drinking, and Nicaragua uses tap water. In Nicaragua, I used tap water purified with iodine tablets and carried in an old rum bottle I had scrounged from a restaurant. Costa Rica's water is safe to drink except if the place you are staying is very old. Then the pipes may be contaminated. However, if the place is not really old and looks clean, I would not be afraid to use the water.

Peel all fruit before eating it. Salads are not safe in the countries where water is not safe because they may be washed in unclean water. The large hotels are accustomed to serving international travellers and businessmen so if you are in need of a fresh salad, spend the money and go to one of the better places. As of late, some places will advertise that they wash all products in purified water. So far, I have never heard of travellers finding this advertising to be false.

In most places, the milk is not pasteurized. Be very careful because there is a lot of tuberculosis in Central America. Calcium tablets are not too heavy to carry and are a good substitute for milk. Yogurt may also be made from unpasteurized milk so, again, be careful.

Use a foot stone to keep the heels of your feet smooth and free from cracks. Keep toenails trimmed to prevent an accidental tear. Wear closed shoes if there are any open sores on your feet. Hook worm is common and can be picked up easily. Tuberculosis is common and spit is often disposed on the sidewalk. Open sores on feet clad in sandals are great places for breeding this type of creepy-crawler.

ILLNESSES
Diarrhoea - The Inca two-step. Montezuma's revenge. Very common.

Don't panic. It may be caused from change in diet, especially the hot spices or the different alcohols. Stay off food altogether for a couple of days, take yogurt tablets and plenty of mineral water. Should it continue for longer, try some kaopectate which is available in most drugstores. Camomile tea (te de manzanilla) is very soothing for a bad stomach, but be careful from where you order it. Make certain that the water has been boiled. Otherwise, stay with the mineral water.

Dysentery or **Amoebas** - This is a different and more serious problem than diarrhoea. Should you be having very loose stools with a lot of mucus and/or blood, you may be in trouble. Bowel movements become strained and painful; fever, muscle cramps and nausea are often present. If this is the case, go to the doctor immediately. This can be a very dangerous condition; death could be quick. Don't be afraid to look foolish - a live fool is a lot better off than a dead one. Another condition that could arise from dysentery is intestinal scarring which will affect your health for the rest of your life. Other intestinal parasites may cause the same symptoms, but it is better to have something unusual checked than ruin your holiday with a serious illness.

Hepatitis - Acute hepatitis is an inflammation of the liver caused by a virus usually transmitted through human body fluids. Symptoms are tiredness, chalky stools, dark tea-colored urine, nausea when eating fried or greasy foods, and yellowing of the skin and eye whites. If you have hepatitis, bed rest is the best and only medicine. Spend a few weeks on one of the spectacular beaches in Central America. However, I heard of research that was done in Nepal (where hepatitis is as common as the house fly) and they did not have one case of hepatitis with a person who had the gamma globulin shot within the previous six months. So, the hepatitis shot is really recommended.

Flea Bites - These will be frequent. Use an antihistamine cream to keep from scratching. Open sores are excellent incubators for bigger diseases in which to mate and multiply. In Panama, the people put moth balls amongst their linen and it helps prevent flea bites. I kept one in my backpack and it certainly decreased the number of flea bites. A faint odor on your bed clothes seems to do the trick.

Chagas Disease - Like hepatitis, chagas disease can become either chronic or acute. This is a parasite that enters the blood stream after the victim has been bitten by a nocturnal, smooth, oval-shaped insect called the vinchuca. It is brownish in color, and about two centimeters or one inch long. The vinchuca has a long, narrow, cone-shaped head, with two antennae that curve under the head and end in the thorax.

The vinchuca is found in thatched roofs or in wall crevices of old buildings. They are not found in areas with an elevation of over 3500 feet or 1000 meters.

The insect usually bites the face of his victim leaving a hard, violet-hued swelling within a week of infestation. The vinchuca inserts its proboscis into the victim and sucks blood for about twenty minutes. This causes its body to fill up and excretion to be eliminated, some of which seeps into the opening of your skin. It is the excretion that carries the larva of the parasite. The larva enters the blood stream and infects the heart, brain, liver and spleen.

In the acute form, there is an elevated temperature, vomiting, shortness of breath, convulsions and rigidity of the neck. Death occurs within three months of the first bite. The chronic form begins with acute symptoms; these subside and the heart is weakened until a severe heart condition occurs ten to twenty years later. This is not a disease to worry about unless you are staying in thatched cabinas at low elevations like on the San Blas Islands or along the Mosquito Coast. Should a suspicious purple sore appear on your face, or any other part of your body that may be exposed during sleeping hours, it may be wise to have the sore checked by a doctor.

Malaria - This is a parasite transmitted by a certain type of tropical mosquito. The parasite enters the blood stream and then the red blood cells. When the parasites have multiplied enough to rupture the blood cell, the victim encounters high fever, chills, delirium and sometimes coma. The best thing to do is to take anti-malaria tablets during your stay in the tropics. The general routine is to take chloroquine for two weeks before going, all the time you are away, and for six weeks after you return. This does not guarantee that you will not get the disease, but it certainly reduces your chances. There are a few chloroquine-resistant malaria strains in some parts of Panama where you will need something like Meflaquine. Before leaving, check with your doctor or health unit for the latest information. But do not neglect this one prophylactic if going into areas where there are mosquitos.

I met a gal who had been on the Mosquito Coast area of Honduras and contacted malaria while not taking any precautions. It was six weeks after she had her bout of tremors that I saw her, and she was still hobbling along with two canes. The tremors had been so severe that they had ripped all the muscles in her legs. She was trying to get home after ruining a wonderful holiday.

Worms - There are so many types of parasitic worms in the tropics that I would not be able to list even half of them. If you have unexplained stomach cramps, loss of weight or a general feeling of sickness, go to a doctor. One way of preventing worms is never to go in bare feet, even in the shower. Be very careful not to put your hands in your mouth and be careful not to eat uncooked vegetables unless you are certain the water used to clean the vegetables has been purified. If the restaurant you patronize does not look too clean, skip the uncooked food. Also, insist on your meat being well cooked.

WHAT TO TAKE

Backpack - A backpack leaves your hands free to carry maps, dictionary, and camera; it is the easiest way to carry a heavy load. Be very careful in crowds as the bag slashers will slash, steal and vamoose long before you notice the weight change. It is often best to go to crowded places after you have a hotel room so you can leave your big pack there.

I find a small pack good for everyday use because it can be worn at the front. This way you can protect it with your hands and it is very difficult to slash or pick. If worn at the back, the pack is much easier for a robber to slip open a zipper. The only drawback with a small daypack is that it gets so dirty that it in turn gets my clothes dirty. It is also harder to wash than a regular, locally made, shoulder sack. Sacks are good, but not quite as comfortable as a small pack worn in the front.

Money Belt - The belts worn around the neck or under the armpit are accessible in public places for both you and the robbers. Waist belts with compartments in them are good but out of fashion for the female traveller. Many people sew extra pockets onto the inside of their garments and use velcro for closing these pockets. In this way, money can be hidden in many different places so that you would never be left without a red cent. Some travellers also put a few bills in their shoes. The safest money belt is the one worn in the midriff area tied tightly around the waist. Its only drawback is that it is hot.

Cotton Dress or Pants - These should be very loose. Skirts should be full and fairly dark in color. They can be draped over a bathing suit or shorts when leaving a tourist area, or dressed up and worn to a concert in the evenings. They are cool and socially non-offending to the local people. Men should wear loose cotton pants and a loose shirt or T-shirt. Cotton is better than denim because it can be washed and dried easier. Cotton shorts should be long and loose, for comfort from heat and to prevent offending the locals. I travelled with a beautiful girl for a few days. She would be a knock-out in North America or Europe but in Central America both her knees and shoulders showed and this made her a "puta" (a whore). Calling someone this is quite an insult in Latin America. Because her appearance offended the locals, I had to abandon her as a companion. I have seen European ladies sun bathing topless and the locals watching in astonishment. This is offending to a conservative society.

Please be careful. It makes your trip much more pleasant if you have the approval of the locals. It also prevents feelings of animosity which often result in violence. For your safety, and the safety of your fellow travellers, please be as conservative as the people you are visiting. Your values belong at home.

Bathing Suit - Neither men nor women should wear the string-type bikini anywhere except along the Pacific beaches of Costa Rica. In most of the countries in Central America, you will see the local ladies wearing a bra under their bathing suits or wearing a dress into the water. For the most part, they are very modest. Showing too much thigh will get you a lot of disapproval. In Costa Rica, however, skimpy bathing suits for either men or women are quite acceptable on the beaches. Wearing a bathing suit on the street of a village is not acceptable anywhere in Central America. Even in Costa Rica, shorts are not well accepted in the towns and cities. Shorts in places like El Salvador are unacceptable. They are worn only by prostitutes unless the shorts are the kind that come to, or below, the knee.

Bed Wear - Use a long cotton shirt or short cotton housecoat. This enables you to walk down the hall to the bathroom at night or in the morning before getting dressed. Again, a dark color is the wisest choice. A light-weight cotton shirt is not very heavy in your pack.

Light Sweater or Fleece-Lined Sweatshirt - It gets cold in the mountains in the evenings. It also gets quite chilly when there is a lot of rain. If possible, get a sweater or sweatshirt with a hood. One time in Honduras, I had to wear my warm clothes to bed because it was so cold and the hotel did not have any extra blankets. The hood on my sweatshirt was a blessing. It is a good idea to roll your clothes, instead of folding them, as this will result in fewer wrinkles.

Camera, Film, Flash and Extra Batteries - Have versatility in camera gear, but beware of weight. Also, be certain that you have good insurance coverage for your equipment as theft is always a possibility. In some places, getting a police receipt saying that the theft has occurred is no problem but in some places, the receipt will cost as much as the equipment that you lost.

Take film and batteries with you because these items are very expensive. A roll of film is about $6.00 US. The quality of developing film in Central America has improved in the last few years, and I found the color to be quite acceptable. However, for a roll of 24, you will pay about $12.00 US. It is cheaper to bring the exposed film home and have it developed in your own country.

First-Aid Kit - This should include bandages, aspirins, kaopectate, antihistamine cream, disinfectant, tensor bandage, mole skin, small scissors, and a muscle pain reliever. There is an antibiotic powder called "Cicatrin" that is excellent for infections. Because it is a powder, it does not deteriorate due to the heat. Many prescription drugs can be purchased over the counter, but if you have a specific drug that you must have, be certain to take enough to last the duration of your trip. Should you lose your medicine it is often very difficult to replace exactly what you have.

Vitamins, Yogurt Tablets - Take only the amount you will need for the number of days you will be there. Don't overload yourself. If you think that vitamin "C" will not be necessary because of all the fruit you will get, think again. I had a fellow traveller come to my rescue in Nicaragua when I got a terrible cold and it started going into my chest. I am certain the vitamins he gave me helped tremendously. However, if your Spanish is good enough, you can always buy vitamins from snake-oil medicine men who sell their stuff on the buses. And all for a very good price!!

Sun Glasses or Sun-Visor - Some people use the Panama hats as a sun visor and they can be purchased in Central America for a very reasonable price. If you are sensitive to the sun you will need glasses. They are expensive to purchase in Central America and a favorite object of theft. It is advisable to have sun glasses well secured to you and do not wear prescription sun glasses as they can be grabbed off your face.

Underwear - Take only a few pairs as they can be washed regularly and hung in your room. If travelling for a long time, they can be purchased quite cheaply anywhere in Central America.

Shoes - Sandals may be used with a dress or pants and are good during the hot days. You may take a good pair from home or purchase the locally-made type. Runners are needed for mountain areas and when feet are not in top shape. Unless you are doing a tremendous amount of hiking in the mountains, boots are not necessary. Rubber thongs may be taken to use in the showers.

Flag Pins - Canadians always take these. They are great for identification and for trading, so take a few with you. The children love them. Give children anything from your country except candy.

Clothes Soap - Pack this in a zip-lock bag. A hard bar of soap is the best for washing clothes. A good hard soap can be purchased in the markets anywhere in Central America. If you are spending a lot of time near the ocean, there is a soap that is good with salt water. It may be purchased in a marine supply store.

DayPack or Shoulder Bag - I prefer the day pack to the shoulder bag because I carry my camera in it. When worn in the front, the weight is better distributed and I can protect it from theft with my arms. It is also very handy if I want to quickly take a picture or get a book out. Worn at the back makes it very accessible to the pickpockets. Purchase yourself a well padded daypack that will be comfortable for long periods of time.

Mosquito Repellent - This is good in the evenings and in bed as I found that the bed bugs don't bite when you use repellent. However, it is of little value against the sand fleas found along the Caribbean.

Moth Balls - I learned this trick from the Panamanians. Put one or two moth balls in the bottom of your pack, near your clothes section and it will certainly cut down on the bed bug and flea bites. The smell becomes unnoticeable on your clothes in a short time but remains strong enough for the bugs to stay away.

Toilet Paper - One roll per month is a good estimation, but take more if you are susceptible to colds. Some places will supply toilet paper for you. The type that you get in Central America is serviceable but thin and rough. However, it is also unbleached. Note also that toilet paper is not to be thrown in the toilet, but in a basket beside the toilet because the sewers are not able to take the paper.

Pens and Note Book - Use this to keep a diary and/or record of the pictures you have taken. One ruin or mountain will look the same as the next one once you get home, unless they are properly labeled and recorded. Pens are fairly expensive in Central America. If you take pens with any type of advertising on them, they are good for trading or as gifts for the children.

Padlock - Often doors don't have a lock, especially in Nicaragua. It is handy to have your own lock plus three or four keys. This way, if you share a room with a stranger, you can use your own lock and give one key to your room mate. If a key gets lost, you have an extra.

Cotton Sheet - Cotton is lightweight, and easy to clean, but the sheet should be big enough to wrap yourself in. Sometimes there is not a very nice room available and the sheet keeps you clean and free from bugs. Some places have only a bottom sheet, and the blanket that you would have on top is not cleaned every day. This again is where your sheet would come in handy. Some places, especially in Nicaragua, charge extra for sheets.

Rope for Clothesline - Thin climbing rope is excellent. It does not tangle and is light weight but very durable. If you take enough, it can be used for other things like shoe laces or tying some of your purchases to your backpack.

Knife - This item is useful for eating lunches, clipping nails, and cutting hair. The Swiss Army knives are excellent as they are lightweight and have many useful gadgets. They are not considered a weapon when crossing borders, but they are a desirable item. I have heard of border guards confiscating them when people try to cross certain borders. I usually try to put it in my day pack and in an area where it will not be noticed too quickly.

Personal bag - Toothpaste and brush, shampoo, razors, foot stone, skin cream, comb, small towel are examples of things you will need. Use only screw top caps as the snap ones can snap open under a bit of pressure and this leaves your pack in one heck of a mess. These items can be purchased in all the countries in Central America so there is no need to take a year's supply.

Ear Plugs - Every hotel is noisy. People are up by 5:30 AM and expect you to be awake also. The acoustics in most hotels is better than in Carnegie Hall. If you are a light sleeper, ear plugs are a must.

Skin-so-soft - This is a bath oil put out by Avon. If you are planning on doing a lot of beach time on the Caribbean, the sand fleas will kill you. Many beachers use skin-so-soft, diluted half-and-half with water as a sand flea repellent. The locals say that any thick oil will keep the fleas from biting.

Compass - A map is much more useful when you have a compass. It may also save you many miles of walking in the wrong direction. It is also an item that causes curiosity by the local children. This is a good way to open a conversation.

Customs Card - This is a card put out by your own Customs Department and has the serial number of cameras and lenses, lists of expensive jewelry or any other items that may be questioned when you return to your country. If you have no proof that you purchased that item in your own country, you may be charged duty again. These cards are issued for free.

Dictionary, Guide Book - A dictionary is essential. You can not talk to anyone unless you are fluent in the language or you have a dictionary. A copy of the first edition of "Chickenbus" is needed in order to flag down buses at night.

Maps - I.T.M.B. Publishing makes the latest and best maps of Central America. They have the whole region for $10.00 Cdn. They have a good one of Costa Rica for $9.00 Cdn. The map of Guatemala includes El Salvador and sells for $10.00 Cdn. The map of Belize is $8.00 Cdn. If you wish to order these maps, you may get them from ITMB Publishing, 736A Granville St., Vancouver, B.C. V6Z 1G3, Canada

Umbrella - If travelling during rainy season, this is a useful item; also it is lighter and cooler than rain gear. An unbrella may be purchased in Central America if you are undecided about carrying one before leaving.

Photocopy of Passport - Photocopy the main page of your passport. If your passport is lost, it is much quicker and easier for the embassy to get you a replacement if a copy is available. Be certain to keep it in a different place than the actual passport. You can have this done in Central America with no problems as there are many photocopy machines for public use.

Articles for Trade - Pens and pencils with advertising, pins from your country, small packages of needles, and small sample lipstick tubes are excellent for gifts or trade. I saw an Avon lady before I left; for a reasonable price, I purchased her outdated samples of lipstick. The peasant women in Central America thought the lipstick was just great. You can also take small samples of shampoo, hand lotion, and so on. Instead of money, often this can be used for tipping. In places like Nicaragua and Honduras, where most people do not have extra money for luxury items, these items are greatly appreciated.

Flashlight - A flashlight is useful to look down dark areas of old buildings and ruins or for finding the bathroom at night. Power disruption is not infrequent and a flashlight is invaluable as there is often not enough candles to go around. Be certain to have a small supply of extra batteries as all sizes are not always available in small towns.

Water Proof Case - This is a small case that can be worn around your neck when you are swimming. It is big enough to hold your money and passport. Excellent if travelling alone because you can take your valuables into the water with you.

Sink Plug - There are no plugs in Central America; if you want to wash clothes in the sink, this is a useful item. Personally, I wash clothes in the shower or give them to the house maid.
A sink plug and water proof case were recommended to me by Al Weeks of Edmonton.

GENERAL INFORMATION

American money is accepted anywhere and better rates can always be obtained for cash in some places. Traveller's cheques are seldom cashed on the black market except for Costa Rica. However, black market money is getting less and less lucrative and therefore, fewer people are exchanging in this manner.

Canadian money may be exchanged in many banks in Central America. In Belize, Canadian and Sterling is acceptable along with some Caribbean currencies. In Guatemala, the Bank of Guatemala in any major city will exchange many currencies including the German mark, Swiss franc, British pound and Canadian dollar. However, the American dollar is the easiest to exchange. I found that Honduran banks do not like to exchange any money, Canadian or American. This almost forces the traveller to exchange on the black market. Of course, Panama uses the American dollar as its currency. In Costa Rica, the American dollar is the only safe currency. The black market rate is good and any bank will exchange a traveller's cheque in US currency. There is only one bank in San Josè that will exchange any other currency than American and the rate is very low.

If changing money on the black market, be aware that you may get counterfeit money in exchange. This could be dangerous. The black market is no longer very lucrative in most countries in Central America. Costa Rica has the most active black market, but other countries have stabilized their currency; it just does not pay enough to keep a black market going. Even Nicaragua has managed to keep the newest currency at a stable rate; thus, people are not interested in US money. In Honduras, it is still easier to change money in some of the shopping stores, as the banks just are not interested in your money. In El Salvador, you must have the receipt from your bank proving that you purchased your traveller's cheques before they will cash them.

In some countries, inflation is high, but the prices rise in proportion to the inflation rate. In the chapters on each country, I will give the exchange rate and the local prices; you should be able to figure out what the prices should be.

Hotels and restaurants are only recommendations. You are advised to ask around. See for yourself what your money will get for you. Some people may require a few more comforts than others so once a feeling for exploring is experienced, try more.

Study the history of all the countries you are going to visit. It makes the trip worthwhile, and gives you many opportunities to ask questions of the local people which will lead to interesting stories that you will remember forever. See book section for a few recommendations.

When in Central America, be aware of the image you will portray. Dress very modestly. This is most important. For an example, if you are in very short shorts in El Salvador, you will be considered a prostitute. When you are having supper, by all means have a drink if you wish, but don't have that extra few. You need your wits about you at all times. If you feel like doing a few extras, go to your room, lock your door, and have a good time.

As for dope, you are advised to stay away from it completely. If you get caught, the jails have a poor reputation and I hear the fleas have jaws the size of donkeys. Human rights in Central America are almost non-existent and you are always guilty until proven innocent. With the increase in tourism, the dopers have also increased and this in turn has caused an increase in the amount of robberies that are now occurring. The behavior of the burned out dopers is disgusting and it ruins the area for the serious traveller.

Central America is cheapest during July and August. Generally, this is the rainy season and it is a bit cooler than in December/January. It usually rains for one hour per day; a good time to rest and catch up on your log book or post cards. The winter months are a bit more expensive but still cheaper than most vacations anywhere else in the world. However, the prices in Costa Rica (now that it has been discovered) are becoming quite high during peak season. Winter is the dry hot season and sun tanning between 10:00 AM and 4:00 PM is just too hot. Tropical sun can be dangerous to white skinned people. Now with the ozone depletion, I do not encourage much beach time in Central America.

If travelling during Christmas or Easter, you must have a reservation or be prepared to stay in the very bottom hotels. These are the most important holidays in Central America and well worth being a part of, but be certain to have a place to stay. Antigua, Guatemala, is one place that is often booked and paid for six months before Semana Santa (holy week).

If you are on a bus that breaks down, don't panic. This happens frequently. Patiently wait until the conductor gives you a partial refund (after all, he *has* taken you part way) and then get into the next vehicle that stops. This could be a truck, bus, car or collectivo. Collectivos are vans that charge a bit more than buses, less than taxis, and go only on main streets. All prices should be negotiated beforehand, except buses which have standard rates. If the collectivos have other people in them, you have less chance of being overcharged.

BOOKS
Central America by Chickenbus - The first edition should be used to flag down night buses. The second edition is still a good all-round guide, but is out of date.
Backpacking in Mexico and Central America - The second edition by Hilary Bradt and Rob Rachowiecki, published by Bradt Enterprises, 95 Harvey St., Cambridge, Mass. This is an excellent book for the backpacker or persons interested in back country adventure by foot

instead of by bus. However, it is good only for suggestions and possibilities. It does not tell you how to get from place to place nor how long the trip will take. It is obvious that these men have not done all the hikes.

South American Handbook - Published by Trade and Travel Publications Ltd., Bath, England, 1986. This is a very good scientific-like document that is heavy, expensive and difficult to read because of the small print. However, it is revised every year and has every bit of information you could possibly want for all of Central and South America. It is lacking personal information telling you what to expect on each excursion.

The Costa Rica Traveler - by Ellen Searby, published by Windham Bay Press, Box 1198, Occidental, Ca., 1988. This is a detailed guide book of Costa Rica only. It is for the middle of the line traveller and is for the person who has a car. It is updated regularly. It has more historical information than Chickenbus.

Guatemala for You - by Barbara B. de Koose, published by Editorial Piedra Santa, 7a Ave. 4-45, Zona 1, Guatemala, 1989. This is a good book that tells the traveller where to go in Guatemala. It has wonderful pictures. However, it is for the car traveller.

Guatemala Guide - by Paul Glassman, published by Passport Press, Champlain, New York, 1990. Written in a chummy, friendly manner, this is a good guide for Guatemala. The author has obviously been to many of the places in the book; he has not just collated information given to him by the tourist bureau. This is the best guide available if you want something just on Guatemala.

Art & Architecture of Ancient America - by George Kubler, published by Penguin Books, New York, New York, 1984. This book gives detailed information on the Mayan culture which, although technical, is not too difficult to read for the non-professional archaeologist.

The Jaguar Smile - by Salman Rushdie, published by Pan Books Ltd., Cavaye Pl., London, 1987. This is a recent and fairly accurate account of the difficulties that occurred in Nicaragua a few years ago.

Time Among the Maya - by Ronald Wright, published by Viking, the Penguin Group of Canada Ltd., Markham, Ontario, 1989. This is a travel story of a man going through Mexico, Belize and Guatemala and interweaving his travels with historical facts about the lives of the Mayan people.

Sandino's Daughters - by Margaret Randall, published by New Star Books, Vancouver/Toronto, Canada. 1981. This is an excellent collection of true stories from Nicaraguan women who fought against the Somoza dictatorship during the Sandinista revolution. It gives the reader an idea of the strong spirit of these people.

Four Keys to Guatemala - by Vera Kelsey and Lilly de Jongh Osborne, published by Funk & Wagnalls, United States, 1961. Although this is an old book, it is an excellent source of information about the

Mayan Indian. Easy to read, it covers marriage, birth and death customs, special festivals, home life, languages, crafts, clothes, art and much more. It will give the traveller excellent background information about Guatemala.

The Fist and the Letter - published by Pulp Press, Box 48806 Stn. Bental, Vancouver, B.C., 1979. This is a great collection of Latin American revolutionary poems, written on one side of the page in Spanish and the other side in English. It is well translated and provides good practice in Spanish for the traveller.

Carlos, the Dawn is no Longer Beyond Our Reach - This is the prison journals of Thomas Borge, translated by Margaret Randall, published by New Star Books, Vancouver, B.C., 1984. This is a short summary of Carlos Fonseca's life as told by Thomas Borge. It is less than 100 pages and easy to read.

Guatemala, From Where the Rainbow Takes Its Color - by Joaquin Munoz, printed by Serveprensa Centroamericana, 1975. The travel information in this book is very outdated, but the book has a good section on customs and culture of the Maya Indians in Guatemala. This book is available in Guatemala.

Doris Tijerino - by Margaret Randall, published by New Star Books, Vancouver, B.C. 1978. This tells of the conditions in Nicaragua suffered by women before the revolution. It is vividly descriptive and gives the reader great understanding of Latin American women's unjust lives. These conditions still exist today.

Sandinista - by Marie Jakober, published by New Star Books, Vancouver, B.C., 1985. Another story about the revolution, this book is pleasant reading as it is written in novel form rather than historical fact form.

Revolt in El Salvador - published by Pathfinder Press, 410 West Street, New York, N.Y., 1980. This is a collection of four stories of the struggles in El Salvador. There is little difference between the struggles of the people in Salvador, Guatemala, Nicaragua or Honduras. It provides the reader with some background of what has occurred in El Salvador before the recent 1992 peace negotiations. It would be wise to leave this book at home.

Blood of the Innocent - by Teofilo Cabestrero, published by Orbis Books, Maryknoll, New York, 1985. This book tells of the struggles the peasants had with the American-backed Contras during the Sandanista regime.

Solidarity with the People of Nicaragua - by James McGinnis, published by Orbis Books, Maryknoll, New York, 1985. This book looks at the lives of people in Nicaragua during their struggles against the American-backed Contras and covers topics such as health care, education, prison system and urban barrio life.
It gives a good picture of the recent struggles in Nicaragua.

Incidents of Travel in Central America, Chiapas and Yucatan - by John L. Stephens, in two volumes, published by Dover Publications,

New York, 1969. This is the famous story of John Stephens and Frederick Catherwood travelling through the Mayan area of Latin America and their discovery of the Maya ruins. There are fabulous illustrations by Catherwood in the book. It certainly gives you an idea of the ruins you will see.

Tikal - Handbook of the Ancient Maya Ruins - by Wm. R. Coe, printed by Editorial Piedra Santa, 12th printing, 1985. If you would like more detailed information on Tikal than what is in Chickenbus; this is an excellent book. However, it is quite expensive and only available in Guatemala.

Guatemala: Tyranny on Trial - published by Synthesis Publications, San Francisco, 1984. This is an excellent account of the oppression of the poor in Guatemala. This is the side of Guatemala that the average traveller does not see. Do not take this as reading material into Central America.

Children of the Volcano - by Alison Acker, published by Between the Lines, 229 College St., Toronto, Ontario, 1986. This is a fairly recent account of the suffering people in Guatemala, Honduras, El Salvador and Nicaragua have gone through. Not to be taken south but certainly worth reading before going. It may give you a few ideas of what to look for while there.

Bitter Grounds - by Lisa North, published by Between the Lines, 427 Bloor St., W. Toronto, 1982. This is older information but will give the reader a good background into the situation in El Salvador which caused twelve years of war and now a peace settlement that the people are not too excited about. There is little available about El Salvador because people that could write about the area had a difficult time getting into the country. Not to be taken to Central America.

Modern Short Stories of El Salvador - translated by Jack Gallagher, published by Direccion de Publicationes del Ministerio de Educacion, San Salvador, 1974. This is an excellent collection of short stories, written in English and available in San Salvador or in Santa Ana. Pick it up while you are there.

Quiches Maya of Utatlan - Evalution of Highland Great Kingdom, by Norman, 1981, University of Oklahoma Press. This is a recent account of the exploration and findings of Utatlan, Guatemala. It is recommended by the museum at the ruins.

COFFEE

Latin America is the coffee center of the world. One should not go there without some type of addiction to the drug. However, coffee addicts go crazy in Central America because it is difficult to get the real thing. There is lots of instant coffee, but you must always ask if there is house coffee before sitting down for a meal. If it is instant, send it back. The stuff is terrible. I take an immersion heater and boil water in my room and then filter myself a cup. But even that is not good coffee because these countries export all the good beans. Costa Rica has some great coffee, and you can get the best Guatemalan export coffee in Central America at the airport in Guatemala City for $2.00 US per pound. I pay about $10.00 for the same at home, and it is not quite as good. The brand I like is Anacafe which comes in a shining brown bag. In Costa Rica, I like the Rey brand, but in Costa Rica it is easy to try different brands and then purchase the one you like the best.

Coffee grows in the fields on shrubs with shining dark green leaves and there are usually large trees growing on the same field and used for shade for the coffee plants. Coffee blossoms are small white flowers that have a strong smell. After blooming, it takes about 6 or 7 months for the green bean to mature and turn a rusty brown. The bean is inside; the brown pulp is what one sees.

In Central America, many insecticides are used on the coffee plantations. I met a couple of Canadian tree planters that wanted to try and pick coffee for a few weeks but theygot so sick from the insecticides that they had to quit. Being tree planters, they knew all the symptoms of chemical poisoning. The pickers are given no education about the chemicals and no protection from them.

SPANISH

The people of Central America want to talk to you. They are very interested in foreign countries, women's issues, foreign customs, the cost of everything from homes to cat food. They may not know where your country is, but they will certainly like to hear about it. The people are friendly and helpful. If your language is not too good, they will be patient and help even more. They will often even pretend to understand your poor pronunciation, just as you pretend to understand everything that they say.

One of the purposes of your trip should be to communicate with the native people. Learn some of the language. One European once told me that he could always tell a Canadian abroad. If they only knew three words of the language of the country that they were visiting, they would use them over and over again. I wish all travellers were this thoughtful.

I have only put in a few Spanish words and phrases. You will notice a few of the words are different than in Spanish phrase books because Central American Spanish is slightly different than the more formal Spanish from Spain. There are also word differences between each of the countries, but that is for the more advanced speakers and beyond the scope of this book. For the beginner, I would recommend using the Berlitz phrase book, after you know all the words that I have listed below. After you have mastered most of what you will need from Berlitz and from this book, you will be ready for some serious Spanish lessons. That is when you will start understanding what is being said to you.

PRONOUNCIATION
Vowels:
A - pronounced as "a" in father.
E - pronounced as "a" in may.
I - pronounced as "e" in me.
O - pronounced as "o" in hold.
U - pronounced as "oo" in food.

Consonants:
C - pronounced as a soft sound when before "i" or "e" as in sink; otherwise it is pronounced as a "k".
G - pronounced as an "h" when it precedes "e" or "i". Otherwise it is hard as in "go".
H - is always silent.
J - pronounced like the "h" in house.
LL - pronounced like the "y" in yellow.
Ñ- pronounced like "n" and "y" together. Niña is pronounced "neenya".
QU - pronounced like "k".
UE - pronounced like the "wei" in weight.
AU - pronounced like the "ou" in ouch.
V - pronounced like a soft "b"

Polite Phrases
Good morning - buenos dias.
Good afternoon - buenos tardes.
Good night - buenos noches
Goodbye - adios
Thank you - gracias
Yes, very good - Si, muy bien.
Please - por favor
Excuse me (when interrupting) - descùlpe
Excuse me (when passing) - con permiso
I am sorry - Lo siento
See you - nos vemos (used by locals) Hasta la vista (used by gringos)

Explaining your needs
I would like - quiero
I am hungry - tengo hambre
I am thirsty - tengo sed
Do you understand English? - entiende ingles?

Time
Today - hoy
Tomorrow or morning - mañana
Yesterday - ayer
Last night - anoche
Noon - mediodia

Afternoon - tarde
Midnight - media noche
What time is it? que hora?
It is one o'clock - es la una punta.
It is quarter past three - son las tres y cuarto.
It is ten to two - dos menos diez.

Numbers

0-cero	1-una
2-dos	3-tres
4-cuatro	5-cinco
6-seis	7-siete
8-ocho	9-nueve
10-diez	11-once
12-doce	13-trece
14-catorce	15-quince
16-dieciseis	17-diecisiete
18-dieciocho	19-diecinueve
20-veinte	21-vientiuno
30-treinta	40-cuarenta
50-cincuenta	60-sesenta
70-setenta	80-ochenta
90-noventa	100-cien (when over 100, ciento y una)
1000-mil	First-primero
Second-segunda	Third-tercero

Colors

Black - negro
Blue/dark blue - azul/azul oscuro
Brown - cafè
Gray - gris
Green/light green - verde/verde ciaro
Pink - rosa
Purple - morado
Red - rojo
White - blanco
Yellow - amarillo

Days of the Week

Sunday - domingo
Monday - lunes
Tuesday - martes
Wednesday - miercoles
Thursday - jueves
Friday - viernes
Saturday - sabado

At the Hotel
I would like a room - quiero un cuarto
Single - sencilla
Double - doble
With two beds - con dos camas
With private bath - con baño privado
With a shower - con ducha
Quiet - tranquilo
Hot water - agua caliente (this is a joke)
Laundry service - servicio de lavanderia
For one night - por una noche
For one week - por una semana
May I see the room? - Yo veo el cuarto?
No, I don't like it- No, me no gusta.
Inn - posada
Towel - toalla
Soap - jabon
Yes, it is fine - si, esta bien.
Wake me up at....in the morning - puede despertarme a las....de la mañana.
May I have my bill? - me de la cuenta? or simply say - la cuenta.

Food
Apples - manzana
Avacado - aguacate
Beans (re-fried) - frijoles
Beef - carne
Beer - cerveza
Bread - pan
Breakfast - desayuno
Butter - mantequilla
Cheese - queso
Chicken - pollo (learn this one!)
Coffee - cafe
Corn - maiz
Cup - taza
Duck - pato
Egg - huevo
Fish - pescado
Fork - tenedor
Fried - frito
Fruit - fruta
Glass - vaso
Ham - jamon
Knife - cuchillo
Lamb - carne de cordero
Lunch - almuerzo

Onion - cebolla
Orange - naranja
Peas - guisante
Pineapple - piña
Pork - puerco/carne de cerdo
Potatoes - papas
Rice - arroz
Salt - sal
Soup - sopa
Spoon - cuchara
Sugar - azucar
Supper - cena
Tea - te
Toast - tostada
Turkey - pavo
Wine - vino (not recommended unless you find imports)
With milk/cream - con leche/crema
Without - sin

Flamingo

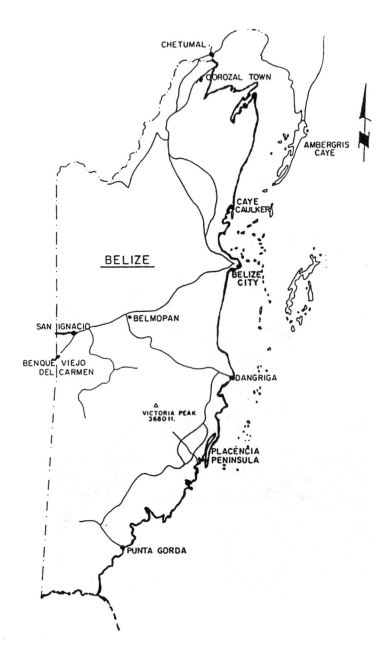

BELIZE

Belize is a delightful, easy-going country. The language spoken is English, the beaches are clean and inviting, there are lazy rivers to canoe, and the people are friendly.

The homes of the locals are small, wood-framed with corrugated tin roofs, and built on stilts. The stilts are necessary because the heavy rains cause flooding. The stilts also make it less probable that snakes will slither into the houses. Shaded areas under the houses are a great relief from the heat for the animals.

The Belizian Barrier Reef is the largest reef in the western hemisphere, stretching 175 miles along the Caribbean. It is second only to Australia's reef in length. The warm, crystal-clear water is excellent for sport fishing, scuba diving, snorkeling and swimming. The white coral beaches are uncrowded and very clean. Belize is becoming an ecological-minded country and as a result has some beautiful parks. Education promotes anti-pollution practices and encourages the local people not to over-fish the waters. The Audubon Society is quite active here.

The eleven major Mayan ruins in Belize are interesting to archaeology enthusiasts. Seven of the ruins are open to the public daily and the rest are accessible only after a permit is obtained from the Department of Forestry or the Department of Archaeology in Belmopan. The limestone systems in the mountains account for the many caves in Belize, some of which have traces of Mayan occupation.

Belize boasts over 500 species of birds, and is truly a bird watcher's paradise. I met one bird watcher in Belize who thought that he was on a different planet. In the two weeks that he was there, he was able to identify more than 200 species of birds. There are also more than 200 species of orchids to photograph.

For the city lover, the larger towns offer movies, museums, cultural events and wonderful restaurants.

HISTORY

The Mayan Indians migrated to Belize as early as 1500 B.C. from the Yucatan in Mexico. It is believed that this civilization crumbled around 1000 A.D. for unknown reasons.

Before the Maya built cities, there were some nomadic hunters and gatherers living in Belize. As the people began to cultivate food crops such as corn, they began living in settled communities. Later, these communities expanded into rich cultures that enjoyed beautiful temples, field tools and kitchen implements, decorative clay objects, religious ceremonies and cultural customs such as music, dances, and games.

Today, there are still ruins of these cities that can be visited. Although not as grand as Tikal or Mirador, they are older, which suggests that the Maya moved southward from Mexico. The temples and town centers are of a similar structure throughout these areas, giving evidence of a related culture. The cities were built around a center plaza with smaller plazas nearby. All plazas had temples around them built on pyramids, and interconnected with small rooms, ball courts and public baths. None of the Mayan cities in Latin America show any indication of ever having used the wheel, so it is believed that the work was performed by human labor.

The altars and stelae found in Belize are not as spectacular as those in Guatemala, but still contain significant information for our modern day scientists to decode.

The Spanish settled in Belize in the 1520's and considered Belize to be a part of Guatemala. The claim to this territory is accredited to explorers Pinzon and Solis, who originally claimed the area for Spain in 1508. However, this was not a favored place to settle, and little development occured until 1638 when British sailors established a settlement in Belize. For the next 150 years, the British built villages around the country.

The British used Belize for the export of logwood and mahogany. The British and Spanish fought over territorial rights until 1670 when they signed a treaty which stopped most of the pirating of the Spanish ships, but increased the export of wood.

As British settlements increased in the Caribbean, protection of the settlers along the Mosquito Coast increased. This began the Seven Year War, which resulted in the Spanish gaining control over the area. However, the British still wanted to have cutting rights to the wood and the Spanish granted them these rights. As the timber was cut down, settlements grew. A showdown came in 1798 when a Spanish fleet appeared at St. George's Caye. A battle ensued and the Spanish were driven away much to the delight of the English. Belize became British Honduras in 1862 and the logging boom began.

The British lumbermen brought black slaves from Jamaica. The slaves worked and lived with their master/owners with production being the main goal. When slavery was abolished in Belize in 1838, many black men continued their employment with their white employers.

The logwood which was used for the manufacturing of natural dyes was soon replaced by synthetic dyes, but the mahogany market increased. This meant that the loggers had to go further into the jungle to get lumber and the task was difficult. Among other British supplies, rum was imported into Belize by the shipload and was drank by the belly load.

As the lumber industry declined, racial tensions grew in Mexico with the Indians fighting both the mestizo and the whites. Later, the mestizo started killing the Indians and the population began to migrate back and forth across the border. This stopped around 1850, and farmers settled in the northern section of Belize.

Boundaries were defined in 1859 between Guatemala and Belize, and in 1862 the area became another one of Britain's colonies. The British set up formal administration in 1871. Immigration continued slowly.

In 1954, the Colonial administration introduced universal voting. In 1964 self-government was achieved under G.C. Price as acting Prime Minister. The country's official name was changed to Belize in June of 1973 and, it gained independence on September 21, 1981. Until 1983, Guatemala claimed all of Belize but, now only claims a small portion in the south.

The boundary disputes with Guatemala stem from an agreement that Britain had with Guatemala to build a road from Guatemala City to Belize City. Britain did not honor the agreement and Guatemala asked for compensation in territory. However, the black population in Belize knew that the right-wing Guatemalan government was not sympathetic to minority groups, especially the visible minorities, and campaigned against a takeover of the area.

After independence, British troops remained in Belize to ensure peace for the people. Guatemala has not challenged the British troups, even though there can be tensions between the Belize and Guatemalan borders.

GENERAL INFORMATION

Belize is a sovereign democratic state with a constitution based on British parliamentary democracy. The Belizian government is headed by a Prime Minister, has a 28 member elected **House of Representatives** and an eight member appointed **Senate**. Five of these appointments are made by the prime minister, two by the opposition leader and one is made by the governor general. There are two major parties in the country; the United Democratic Party, which was in power from 1984 to 1989; and the Peoples United Party, which was previously in power. The Governor maintains responsibility for defence, external affairs, internal security, and safeguarding of conditions of service of public officers and finance, while the government of Belize is in receipt of budgetary aid from the United Kingdom. Local governments are elected councils. The judicial system is based on British Common Law.

The area of Belize is **22,700 square kilometers** (8866 sq. mi.), with the length being about 180 miles and the width being about 85 miles. Belize has 220 miles of coastline along the Caribbean. There are three main rivers in the country with the Rio Hondo forming the northern border between Belize and Mexico. The Sarstoon River divides Guatemala and Belize in the south, and the Belize River   flows through the center of Belize and to the ocean.

The population of Belize is **180,000 people** with a density of 19 persons per square mile. The majority of the people are of

African ancestry and English is the first language although it is often not recognizable to **English speaking** North Americans. **Spanish** is also widely spoken.

The climate is sub-tropical with an average annual temperature of 79°F. Depending on the elevation, the summer high rarely exceeds 96°F and the winter low does not go below 60°F. The rainfall ranges from 50 inches in the north to 170 inches in the south. The rainy season is from June to August, but November through February has frequent warm showers. The north of the country is flat but the southern Pine Ridge area ranges from 1500 - 3000 feet above sea level with Victoria Peak being the highest at 3680 feet.

The flag of Belize has red stripes at the top and bottom with a larger blue stripe in the center. There is a green garland with a white disc in the center of the flag. The national anthem is titled the "Land of the Free".

Education is compulsory between the ages of six and fourteen and is patterned after the United Kingdom's school system. There are over 200 primary schools and two dozen secondary schools in Belize. Although much funding comes from church organizations, the schooling is controlled and standardized by the government. Illiteracy is not extreme with 90% of the population being able to read and write at a basic level. Education standards in Belize are second only to Costa Rica's in the Central American countries.

NATIVE GROUPS

The creoles make up half of Belize's population. The first creoles originated from the Scottish lumbermen and their Jamaican workers. These descendents eventually made up majority of the population.

An interesting group of people that live along the Caribbean coast of Central America are the Garifunas. There are over 50,000 Garifuna living in villages along the coast from Belize to Nicaragua, with Honduras having the largest population.

The Garifuna are a mixture of black African slaves and the Indians of the Lesser Antilles who migrated from Guyana and Venezuela to St. Vincent Island. Near the island in 1635, an English sailing ship capsized, freeing the blacks who then swam to the island. Inter-breeding followed, producing this group of people.

After a few years of settlement, the blacks and the Garifuna engaged in warfare. By 1700, the blacks had become the dominant group, living in the mountains where they became good at guerrilla warfare. They controlled one end of the island.

As conflicts continued, the blacks decided to drive the English from the island. They were quickly defeated. Fearing more problems, the British decided in 1797, to have them shipped to Jamaica and then to Roatan, Honduras. The Garifuna were not satisfied with their new island and soon turned it over to the Spanish.

They then headed for the mainland and settled along the coast. By 1832, there were Garifuna settlements at Stann Creek, Seine Bight, Punta Gorda and Barranca.

The Garifuna are an extremely handsome people. They have smooth dark skin and strong Indian features. Their bodies are big, tall and straight. Their gentle nature is reflected through their dark eyes.

As well as Spanish, the Garifuna speak their own unique dialect and maintain customs and traditions that reflect the mixing of the two cultures. It is believed that the dialect spoken by the Garifuna may have origins in the Swahili, Yuroba, Bantu, French and Arawak laguages.

The Garifuna are Catholic, but continue to tie in many of their Afro-Indian rituals in ceremony. One author I read believes that their religious system called dugu can be compared to the Haitian's voodoo. They use herbal healing methods that may not be recognized by the western medical profession but are useful when usual treatments are unsuccessful. All religious practices include a philosophy of balance and harmony of the spirit.

There are two types of holy men in the Garifuna tradition. The curandero is a healer of physical problems who heals with herbs and natural products. A buyei is a spiritual healer who may be a man or a woman. This person is visited by a spirit called a jiyurujas. If a person is visited by a spirit and fights the calling, the person will become ill. If he/she continues to fight, he/she will die. If he/she submits, he/she becomes a spiritual healer. Once the selected person accepts becoming a spiritual leader, he/she lives in a hut for fifteen days and sees only one woman who is past menopause. Her duty is to prepare anything the new buyei might need.

After the initiation ritual is over the buyei restores equilibrium to the soul during life and the after life. This person becomes the link between this earth and the next. He/she administers herbs and cures to troubled souls but this practice is not learned. He/she knows these cures because of the selection by the spirit world. The buyei may also use animals and dreams for cures. These cures require ritual chanting and dancing. Occasionally, the visitation of a spirit results in a great party where drinking, music and dancing occurs for many hours. The Garifuna believe that freeing the spirit is a great thing.

During a death ceremony, the Garifuni have a confession. This is supposed to be custom which was not derived from the Catholic religion. After death, the deceased's friends dig a hole in the kitchen floor of his home and put his clothes around the hole. Two friends then pour four buckets of sea water into the hole and four buckets of fresh water into the hole. A party is then held in the deceased's home. The same ritual is performed during a birthing ceremony. This is a purification ceremony.

Singing is an important part of Garifuna life. In older times singing was used to pass messages back and forth, to create harmony in the working people, to free the spirit from pain and anger, and to enhance joy. You will find a lot of music around the villages of the Garifua.

Today, many Garifuna live in huts made of palm and mangrove sticks, and the hard wood of the yagua tree they build their homes close to the sea. They believe that there is magic where the land and sea meet. The insides of the houses often have a mud floor and clay-brick dome ovens which are fed by charcoal or wood. There is often a pestle and mortar used for food and herb preparation and always some woven palm leaves which are used to strain and refine yucca. The homes last four to five years if not destroyed by tornado, and are repaired by the men of the village.

Women wash clothes, prepare yucca and pick other fruits such as pineapple, mango, papaya and coconuts for the family to eat. The men bring home fish that the women also prepare.

Although many traditions remain in the Garifuna villages, the 20th century is also visible. The people are leaving and going to the United States or other places for education. There are modern tools and clothes and the villages are serviced by modern vehicles.

LAWS

It is illegal to change money with money changers. This law is enforced!

Motorists should have a valid International Driver's Licence or a valid driver's licence from their own country. This allows one to drive for up to one year before getting a Belizian licence. If you have your own car, you must have a certificate of registration. You must have third party liability insurance in Belize. Drive on the right hand side of the road.

A pet must have a veterinarian's certificate showing that the animal is in good health and have an inoculation against rabies.

It is illegal to camp on the beaches or in park reserves in Belize. It is also prohibited by law to remove or export black coral. The Wildlife Protection Act does not allow the sale, exchange and hire of, or any other dealing for profit in, any wildlife or parts thereof. Export or import of wildlife is only allowed with a permit. Collection of any plants is not permitted without a permit. Picking orchids in the reserves is illegal. Spear fishing while wearing scuba diving apparel is illegal. Removing any archeological artifacts is illegal.

The Belizian government claims that major and violent crimes are low and that the police do not carry firearms.

Getting mixed up in the popular dope trade would be travel suicide. Stay away. I know that many smoke and sniff without getting caught but in my opinion, it just isn't worth the risk.

MONEY

It is illegal to change money with the money changers in Belize but American currency is accepted anywhere. I see no reason to change with money changers unless you have just crossed the border and need a bit of cash.

The Royal Bank of Canada took over the banking business in 1912 and has a number of branches there. There is also Barclays International, the Bank of Nova Scotia and the Atlantic Bank Ltd. in Belize. These banks will change Canadian dollars, US dollars and Pound Sterling with no problems. They will also change some of the currencies from other Caribbean countries. European currencies may be a bit more difficult to exchange as the banks do not get daily exchange rates. As usual, it is always best to carry US dollars with you.

The exchange rate in Belize is $2.00 Belize for $1.00 US. Belizian dollars are not exchangeable in other countries except by the money changers at the borders. Be certain to convert any extra money you may have to a currency you will be able to use.

The banks are open at 8:00AM to 1:00 or 2:00PM daily and some have Friday afternoon openings also. You should keep your exchange receipts in the event you are questioned at the border.

American Express, Visa and Master Card are widely accepted at hotels and shops but there is a surcharge that may be added onto your bill along with the exchange rate. You may get cash advances but there is also an extra charge for this service along with the regular charge by your bank.

VISAS

All visitors must be in possession of a valid passport. British subjects (Commonwealth citizens) and American citizens do not need visas but they must have a ticket of return to their own countries.

All others require visas except citizens from Belgium, Denmark, Finland, France, Greece, Iceland, Italy, Liechtenstein, Luxembourg, Mexico, Netherlands, Norway and colonies, San Marino, Spain, Sweden, Switzerland, Tunisia, Turkey, Uruguay and Venezuela. Everyone must have an onward ticket. This is not usually asked for when you are travelling overland.

Those from other countries may receive a visa at a Belizean consulate or an embassy in their country. If there is not one there, a British consulate may make the necessary arrangements.

You will be allowed a thirty day visitor's permit on entry to the country. However, if you don't have enough money or you look undesirable, you may be refused entry or have your permitted time reduced to two weeks. They may ask to see if you have sufficient funds while staying in the country. Be prepared to show your goods. Your bags may also be searched.

If you wish to stay in the country longer than 30 days, you may apply at the police station in one of the larger towns or at the immigration office in Belize City at 115 Barrack Road (good name).

Personal effects can be brought into the country without any problem. You are allowed 200 cigarettes or half a pound of tobacco products, 20 fluid ounces of alcohol and one bottle of perfume for personal use.

Those wishing to immigrate to Belize are encouraged to do so. The main criterion is that you do not become a dependent on the government. You may enter for agricultural purposes if you purchase a small farm or plantation. You may also enter if you help industrialize the country or if you are or become employed by an established commercial organization.

There are government concession programs and incentives for those interested in investing in Belize. Investors may receive up to 15 years of a tax holiday.

GETTING THERE

Buses to the Belizian border from Guatemala leave Tikal at 6:00AM and 1:00PM and Florez at 5:00AM and noon. Both routes go through El Cruce, Guatemala on their way to Melchor de Mencos at the border. There are no accommodations at El Cruces, although food is available, so be sure to leave early enough so you do not get stuck there. The border crossing may cost anywhere from five to twenty-five quetzales depending on when you cross. If it is after 2:00PM, you will have to pay an "overtime" price.

If coming from Mexico, the Batty Bus Company leaves for Belize from Chetumal quite frequently during the day. The travelling time from Chetumal to Belize City is about five and a half hours. The border crossing here is not unpleasant unless you are going from Belize to Mexico in which case you must get your travelling papers in Belize City before getting to the Mexican border. If you do not, you will be sent back to get them. I have heard of no exceptions.

If flying direct to Belize, there are international services from Miami, Houston and New Orleans in the US. The best deal available at the moment is a Tan-Sahsa ticket to Belize City from Miami for just over $100 US one way. There are other flights that connect the US with Belize via Mexico or Honduras which do not cost an arm and a leg.

If coming in on your own boat, the following requirements must be met:

1. Have a transcript of the vessel's official documentation.
2. Have clearance from the last port of call.
3. Have four copies of the crew and passenger manifest.
4. Have four copies of stores used or a list of cargo on board, or an imballast manifest.

If coming in by ferry, the ferries leave Livingston, Guatemala for Punta Gorda on Mondays and Wednesdays and return on Tuesdays and Fridays. The prices are $5.50 US per person and there is an exit charge for both countries. You can also hire a dory, which will leave whenever it has a full load. I do not recommend hiring a dory however. When I tried it, a storm broke out after 15 minutes at sea. The waves were coming into the boat faster than the boatman could bail, and the motor kept stalling. The mental stress is not worth the day or two saved by not waiting for the ferry.

CONSULATES
British High Commission, Embassy Square, Belmopan.
Telephone: 08-2146/47
Canadian Embassy, 120A New Road, Telephone:31-060 or 44-182
Costa Rican Embassy, 11 Handyside St., downtown Belize City.
El Salvadorian Consulate, 120 New Road, Telephone:44-318
Honduran Consulate, 91 North Front Street,
Telephone:45-889
Mexican Embassy, 20 Park Street, Belize City,
Telephone:30-193
Panamanian Embassy, 3 Orchid Garden, Belmopan,
Telephone: 02-7161

PUBLIC and BANK HOLIDAYS
New Year's Day	January 1
Baron Bliss Day	March 9
Good Friday	March/April
Holy Saturday	
Easter Monday	
Labour Day	May 1
Commonwealth Day	May 24
St. George's Caye Day	September 10
Independence Day	September 21
Columbus Day	October 12
Garifuna Settlement Day	November 19
Christmas Day	December 25
Boxing Day	December 26

BUSES
Riding a bus in Belize can be a joy as most of the major highways are paved and the people do not push or shove. However, the driver may turn his radio up to a nice 3000 decibel level and passengers with radios may start competing for air space. The music is never static; you may get rock and roll up front, reggae in back, Bach in the centre and heavy metal on the sides. Regardless of the combination, it will never be boring.

The average cost of travelling in Belize is $B2. (1. US) per hour. This is a rough estimate. Bus schedules are non-existant for Sundays with some places having no service at all. Be certain to check before planning a travel day on Sunday.

NORTHERN SCHEDULE
Leaving Belize City
Batty buses, every other hour from 4:00AM to 12:00PM and 1:00PM to 5:00PM daily from the station at 54E. Collet Canal.

Venus buses, every other hour from 5:00AM to 11:00AM and from 2:00PM to 6:00PM daily from the station on Magazine Road, nine blocks west of the south end of the Swing Bridge. The 11:00AM bus is an express with stops at Orange Walk and Corozal town only.

Leaving Chetumal, Mexico
Batty buses leave the Chetumal Terminal daily at 5:00, 6:00, 6:30, 8:30 and 10:00AM, and 12:00, 1:00, 1:30, 3:00 and 5:00PM. The 12:00PM bus is express and stops only at Orange Walk town. The 1:30PM bus is an express and stops only at Orange Walk and Corozal town. On Mondays only Batty has a bus leaving Chetumal at 2:00AM.

Venus buses leave Chetumal terminal daily at 4:30, 8:00, 9:00 and 11:00AM and 2:00, 4:00 and 6:00PM.

Leaving Corozal
Venus buses, from the Corozal terminal, daily at 4:00, 5:00, 6:00, 9:00 and 10:00AM and 12:00, 3:00, 5:00 and 7:00PM.

The fares between Belize City and Orange Walk are $B7. ($3.50 US) one way. Fares between Belize City and Corozal are $B12. ($6. US). Fares between Belize City and Chetumal are $B14. ($7. US).

SOUTHERN SCHEDULE
Leaving Belize City:
Z-Line buses from Magazine Road daily at 10:00AM and 12:00, 2:00, and 4:00PM. On Mondays, buses also leave at 6:00PM

James buses, from the terminal at Pound Yard, on Mondays and Saturdays at 9:00AM and Tuesdays, Wednesdays and Fridays at 6:00PM.

Leaving Dangriga:
Z-Line buses leave daily at 5:00AM.

James buses, at 1:00PM on Tuesday, Friday and Sunday and 6:00AM on Thursday.

Leaving Punta Gorda:
Z-Line buses, daily at 5:00AM

James buses, at 1:00PM on Tuesday, Friday and Sunday and 6:00AM on Thursday.

The fare between Belize City and Belmopan is $B8. ($4. US). Between Belize City and Dangriga the fare is $B16. ($8. US), between Belize City and Mango Creek $B26 ($13. US), between Belize City and Punta Gorda $B33 ($16.50 US). Both bus lines stop at Mango Creek.

WESTERN SCHEDULE
Leaving Belize City:
Batty buses, Monday to Saturday at 6:30, 8:00, 9:00 and 10:00AM, Sundays at 6:30, 7:30, 8:30, 9:30 and 10:30AM, from the terminal at 54 E. Collet Canal.

Novelo Bus Service, 19 West Collet Canal, Belize City runs buses on Monday to Saturday at 11:00AM, and 12:00, 1:00, 2:00, 3:00, 4:00, 5:00, 5:30 and 6:00PM and on Sundays at 12:00, 2:00, 3:00 and 4:00PM.

Leaving Belmopan:
Buses Monday to Saturday at 8:00, 9:30, 10:30 and 11:30AM and 2:30, 3:30 and 4:30PM

Batty buses leave Sundays at 8:00, 9:00, 10:00, 11:00AM and 12:00, 1:30, 2:30, 3:30, 4:30 and 5:30PM.

Leaving San Ignacio
Buses Monday to Saturday at 1:00PM, 2:00PM, 3:00PM and 4:00PM.

Batty buses leave Sundays at 12:00, 1:00, 2:00, 3:00 and 4:00PM. The 12:00PM bus runs direct to Belmopan with no stops.

The fare between Belize City and Belmopan is $B5.50 ($2.75 US), between Belize City and San Ignacio $B7.50 ($3.75 US) and between Belize City and Melchor, Guatemala $B9. ($4.50 US).

Leaving Benque Viejo:
Novelo Bus Service, 119 George St., Monday to Saturday at 4:00. 4:30, 5:00, 5:30, 6:00, 6:30, 6:45, 7:00, 9:00 and 10:00AM and Sundays at 6:00, 7:00, 9:00 and 10:00AM.

The fares between Belize City and Belmopan are $B5.50 ($2.75 US), between Belize City and San Ignacio $B7.50 ($3.75 US) and between Belize City and Benque Viejo $B8. ($4. US).

FERRIES
The daily ferry runs to Caye Caulker from Jan's Service Station, 73 North Front St., Belize City and the fare is $B12 ($6. US).

Emile's boat,the "Ocean Star", leaves from the Swing Bridge daily and is only $B10. ($5. US). This family runs a small hotel on the island and has the shuttle boat. They do not supplement their income by fishing, as they are interested in preserving ocean life. Those interested in conservation may want to give this man their business.

There was once a man called "Chocolate" that operated a large boat back and forth to Caye Caulker but his business flourished so well that we now have dozens of Chocolates trying to cash in on the business. The real Chocolate still hangs out at Mom's restaurant.

There are other boats that will take you at odd times if you are willing to pay the price. It costs about $50.00 US for one person in a boat for the one hour trip.

Boats leave Belize City at about 11:00AM. They return daily at about 6:45 and 7:00AM.

There is another boat called the Thunderbolt Express that leaves from the Swing Bridge for Caye Caulker and Ambergris Cay week days at 4:00PM and Saturdays at 1:00PM. The cost is $B15. ($7.50 US). This boat also stops at Caye Caulker on its way back to Belize City. It stops at about 7:45AM daily except Sundays.

A ferry leaves for Puerto Barrios and Livingston, Guatemala on Tuesdays and Fridays at 2:00PM. The ferry leaves Puerto Barrios on the same days at 7:30AM. The cost is about $B12. ($6. US). You should get your ticket in advance to ensure a trip as the boat fills up quickly. After you have your ticket, you must go to immigration and be stamped out of the country. It is your responsibility to see that it is done properly.

If you do not want to wait around for a ferry, you can get a dory to take you across but I do not advise it. Storms break out in the Caribbean frequently and it can be quite dangerous. I did this one time and ended at the Guatemalan immigration office in Livingston looking like a drowned rat. Lucky for me, they felt sorry for me and let me change in their office before being admitted to the country to look for a room.

NATIONAL AIRLINES

There is daily service to Ambergris Caye, Dangriga and Punta Gorda which saves a lot of overland travel but is more air polluting than bus travel. The costs are not high, $20. US to the Caye and $50.00 US to Punta Gorda.

The airlines offering this service are:

Maya Airways, 6 Fort Street, Belize City, telephone: 77215 or 44032.

Tropic Air with the office at the municipal airport, telephone: 45671.

CAR RENTALS

There are many car rental companies in Belize but again, I suggest using buses and being an eco-traveller. Public transportation is so much fun in Belize that you would miss a lot if you went around in a private vehicle. Because four wheel drives are the most common vehicles for rent in Belize, the cost is high. Some of these vehicles cost up to $900.00 US per week. For that price, you could feed half of the school children in Belize for a day which would be money better spent.

TAXIS

The taxi rate in Belize City is government controlled and you may get a price list from the tourist office. Generally, a short trip will cost $B4. ($2. US) or about $B10. ($5. US) per hour if you want to tour. The cost to and from the international airport is $B30. ($15. US) and only $B6. ($3. US) if going to the small plane landing strip close to town.

All taxi fares must be negotiated before you get in so that everyone is clear on the price. Even though there are fixed prices, you must be certain on the details. Any taxi trips out of town would have to be negotiated. I prefer bus transportation.

TELEPHONE

To make a long distance call in Belize, you must go to a telephone office. If you are staying in a higher priced hotel, they will be able to place a call for you. In Belize City the office is at 1 Church St. near the central park. The office is open from 8:00AM to 9:00PM and the service is okay. When talking to a party out of the country, there is a time delay, somewhat like speaking on a radio phone. Calling collect is not a problem, either person-to-person or station-to-station. A station-to-station call to Canada is about $3.00 US per minute; to the US it is somewhat cheaper.

To get an international operator, dial 115. If calling to Central or South America, dial 114. Making local calls are not difficult in this little country but finding a pay phone is. You may have to use a private phone in a store or hotel and then pay a small charge.

TAXES

There is an 8% tax on restaurant meals and on hotel bills. Other than that, there are no add-on taxes for goods in Belize.

The airport tax is $10.00US and crossing the border will cost $B1. ($.50 US).

TOURS

If you would like to have arrangements made to enjoy canoeing, horseback riding, excursions to parks, bird-watching, or nature tours, or anything else arranged before you arrive in Belize, there is a very knowledgeable man who can accommodate you. Contact Hugh Penwarden, Box 429, Erickson, Manitoba, Canada, R0J 0P0.

AMBERGRIS CAYE

The Cayes in Belize are spectacular and a must for anyone visiting the country. There is a price and a style for everyone from the very rich to those who ride chickenbuses. One can fish, snorkel, suntan, swim, eat, drink, skin dive, bird watch, photograph both below and above the water, and just enjoy the local culture.

Ambergris Caye is the largest, most developed, and most expensive of the cayes. It is dominated by the larger syndicated hotels, the profits of which leave the country. If you are in need of a luxury hotel and excellent restaurants on a beautiful tropical island and are willing to pay the price, this is the place for you. You can also find a few cheaper places on Ambergris.

The beaches on this island are not very nice because they are small and usually used as streets.

The easiest way to get to Amergris Caye is to fly. The price is $B40. ($20. US) one way on any one of the 19 daily flights. The flights leave from the municipal airport in Belize City. There are flights from the international airport but they cost a bit more.

The Thunderbolt Express (be instantly suspicious) leaves the Lagoon Side Marina at 7:15AM Monday to Saturday. It also leaves from the Swing Bridge at 4:00PM Monday to Friday and 1:00PM on Saturdays. These schedules may change at any time.

The return times should be checked when at the Caye. There are other boats besides the Thunderbolt and departure times vary. Just ask around the Swing Bridge and you will get a dozen fellows trying to get you onto their boat.

Another good boat that goes back and forth is the Andrea which goes at 7:00AM, Monday to Friday and 8:00AM on Saturdays from the Texaco wharf in San Pedro and goes back to Ambergris at 4:00PM every afternoon.

PLACES TO STAY

This is not a place for the chickenbuser and finding a room for under a hundred dollars US per day becomes a challenge. The hotels away from San Pedro are prohibitive, some running to two hundred dollars a night. Spectacularly comfortable but..... The few listed here are among the cheaper places, but this is not the island if looking for a bargain. Some of the cheaper places in San Pedro run from $B20 to $B60. ($10.-$30. US) but they are basic and hard to find.

Coral Beach Hotel in San Pedro is $B60. ($30. US) for a single and $B90. ($45. US) for a double. The beach location allows for fishing, boating and swimming. There is also a restaurant, a bar, telephone, postal and laundry services. The rooms have private baths and fans. Not much for the money. This is the diver's hang out.

Lily's Caribeña has basic rooms for $B60. ($30. US) and $B80. ($40. US) for a single and double respectively. There is a delightful veranda around the front of the house that looks out to the sea. This is a good place to sit in the evening. The rooms are bright and clean and equipped with fans. Unfortunately, the price has gone up because of renovations that have been done.

Seychelles Guest House is on the opposite side of town from the sea at the south end. There are a few rooms without private bath but with fans. The owners are pleasant and it is nice to live with a family for only $B40. ($20. US) per person per night. However, it is a long way to any type of beach.

Laidy's Hotel in San Pedro is $B40. ($20. US) for a single and $B70. ($35. US) for a double. The rooms have fans but no frills. The hotel is located on a tiny beach so you can at least get some of the pleasures of the sea.

Bird of Paradise

RESTAURANTS

Elvi's Kitchen is that big place with the thatched roof. This is the most popular place to eat even though it is not the cheapest. There is a sand floor inside with a tree growing in the center. The menu has fishburgers and sandwiches that come with fries for around $B10. ($5. US). These are similar to US prices.

The Coffee Shop near the airport is the place to get breakfast. They serve excellent waffles with butter and syrup for $B6. ($3. US) a plate. You get a decent portion.

Leny's Place near the airport turn-off serves good suppers for a decent price (less than $B15. ($7.50 US). The meals are a decent size. They often serve shrimp.

Lily's Restaurant will give you a good meal but the cost will be over $10.00 US. However, she cooks the best sea food on the island. It would be a pity not to enjoy this culinary.

THINGS TO DO

The beaches around San Pedro are not great. In fact they are almost non-existent, so suntanning is not the best thing to plan on doing. There are lots of boats that will take you out snorkeling along the reef and many shops in town that will rent you equipment. This could be a one day passtime, but be aware that the sun is very hot and if you are snorkeling for a few hours in the wonderful cool water, you will not feel the sun burning your skin. This is always a danger in this area.

Bird watching is a favorite passtime in any part of Belize. If you go around the mangrove swamps you have a better chance of seeing some of the larger and more colorful species. Binoculars would be a great piece of equipment to carry and a bird book would help you identify some of the lesser known birds. You must wear good shoes for this.

Hol Chan Marine Reserve is at the very southern tip of the island and is best visited by a boat. Some of the hotels offer tours or you may be able to negotiate a good price with one of the locals. There is a sinkhole and a cave in this reserve. The park has mangrove swamps teeming with bird life, and this protects part of the coral reef from fishermen.

BELIZE CITY

Belize City is a bustling mass of people, cars, boats, whistles, horns and more people. The city has had a bad reputation for robberies. However if you are careful, you should have no problems. Keep your money out of sight and stay out of dark, isolated areas. People travelling alone should be especially careful that they are not conned. If it sounds like an extremely good deal, beware.

I was walking down the street one day with map in hand and asked a man for directions. He was about to answer when an elderly lady said, "Come along my dear, I'm going right there." As I started talking with her, she made it quite clear that I shouldn't be talking to "the likes of him". She also told me to stay inside after dark and to use only the main streets.

I have to admit, however, that I have never had any problems in Belize City. I will repeat her warnings to stay away from dark streets, persistent strangers, and suspicious hockers.

Around Belize City, you will find most of the action in the center of town, at the mouth of Haulover Creek. The Swing Bridge crosses the creek and connects one section of town to the other. The more peaceful part of town is down around the Fort George Lighthouse and surrounding neighborhood. If you get a room closer to the Swing Bridge, it will be a bit cheaper, seedier and noisier.

There has been improvement in the Belize City street sewers, thanks to the Canadian government. They financed a project to have underground sewers installed along the main streets and the people need only to hook up from their houses to the main line. Some people have done this; however, some cannot affort this home improvement and still use the open sewers.

PLACES TO STAY

The Sea Side Guest House at 3 Prince Street is a lovely place just off the ocean. It is very safe and highly recommended. The price is $B18. ($9. US) for a single and $B28 ($14. US) for a double. There is one room with four bunk beds in it and the bunks are $B10. ($5. US) per person. The house is clean and quiet with breakfast and dinner available. German and English is spoken. If you are interested in some special trips, the owners of the Guest House are a wealth of information. This is a real find.

Glenthorne Manor at 27 Barrack Road is a gorgeous old wooden mansion that is a delight to stay in. Go over the Swing Bridge and up Queen street towards the hospital. Turn left down Barrack Road. The cost is $B60. ($30. US) for a single and $B80. ($40. US) for a double. The price includes a breakfast of johnnycake and fish. All of the rooms surround the common room which has a piano and other interesting pieces of furniture. The most interesting is in the family's sitting room and is the actual throne once used by the Queen of the Bay. You may use the kitchen and fridge and there is washer and dryer for use for a slight charge. You will find the owners quite happy to give you the history of this old house.

Golden Dragon at 27 Queen Street costs $B30. ($15. US) for a double with private bath, air con, restaurant and bar. Although the neighborhood is not the classiest, the small rooms are not a bad buy.

North Front Street Guest House is at (surprise!) 124 N. Front Street and is run by a Canadian and an American. The cost is $B16. ($8. US) for a single and $B26. ($13. US) for a double with fans. The place is basic but safe and clean. They have been around

45

for a while which is an indication that they know what they are doing.

Dima's Mira Rio is at 59 North Front Street and is a popular place to stay. This is because of the price and the friendliness of the owners. The price is $B16. ($8. US) a single and $B20. ($10. US) for a double. The rooms are small with a bancita (partial bathroom) in it. There is a nice balcony overlooking the river where you can have a beer and enjoy the action below.

Mom's Triangle Inn has beautiful rooms with private bath, high celings, nice interior decorating and fans. The price is $B50. ($25. US) a single and $B60. ($30. US) a double. One of the reasons you may want to stay here is because of the famous restaurant below. It has been a meeting place for gringos for years. To get there, go over the Swing Bridge, up Queen Street, past Barrack Road and turn right on Handyside. You can get coffee in the morning and there is laundry service.

RESTAURANTS

Mom's Kitchen at 11 Handyside Street. is famous for being the gringo meeting place. If you need information, this is the bulletin board you need to scour. The coffee at Mom's matches the writings on the bulletin board; both are plentiful. The meals here are excellent. This place was originally started by an American lady who knew what people wanted. Good food and lots of conversation. It is still offered today.

The Sea Breezes Bar is just around the corner, towards the water from the Sea Side Guest House. It is at the south end of Forshore Street. This is a safe and pleasant little bar, highly recommended by the locals in the area. The prices are good.

The Nile Restaurant at 49 Eve Street is across from the hospital and serves excellent shish kebabs for $B10. ($5. US). It is a good meal and the portions are large. The place is clean and friendly.

Dits at 50 King Street is the place to stop in for your afternoon coffee break which would be incomplete without some of the delicious home made pastry that is offered here. The prices are low and the pie pieces are large. The lemon pie is recommended.

The Golden Dragon Hotel has a great restaurant which offers Chinese, Belizean or American style foods. It is on Queen Street and Barrack Road. A full course meal will cost less than $B15. ($7.50 US).

THINGS TO DO

The Swing Bridge is the most famous landmark in Belize City. If you want to follow or give directions, it is always from or towards the Swing Bridge. The bridge spans the Haulover Creek, which got its name when the original inhabitants of the area used to haul their livestock over the creek at this spot. The creek, which is actually a branch of the Belize River, became known as Haulover Creek. Today, the bridge is used by both pedestrians and vehicles except during the time it is opened at 5:30AM or 5:30PM to let the boats go by.

Altun Ha Ruins are 31 miles north of Belize City, off the old Northern Highway near Rockstone Pond Village. Altun Ha means Rockstone Pond in Mayan. You must take a Maskall Village Transport truck and get off at the junction going to Rockstone Pond. Once at that village, you only have a couple of miles to walk to get to the ruins. Take the little side road that goes to the west. This is a hot walk and there is no traffic for you to hitch a ride. There are accommodations just past the junction into the ruins which are very expensive. There are some in Maskall Village also. This trip can be done as a day trip from Belize City but you must go early in the morning in order to be on the last bus back to the city before dark. The easiest way to visit these ruins is to take a taxi or join a tour.

Altun Ha is an old city from the Classic Period, around 2000 years ago. Located only six miles from the sea, Altun Ha was an important trading center, and as a link between the sea and the interior. One of the biggest pieces of evidence that supports this theory are the green obsidian blades and figures that were found in a tomb at the site. Since there is no obsidian in the area, but identical types of carvings were found in Teotihuacan, Mexico, the pieces are believed to have come from there. Similar pieces like this were not found inland until a much later date, suggesting that the Mayans traded along the coast first and then moved inland.

The two main plazas are surrounded by pyramids and palaces which have been partially restored. The temples are oval in shape with stairways facing the center square. The rooms at the top of the temple are limestone with false arches. These arches are layers of stone leaning towards each other in a stepped fashion until they meet at a point where they are topped with one last stone. The north plaza has five pyramids and one palace.

The Temple of the Green Tomb is west of the north plaza. When standing on the stairs of the main temple at Plaza A looking toward the center, the Green Tomb is on your right. Canadian; Dr. David Pendergast found over 300 jade pieces including beads, earings, rings, pearls and a book. One of the other tombs disclosed beads of a gold and copper alloy, and sea shells from the Pacific Ocean.

The next plaza to the south has the Sun God Temple on the east side of it. This is the building with many stairs and a room at the top. It is called the Sun God Temple because there are carvings of Kinich Ahau on the sides of the stairs. It is where the nine and a half pound jade carving of Kinich Ahau, the Mayan Sun God was found. This carving is now in the Royal Bank vault in Belize City.

South of this plaza is a reservoir that was fed by natural springs and used by the Mayans.

The ruins are open from 8:00AM to 5:00PM daily and there is a $B3.00 entry fee. There are no restaurants or tiendas close to the ruins, so water is a must and a snack is recommended.

The Holy Redeemer Cathedral is reached by walking north across the Swing Bridge and then making a left turn down North Front Street. The tallest building on your left is the Cathedral which was build in 1857 and, despite hurricanes, most of it remains intact.

The United States Embassy is at the corner of Gabourel Lane and Hudson Street. There has been a US consulate in Belize since 1840. The building was originally build in New England and then dismantled and used as a ship's ballast before being reconstructed 120 years ago in Belize City. The consulate is tucked away in this quiet neighborhood between old wooden plantation style houses that have been well maintained or renovated. Most have lovely old balconies around them where ladies once sat and caught the delightful sea breezes.

The Belize City Prison is located on Gabourel Lane and Gaol Lane. To get there, walk north on Queens Street until you get to Gabourel Lane. Then turn left and continue until you get to the high-walled building. This building was built in 1857 and is still used today. This could be a deterrent from the drug trade for those that have not made a definite decision about that topic. Just past the prison is the city hospital. On the corner of Freetown and Barrack Road is the old clock tower.

Fort George Island is at the south end of Marine Parade. This piece of land was originally an army barrack during the 1850's. After the first World War, the small canal separating the island from the mainland was built, and the area was made into a park and dedicated to dead war heroes. Just past this area is an old lighthouse and the tomb of Baron Bliss. Bliss was a wealthy Englishman who died offshore on his boat in 1926. He left his fortune to Belize even though he had never set foot on the land. The money has paid for the Bliss Institute on Southern Foreshore, which includes a museum and the National Arts Council. It has also paid for buildings, roads and other public improvements. The country celebrates this man's life (death?) on March 9th of every year.

St John's Cathedral is at the southern end of Albert Street. It was built by slaves in 1812 from red brick imported from England. It is the only Anglican church in Central America where four Mosquito kings were crowned. It took slaves 14 years to complete. There is a plaque that sits in memory of those that died of yellow fever in the area, before an inoculation against the disease was discovered.

Government House is one block east of St. John's Cathedral and is a beautiful old manion with immaculate grounds and wide windows that let the ocean winds in. The house was designed by the architect Christopher Wren in the mid 1850's. It was originally the home of the governor of British Honduras but today it is still used to house visiting diplomats and royalty. I could not manage to get a room there.

Belize City Vaults are at the southern end of Albert Street. One must cross the Yarborough Bridge in order to reach them. They now enclose a children's playground. There are about two dozen people entombed here, the last of whom was Gustav Von Olhaffen who introduced the idea of vault-burial to Belize. After his burial, the method was discontinued.

Yarborough Cemetery is found at the south end of Albert Street. Only a few of the early stones remain here, some from as early as 1781. The cemetery was named after the magistrate who donated the property to the city. It was not used after 1870.

The colonial residences along Regent Street on the south side of the city are beautiful. Many of these homes were built by slaves. They have lower stone floors, and timber on the second level, often with shingles. The lower floor was used to house the slaves when they were not at work.

Market Square, just south of the Swing Bridge, at the location of the Supreme Court. This grand old building has a gorgeous iron staircase going from the street to the balcony. There is a town clock on the tower. The original building was built in 1818 and then destroyed in 1878. The second building burned to the ground in 1918 and the governor, William Hart Bennett, was killed trying to save the flag pole from burning. One block to the east of Market Square is the Baron Bliss Institute which has a museum and the National Arts Council.

Moho Caye is a half-mile trip out from St. John's College on Princess Margaret Drive. You can hire a boat or if you are a great swimmer and feel sporty, you can swim.

During recent times this island was used to quarantine people suffering from smallpox and other contagious diseases. It was also used as a cemetery for unfortunates. There are no facilities on this island but it is a pleasant place to visit for the day if you can get a boat to drop you off and pick you up.

BELMOPAN

Fifty miles from Belize City, Belmopan is the capital of the country. The name is derived from the first three letters of "Belize" and the word "Mopan", which is the name of a tribe of Maya Indians. Being the capital of the country, the government houses are the main attraction. They have been built as copies of original Mayan structures. The National Assembly is open to the public. The residential sections are quite a way from the center of town. The hotels are expensive and there is not much else to do but look at the government buildings and birdwatch.

One of the reasons this site was chosen for the capital of the country is that, unlike Belize City, it is inland and protected from the hurricanes which had devestated Belize City in 1961.

PLACES TO STAY

The Circle "A" Lodge at 35/37 Half Moon Avenue is across town from where the bus stops. It is a nice walk of about half an hour. The rooms cost $B50. ($25. US) a single and $B60. ($30. US) for a double. The place is clean and quiet, but a long way from the center of town.

Mike's Grand Hotel is at #5 Santa Elena and is one of the cheapest in town but you do not get much. There are no private baths and little hot water.

RESTAURANTS

There is a restaurant at the Bull Frog Inn just up from the Circle "A" that is fairly good. They do not have anything special but the open breezy atmosphere makes the extra dollar worth while.

The market area has some neat places to eat with some of them being fairly cheap.

THINGS TO DO

St. Herman's Cave is 13 miles south of Belmopan on the gravel Hummingbird Highway toward Dangriga. The best way to get there is to hitchhike or take a taxi. There is no reliable bus service that I know of. When coming from Belmopan, take the first right-hand turn about a mile after the highway department center. Follow this road for about 20 minutes, go up a hill, and then follow the steps down to the cave. The jungle vegetation is green, lush and inviting. Once in the cave, you may see traces of ancient civilizations, but most of the findings have been removed. You will need a flashlight and good shoes if going on this excursion.

The Blue Hole is about two miles past the turnoff for St. Herman's Caves. Once you get back to the highway from the cave, walk for about 45 minutes and you will see a sign painted onto the road that says "Thieves Here". Look for the steps going down to the water; not for the thieves. The hole is spectacular with lush green jungle growing around, contrasting the blueness of the hole. It is believed that the water in the hole comes from St. Herman's Caves. As long as you are walking, you may as well take a nice swim before heading back to Belmopan. A delightful way to spend a day.

Guanacaste Park is opposite the road going into Belmopan and is easy to get to. It is a 52 acre triangle that sits between Belmopan, Roaring Creek and the Belize River. It was named after the huge guanacaste or earpod tree. There are a number of trails that go through the park and early morning birdwatching is wonderful. The park is a rainforest that has many orchids and ferns giving shelter to birds. If in Belmopan, this is a must. You will need a bird book and good shoes.

BENQUE VIEJO DEL CARMEN

This is a border town and, like most border towns, it does not have much to offer. If you are stuck here, there are places to stay, but it is best to pass through Benque Viejo and go on to San Ignacio. However, if you are going to Guatemala and decide to stay near the border, it is more comfortable on the Belizian side.

The town got its name from the men that at one time logged and collected chicle in the area. The "bank" refers to the bank of the river which is the border between Guatemala and Belize.

There are buses going to and from San Ignacio all day long, about every hour. There are also taxis that will take you the final mile to the border. It is not too expensive and is usually the same price regardless of how many are crowded into the car. You will often be approached by money changers in this town.

PLACES TO STAY

Okis Hotel is on George Street. The rooms are $B10. ($5. US) for a single and $B15. ($7.50 US) for a double. The rooms have a shared bath but it is on the main drag and is the best deal in town.

The Roxi Hotel is on #70 Joseph Street is on the street coming into town from Guatemala. The rooms are $B5. ($2.50 US) for a single and $B7. ($3.50 US) for a double. This is the most basic in town. There are no private baths or hot water. The rooms are just a bed and a door. You could stay if there was nothing else.

The Maya Hotel is on the main drag just up from the Okis and in the middle of the three. It charges $B8. ($4. US) per person without private bathrooms. It is okay but I still recommend going into San Ignacio for comfort.

RESTAURANTS

Eat from the vendors around the main square or buy fresh food in the market. There is really not much in town to choose from.

THINGS TO DO

San José Succots is a small Mopan Mayan village just outside of Benque Viejo. Mopan is the most popular language among the Maya people of this region. If you are unable to go to Guatemala and want to see some Maya customs, this is a good place to go. The Indians still dress traditionally, live in white painted huts and are able to live as they choose without the threat of the military coming in and mowing them down during the night. These natives were originally from San José in the Peten of Guatemala but found life in Belize more peaceful.

To get to San José Succots you can get on a truck near the market in Benque Viejo or a non-direct bus to San Ignacio. Ask the locals and they will give you the latest information. It is less than five kilometers on the road toward Benque and could be walked.

CAYE CAULKER

This is a beautiful, friendly little island about 45 minutes from Belize City by boat. It takes 15 minutes to walk from one end of the island to the other. It is the most popular island for travellers and has very affordable prices. The food here is spectacular and a gout sufferer's hell. The usual diet is lobster and eggs for breakfast, lobster burger for lunch, lobster salad in mid-afternoon and then for a change, a mixed seafood dish for supper. The prices for supper usually range from $B8. - $B12. ($4.-$6. US).

Once the haunt of pirates, it is now the haunt of chicken-busers. The residents are fishermen, hotel owners, boat builders and restaurant owners. Originally called Cayo Hicaco, it was named after the palm tree that grows on the island.

To get to the island, there are many boats leaving every day from the wharf by the Swing Bridge in Belize City. There are numerous hustlers just waiting to get you onto their boats and they leave around 3:00PM daily. I would recommend Emil's boat, the Ocean Star, which is $B10. ($5. US). Another wellknown boat is the Thunderbolt Express which charges about $B15. ($7.50 US) per person and usually leaves by 4:00PM daily. These times should be checked out before making definite plans. To return to the mainland, you can get a boat at the dock by the Martinez Restaurant. Check with your hotel owner for times. They usually start around 6:30AM daily and go for most of the morning.

PLACES TO STAY

There are many places to stay on Caye Caulker and I have listed just a few to give you an idea of what to look for. There are not many places at the top end of the scale but the bottom end is loaded. I doubt that you would ever be stuck without a room on this island unless you were extremely fussy.

Tom's Place is at the very east end of the island. The price is $B20. ($10. US) for a double and $B30. ($15. US) for a triple but they will not rent to singles, even if they are prepared to pay double price. She lets single travellers know that they are unwelcome. She does have washing facilities, at $B10. ($5. US) per load, but at that price I would throw away my dirty clothes and buy new ones in Guatemala. The rooms are neat, clean and have a shared bathroom.

The Tropical Paradise is the place to stay for $B70. ($35. US) a single and $B90. ($45. US) for a double which includes hot water. The rooms are immaculate with private baths, fans, and TV. There is also a restaurant on site. The rooms are in a condominium-type building, but there are also some superb cabins for a few dollars more. The cabins are equipped with fridge and air-con. If you are only in Belize for a couple of weeks, this would be a delightful place to hang out and read. The hotel is about one city block before Tom's Place.

Edith's Hotel costs $B20. ($10. US) for a single and $B30. ($15. US) for a double. The place is clean, cheery and friendly. Singles are welcome. The rooms have fans and the beds are very comfortable. You may wash your clothes on a scrub board and hang them on the line, at no charge. The owner, Angelina Novelo, makes the best fresh-squeezed orange juice on the island for $B5. ($2.50 US) a quart.

Shirley's Place, next to Ignacio's, is a delightful place with a gorgeous sandy area where plants grow abundantly and give shade to the vacationing day dreamer. The prices are high for the little rooms at $B30. ($15. US) per person, with some rooms having a private bath for a few bucks more. It is the yard that is the drawing card here.

Deisy's Hotel is $B20. ($10. US) for a single. It has a nice porch to sit on, but other than that it is just average.

Lena's Hotel is just behind Deisy's and has similar rooms but the place is a bit bigger.

Ignacio's Cabins are at the end of the island past Tom's Place. They are cute little cabins with private baths; however, they are all doubles. The cost is $B10. ($5. US) per person. A little way from the center of the island, it is a very pretty, quiet spot. It also has a private beach. The cabin decor is also delightful.

The Mirmer Hotel is in the center of town. The rooms are $B25. ($12.50 US) per person. They are very clean with lots of hot water all day long.

RESTAURANTS

Emma's Place is a must for lobster pies. At $B2. ($1. US) each, they are an excellent snack. Emma's is in a blue house on the second street from the water at the west end of the island. If you can't find it, just ask a local; everyone knows her. She has all her pies ready by noon and they are gone by 2:00PM.

The **Tropical Paradise** is a clean, cheap restaurant that serves excellent meals and is always full. It is the most popular place for travellers and also has a fairly large (for Caye Caulker) menu. The decor is as tasteful as you will find on the island, the fans keep the mosquitoes off, and the hours are predictable.

The **Miramar** is across from Edith's Hotel and has a beautiful patio garden to eat in. The food is excellent, the atmosphere is pleasant, the prices are affordable and the beer is cold.

Aberdeen Chinese restaurant is at the Rivas Guest House and serves excellent Chinese food - if you can imagine a Scottish Chinese place. I thought they might serve stir fried haggis but no such luck; it was regular Chinese food.

THINGS TO DO

This is a lay-about place to visit. Birdwatching is possible. Some people snorkel while others go deep sea diving. You can rent equipment and guides for anything from deep sea fishing to underwater photography. No matter what you choose to do as a passtime, almost everyone tries to escape the sand fleas when they are in season. What the locals in Honduras do is put lots of greasy oil on their skin and the fleas are unable to bite once stuck to the oil. Other people use Skin-So-Soft by Avon to keep the little pests away.

The **Galeria Hicaco** is a little shop, on the first street up from the water, near the east end of the island. The shop contains arts, crafts and clothing made by Ketchi and Mopan Maya, Garifuna, Mestizo, Creole and other Belizian natives.

Tours are available by Ellen McRae, a Marine Biologist, at Reef Ecology Tours. $B35. ($17.50 US) buys a one-hour lecture plus a snorkeling tour along the barrier reef. A three-hour bird ecology tour along the mangroves is offered for $B16. ($8. US) Ellen is a very knowledgeable person and loves to talk about the area, so don't be afraid to ask questions. One of her greatest virtues is her desire to preserve her newly-adopted land.

Snorkeling costs about $B20. ($10. US) for three hours. There are many boats that go out, but I would recommend the ones associated with the Galeria as they would be more apt to be trying to promote the preservation of this wonderful stretch of water.

CHAPEL CAYE or PYRAMID ISLAND

This is one of the wealthiest establishments on the cayes. Pyramid itself is not the most expensive, but it is connected to other expensive hotels and some of the bars, equipment shops and boats that are around the islands. Chapel Caye is a private island with one large establishment which has everything you could want while on a luxury vacation including air-con and hot water. You may also go deep sea fishing with a guide from this hotel. The large, clean rooms run around $100.00 US per day for a double. Meals are about $10.00

US each. There are boats that will stop on Chapel Caye on their way to Caye Caulker but pre-arrangements must be made. This is not a regular stop. You will be charged extra.

COROZAL TOWN

This is a little town of 7,000 people, just south of the Mexican border on the Bay of Chetumal. The town was originally a refugee site for people escaping in 1849 from the Caste War of the Yucatan. In 1955, Hurricane Janet destroyed the old town and today, Corozal Town has a mixture of modern Mexican and wooden Caribbean architecture. It is a laidback place that encourages slow beers, long conversations and developing friendships.

PLACES TO STAY

Nestor's Hotel is the best buy in town and is at #123 Fourth Ave. The rooms cost $B20. ($10. US) per person and although tiny, are clean, nicely kept and have fans. You may go up on the roof for a great view and good pictures. Nestor's also has a restaurant that serves good food.

Capri Hotel at #14, Fourth Street, costs $16. ($8. US) a single with private bath. The rooms are small and dreary and the clientele in the pool hall are noisy on occassion, but the ocean breezes are lovely. There is a restaurant on the premises and the rooms have telephones. This should only be considered if Nestor's is full.

Hotel Maya is a few blocks from the center of town and the rooms cost $B30. ($15. US) for a single. They are clean, fairly large, have fans and private bathrooms. If you get one facing the ocean, you have a real deal. This is a lovely place to stay. There is also a restaurant on the premises.

RESTAURANTS

There are many places to eat in Corozal Town and I cannot even begin to mention all the ones that are good. Most of the hotels have small restaurants that are good. The center of town is where there are the most restaurants that are in my price range.

Tony's Hotel at the south end of town, just on the way into the village, has a great restaurant. Although expensive to stay at, it is worth the walk over to eat. The special of the day is usually of the best price and quality. The atmosphere is delightful and the service is good.

The Kwality India Restaurant, at the highway and 5th Avenue, has a great selection of vegetarian dishes. It is a delight to have a few good meals that are not heavily laden with meat. The nan (East Indian bread) is a nice change after eating tortillas if you have just come from Mexico.

Nestor's Restaurant is not only the cheapest place to eat, but the meals are good and the place is clean. American run, this man knows how to attract business. His restaurant is often full.

THINGS TO DO

Corozal Town Fort is in the center of town. There are four red brick structures at the government administrative offices, west of Central Park. After the refugees left the Yucatan and settled in Corozal, they decided a fort would be necessary to defend themselves against attacks by Mexicans. This venture was not very successful, however, as the town was captured many times by Mexican Mayans.

The Town Hall is a must to visit while in town. There is a painting on the back wall that is simular in style to Diego Rivera's paintings in Mexico City. The mural tells the story of the town of Corozal from the beginning of the Colonial Period to modern times. It was originally painted in 1953 by Manuel Villamor, a Belizian who re-painted it recently, giving it new life and meaning.

The Santa Rita Ruins are Mayan ruins that were built on top of the original inhabitants of Corozal town. The ruins are not the most impressive in Belize, with only one large building still standing. There are a few rooms in the top temple. This building in the central core of Santa Rita is located across from the Coca Cola factory which is on a small road just to the left of the main road going to Mexico. This site was important during the Late Post Classic Period (1350 - 1530AD) and was still occupied by the Maya when the Spanish came in the 1500's. Some of the artifacts found are friezes and murals, pottery and jade, fishing-net sinkers and copper tweezers. Objects found from the Early Classic Period (300AD) were made of sea shells and stingray spines, jade and mica jewelry, golden ear decorations and more pottery shards. The site is open from 8:00AM to 5:00PM daily and there is a small entrance fee.

The Aventura Sugar Mill is seven miles from Corozal on the Northern Highway just past the Adventura Inn at Consejo and a mile before the village of Sarteneja. The mill is on private land and permission must be obtained before visiting it. The chimney of the mill is the most prominent object still standing. Sugar manufacturing operations started in the 1800's.

Consejo village has a couple of expensive hotels along the beach where you can have a swim, eat and drink and then walk or hitch the seven miles back to Corozal Town. This is a pleasant place to spend a few hours. Because the area has not been infested with a lot of tourists, you may enjoy the company of some of the locals.

The Cerro Ruins can be reached by boat from the Corozal docks. You must hire someone to take you south, across the bay. You can walk, but it is a long journey and you will still need someone to take you across the mouth of the river between Corozal and the ruins. During the dry season, between January and April, you can drive on a secondary road. However, I have not gone this way and do not have any information on it.

Cerros dates from the Late Preclassic Period (350BC to 250AD) and was an important coastal trading center. The tallest temple rises 21 meters, about 70 feet, above the plaza floor. Although a lot of evacuation work has not been done here, you can see the remains of a ball court and there is a stone carving. The ruins are open from 8:00AM to 5:00PM and there is a small admission fee.

DANGRIGA or STANN CREEK

Unless you are planning on making this your place of residence while you visit the Cockscomb Basin, Dangriga does not have much to offer the traveller. It is a grubby little town. You should note that buses leave at 2:00PM for Placencia regardless of what the schedules say, but you cannot take the bus out of Placencia to Punta Gorda. You must either return to Dangriga and take a bus, or take a dory from Placencia to Mango Creek (Independence.)

Dangriga was first stettled by the Garifuna in 1823 when life became unpleasant in Honduras. November 19th is the day of celebration for this landing.

PLACES TO STAY

The Riverside Hotel at 135 Commerce Street, is across the bridge from the bus stop. The price is $B20. ($10. US) for a single and $B30. ($15. US) for a double. It is nothing special but it will suffice. The proprietor is friendly and the sitting room is pleasant. There are a few interesting vases and a gorgeous mahogany dining room table. The cockroaches are of the larger variety but the place is quite clean and is the best place in town for the price.

The Central Hotel at 190 Commerce Street, is cheaper at $B15. ($7.50 US) per person with shared bathrooms. It is basic.

The Catalina is one block up (not across the bridge) from the bus stop. Turn left at the corner. This is a dormitory-style hotel at $B15. ($7.50 US) per person.

Pal's Guest House is along the water but the rooms are small and sparce. They cost $B30. ($15. US) for a single with a private bathroom and fan. There are a couple of rooms with shared bath for less.

RESTAURANTS

The Sunshine Restaurant is more expensive than the Sunrest across the street. Both are Chinese restaurants and they both serve a good place. For what is available in town, they are the best choices.

THINGS TO DO

The Fish Market in Dangriga attracts people from all over Belize. Some of the fish found in this market are the yellow tail, silk snapper, barracuda, porgy, grunts and kingfish. This is an interesting place to check out local life.

57

The Post Office in Dangriga is an interesting little building built high above the ground. To find it, walk up the main street on the bus side of the bridge, past the electrical company. Turn left toward the sea and it is on your left hand side. The most interesting buildings in town are the "outhouses by the sea". Walk either way along the shore until you come to a dock with a shack on the end. This is an outhouse! You will notice that the traffic to and from it is fairly heavy.

Cockscomb Basin is also known as the Jaguar Reserve, which the Jaguar Car Co. helps to support. It is found between Placencia and Dangriga on the peninsula. The area became a forest reserve in 1984 and a wildlife sanctuary in 1986. There is a minor Maya ceremonial site from the Classic Period called "Chucil Baalum". The basin sits from 300 to 3675 feet above sea level. The average rainfall is about 100 to 180 inches a year and all of it falls between June and January. This means that the area is defined as a tropical rain forest. Other Species under protection here other than the jaguar include the ocelot, margay, baird's tapir and the scarlet macow.

The average jaguar weights up to 200 pounds and is about six feet long from nose to tail. The jaguar is a nocturnal animal and uses old trails to hunt on. Males have a territory of 11 - 16 square miles and females use about one third of that space.

Also in the park is the unspotted puma which averages about 70 pounds and eats as much as the jaguar. The ocelot weighs about 30 pounds and eats smaller prey than the jaguar. Resembling the ocelot but weighting about ten pounds, the margay eats insects, birds and rodents. Other animals found here are the rayra (a weasel-like animal), otter, deer, anteater and armadillo. There have been 290 species of birds recorded in the area. There are also reptiles and amphibians, including snakes.

To get there, take the bus from Dangriga to Placencia. Have the driver drop you off at the turnoff and you can walk the last eight kilometers. It will take you close to two hours to do this. The walk will get you there close to dark. You must bring your own food to the park. There is some tenting available and there are a few huts that can be rented. There is a slight fee for this service. The park has a small museum that has illustrations of local birds and animals.

If you stay in Placencia and get a morning bus to the road and walk in, you will have most of the day to spend in the park. Then you will have to hitch to get back to Dangriga for the night. Another alternative is to hire a truck for the day. This would run about $150.00 US so it would be necessary to get a group together. The Toucan Hotel at Big Creek (see Mango Creek) has some trucks for rent for $70.00 US per day so you may want to make arrangements there.

To camp in the park you must first obtain a permit from the BAS office in Belize City, at the Pelican Beach Resort by the airport in Dangriga, or at the Wildlife Sanctuary Office in Belize City.

HALF MOON CAYE or LIGHTHOUSE CAYE

This island is 45 miles from Belize City and boats can be hired to get to it. It is a Natural Monument established in 1982 and the first conservation area in Belize. The Caye is eight feet above sea level and 45 acres in area. There is a solar-powered lighthouse on the island which was build in 1848, replacing a previous lighthouse built in 1820. The tower was added in 1931. This is an excellent place to get a good view of the Cayes. Guests are requested to register with the park warden upon arrival. There are maps of the area available. Camping sites and sani-stations are also available.

Half Moon Caye is noted for its Red-Footed Booby, a population of the white instead of the usual brown type. This bird shares the island with the magnificent Frigatebird which has a seven foot wingspan.

Of the reptile family, there is the bamboo chicken, and a red iguana with black bars on its back. This iguana was hunted for it's meat. The wish-willy is a smaller lizard; it is yellow with black bars on its back. It is a mere three to four feet in length. The loggerhead and hawksbill turtles are hunted for meat; the shell of the hawksbill is used for jewlry.

The Blue Hole diving area is near this island. It is an area of underwater caves complete with stalagmites and stalactites which were formed by underground rivers years ago. The roof of the cave broke, leaving this beautiful hole that makes the caves accessible to divers. This area was explored by Jacques Cousteau during the 1970's and is considered one of the more interesting cayes along the coast.

When visiting the island, please stay on the trails in order not to disturb the delicate plant life or the nesting birds. Do not litter. Do not touch any eggs, coral, shells or plants. This reserve is sponsored by the Belize Audobon Society and the Government of Belize.

Sail Fish

HATTIEVILLE

This village is about 16 miles out of Belize City on the way to San Ignacio. It was originally a camp for the homeless people that survived Hurricane Hattie. The refugees liked the area so much that many of them remained. There are about 2500 people here.

MANGO CREEK

You can catch the mail boat from Placencia on Monday, Wednesday or Friday for Mango Creek and then the bus bound for Punta Gorda. The boat will cost you about $B10. ($5. US) per person. Mango Creek is a cute town and the inhabitants are pleasant.

PLACES TO STAY

Hello Hotel is right next to the bus stop and pool hall. It is clean, friendly, and now expensive at $B80. ($40. US) for a double. There are private bathrooms, two tap showers and air con.

The Toucan charges twice as much as the Hello and is next to the airfield at Big Creek. Although not the place to stay, it is a great place to get information and rent a vehicle for around $70.00 US per day. If you want to go to Cockscomb Reserve, this may be one of your alternatives.

RESTAURANT

For the best place to eat, everyone goes to Miss Ella Forman's home. It is the white house behind the restaurant with the Fanta sign. Just go to the door and ask for a meal. You will feel like a hobo out of the Depression until she opens the door. She will serve the meal of the day for $B10. ($5. US) per person and the meal will be very good. Miss Ella Forman and her family are good to their guests. Visiting this place is a must if you are in Mango Creek for any reason.

ORANGE WALK TOWN

There are some interesting excursions from this town of less than 10,000 people. If you don't wish to stay in Belize City, Orange Walk is an alternative for a few days.

There is a small Mennonite community around Orange Walk Town and their presence is noticeable. Their conservative dress and older style of transportation contrast to the Caribe and Mestizo population.

PLACES TO STAY

Jane's Hotel at 9 Baker street or Market Lane No. 1, is at the far end of Bakers Street overlooking the New River. It is a wooden house with small single rooms that cost $B15. ($7.50 US) per person. There are fans in the rooms but the bathrooms are communal.

Mi Amour Hotel is on the main street at #19 Belize/Corozal

Road and has bigger rooms than Jane's, but it is in a noisier location. The rooms cost $B20. ($10. US) per person with a private bathroom. The price includes a restaurant on the premises, a telephone and laundry service.

Camie's Hotel is the pink cement building on the square that has rooms for $B20. ($10. US) per person. This does not include private bathroom but there is a restaurant.

RESTAURANTS

The Chinese restaurants seem to be the best and most reliable for meals in this area, but nothing is very bad or very good. Take your chances.

THINGS TO DO

Nohmul was a major ceremonial site of the Maya and has twin ceremonial groups that are connected by a raised causeway or Sacbe. The twin mounds sit in the middle of a sugar cane field. The site was thriving during the late Preclassic (350BC to 250AD) and Late Classic Periods (600AD to 900AD). Nohmul means "big hill" in the Mayan language. As it was excavated by Thomas Gann of England jewelry, shells and pottery ended up in the British Museum in London.

To get to the site, take a bus from Orange Walk to San Pablo. There are buses going in both directions several times a day. When you get to San Pablo, walk about half an hour (one mile) down the road going west until you come to the site. Ask anyone for directions.

Lamanai is an old Mayan site and it was also a part of the British Honduras Estate Company which had a large mill site there in the 19th century. At present, Lamanai is a difficult place to reach so you must plan on an entire day and you must bring food and water with you.

At present, Lamanai can be reached only by road from San Felipe Village in a four-wheel drive vehicle, or by boat up the New River Lagoon from Guinea Grass or Shipyard. Take a taxi or hire a car from Orange Walk to Guinea Grass or Shipyard. You can also take a boat all the way up the New River from Orange Walk but the boat will be a bit more expensive.

At Lamanai, there are the remains of two churches which were built by missionaries in the 16th century. The older one was built with cut stones similar to the ones the Maya used for their temples centuries earlier. The Mayan Indians destroyed both churches in protest against the Christian religion. The flywheel and other sections of the sugar mill can be seen east of the ceremonial sites. The mill was imported from the Leeds Foundry in New Orleans and installed in 1869.

More than 700 buildings have been identified at the site. There were many children's bones found under one of the stelae here and it is believed that they may have been human sacrifices. The major temple at Lamanai may be climbed by a steep, stone stairway to wonderful views of the surrounding jungle. One of the ball courts has a date from around the tenth century on it which suggests that this city lived longer than many others which declined during the 9th century. The name "Lamanai" means "submerged crocodile" in the Mayan language.

The Cuello Ruins are about four miles from Orange Walk Town on the Yo Creek Road. They are behind the Cuello Distillery. You must ask for permission to enter at the distillery. This is a small ceremonial center that dates back to the Protoclassic Period (about 2500BC). Wood found preserved in a plaster floor has been tested and proven to be from that era. Pottery found here indicates that the Maya did not get their style from the Olmecs in Mexico but may have developed it independently.

At one period around 400BC there was a large group of people that died within the same period. This may have been caused by a plague, an epidemic or a war. A few of the graves had large earthenware pots placed over the heads of the dead. Some of the obsidian and jade found here date back to around 1200BC. This indicates that trade took place large distances from home because obsidian is not available in Belize. A large temple has been excavated and consolidated and is in front of an excavation ditch.

Crooked Tree Wildlife Sanctuary is 33 miles north of Belize City, halfway between Orange Walk and Belize City on the Northern Highway. There is a dirt road going west from the highway which goes for two miles to the old logging village of Crooked Tree. Once there, you may hire a boat from some of the residents to go into the reserve.

The sanctuary came into existence in 1984 for the protection of migrant birds. It is run by the Belize Audubon Society. There is a visitor's center at the end of the causeway with displays of the plants and birds found in the sanctuary.

The inland lagoons, swamps and waterways are ideal for food sources and resting places of the migrating birds. A few of the many, birds found in the sanctuary are boat-billed herons, chestnut-bellied herons, bare-throated tiger herons, black-bellied whistling ducks, muscovys, snail kites, great egrets and black-collared hawks. Also, there are Black Howler Monkeys, crocodiles, coatimundi and several types of turtles and iguanas. Again, if bird watching is your thing, this sanctuary should not be missed, especially in April, May and November when migrations are at their peak.

PLACENCIA

Placencia is a gorgeous little Caribe town with spectacular beaches and good snorkelling. The bus trip down is well worth the effort. However, places to stay at are limited and if all are full, you may have to stay in a local house. This is safe and more interesting than staying in a crowded hotel. If this does not suit your fancy, there is camping along the beach. Placencia also has the infamous "outhouses by the sea".

Getting to and from Placencia can be difficult. If you are coming from Dangriga or Belize City, then it is just a matter of connecting up with the bus. If coming or going from Mango Creek and Livingston, Guatemala, then you need a boat. You may catch the mail boat on Monday, Wednesday or Friday going to Mango Creek at 2:00PM and returning at 2:45PM. There are boats that leave around 9:00AM daily but there may be a problem finding one that has room to take you. There is no definite schedule. The final alternative is to call Miss Leslie at the post office in Placencia at 06-22046. She can usually rustle up a ride for travellers.

PLACES TO STAY

There are many expensive places to stay along the beach going north. The bus gets into town at dark so I would suggest you stay in town for the night and look over the expensive places the next day.

Ran's Travel Lodge is a clean and pleasant place. It is directly across the field from where the bus will let you off. It is a favorite with travellers. Singles are $B17. ($8.50 US) per person or $B10. ($5. US) for a hammock on the porch.

The Sea Spray is up the road from Ran's and on the seafront. It is not as clean as Ran's but it is certainly comfortable. The rooms cost $B20. ($10. US) for a single without bath and some are $B80. ($40. US) for a double with a private bath.

Hello Hotel is right on the beach in the gorgeous white house with the bright blue trim. The rooms are clean and cheery and some have private bathrooms. They all have one tap showers. The cost is $B20 (10 US) for a single and $B35. ($17.50 US) for a double.

L. Lee Hotel is at the pier end of town. When you get to the end of the road, turn right and follow the path for about ten minutes. Do not try this in the dark. The rooms are $B25. ($12.50 US) for a single without bath and $B60. ($30. US) with bath. It is a clean and friendly place.

Miss Lydia's place is a block north of Gene's restaurant. The rooms sparkle with cleanliness, there are fans and no private bathrooms. The owner will let you purchase some of her delicious baking if you ask. This is a delightful place to spend time. If Ran's is full, try Miss Lydia.

Babe's Campground is at the pier end of town behind the Post Office. It is in a lovely spot right on the ocean. The cost is $B10. ($5. US) per tent which includes the use of a shower room.

The Cove Resort is half a mile north of town along the beach. They have four private cabins with two queen-size beds in each, private showers, lavatory and fan. They have screened porches with deck furniture and hammocks. There are two additional cabins with two units each. Each unit has its own bathroom and separate entrance. The rates are $50.00 US per person per day if meals are included and $30.00 US without meals. It is expensive, but if you need a good rest, this may be the place for you. There is also a bar here.

Turtle Inn, a little ways past the Cove Resort, has spotless thatched-roof cabins. A single is $B60. ($30. US), a double $B85. ($42.50 US), a triple $B105. ($52.50 US) and a quad $B120. ($60. US). The inn has solar panel, direct current electricity so you will not hear the hum of a generator. It is your choice whether you have meals included. The trip possibilities from here are endless. Write to Skip and Chris White, Placencia, Stann Creek District, Belize, C.A. for further information.

RESTAURANTS

Gene's is the most popular place in town. The food is good but not cheap. If you are there for breakfast, try the fried jacks with butter and honey. An excellent way to start the day. Turtle is on the menu, however it should be avoided in order to preserve the species.

Kingfisher is a large thatched roof building near the sea. The meals here are not all that cheap but it is a nice place to sit if Gene's is busy.

Tentacles is another bar overlooking the sea at the pier end of town. The sea food is spectacular but the prices are higher than usual.

The Galley serves hamburgers and chips at a reasonable price and is open all day long. The fresh juices offered here are a treat. I like the banana milkshakes for breakfast.

THINGS TO DO

This is one of the most laid-back places in the country and you should plan on being here for at least 48 hours. It will put you into shape for any type of travelling you may wish to do. The area is trying to develop some high priced tourist places but the town offers something for everyone.

The Blue Creek Caves by Blue Creek Village are exciting and beautiful. A vehicle is necessary to get there and the people at the Turtle Inn can help you. After you get to the village, it is about a 45 minute walk to the caves. The cave entrance, or first room, is spectacular and 125 feet high and 80 feet wide. The cave goes back for a few miles, but you must be fit and experienced to go very far. Take a flashlight if you want to see much beyond the entrance. This excursion can also be done from Punta Gorda and it is closer to that village. For more information, see Punta Gorda.

The Blaiden River trip is a wild, spectacular excursion that takes about three hours without stops, longer if you choose. You will see dense jungle foliage, monkeys, alligators, birds and iguanas. Again, the Turtle Inn can make arrangements for you. This trip will cost $320.00 US per day with a maximum of four people in the boat. This includes all equipment, food and transportation from Placencia. If you are a white water enthusiast, you may want to do this.

Snorkeling is good right from shore, but you can go out to some of the cayes for the day. The marine life is much more abundant here than it is around Ambergris Caye. If you go all the way to the coral reef, you will not be disappointed. There are also some diving guides in town that can take you to the better areas around the reef. If you are in need of bicycle, canoe, windsurfer or diving and snorkeling gear, you should go down the beach about a mile to Kitty's place. They have it all and if they don't, they can certainly find it.

Sea Kayaking Expeditions are offered by the Slickrock Kayak Adventure Inc., Box 1400, Moab, Utah. They offer two trips, one for 12 days at $1150.00 US per person and a 7-day package for $875.00 US per person. The trips start from the Belize airport and include camping on the cayes, all boating equipment, safety equipment, all transportation within Belize, all food, and local guides, plus any hotels needed while in transit. There are also extensions available to Tikal in Guatemala or the Jaguar Preserve in Belize.

Seine Bight Garifuna village is about three miles up the coast from Placencia. There is a place to stay in Seine Bight but it may be more comfortable in Placencia. This is an interesting way to see a way of life of people who respect privacy and their traditional lifestyles. If you go, go quietly and do not try to change their way of thinking. Walking is the best way to visit this village. Taking a boat is also a possibility but that would cost a few dollars.

PUNTA GORDA

This is not a very pleasant town but it is where the ferry arrives and leaves from if you are moving between Puerto Barrios or Livingston in Guatemala and Belize. The ferry only runs on Tuesday and Friday afternoons.

PLACES TO STAY

Foster's Hotel will cost $B10. ($5. US) per person per night. It is a dump. All the keys are mixed up in one box and if you can find a key to match one of the doors that is not occupied, then you have a room. Poor old Mr. Foster is 90 years old and it takes him longer to shuffle down the hall than it would take an inchworm to cross the Taj Mahal. The bathrooms are dirty. However, Foster's is usually open whereas most other places in town will not give you a room after dark. The bus arrives in Punta Gorda at around 7:00PM.

Lux Drive Inn on the street by the wharf, next to the customs office, is clean and pleasant. They have only double rooms for $B28. ($14. US). The rooms are pleasant enough but adjoin a bar and can be noisy in the early part of the night.

St. Charles Inn costs $B27. ($13.50 US) without bath and $B32. ($16. US) with bath. They have fans, T.V., immaculate and are highly recommended unless your finances won't permit staying here. The Inn is towards town from Foster's or the bus stop at #21 King Street. Turn left at the first street and go down to the end.

Mahungs is across the street from Billy's restaurant where the bus stops. The cost is $B21. ($10.50 US) per person without bath but the place is very clean. The owners are friendly and the place is often full. The bar across the street can be noisy.

Nature's Way Guest House is on Front Street but far down past the center of town. Keep walking for about a mile. They have a trailer that holds two people for $B20. ($10. US) per person. The upstairs rooms are $B40. ($20. US) for a double without private bath and $B80. ($40. US) for a room with a private bathroom. The place is clean, cheery, friendly and has a restaurant downstairs. The owners have many reference books about the area and a lot of general knowledge. This is a delightful place to stay.

RESTAURANTS

The best place in town is just off the town square. It does not have a name but it is at the far end of the square, on the right hand side when coming from the bus stop. The food is excellent even though the choice is limited.

Billy's Restaurant is where the bus stops. It is noisy but the owners are pleasant. The beer is better than the food.

Nature's Way Guest House is a delightful place to patronize. The food is good and varied. They offer both Belizian and Mayan foods so the adventurous will be lured in this direction. The place is clean and the atmosphere is pleasant. It has not taken long for this place to catch on.

Lucille's Kitchen is around the corner from the Mahung Hotel and has excellent food at a good price. The place is not big and the menu is not extensive but what you get is worth it. Give it a try for lunch.

THINGS TO DO

Lubaantun Ruins are about five kilometers past the town of San Pedro and then another 20 minutes up through a jungle path.

To get to San Pedro, take the bus going to Belize City from Punta Gorda and get off when the bus turns towards Belize City. You can walk the five kilometers to San Pedro or try to hitch. Check on bus schedules before you start out. It is possible to hitch a ride to San Pedro all the way from Punta Gorda if buses are not available. After reaching San Pedro, go around to the back of the church and to the left. Veer to the right, down hill and over a bridge. This will take about half an hour. There is a road going to the left, after the bridge which will take you to the ruins. The road can accommodate a vehicle part way during dry season.

Once at the ruins, ask the watchman to let you pass. The ruins are open from 8:00 AM to 5:00PM daily and visitors are not frequent. The watchman likes to tell you where things are and the stories behind them.

The main structures are along a ridge which is common for this area. The main building, already on a hill, sits 40 feet higher and has great views of Punta Gorda. The plazas and ceremonial center are from the Late Classic Period. The civilization declined around 800AD. The pyramids and residences are made from dressed or precision cut stone blocks that are not bound with mortar. Some of the corners of the buildings are rounded (similar to Mixco Viejo in Guatemala), but the temples on the pyramids have been destroyed. It is commonly believed that this is because they were made with soft materials such as wood and thatch.

The surrounding hills were obviously terraced during the time the area was densely populated and some of the objects excavated include molded whistle figurines, iron pyrite mirrors, jade beads, obsidian knives, grinding stones, fish bones and conch shells.

The word Lubaantun means "fallen stones" in Maya. This is probably what was actually seen in the late 1800's when the site was first reported to the outside world. Little restoration has occured. There are other mounds and ruins throughout the area but none have been seriously excavated. There is another unexcavated site about three miles away along the river. It is called Uxbentun which means "ancient stones" in Mayan. You can go poking around as a junior archaeologist if you wish, and you may be lucky to find something important. Just remember, you are not permitted to remove any artifacts from the country.

San Pedro Columbia is a little Mayan Indian village and if you are unable to go to Guatemala, you will get a bit of the flavor of Maya culture from here, and San Antonio. The people wear traditional clothing and the women's huipiles are similar to those of the Verapaz area of Guatemala, their area of origin. Traditional life can be seen in the way the people farm, the way the corn is ground and the manner in which the food is cooked. It is interesting to walk along the paths of the village and watch life as it has been for centuries.

Nim Li Punit Ruins are on the main road between Punta Gorda and Belize City. Take the bus going either way and ask the driver to let you off at the path. If you are going north from Punta Gorda, once you see the Whitney Lumber Mill, you must get off and take the trail going to the left. The ruins are about one kilometer in. There has been no restoration done to the area. There are no facilities so if you miss the last bus back, you will have to hitch a ride. Check on schedules before heading out.

The ruins were discovered in 1976 and are from the Late Classic Period. Known for its 25 stelae, eight of which are carved, the largest one is 31 feet tall and is the largest in Belize. It was never erected after being carved probably because of an error in the carving.

The stelae date from 700-800AD. An interesting feature of these ruins is the walled ballcourt which is not typical of this area.

Big Falls Hot Springs are on the opposite side of the highway to Nim Li Punit. They are on the Rio Grande and are the only known hot springs in Belize. The hot springs are a popular picnic spot and you may camp there if you wish. Ask directions at the general store if you wish to go there.

Pusilha Ruins are accessible only by boat as are many other unnamed ruins in this area. To get to these ruins, you must get a boat in Punta Gorda that will go up the Rio Moho, wait while you explore, and then bring you back down. In Belize, this will cost quite a bit. I know of no other way to get there.

More than 20 carved stelae have been found in the main plaza. Some of the zoomorphs have jaguars and ocelots carved into them which is not very common. I have not been to these ruins.

SAN ANTONIO

San Antonio Village can be reached by bus from Punta Gorda but you must plan on staying overnight as the bus goes up one day and returns the next.

The village has an interesting history. The Indians escaped from Guatemala in order to avoid military service and heavy taxes. When they got to Belize, they did not prosper. After deaths and disease, a few men went back to Guatemala and stole the statues from the church. They put them into their newly constructed church and life after that improved. Although the Guatemalan people wanted the religious statues returned, the Indians refused, because God had blessed them for their act.

Like San Pedro, it is nice to see the Mayan Indian culture still alive in these villages. If you are unable to get to Guatemala, this is an excellent place to visit.

PLACES TO STAY

Bol's Hilltop Hotel is basic but a very clean place to stay. There are one tap showers, shared bath and alot of friendship for only $B10. ($5. US) per person. You may also get meals here. The only drawback is that you must climb the hill to get to it.

THINGS TO DO

Uxbenka Ruins are about three miles west of San Antonio. These ruins were discovered in 1984 and has more than 20 stelae, seven of which are carved. One stelae is from the Early Classic Period, which makes it quite rare. The site sits on a scenic ridge overlooking the Maya Mountains and the village of Santa Cruz. Before the ruins or on your way back, there is a beautiful waterfall that you may stop at and have a rest. Going on this excursion will take you into the backwoods of Belize.

Blue Creek Caves are along a road going to Aguacate. Ask the bus driver to let you off at the junction and you can walk the rest of the way. This will take you all day and you will have to plan on staying at San Antonio for the night. Once you start walking down the road toward Aguacate, it will take about two hours. Once past the village of Blue Creek, cross a bridge over the river and you will see a little hut where there is a watchman. You will have to register with him.

Follow the trail along the creek for about 20 minutes until you come to a lean-to. Continue along this delightful creek which has every type of vegetation known to Belize. Always stay on the trail. It will follow a dry creek bed and then cross a rocky section. After about 20 minutes, you will see where the water flows from a box canyon forming a waterfall. It lands in a couple of pools and then eventually calms down. You can go for a dip. The cave is visible from here and you may explore it. The first room is about 125 feet high and 80 feet wide. The caves go back for a few kilometers but you must be fit and experienced to go very far. You should have a flashlight with you. Be certain that your batteries are strong. You will need food and water if you are going to do this hike.

This is one of the most beautiful and unexplored areas of Belize and I highly recommend it. Because it is difficult to get to and a lot of walking is involved, I imagine that it will stay pristine for a long time.

ST. GEORGE'S CAYE

This is only half hour by boat from Belize City. Boats may be rented by the swing bridge. This caye is the most famous historical site in Belize. In 1798, the Spanish and the British fought over the claim to Belize. The Spanish lost. British occupation lasted until 1981 when Belize became independent. Although most of the graves and tombstones have been washed away by hurricanes, this caye was the first capital in the country and remains a very important monument in Belizian history.

St. George's Lodge, at $180.00 to $210.00 US is the only place I could get any information on. Fans, fishing, boating, beach rights, restaurant, bar, resort shop, cottages, scuba diving, postal service and laundry service are provided. The price includes meals, however, I would expect room service and fur-lined toilets for that price.

The island is interesting to visit for historical purposes but certainly not to stay on. If you can share a boat with a few others, you may want to make this a day trip.

SAN IGNACIO

The town of San Ignacio has very little to offer the traveller but the excursions that can be taken from here are excellent, for both the outdoor adventurer and the archaeology buff.

The town, often called Cayo, has a sister city of Santa Elena across the Macal River.

PLACES TO STAY

There are many expensive places to stay in the area and I have not even looked at them. If you are interested in the soft adventure tours, you will certainly find a lot in this area. Enquire at Eva's Bar if these are your desires. Otherwise, stay in town.

Hi-et Hotel on #12 West Street, is a good buy at $B12. ($6. US) a single and $B15. ($7.50 US) a double. It is a clean house with a few spare rooms that the family rents out. The people are very friendly and I would highly recommend staying here. It is truly the Hyatt of San Ignacio.

Belmoral is the hotel on the corner where the buses stop. It costs $B15. ($7.50 US) for a single and $B25. ($12.50 US) for a double. There are no private baths. The lady will assure you that there is hot water in the bathroom, but don't believe her. The hotel is noisy, but quite clean.

The Central Hotel at #24 Burns Ave. is $B20. ($10. US) for a single and $B30. ($15. US) for a double. There are no private baths but there are fans in the large, airy rooms. This is the second place I would choose to stay at.

The Imperial is beside the Central and costs about the same. There are a few rooms with private bath for more money but the owners were not receptive to my poking around. Staying there as a single woman may be unpleasant, or I may have met him on a bad day.

Mike's Grand Hotel is on the Santa Elena side of town where they have cheap rooms at $B10. ($5. US) per person without private bathrooms. The price is low but so are the standard.

Jungleview Campground is on the Cristo Rey Road, about 2 kilometers past San Ignacio. It is beautifully set in the jungle. The campsites are $B10. ($5. US) for two people and $B10. ($5. US) for each additional person. Every group of two people can have their own spot at that rate. There is also a very nice, clean cabin for $B25.

($12.50 US) for two. The campsites are by the river. There is a park-like setting for those interested in bird watching. One man I spoke to had recorded over 200 species of birds in the area. Many of the birds here are migrating to or from their summer or winter nesting sites. The woods have numerous orchids. The renting of horses or canoes can be arranged from here. If you want reservations, write to Ignacio and Jeannie Aquirres, Cristo Rey Road, San Ignacio, Cayo District, Belize, C.A.

Windy Hill Cottages, Graceland Ranch has thatched-roofed cottages with private baths, hot water, and great views. They cost $50.00 US for a single and $60.00 US for a double and $10.00 US for each additional person. There is a rec-hut with table tennis, pool table, TV and hammocks. There is also a swimming pool. Tours and meals are available. The cottages are about two miles from town.

RESTAURANTS

As the tourist industry increases, so will the restaurants. There are expensive restaurants attached to the expensive hotels but they always seem uninteresting to me. Scout around San Ignacio. You may find something new that has opened since I was there last. However, the places that stand the test of time are usually the best.

Eva's Bar is the Doña Louisa of Guatemala, the Chico's Bar of Costa Rica and the center of communication in Belize. If you need anything from a group to share a jeep to information on one of the locals, this is the place. There is a well used bulletin board where you can leave or pick up messages and the food isn't that bad either. In fact, the tamales with curried chicken are a delight.

Maxims is the next best place to eat. It is a Chinese cafe, just up the street from the Belmont and the Hi-et on Far West Street. It is a bit pricey but the meals are super.

The Farmer's Emporium is under the Central Hotel and sells fresh bread. You can also get granola and yogurt, fresh orange juice and other goodies that make travel to the tropics worth while. The prices are within reach of chickenbussers.

The Place is across from the Jaguar Inn and serves typical Mexican food at a decent price.

THINGS TO DO

Caracol Ruins are considered to be equal to Tikal in Guatemala. The site is on a plateau in the Chiquibul Forest Reserve. The largest temple is 42 meters above the plaza floor and is called "Canaa" which means "sky place" in Mayan. Archaeologists believe that Tikal and Caracol were rival chiefs. Some of the carvings on the stelae indicate this. They also believe that Caracol was once a more powerful city than Tikal. The name Caracol means "snail shell". One of the unique features of this site are the tombs used for group burials, indicating the graves of lesser nobles. Caracol was inhabited from as early as 300 BC until the Late Classic Period.

To get to Caracol you need a four-wheel-drive vehicle. It is 30 miles past Augustine in the Pine Mountain Ridge. It is best to stay in San Ignacio and get a group together for this trip. You can make arrangements at Eva's Bar.

Before you can enter the site you must get permission from the Department of Archaeology in Belmopan.

Xunantunich Ruins are very well-kept, with the frieze on the main temple being the main attraction. To get to these ruins, take the Novelos bus either behind the Belmoral or in the Central Park by the police station. They will let you off at the ferry which will take you across the river. You may then walk up the fairly steep trail to the ruins in about 20 minutes. The ferry quits at 5:00PM sharp so be certain not to be late returning. The ruins take about an hour to visit and there are no refreshment stands. You will need water.

Xunantunich means "maiden of the rock" in Maya. The city was prosperous until the Late Classic Period of around 850AD. The building, called "El Castillo", is the second tallest Mayan building in Belize, standing at 130 feet above the plaza floor. The most famous frieze sits on the east side of the building and is decorated with astonomy. The one you will see is a restored version of the original one that sits underneath. From the top of El Castillo, the views are spectacular.

When looking from El Castillo towards the road going back to the ferry, the last large temple on that side has Mayan graffiti that may still be seen. (I think it says Grad 825).

Some of the objects found here include a spindle used to make thread, a jewellers shop, flint hammers and stone chisels. The ball courts at this site have not been totally excavated. The ruins of **Actuncan** are just three kilometers north of Xunantunich and it is believed that they were once a suburb of Xunantunich. There is not much there to see, but the pottery found is simular to that belonging to Xunantunich.

Ix Chel Farm is along the Panti Trail just out of San Antonio and is one of the most interesting places in Belize. San Antonio, a Mayan Indian village, is past the village of Cristo Rey. Run by Rosita and her husband, both naturopaths, this herbal research station is becoming world renowned. The Panti Trail's name originates from the path that Don Eligio Panti use to collect his medicines that he shares with his people. Rosita came to Belize in 1983 and convinced the shaman to share the secrets of plant medicine. He has agreed to do this and Rosita is recording this invaluable information.

The Panti Trail has labeled plants so the visitor can see what each one looks like. The uses for each are also given. At the beginning of the trail is the healer's hut where roots, barks and flowers are stored awaiting the needs of sick people. There are over 4000 plants in Belize and about 1500 are used by shaman like Panti for medicine.

At present, the US Cancer Institute is funding the research being done here by Rosita and her husband in the hope of finding a cure for cancer. If you happen to visit the area, please leave a small donation to ensure their work will continue.

Pine Ridge Mountain is a 515 kilometer reserve east of San Ignacio. A four-wheel-drive is needed to get there and the rental is around $150.00 US per day for up to five people. Do not believe the taxi drivers if they say they can get you there. If the area has had so much as an inch of rain the day before your trip, an ordinary vehicle cannot make it. There is a 1000 foot waterfall in the park, which is part of a river that eventually flows into the Belize River. An observation deck has been provided by the Forest Service for the tourists. Further along, the Rio On Picnic Site is a favorite swimming area for both locals and tourists.

Beyond the government campsite at Augustine, are signs pointing to caves. The Rio Frio Cave is about a mile from the camp and is spectacular. It has a 65 foot high mouth that allows enough light to the interior to see without a flashlight. You can follow the riverbed and be able to see other rock formations before coming out at the other side of the cave. It is quite a trip. There are many other caves in the area but be careful going in.

There are camping sites available at Augustine where you can make a base camp so that you can come and go for a few days. However, a car would be necessary.

Vaca Falls are about nine miles south of San Ignacio on the eastern branch of the Belize River. They are lovely with rugged karst hills extending to the banks of the river. This is a difficult trip but well worth the effort.

Canoeing is a popular outdoor adventure in the area around San Ignacio. Canoes can be rented for half a day at $25.00 US for two people. The recommended trip for experienced white water canoers is down the Mopan. A full day will cost $30.00 US for two people. The canoes available are 17-foot aluminum boats. Trips of up to five days down the Mopan and the McAll Rivers can be arranged also. The person to contact for this is Scott Cast, PO Box 48, San Ignacio, Cayo District, Belize, C.A. He supplies gear, maps and drinking water.

Horseback riding can be arranged from either the Jungleview Campground or Windy Hill Cottages. The price is quite high at $60.00 US for half a day and $100.00 US for a full day. This includes horse and guide.

If you would like to have all these adventures arranged for you before you arrive in Belize, there is a very knowledgeable man who can arrange birdwatching vacations, nature tours or adventure trips. Contact Hugh Penwarden, Box 429, Erickson, Manitoba, Canada, R0J0P0.

SOUTH WATER CAYE

This caye is 35 miles south of Belize City and is a quiet tropical paradise. There is only one lodge on the island that I know of, and it is fairly expensive. However, if you are in need of seclusion, this may be your package.

The Blue Marlin Lodge was named for the day that a beautiful 200 pound blue marlin was caught offshore. The lodge offers package deals. For eight days and seven nights at $995.00 US per person, you get two boat dives per day for six days, a room based on double occupancy with a private bath, three meals per day, day trips to Glover's Reef, Queen's Caye, Blue Hole and more. This also includes round trip transportation from Belize City to the island. For five days and four nights on a similar package, the cost is $595.00 US per person. If fishing is your thing, you may have eight days and seven nights for $1295.00 US per person. This package is the same as the diving one, but rather than diving, you fish for 6 full days. This package may also be purchased for five days and four nights at $690.00 US per person.

For further information, write to Blue Marlin Lodge, South Water Caye, Belize, C.A.

Ferry across river

CHICKENBUS TALES

CHICKENBUSES
First printed in the Prince George Citizen, 1991
Not all chickenbus rides are pleasant or entertaining. Some silently tell the stories of the hardships suffered by people in oppressed, third world countries.

The Peten is a remote northerly district of Guatemala which has an official illiteracy rate of 90%. It also has the highest crime rate, the highest infant mortality rate, the highest disease due to malnutrition rate and the highest divorce or desertion rate.

On one bus trip in the Peten, I saw a lady get on carrying a little child of about three years old. The baby was obviously suffering from malnutrition. There were scaly blotches on her skin and her hair was sparse and brittle. The child was unconscious when the mother got on the bus. The unseeing eyes were rolled back their little sockets. The mother carried a baby bottle that contained pop for the child to drink when she woke up.

While we were travelling, the baby died. Everyone on the bus was quite upset with the mother for not giving the baby milk instead of pop. The mother was devastated. Not only had she lost her baby but she was being chastised by her peers. We left her sitting on a curb in a small village, cradling the child in her arms.

I was upset and I thought about the situation for a long time. The illiterate mother had seen the advertising posters for (which are everywhere in Guatemala) for pop, showing beautiful, healthy people with straight white teeth, creamy, clear complexion and glistening hair blowing in the breeze. These healthy people are drinking bottles of pop. The mother probably wanted the same for her child. Not having much knowledge about nutrition, the mother gave her hungry child something that the child liked. It also stopped the hunger pains in the child. I believe the mother did her best. She believed the advertising posters and gave the child pop thinking it would make the child beautiful and healthy. As a result of exploitive advertising and illiteracy, a child was dead.

On another occasion, I was on a bus in the same area and saw two very clean and beautifully dressed children get on. Their shoes were shined and their hair glistened. The little fellow was about nine and he was holding his three-year-old sister in his arms who was holding a tattered little doll in her arms. The little girl fell asleep and the little boy spoke politely to the people around him. When the conductor came around to collect the fare, the little man told the conductor that he had no money. Everyone breathlessly watched to see what the conductor would do. The conductor could see that the little girl was sick with fever and he knew the children were heading for the Belizian border. He gave a sad smile to the child and let them stay on the bus.

As the boy spoke, he told us his age, his sister's age and that the sister had been sick for some time. He told us their mother was dead and he did not know where their father was. The boy said that he was going to the border town where there were relatives that would help him.

This of course was not true. Once at the border, the child would wait until dark and sneak through the mosquito-infested swamps and jungle carrying his sick little sister in his arms. If he got through safely, he would arrive in Belize and the Belizian authorities would help the children. Although Belize is as poor as Guatemala, they have better facilities for their poor people and they do not have a murderous military.

However, if the children were caught by the military in an attempted escape, their fate would be horrid. There have been numerous reports of the tortures and murders that the military commits against street kids in Guatemala.

I found it difficult to believe that humans could be as cruel as the reports I had read declared. But when I was in a town in the Peten, it was a couple of days before I could pinpoint what was different about the village from the last time I was in the vicinity. I soon realized there were no street kids around shining shoes, hustling for a few centavos or scrounging for food. Their absence was conspicuous. The stories about the military flashed through my head and I felt physically sick.

When travelling in the remote areas of a poor, oppressed country, I often see things that are extremely depressing. These visions never leave me but they do give me the incentive to work and try to keep my country from becoming the same.

COSTA RICA

Costa Rica is a beautiful, clean country with easy, hassle-free travel, but it is almost too late to go there. It has been discovered. However, if you need a rest or have only a few weeks holidays, then this is the place to go. There are many inexpensive excursions to Costa Rica.

Not only is travel easy and civilized, but the beaches are spectacular and plentiful, second to none. I could not begin to visit all the Pacific and Caribbean beaches that Costa Rica has to offer, but a nice trip would be to walk the coast of the Nicoya Peninsula. Camping is available along the way and many places offer showers for a few dimes (it used to be pennies before Costa Rica was discovered). Several parks have every type of jungle animal imaginable, including seven species of poisonous snakes. Although conservation is a serious concern of the Costa Ricans, there is still room for improvement. For example, construction of new tourist accommodations on the mountain in Manuel Antonio is destroying the mountain and the scenery.

Climbing volcanos in Costa Rica is a favorite pastime for both locals and travellers. Visiting many of the well-organized museums is also a must. Then, for leisure, one may enjoy the superb restaurants available everywhere in Costa Rica. Because Costa Rica is so clean, one can eat the food from almost anywhere and even drink the water in the bigger centers.

Costa Rica claims to have more teachers than policemen. This makes it the most literate of all the Central American countries. The policemen are unarmed. Politically, it is sound and has made more effort at promoting peace than any other country in the area. The army was abolished in 1948. However they do have a National Guard who could be assembled within a very short time for the purpose of national defence. The National Guard is trained and equipped in US fashion. I feel that Costa Rica is safer than most North American cities of over one million people and would recommend it for anyone.

HISTORY

Costa Rica does not have a very long history. There was an Indian population from around 1000AD until the Spanish colonization. The Indians were assimilated into the Spanish culture and, today, of Costa Rica's population, only about .27% (less than 1%) is pure Indian.

Columbus arrived in 1502, at the port of Cariari, today called Limon. The lure of gold to the north and south caused the Spaniards to move on.

Seven years later, Hernan Ponce de Leon and Juan de Castaneda, both Spanish explorers, made their first journey along

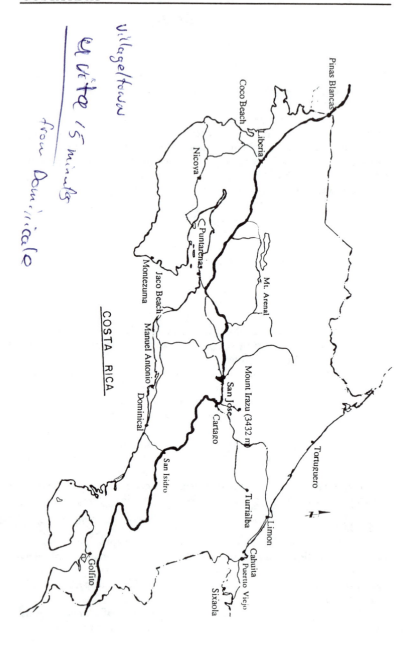

Villageltown
Uvita 15 minutes
from Dominicale

the Pacific Coast and then explored the Nicoya Peninsula. However, Ponce de Leon went over to Puerto Rico and became governor from 1510 to 1512. Later, looking for the fountain of youth, he continued his explorations in the direction of Florida.

While Pedrarias was trying to bring control to the entire Central American area, an unknown explorer called Espinoza headed an expedition up the Gulf of Nicoya. During this time the first Spaniards settled in Costa Rica. Since Pedrarias was more interested in Nicaragua, he concentrated on settling that area first. In 1522, an adventurer names Gil Gonzalez Davila went inland into Costa Rica. He was welcomed by the Indians and was rewarded with a good supply of gold.

In 1524, Francisco Fernandez de Cordoba founded a little village on the Nicoya Peninsula. However, he also was not interested in this area and continued on to Nicaragua. It was not until 1539 that Cordoba, impressed by the rich vegetation and abundant wild life, named the area "Costa Rica" or the Rich Coast.

However, because of the lack of gold, colonization of the area was of no interest to the early explorers. In 1560, Juan de Cavallon penetrated the jungles of Costa Rica and started to colonize the country. Finally, in 1564, Juan Vasquez de Coronado founded the city of Cartago just outside the present city of San Josè. The city of Cartago became the capital of the colony. Coronado became the first governor. A year later, Coronado became the Mayor of Costa Rica and New Cartago.

During the 1600's, Costa Rica became populated with Spanish settlers, English pirates along the Caribbean coast and some Mosquitia Indians from Nicaragua. However, because Spain put strict commercial restrictions on the country, economic progress was slow and difficult.

As an incentive for development, land was given to anyone who was interested in growing and exporting coffee. Settlement increased and the land was developed. Thomas de Acosta is credited for bringing the first coffee plants to the country. After plantations were established and coffee production was stabilized, the coffee was transported from the midlands to Puntarenas on the Pacific coast and then shipped by boat around South America or overland across Panama. From the early days of coffee export, some families became richer than others and a class system developed. This still exists in Costa Rica today.

Later, when the Central American countries wanted independence from Spain, Costa Rica joined them in the incorporated General Capitancy of Guatemala. In 1821, when the General Capitancy dismantled, they joined Iturbide's Mexican empire. Because of poor communications and differing interests, Costa Rica withdrew from the union. Costa Rica then joined the United Provinces of Central America.

In 1823, Cartago, then the capital of Costa Rica, experienced differences with the neighboring San Josè and a political struggle took place. San Josè won and became the capital of the country. San Josè also established the country's constitution.

Juan Mora Fernandez became the first Chief of State and is credited with establishing the first bank in the country and starting the first public schools. Mora also recruited an army of volunteers to chase out William Walker and his filibusters who were trying to form a slavery empire in Central America. Walker was chased back to Nicaragua where he was defeated at Rivas. The national hero of Costa Rica is Juan Santamaria who, as a young boy, volunteered to torch the building where Walker and his men were. Although it was successful, it was a suicide mission.

The last battle fought in Costa Rica was in 1948. The army was controlled by a defeated political party. They battled against the elected officials led by another hero, Josè Figueres. This man tried to prevent future military insurrection by passing a law that allows the president only one term of office. He also disbanded the army.

Today, Costa Rica boasts that it has had forty-four years of free, democratic elections. Oscar Arias, the last president of the country, presented a peace plan for Central America which was adopted with a few modifications. This effort earned him the Nobel Peace Prize in 1987. Costa Rica is very proud of its peaceful reputation.

FACTS

The government of Costa Rica is democratic, and the country has had a constitution since November 7, 1949. The president must be of Costa Rican birth, and over the age of thirty and is elected for a four-year term. He is assisted by two vice presidents and a board of ministers. A second term is not allowed for either the president nor the legislature.

The **Legislative Assembly** consists of 57 congressmen. The provinces are divided into 81 counties which are in turn divided into 415 districts. The Governors of the provinces are appointed by the president. The Council of Government enforces federal laws, conducts foreign affairs and, in general, keeps tabs on the legislature.

The **Judicial** power is based in the Supreme Court. Its seventeen members are elected by the Legislature for a minimum of eight years. The Supreme Court appoints the judges for the lesser courts. The Civil Guard maintains law and order in the country.

Everyone over eighteen is allowed to vote and the government pays for the election campaign costs. The two main parties in Costa Rica are the National Liberation Party and the Christian Socialist United Party. There are many smaller independent parties including a small communist organization. However, the communist party in Costa Rica is not popular.

The **area** of Costa Rica is just under 52,000 square kilometers (20,000 square miles) with 615 kilometers (380 miles) of Pacific coastline and 210 kilometers (130 miles) of coastline on the Caribbean side. At its most narrow part, Costa Rica is only 113 kilometers (70 miles) across; 65% of Costa Rica's borders are on one of the oceans. The three main water drainage systems in Costa Rica are Lake Nicaragua, the Caribbean, and the Pacific Ocean.

Costa Rica is very **mountainous** with the Guanacaste, the Central and the Talamanca ranges running north and south through the country. The central valley has about 3000 square kilometers (1200 square miles) of land and contains the majority of the three million inhabitants of the country. This is also the location of most of the coffee plantations.

The **major volcanos** in the country are Mt. Poas at 2708 meters (8885 feet), Irazu at 3432 meters (11,260 feet), Barva Volcano at 1906 meters (9500 feet) and Turrialba at 3339 meters (10,955 feet). The tallest mountain in the country is Chirripo Grande which stands at a majestic 3819 meters (12,530 feet).

There are three **climatic regions** in Costa Rica. The Caribbean lowlands are hot and humid. Rainfall is between 380 to 510 centimeters (150 to 200 inches) per year, often falling in torrential flash floods. The daytime temperature is around 38°C (100°F). The Pacific strip is much drier and cooler with temperatures ranging from 24°C to 38°C (75°F - 100°F) Rainfall is almost half that of the Caribbean. The Central Highland is the most fertile and pleasant area. Daytime temperatures are between 24°C - 27°C (75°F - 80°F) and very seldom is there more than 190 centimeters (75 inches) of rain per year. Some of the volcanos are over 3000 meters (10,000 feet) in this area, which results in a cool daytime temperature. The Pacific coast has about one hour of rain per day during rainy season and is a nice place to visit at any time of year, but especially December to April. The Caribbean is best visited from July to December.

Costa Rica's **population** is three million peoples, mostly of European stock. Of the Caribbean coast population, 35% is Negro. The native Indian population has been reduced to 0.27%. The pre-Columbian population consisted of the Chorotega, Huetare and Boruca Indians. Today, less than 20,000 natives live on reserves, with the most popular being the Talamanco Indian Reserve just past Bribri in the southeastern region of the country. Other groups are the Guatusos in the province of Alajuela, the Cabecar and Bribri in the province of Limon, the Boruea and Terrabas in Puntarenas and the Nicoya in Guanacaste. There are also a few Quitirrisi and Puriscal in the San Josè province. However, the native culture is not visible. I was on the Caribbean coast talking to a native fellow for days before he told me that he was one of the few natives. He then went on to say that discrimination against the Indian and the Negro was prominent in Costa Rica.

81

Costa Rica's **national flag** has five horizontal stripes of blue, white, red, white and blue. The national anthem is "Noble Homeland, Your Beautiful Flag". The official religion of the country is Catholic, but there are other religions including Protestants, Jewish and some eastern religions.

Costa Rica claims to have a 93% **literacy** rate. This is very high in comparison to the rest of the countries in Central America. All Costa Rican children must complete elementary school but many go far beyond that. Since the 1970s, 28% of the national budget is used for education. 70% of secondary education is received in public schools. The University of Costa Rica was founded in 1940 and is highly regarded by other countries in Central America. Many North American students study in this university. In the 1970s, the National University of Heredia, the Technological University of Cartago and the University by Correspondence were formed and all are operated by the government. In 1977, the Autonomous University of Central America was formed, and it is operated in a similar fashion to North American universities. Its liberal entrance requirements make higher education more attainable for the poorer students in Costa Rica.

Costa Rica has a national **Social Security System** which provides health insurance that covers disability, maternity, and old-age pensions. There are 44 hospitals in the country which are supervised by the government. Because of a fairly decent health system, Costa Ricans can now expect to live to about 74 years of age; this far exceeds the 40 year expectancy age of a century earlier. The infant mortality rate is down from 25.6% in 1966 to 12% in 1986. This is a great improvement.

Costa Rica has 29 **National Parks** covering 530,000 hectares or 12% of the total country. These areas provide shelter for about 12,000 varieties of plants, 237 animals, 848 different types of birds and 361 native amphibians and reptiles. These parks include deciduous forests, mangrove swamps, rain forests, marshes, cloud forests, coral reefs plus many types of forests that are less common. There are also volcanoes, caves and hot water springs. There are beautiful beaches, archaeological sites, waterfalls and rivers in these parks. The sea turtles are a constant attraction as are the pelicans and frigate birds that nest in the country. The sea turtle preserves were the first in Latin America. Today, the turtles are safe on Costa Rican land but once they venture further north, the Mexicans indiscriminately kill them.

Costa Rica has legalized **gambling** and there are a number of casinos in the country. They do not have the number of people that are attracted to Las Vegas every year, but the rooms are a hub of excitement.

LAWS

Costa Rica is very strict about **drug peddling.** Their law states that "Selling, industrialization, fabrication, refining, transformation, extraction, preparation, production, importation, exportation, prescription, dispensing or storing of these habit-producing substances and their byproducts...... will result in a jail sentence of eight to twenty years." The law does not say what will happen to users, but Napoleonic Law is in effect in Costa Rica; this means you are guilty until proven innocent. The prison sentence is eight to twenty years but I imagine a few years would be added on to this time while waiting to get to trial. Even though Costa Rica is a very progressive country as compared to its neighbors, it still has terrible prison conditions as compared to ours. Twenty years is a long time.

A foreign valid **driver's licence** is good in Costa Rica for up to three months. However, extensions can be obtained. Insurance is mandatory and may be purchased at points of entry. Costa Ricans must be 18 or older, or married to get a driver's licence. Foreigners must be over 21 in order to drive in Costa Rica. Those over 13 may obtain a permit to drive a motorbike of up to 90 cc.

To obtain a Costa Rican licence, you have to go to the Direccion de Transporte Automotor at Ave. 18 and Calle 5 in San Josè and fill out an application. You must then take your passport to the San Juan de Dios hospital and have a physical examination. Upon presentation of your medical certificate, passport, four photos of yourself and your valid foreign driver's licence, you will be issued a local permit. However, this is not necessary for just a few weeks when visiting and renting a car.

Seat belts must be used by the driver and any front seat passengers driving in a car. Helmets are required on motorcycles. Highway speed limits are 80 km/hr; infractions are punishable by heavy fines. Hit the old pocket book for best results and it works every time. Right turns are not permitted at red lights unless there is a white painted arrow on the street where the turn is to occur.

Parking is not permitted when the curb is painted yellow, in front of official areas, hospitals or play areas. Parking violations can result in the loss of the vehicle.

Dogs and cats should not be brought into the country without first obtaining a permit. The form, obtained from the Zoonosis Dept. of the Ministry of Health, must contain the name, address and passport number of the tourist importing the animal. The animal's characteristics must be recorded with the destination, date of entry, and how the animal will travel while in the country. The cost is (colones) ¢2.00. The application must be accompanied by an affidavit, signed by a veterinarian, which states that the animal has been vaccinated against rabies no less than 30 days nor more than three years years from the date of the request. There must be a certificate stating that the animal is free from parasites, distemper, hepatitis, leptospirosis and gastroenteritis. Each certificate must be accompanied with a particular stamp, each of which costs a few more colones. If after all this you still wish to bring your pet into Costa Rica, write to the Dept. de Zoonosis, P.O. Box 10, 123, San Josè, Costa Rica, C.A.

Fishing and hunting licences are required if you wish to indulge in these sports. You must present your passport, tourist card, two passport-sized photos plus $10.00 US for each licence.

It is illegal to take **coral or sea shells** from park areas. The collection of plants is also illegal. You have to obtain a permit to stay overnight in park boundaries. Do not buy black coral from anyone except reputable dealers; if it was picked illegally, you will be charged with an offense.

MONEY

The currency of the country is the colon. There are 100 centavos to a colon. The American dollar is worth about ₵1.35 on the street and the American traveller's cheques are accepted by almost anyone. The Canadian dollar brings less than 1:1 at the bank and it is impossible to change Canadian or any other foreign currency on the street. Banco Lyon on Calle 2, Ave. Central in San Josè is the only bank that will accept Canadian currency and British sterling. However, the places out of town will not change any money except American. A few years ago, the National Bank of Costa Rica would change Canadian money but the last time I went in, they assured me they could only change Canadian money if it was from the Bank of America! Be certain to have American dollars. Most hotels in the resort areas will exchange American traveller's cheques. Costa Rica is the worst country in Central America for recognizing foreign currency.

All major **credit cards** are accepted in the higher class hotels, restaurants and shops in Costa Rica, but you can not use your bank card to withdraw money from home. You must make a bank transfer at your bank. Most major banks are represented in Costa Rica.

VISAS

Tourists from Canada or the United States may travel without a valid passport but must get a tourist card which costs $2.00 US. The person applying must have a birth certificate and a picture ID card. If your passport is current, the tourist card is not necessary. The tourist card or visa is available when entering the country. Citizens of the following countries do not need a visa and may remain in the country for a period of 60 days:

Argentina	Israel
Austria	Italy
Canada	Japan
Colombia	Luxemburg
Denmark	Northern Ireland

Finland	Norway
Finland	Norway
France	Romania
Great Britain	South Korea
Holland	Spain

Citizens of the following countries may remain in Costa Rica for 30 days with a tourist card:

Australia	Mexico
Belgium	Monaco
Brazil	New Zealand
Guatemala	Sweden
Iceland	United States
Ireland	Vatican
Liechenstein	Venezuela

Citizens of the following countries must have a visa before entering Costa Rica and it is advisable to apply before arriving. The cost of a visa is $20.00 US.

Andorra	Haiti
Bahamas	Jamaica
Barbados	Malta
Belize	Martinique
Bermuda	Morocco
Chile	Paraguay
China	San Marino
Cyprus	Santa Lucia
Dominican Republic	Saudi Arabia
Granada	St. Vincent
Greece	Surinam
Guadalupe	Tobago
Guyana	Trinidad

Upon leaving, you must purchase an **exit visa** equal to ¢313 or the equivalent amount in US dollars. If leaving with any other status than tourist, the cost is ¢2810. If you have overstayed your time period, the cost is ¢320 per month, or part thereof, plus the cost of the additional visa. If children have overstayed, they must obtain permission from the National Infancy Protection Agency for permission to leave.

A **transit visa** is available for those staying less than 48 hours and the cost is ¢63 per person.

If you enter the country with your own car or boat and wish to leave the vehicle in the country, you must either pay a heavy duty or leave the vehicle with the Customs House or a bonded warehouse.

Personal effects may be brought into the country without question. Six rolls of film are allowed with any reasonable amount of camera gear and all camping gear is allowed. Guns for hunting and all fishing equipment are allowed into the country. Medicines and special foods may also be brought. However, Costa Rica has "communist paranoia" to the extreme and any communist literature or writing will be confiscated. I had a book about an African tennis player; the border guards tried to confiscate it. Apparently, if you are black and have a beard you must be a communist. It is mandatory to present your bags for inspection at customs in Costa Rica.

Those wishing to **retire** in Costa Rica must have a guaranteed pension of $600.00 US per month. There are other laws that have made it more difficult to immigrate. The best bet would be to talk to other pensioners living in the country before making a decision about moving. One of the laws that make living in the country difficult is that you are not allowed to take any profits out of the country. When thinking about inheritance, this may be an important factor. **Time shares** are now a big thing in Costa Rica. The minimum investment that is considered is $25,000.00 US and the profit law also applies to this type of investment.

GETTING THERE

If coming from **Nicaragua** by bus, you may come by either TICA bus or by Sirca Express. However, you must have a ticket out of the country before you will be allowed entry. This is not stringently checked but it is cheaper to have an exit ticket from a bus company of your choice than have to purchase one that the border guards demand. Buses leave Nicaragua daily; it may be necessary to book your seat in advance. There are money changers on both sides of the border.

If coming from **Nicaragua by boat** through the San Juan River, you must have all documents completed by the police in San Carlos before venturing up the river. There is a border post on the Costa Rican side, just past El Castillo. However beautiful, this is a very expensive trip. When enquiring in Tortuguero, the cost was around $700.00 US for a boat. This price would include a few people.

If coming **from Panama**, along the main highway at Canoas, the crossing is busy and requires an exit ticket. TICA bus is the most popular bus and the trip takes about 18 hours from Panama City to San Josè. However, you may also chickenbus down and across for a much cheaper price. This also provides the option of dividing the trip into a few days.

If crossing at **Bribri** along the Caribbean, the crossing is easy; not much is checked other than your passport. This is a great crossing for those going to Panama to shop. You must walk along a railroad bridge across no-man's-land. There are no Costa Rican buses that cross this border and chickenbusing is the name of the game. There are money changers at this border, but they are not as numerous as at the Nicaraguan border.

If **entering Costa Rica by plane** a number of airlines offer excursions into the country at a low price. The onward ticket rule is also in effect at the airport. The rule is not consistently enforced but this can change from day to day. Once outside the terminal, take a bus that passes close to the door on your left. (This is the entrance door to the airport.) Take bus #200 A or B; it will take you down town on Ave. 2 and it stops across from La Merced church on Calle 12. The cost is only 40 centavos. The return bus to the airport is #12 and it stops on Ave. 2 across from La Merced Church. There are banks and money changers at the airport; money changers only change cash.

CONSULATES

Most consulates close at 1:00PM so do your business early in the morning. There are other consulates in the country but I have listed only the Central and North American ones. Most people in the consulates do not speak English; if possible, take a Spanish speaking friend with you. However, consulate employees are accustomed to non-Spanish speaking people and will often be able to communicate with hand signals.

Guatemalan Embassy - Calle 24/28, Ave. 1,
Tel. 22-8991
Honduran Embassy - Calle 2, Ave. Central/2
Tel. 22-2145
Nicaraguan Embassy - Ave. Central, Calle 25/27
Tel. 33-4479
Canadian Consulate - Calle 3, Ave. Central, Tel. 23-0446
El Salvadorian Consulate - Calle 5, Ave. Central, Tel.
22-5536
American Embassy - Apt. 10053, in the suburb of Pavas.
Tel. 20-3939
Panamanian Consulate, San Pedro
(take bus to el Higueròn), Tel. 25-3401

PUBLIC HOLIDAYS

During Holy Week and Christmas week, almost everything, including the banks, is on holidays. Be certain to have extra cash and reserve snacks although the big hotels are always open for meals. Bus travelling is not reliable during Christmas and Easter week. You must check with the bus companies as to when their first and last bus will be travelling.

Costa Ricans have more holidays than Canadians do! There are also special days for special regions. If there is a holiday in a region, I have tried to include it in the information on that specific area.

January 1	New Year's Day
March 19	St. Joseph's Day
March/April	Easter - at least three days

April 11	Juan Santamaria or Battle of Rivas Day
May 1	Labor Day
June (changes)	Corpus Christi Day
June 29	St. Peter & St. Paul Day
July 25	Guanacaste Day
August 2	Virgin of Los Angeles Day
August 15	Mother's Day
September 15	Independence Day
October 12	Columbus Day
December 8	Holy Conception Day
December 25	Christmas Day

BUSES

Transportation in Costa Rica is a pleasure. There are many buses, usually with seats available. The people do not.push and shove. They love to spend time talking while travelling and you will meet many pleasant people. Drunks are not much of a problem and theft is still at a minimum.

Buses from San Josè to:

Alajuela (airport)	Calle 12/14, Ave. 2 Tuasa Bus Co.	Every 15 minutes from 6:00AM - 10:30PM 16 Km. - 20 minutes

This bus goes to the airport. There is a bus every hour on the half hour from midnight to 6:00AM and it leaves from Calle 2, Ave. 2.

Arenal Volcano (Fortuna)	Calle 16, Ave. 1/3 Coca Cola Bus Stn. 130 Km. - 4 1/2 hours	Dep. 6:15AM Ret. 2:45PM

Barva-research Coffee Center	Take bus from Heredia, 2 blocks north of Central Park	Dep. every 15 minutes from 5:00AM to 10:00PM daily

Braulio Carrillo National Park	Calle 12, Ave. 7/9 30 Km., 35 minutes (catch bus on freeway to return)	Dep. every 45 minutes from 5:30AM to 7:00PM daily Ret. same

Canoas (south border)	Ave. 18, Calle 2/4 349 Km., 8 hours daily	Dep. 5:00, 7:30AM, 1:00,4:30,& 6:00PM Ret. 4:00,7:30,9:00AM & 2:45PM daily

Cartago	Calle 13, Ave. Central/2 22 Km. - 45 minutes	Dep. every 10 minutes from 5:00AM to 7:00PM
Cañas	Calle 16, Ave. 3/5 188 Km., 3 hours	Dep. 8:30,10:30 AM, 1:30, 2:15 & 4:30PM Ret. 4:30, 5:25, 9:15AM 12:30 & 2:00PM daily
Cahuita	See Sixaola or take a bus from Limon	
David, Panama	Calle 2/4, Ave. 18 400 Km. 9 hours	Dep. 7:30 AM daily Ret. 7:30 AM daily
Golfito	Calle 2/4, Ave. 18 339 Km., 8 hours	Dep. 7:00AM & 3:00PM daily Ret. 5:00AM & 3:00PM daily
Heredia	Calle 1, Ave. 7/9 microbuses & Ave 2, Calle 10/12	Dep. every 10 minutes, daily, 5:00AM to 10:00PM Dep. every 15 minutes, daily from 12:00PM to 6:00AM
Irazu volcano	Calle 1/3, Ave. 2 in front of the Gran Hotel 54 Km. 1 1/2 hrs.	Sat.,Sun.,& holidays at 7:30AM Ret. 1.30PM
La Cruz	Calle 16 Ave. 3/5 293 Km., 6 hours beside Cocori Hotel	Dep. 5:00, 7:45AM & 4:15PM daily Ret. 7:15, 10:30AM 3:30PM daily
Liberia	Calle 14, Ave. 1/3 217 Km., 4 hours	Dep.7:00,9:00,11:30AM 1:00,3:00,4:00,6:00& 8:00PM daily Ret. 4:30,6:00,7:30AM 12:30,2:00,4:00,6:00 8:00PM daily
Limon	Calle 19/21, Ave. 3 162 Km. 2 1/2 hours	Dep. every hour from 5:00AM to 7:00PM Ret. is the same

Managua	Tica Bus, Calle 9/11 Express, 450 Km. - 11 hrs. Sirca Bus, Calle 7, Ave. 6/8 Express, 450 Km. 11 hrs.	Dep. 7:00AM, Mon. Wed., Fri. & Sat. Dep. 5:00AM, Wed., Fri. Sun., Ret., 6:30AM, Mon., Wed., Fri.
Manuel Antonio National Park	Calle 16, Ave. 1/3 145 Km., 3 1/2 hours	Dep. 6:00, 12:00AM & 6:00PM daily Ret. 6:00, 12:00AM & 5:00PM daily
Monteverde Cloud Forest (Santa Elena)	Calle 14, Ave. 9/11 167 Km. 3 1/2 hours	Dep. Mon to Thur at 2:30PM, Sat. at 6:30AM Ret. Tues to Thurs at 6:30AM and Fri & Sun at 3:00PM
Nicoya	Calle 14, Ave. 3/5 296 Km, 6 hours	Dep. 6:00,8:00, 10:00AM, 12:00,1:00, 2:30, 3:00 & 5:00PM Ret. 4:00,7:30,9:00AM 12:00,2:30 &4:00PM
Panama City	Tica Bus, Calle 9/11, Ave.4 Express, 903 Km., 20 hours	Dep. 8:00PM daily Ret. 11:00AM daily
Peñas Blancas	Calle 16, Ave. 3/5 beside Cocori Hotel 293 Km., 6 hours	Dep. 5:00, 7:45AM & 4:15PM daily Ret. 7:15, 10:30AM & 3:30PM daily
Poas Volcano	Calle 12 Ave. 2/4 34 Km. 1 1/2 hours During the week you may also take a bus to Alajuela and then another bus to San Pedro de Poas and then a taxi or hitch to the top.	Dep. Sundays and holidays at 8:30AM Ret. 2:30PM
Puerto Viejo	Calle 12, Ave. 7/9 97 Km., 4 hours	Dep. 7:00, 9:00AM, 1:00, 4:00 & 5:00PM Ret. 9:00AM, 12:00 & 2:00PM daily

Puntarenas	Calle 12, Ave. 7/9 110 Km., 2 hours	Dep. every 40 minutes from 6:00AM to 7:00PM daily Ret. same
Quepos	Calle 16, Ave. 1/3 140 Km., 5 hours	Dep. 7:00, 10:00AM, 2:00 & 4:00PM Ret. 5:00, 8:00AM 2:00 & 4:00PM
Quesada (via San Carlos)	Calle 16, Ave. 1/3 Coca Cola Bus Stn. 110 Km. - 3 hours	Dep. Every hour from 5:00AM to 7:30PM
Quesada-Arenal-	Calle 16, Ave. 1/3	Dep. 6:00 & 3:00PM
Tilaran	This bus goes around the lake & volcano 101 Km. 4 Hours	Ret. 7:00AM & 1:00PM
Rio Frio (Saratiqui)	Calle 12, Ave. 7/9 97 Km., 4 hours	Dep. 7:00, 9:00AM & 1:00,4:00 & 5:00PM Ret. 9:00AM, 12:00& 2:00PM daily
San Isidro del General	Calle 16, Ave. 1/3 136 Km., 3 hours	Dep. every hour from 5:30 AM to 5:00PM daily Ret. same hours
Santa Cruz	Calle 20, Ave. 1/3 274 Km. 5 hours	Dep. 7:30, 10:30 AM, 2:00, 4:00, 6:00PM Ret. 4:30, 6:30, 8:30 11:30AM & 1:00PM daily
Sarchi	Calle 16, Ave. 1/3 170 Km, 1 1/2 hours	Dep. 12:15 & 5:30PM Ret. 5:30, 6:15AM & 1:45PM
Saratiqui	See Rio Frio	
Tilaran	Calle 14, Ave. 9/11 191 Km., 4 hours	Dep. 7:30AM,12:45, 3:45 & 6:30PM daily Ret. 7:00, 7:45AM 2:00 & 5:00PM daily

91

Sixaola - Cahuita	Calle Central /1 and Ave. 11, 195 Km., 4 hrs.	Dep. 6:00AM, 2:30PM 4:30PM daily Ret. 5:00, 8:00 & 2:30PM daily
Turrialba	Calle 13, Ave. 6/8 65 Km. 2 hours	Dep. every hour from 6:00AM to 10:00PM Ret. same
Zarcero	Calle 16, Ave. 1/3 Coca Cola Bus Stn. 77 Km. 1 1/2 hours	Dep. every hour from 5:00AM to 7:30PM

TO THE BEACHES:

Brasilito	Calle 20, Ave. 3 320 Km. 6 hours From Santa Cruz 64 km.	Dep. 10:30AM daily Ret. 9:00AM daily Dep. 6:30AM &3:00PM Ret. 9:00AM & 5:00PM
Carrillo	From Nicoya 45 minutes	Dep. Mon-Fri at 3:00PM, Sat. & Sun. at 8:00AM Ret. Mon - Fri at 6:00AM, Sat & Sun at 2:00PM
Coco Beach	Calle 14, Ave. 1/3 251 Km., 5 hours	Dep. 10:00AM daily
Conchal Beach	This is within walking distance from Brasilito	
Dominical	Quepos Terminal 80 Km. 3 1/2 hours	Dep. 5:30AM & 1:30PM daily Ret. 7:00AM & 1:30PM daily
Flamingo	Calle 20, Ave. 3 320 Km. 6 hours From Santa Cruz 64 Km.	Dep. 10:30AM daily Ret. 9:00AM daily Dep. 6:30AM & 3:00PM Ret. 9:00AM & 5:00PM
Garza	From Nicoya 65 Km.	Dep. 1:00PM daily Ret. 6:00AM daily

Guiones	From Nicoya	Dep. 1:00PM daily Ret. 6:00AM daily
Hermosa Beach	Calle 12, Ave. 5/7 in front of Los Rodriguez From Liberia	Dep. 3:30PM daily Ret. 5:00AM daily Dep. 11:30AM & 7:30PM Ret. 5:00AM & 4:00PM daily
Jaco Beach	Calle 16, Ave. 1/3 Express 102 Km., 2 1/2 hours	Dep. 7:15AM & 3:30PM Ret. 5:00AM & 3:00PM daily
Junquillal Beach	Calle 20, Ave. 3 298 Km. - 5 hours From Santa Cruz	Dep. 2:00PM daily Ret. 5:00AM daily Dep. 6:30 PM daily Ret. 5:00AM daily
Matapalo	Calle 20, Ave. 3 320 Km. 6 hours	Dep. 10:30AM daily Ret. 9:00 AM daily
Montezuma	Boat from Puntarenas to Paquera; the bus meets the boat	Dep. 6:00AM & 3:00PM daily Ret. 8:00AM & 5:00PM daily
Nosara Beach	From Nicoya 65 Km.	Dep. 1:00PM daily Ret. 6:00AM daily
Palmar Norte	Calle 2/4, Ave. 18 258 Km., 5 hours	Dep. 5:00,6:30,8:30 10:00AM & 2:30 & 6:00PM daily Ret. 5:30, 8:30AM & 3:00PM
Panama Beach	Calle 12, Ave. 5/7 in front of Los Rodriguez From Liberia	Dep. 3:30PM daily Ret. 5:00AM daily Dep. 11:30AM & 7:30 PM daily Ret. 5:00AM & 4:00PM
Portrero	Calle 20, Ave. 3 320 Km. - 6 hours From Santa Cruz 64 Km.	Dep. 10:30AM daily Ret. 9:00AM daily Dep. 6:30AM & 3:00PM Ret. 9:00AM & 5:00PM

Samara Beach	Calle 14, Ave. 3/5 331 Km., 6 Hours	Dep. Mon-Fri at 3:00PM, Sat. & Sun. at 8:00AM Ret. Mon - Fri at 6:00 AM, Sat. & Sun at 2:00PM
	Express	Dep. daily at noon Ret. daily at 4:00AM
Tamarindo	Calle 20, Ave. 3 320 Km. - 6 hours The return bus goes to Santa Cruz first and then you must transfer or	Dep.4:00PM daily Ret. 6.45AM daily
	Calle 14, Ave. 3/5 285 Km. 5 1/2 hours (this is a different route) From Santa Cruz	Dep. 3:30PM daily Ret. 5:45AM daily Dep. 8:30AM daily Ret. 6:45AM daily

From other destinations to:

Cahuita	From Limon 45 Km. 1 hour	Dep. daily at 5:00, 10:00AM, 1:00, 4:00PM Ret. 5:00, 8:00, 10:00AM & 3:00PM
Fortuna	Quesada bus terminal Goes through El Tanque 40 Km. 1 hour	Dep. 6:00, 9:30AM, 1:00, 3:00, 6:00PM Ret. 6:00, 7:00, 9:30 10:00AM, 1:00, 2:30 4:00PM
Fraijanes	3 blocks west of central market in Alajuela	Dep. Tues. to Fri. 1:00AM, 4:15PM & 6:15PM Ret. Tues to Fri. 6:00, 10:00AM,2:00 & 5:00PM
Guayabo	From Turrialba 19 Km. 1 hour	Dep. Mon. to Sat. at 5:00PM
Lankaster Gardens	From Cartego 8 Km., 15 minutes	Dep. daily every 30 minutes from 4:30AM to 10:30PM

Liberia	From Puntarenas 150 Km., 2 1/2 hours	Dep. 5:30PM daily Ret. 8:30AM daily
Orosi Valley	From Cartago, 1 block east and 3 blocks south of church ruins 18 Km. 30 minutes	Dep. Mon. to Fri. every 1 1/2 hours from 6:00AM to 10:00PM Ret. from 4:30AM to 6:30PM - same as dep.
Puerto Jimenez	From San Isidro-by church 250 Km., 5 hours From Golfito by boat from the docks	Dep. 5:30AM & noon Ret. 3:30 & 11:00AM daily Dep. 12:00 noon daily Ret. 6:00AM daily
San Josè	16 Km. 20 minutes from Alajuela	Dep. every 15 minutes from 6:00AM to 10:30PM
San Isidro	Quepos Terminal 80 Km. 3 1/2 Hours	Dep. 5:30AM & 1:30PM daily Ret. 7:00AM & 1:30PM daily
Santa Elena	From Puntarenas	Dep. daily at 2:00PM Ret. daily at 6:00AM
Sarchi	Alajuela, Calle 8, Ave. Central/1 152 Km. 1 1/2 hours	Every half hour from 5:00AM to 10:00PM
Tilaran	From Santa Elena 40 Km., 3 hours This is a very bad road.	Dep. daily at 7:00PM Ret. daily at 12:30PM

TRAINS

The famous jungle train from San Josè to Limon is no longer running. There was an earthquake that dropped tons of earth and rock on the track, and the government does not want to repair this damage. It was a delightful trip in days past.

The electric train to Puntarenas is not as historical as that to Limon, but it certainly is as beautiful. It travels through small villages which are inaccessible by car or bus. The most spectacular section of the ride is through the Barranca valley. The train travels along a deep gorge, around steep ridges and through many tunnels. It is breathtaking both in scenery and in excitement (or fear). The train leaves the station at Ave. 20 and Calle 2 at 6:00AM and 1:00PM every day except Sundays. The cost is about ₡200 (1.50 US) per person and the trip is much more pleasant and scenic than the bus. Highly recommended.

FERRIES

Ferries from **Puntarenas** run all day long. The ferry to Paquera which will eventually take you to the bus and taxi to Montezuma leaves from Los Platanos Docks in Puntarenas at 6:00AM and 3:00PM daily. The ferry returns at 8:00AM and 5:00PM daily. Phone 61-28-30 if further information is required.

The ferry to **Naranjo Beach** leaves daily at 7:00AM and 4:00PM and returns at 9:00AM and 6:00PM daily. There is an extra run on Thursdays, Saturdays and Sundays at 11:00AM which returns at 2:00PM. The ferry leaves from Puntarenas docks and takes about one and one half hours.

The ferry going between **Golfito and Puerto Jimenez** is not consistent. It runs for a while and then is shut down for a while. When it is running, it leaves daily at noon and returns to Golfito municipal docks at 6:00AM. You will have to check while in Golfito to see if the boat is in operation.

NATIONAL AIRLINES

Sansa Airlines has a plane leaving for Quepos, Monday to Saturday, at 8:00AM and 1:35PM, returning at 8:35AM and 2:10PM. The plane for Golfito leaves Monday to Saturday at 6:00AM and returns at 7:00AM. The plane for Tamarindo leaves Monday, Wednesday and Friday at 11:45AM and returns at 12:40PM.

Other destinations available are: Coto 47, Carrillo, Barra del Colorado and Palmar Sur. Most flights take less than half an hour and cost around $20.00 US

The Sansa office is located in Paseo Colon, Calle 24, telephone 21-94-14.

CAR RENTALS

I strongly discourage using private cars for transportation in any country but I also understand that many people come to Costa Rica for only two weeks and do not have the time to get around efficiently by public transportation. Therefore, I have listed a couple of rental companies here that are considered adequate. But if there is any way that you can avoid using private transportation, please do.

If you plan on competing with the macho kamikaze drivers along the narrow (occasionally one lane) roads and wish to rent a car, the cost will be about $200.00 - 250.00 US per week. This is for a compact, no frills vehicle. Gas runs around $2.00 US per gallon and if covering many miles, you should take a car with unlimited mileage.

Your own valid driver's licence is good for up to three months. Insurance runs around $10.00 US per day and is $500.00 US deductible. You must be certain that all marks on the car are registered on the contract, or you may be charged with repairs for something you did not do. During rainy season, you may be expected to rent a four wheel drive vehicle in order to get through some of the mud roads. If planning on driving unpaved roads, be sure to advise the company. Any damage done will not be covered by your insurance if you drive in areas you have not reported.

Companies other than the regular large American car rental firms are:

Economy Rent-a-car at 1007 Centro Colon in Sabana Norte
El Indio Rent a Car at Calle 40-42 and Ave. Central
Elegante Rent a Car on Calle 10, Ave. 13-15

TAXI

Taxis are not expensive and can be taken to all corners of the country. If the price is not negotiated before getting into the car, then ask if the meter (called the maria) works. If the fare is within the city limits, the driver may use the meter but if it is further, then it will definitely be a negotiated fare. If taking an unmetered fare, be certain that you have negotiated a definite price.

The drivers will give you a fairly decent rate if you are not coming or going to some place like the Hyatt Regency. In that case, the fare would be higher because, they would reason, you would have more money. I also found that women could get cheaper fares than men. You may also find drivers willing to take long fares from the bus stations; they are often willing to find more than one person going to a particular destination. If you are not interested in this mode of transportation, let it be known right from the start. Even sharing a taxi is an expensive way to travel.

TELEPHONES

To make a **long distance** call from Costa Rica, just dial 116; an English speaking operator will help you. Station-to-station collect calls are possible from Costa Rica but the calls are quite expensive.

To make **local calls**, the cost is two colones for the first three minutes; then when the buzzer sounds you must put in another two colones for the next three minutes. Calling anywhere in Costa Rica is considered a local call.

Until 1963, Costa Rica was the most backward country in Latin America in the area of telecommunications. The government decided to make this a priority and today, there are over 300,000 telephones in service. The international lines are clearer than in any other Latin American country, and the service is quick and efficient. The telephone company also offers an excellent FAX system which gives access to local and international data bases, sending and receiving of information, the electronic transferring of funds and the storage and sending of information for closed groups. I am not certain if all banks can access the electronic transferring of funds; if they are, you would be able to receive money quicker than in other countries.

TAXES

Resorts, hotels, night clubs and restaurants charge a 23% tax. 13% is the sales tax and the other 10% is the service charge. You may also wish to leave a tip after paying the service charge; this is your decision. In fancier locations, tips are expected; in cheaper places tips are not expected. I do not tip in most of the places I go.

Marañon or cashew nut

ALAJUELA

This is a gorgeous little town just fifteen minutes from San José. It is often the preferred place to stay instead of the crowded, polluted city. However, it is not easy to get into one of the few hotels in the town. The city is also only two and a half kilometers from the airport which makes it convenient if catching an early plane. There is frequent bus service to and from San José all day.

PLACES TO STAY

Hotel Jar Chico is behind the bus station. It is a neat little place which is clean and friendly. The rooms have baths.

Alajuela Hotel costs $22.00 US and is found on the square. The rooms all have large private bathrooms attached to very large clean rooms. Needless to say, there is hot water in this hotel.

Hotel Bosque Mirador is a wonderful place to stay which is about three or four kilometers past Poasita on the road up to the Poas Volcano. The rooms have private baths and the hotel is very quiet. It is situated on a hill, high above San José and out of the city smog. On a clear day, you can see both oceans from the window of your room or from the restaurant on the premises. The cost is ¢1000 ($7.50 US) per person and is worth every penny. However, there is no bus past Poasita and you must walk up the hill. The restaurant serves excellent food which is cooked after you order. I highly recommend this friendly place if you want a very quiet few days.

RESTAURANTS

Selection is much greater in San José. However, if you want to stay in Alajuela, try the **Restaurant La Jarra** which is on Calle 2 and Ave. 2. The restaurant is upstairs and has a very pleasant atmosphere. If you sit on the balcony you can enjoy the park. The prices are not inexpensive but they are reasonable.

THINGS TO DO

Juan Santamaria Museum is named after the national hero of Costa Rica who was born in Alajuela. The museum displays the history of the battle of Santa Rosa where the Ticans defeated the hated William Walker in 1856. Juan was a little drummer boy who offered to carry the torch which set fire to the building where Walker and his men were housed. He died in this battle.

The museum also contains current art exhibitions. The museum is on the central park and is open Tuesdays to Saturdays from 8:00AM to 4:30PM. There is no entrance fee.

Juan Santamaria Park is just two blocks from the museum and has a statue of Juan with his torch. The park is a popular place in which to sit and enjoy Tican life.

Atenas Bird Zoo can be reached by catching a bus to Atenas and getting off at the sign on the right hand side indicating the zoo.

It is across from a tropical plant farm. The zoo has many birds you would not be able to see elsewhere. Although I know the logical reasons for having zoos, I still hate them. However, I must let those interested know their location. This trip would take about half a day from Alajuela. There is a small entrance fee to the zoo.

Bosque Encantado is a delightful park where many Ticans like to spend weekends. It has beautful gardens with sculptured trees plus places to picnic or barbecue. To get there, take the bus to La Garita which stops at the bus stop in Alajuela.

Volcan Poas, Ojo de Agua and the **Sarchi Oxcart Factory** are listed under San Josè even though you must pass through Alajuela on the way to these sites.

ARENAL

The little village of Arenal is just above the beautiful manmade Lake Arenal. This is a fresh water lake with fish. The volcano Arenal is at the far end of the lake; on a clear day it makes an excellent backdrop for this lovely spot. There is not much in this town except a bus stop and a small local hotel. There are no restaurants to mention. If interested in fishing, a place out of Tilaran, is recommended. A road goes along the southwestern shore of the lake. About five kilometers along this road is a relatively cheap place to stay. I do not know the name, but it is the first place you reach. A room with private bath, hot water and a delightful garden to sit around costs ¢2000 ($15.US). You get excellent views of the volcano if you wish to photograph the activity at night. You may also go fishing in the lake and catch your own supper which will be cooked if you ask ahead.

BOLAñOS ISLAND

Bolaños Island is a spectacular and isolated wildlife preserve. This is not a tourist area. The island is tucked away in a bay just south of the Nicaraguan border. To get there, you must take a bus to La Cruz and then a truck or bus to Puerto Soley. From Soley, you must rent a boat to take you the one and one half kilometers from Descartes Point to the island. The driver will wait while you enjoy the island for a few hours if you pay him a fair price. If not, have a good swim.

The vegetation of the island is thick and stunted, growing about two feet high on the rocky soil. Frangipani, alfaje, gumbolimbo, lemonwood, and crown fig trees which can produce up to 800,000 figs per tree grow here. The figs are largely eaten by birds. The vegetation is good for nesting grounds. The island protects the brown pelican, the frigatebird and the American oystercatcher. The northern side of the island has about 200 nests. The frigatebirds nest in the alfaje trees on the southern cliffs. The male frigatebird blows up his bright red neck when he is courting the love of his life. There are also magpies, black vultures, ctenosarurs and some bats.

There is one sandy beach on the island, on the east side, where there are sea snails and clams. It is possible to walk all the way around the island during low tide; otherwise you keep your boat man around to help you get past the cliffs. There are no accommodations on the island nor is there any camping. The closest place to stay would be in La Cruz which has a cheap hotel.

BRASILITO BEACH

Because the tourist trade in Costa Rica is developing so quickly, it is difficult to keep up to date with the latest information on the beaches. Fewer cheap places are available and more expensive American-style hotels are taking their place. The little village of Brasilito has a few stores and some cheap accommodations but this is rapidly changing. On the hill behind the town is the expensive **Hotel Las Palmas** where you may be able to afford a dinner or a beer, but the rooms run at prices beyond our means. However, the air-con and large luxurious rooms are a treat for the upper crusts of Costa Rica.

PLACES TO STAY

Cabinas Mi Posada charges about ¢2000 ($15.US) for a double with private bath and fairly large, clean rooms.

Albergue-Campo de Pesca is in Brasilito. You can camp here if you have equipment or take your chances on one of the five rooms available in the small hospedaje. The cost is around ¢600 ($4.50 US) per person without private bathrooms. The campgrounds are adequate.

THINGS TO DO

The beach is quite nice and beach walking is recommended. Going south, you can reach **Playa Conchal,** which is a beautiful beach made of crushed sea shells. The walk is only about three kilometers and can easily be reached at a slow pace in an hour.

After swimming and walking to the south of Brasilito, you can try walking north to **Flamingo Beach.** The walk is beautiful and a lot cheaper than the cost of a beer at the Flamingo Beach Hotel. The actual beach at Flamingo is also very beautiful. There are many small coves along this shore where you can sit quietly, read a book, enjoy the surf and meditate the wonders of the world before modern development. Beyond Flamingo, about another hour's walk, is the small community of **Potrero.** This is where the bus turns around to return to Huacas. It is always pleasant to walk one way to a beach, have something to eat and drink and then take the bus back. However, check bus schedules before doing this.

101

BRIBRI

This is not a place one comes to visit unless you are sent to work here without any choice. It is a dusty little town where you can catch a bus to the Indian Reserve or to Sixaola and on to the Panamanian border. But, if you should be stuck here late at night, there is a place to stay and a place to eat.

Cabinas Piculino rooms are basic and cheap without private bathrooms or hot water but at least there is plumbing. The rooms run at about ₡400 ($3.US) per person. You may find it better to stay in Bribri and commute to the reserve.

The Chinese restaurant where the buses stop is not very good. You would be better off getting your food from one of the local ladies who may be selling her wares by the bus stops.

THINGS TO DO

Bribri is situated in the Talamanca Mountains, half way between Sixaola and Puerto Viejo. Just past Bribri (a bus goes in this direction twice a day), at Sheroli, is the Indian Reserve. There is nothing at Sheroli, but you can rent a four-legged taxi to go into the mountains. There are herbal doctors who live in the hills; they are quite popular with some Ticos. If you rent a horse, you must take the path that goes across the river and up the mountain to get to the doctors. It is a full day's ride to get there; bring food to eat and a sleeping bag or tent as there is no accommodation.

If you wish to stay within walking distance of the reserve, there are some basic cabins at Suretka, down the road a few kilometers. They are the most rustic of accommodations with no plumbing and very hard straw mats. You must also bring food unless you can get one of the local families to cook a meal for you. To do this, you would need to speak fairly decent Spanish.

Cabinas Piculino in Bribri are also quite basic and inexpensive. At least there is plumbing. It may be more feasible to stay in Bribri and commute to Sheroli if you are interested in being with the Talamanca-Bribri Indians.

CAHUITA

This once sleepy little village, only an hour from Limon which is nestled in a bay on the Caribbean, has been discovered. It is now a swinging paradise for surfers, swimmers, hikers, dancing lovers, gourmet specialists and holiday worshippers.

At one time Cahuita was only swinging on Saturday nights, but now it swings every day at any hour. In the past, there were only two bars/dance halls where people partied on Saturday nights, but now there is a large village full of bars, reggae dance joints and restaurants interspersed between hotels and surfing shops.

Besides partying, Cahuita has a delightful beach but it has dangerous undercurrents during high tide. About one half mile from the town is a safer swimming area. Coral reefs, a short distance out, make snorkeling a pleasure and one can walk for miles along a trail which follows the water. Cahuita National Park is known for its coral reef because this is the only reef bordering the country. The park is also known for some rare varieties of frogs.

To get to Cahuita you may take a direct bus from San Josè from Calle 11, Ave. Central at 6:00AM, 2:30PM or 4:30PM, or you may take a bus from Limon which leaves the center of town once every hour.

PLACES TO STAY

Like many of the beaches in Costa Rica, Cahuita has new places appearing every week. The old mellow little village no longer exists; it is now a tourist mecca. Because of rapid changes it is difficult to name all the good places.

Surfside Cabinas cost ₡1100 ($8.US) with private bath. The rooms are very clean, the courtyard is extremely quiet, the rooms have a fan and the owners are the friendliest in Cahuita. This is the best place in town to stay. I recommend it highly.

Jenny's Cabinas are now ₡1700 ($12.50US) and have been rebuilt. The old screened-in building which let the gentle ocean breezes lull one to sleep is no longer being used. The atmosphere is gone but the view is still beautiful. This is owned by a Canadian gal and has a friendly atmosphere.

Cabiñas Ves are across from the Cahuita hotel and have cabins for ₡1740 ($13. US) for a double with private bath but no fans or screens on the windows. The building is not as nice as the Surfside.

Hotel Cahuita is still a popular spot, but it is noisy with rooms costing ₡1100 ($8.US) for a single with the bath down the hall. The rooms are large, airy and clean. The hotel also has cabins at the back which would be a bit quieter but certainly more expensive.

Hotel Sol y Mar has new rooms and a new restaurant. The cost is ₡1700 ($12.50US) for a double with private bath. This is right downtown where the action is noisy.

Cabinas Correoso has only six units and is very quiet with private bathrooms, clean rooms and is only ₡1550 ($11.50 US) for a double and ₡950 ($7.US) for a single.

Palmer Cabinas is set up like a motel. It is very clean with only a few units. It is along the main street from the bus stop. The back is now fenced-in, but the cost is still high at ₡1500 ($11. US) for a double with private bath. These units are fairly popular.

Moray's is along the road to the Black Beach and has cheaper rooms for ₡900 ($7.US) for a double. This is without private bath.

Tito's along the black beach (follow the signs) has five cabins for ₡1800 ($13.50US) for a double. These cabins are situated back in the jungle and away from the traffic. Not bad and fairly clean.

Jaguar Hotel is a new, large motel-style place which offers rooms with private bath for $20. US per person per day; this includes breakfast and supper. They will pick you up at the bus stop if you have reservations.

Cabinas Atlantia is a beautiful spot on the Black Beach about 15 minutes walk north from the bus stop. The rooms here are ¢2400 ($18. US) for a double. It is a clean, quiet place; a good spot if you are planning a long stay. There are private baths, kitchenettes and fridges in the rooms. There is a nice little garden on the premises.

RESTAURANTS

Again, there are so many new restaurants in Cahuita that it is difficult to stay current. However, there are some tried and true restaurants that have not changed over the years. You may also ask other tourists what they have discovered.

Surfside Hotel also has a small restaurant that operates mostly for its own guests. However, you may go in and have something to eat at a reasonable rate during meal times. Although I stayed there, I did not eat in the restaurant.

Sol y Mar Restaurant is new and their prices are a bit higher, but they still serve super french toast made with thick bread dipped in cinnamon and egg and then topped with maple syrup. Their suppers are also fairly large.

Vegetarian Restaurant owned by Miss Edith is on the way to the Black Beach. One street before the police station, turn right and go to the end. You can also find it by going left from Surfside and walking straight down. The food is excellent. It is made only when you order thus taking a bit of time to cook. You may order in the afternoon for a special hour. The most highly recommended meal is the meal of the day that she prepares ahead of time. Her style of cooking is very good. There is no alcohol served on these premises, but the herbal teas are for medicinal purposes even if you don't have an ailment.

Restaurant Tipico Cahuita down from the Defi has not changed in the last seven years. The food is the same quality as the atmosphere and service. The prices are a tad higher than seven years ago but that is to be expected. Seafood is the best choice offered.

Restaurant Defi is around the corner from the Ves hotel and is new with an excellent atmosphere. Their specialty is pizza, but other foods are also good.

Reposteria Casero by the Black Beach has many natural products such as homemade yogurt and fruit juices. The prices are reasonable, and the food is consistently good.

Hotel Cahuita is a popular place to eat. The food is generally good with shrimp and rice being one of the most popular dishes. However, the meals are not huge.

Restaurant Cahuita Park which is next to the park entrance is a very popular place with tourists, and they often just sit and drink for hours. The entertainment offered by the waiters is well worth the visit, especially if there are some pretty young gals sitting around waiting to be entertained. Prices are not really cheap. This restaurant became popular in the last five years and is consistently good with its meals.

THINGS TO DO

Cahuita National Marine Park is a good place to spend a few days scouting out the animals of the area. There are over 2600 acres (1000 hectares) of incredibly beautiful park. The jungle is a rain forest with wildlife such as the howler monkey, black-eared opossum, spectacled cayman, three-toes sloth, spotted skunk, and coaties. In the swamp areas are iguanas, butterflies and some rare types of frogs. Hiking along the beach is wonderful and you can go about seven kilometers down the beach to Punto Cahuita. Just past the point is Puerto Vargas where the ranger station is located. Along the hiking trail, which follows the beach for most of the way, there are picnic tables.

The coral reef extends out from Cahuita in the form of a fan and covers an area of 1483 acres. The reef is made up of old coral debris, stands of live coral and underwater prairies of turtle grass. So far, 35 species of coral have been identified, including the elkhorn coral which is outstanding because of its size. Among the coral can be found 140 species of mollusks, 44 species of crustaceans and 128 seaweeds. There are also 123 species of fish in this area. This is a lovely park.

The park is officially open from 7:30AM to 4:00PM and there is a slight entrance fee of about ₡150 ($1.US). During the day, there are park rangers to answer questions. However, there are no restrictions to park entry after hours and you may walk freely at any time.   Cahuita Tours offers anything from glass bottom boat rides to bicycles rentals. The office is found on the way to the Black Beach. Bikes may also be rented from Cabiñas Ves for ₡200 ($1.50US) per hour. Bikes are a popular commodity and rentals go early in the morning. Occasionally, they will take a deposit for the next day.

Tours to the reefs are recommended either by snorkeling or in a glass bottom boat. The reef is the largest in Costa Rica and includes the large elkhorn coral in Central America. It is outstanding because of its huge size.

Beaches along the bay are delightful when the sea is calm. There are signs posted where one should not swim because the riptides are too strong. Heed the warnings as many people drown in Costa Rica every year because they panic when caught in a strong current. The Black Beach area is not as nice for swimming and often has strong waves.

The beach along the park starts with Kelly Creek emptying into the ocean. At present, because of the last earthquake, there are many huge logs along this part of the beach. However, clean up has been consistent, and this area will soon be cleared of logs. After the creek is about two kilometers of beautiful, white, sandy beach; about 50 feet back from the water trees provide shade from the sun. This beach is separated from the next one by the point called Punta Cahuita. The trail cuts across the point to the next beach called Vargas Beach; the ranger station is found at the far end of the beach. Swimming is possible along these beaches; plus you may be lucky enough to see animals and many tropical birds. Just heed the swimming warnings. Also, do not leave your belongings unattended on the beach; you may find them missing upon your return.

Hiking tours are offered from Moray's Cabinas. These tours would provide a guided and informative trip through the park.

CAñAS

This is a busy little stopping off center for those going to Lake Arenal, for those wanting to visit Palo Verde Park or for those rafting the Corobici River. There is also a small airport here. This is a bustling little town and tourism has certainly helped its bustle.

PLACES TO STAY

Moderately priced hotels are located along the highway, close to the bus stops. These are clean and acceptable, but more than most chickenbusers like to pay.

Hotel Cañas charges ¢700 ($5.US) per room with a private bath. It is clean and friendly and about the best in town. It is on Ave. 3, Calle 2, close to the central square and other pleasant amenities.

Cabinas Corobici are a bit cheaper and a little bit further from the center of town. They are on Ave. 2 and Calle 5 and rent for ¢400 ($3.US) per person. There are no private bathrooms nor any hot water, but hot water is not needed in Cañas.

RESTAURANTS

Although there are several restaurants, none are spectacular. Because I was usually travelling through, I ate mostly from the ladies around the bus stop.

THINGS TO DO

Palo Verde National Park is 11,623 acres of parkland just a little ways from Cañas by bus. In rainy season it may take quite a while to get there. You must take a bus to Bebedero and then hitch a ride for the last ten kilometers (or walk). Without a pack, it would not take more than two to three hours to walk.

The park runs along the west bank of the Tempisque River and is part of the biogeographical unit known as the Tempisque

Lowlands. These lands are made of floodplains bordered by a few limestone hills and various rivers. The park contains a diversity of habitats such as mangrove forests, river-side forests, thorny shrubland, grasslands, deciduous forest, brackish marsh, limestone forests, savana brushland and evergreen forests. During most of the year, the swampy part of the park is host to a fantastic number of aquatic bird species including all types of herons, storks, egrets, grebes, ibis, ducks and jacanas, not to mention mosquitoes and ticks. The animal life is as abundant as the bird life and includes creatures like deer, armadillo, skunks and monkeys.

Many marked trails wind through the park; as well you can camp here. There are bathrooms (without showers) and drinking water. Some of the lookout points will give you good views of the Tampisque River which is often canoed by the adventuresome.

Rafting the Rio Corobici is possible all year and is a class I or II, depending on the water level. This would be a nice gentle trip for those not into extremely wild adventures. The trip is about ten kilometers of Walt Disney-style river rafting and bird watching. This is a trip that little kids can do; if you wish to avoid children, try another river. The trip passes through farmlands and cattle ranches plus areas with a variety of birds and monkeys. The take-out point is at Bebedero, close to Palo Verde Park. I do not have a price on this trip, but it is a one day, easy trip. If you are interested, contact Rios Tropicales, P.O. Box 472-1200, San Josè, Costa Rica or phone (506)33-6456.

CARILLO BEACH

This quiet, small beach is about an hour walk south of Samara and is a popular spot for fishing trips. There are a few cheap places to stay in the village, but the area is known for the beautiful **Guanamar Hotel** which sits on a cliff overlooking the ocean. However, even a beer is beyond my reach at this hotel. There is even a private airstrip here if you want to land in your private plane.

CARTAGO

The old capital of Costa Rica, Cartago is about 25 kilometers (14 miles) from San Josè. Cartago's first settlement by the Spanish was in 1523. Sitting at the base of Mount Irazu, the town has been destroyed by two earthquakes, one in 1841 and one in 1910. You may get there by either a half hour bus ride or a short car ride (train is no longer available) from San Josè.

This is a delightful, clean little town with lots to do in the area.

PLACES TO STAY

There is really no decent place to stay in Cartago. Some grubby places are located near the train station, but it is recommended to stay in San Josè and commute to Cartago and surrounding area. Accommodations will increase as tourism increases.

RESTAURANTS

The Paris is on Ave. 2 and is the most popular place to eat. It is close to the Basilica and has acceptable food at acceptable prices.

THINGS TO DO

The Ruins of La Parroquia is found in the center of town, on Ave. 2, close to the bus stop. It has been damaged several times; the earthquake of 1910 was the one that left the church in its present state of disrepair. The legend of the ruins says that the church was cursed by God because of the misbehavior of a priest. It was damaged or destroyed by earthquakes six different times prior to 1910 when it was not restored.

Today, there is no roof left and because of its state of disrepair, you can't go inside. However lovely gardens can be seen and photographed from the outside. The old bell in one of the archways is the original Liberty Bell of Costa Rica.

The stone seats on the outside of the building are shaded by old trees and make a pleasant stop while in Cartago.

The Basilica of Nuestra Señora de Los Angeles is the Patron Saint of Costa Rica. The Basilica is a beautiful, huge, old church which is wonderfully decorated. It is about a ten minute walk down the street from the ruins, going in the opposite direction to San Josè. It is easy to spot the huge white domes that decorate the sky of Cartago.

Inside, the Basilica holds an icon of the tiny black Patron Saint enshrined in gold, sitting on the red background of the altar. It is very beautiful. The icon is about two feet high and made of solid gold.

The church itself is in the shape of a cross. The wooden ceiling is built in wonderful geometric designs and framed with tiers and cornices. Also, the cement pillars and the walls are decorated by designs. The two side altars are tastefully decorated. The stained glass windows are exceptional. The pictures of the saints have a white background giving the windows a soft finish.

There are many cases which contain the gifts of those who were healed after asking for help from this Saint. Some of the gifts take the shape of the body parts that were cured by this lady. Many are made of silver and gold. People often approach the altar walking on their knees while asking the Virgin for special blessings.

Behind the church is a shrine where water can be obtained from the Miraculous Spring. This spring is where the image of the black Virgin was originally found. Her special day, August 2nd, is when Cartago has its biggest celebration.

Lankester Gardens are a few kilometers past Cartago. Take the bus to Paraiso and ask the driver to let you off at the road going to the gardens. Walk down the road for about ten minutes. When you come to the fork, take the right hand road. This will lead you to the gardens which are just past the hydro station. The gardens are maintained by the University of Costa Rica and were first started by Dr. Charles Lankester as an orchid farm. There is a small entrance fee of ₡200 ($1.50 US) and the gardens are open from 8:00AM till 3:00PM.

Orchids in bloom all year. You can stroll along the slippery cobble stone paths (bring good shoes) for a splendid, peaceful walk. There are little wells for garbage, ponds, and a very well maintained and labeled garden. The white orchids have a strong and beautiful smell. There are also many different blooming air-plants. If you are unable to do any jungle hiking while in Costa Rica, this is an excellent substitute.

Agua Caliente is a little village that can be reached by walking in an hour. To get there, go to the street that crosses the road to Paraiso. It is calle 10. Continue south along this road until you see a sign that says Agua Caliente. Follow the sign along the highway. You may find it very easy to hitch a ride from here. There are buses but they run infrequently. Once at Agua Caliente, you will find the medicinal springs dammed into a little pool where you can soak. However, I find the heat of Costa Rica incompatible with hot springs. I prefer the cooling effect of the oceans. I do not know what the medicinal purposes of these springs are.

Orosi Valley is a splendid valley that has beautiful views, hot springs, a lake, a wildlife refuge and some colonial buildings but these places are not very easy to access by bus. You must take the bus from the Cartago market and get off when you see something you like. The valley is a lush mountain valley which has the Reventazon River running through it. In the town itself, there is a colonial church which has a small religious museum. The church has been restored and is probably the oldest church in use in Costa Rica. The museum is open from 9:00AM to noon and then 1:00PM to 5:00PM daily except Mondays.

On the way to Orosi, there is a lookout point called **El Mirador de Orose** which gives the best views in the entire valley. The bus may stop for you for a minute, but if it does not stop, then plan on walking either way from Orosi in order to take in the entire magnificence of the valley. It is about a one hour walk to Orosi.

Lacustre Charrarra Recreational Site is on the Cachi Reservoir. You get to the lake by catching the Cachi bus in Cartago. On weekends and holidays, the bus goes all the way to the recreational site but on week days you must walk the last two kilometers. Charrarra is open Tuesdays to Sundays from 8:00AM to 6:00PM. There are basketball courts, volleyball courts, swimming pools, eating areas with barbecue grills, a camping area, rest rooms, a restaurant and a bar. What else would one need when this is combined with Costa Rica's beautiful climate?

The Rio Reventazon flows from the lake eventually tumbling down the 1000 meters to the Caribbean Ocean. The river has lots of white-water on it; some is a Class III. There are many rafting tour groups that offer white-water rafting down this river. The cost is about $65. US per day (high in my books) and includes everything from San Josè and back. There are some people who either rent or bring their own kayaks and make their base in Turrialba in order to spend a few days/weeks playing on this magnificent river.

Tapanti National Wildlife Reserve does not have a bus going all the way to it. You must go to Orosi and stay on the bus to Rio Macho (saves a bit of walking) and then walk or hitch a ride the rest of the ten kilometers to the park entrance. There is some traffic along this road so a ride is possible. You may also take a taxi from Orosi.

Once at the park, there is an information center open from 6:00AM to 4:00PM daily. You may then take some of the marked trails through the park to a waterfall, a swimming hole or picnic areas. The park is noted for its birds that live in the lush rain forest of these Talamanca Mountains. Some of the birds include the Quetzal, eagle, hummingbird, toucan and parrot. The park is open early for the avid bird watchers. However, getting there early in the morning is difficult.

Irazu Volcano National Park - see under San Josè.

Dinner guest

COLORADO

Colorado is for the avid fisherman or for those wishing to go to Nicaragua along the Rio San Juan. The border is open and you can get a boat as far as Castillo in Nicaragua on the San Juan River but the estimated price was $700.00 US. If you are serious and there are a few of you, this may be a grand adventure. There are no places to stay along the way so you would sleep on the boat and bring your own food. The estimated travel time is two or three days.

In Colorado itself, there are expensive places to stay. There is not much to do in Colorado except for the beer drinking after the fishing is done. This is when the stories about the other fish get longer and louder as the night goes on.

You can get to Colorado the same way as you get to Tortuguero or you may fly into Colorado.

COCO BEACH

Thousands of Costa Ricans vacation at this gorgeous little beach which sits between two rocky outcrops. Small islands dot the ocean. If you go on a weekend or during school vacation (January and February), forget about getting a room. You will need your own tent. There are a few hotels here, but the prices are either high or the rooms are cell-like. Girls travelling alone or in twos should watch out for con artists in this area. Stay only in hotels, don't walk on secluded beaches alone and keep your senses about you in the disco or bar. The last bus out of Coco for Liberia is at 6:00PM. If you don't have a room or a tent, be on it.

PLACES TO STAY

Claudia's appears to have enough rooms to house all of Costa Rica, but it is often full. To find it, walk to the square or the street on the water and turn right. There is no sign but you ask at the restaurant. The rooms are ₡1200 ($8.50US) per person. The rooms are clean and have private baths. This is the best place to stay in Coco.

Hotel Rio is the first little hotel on your left if you are going south down the main street from the square. The rooms are cell-like and hot. Rooms near the shower are noisy. Prices are ₡600 ($4.50 US) for a single and ₡1000 ($7.50 US) for a double. The shower rooms are in a separate building.

Campsites are available at this beach. You must follow the signs from the square going to the right. The campsites are not all that clean but there are plenty of showers and bathrooms. If you have gear, this is the cheapest alternatives. The cost is only ₡200 ($1.50 US) per person per night.

Cabinas El Coco are in the center of town, on the beach to the right of the main street. The cost is high at ₡1350 ($10.US) for rooms at the back and ₡1800 ($13.US) for rooms at the front. This is

111

one of the noisiest places on the beach, but also one of the most popular. All the rooms are clean, with private bathrooms and a restaurant downstairs. The drawback is the disco next door. It can't be turned off when you want to sleep.

Cabinas Luna Tica is a real find. It is on the beach and is fairly new. The rooms run from ¢1600-3000 ($12.-22.US) for doubles with private bath. They are clean, comfortable and away from the discos. This may change as development continues. The hotel has a restaurant and is fairly close to the beach. If you want to spend that much money on a hotel, this is a great place to stay. I also liked the owners who wanted non-rowdies.

RESTAURANTS

The Gilmar Restaurant is on the beach, on the south side of the square. This is the place to have camarone (shrimp) ceviche. The ceviche here is the best I have tasted in all Central America, and I would stop at Coco just for a few dishes of this.

THINGS TO DO

Playa Ocotal is a wealthy man's beach only three kilometers south of Coco. It is not for the chickenbuser to stay, but the walk is of interest. The beaches are beautiful and peaceful as compared to the blaring music of Coco. There are two hotels at Ocotal, both costing more than $100.00US and catering to deep sea diving and sports fishing.

Playa Hermosa and Playa Panama are north of Coco. Panama is quieter, cheaper and friendlier than Coco. The tourist office will send you to Hermosa, but it would cost my entire week's budget to stay there for more than a day. It is about an hour and a half walk past Coco; Panama is just beyond. There is a bus that passes both of these beaches leaving from Liberia at 11:30AM, 3:30PM. However, for real beach style fun, Hermosa rents surfboards, bicycles, snorkeling gear and will offer any kind of tour you could possibly imagine.

DOMINICAL

This is a tiny village situated on the Pacific where the Rio Barù terminates. It is quiet, peaceful, clean and unpatronized by tourists. This will probably not continue for long, but if you want a nice spot, this is about the only uncommercial place left in all Costa Rica. Go quickly!

Dominical is about 40 kilometers south of Quepos. From here, you can continue down the coast for 50 kilometers more of sun, sand and beach. All the Pacific beaches along here are spectacular. Those in the area of Matapalo and Utiva do not have hotels or camping facilities, but they are worth visiting. At the river mouth in Dominical you can enjoy beautiful freshwater pools, especially during high tide when the ocean is quite dangerous.

When coming from Quepos, you will travel through many coco-palm oil plantations and little villages like Hatillo. These villages belong to the workers; they have row houses, usually built on stilts, a general store and a large football field which is almost always occupied. There is no reason to stop at any of these villages unless you are curious about labor conditions in Costa Rica.

PLACES TO STAY

Coco Suiza is the best place in the village to stay and costs ¢700 (5.US) for a single and ¢1100 ($8.25US) for a double. It is clean, popular and very difficult to get a room on weekends. It is also the cheapest place in town.

Nayarit is the high class hotel in town at ¢1600 ($12.US) per room with a private bath and fan. However, there is no extra charge for two or three people, so if there are three of you, the price is not too bad. It is clean enough and may be a steal once the village is discovered.

Cabinas Punta Dominical are the beginning of the rush to expand this little village and is found high on the rocky cliff just a bit south of town. The cliff is called Punta Dominical. The hotel has a restaurant and bar and the rooms include fans, private baths with hot water and a nice porch. However, the prices are North American at around $30.00 US a cabin, depending on the season and how busy they are. In low season, the prices can be negotiated. Do walk up there and have a dinner. It is pleasant and friendly, but the hill is difficult to walk up after a day in the sun.

RESTAURANTS

Dominical has a few quaint little places to eat that are on the main street where the bus passes. Take your choice. The other possibility is to walk to Punta Dominical and eat at the hotel.

THINGS TO DO

Fishing is a popular sport all along this coast. You may be able to rent a boat for a better price here than further north. But, this will only be temporary. Once the tourists come, the prices will rise.

The beaches around **Utiva**, 20 kilometers south of Dominical, can be reached by a bus leaving from San Isidro once a day, but I suggest that you hitchhike. Although the road is not all that well travelled, a ride is easy. The beach is delightful and isolated; skinny dipping is still a possibility.

The beach of **Matapalo** can be reached by taking the Quepos bus that far. It is only about 20 kilometers north of Dominical. The beach is off the road a ways but can be reached by walking. However, I would prefer to stay in Dominical.

Barù is the little village at the top of the hill on the way to San Isidro. There is really no reason to walk there unless you need exercise.

FORTUNA

People stay in Fortuna in order to see the active volcano Arenal. Seeing the activity on the mountain is truly a sight, but it is not visible during the day because of the clouds. There are many places offering a trip to see the volcano at night. Other than the volcano, there isn't much reason for people to go to Fortuna.

PLACES TO STAY

San Bosca Hotel is two blocks off the main road going north. The owner charges ₡800 ($6.US) per person for a room with a private bath. It is a nice place to stay and quite popular with travellers.

Hotel Fortuna is in the opposite direction to the San Bosca and has both the king's quarters and the servant's quarters. The owner has rooms for ₡1000 ($7.50 US) for a single and ₡1500 ($11.US) for a double. These are new, large, high ceilinged rooms with private bath and hot water. You can sleep up to four people per room. At present, there are only two large rooms, but the owner is building five more and they should be ready by 1993. There are also cheapies for ₡300 ($2.25 US) per person. They are minimal but certainly clean enough. The owner may close this section in the future.

Hotel Central is on the main street and is adequate for the price. The cost is ₡350 ($2.50US) per person. There are no private bathrooms and only cold water showers.

Cabinas Burio is on the main street. Rooms are ₡1650 (12.25US) for a double including breakfast. The cabinas are just off the street so they offer a bit of quiet. The meals are excellent, and this is a delightful and pleasant place to stay.

Los Lagos Campground is about 12 kilometers (seven miles) from Fortuna, going toward Tilaran and only about one kilometer from the hot springs. It is situated near the park so you can see the volcano from your tent at night. A delightful restaurant, situated under a canvas roof, serves everything from seafood to chocolate cake. This is a good way to see the volcano at night, but you must have camping equipment.

RESTAURANTS

There is only one place to eat in town and that is where the bus stops. It is a fairly large open air restaurant that serves decent food at good prices. I almost drank them dry of banana milkshakes. If you are in need of North American foods, they make excellent french fries. People also wait for the bus here so the place is easy to find.

THINGS TO DO

Volcano Arenal is usually the main reason for people to come to Fortuna. It is a beautiful 5500 foot (1675 meter) perfectly shaped mountain that has been active since 1968. The explosions can occur from about once every half an hour to only a few times in a week. When the explosions are frequent, they are not as huge as when they are infrequent. The gases build up in the volcano and when enough pressure has been built up, the lava bubbles, throwing some over the lip along with huge boulders. You can see the red hot rocks cooling on the sides of the hill. You may also encounter some volcanic dust in your eyes and it can cut your face. The wind pressure also builds up when there is an explosion, causing the dust to travel large distances. Along with the wind, there is usually a huge sound and the earth will shake when there is an explosion. This is an exciting event to observe.

There are tours going every night; they all charge the same price of ₡1000 ($7.50 US) per person. This includes a trip to the volcano and a trip to the hot springs. They stay on the mountain for about an hour and a half. If the night is not clear, you will not see anything and the trip is not worth the money. Be certain the sky is fairly clear before paying your money.

You may also go by yourself, but you must have transportation and I do not know if hitchhiking is possible at night. There is a sign at the road between Tilaran and Fortuna, just about five kilometers from the hot springs, leading up the mountain. A sign at the turnoff says "Parqueo". Continue up this road for about three kilometers until you come to a fork in the road and a large sign at the side of the road. The sign gives some information about the mountain. The left fork goes to the side of the volcano and the one straight ahead goes to the river which has a small building where one could stay. However, be certain to have food and water as there are no entrepreneuring Ticans trying to sell their goodies up here.

I recommend going to the volcano with a group. The price is not expensive, and it is much safer. Although robberies are infrequent, you would make yourself vulnerable if you were alone at night on this mountain. The guides also know the best and safest place to view the volcanic activity. For my money, I would prefer to be safe. Volcanos are great, but they can be dangerous if you do not know what you are doing. We have long given up the practice of sacrificing virgins into the mouth of the volcano, and we have not yet taken up sacrificing tourists even though I am certain some would love to.

Tabacon Hot Springs can be visited on the same trip to the volcano, or you can rent a bike and go there yourself. To get there, take the road toward the volcano's park entrance. The springs are difficult to find. About one mile past the village of Tabacon, and before the park turn off, you will see a curb along the road that is about six feet long. There is a path just past this curb, going to the left (if you have passed the village). Follow this little path in the dense underbrush. It goes down about 20 feet. The "hot" springs are not really hot as this is where the hot and cold water meet but the

115

springs are in their natural setting. This is a nice place to visit during the day.

Fortuna River Water Falls are a wonderful place to visit and stretch the legs for a few hours. To get there, walk west from the bus stop for two blocks (there is a sign) and then turn left. Continue along this road until you have crossed two bridges. The first one is close to town. You will then pass a creek that goes under the road and through a culvert. Turn left at the first road after this. Continue along this road all the way to the end. You will see a sign indicating where to go to the waterfalls. Although you can see the falls from the top of the hill, it is more fun to go down and play in the water. Play downstream from the falls. Wear good shoes on this trip as the trail is rocky and slippery. The one-way trip takes around two hours, so take something to eat and drink.

GOLFITO

This is the longest town in Costa Rica. The main street, which is about the only street, runs along the bay for at least five kilometers. The nicer end is past the fishing section further into the town. Although a grubby town, it is certainly a friendly place. One of the main reasons people come to Golfito is to shop dutyfree. This sport is located at the very farthest end of town.

Buses from San José take about eight hours and the buses often break down on the way down to Golfito. If returning to San José or San Isidro, purchase your ticket in advance. The seats are numbered and if they are sold out, you may have to stand for the entire eight hours. People may purchase reserved seats for as far away as Palmar.

The ferry going to **Puerto Jimenez** and the park leaves every day at noon and takes one and one half hours returning at 6:00PM. However, make enquiries as soon as you arrive as this schedule is unpredictable. One day it runs, the next day it quits; the information given in San José is not accurate.

PLACES TO STAY

Hotel Gulfina is in the center of the bay and costs ₡700 for a double and ₡300 for a single ($2.25 - 5.20 US). As you can see, it is cheaper to have two singles than one double. I think the owner miscalculated when he gave me these prices. There are no private bathrooms and the hotel is basic.

Costa Rican Surf is a large hotel where English is spoken. The cost is ₡1400 ($10.50 US) for a double. The windows are boarded, but each room has a sky light. The rooms have a musty odor. Hot water is plentiful in the showers. The restaurant downstairs is noisy early in the evening. I was never there on a party night, so I don't know if the sleeping guests or the partying guests get first priority.

Hotel Lee is just past the Costa Rican Surf and is ¢270 ($2. US) per person. There is no private bath nor much else for frills. It is basic but okay.

Hotel Gulfito is the best buy in town for ¢1000 ($7.50 US) for a double but there are no singles. The rooms include a bathroom, and the hotel is fresh and clean. It is on the water side of the road.

Pension Minerva is on the water side of the street going towards the shopping area. The cost is ¢250 ($2. US) per person without bath. There is not much there.

Vista Mar costs ¢600 ($4.50 US) for a single with a private bathroom. It is really a nice place, but it is right on the street and noisy traffic starts early.

Hotel del Cerro costs ¢1000 ($7.50 US) for a double with no bath and ¢1500 ($11.US) for a double with a bath. The rooms are small and clean. I think they increased the prices when they saw a gringo with a backpack so be careful. If it is raining, late at night, and many people in town, you can bet the owner will charge ¢2000 ($15. US) for a room without a bath. There are better deals in town.

Cabinas Wilson are over the bridge and past the bus stop. The cost is ¢1000 ($7.50 US) for a double without a bath but the place is clean and friendly. There is a nice yard. This is an excellent deal for the money in Costa Rica.

Cabinas Princesa del Golfo are across from the National Bank of Costa Rica. They charge ¢1500 ($11. US) for a double with a bath. It is a huge old house that is clean and well kept. There is a nice yard and the owners are friendly to the extreme. A great deal.

RESTAURANTS

The fishing boats bring fresh fish to the town on Saturdays; this is the best day to have seafood meals. Restaurants are plentiful so choose what looks good to you.

Hong Kong Restaurant serves good meals at just about any time of day or night. It is just past the Costa Rican Surf. The prices are lower than many.

The Costa Rican Surf has a nice breezy restaurant attached to the premises and serves fairly good food, although it is not cheap. The open air restaurant, which looks out on the gulf, is the most attractive aspect of the place. However, there is really not much to choose from in Golfito.

THINGS TO DO

Golfito National Wildlife Refuge has many plants that are worthwhile seeing; most are usually not seen anywhere else in Central America. One of these plants is from the primitive cycadaceae family. During the dinosaur days these plants were in all parts of the world. Today they only exist in tropical or subtropical regions. They are the ancestors of the flowering plants. These palm-like plants have many tiny palm-shaped leaflets on each leaf stem and the columnar stems are marked by the leaf scars. These plants generally grow less than ten feet tall. The flowers are cone shaped; the female cones are larger than the male cones. There are less than 100 species known to belong to this family of plants and Golfito has at least one species.

To get to the refuge, you walk through town until you get to the soccer field. Turn right and go up the gravel road. It ascends the distance of two city blocks and then passes a few scattered homes before getting up to the top of the ridge. The walk takes about one and one half to two hours, depending on the heat and your energy level. Once you reach the microwave station on the ridge, you may as well continue along the road into the area where there are spectacular jungle plants dotted with many different types of birds, including the entertaining toucan. However, if you are just interested in the view of the gulf and surrounding area, the microwave tower is as far as you need to go. The total distance is eight kilometers, or five miles which is a substantial hike in the heat. Plan on going early when the heat is less intense. The elevation change is about 500 meters (1500 feet). Lots of water and good runners are all that are necessary. A bird or plant identification book may be of value, and camera equipment is essential as the views are spectacular. There are no restaurants on the ridge.

United Fruit Company was once the main employer of Golfito. Today, there is a small   ghost town remaining where the company town once thrived. From 1938 to 1985, United Fruit shipped bananas to all areas of the world but higher taxes, fruit blight and worker unrest (due to low wages) led to the departure of the United Fruit. This is the story all over Latin America. As soon as the workers want some of the profits and the host government wants its share of the profits, the company takes off for cheaper grounds. Today, the United Fruit Company is not operating under that name in Latin America. Other large companies are still emulating United Fruit's practices.

Some of the United Fruit Company's land has been converted to palm-oil production. This does not employ the same number of people so there are some gorgeous old American-style houses sitting empty in the area around the airport. It is a long walk but a pleasant walk until you think of the entire situation that has caused this ghost-town area.

Beaches which are accessible from Golfito include Cacao, Pavones and Zancudo.

Cacao is easiest reached by taking a water taxi from the banana boat dock at the north end of town. It is the lovely little beach that can be seen across the bay from Golfito. You may want to take your chances on hitchhiking along the gravel road to Cacao, but I would suggest taking the boat because road traffic is sparse. Once in Cacao, there is a basic place to stay; as well, decent meals are available. This is a quiet and restfull location.

Pavones is the surfing beach of the southern area. A bus goes to Pavones twice a day from Golfito. Although there are some cabins available, it is better to stay in Golfito and commute as the selection is better. However, be aware that the Pacific coast along Costa Rica has some huge currents and swimming is often dangerous. Be certain to be with friends. If it is only swimming that you want, go to Cacao.

Zancudo is the other beach that can be visited from Golfito; this one is considered the finest in the area for swimming. However, it takes time to get there. You must go first to Pueblo Nuevo and then to Zancudo. You may hitch a ride quite easily on weekends, but during the week, this is quite difficult. There are expensive cabinas for rent and a restaurant is available but, I suggest staying in Golfito and visiting this beach for a day trip.

Playa Cativo is a lovely place if you are looking for a resort. I don't usually recommend resorts, but I have included this one because it deserves more appreciation. Rainbow Adventures have a three level lodge made of native woods which is set in a tropical garden. The backdrop is jungle, and the front view is a coconut palm-lined beach. The lodge offers pick up and delivery to Golfito Airport, all meals and snacks, beer (but not hard liquor), use of snorkel gear, tour of the jungle, clean linen daily, laundry for personal items, fresh flowers and all taxes for a mere $55.00 US per person based on double occupancy. This is a deal if you are just down here for a couple of weeks R & R. Although not included in the price, fishing near the river mouths is excellent. All boat rentals include guides and safety equipment. If you require reservations, write to: Rainbow Adventures, Apdo. 63, Golfito, Costa Rica, telephone (506) 75-0220

Sport Fishing is quite popular in this area, but all ecology-minded travellers will frown at that type of commercialism, so I need not give any information.

HEREDIA

This provincial capital of 30,000 people is one of Costa Rica's oldest and prettiest towns. Built in 1706, and known as the city of flowers, Heredia is the home of the university and a delightful colonial area to visit. Like Alajuela, some like to stay in Heredia instead of downtown San José as it is cleaner and quieter.

PLACES TO STAY

There are quite a few places to stay in Heredia and you should look around if you do not like the one below. However, I find most people like to stay right downtown in San José so I did not thoroughly explore this area. Because of the university, many places offer monthly rates.

Hospedaje Herediano between Ave. 4 & 6 on Calle Central is a nice clean place with a comfortable courtyard. The cost is ¢350 ($2.50 US) per person per night without a private bath and with no hot water. The owners are very friendly and fun to be with.

RESTAURANTS
You are on your own for this area, but there are many restaurants listed under "San Josè" which is only five minutes away by bus.

THINGS TO DO
The Central Park is always the best landmark from which to start. This one has the remains of an old Spanish fortress on one side, and an old colonial church, built in 1797 and still in use today on the other side. The bells inside the church were brought from Cusco, Peru, in the good old days when gold and silver were transported up and down the coast. The fort and church are well worth the short time it takes to see them.

Braulio Carrillo National Park can be reached from here, but it would be a full day trip. If you have taken the bus from San Josè to Limon, along the main highway, then you passed through the most frequently visited section of the park. The park is spectacular from the bus and even more spectacular from your feet. To get to the park, take the bus from Heredia to San Josè de la Montaña, then take the bus to Sacramento from where the trails start. Three buses leave for Sacramento each day. However, the distance between San Josè de la Montaña and Sacramento is about eight kilometers so it could be walked, especially if you are coming down and miss the last returning bus. Expensive hotels are available and a few cheapies are reported to be in the area, but I did not check them. The volcanoes in this park are not the most favorite, but it does have fewer tourists.

The park covers 108,967 acres (44,100 hectares) and is dedicated to Braulio Carrillo, a national benefactor and past chief of state. The park lies in one of the most rugged regions of the country. It covers three different elevations of growth; the most prominent is the rain forest. Fifty years ago, 75% of Costa Rica was covered in rain forest; today, only 25% of the land is rain forest. This is a large and spectacular section of it. The entire landscape is broken up by huge mountains covered in thick forest and separated by steep canyons. In this area the rainfall is high (4500mm per year); this creates rushing rivers and numerous waterfalls. Primary forests cover 95% of the area, and there is reported to be over 6,000 species of plants. To date 333 different types of birds have been seen in the area. So, for a number of reasons, it would be delightful to stay in the park.

Once at the entrance, you will find a small museum. The trails have quite a few lookout points and there are picnic grounds complete with metal barbecue pits. The grounds near the entrance are well kept and there are signs giving directions. The top of Barva Volcano is 2906 meters (9500 ft.) and is thus quite chilly. Running shoes and a warm sweater need to be taken.

There is a small entrance fee to the park. Some routes in the park can take a few days to travel. For more information, talk to the park wardens.

JACO BEACH

When I compare Jaco from ten years ago to the present, I feel sad and no longer want to promote tourism. In the old days, there were two bars and one hotel in town, and the long, six-mile beach was unscathed by humans. Today, Jaco, like so many other beaches in Costa Rica, is a long strip of discos, bars, beach-side restaurants, expensive hotels, tourist agents and rental joints. However, if you want action along with your sun and surf, this may be the place for you.

PLACES TO STAY

Although there is a variety of accommodations, most are expensive. Be prepared to pay a bit more in this area. The two listed here are the best for the money and also the cheapest.

Emily's Cabinas is a small, family-run place that rents rooms for ₡1200 ($9. US) for a double with a private bath. The owner also gives weekly rates and is not real picky about check-out time. The owners are friendly and run a good business.

Cabinas Antonio is the other reasonably priced place to stay at ₡1200 ($9. US) for a double with a private bath. There is a well kept lawn and a nice sitting area in the garden. The rooms are larger than Emily's and a bit cheerier. It is quiet at night as there is no bar attached (at this time).

Hicaco Campsite is close to the beach and offers clean bathrooms, clean drinking water, and rather small tent spots. You can camp here at a reasonable price of ₡250 ($2. US) per day. The restaurant attached to the campsite is excellent for seafood.

RESTAURANTS

Restaurants are found up and down all the little alleys and backroads so scout around and find what looks like good home cooked meals. I was so disappointed to see the changes in Jaco Beach that food was the last thing on my mind.

Jaco Beach Hotel was once the ONLY place to eat in Jaco unless you went to the bar. Now it has been renovated and redone as have the prices. However, it is always fun to visit the other half of our society, and if you can afford to stay in Jaco for a while, you can certainly afford to have a dinner at the Jaco Beach Hotel. The food is more than acceptable.

El Hicaco is the restaurant attached to the campsite. It is excellent for good fish dinners. It is on the beachfront and prices are quite decent.

THINGS TO DO

Surfing is quite popular along this beach. Numerous shops rent equipment but remember that the beach has strong riptides and swimming can be dangerous. I have seen more than one person pulled out of these waters with barely a breath left. Hermosa beach, which is six kilometers south, is supposed to have the best surf.

Cycling is becoming more popular, especially if you want to visit other areas. Rental shops are in town, but book ahead to reserve a bike. The shop next to the Hotel Jardin has decent rental bikes for about ¢800 ($6. US) per day. This does not include helmets.

Carara Biological Reserve is up the highway about 25 kilometers. It is more a bird sanctuary than anything else. Many water birds have been seen here, including woodstorks and spoonbills. Take a bus from Jaco that is going to San Josè or to Puntarenas and ask the driver to let you off at Tarcoles. The road passes between the beach and the preserve and then you must walk the two kilometers (half an hour) to the park entrance. The beach on the other side is gravel and is not a good place to tan. The reserve itself has 4700 hectares of land with the Rio Tarcoles passing through it. There are picnic spots, washrooms and a few nature trails to walk along. If you are an avid bird watcher, this is a great place to visit early in the morning.

Carara protects an important archaeological site where the Huetar culture is being studied. Stone, pottery and gold objects have been found in the graves. If you are interested in this part of the park, you will need a guide. There is a small entrance fee to the preserve which helps maintain it.

Herradura Beach is on your way up to, or returning from, the Carara Preserve. This is a fairly nice, and still quiet, black sand beach that has a few restaurants and places to stay. It is a great place to stop and enjoy part of the day and then head back into Jaco for the night. If you want to camp, there are two campsites at this beach. One is on the road into the beach and the other is right on the beach. However, cleanliness is not why this beach is renowned.

LIBERIA

This is a beautiful, clean and bustling little town. Although it is hot, it is quite pleasant and definitely friendly. If you have just come from Nicaragua and are tired, this is a nice place to stop. Liberia is also a pleasant (and cheap) place to stay if you want to visit a few of the parks in the area.

Liberia is a town of about 15,000 and is the capital of the Guanacaste Province. When you arrive in Liberia by bus, you will have to walk about five blocks to the center of town. If it is late at night, do not walk, but wait for the city bus. It is fine during the day, but a few robberies have occurred at night.

PLACES TO STAY

More expensive hotels/motels are close to the highway; I prefer to stay in the center of town.

Pension Margarita is a great old house which is still renting rooms at a reasonable rate of ₡400 ($3. US) per person without private bath. The front porch is a delightful spot to sit and watch the action. The shower is not really cold because the sun warms the water which sits in a container on the roof. A bonus. Margarita has been running this place for twenty years, and she runs a tight ship. She will also serve a typical breakfast which is more than I can eat for only ₡300 ($2.25 US). The rooms are not luxurious, but everything else makes up the lack of frills.

Hotel Liberia is just off the square and costs ₡450 ($3.25 US) per person and is a good buy for the price. It is friendly and clean. There are no private bathrooms.

RESTAURANTS

The Pekin is just up the road from the Margarita. The owners will change money as well as serve a decent meal, which are quite large.

THINGS TO DO

Santa Rosa National Park is on the road going to Piñas Blancas (the Nicaraguan border). From the park entrance, which is 35 kilometers from Liberia (around one hour), you may either hike for seven kilometers on a flat, paved surface (about one and one half hours), or you may hitch a ride with one of the vehicles. You will find an information center that also sells maps of the area. The people are very helpful and encourage a stay in this most popular of Costa Rica's parks. Entrance fees and camping fees are both $1.00 US.

Santa Rosa has 54,146 acres of land and was Costa Rica's first park. It was established in order to preserve the last battleground of William Walker against the Costa Rican people. Then after the defeat of Somosa in Nicaragua, his land was confiscated and added to the park area to the north; this left a thin strip in the center of the two areas that was still privately owned. In 1987, President Arias added this strip to the park, thus joining the two pieces of land. This strip of park is said to have been the CIA landing strip when the US sent supplies to the Contras during the war against the Sandenistas.

Once inside the park, tent sites complete with bathrooms, picnic grounds and drinking water are available. Just past the campsite, you will find the Santa Rosa Hacienda or interpretive center.

This is a splendid little museum that has old furniture, old pottery, old tools, old rifles etc, all in a 200 year-old house. There is also a display of moths and butterflies. The colonial stone corrals are the sight of the heroic battle of Santa Rosa which took place on March 20, 1856.

When hiking in the park there are trails for every type of hiker, from the long, all-dayer to the "sandals-will-do" type. The park contains petrified forests, mangrove swamps, thorn forests and wooded savannahs. Birds, monkeys, bats, armadillos, green iguanas, white tailed deer, coatimundies and ocelots are just a few of the animals you could see. From October to December, the Ridley, Leatherback and Green turtles come to the beaches to lay their eggs. This is, of course, one of the most exciting natural spectacles Costa Rica has to offer. Because these creatures are well protected, there are many opportunities for nature lovers to get the opportunity to see them.

The next attraction is **Playa Naranjo** where the leatherback turtles nest and **Nancite** where the Pacific Ridley turtles nest. It is 12 kilometers from the park museum and campsite to the Playa Naranjo and then another six to eight kilometers north to Nancite. There is a campsite with toilets and water at Naranjo but Nancite is a controlled site and you must have a permit to go there. However, between September and December, this coast has many large nesting turtles and to see them once will give you a lifetime memory. Hatching occurs during the other months and to see the little critters struggling towards the water is just as thrilling as seeing the big mothers nesting.

If you visit no other park in Costa Rica, this one is a must.

Rincon de la Vieja Park has 54,146 acres of parkland just 25 kilometers from Liberia. The two major volcanos are Rincon de la Vieja which stands at 1895 meters (6300 ft) and Santa Maria at 1920 meters (6400 ft). Rincon de la Vieja is still active but has not had a major eruption since 1966 and 1970 when large clouds of ash spewed forth. Rincon de la Vieja is a composite mountain, formed by the simultaneous eruption of several different volcanic cones which, over a period of time, merged into a single mountain. On the summit, nine sites of volcanic activity have been identified, one of which is active. There are also a large number of fumarles or holes in the mountain where gases can escape. South of the crater is a beautiful seven acre lake with pure, clean water. Hot springs and boiling mud pots dot the volcano. Trails pass the major attractions of the volcano. The first one leaves the ranger station and goes three kilometers to the hot springs which supposedly has medicinal value. After leaving the hot springs, you can go another three kilometers and reach the mud pots. These are hot and smelly but very interesting with their many different colors. If you continue along the trail, there is a fork and the one to the left leads to the fumaroles. The right hand fork can take you to the summit but it is a long way off and would take more than a day of hiking for a return trip to Liberia. If volcanos fascinate you, this is an excellent opportunity to explore.

To get to the park, take a bus or truck through Colonia Blanca and up along the river towards the park. There is no regular transportation along this road so some negotiating must be done. However, as tourism flourishes, so will the free enterprise and some entrepreneuring Tican is certain to supply transportation to the area for a nice little fee. Ask for the park or the Santa Maria Ranger Station.

If pre-arrangements are made in San Josè with the parks service, you can stay at the park headquarters for a small fee. There are also campsites complete with bathrooms and running water. Use of kitchen facilities can also be arranged if you contact the parks service in San Josè (see under San Josè). Outside the park is a Youth Hostel which offers basic accommodations, has running hot water, a restaurant and charges North American prices. If you are not a member of the International Youth Hostel Association, the prices are prohibitive.

Playa Hermosa is north of Coco. Although it is a rich man's beach, the tourist office in San Josè tries to promote it - even if you walk in with a backpack and are obviously poor. You can take the bus from Liberia going to Panama beach and get off here if you wish. There are two buses from Liberia daily, one at 11:30AM and one at 3:30PM. However, you can walk up the beach to Playa Panama and get cheap accommodations.

Playa Panama is at the end of the bus line which leaves Liberia at 11:30AM and 3:30PM daily from Calle 12, Ave. 5-7. Playa Panama is a nice place to stay, quieter than Coco and cheaper than Hermosa. There are a few cabanas for rent, a place to eat that is more Tican than North American, and, of course, a bar. Fresh seafood is often available at this restaurant. How long these little beaches will stay undeveloped is your guess; the way Costa Rica is developing, it is almost too late to go there.

LIMON

This Caribbean port city has lots of friendly, English-speaking people. There is not much to do in Limon itself, but it is a jumping off spot for either direction along the coast. If you do not want the hustle and bustle of Limon and are planning on going to Tortuguero, an alternative is to take the 20 minute bus ride to Moin and stay there. It is quite pleasant.

PLACES TO STAY

Hotel Palice is a clean, big old house where you can get a double room for ¢750 ($5.50 US). There are no singles. It is a safe, clean and pleasant place which is near all the bus stops.

The Park Hotel is right by the water and charges ¢1125 ($8.50 US) for a double with a fan and ¢1750 ($13. US) for a double with air-con and private bathrooms. It is probably the best hotel in town but the owners are not as pleasant as some. As well, their prices have doubled over the last few years. It may have been my gringo face, but I felt unwanted. However, it is also full most of the time.

Hotel Miami is next door to the post office and charges ₡1125 ($8.50 US) for a double with a fan and ₡1680 ($12.50 US) with air-con for a double. Considering the location, I found this building to be very clean and quiet.

Hotel Fung is across from the post office and charges ₡1280 ($9.50 US) for a double with bathroom and fan and ₡1145 ($8.50 US) without a bathroom but also with a fan. Again, it was very secure and fairly clean. I do not know the noise level but imagine it to be quiet as long as you don't have a room on the street.

Hotel Caribe is across from the park. It costs ₡750 ($5.50 US) per person with bathrooms but the rooms are quite small. However, the friendliness of the hotel is worth the lack of space.

Hotel Venux costs ₡500 ($3.50 US) per person without bathrooms. The rooms are small but nice. The building is secure.

Pension Dorita is across from the Cahuita bus stop. The rooms are ₡500 ($3.50 US) per person, but they are small and smell musty. It is a large old place, conveniently placed, and quite popular with some, but I prefer something a bit cleaner.

Hotel Ng is just around the corner and to your left from the Cahuita bus stop. The rooms are clean and secure and include baths at ₡1000 ($7.50 US) for a double and ₡800 ($6. US) for a single without bath. There are only a few singles, but I liked the place for its security and friendly atmosphere.

Hotel Aras charges ₡3000 ($22. US) for a double but this includes air con (often needed in Limon), private bathrooms, a restaurant downstairs and clean, large rooms. The only drawback is the nearby disco which is noisy. If you are an early bedder, then you may not want this luxurious place.

Hostel Moin is in Moin which is 20 minutes from Limon by bus. The hotel charges ₡1200 ($9. US) for a double room complete with private bathroom. The rooms are quite big and the people are very friendly. They have not been bombarded with tourists, so you may get a bit better service if you stay here. A restaurant and bar serves fairly decent meals.

RESTAURANTS

There is a lady near the San Josè bus station who sells empanadas stuffed with jam or cooked fruit; they are excellent. They are usually hot and sold in the mornings. Try and catch her. T h e **Park Hotel** has excellent food, but it is quite pricey. However, you can get food like fruit and yogurt for breakfast.

La Fuente Restaurant is around the corner from the Cahuita bus stop. It is very clean and has reasonable prices, super waitresses and good food.

Restaurant Limonense is across from the Moin bus stop and has decent food at reasonable prices.

Hotel Aras has a restaurant downstairs that serves excellent, substantial meals at a fairly decent price. The service is good and there is air conditioning in the cafe. That alone is often worth a few extra cents.

THINGS TO DO

Tortuguero National Park is a must when in Costa Rica. For complete information, see Tortuguero. Boats can be obtained in Moin, but you should have at least four people for a reasonable rate.

Jungle Train was once one of the great attractions of the area, but the earthquake of January 1992, destroyed many of the buildings, some of the Tortuguero canals, and the ferry to Tortuguero. The earthquake also pushed part of the mountain down onto the train tracks. Thus, the jungle train is no longer running. There are no plans for restoring the ride which was quite historical and extremely beautiful. However, you can visit the train station both in Limon and in San José.

Parque Vargas is near the center of Limon and is a splendid place to go in the early evenings to listen to local music, talk (English) and make new friends. Sloths apparently live in the trees, but I did not see any. Normally sloths only come down from the trees about once a week in order to complete the food cycle of the leaves that they eat. If they are found by locals, they are often placed back into the trees so that no harm will come to them. You can also walk along the seawall that goes part way around the bay. This is a pleasant walk, and the sea breezes are refreshing after a hot, humid day.

Uvita Island is the spot where Columbus landed on October 12, 1502. The island is about a kilometer from the mainland and can be visited by a hired boat. There is really nothing to do on the island, but history buffs may wish to plant their foot on the same spot as Columbus once did. On October 12th, there is a huge festival in Limon and hotel bookings are necessary. The fiesta is big. It is a real Caribe celebration with street dancing, parades and lots of food.

Barra de Matina Beach is just north of Limon, along the canals where you can observe the leatherbacks nesting from February to July, with the peak season being April and May This is only about one and one half hours from Limon; to see this spectacular phenomenon, you may want to hire a boat. You would go to Moin and get a boat there to take you up the river and back for a fraction of the price that it would cost to go to Tortuguero. However, you must convince the fellow to come back after dark.

MANUEL ANTONIO

This has always been one of the most popular beaches in all Costa Rica. It is only three hot hours by bus from San Josè unless you get on the wrong non-directo bus; then it takes five hours. Be certain to check. You can also get here in 15 minutes by plane, and the cost is less than $50.00 US.

There are five beautiful beaches and hotels to suit every budget from the luxurious Mariposa at $135.00 US per night to the youth hostel at $2.50 per night to the campsite on the beach. There are a few Canadian-owned places here as many French Canadians discovered this paradise long ago. Recently, it has been invaded by American entrepreneurs who have opened up many hotels and restaurants along the mountain. Many chickenbusers prefer to stay in Quepos at night and commute the half-hour to the beach each day. There is livelier night life in Quepos.

PLACES TO STAY

Because development is rapidly increasing, it is almost impossible to keep a current guide. The prices are going up as quickly as the new buildings. Manuel Antonio is no longer a cheap place to visit. It reminds me more and more of Waikiki Beach in Hawaii.

The Mariposa is $135.00 US per night, and they only take US dollars from the tourists. It has hot water. Even if you don't stay here, it is nice to visit, enjoy a drink, and see how the other half suffers through life.

The Costa Linda Youth Hostel has rooms for ¢400 ($3. US) per person and is the most popular place for travellers. The only drawback is that it is about a ten minute walk to the beach; unlike the Mariposa, you will not have a private swimming pool. You may use the fridge or cook some of your own meals if you get the large room with a small kitchenette. But this room holds five people. Meals are available but you must order in advance. The banana milkshakes are super and recommended for your morning eye-opener.

Hotel Manuel Antonio is where the bus stops. It has four rooms, all with private bathrooms for ¢1100 ($8.25 US) per night. The rooms are very clean and quiet.

Manuel Antonio Cabanas has a number of places right on the beach. A room with three beds and bath is ¢2000 ($15. US); rooms not on the beach are ¢800 ($6. US). There are no fans. These rooms are quite popular and may be full on weekends. However, they are also popular with the partying groups.

Cabana Espadilla is across from the Costa Linda and have cabins for four people. They cost ¢4250 ($31.50 US) per day. These are beautiful new cabins with private bath and a fridge in each quarter. The yard is pleasant and the cabins are only ten minutes from the beach.

Los Almendros is past the Vila Bar and Youth Hostel, just over the little bridge and to your left. It has a large flowered garden with a row of rooms along one side. The rooms are large with private bath and are cleaned every day. There are chairs on the verandah to sit on and enjoy the evening air. The owners are friendly and, because of their excellent premises, the hotel is always full. The cost is ₡2270 ($17. US) for a room that will sleep three people. A restaurant is on the grounds.

Arbolitas Cabanas are half a mile from Manuel Antonio going back up the hill. They are $35.00 US per night and are very clean with private baths and fans. However, if going through the yard at night, beware of snakes. There are also a lot of crabs and some monkeys in the vicinity.

RESTAURANTS

Like the hotels, the restaurants change every few months. Listed below are a few that have lasted the test of time - usually an indicator of quality.

Vila Bar Restaurant is beside the Costa Linda, has good food, a pleasant atmosphere and quick service. However, in the past few years, the prices here have tripled. It is time to boycott the place and give business to a more reasonable establishment.

Hotel Manuel Antonio is a popular place for lunch. I recommend the chicken soup or the chicken dinner (in case you haven't seen too much chicken since being in Latin America). Their spaghetti dinner needs improvement but if you want North American french fries, they serve the best in the area.

Los Almendros is past the Youth Hostel and the Vila Bar, just over the little bridge and to your left. It has super food and adequate portions. The beef steak is marinated in a lovely sauce and is very tender. The pork chops are also excellent. My eldest daughter celebrated her wedding here and the service was spectacular.

Tienda Blanca is at the end of the street from the Youth Hostel and along the road where the bus passes. Blanca is a delight and will give you the best food, best service and sweetest smile in all of Costa Rica. Be certain to patronize her. She has worked very hard as a single mom all her life. As well, she looks after her aging mother and still has the disposition of an angel. She deserves all the business she can get.

Barba Roja is one and a quarter miles up the hill from Manuel Antonio. Take the 5:00PM bus, have dinner, watch the sun set over the bay, and enjoy a pleasant walk back down the hill to your home. The dinner specials change daily and cost anywhere from $6.00 to $10.00US each. The cheesecake is delicious.

Karahi Restaurant is only half a mile up the hill from the beach. The meals are not spectacular but a T-bone steak is only $6.00 US and a lobster dinner is about double that. It is a nice change to eat here if you are in Manuel Antonio for long.

THINGS TO DO

Manuel Antonio Park is the smallest national park in Costa Rica, with only 1,685 acres. The jungle is full of life and monkeys have the tourists trained. At about 4:00PM, they like the tourists to leave eggs and bananas in the tree limbs for them. But be careful. The monkeys have a funny way of showing their appreciation. If you stand directly under them, they may try and leave their scent on you. Because of its near extinction the Squirrel Monkey is of great interest. If you are lucky, you will see one.

The park also has a large population of hermit crabs. During the full moon, these creatures come out in hordes. The jungle crawls with them. As an example of how thick they are, we left six beach bags on the sand near the jungle while we played in the water. When we looked for the bags, we couldn't find them because the crabs had them completely covered. The jungle crackles with their movement and they look like creeping red waves. No one knows why they roam and romp in the full moon.

Walking around the park is pleasant, but if you want to go past the third beach, you must have a guide. The second beach, near the rocks, is the best place for snorkeling. Watch out for the jellyfish which leave a nice sting when they come in contact with your warm skin. There are also very strong undercurrents along these beaches, so you must be careful when swimming. If you get caught by a current, go with the flow instead of trying to fight it. Scream for help and try to cross diagonally across the current to calm waters. People on the shore will help if you can get their attention. There is also a poison fruit that looks like a green crab apple. It is very poisonous. Even a small bite, without swallowing anything, will leave your mouth and throat burning for hours.

There are marked hiking trails through virgin forest, secondary forests, mangroves and lagoons. The one trail in the park goes over the bluff instead of around it and the views from the bluff are lovely. It is worth at least one trip up to the top. The fauna is quite varied and there are over 100 types of mammals and close to 200 types of birds. The park includes the twelve islands that are just off the coast.

I heard stories about some pretty big snakes in this park. One couple was on bicycles, and a large snake would not let them pass. They threw sticks at it, but it wouldn't move. The couple had to try the trail another day. Be careful as Costa Rica has seven types of poisonous snakes that could ruin your vacation.

The sand fleas are vicious in this park during the early part of the dry season. Use the Skin-So-Soft solution if you are going there. Some of the local people use a thick oil on their skin; the fleas stick to the skin, but are unable to bite. If you find nothing else that works, try the oil technique.

There is a small daily entrance fee to the park. If you wish to camp at the campsite, you will pay an additional fee. The campsite is between second and third beach and has water and toilets. It is an inexpensive way to stay at Manuel Antonio.

MONTEVERDE - see under Santa Elena

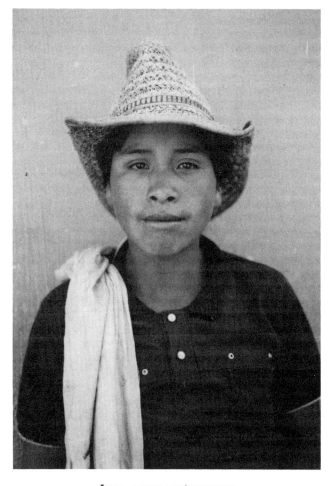

Jorge, a young entrepreneur

MONTEZUMA

Known as Costa Rica's paradise, Montezuma was a small village at the southern end of the Nicoya Penninsula with only four hotels and as many bars. However, like the rest of Costa Rica's paradises, Montezuma has been discovered and is growing faster than this guide. I will only mention a few places; the rest is up to you.

Montezuma's beaches are beautiful, and some of the coves and rocky inlets are deserted. The locals that live in the area are friendly and helpful. Even though the trip in or out is difficult, it is well worth the trouble. Plan on spending a few days soaking up the sun and swimming at the waterfall. It will rejuvenate your travelling spirits. If you have never been to Montezuma before, then by all means go and enjoy. However, if you remember Montezuma from a few years ago, keep the memories and leave the beach for others. You will be devastated when you see the changes.

To get to Montezuma, you must go to Puntarenas. From there, you can take the ferry to Paquera at either 6:00AM or 3:00PM. This ferry is caught at the market place in Puntarenas. Once across the inlet, you will be met by a bus in Paquera. Or, if there are a few of you, you may wish to take a taxi to Cobano, at a price of $15.00 US. The bus is only $1.00 US. The trip is two hours long on a dry, dusty gravel road. Once in Cobano, you can get refreshments, and then catch the taxi for the last seven kilometers to Montezuma. The taxi is about ¢600 ($4.50 US) per person; if it is not available, there is a truck that will take you for about ¢200 ($1.50 US) per person. The entire trip from Puntarenas to Montezuma takes four to five hours, depending on the taxi at Cobano. Leaving Montezuma is a bit tricky. You may take the taxi at 4:30AM in order to catch the 5:00AM bus which meets the 8:00AM ferry. There is also a taxi leaving at noon which gives you the same connections but at a later time. This puts you into Puntarenas at a much later time and may mean staying there overnight rather than getting to San Josè after dark.

PLACES TO STAY

Karen's is before the hotel and is the best buy in town at ¢300 ($2. US) per person. It is a large white house, clean and quiet, and English is spoken. There are communal baths and some kitchen privileges. Karen's also has cabanas down the beach. Ask about them if you are interested. Karen took part in having the Cabo Blanco preserve established and is an avid conservationist. Her cabanas on the beach are on a fair amount of land that has a lot of wildlife. The cabanas are basic, but you will certainly get a glimpse of life in Costa Rica as it was at one time.

Lucy's is down the beach just past the first bay. It is quiet and clean and only about ¢350 ($2.50 US) per person.

The Montezuma Hotel is where the taxi will drop you off. The rooms upstairs, without a bath, are ¢350 ($2.50 US) per person and about ₡150 more with bath. This is complete with fan. The only problem is that the bar doesn't usually close until about 10:00PM; if you are an early bedder, this may bother you.

Arias is between the hotel and Lucy's and is clean and pleasant for ₡500 ($3.75 US) per person.

There is also **camping** along the beach next to the hotel. If you have a sleeping bag, the weather is usually hospitable enough to allow you to sleep under the stars.

RESTAURANTS

Sano Banano is a vegetarian restaurant which is new and probably the cleanest, cheapest and best place to eat. The vegetarian meals are excellent. They also show movies a couple of times a week which you may or may not want to miss - depending on how much you miss home.

Alfredo's is just before Lucy's. This man serves the best fruit salad in Costa Rica. If you let him know ahead how many will be coming for dinner, he will present a veritable feast. When I was there, I got Russian salad, cabbage salad, rice, beans, chicken and a vegetable. For dessert I had fruit salad with ice cream and jello, and coffee. The entire bill was ₡600 ($4.25 US) per person. If you purchase a bottle of wine beforehand, he will chill it for you. This is real Tica hospitality (a Tica is the local term for a Costa Rican person).

The Montezuma Hotel serves tasty meals but the are not spectacular. Often the service is on Costa Rican time, but the staff are friendly and don't rush with the bill either!

Chico's Bar is the social center of Montezuma. If you want to leave in the morning, this is where arrangements are made. If you want to go to the park or find out anything about the area, Chico's Bar is the contact spot. If you just want to make friends and have a few beers, this is the place.

El Pardo Feliz is down from Chico's towards the beach and is another pleasant and well serviced place to eat. The prices are reasonable.

THINGS TO DO

The waterfall is one of the loveliest sites in Costa Rica. It is a twenty minute walk. To get there, go past Alfredo's and Lucy's. Once over the bridge, you will see a small path going to your right. Follow it. If you go as far as the road on your right, you have gone too far. The path follows the creek for about fifteen minutes. You may see monkeys on this walk. The pool at the waterfall is deep and many of the local boys spend hours climbing up the cliffs and jumping in. The water is clean and warm. The sun hits the pool at about 10:00AM.

Cabo Blanco National Park is on 1172 acres at the end of the peninsula. To get there on the four wheel drive road, you can hire a car or taxi for about ₡3000 ($20. US) at Chico's Bar. It is best if you can get together with six or seven people. Another alternative is to walk the 12 kilometers both ways, but this would make a long day in the tropical heat. If you do this, be certain you have plenty of water, as it is hot and dry. I would suggest at least half a litre of water per hour of walking. Most people take the car one way and walk back along the beach. It is a wonderful, scenic walk. When you get to the park, the warden will give a brief introduction and show you where to go. There are marked trails going through the jungle and down to the beach. You may see spider and howler monkeys, small deer, butterflies, birds and much more. The trees with the small spikes that stick out from the trunk have a medicinal use. If you pick a little bark and chew it for three minutes, your mouth will become numb. This is used by the locals for toothaches. The taste is quite bitter but the numbness is unmistakable. It may also be pounded into a pulp and put onto a wound. The walk back from Cabo Blanco is hot so be certain that you have not only a lot of water, but also your swim suit. If you run out of water there are a few farms you can stop at, but the tap water is not cold. The fresh water creeks flowing to the sea were safe to drink from the last time I was there.

There is no camping in this park nor on the Cabo Blanco Island that is just off the shore. The park takes a few hours to visit and the walk back is at least three. Enjoy, as this is a wonderful area of Costa Rica.

There is another story attached to Cabo Blanco that makes the area interesting. It is believed that Captain James Cook, while on a voyage with William Dampier and other pirates, met his death at the gates to Cabo Blanco. Because of his desires, Cook was not buried at sea, but on the coast of Costa Rica, somewhere on the shores around this park. It is believed that the pirates brought the body ashore, dug a shallow grave, placed the body, sword and pistol of Cook in it, drank some rum, spit into the wind, and headed out again after fighting with some local Indians. Today, some locals will tell you that Cook's ghost can be seen on stormy nights, walking the shore with sword and pistol while he watches for more enemy ships.

NICOYA

This is another beautiful, friendly town which can be used as an inexpensive base while enjoying the peninsula's beaches. This quiet town is cooler than the beaches and a convenient center for commuting. In the actual town, there is very little to do.

PLACES TO STAY

Pension Venecia is near the cathedral and is the best place to stay. The cheery rooms and communal showers down the hall are both very clean. The cost is ₡400 ($3. US) per person and singles are available.

Hotel Ali on one corner of the square, charges ¢500 ($2.50 US) per person but is dirty, noisy and smelly.

Hotel Jenny is one block closer to the bus station; if Pension Venecia is full, stay here. The rooms are ¢900 ($6.50 US) per night with private bath, air conditioning, soap and towel and, believe it or not, television. I could walk bare-footed in my room. The floors shone. The owners can give bus schedule information and recommend the best places to go. This is an excellent place to stay.

RESTAURANTS

I did not find any place that I would care to recommend in this town; you are on your own. Be brave. Try one or two Tica-type places. I did eat in a couple of Chinese restaurants and they were okay but .....

THINGS TO DO

Central Park has a colonial church dating back to the 1600's which is still in use. After a day on the beach, it is pleasant to spend the evening in the park.

Barra Honda National Park is close to Nicoya and could be visited for a day trip. The park has 5670 acres; its main attractions are the caves, but you must have a permit to enter, and you must have your own spelunking equipment. The permit must be obtained in San Josè at the Parks Office. There are other attractions to the park such as wildlife, hiking trails, a volcanic cone and nice views from the deciduous forest. Camping is available for those who have permits to enter the caves. The sites have water and bathrooms.

The 60 million year old Barra Honda Hill contains an extensive system of limestone caverns. Nineteen of them have been explored and some contain stalagmites, stalactites, columns, pearls, chalk flowers and needles. The Santa Ana cave is the deepest at 240 meters (800 ft.), but Nicoya is the most interesting. It is believed that it was once a cenote where pre-Columbian human sacrifices were made because human bones plus decorations and utensils have been found in that cave. I have not entered the caves, but if you are a cave lover, bring some equipment with you, visit the park at the beginning of your trip and leave some of the heavier (and less expensive) equipment with the park wardens. They have a difficult time getting equipment; donations are always greatfully accepted.

To get to the park, take the bus from Nicoya to Santa Ana and ask the bus driver to let you off on the road going to the park. It is about a half hour walk to the park entrance from the bus stop. However, not many buses going to Santa Ana each day, so check at the hotel before you make your plans.

Sugar Beach is 39 kilometers in from the road; a bus goes in and out. There are two hotels in Sugar Beach, the Tamarindo and the Portrero. As with all the beaches in Costa Rica, you can find your type of beauty. Some people like long stretches of sand and some like little rocky coves. You will find Sugar Beach to have both and it is still possible to have privacy. The restaurant is on a porch overlooking the beach. It is attractive and expensive. The beach is delightful and has not been over developed.

Nosara beach is 65 kilometers from Nicoya. The bus leaves at 1:00PM and returns at 6:00AM the next day. This presents a bit of a problem for making this a day trip. However, you can hitch a ride fairly easily because there is a good traffic flow to a nearby settlement. There are two basic places to stay in Nosara. The Cabinas Chorotega, right in the center of town, is the better of the two. It is inexpensive but acceptable. The beach itself is a delightful white sandy beach which can be walked for hours. If going south, there are a number of rocky coves perfect for suntanning.   **Playa Guiones** is on this same bus route and is a small beach just south of Nosara. You could get off the bus at Nosara and walk down to Guiones. However, Guiones does not have tourist accommodations.

Garza is a small beach about ten kilometers south of Nosara. The same bus going to Nosara goes through Garza. However, this is a richer and more developed area. There are no cheapies to stay at and the restaurant in town is expensive. The beach itself is on a small bay with a picturesque island in the center. There are rocky coves tucked away among the waves where you can enjoy solitude.

Samara Beach is a beautiful spot with white sandy beaches and soft gentle waves - not high surfing waves. On weekends, buses leave San Josè at 8:00AM and return at 2:00PM, but the ride is six hours one way. You can get a bus from Nicoya or hitch a ride. This is also a nice place to stay for a night or two. The views are beautiful and an aura of tranquility pervades. Punta Samara is a delightful place to stay; it has clean rooms, fans, private bathrooms, restaurant (with edible food), bar (noisy at night) and an ocean view. The prices are ¢1000 ($6. US) per night. If commuting is not your desire, then a few nights here will heal any travelling wounds you have acquired. The Nosara bus will take you to Samara.

OSA PENINSULA

The Osa Peninsula is an isolated and difficult place to visit. I am happy that a few of these places still exist. The peninsula is the home of Corcovado National Park, the Morenco Biological Station and the lesser known Tierra de Milagros private preserve. In other words, the entire peninsula is one park. However, it is hot, humid and swarming with mosquitoes.

To get there, you can take a bus from San Isidro to Puerto Jimenez daily at 5:30AM or at noon. You can also get there from Golfito by the ferry which leaves Golfito every day at noon. However, this ferry is inconsistent. Check in San Isidro or San Josè before planning on taking the ferry.

PLACES TO STAY - in Puerto Jimenez

Pension Quintero is about the best budget place to stay with rooms costing ₡350 ($2.50 US) per person per night without private bath. The rooms are spotless and the owners are pleasant.

Hotel Valentin also have clean rooms but they are stuffy and smaller than the Quintero. The bathrooms are shared; the rooms are only ₡300 ($2.25 US) per person.

Cabinas Marcelina is up the street from the other two hotels. They have private bathrooms and fans for ₡800 ($6. US) a night. Fans are a luxury after being further down the peninsula.

In Las Palmas there are some small cabins, so if you finish there, you know that there is a place to stay. They are acceptable.

Carate is just outside the park boundary and if you get to Puerto Jimenez, you should be able to hitch a ride to here with little problem. There are three Canadians gold mining in the area and they have a couple of cabins that they will rent. These are comfortable.

RESTAURANTS

Agua Luna next to the docks is a good place for fresh sea food. I like fried fish with lots of garlic and when you ask for lots, they provide it. They say garlic helps keep the mosquitoes away; it certainly keeps any friends away.

THINGS TO DO

Corcovado National Park is the main attraction to this interesting but isolated area. You can walk to the park from Carate but it is along the beach and the sand is soft so the walking is difficult. You will also need tide charts as there are places where you could get stuck. Walking overland from Puerto Jimenez to the park could be dangerous if you should stumble upon some undesirable sight. It is rumored that this route is discouraged for reasons the government won't admit. However, I have spoken to people who did walk overland and had no problems - obviously, since they talked to me after their excursion.

There is a four wheel drive that goes from Puerto Jimenez to Carate on Thursdays and Saturdays; the owner charges about $5.00 US per person. From Carate, the park entrance is a few hours of difficult walking along the coast. You must inform the park service that you are going into the park, or you must bring your own food. The cost of staying with the park service is ₡1800 ($13.50 US) per day but includes three meals. You MUST have a mosquito net as the mosquitoes are the large variety imported from northern Canada. A variety of animals and birds live in this park because the isolation protects them. Also, the mosquitoes keep the birds quite fat. It is a damp area (good breeding grounds for mosquitoes) and can be muddy.

A nice circle hike is possible from Carate to the headquarters, through the park, and back to Las Palmas. It is a full day's hike from the park headquarters to Las Palmas and you will be hot, tired and thirsty when you finish. This hike can be done in either direction. You can get a ride either to Las Palmas or to Carate.

Corcovado park has 103,254 acres of rain forest which gets up to 5500 millimeters of rain per year. There are also cloud forests, alluvial plains, swamp forests, holillo forests, herbaceous swamp and mangrove swamps. The 500 different tree species and the flowers are astounding. Some spots have over 100 species of trees in one hectare. There are about 140 different mammals, 370 birds, 120 amphibians and reptiles, 40 freshwater fish and most abundant of all, 6000 types of insects. Crocodiles, jaguar and dantas which are all endangered species plus squirrel monkeys, giant anteaters, harpy eagles, scarlet macaws and red-throated caracaras all live in the park.

The park has five ranger stations where you can camp. Fresh water is available at these sites and marked trails go from one station to the next. If you make pre-arrangements with the park service, you may have meals prepared for you when you are staying at these stations. All sites have bathrooms but not showers. The ranger stations are at Sirena, Los Patos, La Palma, San Pedrillo and Puerto Jimenez. Be certain to go to the ranger station in Puerto Jimenez for a map and instructions. Each station is about a day's hike from the next which could be anywhere from five to eight hours of hot, humid hiking. Water and supplementary food needed between the stations must be carried. Meals must be previously arranged with the park's service.

Morenco Biological Station is a privately-owned nature reserve on the Peninsula bordering on Corcovado National Park. In fact, you can walk here from the park. This area is of special interest to researchers, history buffs, student groups and bird watchers.

To get to the Biological Station you should make reservations by calling the Administration Office, Edificio Cristal, 2nd Floor, Ave. 1, Calle 1-3, San José, telephone 21-15-94 or write the Morenco Biological Station, Apt. 4025, 1000 San José, Costa Rica, C.A.

You can fly from San José by charter flight to Morenco or you may take a bus to Uvita or Sierpe and have the Morenco boat take you to the reserve. These arrangements can be made in advance. The other way to reach the preserve is by walking from Corcovado Park. The rangers can give complete details on this section of the hike. If advance arrangements have not been made, there may not be room at the station for you to have a bungalow; you would be stuck in your tent for another night.

Researchers will be given special rates and considerations because their work is of benefit to both the reserve and the country. If an outline of the study is presented and authorization received, those at Morenco can help with arrangements, guides, field assistants, cooks and horse handlers; as well, they have a tremendous amount of information on the area.

Morenco has a unique approach to conservation as they are trying to bridge the gap between education and tourism. They hope to develop an awareness of the delicate balance and intricacy of natural systems and they have one of the best places in which to do this. Morenco has helped to develop some of the natural parks, biological reserves, wildlife refuges, national monuments and Indian reserves which now comprise 25% of the land area of Costa Rica.

The cabins are dormitory style, four persons to a cabin. The accommodation site is 60 meters above the ocean which ensures a beautiful view from the balcony of your cabin plus a gentle breeze to keep you cool and insect-free at night. With over 6000 types of insects in the area, this is important! Showers and bathroom facilities are in a separate quarter. Meals are served in a dining hall and special arrangements can be made for packed lunches when an excursion is planned. An information center whith a small library, papers of local interest, maps, species lists of the area, and a reference collection of preserved local specimens is available. There are also an archaeologist and a biologist at the site to answer any questions. This entire package is offered for around $100 US per day. The minimum time recommended to stay at Morenco is two days, but if walking in from the park (five kilometers to the south) you may be able to make different arrangements.

Two excursion packages, either for three nights and four days or four nights and five days are available. The three night package includes travel, orientation to flora and fauna, guided nature walks through the rain forest to a swimming hole and an all-day excursion to the Corcovado National Park. The four-night package includes all of the above plus a visit to Isla del Caño, which is a real bonus. These excursions are expensive but you will get to see sights that others will never see while in Costa Rica.

Caño Island Biological Reserve is off the western coast of the Osa Peninsula and just a bit north of the park border. It is 20 kilometers out into the ocean and difficult to access. You must have a permit from the park wardens before going. Camping is permitted and there are water and toilet facilities. You must have a stove and food.

The main attraction to this preserve is the opportunity for snorkeling. The water is incredibly warm and has abundant underwater wildlife. If you would like more information on this area, see the wardens.

Coco Islands are also a park preserve, but they are 650 kilometers off the coast of Costa Rica, at the northern tip of the Galapagos Archipelago in Ecuador. They are inaccessible to most of us. The trip is 36 hours by fast boat one way. However, I mention the park here for its historical ditties. The island is famous for its three pirate treasures from William Davis, Benito "Bloody Sword" Bonito and William Thompson. The last, a result of the sacking of La Lima, is one of the greatest lost treasures in history and consists of many tons of gold. It is also believed that Captain Cook visited this island on his last voyage to America.

Over 500 treasure expeditions to the island have found only a few coins. If you wish to try your luck, you may have found the vacation spot of your desires. However, the natural treasure of the island is far greater. The volcanic islands have about 7000 millimeters of rain a year; this makes it a lush jungle.

PUERTO NARANJA

This is where you will catch the ferry for Puntarenas if you are on your way to or from the Nicoya Peninsula. The ferry goes quite frequently. The little village of Puerto Naranja has an adequate beach, one expensive hotel and one that it a bit cheaper. There is a wildlife preserve 25 kilometers south of here. Otherwise, although a lovely area, it is not yet a touristy area.

PLACES TO STAY

Hotel De Paso costs ¢2000 ($15. US) for a room without aircon. These clean rooms include private bathrooms, clean towels, soap, mirror, clean beds, pleasant service, excellent trips to surrounding beaches (extra). It is an excellent hotel.

Oasis del Pacifico is the big hotel that charges too much and is seldom full. It has a swimming pool, tennis courts, horses, boats, restaurant, bar and disco. If you are interested they may be willing to let you have a room for a bit cheaper - depending on occupancy. Most rooms go for about $50.00 US for a double. However, the restaurant is good and the meals are a decent size.

THINGS TO DO

Curu Wildlife Refuge is just south of Paquera Village and has many interesting wild creatures to see while walking through the small 200 acre forested area. Bird watchers have found many types of birds. A major attraction are the sea turtles. If you are a biology student or researcher, then you may want to visit here as the people that own the refuge are both knowledgeable and helpful. If you are interested in this area, ask about it at the Hotel De Paso.

PUERTO VIEJO

This village is about two hours from Limon and past Cahuita. It is on the ocean, is much quieter than Cahuita, and has not lost some of its Caribbean charm. However, there are many expensive, hotels catering to the Germans; every time you visit the beach, you will see a new hotel being built. This is an excellent surfing area and there is a surf crowd who hangs out here. It is also close to the Talamanca Indian Reserve which makes visiting there convenient.

PLACES TO STAY

Cabiñas Jacarinda is run by a lady named Vera. To find her place "ask anyone, everyone knows me" is what Vera says and this is true. Her place is clean and quiet with mosquito nets over the beds and pleasant decor in the large rooms. There is a communal bath and free information about the entire area. The cost is ₡1200 ($9. US) for a double. This is a good value. Vera is also opening a restaurant on the premises which will serve some of the best food in Costa Rica. I highly recommend staying here.

Cabinas Salsa-brava are on the beach towards Punto Uva. The four rooms cost ₡700 ($5. US) a night and are quite popular. It is difficult to get a room. There are no private baths.

Escapi Cabineño are towards Chiquita Beach and charge ₡3000 (22.US) per night. The beautiful cabins are on the opposite side of the road from the office. They are clean, have patio chairs, fridge, and a private bath. There is a small kiosk where you can purchase and enjoy cool drinks. Although expensive, this place is nice and is owned by Ticans.

Puerto Viejo Hotel is small with basic, stuffy rooms and beds which have mosquito nets for a mere ₡700 ($5. US) for a double. There are no private bathrooms. There is a wonderful ocean breeze. The surfers usually gather here.

Hotel Maritza is on the main drag just past the bus stop and costs ₡1500 ($11. US) for a cabin with fan, private bath, hot water and large rooms. This is a good deal.

Hotel Ritz is run by Vincent, a wonderful man who loves to tell stories to those who have the time to listen. The rooms are ₡700 ($5. US) per night for a double. They are basic without private baths. The hotel is also next door to the bar and is therefore quite noisy. However, even if you don't stay there, go and talk to Vincent. He is delightful.

Hotel Pura Vida is a bit expensive but quite nice. Walk past Vera's, turn right at the corner and go down the path about 100 meters. These rooms have private bathrooms.

Punta Uva Cabinas are a great place to stay. The have large, clean rooms, pleasant owners and charge ₡1000 ($7.50 US) for a double. There is a delightful flower garden to sit in and it is away from the hub of the main part of town. However, it is a long walk past the bus stop, so I would suggest leaving your belongings at Puerto Viejo and walking out to see if they have a room. If they have rooms, you can easily hitch a ride both ways. I liked this place.

Camping is available just past Escapi Cabineño toward Chiquita beach, but the place is a dump, with no running water.

When I asked a price, he was too stoned to tell me how much. This is not where I would want to stay, especially if you environmentally conscious.

RESTAURANTS

There are many place to eat in the area and, as tourism increases, more and more will appear.

Vera's at the Jacarinda is now open and you should be able to get excellent meals. I ate some of Vera's food while I was there, before the restaurant opened, and it was so good that I am pre-recommending her restaurant.

Tamara's Restaurant is near the beach and is the most popular place to eat. The fish is excellent and the milk pie is always sold out early in the day, but the service can be slow and the waitresses can be quite rude. It was here that I decided that male tourists should deal only with women working in the industry and female tourists should deal only with the men. That way, there would be no rudeness nor sexual discrimination.

Coral Restaurant has superb pizza, but the food is expensive. The place is clean and the lemon pie is irresistible. Try some!

Johnny's is by the beach and a popular beer stop. You can also get a decent meal of Chinese food; however, the fish fried in butter is by far his best dish. This restaurant is popular with the locals.

Restaurant Caribe is also by the beach and is both busy and popular. The only way they can get the place cleaned is to close it for a few hours each day. The food is good, the music is loud, the ocean breezes are wonderful and the prices are comparable.

Restaurant Natural is on the way to Punta Uva. It is on a hill overlooking the entire Caribbean Ocean. The drinks are all natural and delectable.

Mix-tica restaurant has poor food and they really do not care if they get your business.

Dudley's Ice Stand is a must. Dudley is a delightful local resident who serves the best flavored ice in all Costa Rica. People come all the way from Limon just to have some of his flavored ice. If you have always wanted to try some, but never had the nerve, this man's products will guarantee you will want it again. Dudley hangs out near the Restaurant Caribe; be certain to ask for him, as his ice is the best I have ever tasted.

THINGS TO DO

Chiquita Beach is a delightful place to visit. To get there, walk along the path just past the Restaurant Caribe, along the beach and through the bush until you come to a huge rock in the water and a cliff on the shore. Just past the cliff (go behind) is a wonderful little bay with a beautiful beach, good snorkeling and lots of privacy. There is no place to eat or drink so take snacks and water.

Punta Uva is five kilometers (three miles) past Puerto Viejo and it is easy to hitch rides both ways during the day. Another option is to rent a bike in Puerto Viejo; these must be booked and paid for in advance. Punta Uva is down the road going the opposite way from Cahuita, past the Restaurant Natural (up on a hill), and over a wooden bridge and then take the first left after the bridge. The bay is large and calm and is the beginning of a biological preserve.

Gandoca Manzanillo Wildlife Preserve covers a large land and sea area from Punta Uva to the Panama border. The main attraction of this park is the snorkeling off the living reef, just a few hundred feet from the shore. The refuge also has the only red mangrove swamp in Costa Rica. This in turn houses different creatures. The natural oyster bed is the specialty of the area. The many birds and animals in the preserve make it an attractive place to visit. You will also see locals building dugout canoes from trees and then taking the canoes out for fishing.

To reach the park, rent a bicycle or hitchhike. Once you get to the end of the road, you will see a wooden house. Beyond this house is a lagoon which marks the beginning of the preserve. The house belongs to Burton who will take you either on a guided tour of the park or take you to the reef. His wife will cook you a meal or you may purchase a beer. This is an oasis in the jungle.

Some people stay in Manzanillo where there are cheap rooms. Others get a group together and rent a vehicle. The very hardy walk. It is a long day (about 30 km) but, without a pack, possible. Be certain to take lots of water. There is a place to get food and water in Manzanillo.

Talamanca Indian Reserve is at Sheroli. To get there, you must take a bus to Bribri, then change for a bus to Sheroli. It is about a three hour ride and is certainly worth the effort. The trip through the beautiful mountains is worth six hours on a hot and dusty bus. Once in Sheroli, you may rent a four-legged taxi and go into the mountains. There are herbal doctors in the hills who will help you and your ails. You must take the path that leads across the river and then up the mountain. You must be completely self sufficient. Carry a sleeping bag and food. It would be an overnight trip. You can hire a guide and rent a horse from the man who lives just up the road from the bus turnaround. You will be able to see his corral. If you wish to stay in the reserve overnight, there are basic cabins at Suretka, down the road a few kilometers from Sheroli. These are very rustic with no plumbing. You must have your own food. This reserve is interesting to visit for a day trip, but the visit is limited to two hours because of bus schedules. There are only two buses a day going to Sheroli.

PUNTARENAS

I have not heard of one person liking this grubby little town. It is dirty, hot and unpleasant which is unusual for Costa Rica. If you are stuck here while waiting to go elsewhere, there is a long, crowded, dirty beach, complete with a few pickpockets, south of town where you can cool off.

However, Puntarenas was not always an undesirable place to be. Before Limon became an important port for the shipping of coffee to Europe, Puntarenas was the most important port. The carts, which are now seen as tourist attractions, were once an important part of the transportation system, and they all ended here in Puntarenas loaded down with goods going to Europe.

Puntarenas is also a sandspit which means that it is a piece of land that was formed by winds blowing the sands until they became a solid piece of land. These spits are common on some of the northern Pacific islands like the Queen Charlottes in Canada. The spits here offer a refuge for many marine birds. Because Puntarenas is built on a long spit of land, there are only five avenues in the town although there are around sixty streets.

PLACES TO STAY

I cannot recommend a good place to stay; everything I looked at was very basic at best. Since the market area is the most central (for example, it you want the 6:00AM ferry for Paquera or are waiting to go to Monteverde), look for a place near the market and get an extra ten minutes of sleep. **The Hotel Cayuga** on Ave 3, Calle Central is about the best place you can find. It runs for about ₡1200 ($9. US) with a private bath for a double complete with air conditioning. There is also a restaurant on the premises.

RESTAURANTS

As in all Costa Rican towns, there are a number of Chinese restaurants available. The best here is the **Mandarin** on the main street. Also, many people eat at the bus stop which is remarkably good. There are a lot of locally owned soda places on the Paseo de los Turistas (along the beach) that serve good food at Puntarenas prices.

THINGS TO DO

San Lucas Prison is an interesting place to visit but this can be done only on Sunday. You can take a boat over and visit the old prison, which still houses inmates. The prisoners will sell or trade their handicrafts for money or items such as toothpaste, cigarettes, razors or other luxuries. Ladies travelling alone should be aware that these are prisoners and they have not been free for some time. Dress modestly for both your sake and theirs. The boat leaves by the Paquera dock at 9:00AM on Sunday and returns at 3:00PM. If you go over be certain to be on the boat coming back!

Beaches going from Puntarenas down towards Jaco are not plentiful at this time but development of the Pacific coast is occurring rapidly and this will soon change. The established beaches are **Doña Ana, Mata Limon, Puerto Caldera, Playa Tarcoles and Herradura**. At present, these beaches have places to stay. You can hire a guide and a boat to do some birding and exploring of estuaries and mangrove swamps. Tarcoles is a gravel beach and Herradura is a black sand beach; none of these beaches are known for their extreme cleanliness. Until ecology takes hold in Costa Rica, this will remain a problem for these more isolated areas.

QUEPOS

This is a swinging little town at night, more so a few years ago than today but still with lots to do. Often people like to stay here and commute to the beach at Manuel Antonio during the day. The first bus leaves for the beach at 6:00AM and the last bus returns at 5:00PM. The cost for the trip is about 25¢ each way. It is also much cheaper to live in Quepos than it is to live in Manuel Antonio.

PLACES TO STAY

Hotel Ramu is now the best buy in town. The owner charges ¢620 ($4.50 US) per person per night without a private bath. The place is cleaner than spotless, quiet and the owner also gives the best exchange rate in town. This is a real find and should be the first place tried.

Hotel Ceciliano is still a popular place to stay, but it is no longer the quaint little building with a wooden porch. It is now an expensive, spiffy place. The price is ¢1500 ($11. US) for two with a bathroom. It is still a family-run business, with a homey atmosphere, always clean and usually full.

Mary Luna is another excellent find at ¢1000 ($7.50 US) for a double with a bath. The rooms are clean and spacious and the owners are friendly. If Ramu's is full, try this one. They are across the street from one another.

Hotel Malinche offers rooms at ¢650 for a single and ¢1200 for a double ($4.50-$9. US) complete with a bathroom. It is another delightful place to stay and these prices are much below Manuel Antonio's price plus it is Tican owned.

Helen's is across from the Ceciliano and charges ¢1500 ($11. US) for a double with a bathroom. The rooms are large and clean and the owners are quite helpful. However, this is also a place that fills up quickly.

Hotel Quepos is expensive for what you get. It is ¢1500 ($11. US) for a small, stuffy, double room. The owners are quite unfriendly so this should only be a last resort. However, the wood floors gleam with cleanliness and polish. The women work so hard keeping the hotel clean that they have no energy left for friendliness.

Majestic Hotel costs ¢400 ($3. US) per person but the place is not all that clean. There are no rooms with a bathroom.

RESTAURANTS

There are a few restaurants to eat in Quepos but the good French restaurant is closed. There are reliable Chinese restaurants plus a few others. The ones along the street beside the water are good but nothing is outstanding. I think Manuel Antonio has the better restaurants in the area.

Restaurant Ana is an acceptable place to eat with hamburgers and sodas being the specialty of the day. Prices are in the mid-range.

Soda Isobel is up the street from Ana and offers some good meals at a reasonable price. The fish dinners are almost always recommended when the restaurants are near the ocean.

THINGS TO DO

Deep Sea Fishing is expensive in this area but you are guaranteed fish. A boat costs $500.00 US for the full day including beer and lunch. A man I know went and caught about six sail fish, had his picture taken and released the fish. Environmentally this is better than trophy fishing. The men also caught some large (I don't know what type) fish for supper which they fried. It was excellent.

Manuel Antonio Park - see under Manuel Antonio. Buses go and return every hour.

QUESADA

If you would like to be the only gringo in town and practice your Spanish, then you may want to spend a day in Quesada. Otherwise, there is little to do here. There is a nice central park area where you can speak to the locals, people watch, and eat and drink at a reasonable price.

PLACES TO STAY

Hotel Conquistador is on Calle Central below the plaza and has spacious, quiet rooms with private bathrooms for ¢1200 -1500 ($9.-$11. US). It is a nice, quiet and friendly place to stay.

RESTAURANTS

There are a few restaurants on the main plaza.

SAN ISIDRO DE GENERAL

This is a delightful town where you may make your base if you want to visit the spectacular Chirripo National Park. Costa Rica's highest peaks are above beautiful cloud forest in this park. To get there, travel along the breath-taking Pacuare River and valley. You will pass Cerro de Muerte (hill of death), the highest peak standing at 11,400 feet, along the Panamerican highway.

PLACES TO STAY

Hotel Chirripo is on the main square and charges ¢1315 ($10. US) for a double with a private bath. It is adequate and may be a bit noisy at night.

Hotel Astoria is on the square and has small cheap rooms. A double without a bath costs ¢800 ($6. US) and ¢1070 ($8. US) with a bath. The rooms at the back of this one story hotel are good.

The Balboa has double rooms for ¢700 ($5. US) with bath. It is nothing special.

The Ideal is really cheap and really grubby.

The Lala is a good cheapie and costs ¢700 ($5. US) for two without private bathrooms. This is one of the noisiest hotels in town. However, the friendliness outshines the noise.

The Ahaneli is ¢1400 ($10.50 US) for a double and is the cleanest in town. The rooms are large, complete with fan and hot water. It is on the main highway going out of town.

RESTAURANTS

Food is not the main attraction to San Isidro.

Restaurant El Tenedor has reasonably priced pizza that is quite good. It is nice to sit on the small balcony and watch Tican life while eating as long as the gas fumes don't persist in ruining your meal.

The Ahaneli Hotel has a restaurant which serves good food when the ladies are working. They will serve coffee and a toasted bun for breakfast for a decent price after you have missed your first attempt at catching the bus to the park.

THINGS TO DO

Chirripo National Park is the main reason people come to San Isidro. The park is 603,000 acres of rich, biological preserve. It has the largest remaining virgin forest. It also has the region's largest hydroelectric potential. There are many different ecosystems at different elevations, with different soil types and climates which are evident. One is the beautiful fern forest. Because there is such diversity, it is claimed this area could feed up to 60% of the country's wildlife. Mount Chirripo is the highest mountain in the country, standing at 3842 meters or 12,606 feet. La Amistad park is part of the area and is the Costa Rican - Panamanian International Friendship Park.

To reach the park catch the 5:00AM bus going to San Gerardo. It leaves from the MAIN square not from the bus station. Many locals will not be able to give you correct information, but they want to be helpful (especially at 4:30AM) so they will often give incorrect information. The bus leaves from the main square.

San Gerardo has basic rooms. If you take the late afternoon bus to San Gerardo, or if you finish hiking late, you will not be left out in the cold.

Check with the park rangers in San Josè and make arrangements for food and lodgings in the park huts. The wardens like to know who is in the park. You will be more comfortable in the huts than camping unless you have camping gear.

Wear good boots and warm clothes if going to the top of the mountain. It is over 12,000 feet and it can be cold even on a warm day. You must have sunscreen because the rays are stronger. The length of time you spend hiking is up to you. The main trail can be hiked in two days with one night in a hut. It is much better to spend three days and two nights or longer on this hike. It is an excellent park to explore; I suggest three days minimum.

The hike takes eight to ten hours to the first hut that sits at 10,000 feet. It is a long way to go in one day and you will be tired at the end of the day. It takes another three hours to reach the top of the mountain where marked trails lead to a few lakes.

Once hiking, you will see the fern forest. Then, you will come to an alpine-like area called the paramo where there is often frost but no snow. In some areas, the brush is very dense. This is because the precipitation is as high as 7000 mm per year. Quetzales have been seen in the park so look for them while puffing to 10,000 feet.

La Amistad Park is a UNESCO (world heritage) park. It is next to Chirripo Park but is not easily accessible. There are no hiking trails or amenities in the park. However, the park has a huge amount of wild life including the Baird's tapirs, anteaters, jaguars, puma, ocelot, and many common animals. There are over 500 species of birds in the park. Some are indigenous to this area. Snakes, frogs and iguanas are abundant and may make you start if you startle them in the dense jungle. This is not a park for the average chickenbuser. If you want more information about this park, contact the wardens in San Josè.

Rio General white water rafting has class III and IV white water. The trip is 75 kilometers (47 miles) from San Isidro to El Brujo on the Panamerican highway. The General is a "play" river with surfing waves for the kayaker or the experienced canoer. There are whirlpool and hydraulic play areas interspersed between gentle flowing areas. The scenery down the river is wild and exciting, and the water is warm in the event of a roll or spill. This river can be rafted with a group or you may be able to rent a kayak from Rios Tropicales, PO Box 472-1200 in San Josè, Costa Rica or telephone (504)33-6455.

SAN JOSE

The capital of Costa Rica is one of the most pleasant cities in Central America. It is clean, easy to tour, and has many sights to see. The vendors are clean for the most part and you may save money by purchasing from them instead of eating in restaurants. If you crave "junk" food, McDonalds and Pizza Hut are in the downtown area.

The city has a population of 275,000 people. It sits at 1200 meters (4000 ft) above sea level giving it a warm daytime climate of around 75°F, but a cool evening temperature. The very center of town is at Ave. Central and Calle Central. The avenues go east to west and the streets go north to south. From Ave. Central north, the avenues are odd numbered. From Ave. Central south, they are even-numbered. The streets are even-numbered west of Calle Central and odd-numbered to the east. This makes address finding very easy.

Costa Rican oxcart

PLACES TO STAY

Pension Otoya, on Calle Central and Ave. 5-7 is the best hotel in San Josè for the budget traveller. The building is clean and safe, and has a lovely garden in the main hall. There are a TV and lounge chairs there. The large, clean rooms cost ¢700 for two and ¢500 for a single ($5. & $3.75 US). The separate bathrooms have plenty of hot water. The owner, Yolanda speaks some English and is helpful. This hotel is the Doña Luisa's of Costa Rica. For reservations call 21-39-25

Pension Americana is on Calle 2, Ave. 1 and still a popular place with travellers. However, the price has gone up to ₡600 ($4.50 US) per person, but they have made no improvements. There are copious amounts of ice cold water and the mattresses are made of hard straw. The hotel puts one sheet on the bed. If you can't get into the Otoya then try this one as they often have vacancies. The rooms at the front are quiet and large with small balconies and 16-foot ceilings. You can leave your bags if travelling for a few days.

Ticalinda is on Ave. 2 and Calle 5, #553. The hotel is difficult to find. Look for a blue door across from the Sixaola Dry Cleaning Shop. There is a tiny sign on the door but nothing that can be seen from a distance. This is the closest to a hostel you will find in Costa Rica. The rooms are fairly clean and secure. You can make sandwiches or snacks in the common room. The cost is ₡450 ($3.50 US) per person. There is no hot water or private bath and the hotel is often noisy. Laundry facilities are available.

Hotel Asia on Ave. 1, Calle 11, just one and one half blocks up the street from Tiny's Bar. The rooms are clean and quiet, and the men speak English. They have hot water. The rooms are claustrophobically small but the hotel is popular with the backpacking crowd. The cost is ₡700 ($5.25 US) for a double.

Doña Alice on Calle 3 and Ave. 6-8 costs ₡450 ($3.50 US) per person and is a dump. There are no private bathrooms. It is certainly as good as Pension Americana.

Pension Salamanca is two blocks from the Ticalinda on Ave. 2. It is ₡500 ($3.75 US) per person and is barely adequate. The little dog in the hotel is cute but barks all night. There is a single room at the back that costs ₡300 ($2.25 US) but the bed has no mattress. There is also no hot water.

Hospedaje Avenida Segunda is on Ave. 2, Calle 9-11 and is ₡600 ($4.50 US) per person. It is clean and secure. If you are tired and the Tikalinda is full, try this hotel. You may look for a different room the next day. A bonus is that there is hot water here.

Hotel Colon on Calle 4, Ave. 1, #150 N is only ₡600 ($4.50 US) per person and is clean and fresh looking. The price is right and the location is great.

Hotel Capital on Calle 4, Ave. 1 is expensive at ₡900 ($6.75 US) per person but this includes a private bath and hot water. If you are in need of comfort and the Otoya is full, this may be the hotel for you.

Gran Centroamericano is on Ave. 2, Calle 8 and is ₡1100 ($8.15 US) per person. It is clean with private bathrooms and pleasant management. The rooms are small and it is often full. The location is excellent.

Hotel Rialto on Calle 2, Ave. 5 was recommended to me by a fellow traveller because it has hot water. A room with a window but no curtains was $500 ($3.75 US) per person. However, it was so noisy that, at midnight, I got up and asked the people in the common room to please stop shouting when speaking. In the morning, I did get to stand under a scalding hot shower for at least 15 minutes. The staff are friendly and helpful and take messages for travellers.

Musoc Pension is on Calle 16 and Ave. 1-3. It is close to the Coca Cola Bus Station. This makes catching an early bus travel easier. The cost is ₡1000 ($7.50 US) for a single without private bath. They have some rooms with private bath at a slightly higher price. The hotel is clean and secure. It is used by many travellers that do not like the cheapies.

Bella Vista on Ave. Central and Calle 19-21 is ₡1850 ($13.75 US) for a double with a bathroom. This is expensive if you are alone because they do not have single rates. It is clean and English is spoken. You may safely leave your pack here while travelling.

Hotel Johnson on Calle 8 and Ave. Central costs ₡1300 ($9.75 US) for a double. The rooms are very clean and there is a restaurant on the premises. This is a real find considering that Pension Americano charges ₡1200 for two and it is a dump in comparison. This hotel is often full.

Hotel Bienvenido is on Calle 10, Ave. 1-3 and is brand new. The cost is ₡1825 ($13.US) per person. It includes a private bath with hot water (from a tank not an immersion heater). There are 44 rooms and the staff speak English. The front door is locked and secured during the night. This is a nice hotel and the owners are trying to establish a good name. I can see them succeeding.

Hotel Marlyn on Calle 4, Ave. 7 charges ₡400 ($3. US) for a single without bath and ₡700 ($5.25 US) for a room with private bath and lots of hot water. The rooms are clean and spacious.

Toruma Youth Hostel is a huge, old, rambling building in Los Yoses, a suburb of San Josè. Because bus service is good, this is a popular place to stay. Walking is not that difficult because the hotel is fifteen blocks from the post office. The hostel is on Ave. Central and Calle 29-31. This hostel is affiliated with the International Youth Hostel Assoc. There are clean, safe, segregated, dormitory rooms. The beds cost is ₡700 ($5. US) per person and you should have a sleeping bag. The price includes breakfast. There are laundry facilities and a lunch counter but no cooking facilities. The large pleasant porch and yard are a drawing card to this hostel. The owners will take reservations. Telephone (506) 24-40-85 or 53-65-88

The Peace Hostel is run by the Quakers and is an excellent place to stay or visit. It is on Calle 15 and Ave. 6-8. The cost of a room is ₡700 ($5. US) per person and includes kitchen facilities. There is a small library for those interested in the world peace movements. Any type of non-violent intervention on any global issues could result in a long and pleasant discussion. This is a great place.

RESTAURANTS

Soda Palace is on 2nd Ave., up from the Pension Americano. The money changers hang around this area. Others are on the same street but closer to the post office. Of all the times I have been in Costa Rica, I have never seen many women in the Soda Palace. So gals, I suggest you patronize as a matter of principal.

Tiny's Bar on Ave. 2, Calle 11 is a popular and pleasant bar where you can meet other travellers. There are a couple of TV's tuned to the sports channel and the atmosphere is relaxed. The meal specialties are hamburgers and chili.

Piano Blanco Bar is on Ave. 1, Calle 10, across from the El Presedentè. It is expensive but clean, friendly and pleasant. It is often frequented by other English speaking people. However, there is no piano.

Amstel Hotel on Ave. 1, Calle 7 is a clean and pleasant hotel to have breakfast. The service is good and the coffee is nonending. The prices are not cheap.

El Calcon de Europa is on Ave. Central and Calle 9. The restaurant serves excellent Italian food with a cheese plate at the end of the meal. The restaurant will be moving around the corner to Calle 9, off Central in 1993. The pastries in this restaurant are excellent. This restaurant is highly recommended while in San Josè.

Promesas Bar on Ave. Central and Calle 7-9 is popular with the gringos. It is just down from the Piano Blanco Bar. The prices are lower than Blanco's and the atmosphere is rowdier. It is a good bar to have a beer and watch the street traffic.

Via Veneto Italian Restaurant is classier than most but if you want a nice evening, this restaurant is excellent. Take the San Pedro bus to Plaza del Sol and walk half a block past the plaza to get there. Wine is recommended with dinner.

Chalet Suizo is half block south of Parque Morezan (by the Holiday Inn) and is excellent. The atmosphere is sophisticated and the food is well prepared. The portions are small.

Key Largo Bar is past the Amstel Hotel on Ave. 1, Calle 7. It is a good bar, but it is difficult to find. It is between the Amstel and the kiosk in Morezan Park. The bar is on the corner. The bar is an old school made into the best pick-up joint in town. The atmosphere is wonderful. There are four bars; one with a band, one with a TV, one with stuffed fish on the wall and one is quiet, eating room. There is a casino upstairs. The old crystal chandeliers, old wood decor and the stained glass windows in the doors give the place a 1930's atmosphere.

Churreria Manolo Chocolateria on Ave Central and Calle 2 or on Ave. Central and Calle 11 are the best breakfast restaurants I know. The fruit portions are large and the coffee is strong. Service is quick and prices are reasonable.

Bella Vista on Ave. Central and Calle 19-21 specializes in Limon-style cooking and is enjoyed by many. The owner speaks English which makes selection easier. The building is old and the floor a bit wonky, but that has no effect on the food.

Chicharronera Nacional on Ave. 1, Calle 10-12 is excellent and cheap. The only problem is it is always full. Chicharrons are pieces of fried pork fat eaten like we eat the bags of dried potato chips. The stews in this restaurant are excellent.

Poas Tabernay Restaurant is on Ave. 7, Calles 3-5. This restaurant offers happy hour with bocas (snacks). The meal of the day costs about ¢200 ($1.50 US) and is usually good. The a la carte menu is more expensive.

Restaurante Beirut is on Ave. 1, Calle 32, is clean and offers excellent food. After eating, walk back to the center of town and shake down your large dinner.

La Hacienda Steak House is on Calle 7, between Ave. Central & 2nd. This restaurant has stood the test of time and is still offering good steaks after twelve years of business.

Restaurant La Macrobiotica on Ave. 1, Calle 11-15 is a vegetarian restaurant which has moved from the other end of the town. Since vegetarian restaurants are hard to find, this one will probably stay in business for a long time. It serves good food at reasonable prices.

The Gran Hotel Costa Rica on the square is a great hotel to have coffee and a pastry at any time. The coffee is nonending and strong.

The National Theatre Coffee Shop has excellent pastries which are enjoyed by non-Ticos. The shop's French hot chocolate is served with heaps of whipped cream, and the expressos are good. It is the old bar style atmosphere that makes the shop appealing. There is local art work on display around the room. This is a great place to rest in the afternoon, practice Spanish (because it takes lots of energy) and consume copious amounts of calories.

Jappys House of Cheesecake is another great place to stock up on calories - especially if you are heading north to Nicaragua where cheesecake is rare. Jappys bakery is 200 meters west of Pops in La Sabana and a good place to stop after touring the museum. They also have good sesame cookies.

Restaurant Kam Wah on Ave. 2, Calle 5-7 is excellent. It is a bit dingy when you first walk in but once your eyes acclimatize, you will be able to appreciate the wonderful (and cheap) meals. The service is excellent and all the meals are good.

THINGS TO DO

The National Theatre is on Ave. 2, Calle 3-5, across from the Gran Hotel and bordering the Plaza de Cultura. The theatre is the most popular landmark in San Josè and is the Tican's pride and joy.

In 1890, Angela Pelati, a prominent opera singer, was in Guatemala on tour, and the Costa Ricans wanted her to perform in their country too. However, there was no adequate stage for her so she did not come. This sparked a campaign to get a theatre built in San Josè. The building was financed through a coffee tax approved by the general population. After many trials and tribulations, the building was completed and the inauguration took place on October 19, 1897.

The plans and metal framework were done by Belgian architects and craftsmen. The Great Hall of Spectacles seats 1040 spectators. The hall is grandly ornamented with baroque decorations over-laid in 22 1/2 karat gold. Maintenance of the theatre has emphasized preservation of the original style. For efficiency, the stage has been modernized with the latest mechanical and electrical equipment. The central soffit or ceiling fresco is a painting done by the Italian painter, Arturo Fontana. It is illuminated by an eighty-five light chandelier made by craftsmen from the Costa Rican Ministry of Public Works. The Presidential Box is located in the exact centre of the balcony, directly over the entrance. The box has a soffit by Fontana which depicts justice and the country. The floor mechanism is a special feature of the theatre. There is a manual winch in the basement which allows the floor to be winched to the level of the stage. This takes twelve men 55 minutes. In days past, it was done so that the theatre could be made into a ballroom. The Lamp Vestibule or lobby is decorated in sculptures and high relief works in Carrara marble. A painting by Aleardo Villa shows the dock workers in Limon in the late 1800's loading bananas and coffee. There is a little girl on the dock who seems to be fascinated with the painter more than the dock workers. This painting is also on the back of the five colones bill. The main staircase is richly decorated with Carrara marble, stucco decorations and gold overlay. The lights are six bronze and crystal candelabra decorated in baroque styling. The foyer is a spectacular hall with three soffits by Vespasiano Bignami; the first depicts the dawn, the centre daytime and the last night. The articles of furniture in the room are replicas of originals and were reproduced in mahogany with 22 1/2 karat gold leaf. The floor was originally made of European pine but was replaced in 1940. The replacement woods are the ten most precious hardwoods found in Costa Rica. The annex Halls are decorated in a style matching the large foyer. "The Shepherd with the Little Girl" is in this area and was painted by the Italian, Indoni, in 1877. This painting was in a collection of Don Jaime's, on exhibition in 1932. When Jaime saw the painting in the theatre, he felt it should stay. He donated the painting to Costa Rica. The main lobby functions as a vast sitting room and meeting place for the public. It is decorated in pink marble. Two of the sculptures in the lobby are by Pietro Capurro representing comedy and tragedy. The third, called "Heroes of Misery" was done by Juan Ramon Bonilla, a Costa Rican. The Renaissance-style facade outside is decorated with three sculptures by Pietry Bulgarelli called Dance, Music and Fame. On the ground level are Adriatico Feoli's statues of Ludwig Van Beethoven and Pedro Calderon de la Barca, a playwright and poet of the 1600's.

The National Theatre was damaged by an earthquake on December 22nd, 1990, and is in the process of being repaired. The entry fee is ¢150 ($1.10 US) and most of the proceeds go toward the reconstruction.

Malico Salizar Theatre is on Ave. 2, Calle 3-4 and is an excellent place to enjoy evening entertainment. The theatre offers dance festivals, ballet, contemporary and classical music. There is a special cultural show called **"Fantasia Folclorica"** which is worth seeing. It is contemporary dance and music telling the history of Costa Rica from pre-Columbian times to the present. The choreography is artistic and the costumes are colorful. I know no one who did not think this production was excellent.

The play itself begins with two men discussing whether there is folkore in Costa Rica. They go through time, seeing the magic of the rain forest, the jungle and the creatures in it. The mixture of native cultures are symbolized by three men, one in gold and the other two in jade. They go on to play the game "volador" (flyer) that came from the Nicoya area. The natives believe the white men that arrive are their long awaited gods of Quetzalcoatl. The Spaniards clash with the natives over a mask belonging to the shaman, but the strongest native survives. The second part shows the horrors suffered by the people during the conquest such as the physical violation of native woman. The next dances are in honor of the Virgin of the country, the celebration of the wheat crops and finally, a wedding. After intermission, dances and traditions indigenous to each region of Costa Rica are performed. A program is for sale at the show and is written in English and Spanish. It gives an excellent interpretation of the play.

The schedule of events is posted outside the door of the theatre and tickets will cost anywhere from ¢200 - ¢500 ($1.50 - $3.75 US). Special events may cost a bit more. The seats are comfortable and the acoustics are good. This entertainment is highly recommended.

The National Museum is on Calle 17 and Ave. Central - 2. It is open Tuesday to Sunday from 8:30AM to 4:30PM. The Bellavista Fortress is an old army fortress with bullet holes in the stone from the 1948 revolution. The museum contains pre-Columbian ceramic, stone jade and gold pieces. It has a religious section, a furniture section, a history section and a local flora and fauna section. This is a well-organized museum. The fort became a museum in 1948 when the army was abolished. There is a small admission fee.

The Jade Museum is on the 11th floor of the National Security Institute on Ave. 7, Calle 7-9. It is open Tuesdays to Sundays,

8:00AM to 5:00PM and there is no admission charge. This museum contains American pre-Columbian jade produced by indigenous Ticans. It also has gold pieces, some pottery and stone carvings arranged according to region and historical time period.

The Gold Museum is located in the National Bank Building under the Plaza de la Cultura on Ave. Central and Calle 5. It is open from 10:00AM to 5:00PM, Tuesday to Sunday and there is no admission charge. The museum has more than 1600 pieces of gold and it is one of the most valuable gold collections in the world. In 1950, officials of the Central Bank started collecting pieces from cemeteries around the world. Later, some of the pieces were obtained from private collections. There is over 20,000 troy ounces of pre-Columbian gold on display. Security is rigid and you must leave your bags at the counter before entering. This is understandable.

The Museum of Costa Rican Art is in La Sabana Metropolitan Park at the west end of Paseo Colon and Calle 42. The museum has a well-displayed collection of nineteenth and twentieth century Costa Rican wood carvings, sculptures and paintings. There are also changing art shows on display. The building was once the International Airport of San José.

National Contemporary Art Gallery is on Calle 15a, across from the National Park. It is a small gallery with a few contemporary photos. It does not take long to visit. There is no entrance fee and it is a pleasant diversion when in the area.

La Salle Museum of Natural History is in the former La Salle High School and is on the southwest side of La Sabana Metropolitan Park. Open Monday to Friday, 8:00AM to 3:00PM, this museum has about 1500 species of flora and fauna from all over the world, including some extinct species. All the pieces were prepared for display in Costa Rica. The museum was opened in 1959 and is worth a visit. There is a small admission fee. Buses go to the museum.

The Crime Museum is located on Ave. 6, Calle 17 in the Supreme Court of Justice building. It is open from 1:00PM to 4:00PM, Monday, Wednesday and Friday. This museum has various weapons, counterfeit money and a bizarre display of weapons used in violent crimes. The philosophy of this museum is to deter crime through the education and display of criminal objects.

The Entomology Museum is credited with being the only insect museum in Central America. I certainly know of no other. The museum is in the Musical Arts building in the Faculty of Fine Arts at the University of Costa Rica. The collection is extensive with the butterflies being the most beautiful (of course). It is difficult to call a spider beautiful. Visiting the university is always a pleasure and going to this museum is a must.

Central Park and the Metropolitan Cathedral are on Ave. 2 and Calle Central. The large, cream colored, stucco church is at one end of the Central Park. There is not an overwhelming amount of decor in this cathedral like in some Mexican churches. The park has a bandstand where musicians often play in the evenings. The children's library is also here. Many buses stop at this park.

The Serpentarium is on Ave. 1, Calle 9-11 and is open daily from 10:00AM to 6:00PM. There is an admission fee. There is a collection of live snakes, frogs, toads, and other cold blooded critters in this museum. It is interesting to view but certainly a relief to know they are all behind glass cages.

Carrillo Park on Ave. 2-4 and Calles 12-14, has a four-foot pre-Columbian stone sphere. These spheres are found throughout Costa Rica and are no more than 1/32nd of an inch out from being perfect. No one is certain of their origin. There is a set of three in the National Museum.

Morazan Park on Calle 7 and Ave. 3 has four different gardens, one being a peaceful Japanese garden. The kiosk in the center is called the "Temple of Music" and is used by musicians in the evenings. The park has been spruced up recently.

Simon Bolivar Zoological Park is on Ave. 11, Calle 7 and is a lovely little zoo for those who like to see animals in captivity. The zoo is open Tuesday to Friday from 8:30AM to 3:30PM and on week-ends from 9:00AM to 4:00PM. They are building a new zoo in San Josè and the animals will be put in large, comfortable cages.

Plaza de la Cultura is where the National Theatre, the Gran Hotel Costa Rica, the Tourist Office and the Gold Museum are located. The plaza is rimmed with hockers selling anything from hammocks to porcupine quill ear rings. The plaza is always full of young people. This area is also famous for the female pickpockets who sensuously rub up against men, bat their eye lashes and make off with their wallets. Ladies will not be excluded by the pickpockets. You should wear your day pack at the front when in this area.

The Butterfly Farm is at La Guacima de Alajuela, half a kilometer south and 100 meters east of the main entrance to Los Reyes Country Club. This farm is simular to the one at Monteverde. It has many species of butterflies in different stages of development. There is a one hour tour of the butterflies' natural habitat. The tour guide talks about the predator and disease problems faced by a butterfly. The butterflies can be photographed at this farm, resulting in great photos that would not be possible for the average traveller.

National Park is on Ave. 1-3 and Calle 15-19. This is a peaceful park with many statues. The best statue is in the center and it is William Walker being driven out of Costa Rica. There is also a statue of the national hero, Juan Santamaria who set William Walker's house on fire during the Battle of Rivas. **The National Liquor Factory** borders this park as does the National Library and National Assembly. There are guided tours through the Liquor Factory on week days at 4:00PM. Samples are given.

Irazu Volcano is 55 kilometers from San Josè and 31 kilometers from Cartago. A visit is recommended. Getting to the volcano is difficult. Take a bus to Cartago and change for a bus to Tierra Blanca. This is about 20 kilometers before the summit. From Tierra Blanca, you can hitch a ride. There is not much traffic during the week. You may also take a taxi from Cartago or join a tour in San Josè. One of the reasons that the government keeps this area inaccessable is because the land is new and growth is delicate. Keeping tourists away helps preserve the new growth.

Irazu is 3432 meters (11,260 ft) above sea level; a sweater is needed when walking around the crater as it is quite cold. Known as the "powder keg of nature", Irazu has a long history of eruptions consisting of huge clouds of steam, ash and scoria. Rocks often fall near the crater during eruptions. On March 13, 1963, Irazu erupted causing tremendous damage to San Josè and the surrounding villages. It is estimated that 40,000 tons of ash were cleared from the streets of San Josè during that year. Winds carried the ash as far as 71 miles away and it was still falling lightly two years later. The main crater is 1050 meters (3500 ft.) and 300 meters (1000 ft) deep. Today, some of the flora is returning to the area. One of the most interesting trees growing in the area is from the mistletoe family. Usually, this plant only grows farther north but due to the rich volcanic soil and perfect climate, it is growing near the crater. There is a trail around the crater.

Irazu has five craters in all. The second largest crater is the Diego de la Haya crater, named after the governor of Costa Rica. In 1723 there was an eruption that Haya reported thus recording the first eruption after the Spaniards arrived. This crater is 700 meters (2300 ft) wide and 100 meters (300 ft) deep. During a clear day, both the Atlantic and the Pacific Oceans are visible from the summit. Irazu Volcano is a wonderful trip even though it is difficult to access. Of all the volcanos, I like this one the best, probably because of the young growth starting on the moonscape. This young cloud forest grouth is characterized by young colonies of Arrayans, a group of plants not common in many places.

Poas Volcano is easier to visit than Irazu. There is a bus on Sundays going to the top. It leaves at 8:00AM from 2nd Ave. and Calle 12, (beside La Merced church) and returns at 2:30PM. On weekdays, you must take a bus to Alajuela, and transfer to a bus going to San Pedro de Poas. From San Pedro you must hitch a ride or walk. It is about 10 kilometers to the top. There is a restaurant at Poasita where you can get something to eat and drink. Between Alajuela and Poasita are run ways of grey-black cotton greenhouses. Because of the climate and volcanic earth, this area grows Costa Rica's best flowers and plants   used for export. This area is good for strawberries and export brings money to the area.

Poas erupted in 1953 and is still active. It is a composite basaltic volcano, 2708 meters high (8900 ft) with a crater one and a half kilometers in diameter and 300 meters deep (1000 ft). Since the mountain is still active, fumes spew from the crater periodically and care should be taken not to inhale too many of the nauseous fumes. The fumes are strong acidic sulfur and chlorine gases. The volcano sporadically emits geyser-like eruptions and has the world's largest geyser. It is only luck if you happen to be there when it erupts.

A lake formed on the main crater in 1963 with large geyser-like eruptions but it disappeared in 1989. The lake water had a temperature of around 45ºC but went up to 93ºC causing a dome glow. The lake then disappeared.

Lake Octu was formed because of a secondary channel when the volcano erupted. You can walk part way around this lake. It is a very nice walk but be certain to stay on the paths as the vegetation is delicate. This lake is past the main crater.

There is a covered shelter, barbecue pits, washrooms, a small museum, a gift shop and a small tienda at the top of the mountain. The information center explains the entire phenomenon of volcanic activity.

Sarchi Oxcart Factory is reached by taking the Sarchi bus from the last bus stop in Alajuela. It goes every twenty minutes. At the factory, you may purchase replicas of the colorful oxcarts found in the countryside. They come in many colors and sizes. Some people use the bigger ones as portable bars in their homes. There are other Costa Rican wooden crafts at Sarchi but the oxcarts are the most popular.

The oxcart was first used in Costa Rica about a hundred years ago, after the Spaniards brought the concept of the wheel for labor. The Costa Rican wheel has no spokes and there are no holes between the radii. It is a compact wheel that could come unstuck from the mud common on the roads. The cart is a combination of the Spanish cart and the Aztec disk (which did not turn because it was a calendar). The wheel itself is not solid but is built by putting angular arcs side by side. The wheel is very strong and requires an elaborate technique to finish correctly. The carts were rough-hewn vehicles with a bar for the harnesses. The harness bars extended from a rectangular support under the axle. The wheels were mounted to the two ends of the axle and were four to five feet in diameter and at least four inches thick. It is not difficult to see how quickly the oxcart changed. Eventually the richer teamsters wanted to show off by decorating their carts with beautiful designs.

During the 1840s, the coffee production and exportation increased making efficient transportation a necessity. Thus, the cart previously pulled by farmers bringing food and fuel from the fields was transformed into something bigger and stronger. The trail to Puntarenas went from San Josè to Alajuela, Atenas, The Monte del

Aguacafe, Orotina, Esparza, Barranca and finally the Pacific port of Puntarenas. The entire trip took 11-15 days.

By 1844 there were over 500 oxcarts in Costa Rica and by 1858 there was about 10,000. Each cart cost 35 pesos and carried between six and seven metric hundredweight of coffee. The convoys became known as the "Cart Train to Puntarenas". The convoys brought secondary growth such as road gangs, highway guards, customs, smithies, pastures, inns, mail and teamsters to the country. It also brought the strongest man in Costa Rica to light. Josè Chavarria lived near Barranca pass, the most difficult section of the route. Chavarria became the number one helper of the teamsters. He was so strong that he could lift a full cart while repair men fixed damages. He also helped the carts out of the mud during the rainy season.

Ojo de Agua is six kilometers from Alajuela. You can catch a bus to the site from Alajuela or from the Coca Cola bus station at Ave. 1, calle 18-20, in San Josè. Buses leave every hour. Ojo de Agua is the most famous swimming resort in Costa Rica. It is a pool that is fed 6300 gallons per minute, of fresh water from an underground river. At the site, there is a pool and an artificial lake, restaurants and a spot to have a cool beer. There is an entrance fee. On week ends there are many Ticos who patronize these pools. Week days may be a bit less busy.

Bungee Jumping in Costa Rica sounds like a hell of a lot of fun! This company has all the safety features that a North American company would so I feel confident recommending it even though I did not personally jump off the bridge. They offer a free fall jump from a bridge 83 meters (275 feet) high with an original New Zealand elastic cord of 400% rebound quality. The jump is from a bridge into tropical wilderness. The jumping area is on the highway between San Josè and Puntarenas, 37 kilometers (23 miles) from San Josè. It is on the right hand side of the road and after the Rafael Iglesia bridge. If you are unable to find it, contact Tropico Saragundi Specialty Tours, PO Box 51-2120, San Josè or go to the office on Ave. 7, Calle Central-1. They will also help you find cheap accommodations, restaurants and other great hiking, biking or boating trips. I think that chicken-busers are really the ones who would enjoy this sport.

SPANISH LANGUAGE SCHOOLS

There are numerous schools in San Josè and many students go to the university for Spanish cultural courses. I will list only a few schools here, but be aware that Costa Rica is more expensive than some of the other countries in Central America. It does not offer one week crash courses like Guatemala does. If school is a priority, be certain to shop around wisely.

Centro Cultural Costaricense Norteamericano has two locations; one is in San Pedro, one and a half blocks north of the fire station "Los Yoses" and the other one is on Paseo Colon, one quarter block north of Kentucky Fried Chicken. Phone 25-94-33 or write to P.O. Box 1489 - 1000 San Josè, Costa Rica. This school offers courses for two month periods. The cost is $130.00 US for daily, two-hour, classes, Monday to Friday. The school will make arrangements for room and board but they must know one month in advance. They offer on-going registration, computer assisted instruction, cultural events, library privileges, and cross-cultural activities.

ILISA-Latin American Institute of Languages offers four levels of Spanish, a maximum of four students per class and a flexible schedule. This school is close to the university. If you are interested, you may visit the school. To get there, go the the church in San Pedro. Walk one block east, four blocks south and half a block east again or telephone 25-24-95. You may write for more information to: P.O. Box 1001, San Pedro 2050, Costa Rica.

Instituto Universal de Idiomas, three blocks east of the National Theatre, Ave. 2, and 9th Calle, on the 2nd floor. Phone 57-04-41. This school offers a three day mini survival course, a two week course for beginners, intermediates and advanced for $155.00 US. They also offer a four week group course for $250.00 US. They have homestay programs and private tutoring. These are about the most reasonable prices I have seen in Costa Rica. Again, there are cheaper prices throughout Central America.

SHOPPING

Central Market is on Ave. 1-3 and Calles 6-8. This is a crowded, noisy and intimidating market. However, there is not much you would not be able to find in this market if you looked long enough and asked enough people. This is not the best place in Costa Rica to shop for souvenirs.

Mercado de los Artesaños on Ave. 1 Calle 11 (across from the Asia Hotel) is a decent place to look for souvenirs with comparable prices to the streets. They do have a nice collection of wooden vases if this is what you are interested in.

Cafè Volio on Ave. 1, Calle 6-8 is the best place to purchase fresh coffee. The small shop is near the central market. They charge ¢250 ($1.85 US) per kilo for fresh coffee. Coffee is a large agricultural product of the Meseta Central and can be seen from the window of a bus on almost any out-trip you will take from San Josè. The plants grow about one to two meters high and have shiny dark green leaves with white flowers and then red beans. There are often large shade trees interspersed among the coffee plants on the plantations.

Artisans Market is on Calle Central between Ave. Central and Ave. 1. This large, two-story building houses many small stalls where you can barter for souvenirs. I found this the most interesting place to shop; it has everything close at hand and the prices are comparable. They also carry some products from other parts of Central America like the beautiful Salvadorian towels.

Apropo is on Ave. Central, Calle 5-7 and is a shop that makes good quality, American-style cotton clothes. If there is something that you like, but it's not your size or color, they will make it for you within a few days. There is both a men's and women's shop. Prices are not cheap, but the quality and variety of styles are worth the price.

The Book Shop on Ave. 1, Calle 3, is a great book shop full of English books. It has excellent maps of Costa Rica with details of the National Parks on the back. The last time I was in, they had many books on Central and South America including Chickenbus ll.

The Book Trade is in the Costa Rica shopping center on Ave. 1a, Calle 3-5, one block north of the Hotel Costa Rica. The book store buys, sells and trades used books in English, French and German at reasonable prices. There are many trashy books but with a bit of luck you will find something worth reading. The owner speaks English and is quite helpful. As his business expands, so will the selection. This is the best place in San Josè to get second hand books.

The Tico Times is the English written newspaper in Costa Rica. They publish some interesting events that are occuring in the country. They also publish a special tourist issue with information pertinent to the first time visitor to the country. If you want it delivered to your home, write The Tico Times, Apt. 4632, San Josè, Costa Rica.

Electrician's nightmare

SANTA CRUZ

This town is on the Nicoya Peninsula and is cheaper than the nearby beaches. You may easily visit the beaches from Playa Grande down to Playa Junquillal every day with little beach time wasted riding a bus. The town is known as Costa Rica's National Folklore City and is famous for its colorful fiestas. They feature delicious native foods and beautiful native dancing; the most famous dance is the Punto Guanacasteco.

PLACES TO STAY

Although there are other places to stay the best place is the **Pension Isabel.** It is a block away from the bus stop in the center of town. It is a quiet and clean hotel with public washrooms. The cost is only ¢400 ($3. US) per night.

RESTAURANTS

The most interesting restaurant in Santa Cruz is the **Tortilla Factory** which looks exactly like any stereotype factory but is in fact a place to eat good, cheap, tipico meals. This is a good way to make certain that the Ticos get your money and you get your money's worth. The meals are all Costa Rican style (no hamburgers) but the taste is exceptional and the waitresses feed you lots, not just an appetizer. This no frills diner is a few blocks from the square and up an alley. Ask for directions to the Tortilla Factory and anyone will help you. It is a great place.

THINGS TO DO

Junquillal is not a swimming beach, but like Dominical, it has not been discovered yet. There are a couple expensive hotels but the beautiful sandy beach is not used by the general public. The area is not good for swimming because the surf is very big. Inshore body surfing, sun tanning, reading are excellent pass times. Locals like to fish off the point and they have been known to get some pretty big fish. Refreshments can be purchased at the expensive hotels. It is best to live in Santa Cruz and commute to this beach.

Guaitil is a small town known for its ceramics. Because Costa Rica does not have much in the way of souvenirs, this is a good place to visit. The art is the traditional work of the Chorotega Indians, and they have formed a co-operative where you may purchase their work. You can also see them working at their art while you are there.

SANTA ELENA

Santa Elena is the village most chickenbusers stay at when visiting Monteverde National Park. The trip to the park is spectacular if coming from San Josè and horrendous if coming from Tilaran. If your bus stops in the village ten kilometers before Santa Elena (coming from Tilaran) there are vehicles that will take you to Santa Elena.

You may also walk. The best and cheapest place to get a ride is at the restaurant. If a man with a big truck is blocking the road and charging more than ¢300 per person, be certain to check at the restaurant. Buses have trouble going all the way to Santa Elena during rainy season. When it is dry, the buses get through. No matter how you get there, the visit to Monteverde is one of the major attractions of the country.

The village of Santa Elena is five and a half kilometers from the park. It is cheaper to stay in the village than on the hill closer to the park. Besides, it is an interesting walk to and from the village. Some people are lucky enough to hitch a ride up the hill but most people walk. The views are spectacular.

When you arrive in town, many ambitious young men will try to take you to their hotel. I checked some of these hotels and they were not worth the price.

The bus leaves Santa Elena at 6:00AM and goes to Puntarenas. The 3:00PM bus goes to San Josè. If you can't get one of the buses, you may hitch a ride down the mountain as there are many vehicles going.

PLACES TO STAY

There are expensive, moderate and cheap places to stay up the hill to the park. If one is full or does not suit your fancy, try the next. You can camp at the park but you must have good rain proof equipment; this is a rain forest.

Santa Elena Hotel is the best place to stay. The rooms are quite small and basic but clean for ¢300 ($2.25 US) per person. You may eat the home cooked meals which are carefully prepared and served for a reasonable price.

Hotel Bueno Sueño offers nice rooms with a private bath for ¢1300 ($10. US) a double and ¢700 ($5.25 US) a single. It is clean and pleasant but doesn't have the warm home atmosphere of the Santa Elena.

Pension El Tucan is a neat place to stay but is about ¢600 ($4.50 US) per person. It is down the hill from Santa Elena Hotel. This hotel would be my second choice if the Santa Elena was full.

RESTAURANTS

Except for the more expensive restaurants on the hill, there is nothing in Santa Elena except the hotel. I recommend the hotel but try other places while walking. You may be pleased.

THINGS TO DO

The Butterfly Farm is the first place to visit on your walk to the park. It is an easy walk one and a half kilometers up the hill and one kilometer off the main road. The farm is run by two Americans that are saving money to purchase more land for the preservation of the cloud forest. The butterfly farm is interesting. The display room has many types of butterflies in different stages of development from egg laying to cocoon hatching. The other part of the farm is outside and under nets. A biologist guide will show you different butterflies and tell you what the butterflies are doing. The net is to keep the critters in. The entire tour does not take long but the cost is $5.00 US per person. This is expensive for Costa Rica.

The Cheese Factory should be your next stop up the hill. It is run and operated by descendents of the original Quakers who first settled in this area after leaving the US. This is an excellent place to watch cheese production. At one time, the Quakers produced about 20 pounds of cheese a day and now they produce over 200 pounds per day. It is shipped all over the country. This shop is a must.

Stella's Bakery is just before the cheese factory and an excellent place to get some baked goods to go with your cheese which you can eat on one of the many trails in the cloud forest. It is so inviting, I can't imagine anyone missing this bakery.

Monteverde Cloud Forest is your ultimate destination and after walking up, take a minute to look at the view below you. It is spectacular, looking at the Nicoya peninsula dotted with volcanic islands. This is a photographer's dream. However, it is a cloud forest which means it is wet all the time. Be prepared for mud and moisture. If you are prepared, your complaints will be fewer.

Monteverde was started in 1951 by eleven Quakers who wanted to be free of the draft in the United States. They loaded some trucks and immigrated to Costa Rica. At that time, they could buy land fairly cheaply; the country was non-violent and had no military so they felt they could make a decent living in this little paradise. They had no idea they would prosper as well as they did. Around 1972, the Quakers decided to put some land into a preserve in order to save the cloud forest. Later, with the help of the World Wildlife Fund, they managed to purchase another 5000 acres.

In 1985, the Monteverde Conservation League was formed and it made an international appeal to raise funds to preserve more cloud and rain forests. One of their targets has been elementary school groups. This collection of land is where you will visit.

The entry to the park is $5.00 US per day; the money goes to the maintenance of the park. The gift store has maps, bird lists, trail guides and posters. There is a limit to the number of visitors the park will allow per day (100) and if you are late, you may have to return the following day. Go early and dress for a rain storm.

Marked trails are in the park and you should be able to see many birds. You will need binoculars, a bird book, rain jacket and good boots. An umbrella would also be valuable. You can pick a cheap one up in San Josè and then donate it to a beggar (or another chickenbuser) when you leave the park.

SIQUIRRES

This is a friendly little town at the summit between Limon and San Josè. It was once a stop off point for those only going part way on the jungle train but now that the train is no longer running, the town sees fewer tourists. There are good places to eat, acceptable places to stay and buses leave for San Josè every hour. This is also where those running the Rio Pacuare end their trip. I like this town and if you want to see something different but pleasant, it is not far from San Josè. The best place to stay is at the **Hotel Central** which is fairly clean, is on the square and charges ₡400 ($3. US) per person. The hotel owners are as friendly as the rest of the town. If you do not like the Central there is another hotel, **the Garza**, on the opposite side of the square for the same price and with the same quality. You will not find the Hyatt in this town. Eat where it suits your fancy.

Rafting the Rio Pacuare is a two or three day trip ending in Siquirres. The put in point is where the road crosses the river, south of this town. The river is a class IV river and the trip is about 30 kilometers long. This was the first river in Costa Rica to become protected. It has wild rapids, beautiful waterfalls and excellent scenery. The first day of the trip has a lovely gorge with fast rapids that are separated by quiet pools. The gorge must be navigated on the first day of the trip and then you can relax on the quieter waters of the river, and enjoy the beauty of the virgin forests and the wildlife. This is a delightful trip. One tour group that offers the trip is the Rios Tropicales, PO Box 472-1200, San Josè, Telephone (506) 33-6455. They will rent equipment.

TAMARINDO

Tamarindo is the beach the tourist office will tell you to visit if you look over the age of 27. Although it is a beautiful beach on the Nicoya Peninsula, it is also popular with the wealthier Ticans. There was heavy investment from that sector of the population in the hope of making a lot of money. The transportation to and from Tamarindo is good. Daily buses leave from San Josè and Santa Cruz; daily flights leave from San Josè. I like to hitchhike in this area to see how the poor rich manage to struggle through a Costa Rican vacation.

PLACES TO STAY

Hotel Doly is near the beach. They have clean rooms, public bathrooms, friendly service and good prices. The cost is ₡500 ($4. US) per person and the owner will convince you her meals are the best in town for the price. I believe she is correct. There are a few other cheap hotels but the expensive (over $10. US) ones have definitely overtaken this area.

RESTAURANTS

Eat where you can find something appealing. **Johnny's Bakery** has fresh croissants and strong coffee which is a must for breakfast. If staying in Santa Cruz, this is a good breakfast stop before going to the beach.

TILARAN

Tilaran is about three and one half hours from San Josè. If going between Fortuna and Arenal from Tilaran, you ride along a rough road that borders Lake Arenal. The lake is a beautiful, large lake periodically dotted with islands. Tilaran is situated high in the mountains, overlooking the entire lake and valley. Tilaran has a constant, cool breeze; the trees grow leaning toward the Pacific.

PLACES TO STAY

Wind Surf is about two blocks from the bus stop and is nice. The rooms cost ₡1000 ($7.50 US) with a private bath.

Cabinas Sueño are up the road from the Wind Surf and cost the same except a double is ₡1500 ($11. US) for the night. The two places are comparable.

Hotel Grecia is on the town square a couple of blocks away from the bus station. The cost is ₡400 ($3. US) per person without private bath and with a one tap shower. It is a pleasant place to stay.

RESTAURANT

El Sueño is the only restaurant I tried in this town and the food was excellent. The prices were reasonable and the service pleasant. Tilaran is a nice town to spend a cool evening.

THINGS TO DO

Windsurfing, horseback riding and fishing can be arranged from the tour guides near the square. I would certainly recommend horseback riding in the area as the scenery is beautiful.

TORTUGUERO

There is only one way to get to Tortuguero or Colorado and that is by boat along the natural canals and lakes which are joined by a few man-made canals. Some people fly to Colorado but the prices are prohibitive. There is a four wheel drive road going a little way along the canals but it does not go all the way to Tortuguero. If you drive the road, you will not get a cheaper boat further up.

To get to Tortuguero or Colorado, you must go to Moin and hire a boat. The best place to do this is at the hostel or the Soda de Coca in Moin. You must barter for a boat; the average price is $150.00 for a boat and it can take four people. This makes it less than $40.00 per person. There was once a government ferry going to Tortuguero but it was damaged in the 1991 earthquake; it has not

167

been repaired. The earthquake (terrimoto in Spanish) also shifted some of the soil on the hills thus clogging up the canals but the locals started working on it a few days after the disaster so travel is possible.

If you sail when the tides are low, you may have to get out and push the boat. Watch where you step. When I did this, I was not back in the boat 30 seconds before I noticed a crocodile sunning himself on a sand bar a few feet from where we passed.

A good boat man will take you up the canals in four to five hours. On the trip you will see birds, sloths, howler monkeys, water dogs (otters) and possibly the odd manatee. It is a wonderful trip and another must when in Costa Rica.

PLACES TO STAY

If you go to Colorado there is good fishing, but you will pay more for a room. In Tortuguero, accommodations are cheaper.

Sabina's Cabinas cost ₡1000-1200 ($7.50-$9. US) per room. They are clean and the owner is friendly and funny. She teases everyone that comes to stay at her place so before you answer her questions, look for the twinkle in her eye. It tells if she is serious or not. The grounds of the hotel are immaculate and on the ocean.

RESTAURANTS

Sabina serves food most of the day and the bar serves booze most of the evening. However, the owner closes early and noise is not a problem. The food is excellent but then there is nothing to compare it to in Tortuguero.

There are other hotels about 15 minutes further on the canal but they cost about $40.00 US per night.

THINGS TO DO

Tortuguero National Park has 46,815 acres nestled between the Sierpe Hills and the Caribbean Coast going north of Moin and to the Nicaraguan border. It is the most important area in the entire central Caribbean for the nesting ground of the green turtle. This is also the home of the Gaspar, a living fossil fish that can be seen in the canals. Seeing the turtles nest or hatch is such a thrill that if you see nothing else in Costa Rica, your trip will worth the time and money spent.

To get to the park, walk south along the beach until you come to the park sign. Follow the trail inland to the warden's office. There are a few displays at the office and the warden will answer any questions you may have - in Spanish. The entry fee is ₡100 (75¢ US). There is a trail through the jungle leading to the nesting beaches of the turtles; as you walk you will be serenaded by the howler monkeys. Young turtles hatch between 5:00 and 6:00PM, at dusk. The older turtles lay their eggs around the same hour. You will see many broken eggs on the beach. They are opened by wild animals or by hatching young. If you sit still, you will see the little guys struggling to the water or the huge mothers struggling out of the water.

If you are there for nesting season, from July to October with August being the peak time, you must sit very quiet and watch. The turtles are huge and they waddle to shore, lay their eggs and get back into the water with little trouble. The thrill of seeing this miracle is undescribable.

It is the greenback turtles that are nesting and hatching in this area and they are hunted for their delicious meat. In order to assist in their conservation, please do not eat or use any turtle products.

Many locals will guide you to the shores in order to charge you a few cents to see the turtles. I suggest that you go to the park and talk to the warden. It is cheaper and just as successful.

Canoe Rides through the canals can also be taken with locals for about ¢300 ($2.25 US) per hour. This trip leaves early in the morning because animals are active at that time. If in Tortuguero for only a short time, I would suggest you do everything, including a few hours in a dugout canoe.

TURRIALBA

This delightful little town is nestled in the mountains, surrounded by wild rivers and lush jungle. People from all over the world come to play with kayaks in the white water of the Reventazon River. This area is a muscle powered sportsman's delight.

PLACES TO STAY

Interamericano has rooms for ¢1000 ($7.50 US) a double and ¢900 ($6.75 US) a single, per night. Walk down the main street and over the tracks to the hotel. The rooms are small and basic but they have private bathrooms with two tap showers.

Hospedaje Prima Vera costs ¢300 ($2.25US) per person for a clean but basic room without private bath and only a one tap shower. Walk past the green building on the park and turn left to find the hotel. It is just past the corner.

RESTAURANTS

There is a little shop down from the park and around the corner from the bus station. They serve the biggest hamburgers in all Costa Rica. The shop has no name but the front is open; there are no doors. This is the best place to eat in town.

THINGS TO DO

Rio Reventazon is a class III river that has year round white water. The river flows through the mountains and into the Caribbean. There are two challenging spots; one called El Gordo

(Fatso) and the other called Hueco Santo (Holy Hole). These white water spots will test your skills and speed the blood flow in your viens. Many people I spoke to brought their own kayaks and spent a few weeks playing on this river. You may join a tour group and do some white water rafting on this river.

Guayabo National Monument is an archaeological site. The ruins are not as impressive as some in Central America but they are important to Costa Ricans. The park was created in 1973 and the original city is believed to have covered 15 hectares. The most impressive remains are a mound that was the foundation of a building and an aqueduct.

The area was inhabited by about 10,000 people from 1000BC to 500 or 600 years before the Spanish arrived. This is not a long time and the reason for people deserting this village is unknown. There have been ceramics, stone and gold artifacts found there. Interesting monogliphs and petrogliphs were also found at the ruins.

The jungles around the site are quite impressive but the site is difficult to access. You must take the daily bus to Santa Terisita which leaves Turrialba at 10:30AM and 1:30PM and walk the final four kilometers to the site. There is a hotel outside the park. La Calzada charges ₡1300 ($10. US) per night for a clean room, no private bath and a two tap shower. There are four rooms for rent but they are seldom full so take a chance if you are interested in the ruins. There is a **restaurant** here so you need not bring food.

You may **camp** at the ruins at the information center. Water, bathrooms, no showers, picnic tables and barbecue pits are available. It would be lonely camping here because it is so remote.

Turrialba Volcano is 3328 meters (11,000 ft) high and difficult to access. There is activity in the mountain even though the last eruption occurred in 1866. The mountain got its name from the white smoke or cloud seen around the volcano. Torre means tower and alba is the white robe worn by priests, thus the volcano looks like a tower that has a white robe around it. If you want to hike on this mountain, you will need a guide. I have heard of a trail going up the mountain but the sources were not reliable so I would suggest you see a park warden in San Josè or a reputable tour guide.

CHICKENBUS TALES

Enrique the Great
first printed in the Prince George <u>Citizen.</u>

Tortuguero (place of the turtles) is on the northeast coast of Costa Rica. It is a national park. The only way to get there is by boat, through the natural canals that run between small lakes and rivers flowing from the mountains into the Caribbean.

We wanted to go there to watch the green turtles hatch but when we enquired at the tourist office in San Josè, the capital city, the man told us that it was impossible to get there and, anyway, the turtles were not hatching. Something about the tone of his voice challenged us. We'd noticed (or thought we did, anyway) that the Ladinos who run the country sometimes don't like sending tourists into areas, like the Caribbean, that are dominated by blacks or Indians.

After a few hours of deliberation, we decided to go and see for ourselves.

We took a bus to Limon, a port near the canals. The people there sent us up the road to Moin where the canals start. After many enquiries and haggling over prices, we finally found a boat that we could afford.

We decided beforehand to pay half the money on departure and the other half when we started the return trip. We didn't want to be left there without transportation. We bargained the price and then the method of payment with the owner of the boat (this is standard practice in Latin America) and finally came to an agreement.

We got into the boat and proceeeded to a check point where we registered with government officials. They took our names, passport numbers and time of return.

Then we stopped for gas.

While gassing up, the owner of the boat told us that he wanted all the money before leaving. This is also standard practice. We decided that (since we had been registered with the officials) this was okay. But then he wanted more. We argued again and were on the verge of cancelling the trip and getting our money back, when another boat came to the gas bar.

Our driver quickly folded the cash we had given him, placed it in his pocket and started the motor.

We weren't far down the canal before we ran into shallow water.

The tide from the ocean had gone out and there wasn't enough water in this section of the canal to float our boat. The boat owner explained to us that the recent earthquake had moved the land and caused these blockage problems. We had to get out and walk the boat up the muddy, shallow water for about a mile.

We got back into the boat soaking wet and covered with mud. We weren't in the boat for two minutes before we passed a young alligator sunning himself on a sand bar. We had asked about sharks but had forgotten to ask about alligators.

The rest of the trip through the jungle was spectacular. We saw otters, monkeys, and a three-toed sloth. There were birds of every size, color and description. The jungle closed in over the canals forming archways of flowers, leaves and vines that shaded us from the sun and amplified the sounds of the insects.

Five hours later, we arrived in Tortuguero in high spirits. We checked into a cabena and then inquired about the turtles and were instantly surrounded by locals willing to be our tour guides. But we declined and went to talk to the park ranger instead. We wanted to be alone with the turtles.

The ranger told us we should be able to see turtles between 5:30 and 6:00 p.m. along the beach. Away we went through the jungle towards the beach with howler monkeys screeching at our passing. We walked slowly along the beach for a long time but saw only dried eggshells. We sat on a log and waited in the rapidly decreasing sunlight.

We saw nothing but skittering sand crabs. With spirits low, sandals in hand and cameras poised, we started back towards our cabenas.

Then Joanne spotted a little turtle struggling down the sand toward the ocean.

He instantly became a celebrity under our flashing cameras. We named him "Enrique the Great". Soon we saw more turtles, dozens of the little creatures, churning their large flippers to reach the water as quickly as possible. We had to stand still so we wouldn't step on any of them.

Enrique was the first to splash into surf. We waved at him and wished him luck.

Enrique, The Great

GUATEMALA

Guatemala, also known as the place from where the rainbow takes its color, is my favorite Central American country. I agree that the rainbow is second to Guatemala for splendor. If my recommendations seem somewhat biased, I don't apologize.

Although Guatemala has a terrible human rights record, the situation has improved some due to international pressure. Recently, the atrocities of the military have been directed to the orphaned street children and, again, international pressure has put the government in the limelight. No government breaking international law likes that kind of negative attention.

The military is visible at all times, but usually polite to tourists. This is changing, however, as more tourists have less respect for the country and flaunt their wealth and naked bodies. The rapes and robberies are increasing as the military has found that it is more profitable to bother a gringo than it is a native Indian. However, for the most part, the female tourist is more likely to be asked for her hand in marriage than to be bothered by the military when out in public during the day. I don't recommend night travel.

Guatemala is rich in Indian culture. The Maya Indians are one of the major attractions in this little country. They are a happy, colorful people that still live in the traditional. Their distinctively designed and colored dress identifies the village that they come from, and their handmade textiles are a treasure for any traveller.

Guatemala has **33 volcanoes** in all, some of which are still active and most of which are a pleasure to climb. There are exciting rivers to travel and spectacular ruins to visit. The Maya Indians used some of the caves in Guatemala for religious purposes and some of these caves are accessible to the adventurer. The jungles are beautiful and inviting. Some of the beaches are nice if you should need sun and sand, but they are not Guatemala's drawing card. However, Guatemala City is only about 6 hours away from the spectacular beaches of El Salvador, now a fairly safe place to visit.

Bus travel in Guatemala is an adventure in itself. There are always buses going in the direction you would like to go. In the outer regions, buses go when full, and full means packed. In the more populated areas, law enforcement officers try to limit the number of people on the buses for safety reasons, but they are not very successful. The law says that everyone must have a seat, but this does not seem to mean that there can't be five or more people to a seat. Also, after the bus is full, the conductor may bring out boards to be put in the aisles, between the seats, for extra people. If there are people standing when the bus passes a police check point, everyone that is standing is told to crouch down so as to appear to be sitting. After the bus safely passes the check point, everyone stands up again. In Guatemala, you never wait too long for a bus and the trip is usually happy, if somewhat crowded.

Guatemala is also clean and cheap in comparison to Mexico. Although the tap water is dangerous to drink, you are never far from a tienda that will sell bottled water or beer. Restaurants are many and varied, and some are exceptional.

There are international travellers in every corner of Guatemala, and you will very seldom be the only gringo in town. Recently, Guatemala has attracted some dopers, drunks and naked sun worshippers. This has caused disrespect from both the Latino and the Indian people and I can only emphasize that if you happen to come across these people, speak out against the disrespect and don't help support their habits. If they are selling their goods to try and get out of a jam, don't buy. If they are unclad, tell them how insulting that appears to the native people, and to yourself in this setting. If they are drunk or stoned in public, don't befriend or protect them. Stay away from these derelicts as they will make travel for the rest of us dangerous and unpleasant.

HISTORY

Anthropologists believe that all American native people migrated from the Orient, over the Bering Sea and down the land mass now known as America. These people made homes for themselves wherever the environment looked appealing and life could be sustained. The Maya of Guatemala were part of that group.

Around 2500BC, these people started cultivating the rich land of Mesoamerica. The Maya settled in southern Mexico, Guatemala, Honduras and El Salvador. The earliest-known society in Guatemala was the Indians in the Los Charcas region of the highlands. They date back to about 1000BC. By 300 - 600AD, the Maya had developed large cities like Tikal and Copan.

The Maya thrived in Guatemala from the fourth century to the tenth century A.D. They continued to build spectacular temples, pyramids and palaces. They recorded their history by carving hieroglyphics of important dates and events on stone slabs or stelae. This advanced society invented and used the concept of zero and they developed a complicated but accurate calendar. The reasons for their decline in the 900's are unknown. However, their priests had predicted the coming of the white man, but they did not predict the holocaust that the white man would bring.

From the 10th century until the Spanish arrived, a few Indian tribes remained in the area, tilling the land, fishing the waters and living a peaceful and pleasant life.

Then, in 1523, Pedro de Alvarado arrived from Mexico with his skilled soldiers and Mexican Indian warriors. He first invaded the Indian cities of Utatlàn and Iximchè in what is part of Guatemala today. Although Cortes gave orders to bring the Christian faith to the Indians without war, this in fact did not happen. From 1523 until 1526, Alvarado ravaged the land and massacred the Indians without mercy. The Indians fought back ferociously but were no match for the advanced weapons nor the ruthlessness of the Spaniards.

The Indians were only one aspect of Alvarado's difficult life. Alvarado's men had to battle dense jungle which contained dangerous wild beasts and malaria infected insects. The changing climates were incompatible with the metal suits of armor the soldiers wore. In the swamps, the land was hot and humid; in the high mountains the temperatures were freezing cold.

The Indians had other problems as well. Because they had never seen a white man nor a horse before, the Indian thought the Spaniard a God and many tried to make peace with the Spanish. The Indians were also divided amongst themselves. Some groups fought the Spanish; some fought other Indians; others tried to ally themselves with the Spanish. This in fact aided Alvarado's invasion.

Although the Indians outnumbered Alvarado's army, and they were accustomed to the area, they were no match against Alvarado. Just outside of Quetzaltenango, at Llanos del Pinal, the national Indian hero, Tecùn Umàn, fought ferociously with his Quichè warriors to the Indian hero's death. He is said to have been killed by Alvarado himself. The story is now told that a Quetzal bird flew over Tecùn Umàn at time of death and covered the Indian's heart with his feathers.

In the area of Iximchè, after many battles and double crossings of the Cakchiquel Indians, the Cakchiquels left Iximchè and started fighting against the Spanish in guerrilla warfare fashion. They continued these battles for six years but never solicited any help from any of the other tribes. When the Cakchiquels were finally defeated, their proud king ended his days washing gold for the Spaniards.

The Kekchè nation, the fiercest of the Indian nations, was never defeated by Alvarado's armies, but was eventually converted to Catholicism by Bartolomè de las Casas, a Dominican friar. This was a fate worse than death in battle because the Indians were rented as slaves along with their land. These packages were given to the early conquistadores. However, Friar Bartolomè de las Casas reported the injustices to the king of Spain and in 1542 King Charles Vth forbade the practice of slavery. However, this law was negated because the Spanish enforced debt servitude, forcing Indians to work for free for a few months every year and by taxing only the Indians.

Alvarado established the first Spanish post at Iximchè in 1524 and named the city Santiago de los Caballeros. But, due to Cakchiquel Indian unrest, Alvarado soon moved on. In 1525, the capital of the area was moved to the Almolonga valley, where Ciudad Vieja is now situated; it prospered until the city was destroyed by a flood in 1541. Prior to the flood, Bishop Francisco Marroquin started converting the Indians of the area to Christianity, but in fact he was enslaving them by making them labor for the church. This was happening in other parts of the country.

In June, 1542, the capital was moved to Antigua in the Panchoy valley where the Spanish believed that the floods would not be able to destroy their city. They built another beautiful and prosperous city which included schools, churches, hospitals and civic centers. Antigua became a lasting colonial city.

On July 29, 1773, more disaster hit. This time earthquakes destroyed the capital. They devastated the city and the ruins remained where they fell for almost 200 years, overgrown and forgotten. However, in 1776, and for the last time, the capital was moved to its present site in the La Ermita valley, the present and delightful spot of Guatemala City.

During this time, Catholicism was very powerful in the area. The priests controlled the monasteries, schools, hospitals, and many of the governing positions. When the capital of Guatemala was moved in 1776, the nobles of the church in Antigua refused to change their position. Antigua had become a beautiful and respected city, comparable to Lima and Mexico City. It wasn't until 1780 that the governing forces finally stopped the opposition and forced the archbishop to accept the new Guatemala City as the capital. This struggle between the king and church resulted in the church losing some power. But, of course, it never lost enough power.

During the colonial period, the General Captaincy of Guatemala included territory which today is Salvador, Honduras, Nicaragua and Costa Rica. In September of 1821, the area became independent from Spain but forcefully annexed to Iturbide's Mexico. On July 1, 1823, after Iturbide's fall in Mexico, Guatemala declared its total independence. But discontent with the first leader, Manuel Josè Arce, soon resulted in Francisco Morazàn, a Honduran, to take control. He fought against the wealthy land owners and the clergy until he was able to succeed Arce. Meanwhile, in other parts of the territory, Mariano Gàlvez abolished religious orders, reformed the legal system and introduced the idea of civil marriage.

Eventually, Morazàn was shot and in 1838, Rafael Carrera took charge of the Federation and became the president of the area. Carrera was in power from 1839 to 1865. He gave special privileges to the nobles, land owners and the church. Carrera also won independence for Guatemala. On March 21, 1847, the territory was officially declared a republic. Carrera also helped defeat the filibuster, William Walker, who had managed to take over Nicaragua at that time. Carrera bestowed upon himself the title of "president for life" but that was the extent of his contribution to the common society. He virtually ignored the needs of the poor.

Carrera also gave the territory of Belize to Britain. The treaty required the British to build a road from Belize to Guatemala City, but the British never fulfilled their part of the bargain. This is still a point of contention with the Guatemalans and they now want

Belize back. This discontent is obvious when crossing the border between the Peten and Belize.

Until 1871, there was little development in Guatemala. In 1871, the Liberals came to power and changes began, but political freedom for the people never came. Justo Rufino Barrios, also known as the "Great Reformer", tried to re-unify all of Central America but was killed in Chalchuapa, El Salvador. The rest of the unions did not want re-unification. Before his death, Barrios built roads, developed a school system, established a national bank, confiscated church property and started a railway system.

After Barrios, the Liberals continued to rule until 1944 when a revolution ousted Jorge Ubico, the dictator of that time. Large fincas were owned by rich men that employed poor Indians to work as slaves. The United Fruit Company had been given huge plots of land which was often confiscated from the Indians because the Indians had no way of proving that the land belonged to them.

In 1898, Manuel Estrada Cabrera came to power and chaos overtook the country. Quezeltenango and western Guatemala were damaged by an earthquake and then further harmed by the eruption of Volcan de Santa Maria. When the 1917 earthquake destroyed Guatemala City, the administration of Estrada looted the treasury and public officials went unpaid. Estrada was declared insane by the opposition (not uncommon in politics) and replaced by a long line of presidents until, in 1931, Jorge Ubico came into power.

Jorge Ubico brought stability to the country and cancelled many of the debts owed by the Indians. Ubico demanded honesty in government but political opposition was strictly repressed. Ubico was a flamboyant dictator and liked having his picture taken (this is pre-tourist times) either while standing in a Napoleonic stance or while riding around on his motorcycle. Ubico fled to Mexico in 1944 during student demonstrations. Others tried to rule in his absence, but they were overthrown by a revolution.

Free elections were then held and won by Juan Josè Arèvalo. A new constitution was written in 1945 and both social and economic development was started. After Arèvalo, Jacobo Arbenez Guzmàn came to power. He developed land; this ruffled the feathers of the United Fruit Company. He was ousted in 1954 by Carlos Castillo Armas, an American puppet dictator.

After many assassinations and coups, Julio Montenegro was elected president in 1966. However, under his dictatorship, the military was actually in power. Since the reign of Montenegro, some military generals have been presidents; charges of fraud and corruption accompany every election.

In 1978, Romeo Lucas Garcia came to power, and the reign of terror intensified. There were assassinations, uninvestigated murders, insurrection, and guerrilla activity. In 1982, Lucas's right hand man was elected, but a coup led by Rios Montt was successful and he took power. However, severe economic problems plagued Guatemala; more discontent and hardship was felt among the poor. In 1985, Marco Cerezo came to power, and he tried to cautiously bring in some reforms. However, the military remains in control of the rural areas of Guatemala where the Indians live. Massacures, tortures, killings and rapes are a constant fear for the poor Indians. In the areas of increasing education and health standards, progress is very slow. Life is better now than it has been for the past 30 years, but tremendous change must occur before the Guatemalan Indians have human rights of international standards.

Today, the military is everywhere in Guatemala but seldom bother the tourist. However, be cautious. If you hear of real trouble in an area by more than one person, stay out of that area. Don't travel in the countryside or alone at night. You can and will have a wonderful time in this delightful, if somewhat troubled, country.

GENERAL INFORMATION

The name "Guatemala" is derived from the Mexican Nahoa Indian word "Coactlmoctl-làn". This word means "land of the snake-eating bird". The bird referred to is the eagle. Gradually, the word was changed to Guahtemallàn by Alvarado's troops and it is not difficult to see the final result.

Guatemala is a republic and claims to have an elected government. The **government** is administered by the executive, represented by the president, who is also the commander in chief of the military. He may serve a four year term and is not eligible for a second term, even through popular vote.

The legislative body is composed of two deputies from each of the **22 districts** in Guatemala. They also serve a four year term. The government must have a two-thirds majority in order to pass a bill. It may also veto the president's wishes. The president appoints the judges that serve in the supreme courts. This makes it easy to see how many people charged with atrocities go unpunished.

Guatemala has **42,000 square miles** of land, is 283 miles long and 261 miles wide. There are 150 miles of Pacific coastline and 50 miles along the Caribbean. The highest of the **33 volcanos** is Tajumulco, 13,845 feet above sea level.

Of the **9 million people** in Guatemala, 50 percent are Indian. The population density is 218 persons per square mile, making Guatemala the second most densely populated country in Central America. El Salvador is the most densely populated. The official **language is Spanish,** but Quichè, Cakchiquel, and Mam are Indian languages that are widely spoken.

The official religion is **Catholicism** but many Protestant sects practice in Guatemala. The Indians have modified the Catholic religion in order to incorporate some of their original beliefs and customs.

Guatemala has a pleasant tropical **climate**. In the highlands above 5000 feet, the evenings are chilly during the dry season and cold during the rainy season. The dry season is November to April, and the rainy season is May to October. The coast can have hot and humid temperatures, sometimes reaching 104 degrees F, while skiffs of snow may be spotted for brief periods of time on the highest volcanos. In Guatemala, altitude is the greatest determining factor of temperature. In the northern Peten region, the rainy season is much longer (usually from June to March), but the Peten is low in elevation so temperatures and humidity are high.

The two **mountain ranges** found in Guatemala are the Cuchumatanes and the Sierra Madres, both originating in the Andes. However, the volcanoes are situated in the Sierra Madres. The two **main rivers** in the country are the Usumacinta, the longest in Central America, and the Motagua, the longest in the country. The Usumacinta flows into Mexico and the Motagua into the Atlantic.

The four **main lakes** in Guatemala are the popular Lake Atitlàn in the center, Lake Petèn-Itzà in the north, Amatitlàn near the capital and Lake Izabal near the Atlantic coast.

The flag of Guatemala has two blue vertical stripes, representing the two oceans. A white stripe between the two blue stripes represents the land. The coat of arms has five volcanoes on it and is found on the flag's white stripe. The **quetzal** bird is the symbol of Guatemala. This magnificent bird belongs to the Trogon family. It cannot survive in captivity, therefore it represents freedom. The bird had religious significance during the Maya period and the Indians continued to keep it part of their traditional ceremonies during the colonial period. The national anthem is a song about the quetzal and Guatemalan money is called the quetzal.

Guatemala **exports** coffee, cotton, cardamom (a herb related to ginger), sugar, chicle (the base for chewing gum), beef, bananas, vegetables, fruits and flowers. Corn, rice and black beans are the home market staples. Some oil has been found in the Alta Verapaz region. Mineral production is not large in Guatemala.

It is compulsory for children between the ages of 7 and 14 to go to **school**. This schooling is free. However, this law is not enforced and in the outlying regions, schools are often not available. Also, many Indian children do not go to school because their parents need their labor. At present, according to official reports, the illiteracy rate in Guatemala is about 50%; in some areas it is over 90%. After the age of 18, boys must serve two years in the military.

THE MAYA INDIAN

This colorful group of people constitutes about 50% of Guatemala's population. The Indians are also the greatest attraction to the tourist. These people, regardless of their hardships, live together as a peaceful and loving race. They are gentle, kind and a delight to be around.

Around 2000BC, the nomadic tribes of Mexico and northern Guatemala found the wild grass called "teocintle" which they cultivated. This was the early plant which eventually developed into the corn of today. From the development of agriculture grew the mighty nation of the Maya Indians which spread from Mexico to Belize, Honduras, Guatemala, and a small part of El Salvador. There are many different descendents of the Maya, including the Quiche, Cakchiquel and Mam Nations. They are discussed below.

The Maya built magnificent cities, first introduced the concept of zero and had mathematical knowledge that predates Europe by 2000 years and India by 1000 years. They also developed a complicated calendar which was based on the movement of the stars. It is one of the most elaborate calendars known to mankind. Like their calendar, the Maya religion was complex, having many deities and ceremonial rituals. Their social life was very moral and roles were definite. Punishment was severe.

Around the year 900AD, this amazing civilization started to disappear. The reasons are only speculation; some attribute disease, climate, earthquakes, and/or soil exhaustion to their demise. However, it is also speculated that some remained in the Peten-Itza area on the island of Tayasal and then migrated and intermarried with other nations living in Guatemala.

Maya legends have been translated and written in Spanish by early priests but the authenticity is uncertain. The legend of the origin of the Guatemalan Indian tribes states that the people left their home called Tulàn in the north and travelled to Lake Atitlàn. They divided into the nations of the Quichè, the Cakchiquel and the Tzutuhil. Another migration ended in the highland's of Huehuetenango and the birth of the Mam nation. The last migration resulted in a group settling in the Verapaz area and calling themselves the Rabinaleros.

Fiesta days

The **Quichè Nation** first settled on Lake Atitlàn, but a chief called Nima-Quichè led his people away from the lake and to the Santa Cruz del Quichè area. The Indians called the area "Place of Old Sticks"; this is now the location of the Utatlan Ruins. It is a natural fortress surrounded by a deep ravine and only one entrance. The fortress ensured security. The priests and nobility lived in the fortress and the common people lived in the surrounding countryside.

Because the Quichè grew so strong, they were divided into 24 different tribes, each with a separate chief. As these tribes grew even larger and stronger, a division was again required. This time the Supreme Chief, who ruled from Utatlan, gave one group, the Cakchiqueles, to his oldest son and he gave the second group, the Tzutuhiles to his second son.

Because of their power, these two groups did not pay attention to their priest's warnings of the coming of the white man. They also paid no heed to the warning of Montezuma, who confirmed the arrival of the white man and his subsequent destruction.

In 1524, Tecùn-Uman, the chief of the Quichès, and 70,000 Quichè Indians gathered near Quezaltenango ready to fight the white invaders. However, their style of fighting and the Spanish use of guns and horses (creatures unknown to the Quichè) soon resulted in defeat for the Indians. Tecùn-Uman was killed by Pedro Alvarado during this battle and the Indians claim that a quetzal bird flew over Tecùn-Uman and covered his heart with its feathers.

The Quichè then invited the white men to visit their fortress in the hope that an ambush would follow. However, when Alvarado arrived, he noticed that there were no women or children around and he became suspicious. The Indians planned that after Alvarado and his men entered Utatlan, they would set the fortress on fire and burn the invaders. However, after Alvarado discovered the plan, he had the chiefs burned in the fortress. In 1815, Anastasio Txul, the crowned Quichè chief, tried to rally his people against the Spanish; he was imprisoned and the Quichè never fought again.

The **Cakchiquel Nation** settled at the spot where the Iximche Ruins are found today. This is only 3 kilometers out of Tecpan. The Cakchiquels got their name from the words "cak" meaning fire and "chiquelep" meaning thieves. It is believed that they stole the sacred fire from the temple.

The Cakchiquels concentrated on building a strong capital city, developing agriculture and enriching their culture when they first separated from the original Quichè. After they grew strong, they started fighting with the surrounding tribes. They were so strong and successful that they almost defeated the Quichè as well. However, just before this happened, the white man arrived.

After the coming of the white man, the Cakchiquels united with Alvarado to fight against the Quichè and Tzutuil Nations. This is one of the greatest mistakes the Indians made. Had they united together against the Spaniards, they could have succeeded in keeping them out.

The Spanish were in America to obtain as much gold as possible. Alvarado had not succeeded in reaching his goal even though every other need had been met. He then told the Cakchiquels that they had one week to collect all the gold and jewels in their kingdom to give to him. If the Indians refused, they would be burned alive. The Indians devised a plan to desert Iximche and burn the Spaniards in the fortress. However, on the chosen day, the Spaniards detected the plan, waged war themselves and defeated the Indians. They became impoverished and bitter enemies of Alvarado.

The Tzutuhil Nation lived on Lake Atitlán between Toliman and San Pedro Volcanos. They were not only fierce warriors, but they had the advantage of being able to use canoes to fight their enemies. As well, they had a 300 foot hill at the base of the volcano on which they could see any approach of danger.

The Tzutuhil Nation was very wealthy because it controlled a rich area of the countryside and traded its desired products for gold. The Spaniards came to the area, fought against the Tzutuhils, and rapidly defeated them. Again, the combination of sophisticated techniques, modern weapons and disunification of the Indian nations allowed the Spanish to win. However, legend says that the Tzutuhils hid their gold in the mountains before being defeated by the Spanish. It is still believed to be there today.

The Mam Nation is found around the Huehuetenango area; the ceremonial center was at Zaculeu. They were fierce warriors and believed to be one of the oldest tribes of the region. Their name means "old men".

In 1525, Alvarado sent his brother Gonzalo to fight the Mam Nation. Gonzalo believed that the Mam were not only extremely wealthy, but that they were getting more powerful each day. It took Gonzalo four months of strong fighting to defeat this group of men. Like other Indian fortresses in the area, the Mam Nation built their fortress on a large plateau protected by a river and a ravine. This was of great benefit when they began fighting the Spanish.

Further south and between the **Sacatepeque Nation** and the Cakchiquel Nation lived the **Poloman Nation** which had come from El Salvador. The Polomans lived at what is today Mixco Viejo, another fabulous fortress. When Alvarado went to fight the Sacatepeque Nation with the help of the Cakchiqueles, they found themselves fighting against the Poloman Nation also. The Polomanes had another tribe, the **Chinautlas**, as allies who also fought against the Spanish. After the Chinautlas were defeated, they offered to help the Spanish (in secret) if the rest of the tribe could be spared. Alvarado agreed. The Chinautlas told Alvarado of an underground escape passage that went from Mixco Viejo to the river. Near the end of the battle, when the Sacatepeque Indians tried to escape, they were caught at the exit point and defeated. Again the story of divide and conquer was successful.

The Rabinal Nation lived in the Alta and Baja Vera Pas region of Guatemala. Their capital was near the village of Rabinal, near the Quetzal Preserve. But today, the fortress, known then as Minpokom, has not been restored.

This is one area that try as he might, Alvarado was unable to conquer. He finally named the area "Tierra de Guerra" (land of war) and gave up the effort.

The priests of that time did not give up as easily. Bartolome de las Casas, a Dominican friar, promised Alvarado that he would win over the Indians for the church as long as Alvarado stayed away for a period of five years. However, it did not take very long before the Indians adopted the new religion and within five years, the king of Spain renamed the area "Verapas" which means "the land of the true peace".

Because these Indians had such high moral standards, conversion to Christianity was quick and easy. One legend tells of a chief who wanted to marry the daughter of the chief of Coban. The Rabinalero was a strong Catholic. On the day of the wedding, the Coban chief gave the couple many gifts acceptable to Indian custom. The Rabinal chief refused the gifts as pagan objects and enraged the Coban chief. War was waged and the town of Rabinal was destroyed along with its Catholic Church; this delayed the work of the Dominican friars.

CUSTOMS AND RELIGION

Although the Guatemalan Indian usually worships in the Catholic church, he has actually blended the Catholic religion with his own to form a unique combination of the two.

The cross of the Christian religion was known to the Maya Indian before the conquest. In the Maya religion, it symbolized the four winds of heaven, the four directions on earth, and everlasting life. In the Christian religion, it symbolizes Christ's sacrifice. Because the Maya Indians believed in the concept of many gods, it was easy for them to understand and accept the concept of a multitude of Christian saints.

The Indians have always had shrines and altars to offer flowers, burning candles, prayers or sprigs of pine; after the coming of the Catholic church, they continued to offer the same to the Christian saints. The prayers may often be heard spoken aloud and, occasionally, in anger if a request has not been delivered by one of the saints.

The church is run by a group of men and sometimes women called the **"cofradias"**. They are responsible for a single saint and they carry out all the duties required for the performance of religious ceremonies in the village. Through the cofradias, the social and political life of the community is controlled. These honorable members hold office for one year and are elected by the elders of the village.

The ceremony for the changing of the cofradia is performed by an outgoing man sitting in a special building with his face to the wall. His replacement enters the building wearing flowers around his neck; the old cofradia rises, turns and the two dance past each other. The new cofradia sits on the bench facing the center of the room while the old one dances out the door. In the daily ceremony of the cofradia, this man will carry the staff while he follows the priest to the altar for the early morning prayers.

The Brujo, Zahori or Shaman is the Maya priest who has all the knowledge needed to heal with herbs, to place or remove a curse, or to give advice on the future. Some of these priests are so powerful that it is believed they can protect a man just by looking at him. When the railway was being built in the Quezaltenango area, the Jacaltenango Indians had fewer accidents than any other village. It was believed this was because their priest was much more powerful than others.

The birth of children, whether boy or girl, is highly celebrated. In many villages, before the child is born, the midwife will take the mother into a sweat house so that her body will be purified before birth. This sweat house may be a communal village one or it may be the private family one. If the mother is very sick, the priest may kill a black chicken and pour the blood over her head and breast. **Names** are often chosen from the Maya Tzolkin Calendar. If they are not taken from the calendar, the child is named after his ancestors or the patron saint of the village.

After the child is born and names given, godparents are chosen. This is an extremely important and respected position. Before the christening, the godfather gives the child an embroidered cap, shirt and hanky. Maya children will never step on the shadow made by their godparents because to do so would be an insult. In turn, godchildren must work for their godparents when they get older. Should the child refuse, the entire village may ostracize the child and his immediate family. The children repay their godparents with gifts when they get older. They may give a year's crop of corn or a cow.

Marriage in the past has always been arranged by the parents. A dowry must be paid for the bride. There is usually a week-long feast where everyone in the village attends. Then the bride goes to her new mother-in-law's house to prove that she can cook, sew and weave; the groom goes to his new father-in-law's home to show he can look after the field and generally provide for his new wife.

After the marriage is approved there is another feast. The bride makes coffee for the guests when they are tired and the groom feeds them. The food that is left over is taken to the new couple's home and must be eaten by them before it spoils. This signifies that the marriage will last. There is a woven marriage blanket that is put inside the marriage hut; it must show the correct blood spots to indicate chastity in the woman (how about the man?) the next morning.

However, these ceremonies change from place to place. Some villages spend a lot of time negotiating and paying for the bride; after which the bride and groom just go home and are married. In other villages there are different customs. But, today, these traditions are changing because there is little money and less national support for the continuation of old customs.

Today, divorce is known to the Maya. If divorce occurs, the children are then given to grandparents and the men marry again. I don't have a clue what happens to divorced women, but I can well imagine. There are cases where a man will take two wives if his first is unable to bear children.

After marriage and life comes **death,** which is not a bad event for the Maya. In days past, they buried valuable treasures with the dead, but today they only bury a few objects such as clothing, a little food, or some tool that the deceased used in his life. The coffin is carried through the village to the cemetery on the shoulders of the men of the town. This is not an uncommon sight in Guatemala.

The **Day of the Dead** is the first of November and it is celebrated by placing yellow flowers around the doorways of houses, lighting candles in the church, and placing bits of food on the graves of the mourned relatives.

LAWS

Napoleonic Law rules in Guatemala. In other words, you are guilty until proven innocent. While proving your case, you must wait in jail. It can take an awfully long time for your case to get to the court room. Guatemala's prisons are not pleasant places to be.

A valid **driver's licence** of your own country or an international licence is needed when taking a car into Guatemala or when renting a car. If taking a car in, you must obtain a permit that is good for up to 30 days and can be re-newed in Guatemala City at the Aduana, Calle 10 Ave. 13-14, Zona 1. The office is open from 8:00AM to 4:30PM, Monday to Friday. You may then obtain permission to have the car in the country for a further 180 days. When applying, you will fill out a form where you must list all spare tires and extra parts for your car. If these are not listed, you may be required to pay duty on them at police checks or when leaving the country. All baggage may be examined at the police check points.

It is still necessary to have your vehicle fumigated at the Guatemalan border when entering. This is done at your expense.

It is illegal to wear or take in military clothing of any kind. Such clothes will be confiscated at the border. Communist literature is also illegal, but now that there is little threat of communism taking over, I don't know what the next paranoia will be.

Pets must have veterinarian certificates stating that they have been vaccinated against rabies.

It is illegal to remove any artifacts from Guatemala.

All forms of drugs are illegal and subject to 3 - 5 years imprisonment if caught. Prison is not a place I would want to spend any time. Although the police are not really tough on tourists at this point, this practice could change overnight. Be cautious!

The military and the police do not get paid great sums of money. They are beginning to learn that it is more profitable to harass a tourist than it is to kill an Indian. If you find yourself in a bind, it is better to pay the small "fine" than to argue your point. Women may be taken to the police station to be "searched" (strip searched) so paying the police may be more advisable.

You are allowed to bring in 3 liters of alcohol, two cartons of cigarettes, a still and/or a movie camera and six rolls of film; however, I have never heard that these laws are strongly enforced.

MONEY

The currency of Guatemala is the Quetzal (Q) which is 100 centavos. At the bank, you get Q5 for one American dollar. A few years ago, the black market in Guatemala did a flourishing business in exchanging money, but the banks now give a better rate than the street, unless you have a lot of money to exchange. Almost all banks will exchange American dollars or traveller's cheques. However, if your currency is Canadian, German, Swiss, Japanese, or British, you will have to change your money at the Bank of Guatemala. At one time this could only be done in Guatemala City but now, you may go to the Bank of Guatemala in any larger town, ask for the daily exchange rate, wait a few hours, and exchange your foreign traveller's cheques. Foreign currency in actual paper money, other than US cash dollars, are equal to monopoly money in Latin America. The Bank of Guatemala is open from 8:30AM to 2:30PM, Monday to Friday.

If you are coming overland from another country, there are money changers at all entry points. However, they will only exchange the adjoining country's currency or American cash dollars. No cheques are accepted at the borders.

There is still a bit of a black market around the post office in Guatemala City, but their rate is not great. It is safer to change at the bank. The market will not exchange anything but currency from other Central American countries and American dollars.

It is always advisable to carry a few American cash dollars on you in the event that you get into a bind. You may have to pay someone quickly or you may get stuck in a small place with no local currency. Everyone knows the greenback.

Other banks will usually exchange US dollars, but I find the Bank of Guatemala the friendliest, easiest to deal with, most co-operative, and it offers the most services to the traveller.

The Bank of Guatemala also operates at the airport and is open from 7:30AM until 6:30PM daily, except week-ends and holidays. It also gives a very good rate.

VISAS

Most travellers need a visa for Guatemala. If arriving by plane, you can obtain a visa at the airport. If travelling overland, there are consulates close to the border in the country you are coming from. All capital cities in Central America have a Guatemalan Embassy where you can get a visa at no cost. However, at present, visas at the border cost Q5 per person.

If your visa expires, you may leave the country for three days and then return for another 90 days. Some border guards will not give you a visa for very long. I had one guard at the Salvadorian - Guatemalan border angry with me because I had a visa from Tegucigalpa; it was not one that he recognized. This made him look foolish so he would only give me a visa for 15 days. Luckily, I only wanted it for one week.

Asking for an extension takes money, a police check, lots of photos, a medical exam, other hoops to jump through and no guarantee that you will get it. If you only need an extra 30 days, apply for a "visa de salida" or an exit visa. This only takes 2 days, Q10 and one picture. If you apply for an extension, it will take days and days.

In order to get a "visa de salida", go to the Immigration Office behind the Guatel office in Guatemala City. Go to the window (13) that says "Recepcion de Documentos Para Control de Extranjeros". When you get the papers to fill out, go to the counter that says "Venta de Sellado, Tembres Fiscales y Fotocopias". This will cost you Q0.50 for the stamp you need. Then fill out your forms. Go to window # 12 "Recepcion de pago" and pay your Q10. Return to window #13 and the lady will take everything including your photo and passport. At this point you must go into the adjoining room on your right . Listen very carefully for them to call your name or a reasonable facsimile. The lady will fill out another form, finger print you and give you a receipt telling you when and what window to return for your passport. Of course, they will have your passport at a different window in the morning but you will just have to be patient and eventually, your passport will miraculously appear.

When you get your passport stamped, be certain that you verify the number of days; also, make certain that your papers are always in order. In other words, don't overstay your welcome as they will nail you for a "fine" that could be more than you are willing to pay.

Some foreigners may obtain a tourist card instead of a visa; and it may be valid for 6 months. However, you must renew your original 30 - 90 day permit (depending on what the official gives you) when you enter the country. This is renewed at the Immigration Office. The tourist card is useful if you do not have a passport. However, without a passport, it is almost impossible to cash a traveller's cheque.

GETTING THERE

There are many overland border crossings into Guatemala, and most are becoming more friendly every year. When coming from **Mexico,** you can take the bus from either San Cristobal or Tapachula. From San Cristobal, the first bus leaves at 7:00AM and there are two others during the day. You can catch a bus at the border for the nearest Guatemalan town which is La Mesilla. There are money changers and places to stay in La Mesilla, and buses leave there regularly for Huehuetenango and then Guatemala City. When coming from Tapachula, the closest towns over the border are El Carman or Tecun Uman. Both have places to stay, money changers and good bus connections to other destinations. Some travellers prefer Tecun Uman, but I have had no difficulty with either the guards or the buses at either crossing.

When **returning to Mexico,** buses leave Guatemala City daily, starting at 7:00AM, for Huehuetenango, La Mesilla and the border. It is 5 hours to Huehuetenango and then 2 1/2 hours to the border. Also, regular buses leave Guatemala City, Ave. 7 Calle 19-44, Zona 1 for El Carman or Tecun Uman.

If coming **from Belize,** you can bus from San Ignacio to Melchor de Mencos. There are places to stay in Melchor, but it is the best to leave San Ignacio early, at 11:00AM, and go to either Tikal or Flores for your first night in Guatemala. Border towns like Melchor are usually boring places. If coming from Belize, the other alternative is to take the ferry from Punta Gorda to Livingston or to Puerto Barrios. The ferry leaves on Tuesdays from Belize and returns Wednesdays; it then leaves Belize again on Fridays and returns Saturdays. If you go to Livingston, it is necessary to take a boat down the Rio Dulce in order to get to a bus. If you go to Puerto Barrios, you can catch a bus (it may be a VIDEO bus) from there to Guatemala City. Leaving Guatemala for Belize can be done in reverse order with no special problems. See "Belize - Getting There".

There are two overland crossings into **Honduras.** They are at El Florido, Chiquimula, Guatemala to Copan, Honduras or Agua Caliente, Chiquimula, Guatemala to Nueva Ocotepeque, Honduras. The Copan crossing is very small and buses into Chiquimula only arrive about once every two hours. Sometimes you can share a taxi with other travellers who are waiting. This crossing is quite pleasant, but there are only small tiendas from which to purchase food or drink and you must get to Chiquimula for accommodations. You can get a visa for Honduras at the border when crossing this way.

When crossing from Agua Caliente to Honduras, it is better to leave Esquipulas early to avoid getting stuck in Santa Rosa de Copan or Nueva Ocotepeque. If you leave early, you can get to San Pedro Sulu, a much nicer town. The last bus from the border to San Pedro Sulu leaves at 4:00PM. This crossing is not difficult, and there is a Honduran consulate in Esquipulas if you should need a visa. If using this crossing, you will have to stay in Nueva Ocotepeque, Honduras or Esquipulas, Guatemala for the night. Nueva Ocotepeque is not a very pleasant town but it is about twelve hours from Tegucigalpa. Santa Rosa de Copan is about 3 - 4 hours from Nueva Ocotepeque and is much nicer than Nueva Ocotepeque.

When going to or coming from **El Salvador,** you can go through Sonsonate to Esquintla, Guatemala or you can take the direct route from San Salvador to Guatemala City. No matter where you are in either country, the main highway is the preferred route. Return to the capital and take a direct bus to and from the other capital. These buses go along the Panamerican Highway. The road is paved, and the trip is quick. However, be certain that you have your visa before going to El Salvador. Guatemala has Consular Offices close to the borders if you need to get a visa on your way into Guatemala.

If you decide to go into or out of El Salvador by the Sonsonate route, you will go from Esquintla to the border along a winding gravel road. The border crossing is slow because they do not see too many gringos along this road and then, on the El Salvador side, you will find the true third-class chickenbus. The road is gravel, and it is about four to six hours to Sonsonate. Since the peace settlement in El Salvador, there will be more traffic to that beautiful and friendly little country and travel will improve. At present, buses for El Salvador are operated by the Melva International Lines, with the terminal at 4 Ave., Calle 1-20, Zone 9 in Guatemala City. The buses leave every hour from 6:00AM until 1:00PM. This gets you into El Salvador during daylight hours. Buses do not run after 8:00PM anywhere in El Salvador.

If **flying into Guatemala,** there are numerous airlines going there. Lacsa goes from New York and Los Angeles to Costa Rica, usually with a stop in Guatemala. Aviateca, the Guatemalan airline (that now charges gringos double to go to Tikal) flies from Miami, New Orleans or Los Angeles. Other airlines that will connect in large centers in the US or Mexico City are Continental, Eastern, Pan American, Taca, Mexicana, KLM, Iberia and Sabena. Once in Guatemala, you will be able to obtain a visa at the airport.

I like to fly from Canada to Mexico City and then bus to Guatemala. This is the cheapest route I can find. If coming from Europe, I also suggest going from New York to Mexico City and then busing down. Delta Airlines offers an excellent fair to Mexico City if travelling from the States. However, if time is short, you can get flights directly from New York or Los Angeles into Guatemala with Lacsa, but it is expensive. I also encourage the boycotting of Lacsa because they charge the gringos double the local fair for travel to Tikal. If this money was going to benefit the country, I would not feel this way. However, the money is going to those who are wealthy.

If entering **Guatemala by boat**, there are numerous ports of entry. Champerico, Retalhuleu close to the Mexican border is open. Further down the coast are San Josè and Puerto Quetzal, Escuintla. These are also close to beaches, but not really nice ones. Along the Caribbean, there is Puerto Barrios, Izabal and Livingston. The ferry from Belize stops at these ports. You can get visas at these places.

Entrance and exit fees for overland travel are usually about Q7 ($1.50 US) and airport tax is about Q50 ($10.US). Borders are open as long as there are buses running but you may have to pay "overtime" charges at some of the more isolated crossings.

CONSULATES

There are too many consulates in Guatemala City for me to list. I will include those likely to be relevant to most tourists in this area. If yours is not listed here, look under "Consolados" or "Embajada" in the telephone book. Many consulates close by 1:30 or 2:00PM. However, if your country has regular business hours that are different, your consulate may stay open longer. It would be wise to telephone the consulate before going out. I have found throughout Central America that government business should be started early in the morning because the simplest procedures seem to take hours.

British Consulate, Centro Financiero Torre 11, Calle 7, Ave. 5, Zone 4, Tel. 321602

Canadian Consulate, Edificio Galeria España, Calle 12, Ave. 7, Zone 9, Tel. 321419 or 321413. Open until 4:30PM

Costa Rican Consulate, Edificio Galarias Reforma, Ave. La Reforma, Calle 8, Zone 9, Tel. 319604

Ecuadorian Embassy, Ave. La Reforma, Calle 12, Zone 10, Tel. 312439

El Salvadorian Embassy, 12 Calle, 5-43, Zone 9, Tel. 325848

Germany, Edificio Plaza Maritima, Ave. 20, Calle 6, Zone 10, Tel. 370028/9

Guatemalan Immigration Office, 8 Ave. 12-10 Zone 1, Tel. 534158 (for exit visa or extension of visa)

Honduran Consulate, Calle 16, Ave. 8, Zone 10, Tel. 373921

Mexican Consulate, Calle 16, Ave. 1, Zone 10, Tel. 683289

Nicaraguan Consulate, Calle 2, Ave. 15, Zone 13, Tel. 365613

Panamanian Consulate, Edificio Maya, Ave. 7, Zone 4, 325001

Peruvian Embassy, Ave. 2, Calle 9, Zone 9, Tel. 318409
Swiss Embassy, Edificio Seguros Universales, Calle 4, Ave. 7,
Zone 9, Tel. 313725
United States Embassy, Ave. Reforma, Calle 7, Zone 10, Tel.
311541

PUBLIC AND NATIONAL HOLIDAYS

Most government places are closed during public holidays
but the small restaurants and tiendas never seem to close for more
than the night shift. Guatemalans have as many holidays as
Canadians!

January 1	New Year's Day
March or April	Easter Week (Wed. to Mon.)
May 1	Labor Day
June 30	Army's Day (of course)
August 15	Asuncion Day
September 15	Independence Day
October 20	Revolution Day
November 1	All Saint's Day
December 24-25	Christmas
December 31	Last Year's Day

BUSES

Galgos and Talisman run first-class buses in Guatemala.
They are similar to all first-class buses throughout Central America.
They run on schedules and everyone has a numbered seat. Second-
class, or chickenbuses, in Guatemala, are an adventure second only
to the exploration of the moon. You arrive at the bus terminal and
look for a bus going to where you want. Because of competition
between bus companies the conductors are more than willing to help
you find the bus you want. The conductor will always put your bags
on top for you, and he never forgets which bag is yours when it is
time to get off.

If you manage to get on the bus early, you may get a seat by
the window. This is about the safest place because by the time you
leave, there will be three adults and a few children in all the two
seaters and (at least) four adults in the three seaters. If the passengers are still in need of more seats, then expect five adults plus kids
on the three seaters. However, this is still not full. The best seats go
to the next group. One cheek is propped up on the two seater and
one cheek is propped up on the three seater and there you sit, as on
a toilet, and there you will squat until you get off the bus.

In places where there are not many guard stations where the
police make certain there are not too many people on the buses,
people will stand. Then, of course, come the chickens. Since chickens are held in high esteem, they get the spot beside your ankle or
just under your elbow. At last, when the bus is fully packed, you will

be on your way. Most Guatemaltecans can sleep standing or in any other precarious position, and you will very seldom hear a child cry. Oh you say, "What about the bathroom on a long trip?" This is no problem. Just tell the driver. He will stop and you may pop behind a bush. This is done quite often for either the men or children. However, I have yet to see a woman accommodated in this fashion. I believe women don't do that?

While travelling, the conductors always manage to get the correct change for your fare. Be certain to count your change, because as tourism increases, so does the possibility of the conductors making a slight mistake. The conductors always know where and when to transfer you to your final destination. They seem to hustle you on and off all the correct buses with the greatest of speed and accuracy. Have faith in them. When going chickenbus style, Guatemala is one of the easiest countries to travel in.

LEAVING GUATEMALA CITY

Amatitlàn - take bus to San Vicente de Pacaya

Antigua - Transportes Unidos bus line, every half-hour from 7:00AM to 7:00PM from Calle 15, Ave. 4, Zone 1, a 60 minute ride, 45 K. Q1.10

Biotopo del Quetzal - take Coban bus. It takes about 4 hours to the biotopo.

Camotàn - take Chiquimula bus

Chichicastenango - Veloz Quichelense bus line, every half hour from 7:00AM to 6:00PM from Zone 4 bus terminal, 3 1/2 hours, 146 K., Q4.75 You may also catch a bus at Los Encuentros for Chichicastenango if you are coming from Panajachel or Quetzaltenango.

Chimaltenango - take Chichicastenango, Huehuetenango, Panajachel or Quetzaltenango bus

Chiquimula - Rutus Orientales, Calle 19, Ave. 8, Zone 1, every 30 minutes from 4:00AM to 6:00PM, 4 hours, 222 K., Q6.35 or take Esquipulas

Coatepeque - Take Tecun Uman or El Carmen bus. It takes the southern route in Guatemala and will pass through Coatepeque.

Coban - Escobar/Mona Blanca bus lines, Ave. 8, Calle 15 & 16, Zone 1. at 5:00 /7:00 /8:00 /9:00 /10:00 /12:00 /14:00 /14:30/ 16:00 /16:30. 6 hours, 219 K. Q6.10 Some of these buses are direct and are on the luxury pullmans.

Copan - take Chiquimula bus and transfer to Vilma bus line

Cuilapa - take San Salvador bus

El Florido - take Chiquimula bus

El Rancho - take Esquipulas, Chiquimula or Puerto Barrios bus

Esquintla - Chatia Gomerana bus line, Muelle Central, Zone 4 bus terminal every 30 minutes from 6:00AM to 16:30PM, 2 hours, 92 k., Q2 You may also take Puerto San Josè, El Carmen, Tecun Uman or Monterrico bus.

Esquipulas - Rutas Orientales bus line, Calle 19, Ave. 8, Zone 1, every half hour from 4:00AM to 6:00PM, 4 hours, 222K, Q6.35

Flores - Fuente del Norte bus line, Calle 17, Ave. 8, Zone 1. at 1:00/2:00/3:00/7:00/23:00, 14 hours, 506 K. Q30. You may make reservations for this bus.

Huehuetenango - Los Halcones bus lines, Calle 15, Ave. 7, Zone 1 at 7:00AM and 14:00PM, 5 hours, 270 K., Q7. You may also take the bus to La Mesilla

Iztapa - Zone 4 bus terminal - many buses leave during the day.

Jalpatagua - take San Salvador bus

Jocotàn - take Chiquimula bus

La Avellana - take Monterrico bus

La Democracia - Chatia Gomerana, Muelle Central, Zone 4 bus terminal, every half hour from 6:00AM to 16:30PM, 2 hrs. 92 K., Q2

La Gomera - take Escuintla, La Democracia bus

La Mesilla - El Condor bus lines, Calle 19, Ave. 2, Zone 1, at 4:00/8:00/10:00/13:00/17:00, 7 hours, 342 K., Q7

Los Amates - take Puerto Barrios bus

Los Encuentros - take Chichicastenango, Huehuetenango, Panajachel, Quetzaltenango, or La Mesilla bus

Mazatenango - take Tecun Uman or El Carman bus

Mexican border - take Tecun Uman, El Carman or La Mesilla bus. The Rutas Lima Co. bus leaves from Calle 8 and Ave. 3, Zone 1. This is a direct bus. It leaves at 6:15AM or 2:15PM. It takes 7 hours and the cost is 8Q. Transportes Galgos also goes to the border from Calle 19, Ave. 7, Zone 1. This bus leaves at 5:30, 10:00AM and noon, 3:30 and 5:00PM The cost is Q8 per person. This is a true luxury liner of the Guatemalan type. You will get a seat! To yourself!!

Monterrico - Cubanita bus lines, Muelle Central, Zone 4 bus terminal, at 10:30/12:30/14:30, 5 hours, 124 K., Q4

Morales - take Flores bus

Oratorio - take San Salvador bus

Panajachel - Rebulli bus lines, Ave 3 and Calle 2, Zone 9, every hour from 6:00AM to 15:00PM, 3 hours, 147 k., Q4

Patzicia - take Huehuetenango or Panajachel bus

Poptun - take Flores bus

Puerto Barrios - Litegua bus lines, Calle 15, Ave. 10, Zone 1, every hour from 6:00AM to 17:00PM. First class pullman leaves at 10:00AM and 17:00PM, 6 hours, 307 K., Q8.50 and 10Q for the pullman.

Puerto San Josè - Transportes Unidos bus lines, Ave. 4 and Calle 1, Zone 9 every 20 minutes from 5:30AM to 18:00PM. 2 1/2 hours, 92 K., Q2. You may also connect from Esquintla.

Purulhà - take Coban bus

Quetzaltenango - Transportes Galgos, Ave. 7, Calle 19, Zone 1 at 5:30/8:30/11:00/14:30/17:00/19:00/21:00

Quiriguà - take Puerto Barrios bus

Retalhuleu - take Tecun Uman or El Carmen, Talisman bus

Rio Dulce - take Flores bus

Rio Hondo - take Equipulas, Chiquimula or Puerto Barrios bus

San Cristòbal - take Coban or Huehuetenango bus

San Lucas Sacatepèquez - see Antigua and Chichicastenango.

San Luis - take Flores bus

San Salvador - Melva Internacional bus lines, Ave. 4, Calle 1, Zone 9, at 6:00/7:30/9:00/10:00/11:00/12:00/13:00, 5 hours, 268 K., Q7.

San Vincente Pacaya - Cuquita bus lines, Muelle Central, Zone 4 bus terminal, at 7:00AM and 4:00PM, 2 hours, 46 k., 1.25Q

Siquinalà - take Escuintla, La Democracia bus

Sipacate - take Escuintla, La Democracia bus

Sololà - take Panajachel bus

Tactic - take Coban bus

Taxisco - take Monterrico bus

Tecpàn - take Huehuetenango, Panajachel bus

Teculutàn - take Puerto Barrios bus

Tecun Uman - Fortaleza bus lines, Calle 19, Ave. 8, Zone 1 at 5:30 and 9:30AM, 5 hours, 253 k., Q6

Tikal - take Flores bus

Totonicapàn - take Huehuetenango, Quetzaltenango or La Mesilla bus

Valle Nuevo - take San Salvador bus

Zacapa - take Esquipulas or Chiquimula bus

FERRIES

Ferries between Belize and Guatemala have a regular schedule. There is also boat service on Lake Izabal, Lake Atitlan, Lake Peten Itza and on the Rio Dulce and El Pasion Rivers.

Puerto Barrios to Livingston goes daily at 10:30AM and 5:00PM. The cost is Q1 per person. The ferry leaves from the foot of Calle 12, on the Amatique Bay. It is often full to beyond chickenbus full. There have been people bumped off the ferry because it was too full and the selection for bumping is lottery style.

You must purchase your tickets in advance by one sailing in town. The ticket office is just across from the customs office. There are also private boats that go to Livingston for a higher price; this is often a more pleasant ride. If you are travelling in a group, this is often the best way to go.

Returning from Livingston to Puerto Barrios, the boat leaves at 5:00AM and 2:00PM and it is the same boat, the same price and the same chickens, I am sure. Be certain to be at the boat early so you can get on; then become inconspicuous so that you won't be bumped off.

Going to **Punta Gorda, Belize**, is a regular ferry going every Tuesday and Friday, leaving Puerto Barrios at 7:30AM and stopping in Livingston at around 9:00 - 9:30AM. It is possible to take the boat only from Livingston but you should try and have a reservation to guarantee your passage. This may be done at the docks or at the Immigration Office in Livingston. You must ask around as this changes quite often. The boat to Belize returns the same day at about 3:00PM.

Travel by private boat is not recommended. Too many people emerge from the beautiful Caribbean Ocean, dripping wet and scared stiff because of the rough, wet ride in a small boat.

The ferry going from Puerto Barrios to Honduras has been discontinued. There are private boats that will take passengers, but it is a matter of paying and waiting. There are also small private boats that will go all the way from Belize to Honduras with a brief stop in Guatemala. This is not the easiest way unless your plan is to travel the entire Caribbean coast all the way to Panama (which can be done if you have the time).

CAR RENTALS

At one time I recommended car rentals, but no longer. The cost is high in Guatemala, running about $70.00 US per day plus the cost of gas and insurance. These are not chickenbus prices. The insurance is also $2000.00 deductible. However, this is not the most environmentally efficient way to travel. It also puts the tourist money into the hands of the big (usually US owned) companies instead of the little working guy.

TAXIS

These are plentiful. It is often easier to rent a taxi than to travel by bus when trying to reach a remote location. You must barter, but if you have any Spanish, you will find the drivers easy to deal with. A trip from the center of Zone 1 to the airport in Guatemala City will run about Q20 - 25 for two people. I once took a taxi out to Mixco Viejo; the drivers wanted the fare but were as uncertain as I as to the distance and difficulty of the journey. They thought they had a great deal at Q75. for a return trip for two people. However, after the gruelling trip out, waiting for us for a couple of hours, and then driving back, we knew that they had badly underestimated. We paid Q100 for the ride and felt that we still had a good deal. Be fair with these people. For the most part, they don't want to cheat you anymore than they want a run-in with the military.

TELEPHONE

To make a long distance call go to the Guatel office in any of the larger towns or cities. You may also call from a private phone or the larger hotel phone offices. You can only make station-to-station calls if you pay for the call in Guatemala. The rates are about $10.00 for calls to North America for three minutes.

If calling within the country, it is very easy. For a call outside of Guat City, you must dial 0 and then the number. If calling Guatemala City from another place in Guatemala, you must dial 02 and the number. Calls are cheap (around a dime per minute) and are easy to do. I have been told that these calls are best done at the pay phones found anywhere rather than the Guatel office. However, I can not say enough about the helpfulness and pleasantry I have experienced at the Guatel office.

The Guatel office is found at Ave. 7 between Calle 12 and 13 in Zone 1 in Guatemala City. In smaller places, either ask for directions or just walk around close to the center of town and look for the blue and white sign. You may also send telegraphs from the Guatel office.

MARKET DAYS

Because of the large Indian population in Guatemala, market days are important. On market days, the Indians come from their villages to sell and trade many articles. It is a colorful event and well worth taking in. The most popular market is Chichicastenango; the bargains are few, but the variety and quality makes this market a favorite for both the tourist and the importer.

The garments that the Indians sell are often very precious to them. Either they, or a member of their family, has worn the garment, and it has taken hours of loving work to make it. Don't insult the Indians by wearing the garments that you purchase unless they are truly gringo clothes. Often the economic situation of the Indians is so desperate that they will almost give the article away in order to provide a meal for their families. Be fair and offer a decent price. If a lady says that she has not eaten for the day, she is probably telling the truth. A dollar from your budget will make little difference to you but it could mean a week's food for an Indian family.

The following is a list of the more popular markets in the country and the days when they are trading. Permanent markets in Guatemala are not as exciting as the special day ones. Some, such as Panajachel and Antigua are permanent because of the large tourist trade.

Sundays	Town	District
	Antigua	Sacatepèquez
	Chichicastenango	El Quichè
	Gomalapa	Chimaltenango
	Momostenango	Totonicapàn
	Nahualà	Sololà
	Nebaj	El Quichè
	Patzun	Chimaltenango
	San Cristobal	Totonicapàn
	San Cristobal Verapaz	Alta Verapaz
	San Juan Atitàn	Huehuetenango
	San Juan Chamelco	Alta Verapaz
	San Lucas Tolimàn	Sololà
	San Martin Jilotepeque	Chimaltenango
	San Martin Sacatepèquez	Quetzaltenango
	San Mateo Ixtatàn	Huehuetenango
	San Sebastiàn	Huehuetenango
	Santa Maria Chiquimula	Totonicapàn
	Tactic	Alta Verapaz
	Tamahù	Alta Verapaz
	Tecpàn Guatemala	Chimaltenango
	Todos Santos Cuchumatan	Huehuetenango
	Tucurù	Alta Verapaz
Monday	Antigua	Sacatepèquez
	Chimaltenango	Chimaltenango
	Zunil	Quetzeltenango
Tuesday	Comalapa	Chimaltenango
	Olintepeque	Quetzeltenango
	Patzùn	Chimaltenango
	San Martin Jilotepeque	Chimaltenango
	Sololà	Sololà
	Totonicapàn	Totonicapàn

199

Wednesday	Chimaltenango	Chimaltenango
	Patzicia	Chimaltenango
	Santa Lucia La Reforma	Totonicapàn
	Santiago Sacatepèquez	Sacatepèquez
Thursday	Antigua	Sacatepèquez
	Chichicastenango	El Quichè
	Nahualà	Sololà
	Nebaj	El Quichè
	Sacapulas	El Quichè
	San Cristobal Verapaz	Alta Verapaz
	San Juan Atitàn	Huehuetenango
	San Juan Chamelco	Alta Verapaz
	San Lucas Tolimàn	Sololà
	San Martin Jilotepeque	Chimaltenango
	San Mateo Ixtatàn	Huehuetenango
	San Sebastiàn	Huehuetenango
	Tactic	Alta Verapaz
	Tamahù	Alta Verapaz
	Tecpàn Guatemala	Chimaltenango
	Todos Santos Cuchumatàn	Huehuetenango
	Tucurù	Alta Verapaz
	Chimaltenango	Chimaltenango
Friday	Comalapa	Chimaltenango
	Patzùn	Chimaltenango
	San Francisco El Alto	Totonicapàn
	Santiago Sacatepèquez	Sacatepèquez
	Sololà	Sololà
Saturday	Antigua	Sacatepèquez
	Patzicia	Chimaltenango
	Totonicapàn	Totonicapàn

PERMANENT MARKETS

	Antigua	Sacatepèquez
	Panajachel	Sololà
	Cobàn	Alta Verapaz
	Chimaltenango	Chimaltenango
	Mixco	Guatemala
	Quetzaltenango	Quetzaltenango
	San Juan Sacatepèquez	Guatemala
	San Pedro Sacatepèquez	Guatemala
	Santa Cruz del Quichè	El Quichè
	Santiago Atitlàn	Sololà
	Totonicapàn	Totonicapàn
	Esquipulas	Chiquimula
	Sumpango	Sacatepèquez

AGUACATAN

This is a village close to the Rio San Juan and could be a stopping place if going to Nabaj or Todos Santos. The bus trip in to the village is on a narrow gravel road which is impassable during rainy season. It passes over a high mountain pass and beside a spectacular canyon. The bus trip alone is a thrill. A visit to the swimming hole at the Rio San Juan becomes a second bonus on this trip. The only drawback is the lack of restaurants. Be certain to ask the price before ordering or you will pay high and get low.

Hospadaje La Paz is the only place in town to stay. It is at the end of town on the main street if coming from Huehue. It is very clean but has no private bath and only one tap showers. The cost is Q15 per person which is really high, but you are at the mercy of the owner as there is no other choice but to leave town.

Rio San Juan is interesting to visit. See the description under "Things to do" (Huehuetenango) as this could be a day trip from there.

Colonial architecture in Antiqua

201

ANTIGUA

Altitude: 1530 meters (5020 ft.) Population: 16,000.

45 kilometers (28 miles) and 1 hour from Guatemala City by regular bus service.

Antigua is a delightful, colonial town that is overrun by gringos. This is not Guatemala in its truest form, and if you want to get away from other travellers, this is not the place to be. I have a Guatemalan friend that was in Antigua on a Sunday and was asked by another Guatemalan why he was there as the week-ends in Antigua are now only for gringos. However, it is a popular place for a reason. It has nice places to stay, lots of things to see, many schools to attend and great restaurants in which to eat.

The original name of Antigua was Santiago de los Caballeros de Guatemala; it was founded by Pedro de Alvarado in 1543. Its original location is at a place now called Ciudad Viejo; you can walk to it from the present site of Antigua. In 1541, after days of torrential rain, an earthquake caused the water to spill out from Volcano Agua's crater and destroyed the village. The town was re-established at its present site.

At the new Santiago de los Caballeros, a prominent cultural society developed building convents, monasteries, churches, a newspaper and a university. This village grew to be one of the most admired cities on the continent, often compared to Lima and Mexico City. Until 1773, the city had many problems. The Church was very powerful and battled for supremacy in the government. American born merchants battled for equality with the Spanish who had more power and money. As the crime rate rose so did the discontent of the people; in 1773, when the Santa Marta earthquakes destroyed the city, it also destroyed the power structure of the area. The quakes left the city in short supply of food and water but in large supply of disease. Martin de Mayorga y Mendiente, Governor at the time decided to move the capital to the present site of Guatemala City. However, the Archbishop, Pedro Cortez y Larraz, insisted on re-building the city where it was. This battle for the capital raged for two years until, on January 2, 1776, the King of Spain declared Guatemala City the official capital of Guatemala.

Mayorga moved many valuable objects from Antigua to the new capital and soon people began to move away also. However, the old city was never totally abandoned and today, reconstruction of some of the old ruins is occurring.

PLACES TO STAY

At peak seasons such as Holy Week, it is impossible to get a room in Antigua unless you have booked and paid well in advance. For example, the Santa Lucia is usually booked 5 - 6 months in advance for Semana Santa.

Private homes - Often, the Spanish schools will provide a home for you, so getting a hotel may be a waste of time and money if you are attending school. The tourist office sometimes has rooms in private houses and the bulletin board at Doña Louisa's may advertise rooms. The boys at the bus terminal will also show you rooms which are quite safe. These fellows get a commission for bringing you to a place.

Santa Lucia is the best place in town to stay. The hotel is clean, cheery, secure and friendly. There is a delightful courtyard for sitting, reading, or visiting. The rooms are fairly small but spotlessly clean, all with private bath and lots of hot water. The muchachas will do your laundry for a reasonable price, and there is a spot out back where you can sit in the sun. It is also always full, so don't get your hopes up. The cost is Q20 for a single and Q30 ($6.US) for a double. It is on Ave. Santa Lucia Sur # 7. This is the main street across from the market. When your back is to the market, cross the avenue, turn right and walk down the street.

Hospadaje Pasaje is half a block past the Santa Lucia on the same street and half as expensive. You can get a room for Q10 ($2.US) per person, but there are no single rooms. The place is very clean with a communal, one-tap shower. It is also very quiet. I also like it because it is away from the center of town.

Hotel Refugio is a typical place with communal shower for Q12 ($2.50US) per person. It is fairly popular with travellers if the Pasaje or Santa Lucia are full. You may use the fridge and make snacks here. The address is 4 Calle, #30

Hotel Doña Angelina is not too bad if you get one of the upper rooms. If you get one without a window, the musty smell will be difficult to sleep with. It is Q25 ($5.US) per person for a single and Q30 ($6.US) for a double. In order to get hot water, you must use the upstairs shower and only put the water on at a trickle. Otherwise, the heating contraption won't work. The hotel is on 4 Calle Poniente, # 33 and across from Hotel Refugio.

Hotel Landivar is just off the main street where the buses stop. Walk one block to the right of the post office on Ave. Santa Lucia to Calle 5 and continue down the street. The rooms are Q30 ($6.US) for two with bath. They are excellent and quiet in the main hotel. However, if they are full, the proprietor may send you to the annex.

Hotel Landivar Annex is new and very clean with a communal, hot water shower for Q30 ($6.US). However, it is close to a popular bar that plays loud music and exudes louder drunks until 2:00AM. Not a place for light sleepers. The muchachas also need some discipline as they start banging on your door as early as 6:30AM wanting you out so they can clean your room. The annex is on Ave. 7 Norte #43

Hotel Negris is basic for Q25 ($5.US) for a double and is okay as long as the rest of the guests are quiet. However, the establishment does not have any control over rowdy guests and you may have to do your own fist shaking if you want some quiet. The one tap showers are communal.

Hotel Los Capitanes is half a block south of the square on the west side, on Ave. 5 Sur #8. It is a large building, above a noisy bar, with a number of rooms. It is Q20 ($4.US) for a single and Q30 ($6.US) for a double with a private bath, two-tap shower, toilet paper, soap and towels. However, when busy, the price increases. This practice is illegal in Guatemala, and you need to point this out to the owner.

El Descanso is on Ave. 5 Sur #9 but only has 4 rooms. The rooms cost Q20 ($4.US) or Q36 ($7.US). This little place is next to the Capitanes and I would imagine just as noisy. However, this is one place that I did not stay in.

Posada de Don Pedro de Alvarado is on 4 Calle and charges Q20 ($4.US) for a single and Q26 ($5.US) for a double. There is hot water and a restaurant at this hotel. I did not stay in this one either, so I have no comments.

RESTAURANTS

Like many places in Central America, Antigua is rapidly changing to keep up with the influx of tourists. Antigua has many restaurants which are excellent by international standards. Try anything that suits your fancy. If you want something quiet (rare in Antigua), then you will have to go to the local places that are a bit out of the way. However, there are some old favorites that have passed the test of time.

Doña Luisa's on Calle 4 Oriente #12, just two blocks east of the square, is one of the most popular places in town. A fabulous bakery offers excellent breads and pastries to be eaten in or taken out. The cakes are popular throughout Antigua, and the restaurant is the best place to get your dish of fruit salad with yogurt and granola for breakfast. It is also a very popular place to sit and meet other gringos in the afternoon or to watch the American cable television. The bulletin board at the entrance is good for advertising everything from goods for sale to adventure trips to rooms to airline tickets. It is also a good place to leave a message for your friends. However, Doña Luisa's is not the cheapest place in town to eat.

Mio Cid at 5 Calle and 3 Ave. Sur is a popular place for travellers. It is a Canadian-owned restaurant that serves excellent food at a good price. I also like the atmosphere - it's for the young.

El Capuchino - on 6 Ave. Norte #10 is an excellent Italian restaurant. The home-made pasta is the best but prices are a tad high. The atmosphere is excellent and the place is clean.

Restaurant D'Rino at Ave. 5 Norte #12 has good food but the drawing card to this place is the wine. The owner brings a keg of good wine from Italy every year and sells it in his restaurant. He puts the wine from the keg into a used bottle, but don't be fooled; it is the real imported wine. His food is also excellent; his specialty is the "pepiàn", his chicken in a mole sauce. This is now my favorite place in Antigua. **San Carlos** is on the square and is excellent for meals. The french fries and hamburgers will satisfy any appetite. The last time I was there, I saw some people trying to get through an order of home baked cake that made my mouth drool. It not only looked appetizing but tasted better than some of Doña Louisa's. This place has been in Antigua for years and has really passed the time test.

Cafè Cafè at 5 Ave. Norte # 14 specializes in local dishes. This is a treat when so many restaurants are international. It is also pleasant and fairly cheap.

Portada Palomar is a restaurant and art gallery. It is on 5 Calle Oriente #3 and is expensive for my style of travelling. However, the food is good and the atmosphere is splendid. I like the archways. If you need an expensive treat, this may be the place. However, the choice of restaurants is so great that it is hard to recommend one above another.

THINGS TO DO

The Square is the most logical land mark in any Latin American town or city. In the old days, this square had no trees or benches and was the hub of activity. Antigua's square was used as a common market for the Indians, for bullfights on special days, for whippings and hangings, and for military parades. The plaza had its first fountain built in 1561 and was not paved until 1704.

Palacio de los Capitanes Generales is on the south side of the square (on your right when coming from the central market). First built in 1550 under the direction of Bishop Marroquin, the building was so poorly constructed that it had to be rebuilt. This was completed in 1764, but the palace was reconstructed again after the Santa Marta earthquakes. In the old days, it housed the treasury, law courts and the Captain General's (the Governor's) office.

Both good and bad generals lived behind these walls. Mayèn de Rueda was so corrupt and cruel that his actions caused the Franciscan Fathers to rebel. The Fathers closed their doors and other sects closed their churches, schools and convents in sympathy, similar to a modern day labor strike. However, the scandal was so extreme that the officials removed Rueda from office; only then were they able to convince the Franciscan Fathers to stay in Guatemala instead of moving to Mexico as they planned. The legend goes that Rueda ended up running around the hills naked and totally insane, eating only herbs and the charitable donations of the Indians.

On the other hand, Diego de Avendaño was so good and fair that after he died, it is said that the people re-opened his tomb and found his hands still in the same physical condition as when he was alive. This was because he had never done any misdeeds with his hands.

Presently, on the reconstructed site, there is a coat-of-arms in the center of the building. It is from Old Castile with the name of Charles lll on it. He was the reigning monarch at the time of completion. Today, you may go to the top of the building, walk around the portals and imagine life as it was 300 years ago.

On the main floor of this building, there are the **police station** and **tourist office.**

Palacio del muy Noble Ayuntamiento or the Palace of the Very Noble Municipality (City Hall) was built in the same style as the Palace of the Captains but is a bit smaller. The city is still administered from these offices. On the front of the building is the city's coat of arms which is St. James riding above three volcanoes, with the biggest one, Fuego, erupting. This building is closed on Mondays and open from 9:00AM to 4:00PM on other days. There is a two hour lunch break from 12:00 - 2:00PM on the week-ends.

Book Museum is housed in the same building as the City Hall. Next to this building was a little house in ruins with a plaque on the door. It said that in 1660, this was the site of the first printing press in Central America and the third in the New World. The press was brought from Mexico in 1660 and completed its first book in 1663. The book was written by Bishop Payo de Rivera in Latin. A replica of the press is now in the Book Museum along with numerous old books and historical items related to the printing business. The museum is open daily from 9:00AM to 4:00PM, closed Mondays and closed12:00-2:00 on week-ends.

Museum of Santiago and Museum of Arms These two museums are in the same building. In the Santiago Museum are many artifacts from colonial days; the big drawing card is the sword that once belonged to Pedro de Alvarado. Behind this museum was the city jail and it was used until 1955. Today, it is the home of the Arms Museum. You will find many interesting artifacts including some weapons used by the Indians before the conquest. These include stone swords, hatchets and maces which were attached to wooden poles.

University of San Carlos de Boromeo is on the west side of the square, opposite the Cathedral. On his death in 1563, Bishop Marroquin left money for the building of the university. However, it was not started until 1676 because some of the other religious groups did not want the competition of a university with their colleges. Originally named College of Santo Tomas de Aquino, it became La Pontificia y Real Universidad de San Carlos Borromeo in 1678. Originally only for Castilians, it was soon changed to educate men of all classes. The university offered degrees in theology, law, philosophy, medicine and the Cakchiquel language. Because of the competition of the colleges, the standards were kept very high. In 1687, the university was granted all the privileges of the Universities of Mexico and Lima.

The university was moved to Guatemala City after the 1773 earthquakes. However, the building was never destroyed and was used for various purposes. Today, it houses the Colonial Museum. The building itself is a beautiful piece of architecture. The carved stone doorway was given to the university in 1843 by the statesman Mariano Galvez. The walls are covered with geometrical designs and the many arches are designed with curves, grooves and tips carved into the plaster.

Colonial Museum has many treasures from colonial days. These are mostly art treasures such as old oil paintings and painted, wooden, religious statues. One room has a great painting that is made more effective by the lighting. It is of two students presenting their thesis to a professor who is at the head of the classroom. The next room has four murals which tell the story of graduation at this university. Many more treasures are in this museum.

The Cathedral was started in 1543, but the present construction dates from 1669 to 1680. However, as late as 1748, it is believed that tiles were still needed to complete the paving and the columns were not covered in tortoise shell. The church was divided into five naves and eight chapels; sixty-eight arches held up the walls and the ceiling of the room which was over 300 feet wide. The high altar was under the dome and was decorated in gold leaf and ivory statues. In the underground Royal Chapel were the remains of Pedro de Alvarado and his second wife, Doña Beatrice, but these tombs have been destroyed by earthquakes. Others that have been buried here are Alvarado's daughter and her husbands, Bishop Marroquin, and the historian Bernal Diaz del Castillo. A bishop's residence was to the right of the cathedral.

The most famous chapel in the Cathedral was the chapel of Nuestra Señora del Socorro. A statue of Nuestra Señora del Socorro was found on the shores of Spain after a storm. The statue, along with two others, had been put into a box and dumped overboard when a ship was in trouble. Francisco de Garay brought the statue with him to Mexico; then Padre Godinez brought it to Iximchè, Guatemala. After a few more moves from 1542 to 1620, she was finally put in a shrine in the new Cathedral. From here she blessed weddings and christenings, prevented earthquakes and volcanic eruptions, and prevented droughts by making the rains fall. At one time, she carried a lizard of emeralds which a daring thief stole. He hid in a tomb under the altar, but the virgin made his cloak get caught in the door. This led to his discovery. I love miracles.

Today, the remains of the plaster walls and cornices are of interest because the grandeur of the past can still be imagined. But the outside of the building is also in fairly good condition and a pleasure to visit. You may go inside the present building at any time.

Church of La Merced is on 1 Calle Poniente and 6 Ave. Norte. The church was originally built in 1552 but was partially destroyed in 1773. The building is spectacular with the outside columns beautifully designed in what is known as a Churrigueresque design. To me, the columns look like they have been draped in fine handmade Spanish lace. The Lady of Mercy is said to have come to Santiago de los Caballeros in a box. When the Brothers opened it, they could smell perfume. The statue inside had a wound from where the odorous liquid was coming. It was used on the sick or maimed for healing purposes. However, other sources say that the gold crowned lady was sculptured by a Spaniard in 1628 and then brought to Antigua. I prefer the first story.

The church is the original home of the famous figure of Jesus of Nazarine sculptured by Mateo Zùniga in 1654 for 65 pesos and then painted by Joseph de la Cerda. It is accredited for several miracles and was finally consecrated by Bishop Bautista Alvarez de Toledo in 1717. Today, the treasures of this church are housed in the Church Nuestra Señora de la Merced on 11 Ave. and 5 Calle, Zone 1 in Guatemala City. However, today in Antigua, there is the worshipped carving of Alonso de Paz of Jesus of Nazarine which is used during the processions of Semana Santa. Next door to the church is the convent which has a wonderful fountain plus a panoramic view of the city's backdrop of volcanoes.

Church & Convent of Las Capuchinas found on 2 Ave. and 2 Calle are the ruins of this church. Completed in 1736, this convent was the first Sisterhood of Central America. The bishop, Juan Bautista Alvarez de Toledo, born in Santiago, and educated abroad, and the first creole bishop of the colony brought five Capuchin nuns from Madrid to start the convent.

The convent had a very modern sanitary system; each cell on both floors had its own private bathroom. What a luxury if the hotels in Guatemala followed the same architecture. The cells opened to a circular central hallway. The yard was full of fountains, patios and gardens. There was also the Torre del Retiro, (retreat) where the nuns spent time every year. It was rumored that they suffered great hardships during this time. Their life was by no means as pleasant as other religious orders in Santiago at that time. After taking their vows, these women had no contact with the outside world. They wore the roughest of garments, slept on hard straw beds and worked long hours for the purification of the soul.

These nuns were also known for their expertise in cleaning linen. Because the Holy members of other orders were not allowed to wear blueing next to their skin, this expertise was used and appreciated by others.

The convent is open daily from 8:00AM to 5:00PM and there is a small entrance fee.

Santa Clara Church & Convent 2 Ave. and 6 Calle. These ruins have more history of falling down than standing up. Originally, this church was built in 1699 and housed five Santa Clara nuns from Puebla Mexico. The convent was sponsored by a rich widow and by donations from private citizens. It took three years to build the first building. Beautifully built, the church, confessionals and convent all faced each other. This enabled the nuns to go back and forth without being seen. Beneath the wood and tiled ceilings were five elaborate altars, all richly carved in wood.

The nuns were known for their baking. One humble nun from the kitchen was elevated to Abbess by her superiors due to a dispute as to who should become leader. The nun's name was Sister Berengaria; her picture is in the Colonial Museum between rooms 6 and 7. The structure was destroyed by the 1717 earthquake and rebuilt again by 1734. This building was even more ornate than the first. The church and convent were again severely damaged in 1773, and in 1874 the buildings were completely destroyed.

Today there is a wonderful fountain in the center courtyard plus an ornate facade with the carved figures of San Migal and San Gabriel. Some arches still remain. This is a pleasant place to visit. It is open from 8:00AM to 5:00PM, closed Mondays, and there is a small entrance fee.

Convent de Concepcion is on Calle de la Concepcion. These ruins are found by walking straight east on 4 Calle. They are the first ones you will see from the bus window when coming from Guatemala City. The ruins are being held up with wooden beams and are pretty well unattended. The convent was first built in 1578 and completed in 1620. The nuns were known for their skilled ability in "women's work" such as cooking, embroidery, singing and knowing the church saints and calendar. (Yuk) However, at one time, it is believed that over 1000 lived in this convent. But I always like the scandals. Sister Juana de Maldonado Paz was a wealthy poet whose rich father gave her a tremendous amount of wealth even though she had taken the vows of poverty. She even had her own large and luxurious cell. When her father tried to make her an Abbess, a rebellion broke out in the convent, and a scandal spread in the city. The poor spoiled woman had to remain a regular nun.

Church of San Jeronimo is just past the bus terminal on 1 Calle Poniente and Ave. Santa Lucia. This building was functioning before 1740 but became the college of Maximo Doctor San Geronimo. In 1718, the king prohibited the establishment of further religious orders. In 1763 it was discovered that this church was built without the king's permission. The church was then confiscated and later used as a royal customhouse.

La Recoleccion Monastery The ruins of these buildings are found behind the bus terminal on 1 Calle and Ave. Recoleccion. This Order was founded by Margil de Jesus who devoted himself to the poor of Latin America. Margil de Jesus, born in 1657 in Velencia, travelled with his friend Melchor Lopez throughout the area on foot, peacefully converting the Indians to Christianity. They assisted in squelching a revolt in Verapaz which resulted in them starting the school in Santiago. The first school, just a small hut, was operating by 1701 under the name of Propaganda Fide y Colegio de Cristo Crucificado de Misioneros. The name was bigger than the hut. However, it was not long before their reputation spread and requests for Margil de Jesus's teachings came from as far as Panama. A huge Monastery was built and then slowly destroyed by succeeding earthquakes. Today the ruins are an excellent place to imagine the wonders of the past. The ruins are open from 8:00 AM to 5:00 PM and closed Mondays.

Popenoe House or Casa del Capuchina is an absolute must when visiting Antigua and is found on 1 Ave. Sur and 5 Calle Oriente. However, this building is only sporadically open. When it is open, I understand that you can go from 10:00AM to 11:00AM and 4:00PM to 5:00PM. However, I have also heard that you can go from 3:00PM to 3:30PM daily. I have never been able to get accurate information about this house. Check at the tourist office or just walk past during those times. If your angel is with you, you'll get in.

The house was originally built in 1634 by Luis de las Infantes Mendoza y Venegas who was then the Justice of the Supreme Court. It passed through many hands and fell into ruin until 1931, when Popenoe and his wife reconstructed the building. There are several patios, vast rooms and lush colonial furnishings. The huge Capuchin cypress in the yard was planted in 1850 and thus gives the house its name.

Some of the green and yellow tiles in the house were typical of the Antigua area long ago. The bathtub is a double structure, one for cold water and the smaller one for hot water which was run from the kitchen.

Raphael Landivar monument and tomb is located on Alameda Santa Lucia. Landivar was a famous Guatemaltecan poet who was expelled in 1767 with the Jesuits. He died in Italy in 1793; and his body was later returned to Antigua for its final resting place. His most famous work, written in Latin, was called Rusticatio Mexicana.

Arch of Santa Catalina is the huge arch in the center of the street on 5 Ave. Norte between Calles 1 & 2. The classic tourist picture is the volcano framed by the Arch of Santa Catalina. It is a good landmark in Antigua.

Market is on Ave. Santa Lucia where the buses stop. If you like the little clay painted birds that are common to this area, be certain to purchase them while you are here. They are made only in Antigua and you may not see them again. Antigua also specializes in the delicate white clay unpainted birds; the white clay is typical to the area. There is a neat shop just past La Recoleccion on 1 Calle del Chajon #21 which specializes in the making of the clay birds. The market also has many stalls with every type of souvenir you may wish to purchase. Prices are not too bad but selection (except for the birds) is better in Chichicastenango. There is another small area closer to town that sells souvenirs for the tourist. You will pass the area when walking around. Check prices before making any offer. Listen to what price the locals start and then follow suit. Bartering is a custom; people who do not play this game are not respected.

In many specialty shops the prices may be a bit higher and fixed, unless you are purchasing in quantity. If you don't feel confident bartering, this may be an alternative. I personally don't like the shops because the money does not go directly to the Indians. They work for a wage and the shop owner gets most of the profit. Whenever possible, I suggest buying directly from the Indians on the street. If it costs you an extra two bits - who cares?

San Felipe de Jesus is a short 2 km. walk from Antigua. To get there, walk north along Ave. Santa Lucia, take a right onto Calle 1a and then an immediate left onto Calle Despengano. Stay on this road all the way to the village. The road will take a slight swing to the east about halfway there. There are buses that go every half hour but the walk is much nicer.

The church in this town was founded in colonial times, destroyed and then rebuilt in the 1850's with materials from the ruins of La Merced in Antigua. Many people come to pray here during holy week in the hope of receiving a miraculous cure from the famous figure of Jesus Sepultado (entombed) which can be seen in the church. The pilgrimages to this church occur during the first Friday of Lent.

The main attraction in this village is the silver factory. The craftsmen make beautiful jewelry for a reasonable price and you can use your Visa card. The shop is called **Tienda y O Plateria La Antigueña** on Calle Jon los Horcones #46. If you can't find the shop, ask the kids. They know where it is.

Santa Maria de Jesus is a village just outside Antigua at the foot of Volan de Agua. The bus doesn't leave Antigua before 8:00 AM so don't get out of bed early unless it is market day when the bus leaves a bit earlier. The last bus leaves Santa Maria at 6:00PM so be certain to be earlier than that if you climbed Mount Agua. It is believed that the Indians in this village moved here from the Quetzaltenango area in the 16th century. The inhabitants are 98% indigenous. There are about 8000 people living in the village.

The town was originally called Aserradero which means lumber yard. This is because the Indians originally supplied the area with lumber. This village is interesting to visit because you may witness the Indians living in the same manner as they have for centuries. The men wear red shirts with flowers and animals woven into the design. The people pray at the church on holy days and Sundays with their colorful clothing and combined native-Christian rituals. There is one very basic hospedaje in the village should you be stuck there overnight. If walking back from Santa Maria, you will pass a little village called **San Juan del Obispo.** The palace of Francisco Marroquin, where the first Bishop of Guatemala lived, is here. This palace is a prominent building which can be seen from Antigua.

Volcan de Agua is climbed from the village of Santa Maria de Jesus. A complete day is needed to climb the mountain as the total change in elevation is over five-thousand feet. Those with camping gear may stay in the stone hut at the top but be certain to have very warm gear as it gets quite cold. When climbing the mountain, you will first come to a small church building which appears to be used more for a refuge than religious worship. The next landmark is a little house where you can buy pop and in-season fruit. The viewpoints between these two landmarks allow you to see Lake Atitlan on a clear day. Continuing, there is another house which is sometimes used for sleeping. Once you reach this house, you have one and a half hours to walk to the top. The air gets thinner so conserve your energy and dress warmly to protect your muscles. The total ascent time is about 4-5 hours; allow 2 1/2 - 3 hours to descend. The top of the crater is 3766 meters (12,307 ft) above sea level and the change in elevation is 1716 meters (5600 ft). This is a full day for any hiker. In 1541, this crater filled with water and flooded Ciudad Vieja killing Doña Beatriz, Alvarado's wife.

Ciudad Vieja is situated at 1519 meters (4984 ft) above sea level and has about 9500 inhabitants. This is the site of the second capital city of Guatemala (the first is at Iximchè) and the actual sight of the death of Doña Beatriz, wife of Pedro de Alvarado.

Prior to their death in 1541, it is believed Pedro de Alvarado and his wife Doña Beatriz lived in this area. Some believe that their actual residence was 2 kilometers to the east at San Miguel Escobar. In August of 1541, Alvarado's wife was alone in the palace when she received the news of Alvarado's death in Mexico. At Doña Beatriz's command, the city went into mourning. On September 9th, she went to the Salon de Saraos and declared herself the new Commander of Guatemala and named her brother Lieutenant Governor. On September 10th, after foiling a plot to dispose her, Doña Beatriz commanded all those suspected of treason to be imprisoned. This did not occur. That night, Volcano Fuego started rumbling. Then, the neighboring Volcano Agua released a torrent of earth, mud and water. Doña Beatriz, with Leonor, Alvarado's first daughter, and eleven ladies in-waiting, went to the chapel to pray. They were found dead the next day. Lady Beatriz was still holding the large crucifix in the chapel. Thus ended the only female rule in all the Americas for over 400 years. Female control lasted a short 36 hours.

In the village are a few stone ruins believed to be the site of the old cathedral. The big tree in the square is believed to be the place the Spaniards had their first Mass after they decided this spot would be the capital city of the area.

Today, you are warned not to walk from Antigua because of the threat of robberies along the roads. I would heed these warnings and take one of the buses which run every hour.

Volcanos Acatenango and Fuego are much more difficult hikes than Agua. Acatenango is 3975 meters (13,041 ft) and Fuego is 3763 meters (12,346 ft.). If you want to visit both on the same trip, overnighting is necessary and you must carry water for two days. That is a lot of weight. Fuego still belches the odd gust of smoke and ash but little fire. Its appearance has changed since the Spanish first arrived. These two volcanoes are spectacular; if you are an avid hiker, they are certainly recommended. Because there are not too many hikers in this area, it is fairly safe, safer than Pacaya at present. Before going, ask around, and if the robberies have increased in this area, go elsewhere. Do not ask for trouble. Let the robbers live there in peace and starvation.

To get to Acatenango, take a bus past Ciudad Vieja and go to Miguel Dueña. You must then continue on foot to finca Soledad. The trail goes up and across from there. When you descend from Fuego, you will arrive at the village of Alotenango.

You may arrange for a guide to take you on this trip. Check the advertisements in Antigua. If there is trouble on the mountain, even a guide does not guarantee safety. A few years ago, guides were in cahoots with the robbers on Pacaya; it was not until there were numerous robberies and a few rapes that the tourists refused to patronize the criminals.

San Antonio Aguas Calientes has a population of 3700 and is at 1550 meters (5085 ft.). The importance of this village is the weaving which is said to be the best in Guatemala. I especially liked the table place mats; the weaving is so tight it looks like it will outlast me. However, the napkins that go with the place mats are so tightly woven that I can't use them; they are much too stiff. I have heard that the weavers can weave your face into a piece of cloth if given a photo to copy! One of these village ladies has travelled as far as Alaska showing the art of Guatemalan Indian weaving. If you ask around, you can meet the lady who went to Alaska; she has newspaper clippings to prove the story.

I highly recommend taking the bus back to Antigua; do not walk. There are many robberies along this road. The last bus returns to Antigua at 5:00PM.

Spanish Schools Choosing a school in Antigua is difficult because there are so many. As soon as you get off the bus, at least a dozen young boys will try to get you to go to "their" school where you can live with a family because "theirs" is the best in Antigua. If you are serious about learning Spanish and not just meeting up with other gringos, then Antigua is NOT the place to enroll in school. However, if you are feeling insecure and need the comfort of the familiar (other gringos), then Antigua is certainly a popular place to spend time.

Centro Liguistico Atabal on 1 Ave Norte #6 is a popular school for beginners. It offers one-to-one instruction, immersion by living with a family, weekly change of teachers and flexible scheduling. The price, for four weeks with room and board, seven hours per day in class, is about $350.US. One week without room and board for seven hours per day is $75.US. and you may have variations between these possibilities. The four-hour courses with room and board run around $250.US per month to four hours for one week without room at $50.US These prices include laundry service and a private room, but they don't guarantee a two-tap shower.

Centro America, Centro Experimental de Español is on Calzada Santa Lucia Norte #33. This school claims to teach as an infant learns. You start simple and work slowly into sentence structure. The prices run from $75.US for one week, four hours per day plus room and board, to $400.US for four weeks, six hours per day with room and board. I like this style of teaching. My Spanish, after years of practice, is at about the six or seven year old stage, but when I am tired, I revert back to the two year old "point and shout" stage.

Professional Spanish Language School on 7 Ave Norte #82. (phone 320-161) was recommended by Mike Shawcross. The Director of this school wrote Spanish, An Easy Way and has been in business for over 15 years. It offers flexible hours and room and board with a family. The school claims that part of the cultural experience when living with a family is to get used to the one-tap shower. I am certain that most of you have had that cultural experience by the time you arrive in Antigua! The school's specialty seems to be teaching professionals workable language. The rates are about $65.US for 7 hours per day for five days, $45.US for 4 hours per day for five days, and $25.US for 2 hours per day five days per week. There is an extra $7. - $10. charge for the books. If you wish to stay with a family, the cost is about $35. per week extra; this includes three meals a day. This school claims that you may obtain university credits for taking its immersion courses. Check if this is possible with your university.

Books - There is a great book store on the square called **Un Poco de Todo** (A Little of Everything) and it has both new and second hand books for purchase or trade. They also carry a good selection of typical greeting cards. The owners speak English or Spanish and are very friendly and helpful.

Casa Andinista, 4 Calle Oriente #5 (across from Doña Luisa's) has a good selection of English books on Guatemala. It is a large quiet store where you can browse without being bothered for a long time.

Swimming is possible at the Ramada Inn, about a ten minute walk south along Ave. Santa Lucia. There is a slight fee. It is a close and pleasant place to have a swim.

Public Toilets are just east off the square on 4 Calle Oriente, and they are clean. There is a slight charge.

Laundromats Because labor is cheap and women usually do laundry for a living, laundromats are difficult to find. If the ladies from your hotel will not do your laundry (always ask when the boss is not around) then there is a laundry service on 5 Calle #8 just past 6 Ave. Norte. You have a choice of hot or cold wash. Laundry service takes one day and the job is excellent. However, again I recommend asking the ladies in the hotel, as this will give them a few extra cents above their meager wages, and they do an extremely good job.

Marathon Run on the second Saturday in November; this run goes from the town square up Mt. Agua and back. The run starts at 7:00AM and takes about four hours for those in shape but would take me four days!! The purpose of the run is to raise money for the fire department. After the run, there is a beautiful rose parade where the winner sits on one of the decorated floats.

International Cultural Festival This has been active for only a couple of years but has been so successful that it is becoming a regular event. In 1992, part of the show was on national television. The festival has music, dancing, theater, cultural seminars, conferences and literary readings. Many Guatemalan celebrities are involved and many events take place on the square. The festival is usually in February, so if you are in the area go to the tourist office for more information. It is an excellent event. Tickets for different events run from around Q10 to Q30 ($2.50 - $7.50 US) depending on the performance. As this event becomes more popular, it will be necessary to get tickets in advance. If you write the Tourist Office in Guatemala City before going to Guatemala, they will send you information. They speak English but I don't know if they will answer you in English.

Semana Santa has been a popular event in Guatemala since the first tourist arrived. You must book your hotel long in advance if you wish to see some of the celebrations. The Easter rituals start on the first day of Lent with parades; statues of saints and Christ are carried above purple-robed processioners. Small processions continue in various locations for the forty days before the actual Holy Week. On Good Friday, spectacular carpets, designed from flowers and sawdust by local artists, line the streets. It takes the artists weeks to make these carpets. Then, on Good Friday, processions pass over the carpets; they become unrecognizable. During this procession, the carving of Jesus of Nazarine is carried on the purple-robed shoulders of believers. At 3:00PM, the time Christ was crucified, the faithful change from purple to black robes.

Other processions and events also occur during this weekend. A popular one is the procession from San Filipe de Jesus. Television crews film this event.

Although Antigua has the most spectacular Semana Santa events, celebrations occur throughout the country. You may see processions, religious ceremonies and festivities anywhere. I was close to the Honduran border one year and saw a procession that was not as colorful or large as those in Antigua, but it was certainly as spiritual. About eight people carried heavy Christian statues, up hill. No crowds made a spectacle of the ceremony.

Church steps at Chichicastenango

CHAMPERICO

Population - 7000, 6 meters (20 ft.) above sea level.

If you are looking for some very hot sun and wish to be away from other gringos, then this is a delightful place. It is about one hour from Retalhuleu along the sevana. The bus that ran from Quetzaltenango to Retalhuleu and then to Champerico no longer runs. I am always suspicious when a place becomes more difficult to access. If you are going to Champerico, plan on staying the night either in Champerico or Retalhuleu. Champerico is the preferred overnight spot. If you want to be here for either Semana Santa or Christmas, you will have to book in advance.

Champerico is a port town which was built in 1872 specifically for coffee export. The beach right at the town dock is not so hot, but you only need to walk half a kilometer to clean black sand and warm water. This is also a popular fishing area. Because few gringo tourists invade this area, the local people are quite friendly.

PLACES TO STAY

Champerico has enough hotels that staying there at any time except Semana Santa and Christmas would be no problem. There are places for the rich and places for the chickenbusers.

Hotel Martita - is on Ave. Guatepeque on the corner of the square. The rooms cost Q23.50 ($4.75US) for a double and Q17. ($3.50US) for a single. Although only about six rooms, they are large, with fans, mirrors and a small desk. The bathrooms are bi-sexual and leave a bit to be desired.

Marimar Hotel is across from the Hotel Martita, and is now the preferred hotel in town, even though the rooms are more basic than the Martita. The rooms are Q12 ($2.50US) for a single and Q20 ($4.US) for a double. As long as you are not a single female, the owners are friendly. There is a restaurant in the center of the hotel where you can sit and sweat.

Hospadaje Recinos is not far from the beach and is Q8 ($1.75 US) per person. This is very basic with beds, a small desk and a small room. There are no fans and no private bath.

Hospadaje Aires The rooms are Q7 ($1.75 US) per person and are very basic, without private bath. There is a delightful porch around the building where you can sit and enjoy the action in the bars below. There are also no fans in the rooms.

Posada del Mar is further in town going back towards Retalhuleu and is a real luxury at Q30 ($7.50 US) for a single and Q40 ($10.US) for a double. This is the place in town where the better off Guatematecans go. It is complete with swimming pool and restaurant.

RESTAURANTS

There are more bars in Champerico than there are gringos. The bars are the western frontier type with swinging doors and loud music. For meals, sea food is about all that you will really want. Cevichi is excellent in this town. There are many little tiendas and beach type restaurants all around the harbor. Your choice is as good as mine.

Monti Limar Restaurant is right on the beach and they have real coffee but you must ask for it to be made. It is one of the first places open in the morning at around 7:30AM. It has large orders of french fries at a reasonable price.

Hotel Martita has a cosy restaurant and the cevichi is excellent as are the shrimp cocktails. The place is clean and the food is safe.

Fruit Juice There is an excellent stand next to Tienda Honduras along the street where the buses go back to the city. It sells pure fruit juices, has a good selection and the portions are big.

The Bars are all along the street where the buses return to the city. There are lots of places to drink and carouse or watch the locals drink and carouse.

THINGS TO DO

Other than laying on the beach, reading a good book, eating lots of fresh seafood and fresh fruits, drinking beer at night and sleeping lots, there is not much else to do in the immediate vicinity. Because the current is quite strong in this area, it is often not advisable to go too far into the water. But, there is a **swimming pool** right on the beach that is clean and less than a dollar to enter for the day. There are also showers along the beach if you are not staying in the town for the night.

CHICHICASTENANGO

Population 3200, 2071 meters (6795 ft.) above sea level.

This beautiful little town comes to life on market days which are Thursdays and Sundays. For the photographer, this is the place to sit in the shade and photograph the Maya Indians at their best. They will crowd the steps of the Church of Santo Tomas and perform their religious rituals as if the travellers were not watching. Some of the character portraits will be spectacular. Please be inconspicuous when photographing. Some people believe that their spirit will be taken away when photographed. Others believe that if the photo is reproduced and then misused, it will harm the spirit of the person photographed. Please be sensitive to their beliefs. There is no proof that your belief is the correct one.

Because Chichicastenango is the largest and most beautiful market in Guatemala, the tourist has helped increase the free enterprise tension. Everywhere one goes, he will be hassled for money, to buy something, or to hire a guide. I still believe the people are poor and need our help, but I hate to see them lose their pride.

Because Chichi is surrounded by a gully, expansion is not possible; therefore, the demands on hotel rooms form price increases. You may wish to stay in Santa Cruz del Quichè which is just a short distance away.

One of the attractions of Guatemala is the colorful, gentle Indian. At present, there are over 500 different Indian costumes, each indigenous to a particular village. The most frequently-used materials are silk, cotton, and wool, depending on the climatic location of the village.

All garments worn by the Indians are worn not only for body protection but for customary significance. The **huipile** is the garment most popular with foreigners. It is the overblouse that is worn by the women. Depending on region, these hand-woven garments have either geometric or animal designs woven or embroidered on them. If purchased, they make spectacular wall hangings. Often people put a mirror in the neck hole. When Indians work in the fields, they turn the huipiles inside out in order to protect them from the sun.

The **fajas,** or belts, are worn by both men and women. These may be as wide as one foot and as long as twelve feet or a few inches wide and a few feet long. Depending on the area of origin, the faja may be intricately embroidered or plainly weaven.

Depending on local custom, the skirts worn by the ladies may be any length from the calf to the ankle. The skirts are wrapped around the woman and tied with fajas. They may be worn either way up. Indian women never iron their garments. They always appear unwrinkled because they are spread out flat on the ground to dry and then folded tightly in the customary fashion.

When in the markets in Guatemala, consider the work these women have put into their garments. The garments have sentimental value and meaning to these people. Do not insult them by wearing the garments in public. If you don't manage to get the lowest price possible, don't resent the possibility that this person's life may be slightly improved at your expense. You have a treasure for those few pennies.

Chichicastenango means the **"place of nettles"** and is named after the plant that grows in the area. Chichicastenango was first settled by the Indians after Alvarado defeated Utatlan in 1524. The Indians migrated to this place because it was protected by canyons as you well know from the bus trip in.

The market is one of the most important reasons people come to Chichicastenango, but if you happen to be there for the **Santo Tomas Fiesta** which occurs in December, (celebrations going from 18th - 21st), you will see many parades and other religious ceremonies. Chichicastenango is the Holy City of the Quichè and Indians arrive from many miles around for celebrations. The cofradias, men responsible for religious ceremony in a town, are especially strong in this village and you may see men with the embroidered wool jackets of their office doing important jobs around the village (See section on Indians in the introduction). If you wish to see typical dress for the men of the region, go to the Mayan Inn for a snack. There you have the men dressed in traditional clothes and someone will constantly be playing the marimba.

On Santo Tomas day, December 21st, children born to maxeños (a bastardization of tomaseños) are taken to the church for a christening ceremony. They will all receive some form of "Thomas" in their name. The day is a happy one, and by the time the sun sets, there will be many men sleeping off their indulgence.

During these celebrations, there is a ritual that is performed by the men. They climb a tall pole which has a large circular wheel on the top. There is also a rope wound around the pole from the bottom up. The men attach themselves to the rope and swing out from the wheel. As they go around, the rope unwinds and they come down to the ground. This ritual is called "Palo Volador" or Flying Pole. It is also popular in the Coban area.

There are zillions of tourists in Chichicastenango on market days, coming by the bus-loads, but leaving by mid-afternoon. My advice is to shop along with everyone else on market day but stay in town for a few days after the tourists leave or move on to Santa Cruz del Quichè. These are delightful towns with lots to see and do which does not involve the bus-loads of gringos from the higher echelons of society than that of the chickenbusers.

PLACES TO STAY

There is everything from the very expensive to the cheapo to the private house to stay while in Chichicastenango. I will not bother writing about the expensive Mayan Inn or the Maya Lodge as the rates are over $50.US per day. With prices like that, no wonder the little Indian gal who is not certain where her next day's meal is coming from wants a few centavos from you.

Hospadaje Salvador on 10 Calle 4 Ave. #47 is a clean and colorful place which is the best in town. The cost is Q10 ($2.US) without bath and Q14 ($2.80 US) per person with bath. There are one tap showers. There are nice places to sit, it is clean and quiet, and it has a long history of success for our type of travel.

Hospadaje Giron is a real find in Chichi if the Salvador is full. It is across from the market. The rooms cost Q30.50 for a double without bath and with very cold water in the shower. It is clean, friendly and quiet.

Chuguila Hotel is really a nice place at a mere Q110 ($22. US) per night for a double. However, the tourist office claims that they are not to charge more than Q40 ($8. US) for a double. I did not bother to argue but chose to stay in a private house instead. The food in the restaurant is fairly good.

House of Pedro is a private house and to get there go up to the street over the town gate going toward Santa Cruz del Quichè. When facing the gate, go left to # 4-36. The cost is Q50 ($10.US) for two but the price can be bartered down. The bathroom is spotless with lots of warm (not hot) water. The rooms are delightfully clean, and you may use the lawn chairs in the back to relax. The owner will get his wife to make you a typical dinner for a price. The extra bonus is that the man speaks English and if you ask, he will give you lots of information about the area.

Jenny Taylor lives in the suburbs north east of town. She is now very old and no longer rents rooms to travellers. However, she still has a house of the Bahi faith.

RESTAURANTS

This is not the best place in Guatemala to get a good meal. If you eat at the Maya Inn or Santo Tomas, you will pay their prices and get small quantities.

Tienda Tapena across from the Chauguila Hotel is not a good place to eat. We tried about three different dishes and all were terrible.

Chaguila Hotel is about the best place to eat if you want to sit down and have a meal. Otherwise, go to the tiendas around the market. In Chichi, this is the best.

THINGS TO DO

The Market is either Thursday or Sunday with Sunday being the busiest and best. There is everything from old huipiles to masks to Salvadorian towels. I highly recommend Chichi to do your buying unless you plan on picking things up from all over Guat and carrying them with you. Although prices may be a bit higher here, buying in one location saves a lot of hassle. You will see what you want from all over the country, and unless it is exceptionally different, you will probably be able to get it in Chichi. When I am certain that an object is not available in this market, I mention it in the section of the town from where the object is from. An example of this are the little clay birds from Antigua.

Church of Santo Tomas is the huge white-washed building on the east side of the plaza built in 1540. If you wish to enter the church, please do so by the side entrance; the front entrance is for the worshipers. It has only recently been decided that tourists may enter the church, so remember that this is a place of worship and a very important place to the Indians. Be inconspicuous!!

On the front steps of the church are the Indians who burn their resin incense, carry their flowers and prepare to enter the church. Once inside, prayers are said at the altar railing and at each of the platforms. Here candles are burned and flowers, petals, pine needles and grains of corn are offered to any of the gods who may be listening. Depending on the offering and where it is made, the people may ask for the cure of an alcoholic or the safe journey of a traveller. There are prayers for health and marriage; the prayers being accompanied by orange marigolds are for the souls of the dead. If a rooster is killed on the steps, it helps the spirit of a dead person go to heaven.

In the parish archives is the Popol Vuh, the sacred book of the Quichè, which was discovered by a Spanish priest. The book tells how the Maya was created from corn because wood made man too rigid and clay made man too soft. The second part of the manuscript is an historical record of the Quichè Indians. At the Popol Vuh museum in Guatemala City is a video about the sacred books.

El Calvario is the church opposite Santo Tomas. This is a good place from which to take photos while being inconspicuous. Compared to the Church of Santo Tomas and the market, there is little of interst here.

Municipal Museum off the market is a nice little museum which has artifacts from the pre, the classic and the post classic periods. Pre-classic is 1500BC to 300AD. There is some lovely carved jade, lots of ceramics from all periods, and many household items. The most impressive is a pure gold disk carved in the shape of a snake's head. After the hustle and bustle of the market, this is a nice peaceful place. There is a small entry fee.

Pascual Idol is a Mayan sacred spot and Pascual is one of their saints. To get there, go to the first big hill south west of town. Take the trail in the direction of Guat City. Follow the path all the way down into the gully, and when you get to the fork, each trail leading up a different hill, take the one on the left called La Democracia. Do not take short cuts up through the bush as there have been robberies reported. You will be hassled non-stop to hire a guide but this is not necessary. If you are lucky, you will see the people celebrating on a special day. If so, please be sensitive to others' beliefs and remain inconspicuous. You will see people offering pine needles, corn or dead chickens to the stone carving. This carving was damaged in the 1950's but has been partially repaired. If you must photograph, be inconspicuous. Maybe with enough respect, we can undo the damage that has been done by insensitive tourists.

The Mask Maker is on the same hill as the Pascual Idol. You may stop and see some of his works of art. He makes the masks for the Indian dancers to rent on special fiesta days. However, if you are looking to purchase, there is a large selection in the market. Often, no one is around the mask maker's house.

CHIQUIMULA

Population - 19,000, 370 meters (1214 ft.) above sea level.

This is a busy little town close to the Honduran border, which you pass through if going to Copan. A one day visit to Copan can be an expensive proposition. The border crossings are expensive; the total price is about ten dollars US for the day. Chiquimula has a few hotels and is of little significance other than for overnighters. If you have limperas after coming from Honduras and want to exchange them, the store in the Almacen Nuevo shopping center will take them but at a much poorer rate than in Honduras. This small shopping center is one block away from the square. Chiquimula means "**Place of the Linnet**"; the linnet is a bird. Chiquimula is busy in January when many pilgrims pass this way on the way to Esquipulas.

PLACES TO STAY

Hospadaje Hernandez is on 3 Calle for Q11 ($2.20 US) per person is still the best place to stay. The courtyard is surrounded with rooms and has friendly owners. Many travellers stay here. The price includes private bath.

Chiquimulja Hotel on 3 Calle 6 #31 just off the square is pretty good at Q20 ($4.US) for a single and Q30 ($6.US) for a double with a bath. However, it is quite noisy; unless I am very tired and can't get something better, I would not go there.

The Dario - just off the main square on 8 Ave. 4 - 40 is Q8 ($1.60 US) for a single and Q12 ($2.40 US) for a double without bath. It is clean but basic and a few travellers recommend it.

RESTAURANTS

The tienda next to Hernandez is an excellent place to eat. It is clean, pleasant and cheap. Other than this and the Chiquimulja Hotel, I would suggest you get some of your food in the market. This is not a town to visit for a feast.

THINGS TO DO

The Copan Ruins in Honduras are a must, but an expensive must if only going for the one day. There are buses going every hour during the day from the town square in Chiquimula. The ruins are not huge and do not take a long time to see. However, they are the best restored ruins in Central America. Every summer, archaeology students from all over the world come to work at the site and help with the restoration. The restoration of the Great Stairway is extremely well done and so is that of the Small Ball Court. On the hill just before the Great Stairway, is a spectacular large carved stone head. For more information on Copan, see that section in the Honduran portion of the book.

The Market is by the square and is really not noted for much. However, if you are looking for some good pottery, the Indians in the region are known for producing some unique pieces. The best reason for staying in Chichimula is not the shopping.

COBAN

Population 14,000, 1317 meters (4321 ft.) above sea level. Regular buses leave from Guat City all day long; the trip takes about 4 hours by pullman (first class). This area often has rainy weather, but the road is good and remains open. Coban means "cloudy place". The nicer hotels are in Zone 2, so when coming by bus, get off before the center and walk directly north one block. Although the Oxib-peck is the hotel farthest out of town, it is definitely the best one for your money.

Coban, a delightful town even during bad weather, was founded by the Dominican Father, Bartolome de las Casas, in 1544. He amalgamated a few of the surrounding villages in order to form this larger pueblo. Prior to that, the Indians were unconquerable. Las Casas' method of conquering was by prayer, song, and gifts of mirrors and useful metal objects. Las Casas also had a promise from the Spaniards not to enter the area for a period of five years. This was respected. The name of Verapaz, or true peace, came from this period in history.

The peace and isolation of Coban continued until the late 1800's when there was an invasion of German immigrants who wanted to farm the lands and control the commerce in the area. Many intermarried with the Indians, and German was not an uncommon language in the area. However, during the Second World War, those who retained their German citizenship were thrown out of the country, and their land was confiscated.

Up until the late 1950's, Coban was so isolated that the people travelled down the Polochic and Dulce rivers to the Atlantic and then did most of their business with Europe instead of Guatemala City. They claimed that it was easier.

Coban is a rich, highly fertile area, that has a constant supply of rain commonly known as chipi chipi. There are lakes and rivers and canyons and mountains everywhere and the forests are abundant with orchids and birds, coffee and cattle. The "White Nun", the national orchid, grows abundantly in the forests. This area is a must for the nature lovers. There is also oil exploration and a hydroelectric dam in the area which spoils the natural beauty, but puts a bit of money in the hands of a few locals.

The Indian dress is different in this area. The skirts are short, loose and pleated. The huipiles are also short and embroidered with flowers. The silver worn by some is of high quality and the chachales or antique necklaces worn by the Indian women are prized possessions. You will have to pay quite a bit if you want one for a souvenir.

If you happen to come to this town on a festival day, you may be lucky enough to see one activity that is unique to the El Quichè area. The men climb a tall, 60 foot pole which has a large circular wheel on the top. There is also a rope wound around the pole from the bottom up. The men attach themselves to the rope and swing out from the wheel. As they go around, the rope unwinds, and they come down to the ground. This ritual is called "Palo Volador" or the Flying Pole. It can be seen in other areas of Guatemala but this is one of the best areas.

PLACES TO STAY

Central Hotel on 1 Calle 1, is a central place at Q26.50 ($5.50 US) for two and it has hot water. It is also clean and friendly.

Hospadaje Maya only has cold water, but the price is only Q6 ($1.20 US) per person. The people are friendly and the rooms are basic but clean. Walk past the cathedral and it is across from the Cine Norte.

Chipi Chipi is across from the Maya. This is dirty and unpleasant, but they claim to have hot water. The price is Q10 ($2.US) for a double. I would suspect the hot water would be the same as the chipi chipi in the area (the rain).

Hotel Rabinajau costs Q45 ($9. US) for two with bath and hot water (sometimes). The rooms are spotless and large. When the lights are working, you can read. The downside is that it is over a very noisy disco that stays open until 3:00AM every day. My suggestion is to stay elsewhere and party here. The hotel is at Calzada Minerva, 5-37, Zone 1, phone 512296

Hotel Monteray costs Q26 ($5.25 US) for two and it is clean and friendly. It is across from Hotel Rabinajau. There is also hot water here.

Hotel La Paz This place has the Guatemalan rendition of the giggling Bowery boys looking after the place. The hotel is clean and pleasant and only Q8 ($1.80 US) per person. This is one I would recommend. It is just down from the Minerva.

Hotel Oxib-peck is Q35 ($7. US) for a double and is on 1 Calle 12-11, Zone 2. This is the find of the century. There is real hot water. It is clean, friendly and affordable. There is a pleasant garden and court yard and the lady speaks a bit of English. There is a restaurant attached with home cooked meals. I wanted to stay here for ever. The name Oxib-peck means "three rocks" in Quichè.

Hotel El Recreo Minerva costs Q12 ($2.40 US) for one with hot water and a private bath. Okay if the Oxib-peck is full. It is on 1 Calle 13-65 in Zone 2.

RESTAURANTS

Restaurants are not the drawing card of Coban. However, there are always new finds so this is one place I recommend that you be a bit daring and try some new ones. However, **Refugio** is a must.

Tirol Coffee House specializes in different types of coffee like expresso, cappuccino or liquored coffees like Monte Cristos. However, the straight coffees are not the best.

Refugio Restaurant is between the bus area and the square. It is crowded, well managed, and has excellent food. It is one of the best places in town. They specialize in Mexican foods.

El Ganadero is a steak house on 1 Calle, Zone 2 with a nice steak menu. The food isn't bad if you need some meat. It is a bit pricey.

Hotel Rabinajau has great pizza and the service is good. Prices are not low.

Kam Mun on 1 Calle 8-12 is a nice Chinese restaurant where you can get an excellent bowl of soup for a reasonable price. The place is spotless and the women never stop cleaning. The service is pleasant and the price is right.

THINGS TO DO

Town Center on 2 Calle, Zone 1, someone thoughtfully made a cement map of Central America on this plot of land. I think it is a feeble attempt to copy the one that is in Guat City.

The Colonial Cathedral of Santo Domingo was built in 1650, and is in good repair. The main facade has a plumed serpent on it; this is a reminder of the Indian beliefs. Inside the door, are beautiful carved wooden panels that were hidden towards the wall for years and then faced with marble. They were re-discovered in the 1970's and put back onto display.

Just inside the door is a huge brass bell made in 1772. While hanging in its wooden tower, it was struck by lightning and fell to the ground, never more to toll.

The main attraction of the Cathedral is the Virgin of the Rosary. Why is it that all female saints must be virgins? Mary Magdaline was not a virgin, but she is not considered a saint. Men need not be celibate in order to be saints! This wooden carving was originally painted, but as the statue grew older, the paint wore off. The church priests wanted the virgen dressed. However, they could not put the clothes on her properly unless they cut her dress; so they decided to cut off the Child's head and arms instead. Although I studied the statue for a long time, I could not understand their logic. Anyway, they cut the child, dressed the lady, and then glued a new head and arms on the Child. It wasn't until 1979 that the statue was restored, with a new head and arms given to the babe and the old one put beside the statue. I don't know which Child is the holy one.

The large cross found at the back of the church is used in the Easter services when the cross is placed at the front of the church and a statue of Christ is put on. The large figure of Christ in the red robes is the most important carving in the town and is used during the Easter processions. This carving of Christ goes to El Cavalaro

Church on the hill for the night of Holy Saturday and returns for the 11:00 AM service on the next day, Easter Sunday.

El Cavalaro Church is on a hill just outside the town. Built in 1559, the church has an interesting history. Legend has it that a hunter frequently encountered a pair of tiger cubs on the hill. One day , instead of the cubs, he found a statue of a crucified Christ. He carried it to the village and placed it in an important man's house. During the night, the figure disappeared from the house and reappeared on the hill. This appearance and disapearance occurred time and time again. Finally, the people built the church to house the Christ. Since then, the original figure of Christ has not returned. The figure of Christ found in the church today was designed by the artist Zuniga.

This church has a huge stairway leading to the building and old tombs in the side of the church, and a graveyard which goes part way down the hill. This latest church was built in 1954. I found this a delightful place to poke around and observe the town. To me this spot is much more characteristic of the natural beauty of Coban than the Cathedral.

San Pedro Carcha is a little village just past Coban, on the way to the Languin Caves. You can take a bus to Carcha and then walk back. This is a nice walk if you wish to spend a day observing the local countryside. The Popol Vuh (sacred book) mentions Carcha; therefore, it is believed that the Indians of long ago settled here before exploring other parts of Guatemala.

The Indians in this village make excellent pottery. As well, they have an ancient kind of foot loom used for shadow-work weaving. The Indians are also known for mask making and mask dancing during fiestas. A small museum is in town; it is only open on weekends, and I did not visit it. Along the route to a waterfall, about half an hour's walk out of town along the river Cahabòn, are picnic tables. **Hospadaje Central** on 7 Ave 4-17 offers rooms and meals if you want a quiet place to stay instead of staying in Coban. The rooms are about Q25 ($5.US) for a double.

Lanquin Caves Two buses run daily to Lanquin from Coban. One leaves at 4:00AM from the main bus depot and takes about three hours to get there. The other bus leaves from the same place at 1:00PM; if you take that one you must stay over night in Lanquin. There are cabins just before Lanquin, at the road turn-off called El Recreo. The price is Q25 ($5.US) for one, Q27 ($5.40 US) for two and Q30 ($6.US) for three.

The road to Languin is 62 kilometers of a treacherous and rough dirt road, often requiring a four wheel drive. However, the road passes through some of the most spectacular country in all Central America. The scenery is a photographer's delight. Early in the morning the mist covers the landscape like a delicate hand giving the canyons a sense of romance which keeps you from thinking of the dangers of travelling along these muddy roads. If taking the bus, you must walk the 2 kilometers from the road to the entrance of the caves, if your shaking knees will allow it.

At the cave entrance is a camping site with barbque pits and nice places to pitch a tent. The river is spectacular with lush jungle growing right into the bright green water. The caves are supposed to be lit by a generator run lighting system but the system does not always work. If you take a couple of large flash lights, you will be able to see a lot. The caves are lighted for about five hundred meters. After that, you are on your own. Rumor has it that they go back for miles. There are ladders and ropes to hold on to for the first five-hundred meters. There are many shapes and colors of stalagmites and stalactites in the cave and it is well worth the trip.

Along the road going toward the town of Lanquin you can see the cardamom plant. Also, you will see a furry red bean-like fruit on some trees. This is a natural red food dye which was in great demand after scientists discovered that the commercial red chemical dye was cancerous. However, a new chemical that supposedly is not cancerous is now used, so the natural colored bean has dropped in value.

Church in Lanquin has beautiful old chandeliers. You will often see Indians praying with candles in hand. Please be respectful.

Sumac Champey is 12 kilometers past Lanquin and is on a four wheel drive road into the valley. There are no buses but you will be able to hitch a ride, especially if you are willing to pay a few quetzales. If not, walking is the only alternative; in order to get there and back in one day, you will have to leave very early from Lanquin. There is a camp site at the river if you want to stay overnight. You must take all your own food whether you are going for the day or overnight. You can also get a tour guide in Coban with a four wheel drive that will take you to Sumac Champey and the caves. If you can get a few people together, this is really well worth the money. I am not a tour person, but sometimes, I must give in and do it the easier way. This is one time.

Once at the Cahabòn River, the sight is wonderful. The gushing, dangerous, roaring river surges down the rocks and into the mountain that you are standing on. The top area of the natural bridge is tiered with soft calcified rock and the water runs gently from one tier to the next. The water is a beautiful clean blue green due to an algae living there; for its protection, soap use is prohibited. A swim is wonderful; the water is cool and will cleanse you after your hike over the kilometer or two of slimy mud to the river. If you can, stay a few days in order to rest in a quiet, secluded and beautiful jungle setting. Be certain to have lots of film.

If you would like to take a **four wheel drive** instead of the difficult bus trip, the cost is about $120. US for the entire day (including meals). If there are four or more people, it may be worth the price. Enquire at 5 Ave 1-37 Zona 3 in Coban or phone 0-511-016 for reservations. If you have time, the owner can sometimes get a few people together to share the costs. This man speaks English and is an excellent photographer.

Tactic is a little town about forty-five minutes by bus from Coban. Buses go about once every hour, all day. Once at Tactic, there is a nice little church with a gold altar and more wooden statues - if you haven't been churched out yet. There are two Hospedajes in Tactic; one of these, the Central, offers meals. However, I suggest you make this a day trip rather than an overnighter.

The Pozo Vivo or "living well" is just out of Tactic and really is not much to the tourist but the Indians consider it a special place. To get there, follow the dirt road across from the Esso Station on the far side of town. When the road runs out, climb over the fence and keep going along the path to the stream and over another fence. You will see the pool which is very small, full of debris, and hardly worth the bother to get there. The Indians believe that the pool rests when there is no one around. I believe that the pollution will make it rest permanently in the near future.

Market scene

EL CRUCE

This is a little village in the Peten area that may be used as a transfer stop only. If you are coming from Tikal and wish to go to Belize, you may need to change buses here. If going to Tikal, you should not need to transfer here. But, if coming from Belize late in the day, you may get this far and be unable to get into Tikal, especially during the rainy season. However, there are no places to stay in El Cruce; there are places to eat and they are pleasant and cheap. If late from Belize, it is better to stay in Melcos de Menchor at the border than to go this far.

ESQUINTLA

37,000 people and 347 meters (1150 ft) above sea level; this town is a very warm place indeed.

This is a bustling little town which is an excellent place to stay if you wish to explore the area or if coming or going to El Salvador. At first glance, it is not the nicest place you have seen, but the people are pleasant and there are a few places to explore. The name is derived from the Indian word Esquintepeque which means "hill of the dogs." The Indians who lived there had animals that resembled dogs.

PLACES TO STAY

Iscuintlan Hotel on 4 Ave. 6-30 has a huge red sign outside the door, but you may have to look for the proprietor in the shop next door. The rooms are Q15 ($3.US) for a single, Q25 ($5.US) for a double and Q30 ($6.US) for a triple. The rooms are clean, large, cheery, and have full length mirrors. The rooms also have two tap showers, with only one tap working; because of the warm temperature, there is only need for one. There are towels, toilet paper and soap for the one low price. The fans work, and the keys are not extra. A man by the name of Carlos owns the hotel, and he speaks English.

Pension Familia is close to the bus stop. It is a dive at Q5.50 ($1. US) per person with private bath. This would be my last choice unless I was strapped for cash.

Colonial Hotel on 4 Ave and Calle 5 is Q10 ($2.US) per person, fairly clean and secure but not quite as cheerful as the Iscuintlan.

RESTAURANTS

Alice Restaurant is around the corner from the Iscuintlan Hotel on Calle 6 and is recommended for good meals. This is the most popular place for both locals and travellers.

Los Pollos is the Guatemaltecan version of Kentucky Fried. If you deviate from the exact order on the menu, you will be charged extra. I ordered mineral water with the special instead of pop and was charged more, so be careful. In the past few years Los Pollos restaurants have improved and are favorites with the locals. The ones that are crowded are the ones that serve the best food. If the restaurant is deserted and it is meal time, stay away.

THINGS TO DO

The Market in Esquintla is noted for its fruit. The fruit is believed to have medicinal values not found in other regions of Guatemala. I think the lush soil and humid atmosphere makes the food taste so good. The market, adjacent to the bus terminal is a very busy place.

La Democracia Although there is a place to stay in La Democracia, I would strongly advise you stay in Esquintla and make a day trip to La Democracia. You will be much more comfortable in Esquintla. There are buses going to La Democracia about once every hour. Check with the locals at the bus terminal as the departure time changes frequently.

The village houses the sculptured stones from the finca and archaeological site of **Monte Alto**. The actual site where the stones were found is on private land and not open to the public. However, around the central park in La Democracia are the unique large carved stone heads found at the finca. They are unique because they are carved only on one side. The faces are large and drooping and the eyes are closed, possibly representing a dead person. Another sculpture found here is of a very fat man with his hands on his stomach. These are similar to some stones found at La Mesas in Vera Cruz, Mexico. Some stones weigh as much as 14,500 Kilos (32,000 lbs), so they are not small pieces. The style of carving suggests an influence from the Olmec culture. Some Archaeologists think these sculptures may be pre-Olmec carvings and that this was the beginning of civilization in Mesoamerica. The dates of these carvings are from 4000BC to about 300BC. Their similarities to the Olmec carvings are definite - but where in the pattern of time they fit is your educated guess.

The Ruben Chevez van Dorne Museum is a nicely kept museum with an excellent solid jade death mask on display. The rest of the artifacts appear to be quite minor although there are stone yokes, grinding stones, large urns and pottery. The museum is a quiet place and is open from 8:00AM - 12:00AM and 2:00 - 5:00PM; the cost is minimal.

If, you get stuck in La Democracia, there is a small **pension** on 2 Calle Norte for Q5 ($1. US) per person. I am not certain if the town or the pension has water. If you have your base in Esquintla, you will either pass through or change buses at **Siquinalà** (Ciquinola) on your way to La Democracia. Siquinalà is a delightful, clean little town and everyone seems helpful. Flowers are everywhere and even the dogs seem fatter. Stop, have a meal and visit here either before or after La Democracia or when on your way to or from Santa Lucia Cotzumalguapa.

Santa Lucia Cotzumalguapa is only 7 kilometers past Siquinalà; it has many head carvings similar to those at La Democracia. This area can be explored from Esquintla but the weather is hot and travel is difficult, so if you are really interested in exploring these ancient heads, I suggest that you stay in Santa Lucia Cotzumalguapa and make it a day trip, starting early in the morning.

ESQUIPULAS

Population 7000 and 950 meters (3120 ft) above sea level.

Esquipulas is about 5 1/2 hours from Guatemala City and on the border of Honduras. If you do not wish to spend the night in Santa Rosa de Copan, Honduras, and are too late to make it to San Pedro Sulu, then stay in Esquipulas. It is an okay little town that has a tremendous number of hotels and pensions. This is often where the Guatemalan government holds its national and summit meetings. In this area, the Maya Indians found ten different types of magic mushrooms. They would dry them and use them only when an important decision was to be made. They would then eat the mushrooms, hallucinate and the decision would come to them. Maybe this is why the present government meets here.

Esquipulas is a holy city because it is the home of the Black Christ which is attributed with granting miracles. Pilgrims come from all over Central America to be cured and blessed. January 15th is the busiest time for holy pilgrims.

Should you need a visa for Honduras, you may obtain one at the Piyaqui Hotel for about Q10 ($2. US). This border will not allow you to cross without a visa if required by those from your country and they do not seem willing to take a bribe. To get a visa at the hotel does not take more than ten minutes.

I find staying in Chiquimula to be closer and quicker if you want to do a day trip to Copan. If you have a lot of time and are going to other places in Honduras, then you can cross here. The trip from Esquipulas to the border is very short (15 min), but then to go to Nuevo Arcadia and back to Copan takes a long time.

PLACES TO STAY

There are so many places to stay in Esquipulas that I can only suggest a few and let you decide. The reason for so many places is because of the visiting dignitaries and the visiting pilgrims. You will not need to worry about a place to stay unless it is around January 15th, March 9th (another holy day) and Holy Week at the end of March or early April.

Hotel San Francisco is on the main street and is Q6 ($1.20 US) per person without bath and Q12 ($2.40 US) with bath. It is neither especially clean nor attractive.

Pension Limus is a small and basic but noisy place for Q12 ($2.40 US) per person. It has rooms with bath for Q30 ($6. US) but this is very overpriced. The pension has clean bathrooms and communal showers, but I could not find a sink in which to brush my teeth.

Casa Norman on 3 Ave 9-20 charges Q15 ($3. US) a single and Q25 ($5. US) for a double. It is a nicer place, and they have hot water.

El Carmen on 3 Ave 8-51 is just a block from Casa Norman and on the other side. It is a bit cheaper at Q10 ($2. US) per person. Again this is fairly clean and not as noisy as the Limus.

El Paso on 7 Ave. 10-37 is a great buy at Q6 ($1.25 US) per person. The place is clean and friendly and is my first choice.

Dario on 8 Ave. 4-40 is the same price as El Paso and of the same quality. If one is full try the other. Neither have private bath, but the honesty of the people is refreshing.

RESTAURANTS

I was not impressed with the restaurants in this town. The **Piyaqui Hotel** will give you excellent service, but the food is nothing to scream about. The restaurant beside the Pension Limus makes an excellent bowl of soup. Try that. Wherever you eat, the prices are high. The ladies in the market seem to be the best cooks in this area. I guess one should come here to pray, not eat.

THINGS TO DO

Pilgrim of Peace Plaza is in front of the Franciscan church on the hill of Morola. It is a bit of a climb; the "stations of the cross" on the way were designed by Father Bernardino Quinonez. They are considered beautiful. In the church at the top are icons also designed by the same priest. The plaza and the church were inaugurated in July, 1979 by Mother Teresa of Calcutta when she came for a visit.

The Basilica is a beautiful white plaster church where the Maya Indians go to worship at all times of year but especially during January 15, March 9th and Holy Week. If you are lucky enough to see a holy ceremony, you will see the men in their white pants and bright red sashes sit in groups and light candles while the women cover their heads with huipiles and cradle children in their arms. When worshipping, the Indians seem in complete harmony with all which is around them. Some Indians walk the entire length of the church to the altar on their knees. They are worshipping the Black Christ of Esquipulas.

Legend has it that an Indian saw a vision of Christ on the spot where the church sits today. The Indians of that time then had Quirio Cataño carve the image of Christ out of some dark wood. This was housed in the local church and the miracles became known when, in 1737, Archbishop Pedro Pardo de Figueroa was cured of a contagious disease. Figueroa then had the basilica built and the Black Christ moved. The archbishop is buried in the church.

There is another story about the making of the Black Christ which is probably more reasonable but not nearly as interesting. The Spaniards of that time arranged the carving of the Black Christ because they had told the Indians that nothing white could be holy. The Indians would be more likely to accept a "god" that was more like them than like the Spaniards.

Regardless of how the statue came into being, it is considered very holy today and receives many gifts of wealth for miracles.

The Market Actually the stalls close to the Basilica are the most interesting for shopping. Straw hats worn by the pilgrims, candies in the form of rosaries or other religious objects, delicious candied grapefruit and the famous gusanos or caterpillars, which are the symbol of Esquipulas, are on display here. The candies are incredible works of art created by the ladies of the town. They are worth the purchase as a souvenir, and not to consume as a candy. My favorite is the sombrero.

FLORES - SANTA ELENA/SANTO BENITO

Santa Elena/Santo Benito is the town with the airport and the bus station; Flores is an island on the beautiful lake Peten-Itza which is joined to the mainland by a causeway. Staying at the bus depot hotel in Santa Elena is cheap and might be more convenient if you are leaving early in the morning, but I prefer to stay on the Flores side as it is cleaner, quieter, friendlier and more picturesque. Besides being a stopping place on the way to or from Tikal, there is a wild turkey reserve, caves to be explored and small ruins to visit. This is a delightful town to spend some time around.

The trip to this area of the Peten can be harrowing on a bus or when hitchhiking but taking a plane is not recommended. The plane company charges gringos double the price it charges locals and the money goes to the rich. Taking a bus lets the money go to the poor people of Guatemala as buses are run by the working class, and the food you purchase will be from the same classes. Travelling by bus allows you to see a realistic picture of the country including the poverty, the oppression and the destruction of the environment. On a plane, you will only see rich Guatemalans or other gringos and learn nothing of the country. The plane also causes more pollution than do the more efficient buses.

The Guatel office is three blocks up on the same street as the causeway, on the Santa Elena side of town. There is usually no line-up and is a good place from which to call home. Remember, there is no station to station collect call from Guatemala.

PLACES TO STAY

The San Juan is at the bus stop in Santa Elena and costs Q6 ($1.25 US) per person for a very basic room. There are no private baths and the showers are the one tap type. They do change Mexican pesos or American dollars here at a fairly decent rate. However, traveller's cheques are a bit more dicey. Try and have cash.

El Dorado on the Santa Elena side is the second choice for the area. The price is Q10 ($2.50 US) per person without bath and the rooms are not too bad. They are basic but not totally barren.

Hotel Peten on the Flores side and at the far end of town is the best buy in town. The rooms are Q16 ($3.25 US) for a single and Q20 ($4. US) for a double with private bath and hot water. The cheaper rooms at Q10 ($2.50 US) per person do not have baths. It is very clean and has an excellent courtyard. The place is quiet and the owner is friendly. He speaks a mile a minute in Spanish, and even if you don't understand a word, he pretends that you do.

Peten Anexo is around the corner from the Hotel Peten and is Q5.50 ($1.10 US) per person with no bath. The rooms smell and the bathrooms are used by locals that are partying all night. This should be the last choice.

The Kun-Kax Hotel on the Flores side is the large hotel right on the lake. The rooms are $18. US but the price is negotiable, depending on business. The owners boast of having hot water; however, they often do not have any water.

Monja Blanca in Santa Elena charges Q10 ($2.US) per person. It is reasonable and has a restaurant.

La Savanah on the Flores side is Q25 ($5. US) for two with a bathroom. Breakfast and supper are included. The large meal at lunch time is not. This is a real steal and would be the second choice after the Peten. The only drawback is that most people like to have a large supper and visit with other tourists during the evening meal.

RESTAURANTS

El Toucan on the Flores side is the one that is most popular at this time but popularity changes frequently. It seems when a restaurant or hotel gets too much business, quality goes down. Ask around when in town.

The Maya on the Flores side is popular with travellers, but I found that they served instant soup here instead of the usual homemade variety found in Central America.

The Jaguar has the highest prices of the popular places, but the food is also the very best in town. So, if you are in need of a good meal and are willing to pay, this is the place.

Mesa de los Maya is another popular place with gringos and you can sit here for a long time and enjoy both your meal and the events of the evening. They specialize in wild meat of the area. Those adventuresome enough to try wild boar, turkey or deer will be pleasantly surprised. The deer is not as strong in flavor as northern deer.

THINGS TO DO

Actun Kan Caves These are called the Caves of the Serpents and are located about four kilometers (2.5 miles) from the town of Santa Elena. The caves are said to be about ten km. (eight miles) in length and have excellent examples of stalactites and stalagmites. To get to the caves, you walk straight out the road that goes up from the causeway. Follow the straight road until the edge of town, take the fork to the left and then to the right. When at the caves, there are guides who will take you through. The caves are wet but well worth the trip. Rock formations look like animals and other sights if you use your imagination. Sometimes you may need to stretch your imagination.

These caves extend about ten miles under the hills and have an exit at the other end. Do not try and go all the way through on your own. I have no information whether you must pass underground rivers or if there are many underground hallways. However, you may go to the other side of the hill and find the exit to the cave where you may enter if you wish. You must have a good flashlight and spare batteries for going into the caves because there is only a small section at the beginning of the caves which has lights. If you want to go further, you are on your own.

Lake Peten Itza is a beautiful lake where you can rent cayucos and visit the three islands of interest. Or, on a warm day, you can go for a swim right from Flores. In the evenings the sunset pictures are magnificent. Try all three.

If going to visit the other islands, I would suggest you hire an Indian to paddle the canoe unless you are quite experienced in canoeing. Cayucos are more like an open kayak and are less stable than a canoe; getting your camera equipment wet would be inconvenient when this far from modern services.

Tayasal is the island where the Maya Indians from Chichen Itza migrated and lived in isolation until 1525 when Cortez passed this way. He had with him some Aztec warriors and two Aztec leaders whom he had killed because he suspected treason. Cortez decided to leave the area and on his departure gave an old horse to the Chief of Tayasal, Canek (almost like Canuk so I have a liking for this chief). This was a new animal to the Maya so they considered it holy. After the horse died, the Indians constructed a replica of stone. This was worshipped until the Spaniards returned again about 100 years later and the dear old Catholic priests ordered the idol destroyed. The Indians tried to take the horse to the mainland in a cayuco, but a storm overturned the boat and the horse, of course, sunk to the bottom.

At the close of the 17th century the island, was overtaken by another Spaniard and turned into a prison island. Today, it is an interesting area to visit. The temple mound is not of great interest, but you can climb a tree to a viewing tower where spectacular pictures can be taken and you can see the beautiful lake in all directions.

Ramonal island is close to Flores and a great place to take a picnic lunch, read a book and enjoy the beautiful lake. Picnic tables are available, or you can just relax under a tree. A wild type of jungle swing called "la garrucha" allows the kids to spend time swinging out and back over the water and lily pads.

Petencito is the third island that you should visit. This is the location of the zoo. Many birds and animals native to the Peten (such as turkeys, parrots, monkeys, foxes, alligators, and deer) live in this area. If if you wish to photograph birds and animals come to the area very early in the morning. There is a bridge that connects the island to the mainland but you cannot go around and back to Flores along the mainland. You must come back and take a boat.

There is also a water slide on Petencito which is similar to the slide at Quetzaltenango. It is a long, smoothly finished, cement structure that sends its riders pummelling into the lake at breakneck speeds. I did not try these slides as I wanted to finish this book. I have also heard that there may be amoebas in the lake so ask before swimming.

Biotopo Cerro Cahui is the turkey reserve just out of El Remate on the way to Tikal. After passing El Cruce, it is the next village. You can catch a bus going past the village of El Remate and then walk from the bus stop to the biotopo. There are 650 hectares (1600 acres) of park to explore with groomed trails and many birds, animals and plants to enjoy. The main bird of course, is the wild turkey of Guatemala (and it is not the same as those in the bars). There is a campsite close to the park where you can pitch a tent before heading off the next day. Otherwise, this should be made into a day trip from Flores. The bus trip is just under an hour.

GUATEMALA CITY

First impressions of Guatemala City should never be the final impressions; this is a city that will grow on you. It took me a couple of trips to the city before I got to know it well enough to like it. One must not consider the pollution from the buses, the bums sleeping in their own defecation, or the pack slashers that try to rob you as all there is to this city. There are wonderful museums, clean shops, great restaurants, pleasant hotels, friendly people, quiet parks, easy-to-understand transportation and entertainment for every taste. One time I visited the city I was so content that I almost missed my plane back home.

Recently, excavations have shown that Guatemala City is built over the ruins of Kaminal Juyu, a Pre-Columbian city. Archaeological ruins have been found covering several miles around the city. Artifacts from these ruins can be found in the National Museum of Archaeology. I can not say enough. Please try some of the ideas I suggest in this book and give the city a fair chance.

237

PLACES TO STAY

There are many places to stay in Guatemala City; it would be impossible to list them all unless my book was only "Hotels of CA." However, the red light district is around 9 Ave and 15 Calle. This does not mean you must stay out of the area; it means be careful of the place you choose. I have stayed in many Hotels in the area; they are fine. Most of the time, I am a woman travelling alone which means I must be just a bit more careful than under other circumstances. Most hotels listed have met my saftey standards.

Chalet Suizo on 14 Calle 6-82 is a small family run hotel. However, it has changed in the last few years. They have destroyed all the beautiful old rooms and made them into comfortable new places. The upstairs is now an open and noisy area of the building. The small rooms next to the bathrooms smell musty. But it is still one of the most popular places for travellers to stay; you should have reservations as the place is almost always full. Call 51-37-86. The prices are Q23 ($4.50 US) for a single and Q32 ($6.50 US) for a double. There are a few rooms for triple and a few with private bath at higher prices. The Suizo also offers a storage service for your big heavy packs at Q1 per day.

Spring Hotel is on 8 Ave 12-65 and just two blocks from the Suizo. Although a bit more expensive than the Suizo, this is my preferred place because it is still a great old building with a wonderful central courtyard to sit, drink, read and/or visit in. There is also a restaurant on the premises that does not seem to cater to the street traffic too much. The rooms are large and some have private baths with lots of hot water. They are clean to the extreme and the owners are pleasant. The cost is Q48 ($9.50 US) for a double with private bath, Q40 ($8.US) for a double without bath and Q25 ($5. US) for a single without bath. This is really a great place to stay. You will make up the lost cash in other places so splurge in Guat City and make your visit more pleasant.

Alexander Guest House on 4 Ave 14-10, Zone 10, phone 78-01-52 is an expensive but wonderful place. The cost is $15. US for a single and $20. US for a double, but it is in a very quiet part of the city and the security in the building is superb. If you need to be in the better area of town for a day or two this is a great find. There are all the comforts (almost) of the Camino Real in the small home environment of a prairie town.

Hotel Bilbao on 15 Calle Ave. 8, Zone 1. This hotel costs Q15 ($3. US) for a single and Q25 ($5. US) for a double without bath. The rooms are big and it is off the main street so it is a bit quieter than some. It is difficult to get a decent room in this area so this one is recommended.

Hotel Centro Americana on 9 Ave and Calle 16 costs Q20 ($4. US) for a single and Q30 ($6. US) for a double. The hotel is clean, with hot water, bright, cheery rooms and it is always full. I have never been able to get a room in this hotel. However, try it; you may be lucky. It is popular with locals.

Hotel Capri on 9 Ave. 16-53 is just up and across the street from the Centro Americana and costs Q20 ($4. US) for a single and Q25 ($5. US) for a double without private bath. There are some rooms that have baths; these cost more. The rooms are clean and bright, but noisy; you must request a room that is at the back. There is hot water all the time; the attached restaurant has good meals and opens at 7:30 AM. However, no matter how often you stay here, the hotel will not keep your pack while you travel around.

Hotel Belmont on 9 Ave and Calle 15 has small dark rooms but is very clean. There are no rooms with private bath. For the area, it isn't too bad.

Hotel España on 9 Ave Calle 15 costs Q15 ($3. US) for a single and Q20 ($4. US) for a double with no private bath. It is one of the cleaner hotels but for a few extra cents, I prefer the Capri.

Fenix on 6 Ave, Calle 11 is clean and pleasant. It is reputed to have hot water and the rooms are only Q18 ($3.50 US) per person.

Pension Meza on 10 Calle Ave. 10 costs Q10 ($2.US) per person. When I walked into this courtyard I thought I was in the opium den of Central America. I do not recommend this if trying to avoid the drug scene. There are many travellers staying here, and the rooms are decorated with psychedelic graffiti. The rooms are also not very secure.

San Diego Anexo on 15 Calle Ave. 7 is fairly clean with a bathroom shared by two rooms. The cost is Q20 ($4. US) per person and the place is safe.

The Colonial on 7 Ave. 14-19 is a delightful old place that is quite expensive, but if you are having a hard time finding a room in Guat City, it is better to pay a bit more than a bit less until you can get into one of the better cheap ones. The Colonial is just across from the side of the Suizo and runs at Q60 ($12. US) for a double. This includes hot water, towels, soap and a restaurant.

Costa del Sol 17 Calle 8-17 is a good and cheap place at Q15 ($3. US) for a single and Q25 ($5. US) for a double. The rooms are clean, the owners are pleasant and there is hot water. I recommended it, but it is often full. Call 53-03-61 if you want to reserve.

Lessing House is on 12 Calle 4-35, phone 51-38-91. The rooms are Q16 and Q26 ($3.25 - $5.25 US) for a single and double. I have not tried this hotel but it is small, and clean with hot water. You are on your own with this one.

Hotel Lito on 10 Calle 1-35 costs Q40 ($8. US) for a double; although I have not stayed here, it has been recommended by others. They claim to have hot water.

Albergue Hotel on 9 Ave. 16-20 cost Q15 ($3.US) per person and is a great place to stay. It is an older building with rooms around a central courtyard. It is popular and cozier than the Capri in the same area.

RESTAURANTS

Canton Restaurant on 6 Ave. Calle 14 has the best vegetable dishes that I have tasted in a long time. The prices are low, the meals are large and the service is good. They also serve soup in a fish bowl!

Los Antojitos on 15 Calle between Ave 6 & 7, just up from the police station is an excellent place to have a shish-ka-bob for about Q25 ($5.US). There are marimba players to accompany your dinner. You must get there early or be prepared to wait as the restaurant fills up quickly; a good indication that the food is good. There is another one on Reforma 15-02 Zone 9 which has an outdoor patio. That one is also good.

Centro Hotel Restaurant is on the 2nd floor, 3 Calle 4-55. This is a beautiful old hotel with rich wood walls, excellent service and lots of real coffee as soon as you sit down. This is truly the North American dream come true. The crepes are cooked in maple butter and are a super way to start the day. This is a very popular place with gringos working in Guatemala.

American Donut Shop 5 Ave. 11-47 has real soft and gooey North American style donuts. The coffee is quite strong, and provides a good mid-day perk.

Cafeteria Zurich on 4 Ave. 12-09, Zone 10. This is the best place for first class chocolate, real ice-cream, or even a banana split and a cappuccino or expresso coffee. The place is heavily guarded with gun wielding hombrès, but don't let that scare you away.

Hotel Pan American on 9 Calle 5-63, Zone l, has an elegant restaurant where the waiters and waitresses wear traditional garb and the decor is done with local art and artifacts. The food is good but a bit expensive. However, the pastry and coffee mid-day is wonderful. The meals are moderate (not big) in size.

Hotel Ritz on 10 Calle 6 Ave. is another excellent place to eat your big meal of the day. The service is quick (for Latin America) the meals are big, and the food is well presented. The restaurant is open at 6:00AM and they have real coffee.

Soya Nutrial on 16 Calle 3-64 is the best vegetarian place in town with reasonable prices. Stay away from the turtle dishes as the creatures are protected. The less market, the more turtles will survive. There is lots to choose from without the turtles.

Europa Restaurant on 11 Calle 5 is a good bar if you want to pick up political information. They serve copious amounts of popcorn with the drinks and the proprietor speaks English. This is a popular place for travellers to gather. They also have a TV plugged into an English channel.

Olave Bar & Restaurant on 9 Calle 8 is a neat little bar if you wish to have a pleasant drink and an excellent dish of ceviche. It is a bit pricey, but certainly worth the extra few cents.

El Establo on Reforma 14-34 is where the journalists hang out. They serve an excellent bowl of home made soup. There is also a **used book exchange** or purchase service here with many books to choose from, from Harlequin Romance to some great classics, although the classics are a bit limited. There is a large supply of American middle of the road, easy to read novels. They cost half the original price and you receive 1/4 the original price for any that are brought in. This is by far one of the best book places in town.

Nais Restaurant on Ave. 7 Calle 10 is an excellent place to have a POT of real coffee and read the local newspapers. They will not rush you and the prices are great.

Celeste Imperio on 7 Ave. 9-99 Zone 4 is a well managed and clean Chinese restaurant with excellent food. Every time I walked past here when going to my consulate, I had to stop in and have something because the food was so good.

Fast food can always be bought at McDonald's, Pizza Hut or Pollo Campero, but why bother leaving home if this is where you are going to eat? Besides, much of the profit returns to the States if you solicit McDonald's or Pizza Hut.

Bank of Guatemala, Guatemala City

241

THINGS TO DO.

National Palace borders the north side of the Central Park or the Plaza de Armas on 5 Ave. between Calle 7 & 8 in Zone 1. The other side of the park (which is in fact two parks) is called the **Parque Centenario.** This is a good place to start your wonderings around Guatemala City.

The Palace was designed by Guatemalan architects Rafael Parez de Leon, Enrique Riera and Luis Angel Rodas. The building was started in 1939 and inaugurated in November of 1943. It cost Q2,800,000 to build and everything was done by Guatemalans. Inside the building, the three floors contain the offices of the president and his executive. Upon entering the building, you will see beautiful murals done by the late Alfredo Galvis Suarez. One attractive mural is of Don Quixote. The stairways and banister rungs are of ornate bronze. The second floor has two exquisite rooms. The **Banquet Salon** is used mainly for press conferences. It has a lovely ceiling of carved mahogany and gold leaf. The two large wall paintings on cloth depict the friendship of the Spaniards and the Guatemalans (a bit mythical). The second one is of Pedro de Alvarado, a conquistador, at Volcan Atitlan. These tapestries are by Carlos Rigalt. When crossing to the **Salon de Recepciones** you will find beautifully tiled floors. In this salon, the president meets with diplomats and ambassadors. The chandelier weighs two tons and has one hundred and twenty lights. It is made of bronze, Bohemian crystal and 14 carat gold. The orchestra sits in the upper balconies. The emblem at the back represents strength and liberty. There are flags down both sides of the sitting area and Canada's is at the very front. The center table is a hand-carved replica of the table in the government house in Spain. In the center of the floor there is a circle. This represents the center of the country. When a speaker stands in this circle, the acoustics are such that a microphone is not needed. From the farthest corners of the room, you could hear a pin drop. From the circle, a measurement of Guatemala is taken, the circle being zero point. The tiles pointing out represent the four directions. The stained glass windows represent the colonial conquest of Guatemala. These are truly beautiful. In the lower halls are cool patios with tiled fountains and lush greenery. Next to the entrance of the palace is an exhibition room. The exhibitions change from time to time; check and see if there is a display of interest to you. You will find the displays very professionally arranged.

The Metropolitan Cathedral is on the east side of the Central Park. It is large and quite austere. There are religious paintings along the many archways and the two large chapels close to the front contain ornate gold leaf altars. One end holds the large marble coffin of Archbishop XV, Mariano Rossel Arellano, who died in 1964. The cathedral also houses the tombs of many other church dignitaries. The church was started in 1782 by Marcos Ibàñez and Antonio de Bernasconi and finally inaugurated in 1868. The building is 320 feet long and 112 feet wide and has been built to be earthquake proof. Many of the art treasures were brought from Antigua after the capital was changed to this site. Next to the cathedral is the Palace of the Archbishop.

The Market and the Plaza de Sagrario are behind the Cathedral on 9 Ave. 6 Calle. The plaza was built after the 1976 earthquake and the three-level market was built below. You will find many things here that you see all over Guatemala. However, I would only use this for last minute items that are common and heavy. If you see something you like in other areas of Guatemala, be certain to purchase it at the time if you can carry it, because your chances of seeing it in the city are slim. This fact is especially true in Guatemala as each area specializes in certain crafts and definitely in certain textile designs and colors. However, if it is going to be difficult to carry around the country, you may get a close facsimile at this market. This market is much cheaper than the handicraft market near the airport and definitely cheaper than any of the shops at the airport (except for buying bagged coffee). This central market also sells food and wares for the locals, so if you want some you can get it here. There is also an eating section in this market.

The Cultural Center is on 7 Ave, Calle 22 to Calle 24. This entire area including the main branch of the Bank of Guatemala, the Social Security Office, the Tourist Office, the City Hall and many other government offices is very modern. The **tourist office** is helpful, and if you have any complaints about tourism, you can appeal to this office. They won't do anything, but they will listen which helps alleviate some of your frustration. Maps and other information are available in English.

The mural in the **City Hall** is by Carlos Merida and is called the Mestizos of Guatemala. The sculpturing on the outside of the buildings are by D. Vasquez, a famous Guatemalan artist.

The huge white building with the blue swerving ceilings is the **National Theatre** and the National School of Plastic Arts. The theatre was designed by Efrain Recinos Valenzuela and holds 2200 people. Inside there is beautiful wooden paneling and marble flooring. The building was completed in 1978. The building next door is the National Chamber Music Theatre and across the way is the Greek Epidaurus style outdoor theatre which holds about 2500 people. The hill where the theatre is located is the **Hill of San José** and was last used for defence in 1944 when revolutionaries ousted Federico Ponce Vaides from power. If you walk around the hill, you can still see part of the fortress.

Museum of Art & Industry on 10 Ave. 10-72, Zone 1 is open from 9:00AM to 4:00PM Tuesday to Friday and 10:00AM to 12:00PM and 2:00PM to 4:00PM on weekends. There is a small entrance fee. This is a small museum containing only three chambers. The first has local paintings; I didn't find then too spectacular. The second has a couple of masks and some nice terra cotta figurines. The third chamber is the music section that has an old hand-carved harp. At first glance, the harp appears a bit crude but you will find the pieces fitting very well together even after many, many years of use. There is also a modern harp to allow you to compare workmanship. The museum also contains samples of marimbas and an old potter's wheel. The old craftsmen did not use nails to create these pieces.

Museo Ixchel of Guatemala is on 4 Ave. 16-27, Zone 10 and is open 8:30AM to 5:30PM week days and 9:00AM to 1:00PM on week ends. There is a fee of Q2.50 per person ($.50 US) Because the number of Guatemalan weavers is decreasing, the Ixchel Museum was founded in 1973 as a private, non-profit organization dedicated to the collection, conservation and research of Guatemalan textiles. Ixchel is the Maya goddess of fertility and weaving. Traditional dress identifies the Indian with his community. Each village has a distinctive costume which varies according to age, sex and social rank. These costumes also vary according to the occasion. Today, women continue to weave their own garments and those of their families on the same type of backstrap looms used by the ancient Mayas. Some weave on the treadle loom which was introduced by the Spaniards. Occasionally you will see some of the Indians dyeing their threads with natural dyes. But these practices are giving way to modern technology, and more and more customs are being ignored.

Today, this museum has three separate sections, one of ethnographic objects, one of paintings and one of textiles. Among the artifacts, there are looms, warping boards and pottery. The painting section contains watercolors of Doña Carmen de Pettersen; these depict different Indian costumes. As well, oils of Andres Churuchich are on display; these depict daily life in Comalapa. The pictures feature present day scenes. These are excellent pictures and an introduction to Indian life in Guatemala. However, this is a small museum and does not take long to go through. A larger museum is planned for the future, and there is a collection box for donations towards this cause.

Popol Vuh Museum of Archaeology at Edificio Galerias Reforma, 6th Floor, Ave. La Reforma 8-60, Zone 9 is open Monday to Saturday, 9:00AM to 5:30PM and costs Q3 ($.60 US). Guatemalan museums never overwhelm one. Again, this is a spacious, well exhibited museum. The museum houses some great pieces of stone and pottery but the main attraction is the replica of the Dresden Codes and the Popol Vuh manuscripts.

The museum was founded by Jorge and Ella Castillo in 1977. Their collection was donated to the Francisco Marroquin University and the museum has been under the jurisdiction of the university ever since.

The Maya first used stone to record history through hieroglyphs and figurines. As their civilization developed and spread, the post Maya Indians started using a writing system on deerskin, tree bark and finally a paper which was folded accordion style and painted in many different colors. Three of these Maya codes exist; one of them is in the Dresden Museum in Germany. A replica of this is in the Popol Vuh Museum.

Later in history, the Popol Vuh or Manuscript of Chichicastenango was found by the priest Francisco Ximenez. The writer is unknown, but the story is familiar. It tells of the beginning of man; how God created four men from some corn paste and when these men went to sleep, they awoke to find four women beside them. These men went out to form the tribes of the Maya. However, one of the men was sterile so there were only three major branches of the Maya, one being the Quichè.

When the original men went out onto the earth, they came to a great body of water and when they struck the water with redwood staffs, the water separated allowing the men to go to the other side onto dry land. I thought it was Moses who spread the waters. The Popol Vuh gives reference to many aspects of Maya legend which is similar to the Christian Bible.

There is a creative video at the museum which is an interpretation of the Popal Vuh done in animation. The story is one of creation that includes the story of evolution, Atlantis, the biblical story of creation, Eve and the forbidden fruit, Noah and his arc (but with only monkeys), the great flood, the Virgin Mary, the Twins of Rome, and Jack and the bean stalk. This is all incorporated into thirty minutes of story. The cost is Q2 ($.50 US) per person.

The library has over 2000 books specializing in anthropology, history, art and native folklore. The library is often used for research by people from all over the world.

Throughout the year, lectures and courses are offered; some include an excursion to a great site or other historically interesting place. Check when in Guat City for new and exciting information about this course. Telephone 347-121 for more info.

A good book store at the museum sells new books on Guatemala and the Native Indians of this land.

The National Museum of Archaeology & Ethnology at Edificio #5. La Aurora, Zone 13 is open from 8:30AM to 4:00PM Tuesday to Friday and the same on week-ends except it is closed for two hours from 12:00 to 2:00PM. The city bus to take is # 5 or 6 and you can catch it on Ave. 10 in Zone 1. Get off at the turn around before the airport, and you can go to the zoo, Aurora Park, any three of the museums or the Artisan's Market. The museum has a copy of the Popol Vuh Manuscript plus many samples of pottery, stone sculptures and other articles used by older civilizations. It starts with small scale exhibitions of life as it began in Meso America, starting with the

Asian migration and cave dwellers. There is a lovely fountain in the center of the building surrounded by old stone carvings. The museum ends with some modern day Maya costumes and objects. This is a spacious, well displayed repository of treasures which is a must. I also suggest seeing this museum at the end of your stay in the country as it will synthesize the country's history.

Museum of Natural History on 7 Ave. and 6 Calle, Zone 13 is close to the Museum of Archaeology. It is open the same hours as the Archaeology Museum and there is no entrance fee. The museum is full of stuffed creatures from all over the world, not just Guatemala. There is also a large rock collection. Unless this is of specific interest, the museum does not take long to visit. However, this may be the only place you will ever see a quetzal, even if it is stuffed. I was quite surprised to see how small the bird really is.

National Museum of Modern Art in room #6, La Aurora, Zone 13 is open the same hours as the other museums on this complex. There is no entrance fee. This is not a large or overwhelming museum and contains only the work of Guatemaltecan artists. The works are well spaced and the lighting is soft. There is a spectacular chandelier at the entrance that once held candles. But, my favorite piece of work was a junkman called Quetzal by Efrain Recimos. He was artistically created of garbage pieces. I hope he is on permanent display.

Aurora Park and Zoo is on Blvd. Liberacion and is close to the Archaeological Museum. You may take bus #5 or 6 to the airport and you can catch it on Ave. 10 in Zone 1. Get off at the turn around before the airport. The zoo is about a block past the other museums. Along the outside of the park is an old aqueduct which is pleasant to sit on, walk along and photograph. This is a very nice area of town, even with the traffic.

I do not like zoos personally, even though I realize their necessity. This zoo, however, houses what appear to be healthy animals which are not terribly overcrowded for a zoo. The animals include water buffalo, jaguars, kodiak bears, elephants, ant eaters, and boa constrictors. It is a pleasant zoo which is both free and crowded on Sundays. There is also a children's park here. You can eat everything from the American hot dog (perro caliente) to a full chicken dinner.

Artisans Market is also in the same area as the Archaeological Museum and the zoo, on 11 Ave. Just follow the signs which take you behind the museum. The market is expensive, but has a good selection. It is a convenient place to shop, especially if you are in a hurry and on the way to the airport. You are guaranteed good quality if shopping here. The market is open from 8:30AM to 4:30PM. They are supposed to take a lunch break, but you can almost always find someone to sell you something.

Natural History Museum & Botanical Garden is at the University of San Carlos which was founded in 1680. The garden and museum are at Calle Mariscal Cruz, Ave. 1, Zone 10. They are open Monday to Friday 8:00AM to 12:00PM and 2:00PM to 6:00PM and are closed from December 1st to January 14th plus all national holidays.

The entrance to the gardens is on Reforma, and you may go in any gate or door that is open. There is no cost. This is a fairly decent display of biological specimens, including deformed animals in jars of formaldehyde. There is one room of snakes that are still alive. The room with the stuffed birds have specimens that are a bit ratty, but otherwise it is an interesting place to visit. The gardens are lovely and well kept, even though they are small. There is a statue of Linnaeus, the man who gave us our system of classification for plants. This is a wonderful place to visit.

Fray Francisco Vasquez Museum & Church is on 13 Ave Calle 6, Zone 1 and is open from Tuesday to Saturday from 8:00AM to 12:00PM and 3:00PM to 6:00PM. On Sunday, it is only open from 3:00PM to 6:00PM. The church has a large collection of paintings of martyrs from the 18th century. The church itself has a wonderfully lit dome. This is a lovely place to visit and see old paintings.

National Museum of History on 9 Calle Ave. 10, Zone 1 is open Tuesday to Friday, 9:00AM to 4:00PM and has a two hour lunch break on week-ends from 12:00 to 2:00PM. There is no entrance charge. This is a small museum of historical artifacts, many of them post Hispanic. There are some paintings and early photos of Guatemala.

Kaminal Juyu Ruins are in Zone 7 and are easily located by taking city bus #17 but it must be the "red 17". You can catch this bus at Ave. 4 and Calle 16 in Zone 1. Ask the driver to let you off and point you towards the mounds. The ruins are at the end of the bus line. These ruins are one of the most important sites of the pre-Hispanic period. The growth of the city has destroyed many of the mounds, but archaeologists believe this is one of the largest sites in the highlands. Kaminal Juyu means "Hill of the Dead". The city dates back to the early Pre-Classic period. From ceramic and stone findings, archaeologists think that the inhabitants had contact with the Indians from Teotihuacan in Mexico. Ceramics and stone sculptures were found here. The architecture and engineering techniques were also similar to those in Mexico. One outstanding fact about these ruins is that they were not built on a hill; so defence was not the purpose of choosing the location.

Only true archaeology buffs or those with lots of time should bother visiting these ruins. They have not been totally excavated but the mounds do look promising. You may find it interesting to visit and observe the excavation procedure. If so, take the half hour bus ride and enjoy.

Although there is no food available at the site, there are tiendas in the area from which you can buy food.

The **National Police** are found at Parque Concordia across from the Chalet Suiso on Calle 14. This is a huge, ugly, stone fortress that I would certainly try to avoid. The outside is foreboding - I can imagine the size of the cockroaches inside.

The **Post Office** is the beautiful pink Moorish style building on Calle 12 and Ave. 7. I have seen some wonderful photos of this building, but have never been able to get a good one myself. You will find Guatel in this area. The Immigration Office is also here if you need to extend your visa (see visa section in Intro). This is also the area where the money changers hang out, but their black market is not doing too well in Guatemala anymore. The bank will give a better rate and will change many currencies, including European money. There is a marimba concert every Friday afternoon at the post office.

Abril Theater at 9 Ave. and Calle 14 is a restored old building originally built in 1915 by Julio Abril. This building has winged lions, Greek style columns, theatre masks, marble flooring, mahogany walls and crystal chandeliers. The painted dome adds to the grandeur of the building. I love old theatres like this.

Church Nuestra Señora de La Merced is on 11 Ave and Calle 5 and was built in 1813. The gold and brown mosaic dome against the white plaster building can be seen for a great distance. Inside is the largest painting in Guatemala, measuring 65 square feet. The picture is an example of the Mercedarian Order during the time of the painting in 1759. The artist is unknown but the restoration was done by a man named Rosales. The sculptures are of the life of San Pedro Nolasco and were done by Alonzo Paz. The painting, the sculptures and the altars were brought from Antigua after the 1773 earthquake when Guatemala City was declared the capital of the country.

The patron saint of this church, The Virgin of Mercy (I'd like to see a female saint who is not a virgin) is also the patron saint of lawyers; the feast day is celebrated on Sept. 24th.

Church of Santo Domingo is on 11 Ave. and Calle 10. It is a beautiful white and cream stucco church. This church is known for its Semana Santa processions which strictly adhere to tradition. Inside the church, the choir room has some excellent carvings and an antique music rack. The building is known to house the finest painting in Guatemala which is an example of the life of St. Thomas of Aquino.

Cerrito del Carmen is an area of the city that is reputed to be the oldest. It was inhabited by Indians before Guatemala City was declared the capital of the country. On the hill is the little church of Ermita del Carmen which was built in the 17th century, destroyed twice during earthquakes, and reconstructed to what it is today. To get there, walk north along 12 Ave. until you come to diagonal #4 and then work your way up onto the hill and the far end of the park.

The area is called Barrio de la Parroquia and people that come from this barrio are considered the truest of blue blooded Guatemalans.

Minerva Park is straight out 6 Ave. Go north, past Parque Morazon, until the road turns into Simeon Cañas. You can take bus #1. This is where the large, 2500 square meter topo map of Guatemala is found. The map is made of concrete and is a huge and excellent picture of the country showing the mountains, rivers, jungles and forests which make travel in Guatemala so difficult. This map was built in 1905 by a Guatemalan engineer, Francisco Vela. This is a must. There is also a "Temple of Minerva" built by a past president so that school children would have a place to celebrate the closing of school for the holidays. I like that guy!

Capilla de Nuestra Señora de las Angustias on Ave. 9, Ruta 6, Zone 4. To get there, walk directly up 7 Ave until you come to a building that has tiers around the top; before the mini Eiffel tower known as the Tower of the Reformer. Turn left. This is a spectacular chapel and very different from anything you will see in Central America. The cement cross on the top of the church sits on a ball which is a replica of the earth. It appears to be falling over (sort of prophetic?) The second cross has blue crystal in the center and gives a beautiful light when the sun shines through. The entire building is either carved out of hardwood or designed in mosaic with stones of marble or crystals. The floor is of polished stone slabs inlaid with brass. The pulpit has a spectacular face of carved wood depicting Jesus preaching to the people. The balconies are all of decorated stone - truly a beautiful church. The building was dedicated to Alvarado, the founder of the city. Originally built by the rich Yurrita family as a private church, it is now open to the public.

Tower of the Reformer on 7 Ave. 2 Calle, Zone 9 is a great landmark in this part of town. It is a reproduction of the Eiffel Tower of Paris and was built in honor of President Rufino Barrios. Barrios was a revolutionary who lived from 1835 to 1885. He became president in 1873. He wanted to unite the five states of Central America into one nation. He was killed in battle in El Salvador trying to achieve this. To commemorate the winning of the 1871 revolution, the bell is rung once a year (June 30). On the top of the tower is a light which warns incoming planes of the tower.

Avenida Reforma in Zone 10 is a delight to walk along. Not only is this where the great hotels, super eating places, and high priced shopping stores are, but the avenue is wide with a boulevard full of statues. Some are: General Miguel Garcia Granados by Durini and erected by President Barrios; Benito Juarez, a Mexican who helped in the independence movement; Padre Miguel Hidalgo, a Mexican who started the independence movement; Dr. Lorenzo Montufar, a Guatemalan philosopher; and Father Bartolome de las Casas, the peaceful Dominican priest who worked among the Indians in the Coban area.

Doctors - Hospital Privado Santa Rita is on 2 Ave. Calle 9 in Zone 1, telephone 29-7-60. If you need a doctor, this hospital has been recommended. The price is not high, less than $20. US for exam, tests and consultation. You need no Spanish, just a dictionary. The doctors are patient and kind. They are also accustomed to tropical intestinal parasites, so rather than suffer through the Inca two-step, go for a visit. Your entire trip will be more enjoyable once you know you are not really dying. You can also contact your consulate for a list of doctors, but they cannot officially recommend a doctor.

Plaza de España is on 7 Ave. just past the Tower of the Reformer. This auto circle has a fountain in the center which was originally at the base of a statue of Charles lll of Spain. During a public demonstration, the statue was destroyed and the fountain was hidden. It was not put back into use until earlier this century and now is the center of this park. There are also tile covered benches where you can sit and read a book. This is also a fairly good place to get a taxi, and they are quite willing to agree on a decent price.

Lago Amatitlan is only 25 kilometers from the city and less than one hour by bus. Although the lake is quite polluted, the area is beautiful; Mt. Pacaya and Agua tower in the background. The lake is about 4 kilometers wide and 10 kilometers long. The lake is dotted with hot springs. Most of the lake is owned by middle class Guatemalan people and access is limited. However, there are a few small beaches where people can access the water. There is also a hydro electric plant on the lake.

The beach called **Las Ninfas** is where you can take a cable car up to the **United Nations Park** and get spectacular views of the lake. You can also take a bus up the hills to the north of the lake where you can get off part way up (at a lookout point) and get superb views. This is not a long excursion, but it is an interesting one. The pictures taken from this area are beautiful. If you continue up the mountain, there is a monastery that sells the best bread in all of Guatemala. They say they got the recipe from Quebec. Ask the bus driver to let you off at the monastery.

The town of **Amatitlan** has a population of about 20,000 people and sits 1190 meters (3900 ft) above sea level. According to archaeologists, it has been inhabited for about 1500 years. There are small ruin mounds close to the village, but nothing that is exceptional. There is also an odd looking old building that was built long ago between the village and the lake. This is the "changing room" for the thermal or steam baths. But, the building is really dirty, and I would not suggest using it. It is the beauty of the lake with the volcanos that draw a person to this spot. Unless you are camping, there is no place to stay at Amatitlan.

Volcan de Pacaya is an active volcano that has been a tourist attraction for longer than I have been going to Guatemala. Although not the highest volcano in the country, Pacaya sits at 2544 meters

(8344 feet) above sea level. It is also not the most difficult volcano to climb. Pacaya has become quite active in recent years, and if looking at it at night, you will see the lava flowing down the sides or see huge boulders being spewed out of its cone. The sights are spectacular. If close to the action, you may feel the ground shake beneath your feet when there is a minor eruption and you will also get covered and slashed with volcanic ash. There are times when the volcano is more active.

In order to climb Pacaya, you should take a bus to San Vincent de Pacaya from Zone 4 bus station. You must also plan on spending the night there. There are basic accommodations in the village of San Francisco and guides can be hired to go up. It will be necessary to take warm clothing for either day or night travel up the mountain. A flashlight and a cloth to cover your face are also needed.

However, there are some difficulties in this climb which are not dependent on your physical conditioning, but in the number of robbers. Some people take a large roll of quetzales in one quetzal denominations to pay off the robbers and then continue up. Other people have had tour guides take them up. These were hired in Antigua. However, the tour guides were in partnership with the robbers, and all the groups were robbed. One group actually had a couple of rapes occur; the husbands were tied up and watching. So, what was once one of the best attractions in Guatemala is now a dangerous one.

You must check and see what the latest information is from other travellers. If a group is going up, it may be safe for you to join them, but it may also be very dangerous. Never consider this climb by yourself. If you have friends that are Guatemalan, go with them. But, be careful. I say, let the robbers have the mountain. Take your shekels and go to Costa Rica and climb an active mountain where it is safe. Once the robbers suffer from a lack of travellers, they will move to a different spot and the travellers can move back onto the mountain.

San Pedro Sacatepequez is about 25 kilometers from Guatemala City and only has a population of about 5000 people. You pass it on the way to Mixco Viejo. Here, Indian ladies wear a huipile that is embroidered with gold birds on a purple cloth. They are especially attractive and many people buy the garments as souvenirs. This village is also noted for its beautiful flowers it grows and exports to other countries.

San Juan Sacatepequez is the next town that you will pass on the way to Mixco Viejo and has a population of 7000 people. The huipiles found in this village are as beautiful as San Pedro's. They are gold and purple, with animals and birds embroidered on them. There are places to eat, lots of buses and a couple of places to stay at San Juan.

Mixco Viejo are wonderful ruins that give one an idea of what fortresses these people were capable of building in days past. To get to Mixco Viejo, you can get a bus at 1 Calle, 2 Ave., Zone 9 at the bus terminal. This is quite a zoo in itself. The buses leave at 10:00AM or 12:30PM. The ride is a tough three hours into the mountains. Take food and water because there is nothing after San Juan. There are pop vendors at the ruins, but there is no guarantee that they will be there. Be certain not to miss the last returning bus as there is nowhere to stay close to the ruins. However, if you have camping gear, you can pitch a tent near the grounds quite safely. However, bring your own food. You may be able to hitch a ride from the ruins to San Juan but this is risky and the distance is about 25 kilometers. The ruins will take at least two hours to visit. The last bus leaves at about 5:30PM but don't take this departure time as gospel truth; ask before disembarking. These are one set of ruins that are not especially easy to get to.

Mixco Viejo was a Pokomam Maya capital sitting between the Pixcaya and Montagua Rivers on a ridge 880 meters high. There are fifteen groups of buildings and more than 120 structures consisting of pyramids, altars and platforms. Mixco was at its peak around the 13th century. The only possible access other than straight up the cliff walls was through a narrow passage that had to be traveled in single file. Mixco was probably a military and religious center; it had nine temples and two ball courts. During festivities, it is believed that as many as 9000 people would be present.

Pedro Alvarado had a difficult time conquering Mixco. He could not find the passage to get onto the hill and lost many men including many Mexican Indian allies. Later some Pokomam warriors from Chinautla came to help the men at Mixco. However, they fought on the Llano Grande, a flat area beneath the hill; they lost heavily. Then, the men from Chinautla told the Spaniards the location of the secret passage that allowed the escape and entry of the Pokomam warriors. Alvarado eventually entered by this way and overtook Mixco. However, today there is no trace of the cave or passageway leading in and out of Mixco.

Excavations began at Mixco in 1954 under the direction of Henry Lehmann. Carl Sapper is credited with lettering the structures in each district. There have been jars, bowls and funeral urns discovered at Mixco; the funeral urns are the most distinct. They were put at the base of buildings with their cremated owners inside. The jars had three holes pierced on one side which depicted the nose and eyes of the dead person. The urns were often decorated with snake motifs in black, red and cream paint. There was very little stone sculpturing at Mixco and stucco was the most common decorative material used. However, the men in this area were experts in making tools of obsidian.

At the entrance to Mixco there is a model of the area with the different districts and buildings. Some of the buildings in the fields are also identified.

The most important structure is pyramid C1 because it has three distinct stages of construction, each of which is shown in the reconstruction. The first has walls of pumice rock and is the fill for the second which has five terraces without cornices and two stairways with 16 steps in each. This structure was the fill for the final pyramid which was 18.25 meters high with five terraces complete with cornices. This pyramid had one set of stairs going up between two ramps.

The two ball courts were both sunk into the ground and were entirely enclosed. There are stairs at each end for the players to enter and exit.

The double pyramids of group B are beautiful. In front of each stairway was a small altar. Each stairway has 19 steps and extends six meters above the plaza floor. In front of one of the pyramids was a stelae which was a rare thing in the highlands of Guatemala.

The trip to Mixco Viejo is really worth the trip. The pyramids, buildings, and location are spectacular. There are no carvings such as at Quirigua but it is unique in its own right.

HUEHUETENANGO
The population is 14,500 and the altitude is 1902 meters (6240 ft) so it is getting high and will be cool in the evenings.

Huehue is not the prettiest town in Guatemala, but there is a lot to do in the area so a few days to visit would be nice. If you are interested in Spanish school, this is a good place because there is almost no English in the area. Huehue is fairly high in the mountains so have a warm sweater for the evenings. Because it is quite a distance from the main centers, you may see Guatemalan life here in a more accurate light than you will in places like Panajachel. At the time of writing, there are few street kids in Huehue, different than a few years ago. Their absence is conspicuous.

PLACES TO STAY
Hotel Mary on 3 Ave. 2 Calle is a good place to stay. The cost is Q21 ($4.20 US) for two without bath and Q25 ($5. US) for two with bath. There is lots of hot water but the acoustics are so good that you can hear the kids down stairs watching TV all hours of the day and night.

Hotel Astoria on 4 Calle 1-45 is the best in town. It is clean, pleasant and inexpensive at Q25 ($5. US) for a double with private bath and hot water. There is a nice place to sit in the center and the restaurant serves excellent food at a decent price.

Zaculeu Hotel on 5 Ave. 1-14 has nice large rooms with a lovely court yard. There are private bathrooms with hot water for only Q35 ($7. US) for a double. There is a nice common room with a TV and piano. There is also a restaurant. However, I have been shown dirty and drab rooms in this hotel, so if you are going to spend the price make certain you get a decent room.

Hotel Central on 5 Ave. 1-33 costs Q11 ($2.20 US) for a double but no private bath. There is hot water and the place is not too bad. There is a small comedor for meal times only.

Hospadaje Roberto on 2 Calle 5-49 costs Q6 ($1.20 US) per person with no private bath and only cold water but it is clean and fairly cheery.

Hotel Vasquez on 2 Calle 6-67 is expensive at Q19 ($3.80 US) for no private bath and only cold water showers. The rooms are clean but small. There is a secure parking area.

Posada Familiar on 4 Calle 6 Ave. Not bad and not good. Without bathrooms, the rooms are 9Q ($1.80 US) for singles, Q16 ($3.20US) for doubles and Q23 ($4.60 US) for triples and with bathrooms they are Q12, 23 & 33 respectively. However, there is only cold water.

Gran Hotel on 4 Calle 3 Ave. is across from the market and close to the bus terminal. The rooms are large and face off the street onto a small square which closes at 8:30PM. The cost is Q30 ($6. US) for two with private bath and hot water. Rooms without bath are Q20 ($4. US) for two. This is not a bad place and the people are friendly.

Hotel Maya on 3 Ave 3-55 is where information is plentiful and friendly. Rooms are basic and cost Q10 ($2. US) per person without private bath and Q14 ($2.80 US) per person with bath. They claim to have hot water; I did not try this place.

Mansion El Paraiso on 3 Ave 2-41 is anything but paradise. The rooms are basic at Q5 ($1. US) per person without private bath or hot water.

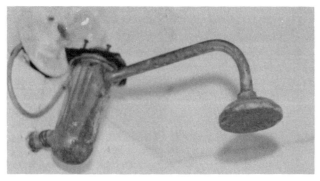

Hot water heater to avoid

RESTAURANTS

Maxi Pizza is one half block from the Mary Hotel and has excellent food and service. The food is baked in a large clay oven in the center of the kitchen area. Don't let the lack of decor scare you away; the fine details have gone into the food and the spirit of the service.

Doña Estercita is just down the street from the Maxi and is a tea and cake shop. This is an excellent snack place after the hike back from the ruins or for dessert after dinner. You will often see a young man bring his sweetheart here for an evening treat. This is a very popular shop with the locals.

The Ebony is also on this main street and is great for breakfast. The orange juice is freshly squeezed and makes a very good eye opener.

Hotel Mary Restaurant on the main floor of the hotel is expensive and the food is okay but not spectacular. However, if you go to the second floor restaurant you will find excellent food. I suggest you try the mush (oats cooked in milk with sugar and vanilla) for breakfast. This is a good example of the popular dish available anywhere in Guatemala. The restaurant also serves fresh juices.

Hotel Zaculeu has a restaurant that serves a choice of two meals for supper; it is excellent. The service is quick and friendly and the meal is large. The price is a bit high.

Cafe Jardin is just off the square and the specialty is hamburger and milk shakes. The food is okay, but the cafe is noisy from the passing traffic.

THINGS TO DO

Aguacatan is a little village of 1600 people, close to Rio San Juan and could be a stopping place if going to Nabaj or Todos Santos. The bus trip in is on a narrow gravel road that would be impassable during rainy season. It passes over a high mountain pass and beside a spectacular canyon. The bus trip alone is a thrill. A visit to the swimming hole at the Rio San Juan becomes a second bonus on this trip. The only drawback is the lack of restaurants. Be certain to ask the price before ordering, or you will pay Hyatt Regency prices and get market food.

Hospadaje La Paz Go almost all the way through town on the main street to get to this hotel. It is very clean but has no private bath nor any hot water. The cost is Q15 ($3. US) per person. It is a nice place to stay.

Rio San Juan There are two routes to Rio San Juan. You can go along the main street to the end where the road curves to the left. Stay on this road until you come to a sign that says Rio San Juan. Turn left and follow this road for about a kilometer. You will find a small sentry post with a road going to the right. Follow this road over a little bridge. You will see a small white church ahead. Keep going for about another five minutes and then enjoy your swim. There are picnic tables (and starving dogs) here. There are also some little bridges and kiosks in the area to give it a park-like atmosphere. To go back, return to the sentry post and turn right. Follow this road to town.

If going the short way from town, turn up the first road before the hotel La Paz. Go up and over the hill. Veer to the right at the first fork. Continue along this road until you reach the Evangelical Temple. Turn left at the first road past the temple and continue down to the river.

The swimming hole is close to where the river flows out of the mountain. The river has been dammed to form a swimming area. Further up there is a pump station, and at the top of the hill there is a huge storage tank.

When walking in this area, you will pass between beautiful garlic crops. You may see the ladies hand scooping water onto the crops. It is a very rich area for growing food.

Parque Central in Huehue is one of the more pleasant parks in Guatemala. There is a nice, plain church which is a relief after the ornate churches of Mexico. There are vestibules down both sides of the aisles that contain beautiful tiny clay statues.

In the main park there is a bougainvillaea tree which grows in a center pot and the branches are cultivated to form an umbrella over some pillars and benches. The intertwined branches are lovely. There is also a map of Guatemala in the square where you can plan some of your routes and then realize why it takes so long to get anywhere. The mountains are incredible.

The locals are very proud of the concert hall on the square. Occasionally there are concerts from here which can be enjoyed from the park.

Zaculeu Ruins are about five kilometers from town and there are buses that leave from the Maya Hotel about once every half-hour. It is nice to ride there (it's uphill) and walk back at the end of the day. The ruins are located in a valley in the Cuchumatanes mountains. The ruins were a fortress belonging to the Mam kingdom. The city was first established in the 10th century and was at its peak during the 16th century when it was defeated by the powerful Quichès. Mam and Quichès are Indian tribes that still have descendents in Guatemala today.

At the ruins, there is a little museum with an urn containing an adult body, originally found under the main pyramid. The main pyramid, sitting at the ceremonial plaza, consists of seven sections that make it look like a wedding cake. There are steps on one side that go to the temple at the top.

There is a small ball court on the site and be certain to look for the miniature pyramid that can be found behind the court. Because the site was a fortification, there are escape passages underground to which the guards will show the entrances if you ask. They exit somewhere in the distance hills. The word Zaculeu means white earth.

These ruins have been restored and when they were re-plastered, they were done in cement. All the original work was covered over, so the appearance from a distance is that of a modern structure. It is not the most attractive ruin in Guatemala, but the surrounding countryside makes the trip well worth the effort.

Chiantla is a village six kilometers north of the city which sits on the slopes of the Cuchumatanes mountains. The town is known all over Guatemala for its solid silver statue of the Virgin de Candelaria. The garments on the statue are made of silver filigrees. Worshippers can be seen here all year around but on February 2nd, pilgrims come from all over to ask for the blessings of the Virgin or to pray for cures. It was sculptured by Quirio Cataño. The painting along the wall tells of the building of the church. There are buses going here all day long.

Español Fundacion Spanish School is at #83 on Calle 5 in Zone 1. It is an excellent school for those who are serious about learning Spanish. The prices are high, 1 week, $100.US, 2 weeks $190.US, 3 weeks $285.US and 4 weeks $375.US. They would like one week notice with a $50.US deposit. These prices include one:one instruction from 8:00AM to 5:00PM with two hours off at lunch, every day. You may go on outings with your professor. You will be placed with a family and your meals and laundry are included in the price. They recommend that you take some schooling, travel for a bit and then return to school. The big advantage of attenting here is the lack of English speaking people in Huehuetenango.

Laundry is on Ave. 8 in Zone 1. The shop is open from 8:00AM to 5:00PM with a two-hour lunch. Laundry facilities are rare in Central America, so it is advisable to get caught up on your washing when here. However, I still recommend having the muchachas in your hotel wash your clothes. It is much cheaper (usually) and they do a splendid job; the extra couple of cents means a lot to the muchachas.

IZTAPA

The population is 1600 and the town is at sea level so it is hot.

This town, located at the mouth of the Rio Maria Linda, is not a very friendly town. The river separates the town from the ocean; you may take a boat across the river for 50 centavos per person. The sand is black and volcanic and the beaches go for miles. The area is not sparkling clean, nor are there many exciting things to do.

Iztapa was the first Guatemalan port to be established. Alvarado had a fleet of ships built here at the expense of many Indian lives. He took the ships to Peru and then Mexico where he was last seen.

PLACES TO STAY

Hotel Maria del Mar is a clean place with a nice swimming pool and excellent service for Q20 ($4. US) per person. This does not include a private bath. If you are in need of heat and sun, the price is right here. The ocean water is not spectacular, but this hotel and its service compensate.

Hospadaje Iztapa is not all that pleasant. The basic rooms are Q6 ($1.25 US) per person and there is no hot water, not that you would need it in the heat of Iztapa.

Huts can be rented across the river and are very basic with just boards going part way up the wall and a board bed with a foam mattress. These are only Q4 ($.75 US) per person.

RESTAURANTS

Hotel Maria del Mar serves the strongest coffee in all of Guatemala. This is a nice place to sit and watch the river. Other places in town are all tiendes and serve mostly typical foods. There are a few nice juice stands on the main streets.

THINGS TO DO

Chiquimulilla River Canal trip is an interesting journey, taking about four hours (longer if going by cuyuco) to the village of Monterrico where you may catch a bus either to Escuintla or the other way to the Salvadorian border. The cost of the trip to Monterrico is about Q20 ($4 US) per person. This is not the most interesting trip in Guatemala, but you will certainly see some wonderful birds, especially if you go early in the morning.

The canal dug during the 1930's is 100 kilometers (60 miles) long and was used as a communications road for years.

LA MESILLA

This is the border town across from San Cristobal de las Casas, Mexico. The money changers will not give you an excellent rate, but if entering Guat, you should change some money here. If you happen to be stuck in La Mesilla late at night, there are places to stay.

Hotel Marisol costs Q5 ($1. US) per person and has a nice garden in which you may sit. The rooms are very basic, with concrete floors and a single bed. There is only cold water in the showers.

RESTAURANTS

This village has two places to eat. The hotel or another tienda; the hotel serves good meals at a very reasonable price.

LIVINGSTON

The population is about 3000 people and the port is at sea level. The town rises 20 meters (65 feet) at its highest point. It does not sound like much, but in the heat of the day, the walk up the hill is very slow. But then, so is everything in Livingston. I found it an effort to eat some of the delightful sea food.

However, Livingston is a wonderful, little, unpopulated town with delicious food, few bugs and clean hotels. Livingston also has a little beach, a nice waterfall, and super food. I spoke with one lady who was detained here because of passport problems, and she felt that she could not have been detained in a better place. The village is on the Caribbean at the mouth of the Rio Dulce. The only way out of the village is up the river or along the coast, either to Belize or Puerto Barrios. The river trip is superb, going back to the main highway. It passes through the manatee sea cow reserve, and it is a thrill if you see one of these large, gentle creatures.

You will see many Rastaferian men and women with their long dreadlocks in this town. These locks take years to grow and are worn with pride. Rastaferians are a group of people that believe in all things natural. Their hair is never combed so it matts, forming the dreadlocks. If these people are caught by the authorities in the village, with any type of drugs the punishment is to have their heads shaved. This is both a humiliation and a waste. You will occasionally see people with bald heads walking around the village.

The ferry to Puerto Barrios leaves at 5:00AM, 7:00AM and 2:00PM but this changes so check while there. Usually, there are signs around town telling you when the boats are leaving. It is often difficult to get on the ferry as it is so crowded; the early one seems to be the best. Although I have never had any trouble, I have heard of others that have; make certain that time is not a deciding factor when you must get out of Livingston. Always give yourself an extra day or so when you have an important date like catching a plane.

The Latigua buses meet the ferry at Puerto Barrios and cost Q20 ($4. US). These are now the infamous video buses; unless you want to watch a cheap, Guatemalan video in Spanish, (telling you how wonderful the military is and how terrible the guerrillas are) you had better take one of the cheaper buses. I find the people in real life much more interesting than the videos.

PLACES TO STAY

Hotel Caribe is a large clean hotel on the same street as the Casa Rosa Hotel. There is a big sign for the Casa Rosa. It is the first street up the hill after leaving the dock. The rooms are still Q5 ($1.25 US) per person without bath and Q15 ($3. US) per person with bath. This is the best deal in town and is a favorite with travellers. However, it can be noisy.

Hotel Viajero is about 100 meters past the Caribe. It costs Q23 for two with a private bath. It is clean and pleasant and the people are really nice to stay with.

Casa Rosita costs Q20 ($4. US) for two with a minimum stay of two days (not hard to do in this place). It is run by a lady from New York, so if you need American English this is the place. It is just past the Viajero and has quite a small sign; if you arrive after dark, you may have to ask where it is.

Hotel Bugo is the last hotel along the same road as the other hotels. The cost is Q45 ($9. US) for two with private bath. Pleasant but overpriced by my standards. I can see no reason to spend that much money unless other places are full.

Hotel Minerva is a great little place to stay. Walk up the main road from the dock to the Happy Tienda corner. Turn left and go a few blocks. Minerva is on a side road to your left. It is Q14 ($2.75 US) for two or Q7 ($1.50 US) for one with a communal bath. There is a nice court yard and friendly people. This is an excellent place to stay.

Hotel Rio Dulce is on the main street and another nice place to stay. The rooms are large and cheery with high ceilings. The building is quite old but very well kept. The cost is Q10 ($2. US) per person.

The Flamingo Hotel is on the beach. You must go all the way through town and follow the road to the beach on the opposite side of the ferry landing. Turn left and go up the beach for five minutes. The cost is Q30 per person with communal bathrooms. It is exceptionally clean and the rooms are excellently decorated with a jungle motif. At one time, this was a good place to stay, but the owner, a German lady, does not get along with the locals, and they give her a bad time. She in turn has turned a bit paranoid and is not fun to listen to. If the hotel is sold (it was for sale in 1991) then it is a great place to stay. If it is still owned by the German lady, find another place unless you wish to stay in your room. I suggest you check it out.

RESTAURANTS

Africano Restaurant is a favorite with everyone and is a bit cheaper than the restaurants on the main drag. They even have barracuda on the menu. To get there, go up the main street as far as the Happy Tienda corner. Turn left and keep going until you see a white mausoleum-like building with a bridge leading to the entrance. The salads and the vegetable soup are good. The coffee is instant so don't bother ordering it.

McTropic Food is next to the Ixchel Tipical Shop on the main drag. This is great for breakfast, especially fruit salad and yogurt. If looking for lobster, it is cheaper here than any other restaurant along the main drag.

Restaurant next to Jugado del Paz has good food, excellent service and is friendly but definitely pricey.

El Malecon on the main drag has the best french fries in town. It is also the town bakery. At 3:00PM each afternoon, fresh baking is ready; there is a steady stream of locals going in to purchase fresh buns. Get in line early if you want some.

THINGS TO DO

Los Siete Altores is a beautiful seven-tiered waterfall about six kilometers from town. A nice dip in the water is refreshing on a hot day. To get there, go straight up the main street and over the hill to the beach. Turn left and keep walking along the beach for about half an hour. You will get to a river outlet. Go towards the sea and cross the river on a sandbar. Continue along the shore for another half an hour. When you see a clump of trees that also goes into the sea, start looking for a path going up off the beach. If you get to the trees, you have gone too far. Go up the path for a bit and you will be there. The second pool is great for swimming. This area is known to be dangerous at night because many robberies have occurred. You should not go here alone for the same reason. Travel in a group, without all your possessions and have fun.

Rio Dulce River Trip is a wonderful trip and well worth the Q25 ($5. US) per person you must pay. There are dorries at the docks; men will hustle you on the street, trying to sell you a trip. Get a group together or you will pay too much. The boats are each able to take about ten people. Some people were afraid to go with the Guatemaltecans because they heard stories about being stopped half way and having to pay more or just being robbed. Listen to these stories. At one time I would have ignored them, but times have changed in Guatemala; if there is trouble in an area, don't go. Take another route and let the robbers starve to death.

Before leaving, make certain that your driver will stop at the places where you wish to stop. The first sight to see is the Rio Dulce gorge where the river flows between beautiful jungle covered cliffs. There are a few settlements along the river. The hot springs are along the river by a rocky shore. This is an excellent place to stop and enjoy the water.

The next stop is the **Chocon Machacas Biotopo** or the manatee reserve. The manatee are wonderful, gentle, huge animals often called the sea cow and they weigh up to a ton. These animals live at river and creek mouths and keep the vegetation in that area from clogging up the flow of water. The animals are so gentle that the locals would just paddle close and kill them. They made a great meal (for many days and many people) but hunting them today is prohibited. The reserve is for both manatees and mangroves; if your boatman stops for you, you may walk along the trails of the mangroves.

You will be at the bridge at **El Relleno** within four hours if you make a direct trip down the river. Then, you can choose between going further up river to Castillo de San Filipe or getting off and taking a bus either north to the Peten or south back to Guat City. If staying at El Relleno, there is a small place called **Hotel Marilu** with your usual basic room for Q10($2. US) per person. Not bad if you can't get a bus going to Tikal until the next day.

Castillo de San Filipe is found near the entrance to Lake Izabal and was built in 1651 in defence against pirates. If you can imagine, the pirates harassed the Spaniards. One of the undesirable seafaring men was Sir Francis Drake. The pirates then burned the fortress in 1686, but it was rebuilt. Because it is a long way from the sea, some pirates were able to get quite a ways inland with no problems. The fort was eventually turned into a prison and used as such until independence. The fortress is in very good repair and takes about one hour to visit. It is a stone structure with a tiled roof and a great old drawbridge. There is a dungeon on the upper level where prisoners were once kept. The park around the fortress is clean and pretty, a nice place for a picnic. Your boatman would be happy to join you for a picnic if you happen to preplan and take some extra food. There is also an expensive hotel nearby, but I much prefer the park.

LAKE ATITLAN - see Panajachel

LAKE IZABAL

Lake Izabal has many expensive hotels close by and many rich Ladinos that visit the area. Once there were manatees and alligators roaming the lake; now the only animal to be seen is man. He is not nearly as friendly as the manatee; this is probably why he is not nearly as extinct.

Lake Izabal is the largest lake in Guatemala and covers 590 square kilometers (228 sq. miles). It is truly a beautiful spot, and I can see why the human animal has invaded the area. The lake is good for fishing and bird watching. You can rent boats and cayucos from the men in the area.

MARIO DARY RIVERA BIOTOPO

Commonly called the Quetzal preserve, this park is one hour by bus before Coban and in my opinion, a visit is a must. It is recommended to stay for the night if you wish to see the Quetzal, the national bird and a truly breathtaking experience. The park has well groomed and maintained trails that take about two hours of easy walking. There is public camping at the park where there are cold private shower stalls and picnic tables. However, to see the Quetzal, you must stay at the hospedaje next door to the park and get up at the break of dawn.

Hospedaje Rancho el Quetzal is the two thatched roofed log houses on the hill just past the park entrance about half a kilometer closer to Coban. It is a delightful place costing Q8.80 ($1.75 US) per person. Each hut sleeps eight people. There is a communal hot water shower in each hut and there are beds for about 4 - 6 upstairs and then more downstairs. The beds only have one blanket and if the cabin is full, and the night is cold, you may not be able to steal covers from the other beds. You may have to sleep with some of your clothes on. Cooking facilities are available; it is advisable to bring food because the comedor serves a small supper of eggs and beans for Q5 ($1. US); it is served at 5:00PM sharp and if you miss it, too bad.

To see the Quetzal you must be up before 6:00AM. The quetzales arrive about 6:10 - 6:15AM and entertain the tourists for about two hours. Pictures are possible. This is a real thrill so be certain not to miss it. The bird is beautiful and unmistakable with its bright red chest, brilliant green back and long tail feathers. The reason you must be up early in order to see the birds is so that you can follow them through the jungle. They always arrive at the hotel at about that time and then go on their usual route. I watched and photographed them for about 45 minutes before I tired out. You must sit outside the cabin and watch the trees in the direction of the comedor and park.

The quetzal nests in old dead trees at an elevation of 1000 - 3200 meters (3000 to 11,000 ft) and the eggs are laid in April or May. During nesting times, it is more difficult to see this magnificent bird. The quetzal eats nuts and small fruits. When you finally see the bird, you will agree that to see this graceful creature glide through the air is breathtaking.

Biotopo de Quetzal is a delightful place to walk around and experience some cloud forest. The reserve is actually 1153 hectares (2849 acres), but only 25 hectares (62 acres) are open to the public. Two routes are available, one called the moss trail, 3600 meters, and the other the fern trail, 1800 meters. I bet you can't tell which plant will be predominant on each trail.

The beginnings of the trails are through secondary growth, but as you ascend, you will be in primary growth; this is recognized by the thinner underbrush. The primary forest is host to lichens, liverworts, mosses, ferns and orchids. There is a side trail off the moss trail to a lovely waterfall that should be visited. As the hike is certainly not strenuous, the side trip is a must. There are strategic resting spots and little signs telling the history of the growth.

Trees which have fallen add food to the soil. They fall because they are so big and top-heavy that the roots are unable to hold them any longer. A strong wind soon blows the trees over. Other trees die on the vine. Their branches start to rot, leaves fall off, and birds such as the quetzal nest in them; woodpeckers (frequently heard) look for bugs to eat from the dead trees.

This is a rain forest. The moisture is carried by the winds which cross Lake Izabal, and the Caribbean. As the winds cross the mountains, the water condenses and turns to rain or mist. For the most part, this water will run-off in streams or gullies, but some will collect in the leaf mould on the forest floor, thus trapping the water for the soil. Some of this water will filter into underground caverns forming the moisture found in caves. The soil in a rain forest is rich in dead and rotting plants and animal remains. This adds food value for new plants. The subsoil is clay and does not hold much water. When water is held it remains in the clay for a long time, thus watering the roots of plants when water is scarce.

There is a tree called Xiu ua li che (post #5) which is over four hundred years old. The name means "grandfather of trees" in Quichè. At the end of the moss trail is a small swimming hole, but I never found it warm enough for swimming.

Posada Montaña del Quetzal is four kilometers (2.5 miles) before the park if coming from Guat City or south of the biotopo. Beautiful cabins are set on the side of a hill overlooking a valley for a mere Q65 ($13. US) per person. However, you will not see the quetzal here. There is a restaurant here, but the food is nothing special. However, if you have eaten at the comedor at the park the day before, this may be a great stop for breakfast before heading off again.

MOMOSTENANGO

The population of Momostenango is about 2700 and it sits about 2340 meters (7700 ft) above sea level. Because of the high elevation and cold temperatures, it is only natural that the people here would be good at making wool blankets. In fact they are known all over the country for their excellent craft. The men produce the ponchos on foot looms while the women are in charge of threading and washing the wool. The wool is washed in the nearby sulfur hot springs in order to make the colors fast.

To get to Momostenango, (means where the monkeys gather) you must change buses at San Francisco de Alto (see under "s") which, and as its name suggests, is high in the mountains and chilly. Buses are not as frequent as the trucks which will usually give you a ride for a few centavos or sometimes for nothing. Momo is one hour from San Francisco. You may also get a direct bus from Quetzaltenango or Iluehuetenango, but they are not very frequent.

PLACES TO STAY

Hospadaje Paclom costs Q5 ($1. US) per person with no hot water except when there is a fire in the stove when the weather is very cold. It is basic with straw mattresses. However, the owners are friendly, and they try hard to please the guests. Meals are not too bad in the comedor, and it is a nice place to sit.

Hospadaje Roxana is across the square just past the church; it is very basic and not quite so clean as the other. Both hotels are the same price. There are frequent drunks roaming the town at night; it is not uncommon to lay in bed and listen to their ranting while they roam up and down the street.

THINGS TO DO

The Hot Springs and Waterfall is a wonderful spot and the Indians claim that the water is very medicinal. I have been told that the area is as valued as the springs in Vichey, France. Walk past the square and straight ahead for 25 to 30 minutes. There is a fork in the road and I suggest taking the left fork over the bridge. You will see a small waterfall, but this is not what you want. Keep going down the road and you will see a path going to the large falls. They are about 50 feet high and empty into a pretty pool. There is one small hot spring bath house here. If you continue down the road for another ten minutes, you will see another path leading down to the river. These are the main thermal baths; the different baths range in temperatures from very hot to cool. Many people come from all over the mountains for the medicinal value of these springs. The area is pretty, and if you are near Momo, the hot springs are a must.

The Market specializes in blankets and wool rugs. The wool is gathered from the sheep and goats that roam in the hills; the women card and spin the wool and then dye it, often with natural dyes. They then take the wool down to the hot springs and soak the wool to fix the color. The men weave the blankets on a large foot loom. This process can be seen in the town. Market days are Wednesdays and Sundays and the town comes alive at these times. Although there is a **co-op** in the center of town which sells at fixed prices, it is more fun to barter in the market. There is also a **fabrica** - a place where they make blankets - which you can tour. They expect you to purchase from the factory but their prices are the same as anywhere else.

Eight Monkey Ceremony occurs on the New Year's Eve and Day of the Maya Tzolkin calendar. In the eve, the Indians gather at the Catholic church to pray for many hours. The next morning, New Year's Day, the Indians go to the altar mounds which can be seen at the upper end of town. Here they offer candles and pine boughs, and they burn incense for the older gods. They also put all the pottery that was broken throughout the year on these mounds. A priest makes these offerings to the gods and in turn asks for favors for the people. These offerings to the gods are also rituals of purification for the new year. This is a colorful and traditional custom.

MORALES

This is a grubby one-horse town of 2200 people, halfway between Flores and Guatemala City. There is nothing here except a few hotels and tiendas. However, if it is raining in the Peten, as it often is, it could take you twenty hours to get from Guatemala City to Tikal so a good night's sleep halfway is a great idea. The lady at the libreria speaks English, so if you need information, by all means stop and visit.

PLACES TO STAY

Hospadaje Libra will rent a single for Q6 ($1.25 US) and a double for Q12 ($2.50 US) without private bath. It is a bit drab, but it will do.

Hotel Harris costs Q15 ($3. US) for a single and Q30 ($6. US) for a double. This hotel has a sign on the main street, but is located off the street, towards the back alley. It is clean and cheery with a private bath and a one tap shower. Don't judge the hotel by its entrance; the rooms are pretty good - especially if you are coming from the Peten.

Hospadaje Simon is across from the Tienda Oriental and has a laundromat. I did not list this place as a choice for accommodations, and when you see it, you will understand why. However, if you are in town for a few hours, you may want to catch up on your washing while you have a bite to eat and a look around.

THINGS TO DO

The Central Park is both beautiful and peaceful. By all means sit and read a book or just smell the flowers. It is an excellent break after Guatemala City. You will find the park on the second street off of the highway; go down any of the side streets.

The Market is to the west of the town center. It is only for those collecting junk such as old irons like our grandmothers used to warm up on the wood stove and of old looking bottles and containers. There were also a few pieces of pottery that the locals tried to convince me were authentic artifacts. However, because I am not an antique expert I cannot tell the difference between fake and real. I strongly suspect when they see a gringo, they bring out the freshly made antiques.

Del Monte, the giant fruit company, has a huge estate in Morales where the important workers may live. It is quite a contrast to the homes around the market. The estate is guarded by men with rifles. There are large spot lights throughout the estate. If you walk around, you may observe the difference between the haves and have nots.

MONTERRICO

The population is under 1000 and is on the ocean; needless to say, it is hot. To get there, take a bus from Guatemala City either to Esquintla or the direct bus to Taxisco. From Taxisco, take the local bus to Avellana. You can take a bus from Guatemala City to Avellana but it is the chicken route and takes about an hour longer. When you get to the Chiquimulilla Canal, a boat will soon arrive to take you to Monterrico. The cost is Q1.50 ($.25 US). On the return, the boats meet the buses. Should you be driving your Rolls Royce, there are boats to take it down the canal.

Monterrico is a seedy little town with nothing to offer but some skinny barking dogs and the nicest black beach in Guatemala. If you want to just lay around, drink beer and eat little, this is the place. Be aware that scorpions are in the area and could be lurking in your clothes. Check shoes and shake clothes before dressing. I found one in the bed, so checking the sheets may also be advisable. On the beach, the surf can be quite strong, so be aware of undertow and never swim alone. The sun here is hot, so if you are just beginning, use lots of sun screen. The constant breeze can fool you into thinking it is not as hot as it really is.

PLACES TO STAY

Hotel Baule Beach is the Hyatt of my price range. The rooms are clean. The beds are cement slabs with foams and mosquito netting. There are private baths and after a day in the sun, the showers feel great (cold)! There is a restaurant at the hotel, but if Nancy, the owner is not there, the staff will tell you to go and eat in town. The rent for one night is Q41 ($8.25 US) for a double. The hotel also has rooms in the main section of the building, a cabaña that sleeps three and another house that has four large double rooms. This is definitely the best place in town to stay. To get there, go along the side walk from the boat, all the way to the beach. Turn left and walk for about five minutes until you see the white house with beach houses to the side.

Hotels There are two other hotels in town and they are very basic. The rooms are small, the beds are cots with straw mats. There are no private baths. However, if you do not want this and can't get in at Baule Beach, then the other alternative is to stay in Taxisco.

PLACES TO EAT

Baule Beach Hotel offers chicken, fish or shrimp. The other restaurants offer the same with the exception of the **Devino Maestro** which occasionally offers shark. Breakfasts are the usual typical eggs, beans and tortillas. This is not the place to come if you want to eat lots. Thank goodness the heat decreases the appetite.

Marañon is a fruit that is common in this area and is ripe at the end of February. This fruit looks like a large red pepper with a huge bean on the top. The fruit is really good. It is simultaneously bitter but sweet. It also has a sour taste which really quenches your thirst. The bean on the top produces the cashew nut. Some famous person wrote "These people are smart; they give us the nut and keep the fruit!" (I think the writer was Viv Lougheed).

THINGS TO DO

Biotopo Montericco is administered by the University of San Carlos. This is both a mangrove preserve and an area of marine studies. Mangroves are tropical trees that grow in the ocean and eventually form swams; a boat trip through the biotopo is wonderful and a must. Bird photography is excellent. Boats can be hired at the dock. Next door to Baule Beach hotel is an area of the preserve with iguanas, crocodiles and turtles. If you make an appointment, a student will take you to the beach to watch turtles lay eggs at the laying time of year. There aren't as many turtles there as in Costa Rica, but as the influence of the preserve increases, so will the quantities of turtles.

NARANJO

This little village is about six hours from Flores and is the waiting point for a boat down the San Pedro River. You must sit by the water and try and find someone to take you on board. Usually, you must wait a day or so in order to get a full boat; otherwise going by yourself is quite costly. The usual rate for a full boat is about $10 US per person, depending on your age, sex and hair color. If travelling alone, a boat would cost about Q300 - Q400 ($60. - $80. US).

Because of the nearby military you will see many military personnel. Keep all conversations light and pleasant and you should be okay. They don't usually bother gringos.

The hotel is basic but great although the bathrooms could use some tender loving care. You can sit in the hotel restaurant and watch kids jumping into the river from the dining room. You may either join them or finish another beer. The restaurant food is excellent, so don't be afraid to fill up with the fresh sweet buns that are available before your boat trip. Considering the isolation, the food here is a real treat.

There are a few stelae and altars around the village that you may wish to visit.

Be certain to see immigration when you are ready to leave. You must get stamped out of the country from this point. However, wait until the last minute before your boat leaves just in case something causes further delay.

The first part of the boat trip, with views of trees and distant mountains, is lovely. Then the river narrows and flows quickly. After travelling by boat for about three hours, you will arrive at the border and your passport will be stamped again. Birds, snakes and other small animal life make the trip very interesting. The far end of the river is swamp and mosquitoes.

Once you get to La Palma, Mexico, your passport will be stamped. There is no problem for gringos going into Mexico, and there are money changers at the border. La Palma is a dump so you will want to get on a bus (or any other moving thing) immediately and get to Tenosique for a beer and shower.

My daughter Fay and her travelling companion, Drew (who was not impressed at the adventure) did this trip. I want to thank them for their contribution to this book. I especially thank my daughter who, by following my footsteps is becoming a wonderful chickenbuser.

NEBAJ

This village has a population of 5000 people and seems to be high in the mountains but is only at 1200 meters (4000 ft). The hair raising experience of getting there makes one think he has passed into the next plane of existence. The unpaved, narrow roads sit along the edge of cliffs almost all the way. The vehicle going uphill has the right of way, and I was never on one of those when our bus passed another vehicle. Buses only go to and from Nebaj once a day from Santa Cruz del Quichè. It is impossible to get good connections from Guat. City.

Nebaj is a little Ixil community that has a long history of terror and oppression. Read the book "Guatemala, Tyranny on Trial" published by Synthesis Publication, San Francisco, for an idea as to what occurs in these hidden villages. The oppression has had its effects on the people but is not visible to us. There are aid programs in the area offering clothing, water and schooling. Nebaj is one of the "model" villages that you will hear about while in Guatemala. The communities of San Juan Cotzal and Chajul are also Ixil villages and are close (relatively speaking) to Nebaj. This area is often called the Ixil triangle and is the only area left in Guatemala where Ixil is spoken.

The Indian weaving in this area is superb. There is a co-op in the town, but I do not know how successful it has been. If you wish to purchase weaving that isn't at the co-op, you will have to bargain with the Indians.

PLACES TO STAY

Pension de las Tres Hermanas is the only place in town to stay for only Q7 per person ($1.50 US). It has a gorgeous, flowered courtyard, clean rooms, warm blankets on the beds and a clean wash area (outhouse). There is a restaurant with real coffee and friendly women. You can sit close to the stove in the morning if it is cold after you finally crawl out of bed. This is really the place to be.

Pension Las Gemelitas is down a couple of blocks and is the second choice in town. There are basic rooms, cold water, and it is not quite as clean as the other. But, it is better than the town square. The prices here are the same as the Three Sisters.

RESTAURANT

Pension de las Tres Hermanas is good but basic and cheap. You have to look around and see if there is anything better for you. There are other places in town but...

THINGS TO DO

Market is not much in this area. It is basically for the convenience of the locals. You can supplement your meals by shopping here and eating some of the fresh fruit, depending what is in season when you are there.

Burial Mounds are just out of town. Walk across the plaza and, keeping your back to the front of the church, walk straight ahead. In about three blocks, turn left and follow the trail. The mounds which are not really much to see are on the right. This is a sacred area used occasionally for ceremonies. This is less than a ten minute walk from town.

Acul is past the mounds and up over the hill. Continue along the trail in the same direction and then start the climb. You will go a long way and this is a tough climb (3000 feet) which will take a few hours. Once over the top, you will come down into the village of Acul. Because of its isolation, it is an interesting place to visit; plus, what else is there to do in Nabaj? Once in Acul, you may go to the finca that makes cheese. Ask the locals for directions. The cheese is supposed to be an excellent Italian type and is sold for a good price. I have not visited there so I can not verify this statement.

Waterfall Walk along the main road to the creek and follow the path along it. This is a delightful walk and highly recommended. It will give you a chance to talk to the people, enjoy this beautiful part of the land, and your walk will have a destination - the waterfall. Take something to eat or drink and read. Enjoy. The mounds and the waterfalls are for the everyday person; Acul is only for the strong and adventuresome.

Stone head at La Democracia

PANAJACHEL

Without the gringos, Panajachel has a population of about 3500 people and it sits at 1575 meters (5200 feet). This town has been re-named Gringotenango by the locals; as the name implies, it is full of gringos. The original name meant "place of the tree killing vine" in the local Maya language. The town itself is situated in a very scenic spot on the beautiful Lake Atitlan, a large crater lake. It is believed that when the crater blew, rocks landed as far away as Ecuador. When visitors arrive, they want to stay for a long time. Many gringos have.

Lake Atitlan is a crater lake which erupted thousands of years ago; the river which drained the lake was sealed by eruptions about 500 years ago. The lake is about seven miles wide by eleven miles long and is framed by the volcanoes, Atitlan, Toliman and San Pedro. In some places the lake is believed to be over 1000 feet deep. There are stocked bass in the lake but the almost extinct "poc", a grebe which is indigenous to Guatemala, is in great danger because the bass eat the young birds. Another one of man's great ideas gone wacko. The bird's nesting grounds are also disappearing; therefore, the poc population is rapidly decreasing.

Lake Atitlan is reached by changing buses at Los Encuentros, going to Solola and then again changing for Panajachel. There are some direct buses from Guat City and there are also buses that go from Los Encuentros to Pana. But, regardless of which route you take, it is very easy to get to Pana. Then, you may walk or take a boat to the rest of the villages around the lake. This is a delightful place to spend at least a week.

Panajachel has every type of restaurant (except large chains) and every class of hotel that you could want. The wonderful restaurants have food that will revive your faith in travel. However, Panajachel is the congregation place for some gringos to gather and party; this has taken its toll on the native population. The gringos walk around half naked, spend wads of money on food, booze and dope, and display appalling behavior. I am truly ashamed to be associated with this group in any way. As a result of the gringo's presence, the Indians have lost their pleasantry. They now resent the tourist and sometimes they steal. Disrespect on our part has resulted in disrespect on theirs. However, the lake is beautiful with volcanoes to climb, small villages to visit, beautiful flowers and birds to enjoy and, if away from the crowds, serenity.

PLACES TO STAY

Fonde del Sol has rooms for two for Q23 ($4.50US) without bath. It is quiet, clean, pleasant and has a large common room in which to read or visit. The rooms with bath are Q40 for two and are spectacular. They are large, clean and bright with toilet seat lids and very hot water all day. This is truly a good buy if comfort is in need. The hotel is on the main street when coming from Solola.

Hotel Galindo is Q60 ($12. US) for two with hot water, private bath and toilet seat lids. The garden in the center of the court yard is claimed to be the most beautiful in all of Guatemala, and I have no reason to disbelieve this. In the restaurant, you will find the best cevichi in Panajachel. The hotel is located on the main road, past the bus stop (just past the curve).

Mi Chasita costs Q19 ($3.80 US) for two without bathrooms, and it is about the cleanest of all low price accomodations. It glitters, and there are no bed bugs. In order to get hot water in the shower, you must ask the owner to turn on an electric switch which is safely tucked away in her kitchen. This hotel is on the main street that goes towards the lake. There is a sign about halfway down the road, directing the way to the hotel.

Las Casitos is across from the market in the old town. It is nice, quiet, and clean with hot water and private baths for Q36 ($7.25 US) for two. This is an excellent deal. Unfortunately, many places near the old town go unnoticed.

Zanahorria Chik Hotel or the "little carrot hotel" is half a block from the cathedral, going back towards the center of the new town. This is a delightful little place which is clean and cosy. The price without bath is Q15 ($3. US) for 1, Q26 ($5.20 US) for two and Q37 ($7.50 US) for three. The restaurant downstairs serves a variety of natural juices for breakfast.

Hospadaje Pana is in the old town across from that Gato Negro Cantina and up from the Zanahorria. The cost is Q18.70 ($3.75 US) for two with hot water but no private baths. The owner also has a small place where you can have drinks.

Hospadaje Eli is new and just past the Pana. There are only four rooms with general bath and hot water. They charge Q18.70 ($3.75 US) for two and if you want quiet and privacy in Pana this is the place. Because it is new, I don't know how good it will be in the future.

Santander is just before Mario's. There are no private baths and no singles. The price is Q18 ($3.75 US) for 2, Q22 ($4.50 US) for three and is a favorite for many travellers, but I find it dark and depressing. I think there are better places in town.

Maya Palace is right on the main drag by the bus stop, but is not recommended as the acoustics are so good that you hear everything that goes on in town all night long. It is also expensive at Q50 ($10. US) for a double per night. They do have private showers and lots of hot water.

Casa Linda is on a side street behind the Maya Palace. The cost is Q30 ($6.US) for a double. It is clean, friendly and quiet. There is, sometimes, hot water in the morning. There is a lovely garden to sit in during the day. The real problem with this hotel is the unreliability of the water. The hot water goes off and on, and sometimes there is no water at all.

Santa Elena Anexo is at the lake-end of town. Just walk down the main street. It is a neat little red and white place that is very clean. The price is Q10 ($2. US) per person.

Marios is a favorite with travellers. The rooms cost Q10 ($2. US) per person; they are clean and safe. If you ask the owner, he will provide hot water by stoking the stove and heating the pipes.

RESTAURANTS

La Unica Deli is on the bus route but up past the fork. There is a beautiful garden in which to sit and the food is excellent; fresh buns, real butter and homemade yogurt. Everything is spotless. This is not usually a supper spot but is excellent for breakfast and lunch.

The Circus Bar is on the left hand fork of the bus route. This is "the bar" in town, but only on weekends. There is live entertainment and most tourists visit for an evening or two. There is a cover charge on weekends. For desert, try the Calypso: kahlua, cognac, ice cream, whipped cream and chocolate syrup.

The Vegetarian Restaurant is down from the Circus. The portions are very good, but they are small. They have a weekly rotating menu; the lasagne is excellent.

The Last Resort is one of the better places to eat. To get there, turn left at Mario's. They serve a huge meal with seven different kinds of vegetables. Prices are reasonable, but please, don't insult the waitress, or you will starve to death before she serves you. If you are eating sit at the tables; only if you are drinking do you sit at the bar. If you have been in Central America for any length of time and need some meat, the filet mignon is a great treat.

El Patio is the restaurant in the center of town on the main street where all the gringos go for everything from American news to backgammon to supper. The meals are good, and the coffee is excellent. If you should need a money changer, this is the place. Otherwise, try the barber shop. The bank only changes American traveller's cheques.

Hotel Galindo is a nice place to have a meal. It is a tad expensive, but the ceviche is excellent. The atmosphere is nice, and the service is very good.

Fonda del Sol is the hotel on the main street, before the Maya Palace, and the food is very good. The portions are quite large and many gringos eat there. Prices are not out of line.

The Blue Bird is another excellent place to eat where you can get a lot for a little. Pizza and stuffed peppers are my favorite from this place. This is a popular place and often full of travellers.

THINGS TO DO

Cycling The return trip around the lake to Santa Catarina and San Antonio is only about 25 kilometers; certainly not a difficult day. Bikes may be rented from a shop past the Last Resort or from another shop which is on the main bus route. Walk towards the market and the shop is on your left hand side. The prices are about Q10 per hour, depending on your ability to bargain. The bikes are ten speeds, and generally in fairly good shape.

Santa Catarina is only about five kilometers away and you can either walk or cycle. It is a little village where Indians wear only traditional dress. The purpose of visiting here would be for the exercise, not the excitement.

San Antonio is beyond Santa Catarina, and the ride is pleasant. The peaceful countryside makes the trip pleasant; it can be walked or cycled. Walking to and from San Antonio would be a difficult day, but there are frequent buses between here and Pana. There are a couple of expensive hotels in the vicinity of San Antonio - not our type.

Hiking around the lake is a wonderful way to enjoy some of the real Guatemala. There are many ways to do this. A day hike would be to San Jorge and back to Pana or the other way to San Antonio and Santa Catarina (see above). Another is to go to Santa Cruz and then continue around to Santiago. This would take a couple of days. Hiking some of the volcanoes is also a possibility by making Santiago your headquarters. For specific directions see below. All these trips can be supplemented by taking a boat from one destination or the other.

Hike Around Lake Atitlan

The Hike to San Jorge is an easy day hike. Go to the Vision Azul Hotel on the road toward Solola. Turn down the road towards the hotel and continue past the hotels to the two abandoned condo buildings by the lake. These buildings were built by a group of rich Ladino men. However, before completion, they ran into many problems, one of them being that the buildings were sinking into the ground so they had to be condemned. When you come to the buildings, there is a road that goes towards Santa Cruz. Continue along this road and it will soon turn into a path. This path goes all along the side of the mountain and in some places is a bit dangerous. Be careful. The path goes down to the lake at the river flats and has a nice pebbly beach. From there, the Indians say the trail is very dangerous if going to Santa Cruz. I recommend going down through Solola instead of this way. However there is an excellent road going to San Jorge. The village of San Jorge is a pleasant little village where one can still see life without the tourist. When you are on the flats, you will see the road going up the hill. Take that to get to the village and then back onto the road going to Solola.

Solola to Santa Cruz is the best way to get to Santa Cruz. Go to Solola, walk through town and over the bridge at the far end of town. Ask for the bridge or road to Santa Cruz. Then, follow that road all the way. It is a beautiful, pleasant, hot trip which requires two to three hours. Returning would take much longer, especially in the heat.

Santa Cruz has a small basic hospedaje plus a few cabins owned by an American. However, these places are often full so give yourself enough time to either catch a boat or walk further to San Pedro. The rooms at Santa Cruz cost Q20 per person; if all the rooms are occupied, you may be able to share with another gringo.

Walking from **Santa Cruz to San Pedro** is pleasant and wonderful. I recommend it highly. The walk which takes six or seven hours is along an excellent, undulating gravel road. Food and drinks are available at the villages along the way but there are no places to stay. San Marcos is known for its coffee and San Pablo is known for its rope. At San Pablo you can see the men soaking, scraping, twisting and drying the leaves that make the rope. This is an interesting process. The people along here are camera shy so please be sensitive.

Walking from Santa Cruz, you will first pass **Tzununa** which has a population of less than 1000. This village is reputed to have the best fruits in all of Guatemala; if possible, buy some for your long day.

San Marcos is the next village, followed by San Pablo and then San Juan. At this point, stay along the lake as the road ascends. The lake route is easier and you may be able to go for a swim. Enjoy your walk, talk to the people, and start dreaming about the beer you are going to drink when you reach San Pedro. Once at San Juan, you only have about half an hour left to hike.

San Pedro to Santiago can be hiked along the road behind Volcan San Pedro, but it is 16 kilometers of uninteresting dirt road. There is a much shorter and more pleasant trail around the front of the mountain. When you get to the peninsula, try and get someone to row you across rather than walking; if this is not possible, you will need an extra hour to walk around the peninsula. The trip around the front of the volcano is around four to five hours. Like San Pedro, Santiago is not a pleasant place to visit because the tourists have created a negative effect on the Indian. This and the oppression the Indian has suffered have caused unpleasant results. Walking around the rest of the lake in this direction is not fun as it is a long hot road. Take a boat back to Pana from Santiago.

SAN PEDRO DE ATITLAN

San Pedro was once a wonderful, sleepy village that most people did not visit. However, the drug burn-outs have found it and again, I recommend that this place be avoided. It is really too bad, and I can only feel ashamed and sad.

PLACES TO STAY

Chuazanahi El Sol is Q16.50 ($3.25 US) for two or Q7.70 ($1.75 US) for a single. Baths are available, but the water is cold. The rooms are clean. The hotel which is on the lake, has wonderful views. Barbeque facilities are available for your use.

Hospadaje Tikaaj is closer to the dock and is Q7 ($1.50 US) per person. It is not as nice as Chauzanahi but is definitely acceptable. If you want to stay for an extended period, you can get better rates.

RESTAURANTS

Comedor in Chuazanahi has excellent banana pancakes served with a chocolate sauce. These are the best in Guatemala; every time I think of them I get a craving for more. They are also the only reason to go to San Pedro.

La Ultima Cena (the last supper) is up the hill from the hotel. Take the right hand fork past the cathedral. There are three pictures at the entrance: one of the Last Supper, one of Jesus, and the best one, of two tigers. Gringos eat here but I found the service slow, the meal small - certainly nothing to write home about. Be certain to purchase some buns at the panaderia just before the restaurant. They will delay your hunger pains while waiting for dinner in this restaurant.

THINGS TO DO

Hike San Pedro Volcano. This is the smallest of the three volcanos and sits at 3000 meters (under 10,000 ft.). However, the mountain is heavily covered with vegetation which makes it difficult to see the views. There are better hikes in Guatemala. If you decide to go, ask for directions in town. It takes about three or four hours to ascend and a few hours to descend.

SANTIAGO de ATITLAN

This is a wonderful little village on the far side of the lake. I like the village despite its latest tale of horrors. The military went into the village just before Christmas 1990, and killed many women and children. This is not an unusual event in Guatemala, but this time the Indians got to the foreign journalists before the government did and international attention was focused on the town. Now, you may see graffiti with the word "Santiago" printed. The "t" is made in the shape of the Christian cross and has droplets of blood dripping from the cross. Military men were charged and convicted of the crimes. However, it does not take much imagination to figure out what will really happen to these men. Indian life in Guat is worth less than the falling coffee market.

Santiago is full of ladies weaving and selling their goods. The ladies of this village are noted for their head dress known as a "halo". It is a strip of embroidered material that is ten meters long and is wrapped around and around the head, holding up the hair. These head dresses are very attractive.

When arriving at Santiago by boat, you will see the ladies washing clothes in the lake; the scum from the soap deters swimming in the lake for conservation minded people.

Santiago has a special service on Good Friday. The people re-enact the crucifixion of Christ, put his body in a coffin, and parade the coffin through the streets. This is a very colorful and religious event. Santiago also has a carving of Maximon, a cigar smoking saint who is usually not highly revered in other villages during Easter but is actually part of the Easter celebrations in this village. The treatment of Maximon caused some problems a few years ago; the president of the country intervened on behalf of the people, and they are again able to have this unpopular saint as part of their Easter ceremony.

PLACES TO STAY

Pension Rosita costs Q8 ($1.50 US) per person and is past the market by the school. It is basic with communal bath and cold water.

Chi Nim Ya is below the market on the lake side of town. It is very clean for Q10 per person ($2.50 US). There are also a few rooms with private bath for double the price. There is only cold water.

RESTAURANTS

Xocomil Restaurant is clean and the food is good. It is up the hill from the Rosita. Xocomil is the name of the wind that comes up on the lake every afternoon and takes away the bad spirits.

El Gran Sol is a little place that has a view to accompany the food which you will enjoy. There are not many special places to eat in Santiago. If you want quality food, you will have to go back to Panajachel.

THINGS TO DO

Hike Toliman Volcano This is a good hike to over 3000 meters (10,000 feet). It takes at least five or six hours to go up and then, if you have any strength left in your legs, another four or five to come down. The hike starts at 1600 meters (5200 ft.) so you are half way up at the starting gate. However, to gain 1400 meters is a long and difficult day, even without a big pack and in cool weather. Once up over the 8000 ft. level, the temperature will start to cool. Before climbing this mountain, ask around to make certain there has been no trouble in the area. Do not hike in this area alone and be certain to take lots to eat and drink. There are no restaurants on the way up.

POPTUN

This is a grand stopping place when on the way to Tikal. Although the sites in this village of 6000 are limited, the caves in the area are interesting to visit. There is a military base here so you will see a lot of guns, and you may be occasionally checked. The Finca Ixobele received international attention when the owner was tortured and killed by the military for unknown reasons. His wife insisted on the American government's intervention after the death. This event occurred close to the time that the military massacred some people in Santiago de Atitlan, so there was some bad press for Guatemala for a while. The wife of the finca owner received some money as compensation for the deed, and some military officials were tried and convicted. However, I am very skeptical as to what really happened to the officers. The real cause of the murder is not known despite numerous rumors. The most likely possibility is that Mike, the deceased, saw something the military did not want him seeing. This is a good lesson in only going where others say it is safe. There have been other disappearances in Guatemala and I would hate a carrier of this book to suffer the same fate.

PLACES TO STAY

Hospadaje Poptun is in the town of Poptun. The price is Q10 ($2.40 US) per person and the rooms are simple and clean. This hotel is available if you can't get to the finca.

Finca Ixobele is about three kilometers before the town of Poptun. The bus drivers will let you out at the end of the road which goes to the Finca. The Finca is a lovely guest ranch that costs Q10 ($2.40 US) per person. It can accommodate at least five in this building and the same number in another building. The beds are large, soft and very warm. The buildings are similar to the type younger children sleep in when at camp. There is also camping available at Q4 ($.75 US) per person; people camp in huts that are raised from the ground. If the accommodations are full, the proprietor has extra sleeping bags and a couple of cleaned-out chicken coops that he will allow people to use. The owner never turns a person away. At one time they had fifty people to accommodate; it was a bit crowded, but not a single person complained.

The main house has parrots for pets; they will gladly eat your leftovers. However, one parrot doesn't like crusts. Breakfast and lunch may be ordered for a very reasonable price. A family-style dinner is served at 6:30PM. There is no choice for dinner, but it always includes a fresh salad. It is an excellent meal and second helpings are available at no extra charge.

Since the owner Miguel (Mike) was killed, I do not know how well the place is operating. I understand that friends are now running the place.

THINGS TO DO

Maya wall carving is in the village. It is very attractive. The market is small and does not take long to visit.

The Caves are the greatest attraction to the area. One trip is a two hour hike through deep, slimy mud, steaming jungles and coffee plantations. This cave has three rooms with pools of water; one room vampire bats. The owner of the finca will give you a map to follow in order to get there.

The second cave trip takes all day and must be done with a guide. This cave has a pool of water that one must swim through in order to get into the cave. This is a favorite. However, it may take a day or so to arrange the trip, so allow yourself enough time. You can organize this trip from the finca.

The third cave trip is a three day hike through the jungle with guides and donkeys. The cave has many original Mayan drawings. Some of the artifacts found there are thought to be from about 300 BC. There is a nice photo album in the finca that has pictures of all three hikes.

With Tikal and Chichicastenango, I feel that this place is a must.

PUETRO BARRIOS

This is a bustling little Carib town of 25,000 people which is neither spectacular nor interesting. In fact, it is hot, humid and boring during the day. I understand that the night life is more active. But, it is a jump off spot for ferry, train and bus exchange. It is also fairly close to Lake Isabel. Therefore, there are many hotels and restaurants. Seafood is the specialty of the day.

Puerto Barrios was named after president Justo Rufino Barrios who is commonly known as the "Great Reformer". Too bad he didn't have more of an influence on this town.

The ferry leaves for Livingston at 10:30AM and 5:00PM daily. It leaves for Punta Gorda, Belize on Tuesdays and Fridays. If you want to pay the price, many private boats go to Honduras, Livingston and Belize.

PLACES TO STAY

Hotel Caribeña on Ave 4 between Calles 10 & 11 costs Q10.50 ($2.20 US) per person and looks like the best buy in town. It is clean and cheery. A good place.

Hotel Palaco de Cine is a great rambling old building that has rooms for Q5 ($1. US) per person but, of course, no private bath. This is a popular place to stay.

Hotel Europa on 8 Ave, 9-84, phone 480127. This is a great place for Q25 ($5. US) for a double.It is also clean and cheery and always full, so you should book ahead. If you do not want to stay in Quirigua and arrive late . phone and reserve a room.

Hotel **Tacana** on 8 Ave costs Q33.55 ($6.75 US) for a double with bath and Q14 ($2.80 US) for a single. This is a nice place but a bit pricey.

Xelaju Hotel is another great big rambling building near the bus terminal that runs at Q5.50 ($1.25 US) per person without private bath. Of course every place in Barrios is only a one tap shower; this is all that is required here.

Pension Nineth along the tracks costs Q5 ($1. US) per person. It is quite friendly, often full but quite drab. This is only with general bath.

RESTAURANTS

Hotel **Caribeña** serves great banana milk shakes to start your day but forget the coffee - it is instant.

Hotel **El Norte** had meals that are large and reasonable in price. This is okay.

Pier The places along the docks near the ferry are about the best places to eat. Prices are low and the quality is high. There is more spice used and indigenous cooking is available.

THINGS TO DO

Get on a bus or a boat.

PUERTO SAN JOSE

San Jose is a bustling little port town of 10,000 people which sits on the Pacific coast. There are black sand beaches, but I would suggest that you stay on the bus another half an hour and go to a quieter spot like Iztapa. However, if you need money, San Jose is the place to exchange as Iztapa does not have a bank.

PLACES TO STAY

Posada Quetzal has nice little huts that are clean. They are building more new ones. They run a bit more than Q25 ($5. US) per person. This is with private bath.

Hotel Azule is on the main road to Esquintla and is very clean, with a swimming pool, restaurant and hot shower but they charge a high price and who wants hot water in this heat?

RESTAURANTS

I cannot recommend better places to eat than the cafes and comadors along the beach. The sea food is always good. The prices are a bit higher than some smaller towns but there is more variety of fish.

THINGS TO DO

Go to the beach. The sand is black but San Jose is a port town and it is not my favorite beach. Other than sunning yourself, you may go to the market, eat, sleep, get money and drink beer.

QUETZALTENANGO or XELA or XELAJU

Xela is a beautiful town, second largest in Guatemala with a population of about 65,000 people. Xela sits at 2333 meters (6750 ft.) above sea level so the temperature may be a bit chilly. During the rainy season, it is very cold. The name Xelaju is from the Quiche Kingdom and means "under the ten hills" which accurately describes this city. Quetzaltenango means place of the quetzal.

It is near here that Pedro de Alvarado defeated Tecun Uman, the famous Indian leader. You will find a statue of this proud man in town.

Xela is a rival of Guatemala City and is often the home of famous poets and writers. The light air increases brain activity on the right side of the cranium.

At one time Xela was aligned with Mexico but later joined the Federation of Central America as the capital of the state of Los Altos. This was eventually amalgamated into the state of Guatemala. After a few skirmishes, Xela became the capital of the state of Quetzaltenango.

If you are planning to attend a language school, Xela is a great spot. There is little English in the area and there are many close and interesting excursions.

When you arrive, you will find the bus stop at least two kilometers from the town square. It is best to take the bus into town; walk toward the center of town and take bus # 7. If you want to take this bus to go to either the first or second class bus station you catch it on 13 Ave, 7 Calle, just behind the square, across from Hotel Kiktem-ja (around the cine).

PLACES TO STAY

Casa Kaeler on 13 Ave, Calle is the best buy in town for a double. The lady tries to get all she can so be careful. She charges Q29 or 33 ($6. or $7. US) for a double and just over half for a single. In slow season, she may barter. There are some private baths and there is hot water anytime. One must have a match to light the tank which gives instant hot water. You may wash and hang your clothes in the courtyard. The building is not overly warm. The muchachas that work here are wonderful and if you can sneak your laundry to them without the grand dam finding out, please do. They do not over-charge, do a fine job and need the money.

Radar 99 is next door to the Casa Kaehler on 13 Ave, Calle 3. They charge Q7.70 ($1.50 US) per person with hot showers down the hall and no private baths. This place was once very dirty but they have cleaned up their act and it is now clean and pleasant. If Casa Kaeler gives you a bad time, go here.

Casa Swiza on 14 Ave. and Calle 2 is fairly decent. It is not what I call spotless, but you will be safe and the water is hot all day.

The rooms are large with private bathrooms. There is also a restaurant. If you wash clothes, you may hang them in the courtyard. A single costs Q20 ($4. US) and a double is Q35.40 ($7.US). Be careful with your change here as the owners have a tendency to forget to return the correct amount.

Modelo is directly across the street from the Suiza but is quite expensive. However, if you are cold, weary and/or miserable, it may be worth your money to warm up in this chilly town. A double room is Q75 ($15. US). All the rooms have a fireplace and a private bath with hot water. The beds are soft and have thick wool blankets. There is a first class restaurant in this hotel.

Gran Hotel Americana has singles for Q39 ($8. US), doubles for Q49 ($10. US) and triples for Q54 ($11. US). The rooms are clean with private bathrooms and hot water. There is drinking water in the hallway if you want to make coffee in your room.

Hotel Quetzalteco on 12 Ave, 3-06 costs Q8 ($1.75 US) per person without bath and cold water showers only. There are better places for this price. However, the owner is quite pleasant and very accustomed to gringos.

Pension San Nicolas on 12 Ave and 3 Calle costs Q 11 ($2.20 US) for a double. The rooms are large but there is only cold water in the shower. There is a pretty patio in the center of the hotel. This is one of the better places in Xela.

Pension El Aquila costs Q4 ($.80 US) for a single, Q6 ($1.20 US) for a double and Q9 ($1.80 US) for a triple. These are small dark rooms and not very clean. Stay here only when desperate.

Rio Azul on 2 Calle 12-15 costs Q40 ($8 US) for a double with private bath and hot water all day with the immersion type heaters. Very clean and bright. This would be my second choice in Xela.

Hotel Kiktem-ja is on 13 Ave. and Calle 7 and just up from the cinema, one block from the square. It is a grand old building which has been very well kept. It was built in the traditional old Spanish fortress style and the rooms are situated around a courtyard. There are private baths with hot water from six in the morning until one in the afternoon. The cost is Q58.50 ($11.50 US). I quite liked this place as it is peaceful and clean. If you want an alternative to the Modelo, then try this one.

RESTAURANTS

Pension Boniface costs Q200 to stay for the night. Suppers look good but are quite pricey. Due to prices, beer is untouchable. Generally, it is not recommended for the chickenbus crowd; however, the restaurant serves the best plate of hotcakes in Xela with all the coffee you can drink for 10Q ($2.US).

Restaurant Arthurs is between Casa Kaeler (up the hill and turn left) and the Modelo. This is a small but good restaurant with very reasonable prices. They serve salad dressing, which is a treat in Guat, with their salad!

Restaurant Americana on 14 Ave 3-45 has a great cup of coffee with refills. The omelets use processed cheese, but the fruit salad is genuine. Good place.

Shanghai Restaurant is just off the square, next to the luxurious Plaza Hotel. Good food (Chinese only) at reasonable prices. Meals are not huge, but they are sufficient after a day's hiking. Fast service makes me believe it is pre-prepared.

Hotel Modelo on 14 Ave is recommended for superb meals. The service is quick, the meals are large and tasty, and the hotel is spotless. For these services you may have to pay a bit more.

Bombonier Pasteleria on 14 Ave and Calle 2. This is a nice place to have coffee and a real doughnut at midday. The doughnuts are recommended, and the service is excellent.

Cafeteria El Kopetin on 14 Ave, 3 Calle has good food and the prices are reasonable. The service is perfect. This is a good place to have a leisurely dinner.

Grizzly Pizza is on 14 Ave and is recommended by all the locals as the place to eat. The pizza is good and the service is not too slow as long as all the teenagers are not having their pizza at the same time. If they are, then the service seems to go to the best looking boy, not the highest tipper. They will turn down the music if you ask.

Taberna de Don Rodrigo on 14 Ave is an excellent bar for small snacks and a beer. The dark beer here is good. They also serve bocas, but they will charge you extra. Unless you want bocas, be certain to refuse them. However, this bar has withstood the test of time and is still offering the same quality service as it did many years ago when I first came to Guat.

THINGS TO DO

Central Park is one of the nicest in Guatemala. The new cathedral has been re-built beside the old one which now has only an outer face. The rest has been destroyed. The new cathedral has beautiful solid silver altars and a very ornate chapel. Two of the alcoves contain hand-carved cases, made of many types of hard-woods, which contain statues of Jesus. The wood is beautiful, some being local cedar and some being Honduran hardwood.

Municipal Museum is open Monday to Saturday from 8:00AM to 12:00PM and 2:00PM to 6:00PM. It is on the south side of the central park. This small museum includes interesting natural history, archaeology and botanical displays. The most interesting section is downstairs where they have musical instruments and fiesta masks. There are often art exhibitions held next door to the museum; these are well worth visiting.

The Government Buildings (Palacio Municipal) are next to the cathedral and, except for the courtyard which contains a modern sculpture of Tecun Uman, the patron saint of Xela, are of little interest.

The Bank of Guatemala on the square will change foreign currency other than American. Go as soon as it opens, and tell them you want to change the type of currency you have (in traveller's cheques only) then they will call Guatemala City for the exchange rate. Return in a few hours and they will joyfully do business with you.

Cultural Building 1 Calle and Ave. 14 is a beautiful old Greek style building with Doric columns in the front. The sculpturing on the walls includes many Indian musical instruments. There is a lovely fountain and a marble bust of Ozmundo Arriola, the poet laureate of Xela. On the other side of the building is a marble bust of Jesus Casille, who resurrected an interest in the music of the Maya Quiche Indians. He died in 1936.

Cerro El Baul is a lovely national park overlooking the city. You may either walk or take a taxi for a few quetzales; the view is wonderful. On Sundays, there are concerts on the hill, and you may use the barbecue facilities provided. There is no camping on the hill. There is a giant slide for children and the adults also seem to enjoy it.

Lake Chicabal is a wonderful hike and can be done in two ways. You may take the San Martin de Chile Verde bus to the village of San Martin. The Indian dialect here is said to be so different that other tribes do not understand it. The ride is one hour. Take fluids to drink as the hike is two to three hours with an elevation gain of around 500 meters (1600 ft). You will start at 2377 meters (7800 ft) so you do go up quite high.

Take the path behind the church and wind your way through the village until you come to the main trail which runs along the fields. Follow this for about an hour and a half, crossing quite a few small bridges. The trail passes many Indian houses where you may see corn drying, wood being gathered, weaving or washing being done and many friendly people trying to talk to you. When you come to a second settlement, you will find a church on your left, followed by a school which has a water tap across the trail from it. This is where you turn and go directly up to the ridge. When at the top, follow the trail that has obviously been used for centuries because it is about half meter below the surface of the land. Follow this down into the valley, through corn fields, veering to your right until you come to a main road (unpaved). Turn left and go up (again). You have only about half an hour left. You may follow this trail back out to the main road where you can catch the bus back to Xela. However, at the lake, the water is a wonderful green-blue and there are crosses found around the lake which serve as altars. Please do not touch any of the crosses.

If you want to go to the lake the easier way, but miss much of the isolated village life, ask the driver to let you off at the Laguna de Chicabal Road which is past San Martin Chile Verde. I much prefer to go the other way.

Aguas Caliente de Georginas are a must. These hot springs are found high in the mountains in one of the nicest settings I have ever seen. The pool is tucked into a corner of the mountain with a high rock wall behind it. The statue in the center is new, and maybe the hot water will one day melt her. The springs were much nicer before they decorated.

To get there, hire a taxi behind the cathedral in the central park. It should cost about Q30-Q50 ($6.-$10. US) for a one way ride. You may also take a bus to the village of Zunil and walk the rest of the nine kilometers. This is okay if you start early in the morning or stay the night on the mountain. The huts at the hot springs cost Q50 ($10. US) for a double and have been recently renovated and cleaned. They have thermal tubs in every bungalow. There is also a place to eat at the hot springs but it isn't fancy. It is easy to hitch a ride both up and down the mountain from Zunil.

On the way to the hot springs there was a village where the government conducted geothermal explorations. Late in 1990, the mountain blew up, burying ten houses and killing 28 people. Now the Indians of that area do not want geothermal power. You can see this accident from the road you will be walking on; watch for a place across and below your route. It is obvious that the mountain has partly blown away from the side of the hill.

Rock Climbing can be done near Xela. Charles Montgomery of Duncan, B.C. writes about climbing:

The high point of my travels! Near Quetzaltenango is the only decent rock climbing in Guatemala, on a spectacular crag thousands of feet above the valley. The two experienced climbers in Xela are anxious to show travellers this breathtaking crag, in exchange for climbing gear or a small donation to help pay for their future expeditions. Contact:

Miguel & Luis Arango Morales
4 Calle, Diagonal 3-67, Zona 1
Quetzaltenango, Guatemala

These two men are experienced rock climbers, exceptionally generous and friendly. Climbers, donate new or used "Friends" or "Cumalots" (#1,2,3) and webbing. This would be appreciated as good gear is very expensive or unobtainable. If you are not going to take gear, then contribute Q50 ($10 US) for a wonderful day with a couple of locals that know where it is at.

Salcaja is a village which is half an hour from Xela and 2329 meters (7600 ft) above sea level. The church of San Jacinto is an example of colonial architecture and is one of the earliest Spanish structures built in Guatemala. The village is also noted for its liquors called "caldo de frutas" and "rompopo". Be certain to try at least one of these delectable drinks. This village is also one place in Guatemala where you will see footloom weaving done by the men. The quality of the work is excellent and should be purchased. Tuesday is market day in this village.

Almolonga is a village four kilometers south of Xela and is noted for the beautiful gardens from which Xela's market receives many goods. There are hot mineral baths in the village, but they are all establishments where one must pay. The three known to me are Cirilo Florex, El Recreo and Villa Alicia. Market days are Wednesday and Saturday, and the leather goods are said to be of high quality.

San Cristobal Totonicapan is only half an hour from Xela. The old Franciscan Church in the town has an excellent example of preserved colonial art. The altar is of chiseled silver and Venetian crystal. Sunday is market day and a good time to purchase some of the hand-woven textiles from the region. The prices are better here than in some of the more popular places. There is a cheap hospadaje in which you may stay if you should want to (I don't know why).

Zunil is a little village only half an hour from Xela. You catch a bus at the main bus station in Xela. They go frequently. Zunil is located on the Salama River and boasts of having the highest geysers in the country. The water in the hot springs is 45ºC. There is a small hospadaje, Aguas Gorginas, which has rooms for Q12 ($2.50US) per person. The rooms are basic with no private baths.

Zunil is noted for its treatment of the saint Maximon. They dress him like a cowboy, feed him booze, light cigarettes for him, and when they think this effigy is drunk, change him into pajamas and put him to bed. On other special days, they dress him accordingly and continue to include him in the celebrations.

Olintepeque is about fifteen minutes from Xela by the Xequijel River. The town is of interest because this is the sight of the bloodiest battle between the Spanish conquistadores and the Quiche Indians. The leader, Tecun Uman, fought until he was killed and the water ran red with blood. The word "xequijel" means blood in Quiche.

SPANISH SCHOOLS

English Club of Quetzaltenango is on 3 Calle and 15 Ave, Zone 1, near the post office. Telephone 8903. They also teach classes in Quiche and Mam. The course includes five hours of study, room and board (three meals a day), washing of clothes and any materials used in class. The cost is $100.US per week with no discounts for longer stays.

International School of Spanish offers the same services as the one above but the prices are $75.US for each week, $55.US per week without room and board and $50.US per week for classes only but for four hours daily. For more information go to 8 Ave, 6-33, Zone 1 or telephone 4784.

S.A.B. Spanish School is one that is in the center of town and offers room and board with a modest family at $125.US per week. If you would prefer living with an upper middle class family, the cost would be $50. per week higher. You also have the choice of taking lessons only, no room and board, for $60. US per week. There are separate classes for beginners and for advanced students. This school also has specialty classes for anthropologists, sociologists, doctors, nurses, missionaries, volunteer organization workers, travel agents, hotel employees, airline personnel, translators and so on. If you are looking for advanced learning, this may be the school you need. For further information, contact the school at Apartado Postal 187, Quetzaltenango.

Instituto Central America is on 1 Calle, 16-93, Zone 1 and was highly recommended by some people including Allan Weeks from St. Albert. To enquire, telephone 011-502-961-6786. The school offers a home with a family plus language instruction with experienced teachers, on a one-to-one bases. The school also offers Cultural Conferences weekly and occasional field trips to local places of significance. The school is small enough to provide a sense of community and support. They only take ten students. This is where those that are truly interested in learning Spanish should first try.

QUIRIGUA

This is a very small town of 1300 people just three kilometers from the Quirigua Ruins. The town itself is quite friendly. The only place in town at which to eat or stay is the Hotel Royal, and if you can, avoid staying there. There are very few street stalls. The location of the town makes it very hot; the walk to the ruins is hot but interesting.

PLACES TO STAY

Hotel Royal charges Q50 for two with private bath and Q25 for two without bath or fan. The place is clean but basic. The owner has the attitude she is doing you a big favor for being there. I felt very unwelcome and uncomfortable here. The final straw (not on the bed) was that according to the government, this lady is only supposed to charge Q10 and Q15 ($3. US) for a room. She does not post her rates and she does not give receipts. I really recommend going elsewhere.

Hotel Santa Monica is just three kilometers down the road, closer to Guatemala City. The hotel is behind the Texaco Station. They have new and clean rooms for Q25 ($5.US) per person. This includes a private bath. Get a room at the back so that the traffic will not bother you plus you have a better view.

RESTAURANTS

Hotel Royal is the only place at which you can sit and eat. The food is okay but not anything more. There are ladies that sell things on the street that may be better. However, there is no market in the area where there are real stalls.

THINGS TO DO

Quirigua Ruins To get to the ruins, walk left from the hotel, past the post office, down the hill to the tracks. Follow the tracks that veer to the right and through the center of the banana plantation owned by Del Monte. Going this way is quite short. If you miss the curve and end at the gravel road, turn right down the road until you get to the entrance. Both walks go through the plantation. The bananas are bagged to prevent bruising.

Once at the ruins, you will find a well kept national park that has some spectacular stelae and zoomorphs. They are all covered with thatched huts for protection and arranged in the main plaza of the old city. The stair case is well reconstructed and interesting as it has two ramps that are slopes with only some sculpturing in the center instead of stairs. This is similar to Chinese style, in which the king was carried over the ramp. Only the peasants or slaves walked up the stairs. This ruin is excellent.

Quirigua is similar to Copan in its style of stelae and carvings. Quirigua is believed to have been settled around 200BC; the people traded constantly with Copan. Quirigua was first discovered by Stephens and Catherwood; they made fabulous drawings of the stelae and zoomorphs. The Carnegie Institution and other US universities have conducted excavations here.

One stelae in the courtyard stands 26 feet high and is carved all around. The detail in the carving will keep you busy for hours interpreting. There is also one zoomorph that, to me appears to be a turtle. There are many different types of carvings around the main figure.

If you are unable to get to Copan to see some of the excellent ruins there, be certain not to miss this ruin.

There are small tiendes outside the ruins where you can get something to drink and a few snacks to eat. The walk back will be hot.

RETALHULEU

The population of Retalhuleu or Reu for short is 22,000 people and the town sits only 240 meters (790 ft) above sea level. It is hot and humid but not as bad as along the coast.

Reu is where you can change buses for Guat City, Coatepeque, Xela or the border. Reu is a friendly place because tourists are a rare phenomenan. The central park is attractive. You could stay here for a day with no problem. However, the population is mostly Latin, not Indian.

PLACES TO STAY

Hotel Hillman is on Ave. 7, 7-99, Zone 1. The rooms are Q16 ($3.25US) for a double and Q12 ($2.50 US) for a single. The rooms are small and without bath. There is a garage in which to park your chickenfleas. The owners are friendly.

Hotel Pacifico is on Ave. 7 just up from the Hillman and on the same side of the street. The cost is Q6 ($1.25US) per person without bath. This place is really basic and the owners think gringos should go first class, not the cheapest class.

Hotel Astor is on 5 Calle 4-60 and is more expensive from the other two so you will get quite a bit more. The cost is Q30 ($6. US) for a double with a private bath, towels and friendly owners.

RESTAURANTS

There are a few but nothing that I found that was exceptional. You are on your own here. This town is fairly close to Champerico where there is lots of sea food so my interest was not in eating pollo in Reu.

THINGS TO DO

Parque Central is pleasant with lots of shade trees. The cathedral was build in the 1700s and the silver ornaments that are in the church were donated by the Indians in 1720. There is also a pretty fountain one block away from the square.

Reu is about one hour from Champerico and there are frequent buses. If Chamerico is not where you want to spend the night, (it is hot) you may want to return to Reu after supper. There are buses going all day.

Happy family

SACAPULAS

This little town of less than 2000 sits at 1200 meters (3800 ft) above sea level. This is an interesting village because the Indians are quite unique in their choice of jewelry. They wear silver adornments with colonial and Peruvian coins attached. The ladies wear huipiles which have geometric designs on a white background. Some like to wear lace. The white is to reflect the hot sun's rays.

The Indians in this area extract salt from the mud using a primitive method. They dig the mud and the salt from the river bank of the Rio Negro and then, by drying and filtering, they extract the mud and are left with the salt.

PLACES TO STAY

Pension Gloris is the only place to stay in town. It is a basic, no frills place for Q5 ($1. US) per person. It is clean and safe. There are a few comedors in town where you can get a meal.

THINGS TO DO

The Colonial Church was built in 1554 and has some lovely silver treasures. The convent housed Bartholomè de las Casas, a Dominican friar and bishop, who was a great protector of the Indians. Too bad he wasn't still alive today!

The bridge built by las Casas in the 16th century over the Rio Negro is long gone. Its construction was quite a feat at that time because of the swiftness of the water. Today, there is a modern bridge near the same spot and it is named after las Casas.

There are communal **hot springs** near the village which you may visit. The people dip the water out in buckets and take manual showers instead of jumping into them. This is not a cold village, and hot springs in a warm climate are not quite as attractive as they are higher in the mountains. The climate here is hot; therefore, these hot springs don't have as much appeal as when in a cold climate.

SANTA MARIA DE JESUS - see Antigua

SANTIAGO DE ATITLAN - see Panajachel

SAN PEDRO LA LAGUNA - see Panajachel

SAN MARCOS/SAN PEDRO

These two towns are known as the twin cities; from what I could tell, San Marcos is the wealthier section. The population of the two towns is about 20,000. About two kilometers separates the two cities. If you are going to climb Mount Tajumulco, this may be a desired place to stay. From here, it is still a three hour trip to the mountain. The town itself has a busy market but there is a lot of plastic junk for sale.

PLACES TO STAY

Hotel San José costs a mere Q3 per person, but the place is small and dirty. It does have very warm blankets on the beds. There are lots of chickens and ducks in the courtyard, which is a change from the usual array of flowers.

Hotel Bagod is on 5 Calle 3-55 and costs Q9.50 per person ($2. US) and the rooms have private bathrooms. The showers have the immersion type heaters. The rooms with bath are on the 3rd floor, all have tiny balconies and are very clean. The rooms without bath are only Q6 ($1.25 US) and are small.

Hotel Posada Don Luis is on 3 Calle 2-35 and costs Q15 ($3. US) for two and Q20 ($4. US) for three. This is a very secure building. All rooms are without bathrooms. The showers are immersion-type heaters and look a bit dangerous. There is a lovely laundry tub in the hall where one can do washing. There is a restaurant next door.

Pension Terminal is rented by the hour if anyone is interested.

Pension Victoria is on 4 Calle between 8 & 9 Ave. The rooms cost Q5 ($1. US) per person and the building is clean and secure. There is a nice courtyard and a pleasant owner. This is definitely the place to stay.

Maya Hotel As soon as they saw gringo, the price went up. Mom mumbled something around Q8 ($1.60 US) per person, but Papa quickly corrected her. It was Q15 ($3.US). They do have hot water, and it is not right downtown but across from the Maya Palace which is the government house.

Pension Mendez is on 4 Calle 5-45, just off the square, and has rooms for Q3 ($.60 US) per person without bath or hot water. The main attraction is the friendly management.

RESTAURANTS

Cafe Las Brasitas is right on the square and is excellent. The chicken de cebollita is the best I have tasted in this country. The meal was worth coming to visit the town. The cook served the chicken with crisp french fries and with freshly cooked spring peas. I knew they were fresh because I saw him bring them from the market after I ordered. The service was upper French Restaurant style. Good place to have a good meal.

THINGS TO DO

There are **hot springs** just out of town which are worth visiting, even if you do not use them for bathing. From the town square in San Pedro, go towards the canyons. Ask if unsure. Follow the road down into a gully and then up the other side. There are many people going here all the time, so just follow them.

To climb **Mount Tajumulco** you should make your base here at San Marcos/San Pedro. Then, you must be on the first bus going towards Ixchiguan or even as far as the turn off for Tejutla. This is a three-hour ride. Then, you have a few choices. You may walk from the junction of the Tejutla turn off. You may hike or hitch a ride to around kilometer 26 along the road and then head up the mountain. You may also go to the village of San Sebastian and then up to Horqueta which lies between the two peaks. I have never done this hike and only have hearsay as to how to do it. From the start of the hike to the lower crater (there are two) it should not take you more than three or four hours up, but down is also difficult because you must pick your way along boulders.

Mt. Tajumulco is the highest mountain in Central America and sits at 4,217 meters (13,835 ft) above sea level. That is a very long way to hike up in one day; altitude sickness may become a problem. However, if you stay in San Marcos for the night, you will start at 2398 meters (7800 ft) which is more than half way up. Then, the bus will take you up to 3100 meters (10,200 ft) which only leaves you just over 3000 feet to climb. Once over 10,000 feet, the air becomes thinner and the walking much slower. This is not a hike for inexperienced hikers. The temperature gets very cold. You must carry food and lots of water which helps alleviate altitude sickness. Also, you must be able to get back down to a hotel before evening. Before you leave for this hike, be certain to know what time the last bus returns to San Marcos/San Pedro.

Tajumulco is a very old mountain. It is believed this mountain sits on a second mountain. There are two complete craters on this mountain. The second one on the eastern slope, is the higher of the two. If you decide to do this hike, ask many questions around the area before going. I have heard of no robberies on the mountain because it is not a popular hike for gringos. It is also quite difficult to access. Under any circumstances, do not go alone.

SAN FRANCISCO DE ALTO

This interesting village is one hour from Huehuetenango and sits high in the hills. It is clean and friendly and is a bus changing place if going to Momostenango. In order to get to the bus stop for Momo, go all the way through town to the far end. Stop for a meal on the way. The market sells a lot of good quality jute products.

PLACES TO STAY

Hotel Vista Hermosa is the best of the two places in town with rooms at Q8 ($1.75 US) for a single and Q15 ($3. US) for two without bathrooms. The cost is Q17 ($3.40 US) for two with bath. You may wish to commute back and forth from Momo, because these places are better than what you will find in Momo.

San Francisco de Asis Hospadaje is basic and dirty and generally unfriendly. The cost is Q5 ($1. US) per person. The only positive thing about this place were some nice murals in the hallway.

THINGS TO DO

Other than just exploring the tiny villages scattered around the hills or going on to Momo, I know of nothing to do in this area.

SAN PEDRO DE ATITLAN - see Panajachel

SANTA CRUZ DEL QUICHE

This lovely little town has a population of about 9000, sits at 2000 meters (6500 ft) and is chilly at night. This is still a town from the old Guatemala with friendly people and no hustlers or money changers. It is very peaceful. I would highly recommend this village which is just half an hour past the expensive Chichicastenango.

PLACES TO STAY

Travel House on 2 Ave. 7-36 is Q11.70 ($2.40 US) per person. The rooms are without bathrooms, but the showers have hot water. This is the best in town and I highly recommend staying here.

Hotel San Pascual is on Calle 7 and costs Q7 ($1.40) per person without bathrooms. When there is enough power, there is hot water; however, being so far north, the power is often not strong enough to heat the water. The results are obvious.

RESTAURANTS

Cafe Musical is good only for the soup. Other foods are fried in rancid grease and not really edible. I didn't find many places to eat in this town that were good, but maybe you can discover one.

THINGS TO DO

Ruins of K'umarkaaj or Utatlàn. This ancient city was once the capital of the Quiche kingdom between 1250 - 1523AD. In 1523, Alvarado trapped the people inside the city and destroyed the city and people by burning it. The remaining site is a wonderful place to visit.

To get there, follow the road out of town away from the market; ask people and they will point. While walking, veer to the left past a farm then follow that road down and back up again. It is three kilometers from town. You will see a peasant farm with one of the old buildings in the background, but you must go further. There is a tiende across from this farm. Go down the hill; the park on the flat hill in front of you is the site of the ruin.

Visit the small museum which has a small scale model of the old city. There are also some copies of artifacts found in the area. The grounds are lovely and the remains of a few old buildings are visible. Unfortunately, the government has planted trees on the site, and the roots are damaging the remaining structures. The greatest attraction of this ruin is the escape and communication route which goes through a cave below these ruins. To visit, walk to the end of the road past the museum and down the hill. Be certain to take a flash-light when you enter the cave which is hand carved and quite nar-row. It goes for a long way. The Quiche mainly used it as a communication route with other villages.

SANTA LUCIA COTZUMALGUAPA

Population 15,000 and 356 Meters (1150 ft.) above sea level. Because of the elevation and proximity to the ocean, this area is very hot and humid. You should walk or travel slowly and early in the morning. The mid-day should be spent resting in the shade with a cold beer in hand.

This is a pleasant town and if staying here instead of Esquintla, you will not have any problems finding everything you need except good bus service.

PLACES TO STAY

Hotel El Camino on the main road on the far side of town and across from the expensive Santiaguito, the El Camino has rooms for Q20 ($4. US) for a single and Q30 ($6. US) for a double. It is a wonderful place to stay, has a good restaurant and for a price, you can use the pool across the street. There are fans in the rooms, they are clean (the rooms not the fans) and the place is friendly.

RESTAURANTS

There are many places in town to eat including two expen-sive hotels.

THINGS TO DO

Going to the three archaeological sites near Santa Lucia is difficult and the weather is always hot. You may want to get together with a few people and hire a car for the day. In that case, you will have lots of time to see the sights plus sit in the afternoon shade and drink a beer. One of the frustrating facts about these stone carvings is some are fake and some are real; how one tells the difference is beyond my ability. Also copies from one site are on display at another site. These facts could be a deciding factor on whether or not to visit.

In the town square are a few carvings but they are fakes. We know this because some have steel rod reinforcements in them - something that the Olmecs probably did not use. Although the stone heads are fakes, the people in this town are laid back and pleasant. Of course, if you talk to the people they will tell you that the heads are real, which in fact they are. They are just not authentic.

To visit the four fincas where the heads have been found, you will have to walk about twenty kilometers in all. That makes for a long hot day with the longest and hottest walking being around the El Baùl finca. However, you may take a bus to the Finca El Baùl and then walk or hitch back. Once back on the highway, you can take a bus or hitch to the other two fincas, depending on traffic, bus service and the time you have.

Finca El Baùl If walking you should take 4 Ave. until you come to the Calvary Church. Take the paved road to the left and not the dirt one that is almost straight ahead. If going in the morning, it is more than a one hour walk to the finca. In mid-day, it would take about two hours. Once at the finca, you will see lots of stone carvings, some of humans, some of animals, some with arms and legs, others without. Poke around the entire yard and you will see many stones that are of interest and some that make great photos. I really liked the stone tiger sitting up, paws in begging position, large teeth non-threatening. There is also a ball player without his head that makes up a lovely stelae. Rest under a tree before continuing on foot to other sites.

Archaeologists have two schools of thought about these stones, some believing these carvings are from the Olmecs, others believing they are from an earlier civilization. I certainly believe that the Olmecs had an influence in this area because these stones are similar to those in Mexico. I also think that the Indians came to this area in order to convert the coastal pagans to their sophisticated beliefs.

After you have enjoyed El Baùl, start down the road for less than half an hour to where the sign points to **Ingenio Los Tarros,** just before the bridge. The sign faces the other direction, but if you cross the bridge, you have gone too far. This area is a must if you have gone to El Baùl. Turn left at the sign and walk for about 15 minutes. You will come to a crossroad; take the right hand trail and veer to the right at the first fork. You want to be on the hill you see in front of you. This is a ceremonial mound which has not been excavated or restored. A path leads up the hill going a bit to the left. You can not get lost at this point. Once at the top, you will walk along and all of a sudden come upon this incredible huge, stone face which has a missing chin. Indians still worship here and you may see candles and incense burning. On the other side of the clearing is a stone stelae with round glyphs and a warrior in the center. This is a holy place for the Indians of the area (thus the candles) and it has the same atmosphere as Pascual at Chichicastenango. Be careful with cameras if there are people worshipping here. I often think how offended we would be if some foreign tourist came up to us during a church service and started snapping pictures of us on our knees. Yuk.

Return as you came to the paved road and go back to the turn-off where the Calvary Church is. Take the left-hand dirt road (if coming from the Finca El Baùl, opposite to the direction of town) and walk just a little way until you come to the caretaker"s hut. This is the **Finca Bilbao.** There are kids around that will show you the way, for a small fee, to the three stone sculptures which are in the sugar-cane fields. I recommend paying rather than going alone, but if you want to go alone you can. The first stone is about 10 minutes slow walking up the road until you see a path into the fields on your left. There is a large warrior hidden in the shade of the plants. The next carving is about another five minutes up the road on the next left hand path. Here you will find the carving known as Governor No. 1. It is supposed to be one of the best in the area. Dressed in the knotted loin cloth of authority this governor is offering something to someone. Other carvings of vines and fruits are around him on the same stone. This is definitely indicative of the Olmec Indians. You must go back to the caretaker's hut in order to see the last carving. Take the road going to the left when facing the hut and walk for less than two minutes and then turn right at an opening in the fence. A carving of the same Governor No. 1 is there; supposedly now he is friends with the Spaniards. However, you are allowed to make up your own story about these carvings. After all, you walked through the heat to get to them.

Return to the main highway and go in the direction of Escuintla. About 20 to 30 minutes down the road, you will see a road going to the left that is lined with beautiful palm trees. This turn off is just before the Esso Station. This will lead you to **Finca Las Ilusiones**. The first carvings in the yard are not originals. There is a small museum on the finca but you must get someone to let you in. This is a private place and courtesy is required; go at respectable times and don't touch the artifacts. I have heard that sometimes people are refused entry. I always feel intrusive when visiting private places.

Further down the highway, about one hour of slow walking, is the **Finca Pantaleon** with sixteen large stone carvings from this finca and the Finca Santa Rita. The figures are delightful and nicely displayed. One carving shows the humor of old sculptures because the face is winking. I am glad that humor was not missing amongst a group of people who had some very violent rituals, such as making sacrifices after a ball game.

This finca is quite interesting; it is a town within itself with school, church and stores. You may visit the sugar refinery if you get permission. I have not visited it.

SANTIAGO DE ATITLAN - see Panajachel

SAYAXCHE

This is a grubby little town about two to three hours (depending on the road) out of Flores. It is only for those that are real archeaology buffs or professional travellers. The town is across the river from the bus stop. For a small fee you can hire a canoe to take you across. Watch what everyone else is paying and pay the same.

The hotel is the **Guayacan** which charges Q25 ($5.US) per person. The rooms are clean, and the building is in good shape. There is a restaurant which serves good meals. There is another hotel in town but I have no idea of its quality.

To access the many ruins on the Rio de la Pasion you must hire a boat. I will list only the ruins that are accessable and you will have to make your own decisions. Unless you can get a few people together, it will not be cheap. Although increasing yearly, visitors are rather scarce right now. Be certain to know what is going on in the area before going there.

If you go to Lago Petexbutun, you will be able to see **Tamarindito and Aguatica.** To see **Los Pilas**, you must take a boat down the Rio Chacrio and then hike; I do not know the exact direction so you will have to ask. The trip down the beautiful Rio de la Pasion will take you past the village of Buena Vista and to the ruins of **El Caribe and Altos de los Sacrificio** which are on the Mexican border.

There is another day trip that can be made to **El Ceible** by road from Sayaxche and then back again. There is no place to stay in El Ceible. As this area increases in popularity, so will services but currently, you will often feel like the only gringo in town.

The river trip down the Rio de la Pasion to the **Usumacinta** should not be done from this point. It is a long and difficult trip. You must make certain all your papers are in order before going. Although I am not a "tour" person, I suggest joining a tour for this trip. If you want a delightful but difficult trip by water into Mexico, then go to the village of Naranjo from Flores and then down the River San Pedro to Las Palmas on the border and then into Tenosique, Mexico. This is a much cheaper trip and quite beautiful. However, you will not see as many ruins as you will along the Usamacinta.

SOLOLA

This is a delightful little town away from the hustle and bustle of Panajachel. It has a colorful traditional market unlike the markets in Pana, which caters to the gringo. In Solola, an old church is in the process of being restored.

PLACES TO STAY

Cafetin Hotel is right on the square and is Q28 ($5.50 US) for two without bath and Q40 ($8. US) with bath. It is a large, bright and clean hotel. The restaurant serves decent food at a much better price than any in Pana.

Santa Ana Hotel costs Q30 ($6. US) for two without bath. Showers are one tap. It is clean, quiet and pleasant. There is a nice garden attached.

Hospadaje Paisaje costs Q15 ($3. US) for two without bath or a two tap shower. It has a pleasant patio, and the building itself is an attractive old structure.

Hotel **Tzoloj-ya** costs Q27.50 ($5.50 US) for two with bath and hot water. This is a very secure building. It is also clean and pleasant and a definite treat if you are unable to stay in Pana. This hotel is found on the road going towards Pana.

RESTAURANTS
Hotel Cafetin on the square has good meals and pleasant people. The food is cheaper than in Pana.

THINGS TO DO
Virgen del Carmen is the new church in town but, it has the old bell from the church which is presently being restored. This church was erected by the Franciscan Order in 1541.

The Market is on Tuesdays and Fridays and is very colorful indeed. There are people that come from as far away as Chichi and the far side of the lake in order to trade. The market is not as large as Chichi's but certainly worth the visit.

Hike to Santa Cruz. Cross over the bridge at the far end of town and then follow the road. It is a pleasant trip which takes two to three hours one way. Once in Santa Cruz, you can keep hiking, return to Solola, take a boat to other places on the lake or stay in Santa Cruz. For more information, see "Santa Cruz" under the hiking section in Panajachel.

TAXISCO
This is a bustling little town which is a bit cooler than Monterrico. You can stay here and commute to the beach. Taxisco was here before Alvarado came to Guatemala; there is nothing really significant to be seen in the area.

The hotel in town is great. It has large clean rooms, private baths and a swimming pool. It is very quiet and pleasant and the cost is only Q15 ($3. US) per person.

The restaurant serves good food for less money than in Monterrico. The banana pancakes are great. The owners want your business and are willing to please. I would rather stay here than at one of the poorer hotels in Monterrico.

TODOS SANTOS
This village has a population of 1500 people and sits at 2450 meters (over 8000 ft.) so the temperature is anything but hot at night.

Todos Santos is one of the most difficult towns to access in all of Guatemala; being there gives the traveller a tremendous amount of satisfaction. The long trip on a winding and narrow dirt road through the Cuchumatanes Mountains, is virtually a cliff hanger, so be prepared. However, the scenery is spectacular; sit by a window in order to appreciate the view. To get a window seat, get on the bus early. Buses leave from the Maya Hotel in Huehuetenango at 4:00AM or 1:00PM. Although only 45 kilometers from Huehue, the trip takes more than two hours, so that gives you an idea of what the road is like. Also, if there is any trouble in that area, the locals in Huehue will tell you not to go. If this happens, take the free advice. They know. The military can be a bit unpleasant in the back country.

Once in Todos Santos, you will notice the brilliant coloring of the local dress: mostly red and some white (my favorite color). Wool capes are worn to keep away the cold. Traditional dress and custom are rigidly adhered to by the people in this town; it is one of the nicest places to watch life as it was in decades past. Some Indians still use the Tzolkin Calendar of 260 days. However, they also use our calendar for their Spanish feast days.

The main feast day in Todos Santos is November 1st, All Saints Day which starts on Hallowe'en with a trip to the cemetery to leave the spirits some food. The children then steal the food. This sounds like more fun than what we do in North America. The adults feast and drink all night. Then the next morning, they start a horse race that requires the rider to run, bend down and take a swig of alcohol, and then ride the horse again. This continues until inebriation takes over.

PLACES TO STAY

Hospedaje La Paz is close to the bus stop and has very basic rooms for Q10 ($2. US) per person. There are no private baths and no hot water. In these cold temperatures, I would be reluctant to have a cold shower. The rooms are small and basic - very basic with straw mattresses. Keep your clothes on at night.

Hotel Lucia is the only other place in town where you can stay. It is as basic as the other one. There are meals available at this hotel.

THINGS TO DO

The **Market** is quite quiet but there are co-op stores which will sell you weavings at a fixed price. There are a few other shops around and above the market which will also sell local goods.

Tojcunanchèn Ruins are not really ruins but are unexcavated mounds where the Indians still worship occasionally. They are south of town, up on the hill and overgrown with trees.

TOTONICOPAN

This is a small town of 7500 people and sits at 2500 meters (8200 ft) so it is cool at night. Saturday and Tuesday are market days; Saturday features the larger market. This is a nice town.

PLACES TO STAY

Hospadaje Centra costs Q4 ($.80 US) per person plus Q1 for each hot shower. It is very basic but decent. It is on 8 Ave on the way to the hot springs.

Hospadaje San Miguel on 8 Ave. is close to the central park. The cost here is Q7 ($1.75 US) per person; it is clean with hot showers but no private bathrooms. This is the best in town.

RESTAURANTS

Pollo Churchill is the best in this town but its certainly not great. I would suggest eating in the market or getting your own food. This is the only drawback to the entire town - no place to eat.

THINGS TO DO

The Hot Springs are interesting because they are actually a bath house in which the Indian women and children bathe. If you wish to visit, go southwest down 10 Ave to the Agua Caliente Zona.

Follow the road into the valley. Many ladies will be going and coming from that direction. Once you get there, please do not bother the people. Be inconspicuous. If you want to watch, go to the bridge and watch from there. Do not disturb the people and do not photograph. There is also an old laundry area where the ladies used to clean clothes and gossip. The water in the laundry is a bit warm. This is interesting to inspect.

The Cemetery has many Mausoleum-style tombs. Some have entrances to the actual grave sites underneath the Mausoleums. It is a fascinating grave yard.

TIKAL

The main reason for going to the Peten would be to visit these magnificent ruins. Not only is the ancient city of the Maya spectacular, but the tranquil setting captures the imagination of all who visit. This is truly a must if you are anywhere in Central America. These ruins are second to none, including Machu Pichu in Peru and the Great Wall in China.

PLACES TO STAY

The Jungle Inn offers rooms in a bunkhouse-style building for Q25 ($5. US) per person. It is a plywood shack. The showers are in a different building and are clean and cold. There are also cabiñas for rent which have private baths; these cost a bit more and are quite nice. For chickenbusers, this is the most popular place to stay.

Tikal Inn is more expensive at Q50 per person ($10. US). It is a bit run down and I would use it only as a last resort. The proprietors are unfriendly. I think they want the really big spenders.

The Campsite is near the entrance to the park and is new. There is running water, toilets and thatched huts to string a hammock under. You can rent hammocks at the restaurants across the street. The campsite is a great improvement to the area.

RESTAURANTS

Comedor Tikal is the first cafe along the main road going from the ruins. It offers a typical meal and is the cheapest of the three restaurants.

Corazon de Jesus is the second restaurant with two items on the menu, frijolis or chicken. The prices are in the medium range. However, if there are a few people in this restaurant during the evening, and you look like you will be staying until dark, the local men will bring in their marimba and play music until the lights go out. You will need a flashlight in order to find your way home.

Imperio Maya is the third restaurant along the strip and offers three delectable choices: beans, chicken or eggs. The prices match the menu - large.

The Jungle Inn has remodelled the dining room and they have made a lovely sitting room. This is an excellent place to eat if you are prepared to pay a large bill.

THINGS TO DO

The Museum was completed in 1964, is small and has a minimal entry fee. Looking at the limited displays, it is evident that these Maya used neither metals nor beasts of burden. The remains of tomb number 116, found under one of the pyramids, are on display in the museum. The jade ornaments found with the body are also on display. For those who are camping out, there is a poster with pictures of local bats.

The Ruins - At last!! You have made it over some of the most horrendous roads in the world (excluding Nepal) and you are about to see a spectacular site. Take your time and listen to the ghosts. Enjoy the sounds and the heat. Ignore the mosquitos. Use your imagination and go back in time a thousand years.

The park is 222 square miles or 575 kilometers square and it has more than 3000 buildings including residences, palaces, shrines, terraces and causeways. Over 200 stelae and altars have been found in the area.

It is believed that Tikal was occupied for about 1000 years, starting in the Pre-Classic period (600BC) and flourishing through the Late Classic period (550-900AD). There is a magnificent cedar (ceiba) tree just before the entrance to the ruins. It is believed that these trees were sacred to the Maya. There is also a large aquaduct which was restored and supplies the town's water.

The Great Plaza has Temple 1 on the east, Temple ll on the west, and the North Terrace with a 230 foot long stairway on the north. Behind the North Terrace is the North Acropolis. The first Plaza floor was laid about 150BC.

Temple 1 is certainly spectacular; the visitor must climb the stairs up the pyramid to visit the altar at the top. It is amazing to think that the Maya carried the stones manually up these stairs to build the temple. Temple 1, often referred to as the Temple of the Jaguars, is 145 feet above the plaza floor and was built around 700AD, making it newer than Temple ll. After you reach the temple at the top, you will notice some wood lintels above the entranceway. These are made of zapote, a rot-resistant wood found in the Peten. On the lintels, one can barely make out the carving of a priest and a serpent. Inside, there are also red handprints visible. They are believed to have been put there after 900AD, but no one knows why. Inside the pyramid are many tunnels and Tomb 116, the wealthiest tomb found in Tikal to date. This tomb was built after the temple was completed, but before the decline of the Maya culture.

Temple ll, also known as the Temple of the Masks, is about 125 feet above the plaza floor which makes it a bit smaller than Temple 1. The date of this temple is a little before 700AD. There is an interesting display of graffiti in this temple, some put there by modern day vandals and some from the Late Classic and Post Classic periods. Be certain to see these as they give one a good idea of the average citizen's interpretation of life in those days.

Plaza and Terrace monuments include many stelae and altars, most of which are from the Post-Classic period. Some of the older stelae were reconstructed during the Post-Classic period when the Indians tried to revive their position in Tikal. The early Classic monuments were not considered permanent. After the Indians decided the stelae and altars were no longer of value, the carved figures were smashed as if to destroy the person completely. Some believe that when a family line lost succession, the carvings were then destroyed. Doesn't sound too different from today.

North Acropolis is about 40 feet above the plaza and is the most complex structure excavated. This is the last of about a dozen earlier structures, all built one on top of another. The earliest of these was built about 200BC and the final structure is believed to be from about 400AD. Many tombs have been excavated in this area and many treasures have been found, but beneath one of the south temples on the acropolis the Maya dug a tomb into the bedrock (burial #10). Here they buried a priest with some of his men, turtles, crocodiles and pottery. Some of the contents of this tomb are in the museum in Tikal.

The Great Plaza Ball Court is just south of Temple 1 and is one of the smallest courts ever found.

Pyramid 73, at the southwest corner of the plaza, south of Temple ll, is a flat pyramid. Archaeologists believe that the temple on top was a thatched building similar to that found in the graffiti on Temple ll. Below this temple was a tomb containing a single person accompanied into the afterlife by many clay vessels and a three-and-a-half pound carved jade jaguar.

The Central Acropolis on the south side of the Great Plaza is about 700 feet long and covers four acres of ground. It contains six palaces or courts ranging from one to three stories in height. These are from the Late Classic period. There is a deep ravine at the south side of this acropolis which is believed to be the reservoir which supplied water to the area.

The East Plaza is north of the Central Acropolis and east of the Great Plaza (aren't you glad you have a compass?). There is a steam bath in this plaza. It has a very low doorway and narrow channel in order to keep in the steam. There are benches and a fire pit at the rear end.

The Market place is in the center of this plaza and is considered to be the public market. Between here and the back of Temple 1 is a Late Classic period ball court.

Temple III is on the southwest corner of the West Plaza and is not totally uncovered. This temple is 180 feet high, has two rooms and is from the Late Classic period. The inside doorway has a lintel with a carved figure of a fat man clad in jaguar skins. It is difficult to get to this temple room but the carving makes the effort wothwhile.

Temple 11, Tikal

Temple IV at 212 feet is the highest standing aboriginal structure in Pre-Columbian America. One must climb up vines and roots and primitive ladders in order to reach the 40 foot thick walls of the temple proper. There is a ladder for the brave to climb all the way to the roof comb of this temple. From here, one can see the other three magnificent temples jutting above the jungle. If you have the time, take yourself to the back of this temple and relax. You may be lucky; if you sit quietly for a while, the monkeys may come to entertain you. However, there are no howler monkeys left in the area because an epidemic killed them off in the late 1950's

Temple of the Inscriptions is a long way from the main ruins. You must take a beautiful twenty minute walk through the jungle. As long as you have insect repellent, it is certainly worth the effort. If you are very quiet while at the temple you may see many monkeys. It is a thrill to sit alone on the steps and have these comical creatures entertain you. The roof comb of the temple itself has some interesting panels of glyphs.

The Plaza of the Seven Temples is from the Late Classic period and is found just to the west of the South Acropolis. These temples are interesting because the sculpturing here has skulls and crossed bones. On the south side of the group, the upper facades are decorated with human heads.

The stelae and altars at Tikal show life for the Maya as somewhat bloody. The carvings depict men being sacrificed or bound and killed by arrows.

Should you want more information on these splendid ruins, purchase the guide book "Tikal, A Handbook of the Ancient Maya Ruins", by Wm. R. Coe. It is available at the Jungle Inn or the museum for about Q50 ($10. US) This book also includes a map of the ruins. No dogs or guns are allowed within the park.

ZACAPA

This town is about two kilometers off the road and is next to a military camp. The bridge going into town is over the Rio Hondo. The town has about 12,000 people and is less than 1000 feet above sea level so the temperature is quite warm. Although the name means "a patch of grass", I couldn't find it.

PLACES TO STAY

Hotel Leon is on the edge of town and will not rent singles. The rooms are Q12 per person ($2.50US). It is very clean but not too friendly.

Hotel Central is opposite the market in the center of town and is the best place to stay. It is clean, friendly and has a very attractive atmosphere. Its only drawback is its location; if you have to catch an early bus, it is a long walk.

RESTAURANTS

Go to any of the typical tiendas around the square. Most will serve an excellent meal at affordable prices. There are no spectacular restaurants to recommend.

THINGS TO DO

There are hot springs about 30 to 40 minutes from town. I have not visited them and no one has raved about them. You will have to ask for directions in town.

CHICKENBUS TALES

Rooms
printed in the Prince George Citizen in 1992.

During my travels, I have stayed in some interesting rooms, varying from the luxurious to the primitive.

When I was in Ireland, I stayed at a Bed & Breakfast that was really different. There was yellow and black, striped wall paper on one wall, red and black, checked paper on the second wall, and pink flowered paper, some of which was coming off, on the ceiling. The other two walls were painted in matching colors. However, I never can remember what colors. The room contained a beautiful old dresser, a double bed, a window with curtains to match the painted walls and a door behind the dresser. If someone wanted to leave or enter the room, the other person (I was sharing the accommodation) would have to sit on the bed. I became curious about the door behind the dresser.

After spending a night in the claustrophobic room, I decided to snoop around the house. The room next to our's was huge, containing four beds, a couple of dressers, an end table beside each bed, a fireplace and an adjoining bathroom. I also noticed a door that had a chair in front of it. When I checked it out, it was the door leading to my room which in fact was originally a closet.

Because Europe is so crowded, rooms are usually smaller. I rented a room in Paris one time with two other gals. This room was as small as the closet in Ireland but it had a private bathroom. The bathtub was small and square with high side walls. When one of my friends who is quite tall tried to sit in the tub, she had to hang her feet out the edge. Trying to wash in that position was quite a task. If anyone wanted to go to the biffy, they would pull the folding door sort of shut, move the bidet (the plumbing was flexible rubber tubes) into the bathtub and then sit side-saddle on the toilet. Getting out was the same process in reverse. Once back in the room, there were three beds(which we had to walk across) a TV (hanging from the ceiling), two chairs (where we put our backpacks), a small writing desk that was unmoveable (cluttered with books, cosmetics etc.) and a balcony where we sat our wine glasses.

When in Mexico Joanne and I were miffed at the bus company because they had ripped us off for our last 500 pesos. This caused great inconvenience so when we had a chance to get even we took it. What happened was the bus went past the stop that we had paid for so we just quietly stayed on. It was going in the direction that we eventually wanted to go anyways. We arrived in a little town, late at night with a very apologetic bus driver. He wanted to take us back with him but we felt quite good at having gone the extra two or three hours for free.

We went to the only hotel in town and asked the price. The fellow at the desk told us 1000 pesos but mama in the background corrected him and said 1500 pesos (that is about 75 cents Canadian). We took the room, site unseen as there were many transport truck drivers staying there and we took that to mean that the place was okay.

The room we got was horrid. There were no screens on the windows and the curtains were ripped, dirty and hanging askew. The bathroom had a sink and toilet but when you washed your hands, your feet also got a soaking. There was no drain pipe. The toilet was unusable. The bed was dirty and only partially covered with a sheet. One cockroach was so big that I felt physically threatened so I threw a towel over it and squished it with my foot.

We decided to push the bed into the center of the floor, leave the light on (bugs move less in the light), and pull out our hostel sheets to sleep in. We would not remove our clothes. I think our rationale was that we could make a quicker getaway.

It was not long before there was a knock on the door. When I answered, a shocked-looking fellow apologised, said that he was looking for his friend Hector and quickly walked down the hall. We tried to settle in but there was soon another knock on the door. We told this fellow to buzz off. We placed a dresser in front of the door for security. However, the knocks continued every fifteen minutes or so until about two in the morning. This made us start to wonder.

Then it hit us. It wasn't just the knocking. I remembered all the truckers downstairs and even our bus driver's reluctance to leave us in the town. We were in a Mexican house of ill repute and the way of advertising for business was to leave the light on.

After realizing that we were the lowest paid of all guests to stay in that hotel that night we snuck out the door and drank coffee at the all night cafe across the street. The ladies in the cafe had been watching the action all night and were still laughing.

As I get ready to leave my cosy little house in Prince George for another three months of travelling again, I wonder what type of adventures lay ahead this time. I don't mind cramped quarters, I don't mind a bit of dirt and I don't even mind the music of dogs barking and chickens squaking. But I really don't like to stay in houses of ill repute.

HONDURAS

Honduras, the second-largest country in Central America, has many interesting and unique sights. Though poor, it has an excellent and efficient bus system which uses spacious Mercedes Benz vehicles. From the large, tinted glass windows, the traveller can see the magnificent mountains and valleys covered with pine and cedar trees.

Honduras does not have any active volcanos; therefore, the earth is not replenished with nutrients and it doesn't have as much lush jungle nor as many subsistence farmers as in other countries. The poor conditions of the soil compound the poverty of the country. Honduras is also the most sparsely populated country in Central America with only 37 people per square kilometer (96/sq.mi.).

You will find three major types of people in this country. The first are the negroes along the Atlantic coast who are wonderful. They don't see many tourists and this makes them trusting and friendly. The second are the Indians in the interior, located west of La Ceiba and south towards Nicaragua. The main groups of Indians found in Honduras are the Mosquito, Chortis, Pipiles, Lencas, Guajiquiros, Xicaques and Tahuajes. The third type is the Mestizo which is a mixture of Spanish and Indian. These are the majority and are quite friendly and helpful. It is not unusual to strike up a conversation on a bus and be invited to someone's home for dinner. These people are friendly and curious and want your friendship.

When travelling in Honduras, you will find many military checks; some of them can be tense. Don't carry any drugs and be certain your papers are in order. The checks occur so often that it can take from one to six hours to go a hundred miles. However, the sun shines, the ladies sell food and drink and the people display a great sense of humor.

The wealthier Hondurans vacation on the Bay Islands which are on the Caribbean coast. The islands are truly beautiful, and they are inexpensive; they also have all the water sports that would be available at any first class resort.

Travel into backwoods areas is difficult as there are few roads and less transportation. If you prefer river trips, you are safe boating or rafting with an Indian guide in the isolated Gracias a Dios or the Mosquita districts.

Honduras is a great destination for the traveller; also it is less costly than Costa Rica or Panama. When walking the streets of Tegucigalpa at night, many Hondurans are also walking around and no one seems fearful. Robberies are relatively rare. The buses are not as crowded as in neighboring countires. All in all, if you are looking for an outdoor adventure with few tourists, Honduras is the country to visit.

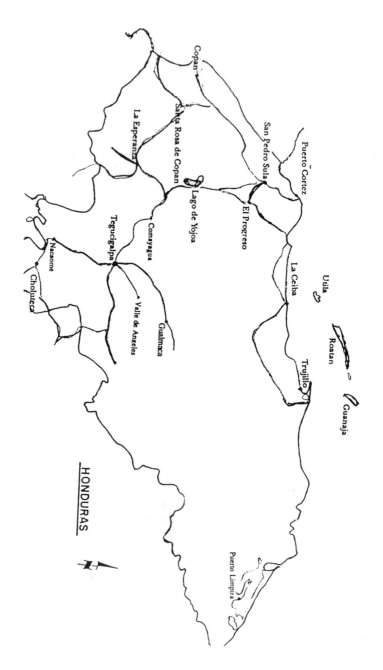

HISTORY

The aboriginal tribes, migrant hunters and gatherers, go back to about 7000 BC. By the year 2000 BC, these people had developed farming methods and a political structure, built magnificent buildings, and developed beautiful arts and crafts.

We eventually called these people the Maya Indians. They covered a large portion of Mexico and Central America. They thrived until around 900 AD when their population started rapidly declining and their beautiful cities fell to the jungles. Small tribes of Indians continued to live in Honduras until the Spanish came.

In 1502, Columbus first landed on the Island of Guanaja (which is now part of the Bay Islands) and then went over to the mainland where the city of Trujillo stands today. He called the land Honduras which means "deep waters".

Settlers to Honduras soon enslaved the Indian population. Gonzales Davila tried to colonize the territory but Cortez sent Cristobal de Olid from Mexico to Honduras to forcefully seize the land. De Olid succeeded but instead of taking the land for Cortez, he took it for himself. Displeased, Cortez came to Honduras to settle the problem himself; he found de Olid dead. The struggles for control continued between the settlers and the leaders of Panama. They all wanted the gold and silver from the country.

In 1536, Don Pedro de Alvarado arrived in the area of San Pedro Sula. Here he fought the famous Indian called Lempira, who gave him a good run for his money (or gold) as he fought with his 30,000 men against the Spanish. It was by trickery that Alvarado's captain, Alfonso de Caceres, was able to entice Lempira out of his fortress and kill him, thus defeating the Indians. Today, Lempira is the national hero, and money in Honduras is named after the Indian. Caceres then went south where he established a city by the name of Comayagua; this became the first capital of the country.

In 1539, Honduras became part of Guatemala. It was divided into two provinces, Tegucigalpa and Comoyagua. The gold and silver mined by the Indians under Spanish authority, kept the Spanish in the area. When they had exhausted the supply of Indian slaves, the Spanish imported Negro slaves by the thousands. However, it was not long before the pirates of the high seas discovered that the Spanish were sending riches home from the area. The pirates then settled along the coasts of Honduras. There are many traces of these colorful men in the jungles of the Mosquito Coast and around the Bay Islands.

Along with other Central American countries, Honduras received independence from Spain in 1821. The leader of this separation was Jose del Valle of Choluteca, a Honduran lawyer, writer and economist. The province then joined Iturbide's Mexican Republic. This did not last long and Honduras fell under the jurisdiction of Francisco Morazan and the United Provinces of Central America.

The countries fought to stay together for eight years but eventually disintegrated into individual republics. Those that wanted a strong, united Central America tried to put Morazan back into power, but anti-union forces killed Morazan on September 15th, 1841, just 21 years after independence from Spain had been declared. Today, Morazan is called the defender of Central America and is considered a national hero.

Like most other Central American countries, the struggle continued because the people wanted more wealth and better living conditions. It was not until the 1950's that Ramon Valleda Morales tried to build roads and schools, change labor laws and improve social services for the poor of Honduras. Ten days before the national elections of 1963, a military junta took control of the country and ousted Valleda. By 1965, a new constitution approved and a new president elected. This was Colonel Oswaldo Lopez Arellano. He tried to encourage foreign investment and received several loans from other countries. Thus started the foreign debt of Honduras.

In 1960, Honduras had joined a Central American common market. At that time, it exported food to El Salvador. Salvadorians, being from a more densely populated country, often emigrated to Honduras, sometimes illegally. In 1969, a soccer team from each country were at a game; frustrations were irritated by a passionate game and war actually broke out. The newspapers dubbed this the soccer war. This war ended, but relations have never mended.

Honduras has also had serious clashes with Nicaragua. Nicaraguan rebels, known as the Contras, used Honduran ground for training. Both the United States and Honduras had a dislike for the left-wing Nicaraguan government and aided anyone who attempted to overthrow the government. Eventually, due to the war and the American embargoes, the Sandinistas of Nicaragua lost power. Today the borders between Nicaragua, El Salvador and Guatemala are easily accessible for the traveller.

At present, there is an elected president in Honduras; however, he is ruled by strict military control.

GENERAL INFORMATION

Honduras adopted its constitution in 1965. It has an elected president and an elected legislature. The responsibility of the legislature is to create laws. The cabinet is appointed by the president, but the key positions are held by the military and they have the power to overthrow any bill. The president is elected for six years and can not run consecutively. All **literate** citizens over the age of 18 years are eligible to vote.

Honduras is **112,000 square kilometers** (43,000 sq. miles) large and has a population of **4.2 million** people. This makes the country very sparsely populated, with **37 persons per square kilometer.** There is **615 kilometers** (382 miles) of Caribbean coast line and

124 **kilometers** (77 miles) of Pacific coastline. Because the Pacific coast is quite small and unsuitable for posts, Honduras uses the island of Amapala in the Gulf of Fonseca as its only Pacific port.

The climate of Honduras is mainly tropical, but it gets cold in the highlands during rainy season. The highest mountain is about 3100 meters (10,000 feet). However, Honduras has built its paved roads over the tops of its mountains. The Mosquito Coast in the northeast is a hot, wet area and is somewhat unaccessible. The **rainy season** is from May to December for most of Honduras but it extends to about February on the Bay Islands. The rain causes problems in the highlands where roads often wash out. Also, the rain can become very cold at higher elevations.

The flag of Honduras has two blue horizontal stripes at the top and bottom with a white stripe in the center. There are five stars representing the five countries that formed the Central American Union in the 1800's.

Honduras requires all children between seven and twelve attend school, but this does not happen. There are not enough schools in the rural areas. This results in an official **50% literacy** rate in the nation.

INDIANS OF HONDURAS

There are seven distinct groups of Indians in Honduras. As well, on the Caribbean coast, are the Garifunas. For information on the Garifunas, look under the section in Belize.

The Lencas or Guajiquiros were a well defined group long before the Spaniards came. They were an agricultural people who had a social structure dependent on economic levels. These Indians settled around the states of Intibuca, Lempira and La Paz.

The Jicaques are also known as the Tol or Tolpan and were located in the Francisco Morazan and Yoro states. Under years of Spanish dominance, native traditions have been lost. Groups of workers in the country are encouraging these Indians to regain their culture and traditions. In some cases, this is successful.

Mosquitos are a group of Indians who live in the Gracias a Dios state of Honduras. It is believed that a ship full of slaves was washed ashore at the Cape of Gracias a Dios and the survivors intermarried with the local Indians in the area. Today we have a mix of the two cultures. These Indians extend to the Caribbean coast in Nicaragua. They are economically suppressed.

Chortis Indians are found in the Ocotepeque and Copan states. Their gods were the strength of their tribal structure, taking care of every aspect of life.

The Payas are found in the Olancho region of the country. Today they are mainly Catholic. They were converted to Christianity in the 1600s by the Franciscan Friars.

The **Sumos** (not from Japan) live around the Gracias a Dios and Olancho states. Very little is known about them. They are probably a disgruntled group who broke away from the Payas many years ago.

The **Chorotegas** are found in the state of Choluteca and have lost their native traditions and customs.

LAWS

Due to the military control of the government, this country is not one in which to break the laws. You can be held without explanation for six days in a Honduran prison, and calling home once a day would not be considered a human right.

It is illegal to carry any type of weapon into Honduras.

It is illegal to remove artifacts from Honduras. This is not a great problem as everything in Copan is carefully guarded.

It is illegal to carry any type of subversive literature into Honduras. However, I found that the border guards are not checking much since relations between the countries have improved. However, when the Sandinistas were fighting the Contras, literature was often confiscated under unpleasant conditions.

Be certain to have all information marked on the insurance papers. If you end up with scratches on your car not noted on the insurance papers, you could be a guest of the government for the specified six days because they will have assumed you have had an unreported accident. You should have an International Driver's Licence in order to drive in Honduras.

MONEY

The Limpera (limp) is the name of the currency used in Honduras. There are 100 centavos per limp. Money changers at the border pay higher for a dollar and it is simpler than bank exchange. The black market is a necessity in Honduras as the banks have an excellent system of frustrating the ordinary traveller. They may say you can exchange foreign currency in traveller's cheques. However, after about one hour in a line-up, you will find that this is not true. For the foolhardy, certain banks will change Visa cheques and other banks will change American Express. Heaven knows what they will do with Thomas Cook! Some banks will exchange American money, but most will not. The legal exchange rate is **4.50 limpera per US dollar** but you may get as much as 4.75 limp, depending on how much you are changing and how well you can barter. The City Bank in Teguc will exchange American Express. The Banco Atlantida say that they will exchange money but I could not get Canadian money exchanged. The Banco Fivensa will exchange Visa cheques. However, the best place in town to change money is at the Mercado M & M (mas por menos) (more for less) on La Paz, past the Guanacaste Tourist Office. They give the best rate in the country, sell the cheapest goods in town and are hassle-free.

In 1918, the legal money was the peso and the exchange was 2 pesos for one dollar US. At this time, US money was considered legal tender. In 1926, the Limpera replaced the peso but US and Guatemalan coins were still used in Honduras. In 1949, Honduras started minting their own coins and no longer used Guat or US money. However, it was not until 1954 that US money was no longer accepted in Honduras. At that time, the exchange rate became 2 limps for 1 US dollar. The black market became popular as it paid a higher price. Today, the exchange rate is 4.50 limp per 1 US dollar but the black market pays a bit more. With the end of the war, the black market's fate is uncertain.

VISAS

Visas or tourist cards are required for many countries; they are easy to obtain. The border guards are pleasant, and it is very easy to cross from one country to the other. You will be allowed to enter for one month and may renew your visa for up to six months at any immigration office in the country. If you overstay your visit, you will be charged 10 limp for every month.

Conditions have changed since the last printing of this book; on this visit I found border crossings a pleasure. At one time, I warned people about immigration undercover men lurking around trying to catch illegal immigrants (including me) but today, the only border which is a bit tense is the Salvadorian border. Coming from Nicaragua, I was almost welcomed with a band and red carpet. However, I never fail to tell the border guards how happy I am to be entering their country; if leaving I always tell them what a wonderful time I had and that I will be returning very soon. Of course, the Copan border guards are so accustomed to many short term and long term visitors that crossing there is easy.

GETTING THERE

When going overland from **Guatemala**, the buses to not go into Honduras. You will change at the border. An onward ticket is not necessary. During the day, there are many buses and connections going in every direction in Honduras. If you arrive later than 4:00PM, you may have to spend the night in one of the border towns and resume travel the next day. Border crossings are not difficult.

Crossing at Copan is the easiest because of the large numbers of travellers. Some only get a visa for the day or a couple of days, but this is a waste of money. Honduras is a wonderful place to visit so keep travelling for at least a few days.

Crossing from Ocotepeque to Aguas Caliente is okay but the town of Ocotepeque is small and dusty without too many comfortable places to stay. People cross from here to El Poy, **El Salvador**; this is an easy crossing.

If going to or from **Nicaragua,** you will cross at El Paraiso or San Marcos de Colon. The border guards on the Honduran side are wonderful. They made me feel so welcome I thought I had landed on Canadian soil. My bags were not searched and I was not questioned about subversive literature. I only had to pay five limps to get across and the guard was very patient while I changed money and ran back and forth to get the right amount. There are money changers here that give a decent rate. There are also frequent buses going to and from the border during the daylight hours. If you go along the Mosquito Coast by boat, there is no place to check out of Honduras and into Nicaragua. At present, this is not an advisable route.

If going into **El Salvador,** you may either go in at Ocotepeque or at El Amatillo. The Honduran border guards are great, and there is no problem. Be certain to tell them how happy you are to have been in their country, and that you are anxious to return. This small appreciation makes everyone happy and eliminates any hassles. Once on the Salvadorian side, you can then tell them how happy you are to be in El Salvador. White lies go a long way at borders. I was not searched at any of these borders in 1992.

Flying into Honduras requires an onward ticket for everyone except nationals. Be certain you have one, or you will not even be allowed on the plane. Airlines going into Honduras from other countries are Tan, Sahsa, Challenge International and Taca International. The domestic airlines are Lansa and Sahsa. Both are available at the international airport. All airlines now require payment in US dollars if the flight is originating in Honduras. The airport tax is 50 limp ($10. US).

There is still **no ferry** service between Belize and Honduras. However, you can get a dory to take you back and forth. This can be really tough because the seas can change rapidly. I once tried to cross the Caribbean from Belize to Guatemala in a small dugout canoe; fifteen minutes after we left, a storm started that I shall never forget. By the time I got to Guat, cold, wet and miserable, I swore I would never get into another canoe again.

CAR RENTALS

This is one place that you can help save the environment. Take public transportation. With public transportation, you will have more contact with the local people, have a better chance to practice the language, eat the food and enjoy Honduras for what it is; a country full of delightful people.

CONSULATES

There are many, consulates and/or embassies in Honduras. You can locate them in the phone book under Embajada or Consulado. As of 1992, the following were listed:

Argentina
Belgium
Belize
Bolivia
Brazil
Canada
Chile
China
Columbia
Costa Rica
Denmark
Dominican Republic
Ecuador
England
Finland
France
Germany
Greece

Guatemala
Israel
Italy
Jamaica
Japan
Korea
Mexico
Netherlands
Nicaragua
Norway
Panama
Peru
Philippines
Spain
Switzerland
United States
Uruguay
Venezuela

NATIONAL HOLIDAYS

New Year	January 1
Easter	Thursday, Friday, Saturday in March or April
American Day	April 14
Labor Day	May 1
Independence Day	September 15
Francisco Morazan's Birthday	October 3rd
Discovery of America	October 12
Fuerzas Armadas Day (army)	October 21
Christmas	December 25

TRANSPORTATION

At present, there are no bus schedules available for Honduras. Generally, there are many bus companies competing for business between the major centers. During the daylight hours, the bus service is frequent To smaller towns, the buses may go only once every few hours depending on the area and road conditions, but I have never seen an area serviced less than once every three hours during the dry season. During the rainy season, there are fewer buses on the mud and gravel roads. The competition between the companies permits easy travel. Most companies have different locations in the cities for their terminals. You may shop around for better prices, it is probably not worth the time.

You will find that the bus drivers pick up extra customers along the highway even though the bus may be a first class, numbered seats only bus. This helps supplement the drivers' meager

315

incomes. Recently, the government put a stipulation on the number of passengers allowed on the larger, longer distance buses and there are never any passengers standing. The smaller, more local, buses may be packed and still have room for one more. If travelling to El Salvador from Teguc, the buses start leaving at 4:30 AM. In the past, they finished leaving by noon; since the peace settlements in El Salvador, this may change. You can always take second class buses to the border. No Honduran buses leave the country. You must walk across all borders and then get local transportation in the next country.

Hitch-hiking is common and fairly safe. I hitched for a few hours in the Gracias area, but was unsuccessful. For information on hitch-hiking, talk to other travellers.

Local buses in Honduras are cheap and easy to use. Even the airport bus in Teguc is a breeze, stopping right at the terminal door. It is highly advisable to take the bus rather than a more expensive taxi. You can ask at your hotel for which bus number.

Buses leaving Teguc are found at the following locations:

Ampala	Che at Mercado Belen - 1 bus per day
Cedeño	Mercado Belen - 2 buses per day
Choluteca	Mi Esperanza on 6 Ave. between Calle 24 & 25 - 11 buses per day
Comoyagua	Catrachos at Mercado Belen - every hour
Danli	Emtra Oriente on 6 Calle between Ave. 6 & 7 -4 per day or Discua-Litena at Mercado Jacaleapa
El Amatillo	Mercado Belen - buses go often
El Paraiso	Same as Danali
Jesus de Otero	Emtra Oriente at 6 Calle between Ave. 6 & 7. There is one bus per day.
Juticalpa	Aurora on 8 Calle between Ave. 6 & 7 - 8 per day.
La Ceiba	Go to San Pedro Sula first - do not take Traliasa
La Esperanza	Joelito on 4 Calle between Ave. 8 & 9 - 1 bus per day

La Libertad	7 Ave. between Calle 5 & 6
La Paz	Florez on 12 Calle & 8 Ave. - 4 per day
Leparterique	4 Calle and Ave. 8 & 9 - many per day
Marcala	Lila on 7 Calle between Ave. 4 & 5 - only one per day excluding Sunday
Minas de Oro	Dias Donavil on 10 Ave. and Calle 4
Nacaome	Same as El Amatillo
Ojojona	4 Calle between Ave. 8 & 9 - many per day
San Lorenzo	Mercado Belen and many every day
San Marcos Colon	Mi Esperanza on 6 Ave. between Calle 24 & 25 - 5 buses per day
San Pedro Sula	Saenz at Calle 12, between Ave. 7-8 Hedman Alas at 11 Ave. between Calle 13-14 El Rey at 6 Ave., 9 Calle Norteños on 12 Calle between Ave. 6 & 7 - buses every 45 minutes all day
Santa Barbara	12 Calle & 8 Ave. on Tuesday, Thursday and Saturdays only.
Santa Lucia	Mercado San Pablo - every hour
Valle de Angeles	Mercado San Pablo - every hour
Yuscaran	Mercado Belen

In the north, is a railroad system which is reported to be reliable. The passenger coaches are a bit slower than the buses. You can go from San Pedro Sula to La Ceiba on the railway.

You can also travel by boat along the Mosquito Coast of Honduras, starting at La Ceiba and going as far as Cabo Camaròn where the winds are so strong and unpredictable that going around the point could take you a few days or even a week. Going that far is exciting and interesting.

TELEPHONES
International calls must be made at the Hondu-tel offices. They do not permit station-to-station collect calls. Person-to-person calls are expensive. Most calls suffer from poor connections but the

services are improving all the time. The service seems to improve when you pay for the call in Honduras but the prices are much higher.

BAY ISLANDS

There are three main islands in the group called the Bay Islands. This is where Columbus came in 1502 on his fourth journey to America. The islands are between 35 and 70 miles off the Honduran mainland and look like a group of emeralds dropped in a tropical paradise. The main islands are Utila, Roatan and Guanaja, but there are also little islets called Helene, Morat, Barbareta, and the Cochinos.

The islands are an extension of a mountain range coming from Honduras; they extend up to 1300 feet above sea level. The underwater reefs often pass close to shore. Common features of the reefs are huge fissures, clefts, extensive caverns and ledges. There are walls, drop-offs and 100 foot pinnacles. Marine biologists claim that 95% of all known Caribbean corals are on the Bay Islands. These features attract people from all over the world for underwater diving.

English is spoken in this area, but it is spoken with an accent that requires intense listening in order to understand.

To get to the islands take one of several planes that come and go daily from La Ceiba. However, they don't fly in bad weather because of their past history of crashes. The cost is L82. ($16.50 US) for a fifteen minute flight. There is also a large number of boats that come and go, but these are not very safe for travellers. It is reputed that once you are on the ocean, you will be asked for more money. If you are travelling in a group, you may avoid these hassles.

If you are coming from Tela or San Pedro Sula by bus, and you want to go directly to the airport before going into town, ask the driver to let you off at the airport turn-off. It is only a five minute walk from the highway to the terminal. They will tell you that it can't be done but this is untrue. If going the other way, take a bus toward Tela or San Pedro Sula and do the same thing. Taxis cost L10 for one way.

A boat operated by a Captain Cooper of the Tonia who sails to and from Utila and Roatan on Mondays has been recommended. He occasionally returns on Tuesdays but this is dependent on weather. The cost is L20 ($4.50 US). He occasionally sails on other days but this is unpredictable. The cost of the airline flight is so inexpensive that waiting for a boat is a waste of time and money.

Sand fleas have infested all the islands. They are so numerous that after I stayed in a house for one night, I looked like I had smallpox. I had no choice but to leave. I have used insect repellent and oil, but nothing seems to work. Some people claim Skin-So-Soft by Avon is an effective prevention, but it didn't save me. You may rub yourself down with a large amount of greasy cream. The locals say this will cause the insects to stick to the oil and thus be unable to bite. Lemon juice which is squeezed on the bites is supposed to take away some of the itch. If you are staying in a cheap place, and you are bothered by these insects, then the islands are not the place for you. Travelling around Central America with scratched sand flea bites can be quite dangerous to your health. You may have a better time at Tela on the mainland or over on the Pacific beaches in Guatemala or El Salvador.

Roatan, Honduras

GUANAJA

This island is for the wealthier tourist. It has large, beautiful resorts with expenses to match; this is where the upper-crust Hondurans will be found.

Originally called Bonacca Island, this 55 kilometer (34 miles) piece of land was Columbus' arrival point on his fourth voyage to America. At that time, the islands were densely populated with Paya Indians who had lived on the islands for centuries. The Indians were taken to the mainland to work in the mines and fields, and the island became inhabited by pirates. These fellows found the islands easy to defend; fresh water and food were readily available. The island was excellent for rest and recuperation.

These islands are beautiful, with clear mountain streams cascading down the hills between the pines and palms. Cool winds provide a comfortable temperature; no poisonous snakes or dangerous animals lurk on the islands.

The main town on the island is Bonacca Town. It is often called the Venice of Honduras because most of the houses are built on stilts and boats are used for transportation. The other two main towns on the island are Savannah Bight and Mangrove Bight.

PLACES TO STAY

The Miller in Guanaja costs L30. for a single and L40. for a double ($7. & $9. US). These are without private baths. There are 28 rooms and it is one of the cheaper places to stay. If this is full, ask the locals if they have a room that can be rented in their homes.

El Rosario is the other place to stay. The cost is L90. for a single and L100. for a double ($20. & $22. US). With only five rooms to rent, the hotel is very small.

THINGS TO DO

The cave on Marble Hill is a must. This is the cave that was inhabited before Columbus came to America. There are artifacts, burial sites, shrines, and pre-Columbian home mounds. It is illegal to remove any artifact from the country - even if the Indians try to sell these "yabba-ding-dings" (as they are locally called) to you at a good price.

Guanaja Marine National Park consists of 90% of the island and the surrounding reefs. Although expensive, it is a delightful.
The cays accessible from Guanaja are Los Cayos, Pine Ridge, Michael's Rock, Sandy Bay and West End. Unbearable sandflies inhabit this island.

ROATAN ISLAND

Roatan island is 53 kilometers (33 mi.) long and four to five kilometers (three mi.) wide. The average temperature is 80ºF; October and November are the rainy months.

The British built three forts at Port Royal which had one of the deepest bays in the Caribbean during the 18th century. The remains of these forts can still be explored today. The British who lived on nearby St. Vincent Island transported 5000 Garifunas (a mixture of Negro and Indian) to Roatan in 1797 and left them stranded. These are the ancestors of the handsome people living there today.

The British gave the islands back to Honduras in 1859, even though Honduras had little interest in them at that time. Today, the uniqueness of the area has caused an influx of tourism and Honduras has great interest in the area.

Roatan is the most developed of the islands and has the nicest beaches. There is some unreliable electricity at the expensive hotels.

COXEN HOLE

An appropriate name, this little village is about a ten minute walk from the airport. As well, mini buses go to French Harbour and West End. These cost L5 to West End, the location of the good beaches. It is a lot cheaper to sleep and eat in Coxen Hole during the night and travel by mini-van during the day. There are also fewer sand fleas in Coxen Hole. In the village is a Hondu-tel, post office and a grocery store that sells a small English newspaper.

PLACES TO STAY

Sunrise at Sandy Bay has rooms for L60. per person ($13.50 US). This is a small place with only 12 rooms. The beach in this area is spectacular.

El Paso in Coxen Hole is on the main street and costs L30 for a single, L40. for a double and L50. for a triple ($6.75, $9.,& $11. US). This place is often full. If it is full, keep walking down the street and you will find some other accommodations.

Robert's Hill in the West End costs L20. per person and is very basic. This is often full, and is not the most popular of cheapies but the food here is excellent. They also exchange money. **Airport View** at Coxen Hole, close to the airport and only a ten minute walk to the center, costs L60. for a single and L70. for a double ($13.50 & $15.50 US). They do have air-conditioning and the rooms have a private bath. This is an okay place, but I prefer some place closer to the center of town.

El Coral is on the main street and is one of the most popular places to stay because it is so clean and friendly. The cost is L30. for a single and L40. for a double ($6.75 & $9. US).

Allen's is further down the street and just over the bridge. It is clean with bancitos (toilet & sink), or without bathroom of any kind for L25. ($5.55 US) per person. However, it is not as friendly as other places on the island. But then I found West End friendlier than any part of Coxen Hole. However, the sandfleas are friendlier also.

Sheila's in Coxen Hole is also an inexpensive place to stay at L25. ($5.55 US) per person. It does not have bathrooms, and the place is about the same size as Allen's.

Jimmy's at the West End is right at the very end of the road and is the friendliest and best place to stay, but it is always full. I liked Jimmy and I liked his philosophy. Even if you can't stay there, it is a delight to talk to the man. Jimmy charges L15. per person ($3.50 US). The building is built quite high on stilts and is very basic. There are showers down the hall and everything is clean. He has a place to sit and enjoy the breezes and have a beer or a pop. This is the place!! You must tell him that if he changes his place, he will not be given this great review in the next book.

Ocean View Restaurant at the West End has a couple of rooms at the back where you can stay for a reasonable price. They have a great crop of sand fleas; unless you have a mosquito net or are not affected by fleas I would not recommend staying there. Ask around for a place to stay if this is full.

Miss Effie's House at Sandy Bay is the best place on the island besides Jimmy's. The rooms are clean and Effie is a delight. The cost is only L15. ($3.50 US) per person. However, like Jimmie's, this place is often full. Give yourself a lot of time to look for a place while on the island.

PLACES TO EAT

Ocean View Restaurant in the West End is the best place to eat. Julie, the owner, has some difficulty keeping waitresses; if service is slow, you may want to help. Another solution is to eat when others are not. Her T-bone steak is very popular and her prices are more reasonable than most places on the island. You can eat dinner and watch superb sunsets from her porch.

Amigo's is the other popular place to eat in the West End. The restaurant sits on the water; you can enjoy the superb island sunsets and feel the trade winds cooling your burning skin. The food is good and the prices are slightly higher than Julie's.

Burger Hut in Coxen Hole is clean and okay. The burgers are not super big, but they are acceptable. However, it is not the cheapest place in town.

Golden Gate Restaurant in Coxen Hole is the best place to eat. The prices are cheap (for the Bay Islands) and the servings are large. The food is well spiced and quite palatable.

Sunshine Hotel at Sandy Bay is a good place to eat. Overall, there are not many choices in this area, so you will be happy with this find. The prices are reasonable.

THINGS TO DO

Deep Sea Diving is the most popular sport on the islands. This is one of the most spectacular places on the planet for diving.

After divers complete a dive it takes hours for them to return to earth. The excitement is soon transmitted to all. There are excellent places to rent equipment; plus, there are knowledgeable guides available. Definitely recommended.

Snorkeling is the next best activity; the reef is so close that you can see an array of sights very quickly. Rental equipment is available all over the island. The best place to snorkel is at Sandy Bay. Just walk to the end of the pier, flop into the water and swim directly out for about a hundred yards. Go just beyond and enjoy the sight. It is spectacular. Even if you are not a diver, snorkeling is a must.

Glass Bottom Boat trips are becoming very popular around the islands, and it is not all that expensive. During off season or with a group, you can get on the boat for a reasonable price which is under $10.00 US. This is not a budget travel price, but then this is not a budget travel area.

Deep sea fishing is another sport which is growing in popularity. It costs about $100.00 US per day for four or five people. This is beyond my budget; as well, deep sea sport fishing opposes my belief in the preservation of the environment. I can not see killing as a sport.

Horses and Motorbikes are available for rent for a small fee in both Coxen Hole and West End.

Hiking is not really hiking in this area. You can hike around the **Carambola Botanical Gardens** which are beautifully kept and well worth the quiet walk. They are between Coxen Hole and West End. You may also walk along the beaches; the West End is the best area for this. Sun tanning seems to be a better sport than hiking.

Fantasy Island is a resort that should not be missed, even if just to look. It is fantasy. The rooms run from $80.00 US to 170.00 US depending on the amount of luxury you want. The cheaper rate includes transportation to and from the airport, a cocktail upon arrival, air conditioning and ceiling fans, private balcony, color TV, and cablevision, wall to wall carpets, fridge, and use of the canoes, kayaks, and windsurf equipment. Chickenbusers should go and at least have a drink.

Barbareta Marine National Park is at the extreme east end of the island and includes the Islands of Barbareta and Morat. The park extends as far west as Port Royal. Diamond Rock has a tropical forest and a few crocodiles.

UTILA

Utila is the closest and cheapest island; it also has the largest swamp area and therefore, the most mosquitoes and sand fleas. The insects are so overpowering that some travellers spend their whole time hiding in the local bar. The next day, they aren't certain what bit them, so they repeat their pattern of living.

Henry Morgan, the British pirate died and was buried on this island.

Today, Utila has a telephone service and post office, electricity and water. There is even a bank which is open regular bank hours and changes traveller's cheques. The scarcity of vehicles on the island makes it very peaceful.

The gallery owned by Gunter, from Austria, is delightful to visit, and Gunter knows all there is to know about the island. If you catch him when he is not too busy, he will give you information.

PLACES TO STAY

The Monkey's Tail is the place to stay as it is cheap, basic and clean. However, until the new addition is completed, it is often full. To get a room, enquire at the store after the Bucket of Blood Bar. The cost is L6. ($1.25 US). This is the most popular place to stay.

Trudy's is the another popular place to stay, but it costs L30. ($7. US) per person. You don't get a private bath.

Captain Spencers is L10. ($2. US) per person and is on the main street. It is basic but expensive. However, if the Monkey's Tail is full, you may have to stay here.

Palm Villa costs L10. for a single and L15. for a double ($2.50 & $3.25 US). It is very clean and is providing competition for the Monkey's Tail. It is across from Cooper's dock.

RESTAURANTS

Selley's is up the path from the Monkey's Tail and is the most favored hang-out. It is family owned and the family treats everyone as family. It is cheap, relaxing and the best place in town to eat.

M & M's serves the best breakfast in town (not M&M chocolate). It is the green building on the main drag so it's not too difficult to find.

The Bucket of Blood is the most likely place to meet other travellers who are beer or rum drinkers. The restaurant is owned by a 70 year old man, Clifford, who is married to a 25 year old woman. While you drink your beer, you can enjoy their tales.

Big Mama's Cook Shop will give you, for a reasonable price, the biggest and best tasting meals on the entire island. Big Mama will also prepare take-out lunches for all day excursions. These are well worth the price.

THINGS TO DO

A Pig Feast is held in town every Sunday evening and gringos are welcome to attend. This is a must according to Greg Cornell of Vernon, B.C.

Pumpkin Hill Beach is on the north side of the island. Walk past the Monkey's Tail and stay on the trail for about 45 to 60 minutes. It is a nice beach with some snorkeling. There are many sand fleas. Allan's Cabinas is the place to stop for refreshments.

The Cays are a must. There are some privately owned cays that cost a fortune to visit for a day; I will not mention them.

Diamond Cay is privately owned but can be rented for around $10.00 US per day. That price I can live with. Submerged next to the wharf is an old cannon.

Water Cay has campsites for L5. ($1. US) if you have a hammock and bring your own food and drink. There are no services on the island. To make arrangements to visit, go to one of the equipment rental shops in town. This is a government-owned cay and is a marine and bird sanctuary. It is also popular for the adventuresome or those who really love sand fleas.

Jewel and Pigeon Cay are the main islands, which are joined by a bridge. There are a few guest houses and places to eat and drink. Otherwise, it is expensive for what you get. Electricity is available for a few hours every day. You must rent a dory or a canoe to get back and forth. The cost is debatable; I have paid as little as L5. but have heard of some paying L15. so barter and see what everyone else is paying.

CHOLUTECA

Choluteca is the largest town near the Nicaraguan border. This town of 100,000 people is one of the oldest communities in Honduras, and it has continued to grow consistently for 350 years. Founded in 1535, it was first called Villa de Jeres de la Frontera, then Choluteca Malalaca. In 1825, it was the first political division in Honduras.

This town was the home of Honduran poet, economist and politician, Josè Cecilio del Valle, who gave strong opposition to the Mexican government against the annexation of Central America to Mexico. It was also the home of former president Dionisio de Herrera, the first leader of Honduras.

It is a very hot area because it is close to sea level; a room with a fan is a must. June and September have the most rain; if you like thunderstorms, then June is the month to visit. Choluteca is only about five hours from Teguc; unless you wish to visit the beach of Cedeño on the Bay of Fonseca you can visit on a day-trip.

PLACES TO STAY

Hotel Pierre on Ave. Valle and Calle Williams is fairly large and expensive. The cost is L40. for a single and L55. for a double ($9. - $12. US) However, there is air con and private baths. It is clean and close to the center.

San Carlos is on Bolivar El Centro and the cost runs around L15. for a single and L30. for a double ($3.25 US) per person. There are no private baths, but it is in the center of town.

Lisboa is also on Bolivar El Centro and runs at L30. - 40. for single and double ($6.50 - $9. US). Compared to the same price in Teguc, this is high. However, it is close to the Mi Esperanza bus terminal and only a few blocks from the market. It is clean, rooms have private baths, and there is a restaurant.

Hospedaje Central on Bolivar Corveta is a cheapie costing L16. per person ($3.50 US). There is no private bathroom in this hotel, and I found the owner quite unpleasant. But, if the San Carlos is full, it is the cheapest accomodation.

RESTAURANTS

You are on your own here. However, the town is a fairly good size so finding a place should not be too difficult. I did go to the **Padrino** which is known for its Italian food and is only a few blocks from the market. If you are in town around meal time, you may want to eat before heading out.

THINGS TO DO

Casa de la Cultura was originally an old church built in 1643. There is a baptismal stone in the building with the date inscribed. This museum is a must, especially if coming from Nicaragua, as it is nice to see artifacts fairly well preserved.

Playa de Cedeño is only a two hour trip from Choluteca; buses go there often during the day. The beach has no facilities except for a few small tiendas and some nonhuman hotels. But Cedeño is worth the trip because it is lovely. You can see the islands on the bay, enjoy safe swimming and wander through the interesting fishing village. Talking to the locals here can be pleasant but you must speak Spanish. Be certain not to go during the holiday season as it will be crowded. You can stay in the nearby village of Mojaras. It is in much better shape than any in Cedeño and is only a few minutes away by bus or truck.

Punta Raton is another little place on the coast that is a delight to visit. However, only two buses per day go there. If you do not wish to stay the night, you must return to Choluteca no later than 4:00 PM. Punta Raton is smaller than Cedeño but a few small hotels are available. Water to drink and wash with is scarce. A wildlife refuge one kilometer south from the village has birds, iguanas and during the autumn, large turtles nest in the area. However, this part of the beach is closed to visitors during nesting time. This is a nice place to spend a day. Visit the refuge, eat in the village, sun tan on the clean beach and practice Spanish with the people.

Orocuina is a little village north of Choluteca noted for its handicrafts. Mud pottery in the form of jars, cooking stoves and ashtrays are the most popular. The town is also known for its bamboo furnishings, woven palm, and decorative objects made from animal horn. If you want to purchase any items of this type, you will find it less expensive here than in Teguc. You can also hitch a ride on trucks going in the direction of the hot springs. These are not especially large nor extremely well-known but you may enjoy them. However, plan on staying in Choluteca rather than near the hot springs. You will be much more comfortable.

COPAN

This little village is delightful to visit and friendly if staying longer than the morning. The ruins are the major tourist attraction. They are considered to be the best restored ruins in Central America. Although the site is small, it is beautifully kept. The stelae from the ruins are considered the best in all the Maya world.

If coming from Guatemala for one day only, you will find the border fees quite expensive as you must pay exit and entry fees for both countries. You will also miss the pleasure of getting the true feeling of Honduras. I like this country and the more I explore; the better I like it.

If coming from Guatemala, change quetzales with the money changers at the border and get enough for yourself until you get to San Pedro Sula. The rate is okay but not great. If you have to change US dollars, you will get a very poor rate in this area.

Stone carving at Copan

327

PLACES TO STAY

Hotelita Brizas de Copan is on the hill near the bus station and is a beautiful little place for L15. per person ($3.50 US) without bath. It is clean to the point of sparkling. The owner is very friendly.

Hotel Marina is expensive at $25.00 for a single without bath. It is usually full of people who are working at the ruins. It is on the corner of the square.

Anexo Marina is on the main street and is much cheaper than the older sister hotel at L12. for a single and L20. for a double ($2.75 & $4.50 US). These rooms are also without a private bath. There is a delightful courtyard in which to sit and enjoy siesta time. However, be certain that you have your own lock for this place as there are stories that things have gone missing.

Hotel Paty is just down the street and across from the Brizas. It is L20. for a single and L30. for a double ($4.50 - $6.75 US). The rooms are clean and it has a restaurant which is popular with the locals - always a good sign that the food is acceptable.

Hospedaje Los Gemelos is also on the main street and is considered to be by some, the best place in town. The rooms cost L8. per person ($1.75 US) without private bath or hot water. The place is clean and pleasant.

RESTAURANTS

Often a well patronized place becomes a bit shoddy because the owners know they have a good reputation. This really bugs me, and I suggest you be adventuresome and try different places. In Copan, if you want to meet people, you will probably have a better chance of meeting people at the ruins than in a restaurant. However, the cafeteria at the ruins is terrible.

Hotel Marina is an excellent place to eat. They serve a daily three course meal for L20. and it is worth every penny. The meals are large, nicely presented and well prepared. However, they are not cheap.

Hotel Paty is the next best place to eat. You may get the typical meal of the day for about L10. Again, not cheap for what you get, but definitely substantial.

El Viajero is an excellent place to eat and is fairly new. It is considered the best deal in town by some as the meals are large, well prepared and not too expensive.

THINGS TO DO

The Copan Ruins are the only reason to visit Copan. Be certain to walk the mile to the ruins as there are stelae along the road which are worth seeing. The walk is easy and pleasant. The ruins are very well restored and the grounds are beautifully kept. There is a small display room at the entrance to the ruins that gives some description of the site.

Many of the stelae in Copan are beautifully preserved. Some have faces of deities, some have toothless old men and some have the faces of the death god, without skin. There are perfectly carved hands, conch shells, feathery designs and tassels. As you wander through the site, the stories told by these stone books are satisfying to every interpreter.

It is generally agreed that Copan reached its peak around 450 - 800AD, but there are indications that people lived in the area as early as 2000BC. Found on the banks of the River Copan, the site is in a fertile valley with a pleasant tropical climate. Sitting 2100 feet above sea level, the area is hospitable to the Chicozapote tree which produces an extremely hard wood which was used for the lintels in the temples. These lintels are still in good condition. The valley was also suitable for growing corn, the main staple of the Maya civilization.

Copan was a major trading center in Central America. Objects have been found from as far away as northern Mexico and southern Columbia. However, Copan was more important for its scientific contributions to the Maya world. Altar Q shows sixteen people facing a central date. It was believed that this day was when the Maya scientists accurately calculated the length of the year, worked out eclipse tables, and timed the orbit of Venus. However, today, modern scientists believe the carving to represent the Royal lineage of King Madrugada.

In 1838, Stephens and Catherwood discovered Copan and purchased the ruins from a local farmer for $50.00 US. Even then the Yankee dollar was desirable! They later wrote about the area in the book "Incidents of Travel in C.A., Chiapas and Yucatan." After Stephens, Maudsley came to explore the site but in doing so he removed many of the artifacts to the British Museum. In this century, the Peabody Museum and the Carnegie Institute did extensive restoration on the area. In 1952, the National Institute of Anthropology and History has assumed responsibility for the site.

The Great Plaza is the first area you see upon entering the park after passing beautiful macaw birds at the entrance. The plaza has stone seats on three sides and many stelae on the floor of the square. The offering chamber beneath Stelae A is open. This is where offerings were placed. The hieroglyphs represent Tikal and Palenque. Stelae B's hero has a beard; a beard is a rarity. Stelae C is different on both sides. Stelae F is a ball player and Stelae G has the most recent date inscribed. Stelae H has a skirt; it is uncertain where this lady came from. There was a gold statue from either Panama or Columbia found underneath her.

The Central Court is between the Great Plaza and the Ball Court. This is the location of Stelae 3 which is the tallest of all the stelae in Copan.

The **Ball Court** is one of the largest found in all the Maya cities. It has the date 775 AD inscribed on it. There were two earlier ball courts under this one. These are the sites where players played only for the nobility; the winner donated his heart on the altar for the final glory. After this ultimate high, the rest of his rewards would be obtained in the next and better world.

The **Hieroglyphic Staircase** is the most spectacular piece of work at Copan. You will not miss it as it is so unique. The structure has a staircase ten meters wide and 63 steps high. Each block has a separate hieroglyph and there are a total of about 2500 glyphs. Don't bother trying to count. When the archaeologists put the stairs back together, they were uncertain of the exact order, so the story in the glyphs may never be interpreted. An earthquake destroyed the original stairway. Today, scaffolds indicate that more restoration is taking place.

The dates on the stairway are between 544 and 756AD and one of the stairs has the Star of David on it. At the top of the stairs is the "Old Man of Copan" sculpture which is great.

The **Museum** is in the town of Copan. It is small and does not have a large or extraordinary display. The greatest attraction is the skeleton of a six-foot-tall man. This is a very tall person for that culture. It is believed to be from around 400AD. Should you miss the museum for some reason, it will not be a great loss. However, it is larger than the one at Tikal.

I did learn in this museum that colors were of great significance to the Maya. Not only do they use many bright colors in their dress, but their religion was also associated with color. For example, the east was represented by the color red, the west was black, the north was white (snow?) and the south was yellow. Green is the most sacred color of all, representing new growing corn, water and all things precious. Thus, jade was the most highly valued stone.

Blue Hill National Park (Cerro Azul) is a rain forest park that is only ten kilometers from Florida, on the way to La Entrada. The town of Florida has one basic hospedaje and a few comedors. You may be able to hitch a ride on a ten kilometer dirt road into the park. The park covers 150 square kilometers of rain forest and has a little lake near the top which is at 1800 meters (6000 feet) above sea level. There is an attractive waterfall at the lake. It is also a place where many migratory birds stop and bird watchers haunt. The top of the mountain is about 2285 meters (7500 ft); it is almost impossible to reach because of the steepness.

Spanish Schools are not all that common in Honduras, but there is one in the town of Copan called Ixbalanque Escuela de Español. It offers one to one instruction with a maximum of ten students in the school. The cost is $125.00 US for four hours of classes, five days a week and it includes room and board with a family. The cost is only $85.00 US per week if not living with a family. Extra lessons cost $17.00 US per hour per week. This is fairly high in price, but the area is delightful and you have a better chance of learning Spanish here than in a place like Antigua, Guatemala.

COMAYAGUA

Once the capital of Honduras, Comayagua is known as the "city of churches". It is about one and a half hours from Tegucigalpa and is halfway between the Pacific and Atlantic. The city was founded by Alonzo de Caceres in 1537 and was the capital city of Honduras before Tegucigalpa became the capital in 1880. This change came about when President Marco Aurelio Soto married an Indian girl in Guatemala and made her the first lady. The people of Comayagua would not give her the honor her husband wanted so Soto moved the capital to a different site where his bride would be respected.

The town itself is not extremely friendly, but, like anywhere in Honduras, there are some delightful people. Ignore those who are unfriendly and continue in a positive manner.

To get there, take any bus going to San Pedro Sula, get off at the Comayagua turn off and walk into the town. It is about a ten minute walk.

PLACES TO STAY

There are many hotels on the main street leading to the highway, but I didn't check them all. The hotels around the market are usually by the hour; and the owners were not interested in talking to me.

Nory Max is off the road going to the highway and half a block to the left when walking towards town. The cost is L32. ($7. US) for a single room with private bath; it is excellent. It is sparkling clean, has a small balcony with well tended plants and a small restaurant.

Hotel Americana is closer to the center and is L27. ($6. US) for a single and L32. ($7. US) for a double with a private bath. Very friendly owners. It is clean and nice but not as exceptional as the Nory Max.

Hotel Honduras is just around the corner from the Americana and costs L10., L15. and L20. ($2.25, $3.50 & $4.50 US) for a single, double or triple. The rooms are small, clean, and basic, with ceiling fans. The bathrooms are clean, and the owner is very pleasant. The hotel is only three blocks from the market.

Hotel La Libertad is on the central square and costs L12. ($2.75 US) and L20. ($4.50 US) without bathrooms. It is recommended by some as the best in town. I did not try it.

RESTAURANTS

Chinese Restaurant on the square is very good. The food is not the best in Honduras, but I think it is the best in Comayagua. The prices are reasonable.

The **Nory Max** has a little restaurant and the food is very good. The prices are a bit higher than around the square, but the place is really clean. They have real coffee.

THINGS TO DO

The major tourist attraction of Comayagua is visiting the churches. Put yourself in "church mode" and enjoy.

The **Cathedral** on the main square is actually the second cathedral of this city. It has been the main cathedral for three centuries and is often considered the finest building in the country. It was built from 1685 to 1715. The building was first suggested by the Bishop Gaspar de Andrada in the early 1600s. Indian designs of palms, flowers and ears of corn are prominent on the first floor facades. Around the door are plants that extend upward to two angels. Several other symbols around the building do not come from the Catholic religion.

The crucifix, a gift from King Philip IV of Spain, was made by sculptor Andres Ocampo. The altar of Señor de Salame was made by Vincente Galvez as was the altar in the main cathedral in Tegucigalpa. The beautiful design of this church makes it a "must" to visit.

La Merced Church the first cathedral in Honduras was built between 1550 to 1558. It held this honor for over 50 years. The church was started by Cristobal de Pedraza, a monk living in the area. The square in the front of this church was the first square built in the city.

San Sebastian Church was built in 1568 and now houses the tomb of president José Trinidad Cabanas. Other than visiting the tomb, there is no reason to go into this church.

San Francisco Church was built in 1569 and has the oldest church bell in all Central America. The bell has the inscription "Fundida 1464, Alcala".

San Juan de Dios, built in 1590, was destroyed by an earthquake. It is the site of the Inquisition of Honduras.

Children's Park behind the cathedral has the remains of an entrance-way which is dated 1739-1741. It is a lovely park and the archway is uniquely designed.

Archaeological Museum is closed Monday and Tuesday. The rest of the week it is open from 9-12AM and 1-4PM. There is a small entrance fee. It is a tiny museum with only a few artifacts. The most interesting are the artifacts found at Salitron Viejo in El Cajon. The museum does not take long to visit. The museum is one block past the main cathedral.

Colonial Museum costs L3. to enter; this is expensive for Honduras. However, it is very tastefully decorated and the displays are interesting without being overpowering. There is some beautiful religious jewelry embedded with emeralds. Many of the objects sit behind the small gift shop. These pieces need only be dusted and displayed in a more prominent location.

The Clock on the main square is one of the oldest in the world. It was made by the Moors in Seville, Spain, in the 12th century. King Philip 11 donated it to Honduras. The clock still tells accurate time.

Mount Comayagua National Park is 13 kilometers east of the city. You can take a bus. There is no information as to the size of the park nor the elevation of the mountain. If you are bored while in Comayagua, you may want to explore this little area.

La Paz - see under La Paz as this could be a day trip or an overnighter.

CATACAMAS

This is an interesting town in the district of Olancho and close to the Rio Tinto. The end of the road past Catacamas goes to Dulce Nombre de Culmi which leaves you quite close to the eastern end of the Mosquitia. There are restaurants and a couple of small hotels in this town; as well, you will find a bank that will not change your traveller's cheques. The church in the center of town is worth visiting.

PLACES TO STAY

Colonial Hotel is on the main street and is the cheapest in town at L10. ($2.25 US) per person. It is not luxurious, but is clean and pleasant.

Hospedaje Oriental is on the lower section of Boulevard San Sebastian. The rooms are about L15. ($3.50 US) per person, and you get a few luxuries such as a chair in your room. There was even a mirror in one of the rooms. The rooms are clean enough to stay in.

Hotelito San Josè is right on the park and only costs L5. per person. There is no private bath nor is there a swimming pool.

Hotel Moderno, also on the main street is more expensive at L15. ($3.50 US), but may be more your style. It is quite comfortable, but it only has a few rooms. This makes the place very homey.

THINGS TO DO

Agalta Park is a little ways north of Catacamas but is said to be difficult to reach. There are two hills that you can climb in the park, the highest being 2590 meters (8500 feet) above sea level and the lower one being 2485 meters (8200 ft.) high. One of the interesting aspects of the park is the abundance of different reeds and canes. There are also caves with underground rivers. I have not explored this park; if you wish to visit, you will find it difficult to find information. The locals say it is very beautiful.

DANLI

This is a pleasant little town you may pass through enroute from Los Manos on the Nicaraguan border. After Nicaragua, this town is a treat and should be visited. The bus station is about a half hour walk from the center of town. If you walk directly along the main street leading to the central park, you will pass a great place to eat and drink.

PLACES TO STAY

Hospedaje San Cristobal is on the main street about three blocks before the park and next door to a burger place. This has been recommended to me by a few travellers. The cost is L15. ($3.75 US) per person without private bath.

Las Vegas Hotel is in front of the bus terminal and rents rooms for a mere L15. ($3.50 US) and L25. ($5.50 US) for a double. It is acceptable.

Esperanza Hotel is three blocks from the central park, just before the shell station. It costs L20. ($4.50 US) and L30. ($6.75 US) for a double. It is a fairly large place and quite acceptable.

Hotel Danli is around the corner from the Esperanza and is recommended. The cost is L10. ($2.25 US) for a single and L20. ($4.50 US) for a double. There are no private bathrooms and hot water is not needed as it is quite warm in this area. However, there is water.

THINGS TO DO

The Central Park has a wonderful little church built in 1750. The municipal building has a small museum which you should visit. You will not need to plan a long visit. Danli celebrates the National Corn festival in August; if you are in the area, it is quite a gala affair which you will enjoy.

Honduran-American Cigar Factory can be toured if you are interested in good cigars. You can only purchase packages of cigars and the cost is not low. The factory is about two kilometers from the center. You must go back towards the bus station and when you come to the cemetery, turn right and keep going. You will soon come to the factory.

Teupasenti is a village that is north of Danli. It is worth a visit because of the proximity of two pretty waterfalls. Take a bus to Teupasenti and then walk towards Chile and the river. The two falls are about 40 meters (125 ft) high.

EL AMATILLO

El Amatillo is on the border with El Salvador and is worse than Nacaome. It is very small, dusty (muddy in rainy season) and hot. The people are friendly but if there are buses, keep going. There is a hospedaje just before the bridge, but I didn't bother to visit it.

EL PARAISO

This is the first substantial town after leaving Nicaragua and entering Honduras. It is small and not really very pleasant. Unless it is late and you are tired, I would suggest going on to Danli. However, if you must stay, there are some basic hotels and a few places to eat. It looks like a frontier town of the old wild west.

Buses go from El Paraiso to Danli and to the border. You may also get a direct bus to Teguc from here. Take the Discua-Litena because it stops in Comayaguela, near the center of Teguc. The other bus stops at the top of the hill before going into the center of Teguc and a taxi will cost you quite a bit, especially if you are a gringo. However, if it is early in the day, you could use a city bus once in Teguc.

PLACES TO STAY

Casa Familiar is on the Boulevard El Calvario and costs L5. per person ($1.25 US) Needless to say, there are no private baths or room service.

Hospedaje Paraiso is on Boulevard San Isidro and costs L10. ($2.25 US) per person. This is a cheapie.

Hospedaje Ninoska is on the central park. This is the classiest accommodation in town and runs at L12. ($2.75 US) per person. This is small and friendly. If you are enroute to or from Nicaragua, this is heaven.

PLACES TO EAT

The typical comedors will have at least the meal of the day which is fried plantain, re-fried beans and eggs with cheese and sour cream. You will not get an eight course gourmet meal in this town.

EL PROGRESO

El Progreso is a bustling little town between the Quemado Mountains and the Ulua River. It was an Indian village known for its importance in the river trade. Today it is a flourishing commercial center. However, it does not have many tourist attractions.

PLACES TO STAY

Emperador is okay for an inexpensive place to stay. It includes a private bath and a one tap shower for L20. a single and L30. for a double ($4.50 & $6.75 US), but it is not the friendliest place. **Honduras** is on the main street opposite the municipal offices. The cost is only L20. for a single and L30. for a double ($4.50 & $6.75 US). This is the best hotel if you want to be in the center of town.

Las Vegas is on Calle 11 and Ave. 2, on the road going towards Tela. It is fairly large and costs L25. for a single and L35. for a double ($5.50 - $8. US); it has private bathrooms.

THINGS TO DO

An old **bronze cannon** may be seen across from the Notre Dame School. It was found near Tela and is from a ship which sank in the Caribbean in 1524.

Santa Elizabeth School is a craft center where Hondurans learn the craft of carving. People may purchase quality wood carvings at a reasonable price. There are souvenirs and articles of furniture carved from mahogany and cedar. You may also order articles which can be sent home or picked up at a later date. Many of the carvings on display are not for sale.

La Mina is a wonderful swimming hole and waterfall. Take a bus going to Yoro, Olanchito or Santa Rita and ask the driver to let you off at the road going to La Mina. Get off and walk towards the river for about one kilometer. The waterfall is about 100 feet high and is a pretty place to spend a few hours.

Pico-Pijol National Park is on the road between Yoro and El Progresso. Take the Yoro bus and get off at Chancara and then take a truck to Subirana. The park is ten kilometers south west of the town of Subirana. You can get a truck to go in that direction once in Subirana. The park is reported to have Quetzales. The park is a rain forest which sits 2282 meters (7500 feet) above sea level. If you are planning to visit for a day trip, you must start early in the morning as there is no place to stay near the park.

Clay oven

GRACIAS

Gracias is a beautiful little town tucked away in the mountains. However, during rainy season, travel is difficult. The buses don't run from Gracias to La Esperanza regularly; sometimes they don't even run between Santa Rosa de Copan and Gracias. You can try to hitch a ride if you dress modestly. These people are poor peasants, and they generally don't trust gringos who are unconventional.

Gracias banks do not exchange any traveller's cheques but you may be able to find someone to exchange American cash.

Gracias was first settled in the 1500's. Francisco de Montejo became the first Govenor of Honduras and Gracias became the first capital. The palace on the park was the original home of Montejo as governor. In 1537, Lempira was defeated and Alvarado came to replaced Montejo as governor. Montejo then went to Mexico. The town remained the capital of Honduras for a short time after that.

PLACES TO STAY

Hotel Eric is the lovely pink building directly across from the bus station. There is no sign, but go into the drug store on the corner and ask for a room. They will rent you a room for L15. ($3.50 US) per person. They are large, clean, bright and have towels and soap. However, there is only cold water; if you are there for rainy season, you may not appreciate the cold water.

Hospedaje San Antonio is about the same size as the Eric with fewer services. The hotel is basic without private bath. It is on the main square and is only L10. per person ($2.25 US).

Pension Herrera is next to the bus station and is probably the least expensive in town, but it is noisy, dirty and to be avoided.

RESTAURANTS.

Club Social is the best place to eat. The food is good, the price is right, the service is friendly and the decor is great. Its decorations, with bright red curtains and black trim, make it look like a gold rush brothel.

THINGS TO DO

El Presedente Hot Springs are the main reason anyone would take the long gruesome ride into Gracias. To get to the springs you may walk by going out the road towards La Esperanza but the walk is quite long, about three hours one way. If you want to walk, go past the central park and back to the road to La Esperanza. Walk along the road until you pass the bridge and then continue for another 20 to 30 minutes. After you pass a house on your left, take the path to the right. Continue along this path up and over the hill until you come to an intersection and then turn left. Continue up the hill and then down into the hot springs. You may ask for directions while walking. I prefer to take the taxi one way.

If you get someone in town to drive you, the price is L20. ($4.50 US) one way, and the driver will return for you. The springs themselves are very nice; they are hot and have three pools. One is tepid which is for swimming, one is for soaking which is exceptionally hot and excellent and the third one is cool and is for children to play. There is a change room but no restaurant. Many of the locals sit in the pool and enjoy the local beer.

The Castle on the hill in Gracias appears to be the local prison at first glance but I am told by locals that I would find the post office located in the building. It is an interesting fortress tucked way back in the hills.

Celaque National Park can be reached out of Gracias. Celaque is the highest mountain in Honduras standing at 2849 meters (9350 ft) above sea level. "Celaque" is an Aztec Indian word meaning "the water of cold ice". If you wish to visit, go early in the morning and take everything you will need for the entire day. It will be a difficult but beautiful climb. To get to the trailhead, go past the cemetery, turn left and then take the first street on the right. Then continue straight past the church and keep going, don't turn off anywhere.

It will take at least three and half hours to the park entrance where you can camp if you have gear. Otherwise, just continue up the trail.

After walking through the rain forest, you will eventually come to the plateau at the top; this plateau is almost perfectly circular. The highest river in Honduras starts up here; from these crystal clear waters come nine other rivers which supply almost 100 communities in Honduras. From the plateau you will have a spectacular sight of the valleys. Even if you don't go all the way to the summit, it is a delight to walk around this area. If you like Gracias, then spend an extra day in the area and enjoy the park. This park can also be reached from La Esperanza.

Erandique is an interesting little town. The people will willingly sell you all the opals you can possibly carry and all for a good price. Although there are places to eat and a hospedaje where you may stay if stranded, it is only recommended to visit here for a few hours during a day trip. To reach Erandique, take a bus towards La Esperanza and get off just before San Juan. Then either hitch or catch a truck. It is an interesting frontier town.   There is a church built in 1524;   many precious stones were found there. The custom of selling precious stones in the town may have originated from that time. About two kilometers out of town is a river where you can swim. If you continue up river, you will see a delightful waterfall.

LA CEIBA

La Ceiba, a beautiful, friendly town, is a mixture of Caribe and Ladino cultures. Many Ladino tourists visit this town and there are only a few gringos. The beach is so-so. One needs to walk east of town about one or two kilometers in order to enjoy fairly clean water. Many on-the-beach restaurants offer drinks or seafood. Locally called Ceibita la Bella, "little Ceiba, the beautiful", it was originally a banana port but is now the tourist port. If you want a boat to the Bay Islands or down the Mosquitia, this is the best place to get it.

The bus depot is a long way from town; it takes about half an hour walk or you can take an expensive taxi. To get to the airport, take bus Colonial de Mayo and get off at the airport. You will have to walk one city block to the terminal.

Change money and traveller's cheques at Supermarket Costeños, which is by the train tracks. They give a good rate without any hassles.

PLACES TO STAY

There is a variety of hotels in La Ceiba; these are only a few of the more popular. They give you an idea of the prices in La Ceiba. During the carnival in May, (Fiesta Isidra during the third week in May), the hotel prices double.

The Granada on Ave. Atlantida and Blvd. El Centro costs L32. for a single and L42. for a double ($7. - $9. US). Although I didn't care for the "modern art" on the walls, all the rooms have brightly colored, clean sheets. There are private baths (one tap) and a fan in the rooms. The hotel is in the center of town.

Ligeros Hotel is across from the Granada on Calle 5. It is L16. and L30. for a double ($3.50 - $6.50 US). The hotel has clean rooms and is very friendly. Each room has its own bathroom.

Dorita is also in the same vicinity and rents for L35. a room ($7.75 US). The rooms have private baths; the place is clean, but there are no singles.

Arias Hotel is along the tracks and rents for L10. ($2.25 US) per person without bath and with cold water. It is basic but certainly clean enough. Is is also safe and popular with Chickenbusers.

The California is in the middle of town and is excellent but slightly expensive. The rooms cost L20. ($4.50 US) without bath and L35. ($7.75 US) with bath. The hotel is very quiet and friendly.

Los Brisas is close to the beach on Calle 1A, the street with the first bridge going over the creek. It is also on the Caribe side of town. Rooms are L20. ($4.50 US) per person with air conditioning and L10. ($2.25 US) without air con. If you want a private bath, it costs an extra L10. ($2.25 US). Due to the attached disco, it may be a bit noisy on Saturday night. This is the fun side of town.

Amsterdam 2001 is also on the Caribe side of town, on Calle 1A, and has a laundromat. This is often a welcome feature when in Central America.

RESTAURANTS

Since this is a vacation spot, there are numerous good restaurants. The ones situated along the river are very romantic and many serve good meals. The ones along the beaches serve excellent seafood, but may be a bit pricey. The restaurants in the hotels usually have good food at fairly reasonable rates. Irregardless of your budget, you will not go hungry in La Ceiba.

THINGS TO DO

La Ceiba is both a vacation spot and the jumping off place for the Bay Islands. The best plan for La Ceiba is to swim and sun tan all day, eat a romantic meal just after dark, and then visit the many discos. The discos are the central action; the ones in the Caribe section of town are especially great.

Corozal is a Garifuna village sixteen kilometers east of La Ceiba. Buses go regularly. If you should decide to walk along the beautiful beaches one way, it will take about six hours. There are places to eat in Corozal and the people are very friendly.

Hike to Trujillo can be started at Rio Esteban. There are two buses a day going to the Rio Esteban. If you walk all the way, the hike takes two full days. There are no places to stay so you will need camping gear, but there are places to eat. You may wish to take a boat or canoe up the coast to Trujillo; these can be rented, with a guide at Rio Esteban.

Pico Bonito National Park is near La Ceiba but it is a difficult park to enter. You must have hiking equipment and be totally self sufficient. Although named the "Cordillera Nombre de Dios" by the Hondurans, I think it should be translated as "God's country". Although, you may not be able to enter the park, you can play in the periphery and visit a waterfall on the Rio Maria. The walk is less than an hour (uphill). The highest mountain in the park is at 2435 meters (8000 ft).

LA ENTRADA

This is where you change buses if going between Copan and Teguc or San Pedro Sula. It is a dusty (muddy when wet) little town which does not have much to offer.

PLACES TO STAY

Tegucigalpa Hotel is at the far end of town, opposite the bus stop. It is basic with a one tap shower for only L15. ($3.50 US) per person; it is the best in town.

Hospedaje Maria is behind the Shell Station and costs about

L10. ($2.25 US) per person. There is no private bath; it is basic and inexpensive.

THINGS TO DO

The museum, although small, is worth a visit. Stone carvings found in the area and interesting clay pottery are displayed. Ten minutes are all that's needed to visit the museum; you can stop in while waiting to change buses.

LA ESPERANZA

During the rainy season, travelling between Gracias and La Esperanza is difficult. Buses and trucks only run when the road is dry; it is a delightful trip. A few villages close to La Esperanza may be visited; however, it is much more comfortable to move on to the main highway.

PLACES TO STAY

La Esperanza Hotel is between the market and the park. It is clean and pleasant with bath for L20. ($4.50 US) per person. This is the best hotel.

Hotel Mina is closer to the market, up from the La Esperanza, and is the next best hotel for half the price. It is clean and friendly but without private bath. The cost is L10. ($2.25 US) per person.

RESTAURANTS

The Magus is the only restaurant in town which serves good food at a reasonable price from a clean kitchen. It is half a block from the square in the opposite direction of the police station. If you do not eat here, you may have to eat at the market.

THINGS TO DO

Indian Center for Handicraft Instruction is a delightful art school which welcomes visitors. It specializes in "Bayal" which is the art of making woven objects out of lacquered cane peelings.

The other art specialty is called "Tuza", the making of dolls, flowers and other decorative articles from corn husks. The tuza is often dyed different colors.

Yamaranquila is a delightful and friendly village half an hour down the road from La Esperanza. You should take a bus one way and walk the other in order to enjoy the countryside. The friendliness of the people in this area is exceptional for Honduras. The walk should not take you more than three hours, unless you spend a lot of time talking to the locals. The presence of tourists in this area is unusual; the locals are patient and answer the same questions over and over again. After you go through the town, continue as far as the bridge and then turn left along the path. Take the path on the village side of the bridge. Continue along for a few minutes and you will come to a delightful waterfall and a great canyon. If you go to Yamaranquila, you must visit the river.

LA PAZ

This town is friendlier than Comayagua and can be visited as a day trip or an overnighter. A tour of La Paz, Tutule, La Mora and Marcala then back to either La Paz or Comayagua is recommended.

PLACES TO STAY

Hotel Ali is the best at L20. ($4.50 US) per person with a private bath. They also have rooms without bath. It is clean and friendly.

RESTAURANTS

La Elegancia is the best in town. It is quite clean and you will receive good service and be charged the same price as the locals.

Hotel Ali also serves meals and may be a good place for breakfast.

THINGS TO DO

Tutule is a village you will pass through enroute to Marcala. It is a Guajiquiros Indian village; market days are on Thursday and Sunday. Although the market is pleasant, it can't be compared to those of Guatemala.

Marcala is a village a few hours away from La Paz. The area is beautiful; oranges, bamboo and coffee grow in abundance. The bamboo resembles huge green feathers fluttering in the wind and I can see why the Chinese revere this plant so much. The bus ride to Marcala is quite beautiful as it passes through mountains, rivers, steams and hills.

PUERTO LEMPIRA, THE MOSQUITIA COAST

This is the most undeveloped and isolated area in Honduras. It is not advisable to go into this area alone, especially if female. I spoke with men who have adventured into this area alone, but they were big, young and Spanish speaking. If you wish to explore this area, you will have to be your own guide; the scope of that adventure is beyond the limits of this book. I am only giving a limited amount of information here.

The Mosquitia was first inhabited by the British; there are many grave sites, old churches and rusting remains of ships, cannons and pieces of sailing equipment. Only a guide would be able to show you where these artifacts are located.

The best way to explore the Mosquitia is to get a boat at La Ceiba and travel along the coast to Puerto Limpera. Regular boats go once or twice a month; as well, smaller boats go when full. Along the coast there is a place before Puerto Limpera where high winds and strong currents make passage difficult. Often boats must wait a few days or even a week before being able to continue.

Another way of travelling in the Mosquitia is to go by boat along the river with the native peoples of the area. I knew one fellow who took a cayuco along a river to the coast and then caught a boat back, but it took him almost a month for the circle trip.

There are regular weekly flights to Puerto Lempira from La Ceiba. Although expensive, about L150. ($35.US) the experience is not as much fun as overland travel. Accommodations are very primitive everywhere, especially in locations away from Puerto Lempira.

Two outfitters arrange tours of the Mosquitia Coast. One is Cambio C.A. which offers Eco-Adventures for $728.00 US for eight days of travel. All expenses are included and much of the travel is by canoe.

The other outfitter who offers tours is Trek International Safaris, P.O. Box 19065, Jacksonville, Florida. This outfit offers hunting and fishing tours; they must have a minimum of ten people.

PLACES TO STAY

The **Modelo** is basic and small but certainly not inexpensive. No private bath nor hot water. The other place to stay is the **Teresita** which is even more basic. However, if you travelled by boat this will feel like the Hyatt.

THINGS TO DO

Laguna de Caratasca Biological Reserve starts at Puerto Limpera and goes along the coast to the Patuca River. This swampy jungle area is teeming with wildlife such as alligators, giant sea turtles, birds and other jungle creatures.

The Cayos Misquitos Biological Reserve includes the cays and rocks just off the coast; some are as far away as 80 kilometers. There is no human habitation on the cays. They can be visited by hiring a fishing boat.

NACAOME

This is a hot, grubby little town. You may have to stay here enroute to or from El Salvador as many buses cease to run by 6:00PM. Hotels are basic and are all about the same quality and price.

NUEVA OCOTEPEQUE

This dusty, dreary little village is tucked away in some of the most rugged country in Honduras. The setting is truly beautiful with high mountains, narrow roads, steep drop-offs and koma-kozi drivers. If enroute to or from Agua Caliente, Guatemala or El Poy, El Salvador you may want to rest here. It is six or seven hours to San

Pedro Sula, you should be rested before journeying further. Guatemalan and El Salvadorian consulates are in this village.

PLACES TO STAY

Sandoval Hotel is the best place. They charge L20. ($4.50 US) per person for a private bath and two tap shower. It is clean and pleasant. A restaurant in the hotel serves excellent food.

Congolon Hospedaje is where the Congolon bus stops. Although dreary, it is clean. They charge L20. ($4.50 US) per person; for the same price, the Sandoval is much better. There are one tap showers in the private bathrooms. The owners will try to avoid renting to the gringos; when they do, they are almost certain to get the worst rooms.

Hotelito San Juan charges only L8. ($1.75 US); it is reasonable for the price. There are no private baths and the showers need some cleaning. The owners are very friendly and helpful.

San Antonio Hospedaje is very, very basic and the rooms are clean. The cost is L8. ($1.75 US) per person; extra blankets are provided. However, the bathrooms are terrible. Plan a shower for your next stop.

Mini Hotel is better than some in town, but they are often full. They charge L5. ($1.25 US) without bathrooms and only one tap showers.

RESTAURANTS

Many comedors are available but if it is a holiday, they will be closed. I found the Sandoval to be the best to deal with.

Sandoval Hotel is open at 7:00AM. The food is excellent, the people are friendly and the prices are reasonable.

THINGS TO DO

Trifinio National Park is reached from this location. This park is jointly administered by the Salvadorian, Guatemalan and Honduran governments. The purpose of the park (other than conservation) is to promote brotherhood and peace between the three countries. The purpose has not been achieved.

The total park covers an area of 54 square kilometers; 20 square kilometers are in Honduras. The mountain Montecristo is the divisional point of the three countries: it sits 2419 meters (8000 ft) above sea level. The deforestation in the area is terrible, and mud slides are common.

Hot springs are only two kilometers going west from town, towards Guatemala. There are three bathing pools. These springs are not often visited as tourists tend not to spend much time in the area.

Salvadorian consulate is on 5 Calle and 2 Ave. However, acquireing a visa is quite a challenge. It will cost at least $30.00 US for the "police search", the paper work and other "expenses".

A **Natural Museum** is in town and is open weekdays from 9 - 12:00PM and 2:00 - 4:00PM. There is a small entrance fee. The museum is quite small with a minimal number of dusty creatures on display.

PUERO CORTES

This town is the main Atlantic port. It handles Honduran imports and exports and some of El Salvador's imports and exports. The town itself is hot and bustling. It is an excellent place to stay and visit the beautiful beaches in the area.

PLACES TO STAY

Hotel Tuek San is on the square. Although it appears somewhat seedy, it is one of the better hotels. It is clean and has private bathrooms for L30. ($6.75 US) per person. A restaurant serves good food.

Hotel Mr. Ggeerr (not a joke) is on 2 Ave. and 9 Calle. It is the nicest place to stay. He charges L20. ($4.50 US) per person, and he is friendly. Some rooms without private baths. The restaurant serves decent food.

Los Piratas is basic and friendly for only L10. ($2.25 US) per person. The owners are very helpful. Only cold water showers are available; given the climate, cold water suffices.

RESTAURANTS

Restaurant Tuek San on the square serves decent meals for a decent price.

Restaurant Mr. G's at the hotel of the same name is good for a meal. It is clean.

THINGS TO DO

Omoa is twenty minutes past Puerto Cortes. It is a must to visit the fort and museum. Although the setting is not as nice as Trujillo, the fort is better preserved and destroyed sections are being restored. The museum at Omoa is also being renovated and more objects being displayed.

Fort San Fernando de Omoa was built in 1759 for a mere two million pesos. It was built as a fortress against pirates. Some of the stone used for the building is actual coral taken from the Zapotillos Island area. After pirating became unfashionable, in 1909, it was used as a jail. Now it is a museum. Next to the fort is the lake called Laguna de Centeno; this occasionally spews volcanic fumes.

A delightful beach a kilometer or so past the fort allows you to enjoy some rays before heading back. There is no place to stay at Omoa. Also, restaurant food is scarce.

The road between Puerto Cortes and Omoa goes along the coast and is dotted with beautiful wealthy homes. A few luxurious hotels are along the route but they are not for the chickenbusers. Most of the beaches along this strip are private. The beach at Omoa is beautiful and should be visited.

SAN MARCOS DE COLON

This is a little town outside of Choluteca and close to the Nicaraguan border. If planning to go to Nicaragua, I would suggest that you have your visa in advance.

San Marcos has many places to stay and is a relatively pleasant spot. Some like this town better than Choluteca. For a small fee, you can take a taxi or a truck to the border.

There is nothing to do in town except getting psyched for Nicaragua. The border town in Nicaragua is Somoto; from there, buses travel to Esteli and then Managua.

PLACES TO STAY

Hotelito Mi Esperanza is inexpensive at L9. ($2. US). There are clean sheets on the beds; bathrooms are in the courtyard. However, there are no towels, no soap, no toilet paper and there is lots of noise if your room is close to the bar. Be careful.

RESTAURANTS

Pollo Frito Bananza has chicken (again) and chips for a reasonable price of about L4.50 ($1. US). Since there is not much to choose from this is a safe place to eat.

Breakfast can be bought at a restaurant close to the center of town; it is the only one open early. In the restaurant is a sign which states: "Show your culture and not spit on the floor."

Hand-made wheelbarrow

SAN PEDRO SULA

With a population of 110,000 people, San Pedro Sula is the second biggest city in Honduras. It has a pleasant, tropical, climate all year, an average temperature of 79ºF, and cool mountain breezes.

Founded in 1536 by Don Pedro de Alvarado, it was originally called "The Village of St. Peter of the Port of Horses" - slightly long winded. The words were slowly dropped and Sula comes from the Indian word "Usula" which means "valley of the birds". The town has a terrible history of misfortune. It was burned and looted by pirates in 1660, twice destroyed by floods, and then becoming a favorite breeding ground for typhoid fever. However, with the change of name came the change of luck; today it is a lovely, bustling town where progress can be seen on every corner.

PLACES TO STAY

Hotel San Pedro on 1 & 2 Ave., 3 Calle is L38. ($8.50 US) per person with a private bath, two-tap shower and clean sheets. However, it is very dreary with numerous ants on the floor. I also found a huge worm in the toilet - enough to turn anyone off. However, it is not the worst hotel in San Pedro Sula.

Hotel Terrazo is L30. ($6.75 US) for a single and L48. ($10.75 US) for a double. This includes a fan and water. It is fairly clean and cheery. It is on Ave. S.O. and 4 & 5 Calle. It has a restaurant with very poor service.

Gran Hotel is on the square; if you are tired and need a real treat, try this place. A double room is a mere L175. ($40. US) but the price is negotiable. However, if you are a gringo, the manager will tell you the price is double that; he will then give you a real deal because business is low. If you are willing to barter, you will then get it for the regular price. It has a wonderful pool, excellent dining (with red wine available), and excellent service. The employees speak English. You may change American travellers cheques, have laundry service, enjoy rooms with television and telephone and at the end of the day, feel like a million dollars (less $40. US). At least go in for a meal and a pleasant drink at the bar.

Hotel Brazilia on 6 & 7 Calle and 2 Ave. S.E. is the best buy I could find. When you get off the Norteño bus, go to the first street and turn towards the tracks. You will see it from the corner. Go over the tracks and turn left. Hotel Brazilia costs L15. ($3.25 US) for a single and L20. ($4.50 US) for a double. There are clean rooms with bathrooms and some even have little balconies. When I was there this year, they were re-painting again.

Hotel Parador is right next door to the Brazilia and costs L20. ($4.50 US) per person. It is also very clean and cheery. Given these two choices, you need not stay in a dump nor live above budget while in San Pedro Sula.

Hotel Paris on 2 Ave. 3 & 4 Calle is a cheapie for L10. ($2.25 US) per person with no bath; it is also noisy. This is only a so-so hotel which was popular quite a few years ago.

La Siesta on 7 Calle and 2 Ave. is across and up from the Brazilia. It is certainly acceptable at L24. ($5.50 US) per person. There are private baths and large clean rooms which have mirrors. The workers are pleasant.

The Ambassador is on 7 Calle and 5 Ave. and is a real treat for only L37. ($8.25 US). If you are in need of luxury and can't afford the Gran, I recommend this. It is very clean, with good service and real hot water. There is a restaurant in the hotel and you can get beer from the fridge at any time. The rooms also have telephones and some have TV. The service in this hotel is very pleasant.

RESTAURANTS

Chinese Restaurant on Calle 3, two blocks before the square, is an excellent place to eat. This clean restaurant has good service, inexpensive meals and large portions.

Italia near the Gran Hotel is good for some pasta. The meals are more expensive than market food but of higher quality.

Gran Hotel is a great place to have a drink and/or a salad. Here you can trust the quality of the food. The cafeteria is also clean and the prices are reasonable.

The Ambassador serves good, thin pancakes for a reasonable price. The restaurant itself is quite small and drab, but the workers are very pleasant and friendly.

Pizza Hut near the square is awful. It is cafeteria style and very expensive. There are much better places to eat in San Pedro Sula.

THINGS TO DO

The Cathedral on the square is a huge austere building with mural paintings in the dome and on the walls. One side has a plaster statue of Jesus surrounded by many donated plaques giving special thanks for the miracles He has performed for the believers. Outside the church, beggars also look for a miracle, preferably from your pocket.

Camping or hiking is available in the nearby park of Palmirola. This mountainous park is full of pine trees. For northerners who are nostalgic for familiar terrain this is a great place to visit even though the pines are different than those in North America. There is a campground and several hiking trails in the park. To get there, take a Sula #5 bus and ask to go to Palmirola.

Waterfall Pulhapanzak on the Rio Lindo is a pleasant, all day hike. Take the bus going towards Teguc and get off at El Mochito. There is a small pop stand at the road turnoff and a few small comedors further up the road. This is close to Lake Yojoa. The gravel road into the falls (there is a sign) is ten kilometers and there is no bus. You must hike or hitch a ride; these are very easy to get. Do not return too late in the day because, if you do have to walk, you will need at least two and a half hours to return to the main road. At the 45 meter high falls (some brochures say 100 meters) is a park with a small entrance fee. Picnic tables are available at this lovely spot. Maya ruins are at the falls, but they are only about 50 - 70 years old. Not quite antiquity. However, it is believed that the Maya used this area as a sacred place.

Central Cultura San Pedro on 3 Calle and 8 Ave. has a nice little art gallery with art from all over Central America. They also have a local theater where plays are performed. This Center is also the school for the artists and actors of Honduras.

Spanish Club on 8 Calle and 1 Ave., over the tracks, is a neat little club where you can drink, play foozeball, play pool or just visit. The people who run the club are friendly and welcome foreigners. One daughter speaks fluent English and enjoys practicing English with travellers.

Cusuco National Park is a rain forest area which was proclaimed a park in order to protect San Pedro's water supply. It is a small park with mountains that are 2242 meters (7350 ft) above sea level. The park is 20 kilometers west of San Pedro. You go to Cofradia and then change for a truck going towards the park.

SANTA BARBARA

This hot little frontier town is tucked away in the mountains. It is usually bypassed by tourists but really deserves a visit. Santa Barbara is between San Pedro Sula and Santa Rosa as the crow flies. However, you must travel on a secondary road in order to visit the town. This means slower travel, but more relaxation.

PLACES TO STAY

There is not much variety in Santa Barbara. I will list a few, but I have not checked them.

Hotel Ruth on Calle La Libertad costs L17. for a single and L27. for a double ($3.75 - $6. US) It is in Barrio Abajo. It is quite small with only a dozen rooms.

Hospedaje Rosilei on Calle La Paz, also in barrio Abajo, charges L10. ($2.25 US) per person. There are no private baths. Only cold water is needed in this town so, that is all you get.

Boarding House Danny is in Barrio La Curva and costs L25 per person (5.50 US). I do not know if this includes meals.

THINGS TO DO

Museum in town is open every day except Monday. It is small, but has a few interesting artifacts. It only takes a half hour to visit the building.

San Vincente Hotsprings and Pencalique Waterfall can be reached from Santa Barbara on a day trip. Take a bus to Zacapa; this will take you about an hour. From Zacapa (where there is a nice church) take a bus or a truck to Azacualpa and then on to the hot springs at Cerro Cargamon. The springs are nice and not patronized by too many gringos. From there, walk for about an hour to the waterfalls on the river. Go in the direction of Atima and keep asking for directions. The waterfall is very high and quite beautiful.

SANTA RITA DE COPAN

Between La Entrada and Copan, this lovely little village has a colonial style church, a quiet park and a little market. You could get off the bus and have lunch or just snoop around for an hour or so before continuing on to Copan. There is a delightful creek running through town; this is perfect for dipping your feet or just daydreaming. There is a small hospedaje in the village and a few typical restaurants. The people are very friendly and love to hear stories about your country. Because most travellers just pass by, this quaint little village is often overlooked. By all means, take an hour or two to discover something different.

SANTA ROSA DE COPAN

Santa Rosa is a delightful, little colonial town tucked into the mountains at 1100 meters (3600 ft.). There is actually two parts to the town, one at the bottom of the hill and the second quite a ways up the hill. It is nice to stay at the bottom and have dinner at the top. The walk makes you earn your meal.

PLACES TO STAY

Hotel El Rey is across from the bus stop and easy to get to. They charge L15. ($3.50 US) per person without bath. Okay but not the best.

Hotel Mayaland is at the other end of the street from the bus stop on Boulevard Miraflorez. They charge L25. (5.50 US) per person and they have private bath. Not a bad place to stay.

Hotel Elvir is kitty-corner from the park and some consider it the best. The cost is the highest at L32. ($7. US) per person. This includes private bath, and the place is quite clean.

RESTAURANTS

Hotel Elvir has an expensive restaurant with decent meals. Other than this, there are very few choices.

THINGS TO DO

The Grave Yard is the prettiest one I have seen in Honduras. It is a mini Santa Rosa and sits on the side of a hill overlooking the real Santa Rosa. I wonder if the dead are put in graves similar to the houses they lived in while alive.

TELA

This is a delightful Garifuna beach town with nice, inexpensive hotels, good restaurants, no undertow in the water and no sand fleas. For my money, I prefer Tela to the Bay Islands. There is more to do, it is less expensive, and the people are just as wonderful.

Originally a port city, the town is divided into two sections, the old, which is east of the Lancetilla River, and the new, which is west of the river. The clean beach is about 30 kilometers long. During Semana Santa everything doubles in price, noise and dirt.

Tela was the headquarters of the United Fruit Company before they moved to El Progreso and then La Lima. However, the headquarters were abandoned except for the small railway line. The fruit company moved to richer land.

PLACES TO STAY

Tela has a variety of hotels. The ones farther away from the beach are generally cheaper. Around the bus station are a few "by-the-hour" places which I recommend you avoid.

El Presedente is just off the square and costs L38. ($8.50 US) for a clean room with bath, two tap working shower, and fan. You can get air con but it is more expensive. The people are friendly, and service is good. The attached restaurant is expensive and not worth the price. Rooms on the street are very noisy at night as the acoustics are complimentary to street traffic. If you always wanted to stay in an El Presedente hotel and couldn't afford it, this may be your chance.

Hotel Hondueño is very basic for a mere L15. ($3.50 US). There are no private baths, and it is not too clean. You can also get rooms by the hour.

Hotel Playa is near the beach and next to the Atlantico. It costs L32. ($7. US) for a room. It is clean and has private bath. It is a gorgeous old wooden building and it has a pleasant owner. If you are planning some time in Tela, this is a neat place to stay.

Hotel Atlantico is right on the beach; a beach room could be quite romantic. The cost is L62. ($13.75 US) for a room which is much too steep for me. Romantic rooms are useless when travelling alone.

Hotel Mar Azul on 4 Ave. has single rooms without bath for L15. ($3.50 US) and L32. ($7.25 US) for a double with bath. Although a bit dingy, it is clean and pleasant and has a nice yard. It is also away from the bars, and therefore quiet.

Hotel Caribe is closer to the highway is clean and quiet with beautiful rooms at L38. ($8.50 US) per room. The rooms have private bath and hot water. This place is quiet.

RESTAURANTS

Considering the size of Tela, there are not many excellent

places to eat. There are a few comedors but these are often patronized by drunks.

Luses del Norte just a block up from the beach is the most popular place to eat. The meals are substantial and good. The place is clean, the prices reasonable. The place is owned by a Canadian who is married to a Hondureño.

The Asia on the same street as El Presedente serves the best sweat and sour in all of Honduras. The portions are large and the food is excellent. The service is good, prices are reasonable and the restaurant is clean. This place is highly recommended. I have occasionally stopped in Tela just to eat here.

Jardine Corona next door to Super Mercado Maria serves excellent liquados, the fruit drink with milk being the best. This is a good place for breakfast.

THINGS TO DO

Playa de la Triunfo de la Cruz is for those who love historical sights. The Spanish first landed in Honduras at this site. Francisco de las Casas and Cristobal de Olid, two of Cortes's captains, fought a bloody battle in 1524 on the Bay of Tela between San Pedro and La Ceiba. The beaches on this bay are beautiful but there is no place to stay.

Triunfo is close to Tela. You can get a truck that goes about once every hour or two. After the first one at seven, the rest don't have a schedule. Triunfo de la Cruz is a Garifuna village and has some incredible herbalists living there. These herbalists have a good reputation throughout Honduras for their medicinal knowledge. The truck takes about 15 minutes, and you can easily walk back along the beach. There are a few places to eat at Triunfo.

La Ensanada is a beach between Tela and Triunfo where the English once hid from the Dutch pirates. It is a beautiful beach.

Lancetilla Botanical Gardens are about a one hour walk from the beach in Tela. Go early in the morning and you will see many tropical birds around the 3200 acres of gardens. There are an abundant number of Tucans. The walk through the gardens is beautiful and a must. The gardens are well kept and well labeled. The creek running through the land is great for cooling your feet.

The gardens were first started by Penonome, a man who worked hard for the preservation of natural land. He eventually retired and died in Guatemala; his house is on display in Antigua.

There is a small entrance fee, but if you go before 8:00AM, they will not charge you. At the gardens is a tienda and an information center with a small map. There are also dorms for rent for L10. ($2. US), but they are not always open. Check at the gate before hiking in with a big pack.

To get there from Tela, walk along the highway towards San Pedro, past the oil storage station, over the bridge and then turn left.

If you take a taxi, the cost is about L3. per person, one way. The driver will take you right to the garden, but you will miss the delightful walk.

Punta Sal National Park is to the west of Tela and in the middle of the bay of Tela. The park is between the Laguna de los Micos and the Ulua River. The point itself is a coral reef. Away from the ocean, the area is swampy and houses many different species of wildlife and birds.

To get there, you must get a boat at the Lancetilla River in Tela. Locals will take you by boat or canoe for a small fee. However, getting back on the same day is almost impossible, as the walk along the beach is long and hot. There are two villages past the point where you can stay with locals, but I did not stay in either. However, the park is a delight and a must for those who have camping gear.

The Book Store in Tela is worth the trip to town. At the restaurant Luses del Norte, just a block up from the beach, the Canadian owner knows the value of books to travellers. He has a small room at the restaurant with a variety of books. As he gets more customers, the books will improve. He will trade book for book; plus, you pay one limpera. You may also borrow a book for L20. ($4.50 US); when you return it, you get L18. back. This little book store will do very well.

SIGUATEPEQUE

If you don't want to stay in the bigger places like Teguc or San Pedro this is a nice little town. However, accommodations are not the best. There is an English school here so some American teachers are around the town.

PLACES TO STAY

International Gomez in the center of town costs L15. & L20. ($3.25 & $4.50 US) for a single and double. It is not so hot but is the cheapest of the three in the center.

Boarding House Central is a 20 room hotel which costs L20. & L30. ($4.50 & $6.75 US) for a single and double. It is clean but no hot water is available.

Hotel Versalles is also in the center and is the most expensive at L40. for a double ($9. US). However, you do get a private bathroom for this price.

RESTAURANTS

Hop on a bus, go out to the lake, and eat at one of the comedors.

THINGS TO DO

Cerro de Celanterique is a hill just out of town where you can have a quiet, pleasant picnic away from the noise and sounds of the big cities. Although the hill is only 1200 meters (4000 ft), it good views of the valley. There is a children's playground in the park.

National School of Forestry is in the town and is famous throughout Honduras. You may visit the school and view the methods being used to improve forestry conditions. The men at the school are pleasant and will gladly take you for a tour. You will need to speak Spanish.

TEGUCIGALPA

Tegucigalpa/Comoyaguela are actually two cities separated by the Choluteca River and joined by a series of bridges interspersed every few blocks. Teguc is not a beautiful city, but it does have some tourist attractions. Like most large cities in Central America, it takes a few days to get to know the city before one feels comfortable. If staying in Teguc, there are cheaper hotels on the Comoyaguela side of town, but it is more convenient to stay on the Teguc side. Most of the out of town buses stop on the Comoyaguela side, and it is about a fifteen minute walk to the Central Park on the Teguc side.

Teguc began as a small mining camp in 1539 and by 1880, grew to become the capital. This happened by accident when the leader of the country, Marco Aurelio de Soto, brought his Indian bride to Comoyagua, the capital at that time. The snobby people would not accept her so the president moved the capital to Teguc.

Tegucigalpa is an Indian word meaning silver hill. Teguc is hill and galpa is silver. Since the area is not prone to earthquakes, this city has never been destroyed. The city has continued to expand into the hills.

In 1578, the city was called Real de Minas de San Miguel de Tegucigalpa (a bit longwinded even for Ladinos). In the middle of the 18th century, the name was changed to Real Villa de San Miguel de Tegucigalpa and Heredia by the president of Guatemala. On the 17th of June, 1762, the title was confirmed. Then on the 17th of July, 1768, King Carlos III presented the coat of arms for the city. Honduras was declared independent on the 15th of September 1821, and the name of the city was then changed to the simple Tegucigalpa. It was not until 1880 that the city became the capital.

Teguc is 935 meters (3100 ft) above sea level; it is warm during the day and cool at night. The town is not exceptionally friendly but there are great restaurants. The center street, which has no vehicle traffic, is a fun place to hang out.

PLACES TO STAY

There are many places to stay in Teguc and I only list a few of the more popular hotels. I have stayed in most of the ones listed except the Honduras Maya, which would break my budget. However, I can well imagine what it would be like if I could afford to stay there.

Hotel Granada on Ave. Gutenburg 1041 in the Guanacaste Barrio is about the best in town for its price. It is clean, with private bath, hot water, excellent service (cleaned every day) and the price is good. They charge L28 for a single and L32. for a double ($6.25 & $7.10 US) and it is worth every penny.

Hotel Iberia on Calle Los Dolores on the Teguc side of town is expensive at L38 for a single and L43. for a double ($8.50 & $9.50 US) with private baths. It is clean and away from traffic; as well, it is right in the center of the city.

Hotel Marichel is also on Calle Los Dolores and is just before the Iberia at L25. and L40. ($5.50 - $9. US). This is not too expensive considering there is a private bath in the room, and it is in the center of town.

Hotel MacArthur on Ave. Lempira and 8 Calle #454 is now a bit overpriced at L55. for a single and L70. for a double ($12.25 - $15.50 US) with a private bath. However, the management at this hotel is friendly and will watch out for any of your needs. They have a variety of information available for the traveller.

Hotel Tegucigalpa on Ave. Gutenberg 1645, just a few blocks up from the Granada, is a bit dingy but it is cheap. The rooms cost L20. ($4.50 US) without private bath and no hot water, but it is a favorite with some of the travellers because it is quiet and reasonable.

Nuevo Boston on Ave. Jerez is clean and looks really good. The cost is L30. for a single and L40. for a double ($6.50 & $9. US). I have not stayed here, but it seems quiet. Rooms are fairly large with private bath and two tap showers. I don't know if they work.

Punta del Este on Ave. La Paz 2408 near the US Consulate, rents rooms for L30. for a single and L50. for a double ($6.50 & $11.US). It is a wonderful old house which is clean and pleasant. You would be close to the consulates and great restaurants and away from the center of the city.

Excelsior is half a block below the Honduras Maya on Colonia Palmira. If you sleep in the Excelsior and drink at the Maya, your budget may be able to survive Teguc. The Excelsior rents rooms for L35. and L50. ($7.75 & $11.US) with private bath and hot water. It is a clean hotel with pleasant owners.

Hotel Condesa is on 7 Ave. 12 Calle on the Comoyaguela side. Although the rooms in this hotel are small, they are clean with private bath and hot water all day. It is privately owned and operated and well looked after. The owner also speaks a little English. The cost is L25. and L40. for a single and double ($5.50 & $9. US).

The San Pedro on 6 Ave. 7 & 8 Calle costs L20. & L30. for a single and double ($4.50 & $6.75 US) with private bath and no hot water. There are rooms without bath for a bit less. The place is just okay.

Hotel Ticamaya on 6 Ave and 8 Calle, across from the San Pedro, is just as clean but a few limp cheaper. Places closer to the market are cheaper and sleazier; I recommend avoiding them.

Honduras Maya on Colonial Palmira costs a mere L565 per person ($121. US) and is a fun place to observe. Pleasant rooms are available in which to sit, relax, have a drink and watch the richer Hondurans.

RESTAURANTS

Being a metropolis, Teguc has every type of pizza parlor, hamburger joint and fried chicken place which you can imagine. Some are excellent and some are terrible. There is a 7% tax on food and pop and a 10% tax on other drinks, cigarettes and liquor.

El Patio near the town square on Ave. Los Dolores NE and half a block off Peatonal (the street blocked off to traffic) is my favorite supper restaurant in all of Honduras. The shishkebab is the meal I recommend. The waiter first serves beans and tacos on a charcoal brazier. This is followed by a wonderful salty cheese also on a brazier. You finally receive your meat with rice and salad which is safe to eat. Lastly, the bill is within reach of most travellers. The quality of the food and the service has remained constant over the years. The atmosphere is also excellent.

La Terrazita de Don Pepe on Calle La Fuente in the center of town is a great place to eat pasta. The spaghetti and meat sauce is excellent. The service is good. An indication that the food is good is the popularity of the restaurant with the locals.

Gouchos Restaurant on Ave. La Paz close to the ostentatious US Embassy, is one of the best restaurants in Teguc. It serves excellent food from Paraguay. This restaurant is also patronized by the upper class Hondurans; this indicates the quality.

El Escorial on Calle Salvador Mendieta is excellent with an especially nice atmosphere. It has good food, good prices and a bar where you can enjoy a drink. Interesting art work adorns the walls.

Greek restaurant next door to El Escorial on Calle Salvador Mendieta is a ripoff for gringos. They overcharge and then try to shortchange you because they think your Spanish will not be good enough to argue.

Pizza Hut in Teguc is the best on the continent. They have the thickest pizza you can possibly imagine and the quality of the crust is excellent. I don't usually like to patronize franchises, but this one is an exception.

Dunkin Donuts are all over town, if you are into donuts and good coffee which can be difficult to find in Honduras. After I returned from Nicaragua, I couldn't resist eating at least six chococrema donuts in one day. They are really good.

Duncan Maya on 6 Ave. 5 Calle is excellent for hamburgers. It is clean and the price is reasonable. Give it a try.

Restaurants along Ave. Morezan in the consulate area of town are excellent. There are both franchised and private restaurants. Many of them have an excellent atmosphere, and the prices are not too high. Stroll around and explore. You will find something to satisfy even the pickiest of palates.

THINGS TO DO

Tourist Bureau is on the square in a little booth. At one time, it was a large building on stilts. The bureau sells a half-decent map of the country, and the city map matches the street names. They also have information for the tourist and are more willing to talk to people. The tourist office on Ave. La Paz, in Guanacaste barrio, is excellent. It is not a long walk and the information they give is invaluable. They also speak English.

The Cathedral of San Miguel and Central Park are both a delight to most Hondurans. With its gold leaf baroque, the central altar in the Cathedral is striking. This church is more decorative than most churches found in Central America. The gold plating was completed during the 18th century but the church was completed in 1782. The art work on the altar was done by the Guatemalan artist Vincente Galvez. There is also a tablet of 22 pieces of silver with the sacrament of the saints on it. On the right side, when first entering the church, is a large stone font with a unique design. It was made, in 1643, from a single block of stone and was used for the baptizing of the Indians.

Numerous beggars are outside the church. The square facing the church has a statue of **Francisco Morizan** on his horse. He was a popular general and politician between the year 1827 to 1830 and 1836 to 1839. The pigeons have done most of the decorating on the statue and in the square. It is a unique experience to go to the square just at dusk and listen to the black birds saying good night. The sound is actually deafening.

Iglesia La Merced is a beautiful church built during the 17th century. Stupendous panels made during the 18th century in the rococo style of the Galvez school of art adorn the walls. This church is a must and is one block south of the central park. The park area is a delightful place to sit and photograph the action which occurs on a regular day in Honduras.

Iglesia El Calvario was constructed in 1746. The stone cross comes from the Church of San Francisco. The church was built beside one of the first cemeteries in Honduras. The church is on 2 Ave. 5 Calle.

Iglesia de San Francisco is on Calle 4, four blocks from the central park. This is the oldest church in Teguc, built by the Franciscan brothers in 1592 and redesigned in 1740. The gold altar pieces and the oil paintings are from the 18th century.

National Palace is on Calle 4 & 5 between Ave. 3 & 4. It was originally a convent, then became a hospital, and in 1934, it became of government center. It is a lovely old building.

Post Office is across from the national palace. It was originally an orphanage and then became a medical school.

Presidential Palace is on the banks of the Choluteca River just down from the park. It was constructed in 1919 and looks like a prison more than a palace. It has been used as a fortress during some of the revolutions.

Iglesia Los Dolores is just three blocks up from the river on Los Dolores and was constructed in 1732. The decor is different because it is complimentary to the black and Indian people of the area rather than the Ladino. The gold altar was sculptured in 1742. The ceramic tiles on the walls are beautiful.

Puente Mallol is just below the Presidential Palace and is the oldest in Teguc, being built between 1818 and 1822. Of the four bridges going over the river, this is the most historic one.

Artesans Market in Comoaguela is on 15 Calle 2-3 Ave. and has handicrafts from all over the country. If you are unable to pack things around with you while you travel, this is a good place to shop. Across from the market is the park of the Unknown Soldier. This commemorates men killed in the war of 1969 with El Salvador. The obelisk was constructed for the independence of Honduras in 1821.

The Market in Comoyaguela is just over the bridges on the Comoyaguela side of town. It covers several blocks, and is noisy, crowded and dirty. You may find anything: plastics, clothes made in Taiwan, and food of every description. However, don't be in that area at night. As there are many hiding places for robbers, it is quite dangerous. If you must pass by the area after dark, walk down the middle of the road. This way, you can see in all directions. Or, better still, take a bus or taxi.

The Museum of Archaeology is a difficult building to find. You must go all the way down from the square to Calle Morelos. Turn right and go up the hill. The museum is a large blue residence that once belonged to President Julio Lozano Diaz. The man donated the building to the country in 1981 to be used as the main museum. It is open only from 8:30 AM to 3:30PM, Wednesday to Sunday. If you are in the area at the time it is highly recommended. Just going through the building is a delight.

Park of Kukulcones or Concordia Park is on Paseo Miramese between Calle 8 & 9 and down from the Museum of Archaeology. This is a beautiful peaceful park with a huge Maya stelae and a replica of the pyramid of Kukulcones. It is by far one of the more peaceful and attractive places in all of Teguc. The park was constructed in 1880 with stones from Indian villages.

Peace Monument sits on top of a hill called Cerro Juana Lainez in the center of Teguc. You can get to it by walking along Ave. Morezan. It gives a spectacular view of the city. The circular kiosk is nice to sit under, have a pop, read a book and watch Teguc.

Mercado M & M (mas por menos) on Ave. La Paz just past the bridge in Guanacaste Barrio gives an excellent rate for travellers cheques without hassle. Just show your passport and wait a few minutes while the gal at the desk finishes arranging her date for the evening and you get your money.

Book Village at Los Castaño shopping center on Ave. Morezan has English books at a reasonable rate. Although some used books are available, most are new classics. Prices are not really inflated.

La Tigra National Park is for the hiker and can be visited for one to three days. This 18,700 acre area was the first rain forest made into a park in Honduras. To get to the park, you must stay in San Juancito overnight. You get a bus to San Juancito at the Mercado San Pablo just past the US consulate on Ave. La Paz. The bus takes one and a half hours. There is one basic place to stay which has straw mattresses, cold water, no private bath and no other luxuries. Although there are no restaurants in town, there are comedors and a cafeteria by the bus stop that serves enchaladas and tacos.

To go to the park, walk past Hondutel, take the first sharp left turn and go straight up. The park entrance is at Rosario about one to one and a half hours up. You can get drinks there. Continue up, past the park administration office and on to the beautiful waterfalls. This is another one to one and a half hours. At Rosario, you can also take the Aguacatal trail which meets up with the main trail, but you miss the park headquarters which has some interesting information. Some of the buildings in this area date back to the old mining days and are interesting to explore. As you go further into the hills, there are more sights to enjoy.

To go up and over takes about three hours once you have passed the waterfall. If staying in San Juancito, you can do this in a day. You should take some snacks and water as the few homes are quite far apart. Running shoes are sufficient for this hike.

The hike to Guaimaca is delightful. It will take you two to three full days. There are old mining shacks to explore and stay in. I met a fit young man who hiked across in two days. Three days are more realistic and four days are preferred if you have the time and want to explore. There are a few private homes to get food but you should take most of your own.

Leaving San Juancito, you must catch the last bus at 3:00PM. Walk up to the highway, about two kilometers back towards Teguc to catch the bus. The park is a beautiful and interesting area and certainly recommended for those who like to walk. Whether you are going for a few hours or three days, the trip will be rewarding. I heard it is easier to get to the park from San Carlos, but I could not find further information on this route. If you are interested in further exploring the park, ask the people at the tourist office.

Santa Lucia is a delightful town that is only a couple of hours on the walk back to Teguc. You can take a bus from the station across from the San Filipe hospital and behind the Esso Station. This is on Ave. La Paz. You get off at the road going to Santa Lucia and walk in. It is not far; the town is a pretty colonial town with small winding streets and a couple of nice restaurants. The church has a black statue of Christ given to the town by King Philip ll. The town was originally a mining town during the 17th century.

Santa Ana is a village out of Teguc about two hours one way. The reason for going to Santa Ana is for the hot springs just past the town. You go through the town and then take the road about one kilometer past the village. There is a sign. The hot springs are about another 45 minutes up this road. They are called San Buenaventura and are delightful with three different pools all with different temperature. As well, there is a waterfall. This is a peaceful and pleasant place to visit which Hondurans are very proud to share with visitors.

TOCOA

The only reason to go to Tocoa is to pass through on the way to Trujillo. If necessary you can stay at the Hotel Esperanza which costs L25. per person. There are a few other places in town, but this is the best with private bath and clean sheets. There are a few places to eat in Tocoa; the ones most popular are the franchise places like the pizza place. The town is hot and dusty with lots of traffic.

TRUJILLO

Trujillo is in a gorgeous setting. It is built on a cliff with a beautiful white beach below and the Caribbean Ocean lapping at the shore. The background has high, lush mountains accessible to the adventuresome. Originally built as a fort to keep the pirates out, the castle is now in the center of town and the town has grown around it.

The town was founded in 1525 by Juan de Medina. It was used as a resting place of Cortes' when he was chasing Cristobal de Olid from the Yucatan. It is one of the oldest cities in Central America.

This historic little town is the site where the famous William Walker was killed in 1860. The cemetery where he was buried is in town. This is also the spot where Columbus celebrated his first Mass after reaching America.

PLACES TO STAY

Hotel Central is on the main street in the center of town and is very friendly but basic. There are no showers in the rooms and only cold water in the bath. The cost is L14.($3.25 US) per person. They are often full.

Hotel Colonial charges L75. per person ($17. US) but the owners are so unfriendly that I would not stay there even if it was free. However, the rooms are delightful with clean sheets and hot water. It is fairly quiet.

Hotel Catracho is up three blocks from the Colonial. At this point, turn left and walk two blocks past the microwave tower. The rooms are clean and large with private bath but only cold water. They cost L18. ($4. US) per person. The place is friendly and quiet. There are no chickens or dogs.

Hotel Trujillo is past the cemetery and just up the hill. The rooms are L25. per person ($5.50 US) with private bath but cold showers. The rooms are sparkling clean and the owner is friendly. I really liked this place.

RESTAURANTS

The Pantry Restaurant is excellent. There is a variety of well prepared food. The prices are also good.

The Granada is the second best place to eat. The service is good and the people are very happy to get your business. It is a bit more expensive than the Pantry.

Restaurants along the beach are your best bet but if you are tired, you may not want to walk back up the hill to get to your hotel. On the other hand, it will wear off your supper.

THINGS TO DO

Fort Santa Barbara was built in 1590 as a protection from the pirates. The fort is in good shape with a few cannons and other artifacts laying around. The entrance to the fort is in excellent condition.

Cemetery is a must to see the gravestone of the famous filibuster, William Walker. There is no prophetic inscription on the grave; I expected there might be some rot around the stone to indicate his personality.

The Museum is past the cemetery. Keep walking and when you come to a fork in the road, take the middle one past the church you can see. The museum charges L2.5 per person and it is the largest secondhand junk shop I have ever seen. They have everything from a crashed airplane (without the pilot) to old typewriters, money, ship parts, chairs, unidentifiable artifacts both real and fake. The objects are not well displayed and is quite funny. You can also go down to the river where water runs into two swimming pools. There is a bridge over the creek.

Lago de Guaimoreto is about a two to three hour walk from Trujillo along the beach. It is a fresh water lagoon that is steaming with wild birds. The lake is surrounded by mangroves and the center has a small island which is popular with the bird population. There is supposed to be good fishing in this lake.

Puerta Castilla is a little town across the bay. This is where Columbus actually landed, in 1502 after leaving the Bay Islands. The first church service was celebrated there on August 8th of the same year. Today it is mostly a port.

VALLE DE ANGELES

Valle de Angeles is a gorgeous little artisan town. You can see the people making their crafts in the shops or visit the school for artists. The streets have cast iron signs painted with the street names. This adds to the uniqueness of the town.

PLACES TO STAY

Posada de Angel charges L25. ($5.50 US) per person. The rooms have private bath and are clean. There is a delightful court-yard in which to sit in the evenings. It is a nice place, and the only place to stay in the village.

RESTAURANTS

Adventista Hospital on the road towards Teguc serves wonderful vegetarian meals on Fridays and Sundays.

Restaurant Valle Angel is just past the hospital and is a great place to eat. There are typical Honduran meals available which are cooked to perfection.

THINGS TO DO

Church on the square is restored with a new patchwork marble altar, and the ceiling is made with new Honduran wood interspersed with the old wood. The effect is unique.

Artists School is just down the hill from the square about half a block. They will show you the process of learning and making pottery, leather sculpturing, wood carving and other artsy endeavours that they teach at the school. The school is on vacation during December, January and February but you can still visit during these months. There is a store at the school; the prices are fixed but fair.

Pabellon de Artesana is a large shop with all types of local crafts. The most outstanding are the wonderfully carved wooden chests which are covered in leather. They sell for around $80. US.

The Park near the town is a pleasant place to visit before returning to Teguc or going to bed. To get there, turn left on the dirt road before the restaurant Valle Angel (after the hospital) and then take the first right hand road. Go straight. The road becomes a path, goes down a hill, over a small wooden bridge and back up the hill on the other side. You will go past country homes but continue straight. The path follows a small creek and then goes up into the park. The entrance fee is one limp plus one limp more if you want to swim in the clean pool. There are barbecue pits, bathrooms, a restaurant, soccer field. You can camp here if you have permission from the tourist office at the park. There is a brown lake which was formed by daming a creek. The park is very peaceful with a variety of birds in the pine trees. The walk to the highway is not far; you can catch a bus back to Teguc until 5:00PM when the last one leaves.

YOJOA LAKE

This is a beautiful lake, 22 kilometers long, directly south of San Pedro Sula. Although the shore is swampy, the lake itself is clean and pristine, tucked away in the mountains. It is believed that animals such as pumas, monkeys, jaguars and ocelots can be found in the jungles close to the lake.

PLACES TO STAY

Los Remos is the most popular place on the lake to stay for only L25. ($5.50 US) per person. This includes a private bath and there are clean sheets on the beds. You must ask the bus driver to show you where to get off. The hotel is close to the south end of the lake.

Agua Azul is right on the largest section of the lake and costs L40. ($9. US) per person. This is also a very popular place to stay. There is a restaurant attached to the hotel. Rooms with private baths are available.

RESTAURANTS

You may eat at Agua Azul, but I would recommend that you try one of the many stalls along the road. They are delightful and serve fresh fish. Some specialize in one typical dish while others specialize in another. Look where the locals are eating and use this cue as a guide.

THINGS TO DO

Boats may be rented at the south end of the lake. The lake has been stocked with bass and I understand that some are fairly large. Bass are fun to catch because they give a good fight.

There are some minor **Maya ruins** on the north end of the lake which you may explore. I have not seen them, but I suspect they are about the same as the ones at the Pulhapanzak waterfall.

Santa Barbara Park has the second highest mountain which sits at 2744 meters (9000 ft) and is close to the lake. However, it is not possible to go to the top in one day. If you wish to go up, the best way is to go to El Mochito and start your ascent from there. This park may also be reached from the other side from the town of Santa Barbara. However, I have heard this side is the nicer.

YORO

The origin of the name of this town is interesting. It was originally called Hacienda de Oro (house of gold), then Santa Cruz de Yoro and then Villa de Santiago de Yoro. The name Yoro probably comes from the Mexican meaning of the word "center".

Yoro is at the end of a good road; everything past here is somewhat unaccessible. Excursions from Yoro are slow.

PLACES TO STAY

Nueva Jerusalem is three blocks above the market and is the best place to stay. It is fairly large and costs L25. for a single and L35. for a double ($5.50 - $7.75 US); they have private bathrooms.

THINGS TO DO

Yoro National Park is just south of town. You can catch a ride in a truck close to the entrance. This park is the second largest rain forest in Honduras. The area is inhabited by the Xicaque Indians. There are many hikes in the park; you can spend as much time as you wish in the park. The parks in Honduras are not easy to reach, nor are there convenient places to stay, so you must be prepared to either return to your hotel in the evening or camp out.

Volcan de Apaya is also south of Yoro. This mountain has a cave close to the top where there is underground water with fish. At one time held sacred to the Indians, today it is an interesting place to visit. I have no directions, so you must ask in Yoro.

CHICKENBUS TALES

MARKET PEOPLE
first printed in the Prince George <u>Citizen,</u> 1992

Latin American market people are more interesting than North American sales clerks.

I often stopped at markets in Honduras to have a drink while waiting for a bus. My presence caused curiosity among the locals and it was never long before someone talked to me.

One young brazen watch seller started a conversation in the market. Carlos was 16 years old, dressed as sharp as any young middle class North American school boy. He had flashing dark eyes, black curly hair and a winning smile. He was handsome and knew it.

Carlos was working, selling cheap Hong Kong watches, batteries, calculators and many other objects that he carried on a tray, through the buses. He was earning money to pay for his education. While we were talking, he spotted another bus rolling into the station. He quickly darted away trying to sell his products. It was his charming smile that netted him a sale, not the quality of the product.

I was walking past another market, on another day when a lady about my age invited me to sit down at her stall and have a chat while she made tortillas to sell. She said her name was Irene as she lit a cigarette and wiped her hands on her dirty dress. We got over the formalities like where I was from and where I had been, how old I was and how many kids I had. This led to what interested her the most.

Irene was interested in woman's issues and life in Canada as compared to life in Honduras. I explained that birth control was widely practiced and many women chose to work instead of having children. We discussed different customs and the freedom of women in our society.

Irene told me that there, the men wanted many children and that birth control was banned by the pope. She said the men would produce the children and then "Pista!" (runaway) and Irene would slap her hand, pointing down the road. She laughed heartily at this but with sad eyes. Neither the men nor the pope looked after the children.

Soon, Irene's children started gathering around to listen to the strange gringo talk to their mom. Each of her five children had at least two friends with them so I had quite an audience.

I talked to Irene's kids trying to emphasize the importance of school and it wasn't long before they were competing with each other for attention. I left Irene's oldest boy very puzzled when I asked him if he wanted his beautiful young bride (yet to be found) to end up like many women in his country. His young wife would soon be old and worn out from bearing too many children at too young an age and having to work all day for a few measly cents. She would be too tired to be friendly and romantic at night. Since he was 14 years old, I could appeal to his romantic side easier than his realistic side.

I left Irene smiling happily while making more tortillas. She had accepted her fate and said there was no sense in crying as we would all end up in heaven eventually. But Irene's son was quiet and pensive. Hopefully his future wife's life would change even a little.

My favorite market people are the snake-oil medicine men. They usually get a captive audience by preaching on a moving bus. They jump on at one stop , give their quick line, sell to anyone that will buy and hop off at the next village.

The snake-oil medicine men have pills, creams, capsules or salves that will cure anything from headaches to athletes foot, infertility to insanity. One medicine man was so talented that he could skillfully mimic each condition that he professed to cure. Some men had anatomical models to be able to show the audience the route of the pill or salve they were selling or the cause of the pain they were curing.

For children the medicine men usually recommended creams for cures. Put it on at night and the cure is evident by morning. These creams cured teething problems, colic, bronchitis and foot deformities. Just rub it on. I was relieved that the cures were topographic as they would probably do less damage this way.

Although market people are very entertaining, I am really glad that I don't have to make my living in Latin America's free enterprise system.

NICARAGUA

NICARAGUA

Until very recently, Nicaragua was the most politically alive country in all of Central America. International travellers were everywhere enthusiastically doing everything from picking cotton or coffee to filming documentaries. Freelance photographers and journalists were trying to counteract all the bad publicity Nicaragua has received in the last few years. Brigade workers were willingly donating their time and money to help in the fields, making friends and then spreading the word of their successes. Church groups were trying to give the Nicaraguan people another candle of hope. You could feel the country buzzing with hope and enthusiasm from the moment you entered until long after you left.

Today there are still brigade workers and the odd journalist working in Nicaragua, but the lifeblood has been drained. The volunteer workers can not get much funding. Poverty is extreme for some. Large expensive cars in Managua are driven by those who went to Miami or Houston during the war. Although the country is poor, the people remain a happy race.

Nicaragua is not without its scars of war. Poverty pervails. There is no longer inflation (for about six months). There is little variety in the markets, and what is available is expensive. Stores have American-made secondhand clothing, but the people do not have the money to purchase it. However, the children still play a mean game of baseball, in the battered, unpaved streets, sometimes using a stone wrapped in an old rag and tied with some string for a baseball. Some children still have swollen stomachs. The buses are crowded, but much improved compared to the days when the Sandinistas were in power. There are now car parts available in order to repair the taxis. However, taxis still operate on the collectivo system.

But, everywhere are smiles. The people want to talk to you. They want to know what you think of the new government, of the economic situation and of them. They are friendly. Most of all, you are still quite safe in Nicaragua. The government will not allow you to go into zones which still have skirmishes. They do not want you to see this. Many of the army personnel are now unemployed. They are often drunk in the streets.

Travel in Nicaragua is still fairly difficult. There are buses, but often they are crowded. Large trucks with wooden seats are used for transportation. The food in Nicaragua is very expensive, especially if you are a gringo. Many restaurants are full of English-speaking Nicaraguans.

Although a country of dicotomies, you will come away exhilarated. You will meet many intelligent and interesting people, and after a visit to Nicaragua, your outlook will be enriched.

HISTORY

Originally, the Matagalpa, Sumu, Rama and Mosquitia Indian tribes lived in the area. These tribes were invaded by the Mesoamericans who perfected a political system with hereditary class systems and organized large townships. Weaving, pottery and gold smithing were the livlihood of the people in these cities.

Nicaragua got its name from the Indian chief, **"Nicarao"**, who lived there when the Spanish arrived in the early 1500's. Because of the large body of water near the Indian villages, the area was called Nicarao-agua (the water of Nicarao). It is easy to see how we got Nicargua from these two words.

Columbus first came to Nicaragua in 1502, but it wasn't until twenty years later that the Spanish started to settle there under the leadership of Gil Gonzales Davila. Later, Francisco Cordoba founded two sites, Leon and Granada, because Indian labor was close to these areas and construction would be cheap.

The Caribbean coast of Nicaragua has a history of famous British pirates such as Francis Drake and Richard Hawkins attacking the Spanish fleets but there was little settlement in the area. The British did try to rule to Mosquitia Indians until the middle of the 1800's but neither contributed anything to each other's welfare.

Nicaragua became part of the Central American states in 1821. There was the usual struggle between land owners and clergy for power which caused many battles and government changes. After Iterbide's fall in 1823, Nicaragua joined the United Provinces of Central America with Guatemala, Honduras, El Salvador and Costa Rica.

Leon, a liberal center often disputed with Granada, a conservative center and in 1838, the liberals declared Nicaragua an independent republic. William Walker entered Nicaragua in the middle 1800's and tried to gain control of the country. He succeeded and, in 1856, became a liberal president. However, Walker had taken away land belonging to the American Vanderbilt and the Americans showed their power by backing the conservatives and ousting Walker. Walker was later hung in Honduras.

In 1893, another revolt brought the dictator, Zayola, to power and he harshly ruled for the next few years. In 1910, Diaz came to power and looked to the United States for financial and military support.

The Bryan-Chomorro Treaty of 1916 gave the Nicaraguans three-million dollars for the right to build a canal between the Pacific and Atlantic Oceans, to lease the Corn Islands and to establish a military base on the Bay of Fonseca. This caused another revolt against the Americans and the United States decided to build a canal in Panama instead.

This was greatly resented by the Nicaraguan people and Augusto Sandino became a leading rebel, a hero who started the rebellion against US domination. Samosa became the leader of the National Guard, a US marine-trained force, and had Sandino killed.

The Samosa family ruled Nicaragua from 1937 until 1979 with the help of the United States government. Samosa supported American investment and the resulting exploitation caused much unrest among the peasants.

Finally, in 1979, the Sandinistas took power and reforms in the country were started. The people were jubilant. The Americans were hostile. The American government supported the Contra rebels who had their bases in Honduras. This caused great hardship for the Nicaraguan people. However, the Nicaraguan people did get some aid from Cuba and the Soviet Union. This has changed since the fall of communism in the eastern block countries. Today, there is a right wing government back in power trying to push the country back onto its feet but the struggle will be difficult.

FACTS

Since 1984, Nicaragua has had free elections. The President and the **National Assembly** are elected by the people and the Cabinet is chosen from the Assembly by the President. This is official dogma.

When entering Nicaragua, it is no longer necessary to change money at the official rate. The government has tried to settle the inflation problem by printing new cordobas (again) and keeping it secure beside the US dollar. It is illegal to trade on the black market in Nicaragua but, ironically, they will only accept US currency when paying for a visa at the border. The cost for some nationalities is $25.00 US but others need to pay only $2.00 US entrance fee.

The area of Nicaragua, the largest of the Central American countries, is **130,000 kilometers square** (50,000 sq. mi.) with **350 kilometers (215 miles) of Pacific coastline** and **500 kilometers (300 miles) of Caribbean coast line**. The population is about **3.5 million with a density of 72 persons** per square mile. Most of the population is Spanish speaking, Roman Catholic and Mestizo. The Nicaraguan dialect is very difficult to understand because they have a tendency to leave off the endings of words and they speak very rapidly.

The climate of Nicaragua is tropical with an average temperature of 27ºC (80ºF) along the Pacific coast. Managua is hot all year and the only relief from the heat is the constant breeze created from Lakes Managua and Nicaragua. The central region of Nicaragua is much cooler than the coast because it rises up to about 2450 meters (8000 ft) above sea level. Rainy season is from May to November in Nicaragua except for the Caribbean coast which is very hot and humid with no definite rainy season. It rains all year.

The flag of Nicaragua is two blue horizontal stripes with a white stripe in between. The white stripe has the coat of arms in the center. It is a triangle with the five volcanoes, a rainbow and a red cap. The cap stands for liberty, the rainbow for peace and the triangle for equality.

When the Sandinistas were in power, **education** and medical care in Nicaragua was greatly improved. They built numerous rural schools and a literacy program was put into effect. There were many outpost clinics set up. Today, because of financial difficulties, many of the government programs are being discarded. Children must go to school between the ages of six and twelve but this law is no longer being strictly enforced. Many areas do not have teachers. The outpost medical centers are receiving less and less money and medical neglect is becoming more prevalent again. It is sad to see. I do not blame the Chomorro government for the decrease in services because they have no more money than the Sandinistas had. The one advantage they have is that the US government approves of the leader and therefore has stopped the war. Sick politics.

LAWS

Black market money is not popular at the present time. However, if inflation takes a running leap again, this will change. It has always been illegal to exchange on the black market in Nicaragua.

You must have in International Driver's licence in order to drive your car in Nicaragua. Because there is little traffic, it is very easy to drive in this country. There are still some gas problems but this is improving daily.

Do not remove artifacts from the country as it is illegal - the same as in any other country.

Helmets are required for motorcyclists and cars must be fumigated upon entry.

Prostitution and robbery are on the increase in Nicaragua. Corruption in the police force is not too bad at the moment but as poverty and unemployment increase, so will the corruption.

There is a 15% sales tax on hotel and restaurant bills. Then there is a 10% expected and sometimes enforced gratuity.

MONEY

The currency is the cordoba which is made up of 100 centavos. The exchange rate is ¢5.00 for $1.00 US. I do not know how stable this money will remain but other than food, little has changed price wise in Nicaragua. I changed money in 1992, and the cordoba had risen to ¢5.30 for $1.00US so I can not say whether there will be stabilization.

There is no problem changing money in a bank but some banks will not exchange traveller's cheques. They do give you a complete check when you do change so be certain to have your passport complete with a valid visa. It does not usually take more than half an hour to exchange money.

At one time many places charged in American dollars but this is no longer so.

VISAS

Those requiring a visa may obtain it at the border. This does take a long time as the officials want the traveller to realize how important they are so they slowly look at each document and stamp that you may possess. Then they confer with other officials just to make the traveller feel uncomfortable. The official then returns, slowly shakes his head and asks you for some money. The cost of a visa is $25.00 US plus there is also a $2.00 US entrance fee. The entrance fee is for all nationalities. Those from Belgium, Denmark, Spain, the U.S., Finland, Great Britain, Guatemala, Greece, Holland, Hungary, Ireland, north or south, Lichenstein, Luxemburg, Norway, El Salvador, Sweden and Switzerland are exempt from the $25.00 US entry fee. Those wishing to only pass through the country may receive a 72 hour transit visa for the country. It is now easy to get through Nicaragua in 72 hours as the bus system has improved. I was not asked for an exit ticket when I entered Nicaragua and I have heard of no one needing one.

If flying into Nicaragua, you must have an exit ticket. This may be overlooked if you can show that you have enough money to get out of the country.

GETTING THERE

The following airlines go into the country: Aeronica, Aeroflot, American Airlines, Aviateca, Continental Airlines, Copa, Cubana de Aviacion, Iberia, Lacsa and Sahsa. Airlines that have offices in Nicaragua are: Argentina, Air France, British Airways, KLM, Lufthansa, SAM, Sabena, Varig and Trans Continental. If coming from Europe, the trip through Cuba can be a very trying experience. They often get papers and reservations mixed up and people end up paying exorbitant prices in order to finish their flight. At present, I would recommend avoiding that route. The extra hundred dollars you may have to pay in the beginning may save you up to $500.00 US in the end.

If travelling overland, you may chickenbus to the border from Salvador, Honduras or Costa Rica and then chickenbus once you are in the country. Transportation has improved in Nicaragua . Although buses are very crowded, connections are still good at the borders. Taxis or collectivo buses leave all day from all border crossings. Money changers are at the borders, and I found the exchange rates better in Nicaragua than Costa Rica or Honduras.

The TICA bus goes from Costa Rica to Managua for about $45.00 US. It is much less expensive to go with Sirca and this company is as reliable as TICA. If going to Costa Rica, the return ticket from Managua on Sirca is about $2.50 US. The ticket may be purchased from the Altamira D'Este Terminal, two streets south of Vicky, in Managua. If going to Costa Rica, it is necessary to have an exit ticket from Costa Rica. If you do not have one, the border guards will make you purchase one at the border; of course, it will be the expensive one. If you do not use the Sirca ticket, at least you are not out a tremendous amount of money. Before purchasing your ticket, be certain to have your visa if you require one, or you won't get a ticket. If going to El Salvador or Honduras, you do not need an exit ticket. They just take your entrance fees and smile.

The ferry route via the Bay of Fonseca from El Salvador is open again. The ferry goes three times a week and leaves for La Union on Tuesdays and Thursdays at 6:00AM. Be certain to get there early in order to get a ticket. This is a beautiful trip and highly recommended.

CONSULATES (Managua)

British Embassy on Calle Principal and 2A Casa a la Derecha, Primera Etapa.

Canadian Consulate, 208 Calle Deltriunfor, Frente Plazoleta Telcor Central,

Costa Rican Consulate is on Gallo and Villa Sur, half a block from the lake.

El Salvador is on Las Colinas, Pasaje Los Cerros #142

French Embassy is on Carretera del sur (about five miles out)

German Consulate is near the Plaza España

Guatemalan Embassy is on the road to Masaya, about five miles out.

Honduran Consulate is on Planes de Altamira #29

Panama Embassy is in Pancasan at the Hotel Colon, one block south and one and a half blocks towards the lake. Etapa Vlll #61

US Consulate is about two miles out on the Carretera del Sur.

PUBLIC HOLIDAYS

New Year's Day	January 1
Democracy & Reconciliation	February 25
Holy Week	Thursday to Sunday in March or April
Labor Day	May 1
Mother's Day	May 30th afternoon
Liberation Day	July 19
Santo Domingo Celebration	August 1st and 10th in Managua
Battle of San Jacinto	September 14
Independence Day	September 15

Day of the Dead	November 2
Purification of Mary	November 8
Christmas	December 25

TRANSPORTATION

Transportation has greatly improved since 1988. Regular buses or trucks go to almost all places. If there is trouble in an area, the bus driver will inform you that you should not go into the area. He may even refuse to take you. There are many robberies of buses and trucks on the road to Rama. You may often have to stand on a crowded bus, but it is no longer a matter of fighting for your life to get on the bus.

BUSES

The buses in the city are still quite crowded. Robbers who are very good at picking pockets and slashing packs frequent the buses. One lady had her blouse slashed and her moneybelt zipper partway opened before she realized something was amiss. If travelling on the buses, be careful.

The trucks which travel out of town are safer than buses and less crowded. Some of course, are as crowded. You must go to the appropriate bus station that has buses going in the direction you wish to go. Local people will tell you where to find the trucks.

TICA bus station is two streets east and two streets south of the Dorado Cine.

SIRCA bus station is at the Altamira D'Este terminal two streets south of Vicky.

Buses leaving from Israel Lewites Terminal going **west** of Managua:

Carazo	5:30AM - 8:00PM	every 20 minutes
Chinendega	6:30AM - 4:30PM	every hour
Citalapas	2:00PM	one bus
Corinto	6:30AM -4:30PM	every hour
Cuajachilo	7:00AM - 5:00PM	every hour
Diriomo	7:30AM - 7:00PM	every hour
El Caimito	12:30PM - 5:00PM	two daily
El Crucero	5:00AM - 6:00PM	two daily
La Paz	7:20AM - 6:20PM	every hour
Las Pilas	2:30PM	one daily
Leon	5:30AM - 7:00PM	every 20 minutes
Leon by the old road	6:00AM - 6:00PM	times vary
Los Aburtos	2:00PM	one daily
Los Brasiles, Mateare	6:40AM - 5:50PM	every hour
Los Cedros	10:00AM + 6:00PM	two daily
Los Chocoyos	2:30PM	one daily
Masatepe	6:30AM - 7:00PM	every hour
Monte Tabor	6:00AM - 6:00PM	every 30 minutes
Nagarote	6:00AM - 7:00PM	every hour

Nejapa	6:00AM - 6:30PM	every hour
Pochacuape	2:30PM	one daily
Pochomil	7:00AM - 6:00PM	every 45 minutes
San Rafael del Sur	7:00AM - 6:00PM	every 45 minutes
Villa Carlos Fonseca	7:15 AM - 5:45PM	every 45 minutes

Buses leaving from Huembes Market going **south east or north** of Managua

Diriomo	7:30AM - 7:00PM	every 30 minutes
El Cacao	11:40AM	one daily
Esteli	4:00AM - 5:00PM	every 30 minutes
Granada	5:00AM - 10:00PM	every 15 minutes
La Concepcion	5:00AM - 7:00PM	every 30 minutes
Masatepe	8:00AM - 7:00PM	every hour
Masaya	5:00AM - 10:00PM	every 10 minutes
Matagalpa	4:15AM - 4:45PM	every 30 minutes
Ocotal	5:00AM - express	one daily
	8:45AM + 2:00PM	two daily
Rivas	5:00AM - 6:00PM	every 30 minutes
Santo Domingo	6:10AM - 6:50PM	every 40 minutes
Somoto	7:00AM - express	one daily
	1:00AM + 12:00 + 2:00 PM	three daily
Ticuantepe	5:30AM - 10:00PM	every 20 minutes
Veracruz	6:00AM - 6:50PM	every 40 minutes

Buses leaving from the Ivan Montenegro Market going **east** of Managua:

Boaco	5:00AM - 4:30PM	every hour
Camoapa	7:30AM + 2:00PM	two daily
Jan Josè Remates	12:30PM	one daily
Juigalpa	5:20AM - 5:30PM	every 30 minutes
Nueva Guinea	3:30AM - 10:30AM	six daily
Rama	2:30AM express	one daily
	4:00AM - 11:30AM	varies daily
Sabana Grande	6:00AM - 7:00PM	every 25 minutes
San Pedro de Lovago	1:30PM	onc daily
Santa Lucia	10:30AM	one daily
Santo Domingo	12:30PM	one daily
Santo Tomas	12:00PM	one daily

Buses leaving from La Piñata central market for:

Granada	7:00AM - 8:00PM	often
Jinotepe	7:00AM - 8:00PM	often
Masaya	7:00AM - 8:00PM	often

FERRIES

The ferry from Nicaragua to El Salvador across the Bay of Fonseca leaves Tuesdays and Thursdays at 6:00AM from Potosi. You get to Potosi from Chinendega by truck.

Although no regular ferries go from Bluefields to the Corn Islands, there are many private boats available. During the week is the best time as everyone likes to party on the week-ends and it is more difficult to arange transportation. Boats to the Mosquitia Coast leave during the week.

Banana boats & ferry

TAXIS

In town taxis operate on the collectivo system. You must have a map and know where you are going; you transfer taxis the same as you would a bus. Try to share a taxi with local people, and you will pay the same price as the locals. If you are the first person into the taxi, you will probably pay more than the locals unless you know the price. If you wish to rent a taxi for a few hours, you may do so for a substantial fee.

HITCHHIKING

Hitchhiking is possible but usually not necessary, as public transportation has improved in Nicaragua. However, in the smaller towns and more remote areas, hitchhiking is the most practical means of transportation. I was never asked to pay for the service, but you may be asked for a few cents. This was the custom in the past and

it may be in effect in certain parts of the country. You may often be
offered a ride in a horse or oxen drawn cart.

TELEPHONE

Local calls are unreliable; international calls usually have
static on the line. It is expensive to call from Nicaragua, but you may
call collect or station to station. To get an international operator who
speaks English, call 116. If calling direct to the US, dial 64. National
information is 112; international information is 118. If you are paying for the call, you must go to a CORTEL office in any larger town.

ALTA GRACIA

On the island of Ometepe, in Lake Nicaragua, are the two
towns of Alta Gracia and Moyagalpa. Of these two major towns, I prefer Alta Gracia to Moyogalpa. Alta Gracia has a nice town square, and
the people are very friendly. The church is often decorated with
many flowers. The bank in Moyogalpa will not change anything but
US cash. There is no bank in Alta Gracia.

There are two island legends. First, if you eat the fish from
the volcanic lake, you will never leave the island. Second, if you curse
the island then the island monster will get you. I don't know what
happens after he gets you.

PLACE TO STAY

Ramon Castillo's Hospedaje is the only place to stay.
It is very clean and quiet, and Ramon will tell you anything
you want to know about the island. He also has some knowledge of local herbal medicines. He speaks very rapid Spanish
and you may have to frequently ask him "mas dispasio". The
meals are really large and tasty. The rooms cost ¢12. ($2.50
US) per person; the beds are very hard.

THINGS TO DO

Lava Beds can be reached in a few hours; a visit is worth the
walk. Turn left from the front of the Hospedaje and go straight, past
the main road, past the cemetery, and keep going. After about 20
minutes, start veering your way towards the mountain. Ask the locals
and they will show you. All you need to say is "lava". After you have
explored the lava bed, continue up until you come to a nice hill with
a spectacular view.

The docks and the **boat to San Carlos** are about two miles
away from the town. The boat leaves at 6:00PM on Tuesdays and
Thursdays and returns the following days. You must walk past the
square on the east side, then follow the road down to the water. It is
easy to get a ride on an ox cart. The beach nearer the port has nice
brown sand and is dotted with volcanic rock. Although the beaches
are not very large, they are certainly pleasant to visit.

Rio Siniope, Urbyte or Tilque are all the same river. They are found close to the village of Magdelina which is accessible by truck. The last truck returns to Alta Gracia at about 3:00PM; you should be on it as hitching a ride is not very reliable after that time. The water is supposed to have medicinal value. You can see the vines shading the crystal clear, cold water and the ladies who wash clothes using special plant roots instead of soap.

The Petroglyphs can be reached by taking a truck to Balque. Asking them to let you off in front of the Callejon (which means alley) de Magdelina. It is a narrow path going up the hill. Follow it for about 15 or 20 minutes. You will come to the small settlement of Magdelina. There, you must ask for someone to show you the location of the rocks. I spoke with Ernest Castillo, the brother of the man who has the hotel in Alta Gracia. However, when I spoke with Ernest stating a price to put into this book, he elevated his price to an unreasonable amount. I would seriously not consider paying more than ¢10 per person for the trip. If you are unable to hire someone at Magdelina, then go on to La Cuchios which is further along the path. Ask some of the young boys to give you a tour. If both these methods fail, talk to the ladies at the tiendas near the road. They will definitely be able to help you find a guide for a reasonable price.

The glyphs are about 20 minutes away from Magdelinas, through the jungle. There are about 24 rocks with inscriptions on the rocks. A delightful one is of a dragon, another of a fish, a flower and a great one which has a face. There are some designs that look similar to designs found in the Nazca Lines in Peru. This is an excellent trip.

The beach is about one kilometer before the path to Magdelina and is a must for an afternoon. The beach is about two kilometers long, dotted with palm trees, and as clean as a whistle. Help keep it that way.

The volcanoes are Mount Maderia which is 1600 meters high and has a beautiful blue-green lake at the top. Concepcion is 1700 meters high and is still active. It is best to hire a guide as the trip is quite long. Even though Concepcion is easier it is higher. I did not climb these mountains, but there are many men willing to take gringos for a small fee. The island is so laid back and pleasant, that I recommend looking into the climb if you need an excuse to stick around.

BLUEFIELDS

This is a delightful little Caribbean town. Most who make the arduous trip usually enjoy it. The journey to the Corn Islands, is difficult and two weeks should be planned for the return trip. There is no regular ferry and you must wait for a private boat to come along which has enough room for you. Some people have waited four days for a oneway trip. It is possible to fly both to Bluefields and/or the Corn Islands from Managua. But, during the winter there are often delays due to bad weather. The road to Bluefields via Rama is reputed to have many robbers on it but I travelled it a few times with no problems. Once you are in Rama, you must take a boat to Bluefields. There are boats going all the time. The fast expensive boat (¢100. or $20. US) may take anywhere from two to four hours and the slow, cheap boat (¢20. or $4. US) can take up to nine hours.

PLACES TO STAY

Hotel Hollywood is great. Turn left from the docks and head up the street past the market area. It is a large old house with high ceiling rooms and a pleasant porch. There is also a restaurant downstairs but it is more expensive than others. The owners will let you use their telephone to make international calls. The cost is ¢40. ($8. US) per double room and ¢35. ($7. US) for a single. This is without private bath.

Hotel Dorado is across from the Hollywood and is quite a dump. The halls are dark, dingy, and dirty; the rooms are not much better. The price is the same and sometimes higher than the Hollywood. However, it is popular with many of the locals.

Hotel Claudia is beside the **Maria Maus.** You turn left before the Hollywood. These are okay but a bit noisy because the market is directly below. The cost is ¢40. ($8. US) for a double and ¢30. ($6. US) for a single. There are no private bathrooms and the taps are single. They are about the same for cleanliness. I liked the people in the Claudia better than the Maria Maus but that may have been my luck.

Costa Sur is up one street from the main street, away from the bay. It is very clean and pleasant and costs ¢50. ($10. US) for a double and ¢40. ($8. US) for a single. There are no private bathrooms here either.

Cueto is in the Santa Rosa barrio and a long way from the center of town. The cost is much the same as those in town. The rooms are small and the one tap bathrooms are not in your room.

El Velero is also a ways up from the docks; water is a problem. The rooms are bigger than the Cueto and the owners are quite friendly; I prefer to be closer to the center.

Mini Hospedaje is up a side street. When walking toward the Hollywood, turn right and go for two blocks. The rooms are basic but cheap. There is a restaurant on the premises.

RESTAURANTS

Hollywood Restaurant serves good food and is very clean. However, a large bowl of soup costs ¢20. ($4. US) and a beer costs ¢7.50 ($1.50 US) There are cheaper places to eat.

Bella Vista Restaurant is on the water. Walk down the main street past the Hollywood to the end of the street. Then turn toward the water. For ¢30. ($6. US) you can get a chicken dinner with all the trimmings. Beer is ¢6. ($1.20 US) per bottle. It is nice to sit on the balcony and enjoy the breezes while eating and drinking.

The **Mini Hotel** has a restaurant that serves good typical food. I am not a connoisseur of gallo pinto (beans and rice) but it was priced correctly.

THINGS TO DO

Rio Escondido is the river which you will take when going to Bluefields. The first hill on your left when leaving Rama is where a large boat landed during the 1988 hurricane. It must take quite a wind to lift a boat that high. The river is wide and pleasant. The shore is dotted with Mosquitia Indian's shacks, and the shores are lined with small cayucos, their only method of travel.

Pearl Lagoon is a small, clean and friendly little village up the Mosquitia Coast. It is four hours away by slow boat and one hour by fast boat. There are boats going every day and this is a delightful trip. There are no accommodations. It is very clean with grassy walks and pleasant people. You could probably get invited to stay at someone's house for a very small fee. It is a pleasure to enjoy the lack of hustle, bustle and dirt.

CHINANDEGA

Since the ferry across the Bay of Fonseca is operating again, traffic has again increased through Chinendega. The town is not really beautiful, but it is better to stay than the little port town of Potosi.

PLACES TO STAY

The Glomar is one block before the market and is about ¢10. ($2. US) per person. The rooms are quiet and colorful, with bright orange walls, rust red tiles and barn-red doors. There is a cream colored strip to offset the clashing of colors. The rooms have fans and a few rooms have bathrooms. The public bathrooms are in better shape than the private ones.

Hotel Chinandega is half a block before the Glomar; it is very basic for the same price. The staff are friendly and cheerful. There are fans but no private baths.

RESTAURANTS

Corono de Oro is a wonderful Chinese restaurant which serves great shrimp chow mein. After a meal, your body will be replenished with needed vitamins and minerals. If you enjoy soups, don't order both a soup and a meat dish, as the meal will be too much. This is the place to eat.

Pizza Caliente is two blocks past the cathedral; it has fairly good pizza but does not have cold drinks or cold beer. The prices are reasonable and they allow the beggar children to finish anything you can't finish.

THINGS TO DO

Volcan San Cristobal is still an active volcano; it can be climbed with a guide. There is a guide available half a block away from the market, past the Gilmar. He does not have a sign, but everyone knows who he is; just ask. You should not go onto the volcano without a guide.

Beaches along the Pacific can be very secluded and beautiful. Jiquilillo is one of the beaches that is not a port. It has some restaurants and a few places to stay, but I have no further information. Now that the war is over and things are returning to normal, it is a good idea to see these beaches before it is re-discovered.

Puerto Corinto is one of the largest ports in Nicaragua and handles 60% of the country's business. Very good fishing is reported in the area. Boats can be rented in town. There is also a beach about half a mile from the center of town which is clean and not crowded. There are places to stay in Corinto, but most prefer to commute back and forth from Chinandega. The seafood in this area is always fresh and good to eat. However, it is expensive.

CORN ISLANDS

These are the Hawaii of Nicaragua, the lost paradise, the other world and one of the most difficult places to access. Maybe this is why it has so much beauty. Isolation and lack of facilities are the best drawing cards of these islands. Since the damage caused by the hurricane of 1988, things have not been totally repaired.

You can catch a boat from the Cocotera - the factory about two kilometers up the street in Bluefields. Turn right from the docks and ask for "Empresa Cocotera". You will wind your way up the barrio. You must ask early in the morning if you can go on a boat. It takes about six hours and can be dangerous in bad weather as the boats are not in perfect condition. There is also a boat that goes from the main dock about three times a week. You definitely need time to get out to the islands. Getting back is the same procedure. You may have to wait a few days while a storm passes or until a boat comes by and has room to take you to the mainland.

PLACES TO STAY

There are some places to stay. Not all have been restored since the hurricane. There is a government hotel which includes meals, but it is quite expensive. The most common places run about ¢25. - 40. ($5-$8. US) per person and are very basic. Coco Beach is a nice place to stay, but the best beach for swimming is across the island at Long Beach.

ESTELI

This is a lovely, bustling little town. The people are friendly and fun. The bus stops at the market at the top end of town. There is a long strip of hotels.

PLACES TO STAY

El Chicito is the very closest to the bus stop. It is pleasant and popular. It has one tap showers and no private baths. The cost is ¢15. ($3. US) per person.

San Ignacio is about the worst place to stay. It has straw mattresses and is grubbier than the rest. The cost is ¢15. ($3. US)

San Francisco is another little place for ¢15. per person, and is one of the more popular places for backpackers to stay. There are no private baths and only one tap showers. Basically, it is the same as all the rest.

Florida is very friendly and often full. It is just off the main strip. The cost is ¢15. ($3. US) and it is the usual one tap shower.

Bolivar has a nice garden and is fairly clean, but all is relative. It also costs ¢15. ($3. US) per person. The owners here are very friendly and helpful.

Hospedaje Segovias is one street to the left of the market and is expensive at $25. ($5. US) per person. The building is new and the yard is still not finished. This may improve with time. The older rooms in the hotel are cheaper but they are my last choice.

Hotel Mariela is behind the market, towards Managua, and is the cleanest and most comfortable at ¢20. ($4. US) per person. This is the best place in town. It is clean and the owners are very friendly, the rooms are quiet, and the price is right. There are fans in the rooms.

RESTAURANTS

There are quite a few restaurants on the main street. **The La Plancha** has good, basic, typical food but I would advise you to try anything that strikes your fancy. There are no exceptional restaurants in Esteli.

THINGS TO DO

Salto de Extanzuela is a nice waterfall with a fresh, clean pool at the bottom. It is deep enough for a pleasant swim. However, at the end of the dry season, it is a slimy hole which should be avoided. During rainy season, there are lots of trees and blooming air plants. You may walk to and from this refreshing place from Esteli.

To get there, walk along the highway going to Managua, past the police station and a granary. There are a number of smaller granaries in the field. The road which passes these granaries and then goes off to the right is where you want to walk. The walk is uphill past small farm settlements; the views are very pretty. Walk for about one and a half hours, mostly up. Pass a small bridge, go around the hill in front of you and then down the hill. After about one and a half hours from Esteli, you will come to a group of houses (three or four). There is an obvious road behind a large gate. Go through the gate and down the road for about two minutes. Be certain to close the gate as there are cattle inside. You will see a small path going down the hill. This leads you to the waterfall and swimming hole.

Town Square is at the opposite end of town to the bus terminal. You must walk at least two kilometers to get there. The square has an old Indian carved rock or petroglyph. Because it is exposed to the elements, I imagine that the carving will wear away fairly quickly.

The Cathedral has been renovated. The altar has a lovely statue of the Virgin robed in white and gold. This is very pretty and not overdone. There is an abundance of natural wood visible in this church.

Gallery of Heroes and Martyrs is across from the fire hall, just one block off the square. There are many pictures of those who dedicated their lives to the revolution. There are also pieces of clothing, some guns and shells, and personal items saved from the heroes. It is not particularly interesting, but what else is there to do in Esteli?

The post office is just around the corner from the fire hall. There is usually a blue and white sign saying "Cortel" or "Telcon".

GRANADA

This is Somosa's old hang-out. The money spent in this town will show for a long time. There are magnificent old colonial houses, the streets are beautifully paved and there are some wonderful old churches to visit. Granada has not been damaged by the revolution nor does it suffer from natural disasters. It is truly a beautiful town.

Granada sits on the northern section of Lake Nicaragua, the only fresh water lake in the world that boasts of having sharks. The lake is 160 kilometers (100 mi) long and 75 kilometers (45 mi) wide. Lake Managua drains into Lake Nicaragua by the river Tipitapa; then, Lake Nicaragua drains down the Rio San Juan and into the Caribbean. The route from the Caribbean to Granada was used by famous pirates like Captain Morgan and Sir Francis Drake. They took many sacks of loot from this beautiful and rich city.

Granada was founded in 1524 by Francisco Hernandez de Cordoba who came from Panama looking for gold from the native Chief Nicarao. It developed into a rich, conservative area which was always in conflict with the liberals of Leon.

William Walker fought against the Central American republics which were backed by Vanderbilt. When the situation got beyond his control, Walker set the town aflame and fled. He later landed in Honduras where he was hung.

The park at one end of town has a beach frequented by both locals and tourists. Granada is the nicest town in all of Nicaragua.

PLACES TO STAY

Hospedaje Los Ojos is before the park on La Cazada, the main street. The cost is ¢20. ($4. US) per person and is comparable to the other hotels in town. However, if you like to be closer to the center, you may want one of the other hotels. There is no hot water.

Hospedaje Vargas is also on La Cazada, after the central park. It has small dark rooms for ¢25. ($5. US) per person and a communal shower. The staff is not friendly.

Hospedaje Cabrera is across the street from the Vargas and is the same price. This is a clean, but not first class, place. The rooms are only partitions and the springs on the beds squeak whenever anyone turns over. However, of the three cheapies, this is the best.

The Granada charges $40.00 US for a room. It is quite a beautiful place and the rooms are situated around a pleasant courtyard. There is a restaurant, bar, cafeteria and excellent service. The hotel is on Calle Calzada, in front of the Church of Guadalupe.

The Alahambra is even more sophisticated than the Granada and has a lovely balcony around the central square. It is nice to sit here and enjoy the activity in the square. The rooms are a mere $35.00 US per night. The Alahambra is on the central park.

RESTAURANTS

Cabaña Amarilla is down by the park. There are many places to choose from along the walkway, but this is one of the best. It has a few selections on the menu and the food is good. Eating in Granada is expensive.

Drive-in El Ancla is across from the Granada hotel. It is clean and reasonable. The french fries are excellent, but don't bother with the hamburgers. The salads have a hot sauce on them; they require ten bottles of mineral water to extinguish the flame.

The Market is often a better place to eat if you are on a budget.

The Alahambra or Granada are both great places to eat and they have great price tags attached. I would recommend eating at the park rather than paying the high prices these hotels charge. But, if you need something luxurious, which may be so when in Nicaragua, then try either one of the hotels.

THINGS TO DO

Central Park is a lovely park bordered by the cathedral and old colonial buildings. The park itself has huge palm trees and manicured ornamental shrubbery. There are fountains and a beautiful kiosk in which to rest. I felt at peace in this delightful city. At one end of the square is the war memorial from 1821 to 1921 beside a Sandinista revolutionary statue. Depending on which government is in power, one of the revolutionary statues may disappear!

Church of St. Francais is run by the Franciscan Friars; you must be taken through the church by one of the brothers. Ring the bell, and they will be glad to help you. The graveyard at the church is interesting and worth the visit. The church itself was built in 1856. The bell tower has some lovely old religious figures such as Saint Francis, Saint Peter and the Virgin. It was originally carved by Indians from the area. There is a small collection of prehispanic sculptures at the church.

Church of La Merced was built in 1781, destroyed in 1854, and rebuilt in 1862. The carved wood statues of Jesus and the Virgin were brought from Spain 300 years ago. This is a delightful little church.

The National Park is on the lake at the end of the city. Here, you will find the locals eating great food and drinking copious amounts of rum. The beach goes for about two miles and is lined with a walkway, change houses, mango trees and restaurants. At the far end of the lake, you can take a small boat to the islands. This is a delightful trip. The park also has "Mylinche" trees which produce a yellow flower in the spring. Although you will see these trees everywhere in Central America, they are most abundant in this park.

Las Isletas or the "little islands" are a group of small islands on the archipelago near the south end of the lake. There are about 300 islands in all. Some were inhabited by rich Granadian families; they built large homes complete with swimming pools. The area may return to a wealthy suburb with the new government. Some islands are small rocky upcroppings with nothing on them. You can hire a boat to tour the islands. This will be less expensive if you go as a group. The trip takes a few hours.

You may take a **boat to San Carlos or Isla de Ometepe** from Granada. It leaves Tuesdays and Thursdays and returns on the following days. The tickets go on sale at 8:00AM at the wharf located near the National Park gate and the boat sails at 10:00AM. The boat arrives on the island of Ometepe between 6 and 8:00PM. If you wish to continue to San Carlos, you will arrive there at about 3:00AM

The boat is always crowded and getting a place to sit or sleep is difficult, especially for gringos. If you are sitting on the deck which you may very well have to do, you will need some type of pack cover and some plastic sheeting to put underneath you. It is more comfortable to sit on the back deck than inside as the air is fresher. However, you must find a spot where you will be out of the wind. There is a small confectionery on the boat where you can get junk food and some pop. I would suggest bringing food along. If you go to San Carlos, you should plan on staying on the boat until daylight. The captain allows this. Just curl up and sleep until morning.

JINOTEGA

This is a lovely little mountainous town and, if coming or going from Honduras, you may wish to stop here. The town is close to a lake which was formed when the river was dammed for hydro power. However, in 1992, the area was temporarily closed to travellers because of guerilla warfare in the hills. The information here is not new.

PLACES TO STAY

The **Moderno** is in the center of town and is about the best for the traveller. It costs ¢25. ($5. US) per person. The rooms are basic without private bathrooms. There are places to eat around town, but nothing is exceptional.

THINGS TO DO

The area specializes in black ceramics and marble sculptures; these may be found at different locations in the town.

You may go on a guided tour through the mountains on horseback. Horses may be rented from the Selva Negra Hotel just out of town. This is fairly expensive.

You may go fishing in the lake; small boats can be rented. However, the trip around the lake on the way to Esteli is now closed. It may open in the future. The locals will be able to give you information on this.

JUIGALPA

Juigalpa is a grubby town with few friendly people. However, this may be because I was tired when I was there. If trying to avoid Managua, or if going to Bluefields or San Carlos, this is a good overnight stop.

PLACES TO STAY

Pension Balon is just off the square. Walk past the bank to the far side of the square, not where the buses stop. Turn right, walk half a block and you will see the hotel. The cost is ¢20. ($4. US) per person. It is clean enough and very quiet.

The **Angelita** is past the square towards the post office. Walk about two blocks. There is a sign. The hotel is small and clean with a little garden in which to sit. The cost is ¢20. ($4. US) per person without private bath. The beds are comfortable.

The **Central** is close to the Angelita, but is not quite as comfortable as the Angelita. I quite liked the place for ¢20. ($4. US).

RESTAURANTS

The little restaurant on the left hand side when facing the post office and one block before it is excellent. The hamburgers which are tacos stuffed with meat are delicious. She does not serve beer, only pop. Service is good, the restaurant is clean, and the prices are not gringo prices.

THINGS TO DO

The Gregorio Aguilar Barea Museum is past the Cultural building and down that street about five blocks. There are many large, old stone carvings in the courtyard. Inside the museum are statues, petroglyphs, fossils and ceramics from Nicaragua. This is considered the best museum in Nicaragua.

LA BOQUITA

This is a tiny little beach developed by the tourist department. It is 65 kilometers from Managua and where a river flows into the ocean. It is a delightful little spot. The tourist center is in the center of town and has kiosks, bungalows, bars and restaurants. The most expensive hotel in town is the La Casona which has rooms with private bathrooms and clean sheets. This is a nice beach to visit when in Nicaragua. The entire Pacific coast is spectacular.

LEON

Leon is a nice town to use as a central location when visiting the area. Leon is the intellectual center of Nicaragua; it has a university and a few religious colleges. Leon was the first city in Nicaragua to develop a university, much to the pride of the local people. It also has the largest cathedral in all of Central America. Leon was once the capital of Nicaragua, but the capital was moved to Managua because Managua is the halfway point between the conservative city of Granada and the liberal city of Leon.

Leon was first built at the base of Momotombo, but moved after it was destroyed in an earthquake. Leon then ruled as the capital of Nicaragua for almost 300 years. Today, the city is not as elegant as Granada, but is still an interesting place to visit.

Leon is not only known for educating intellectuals and housing famous poets like Ruben Dario, but it also is the spot where Hernandez Cortez was hung by Pedrarias in 1526. However, that spot would be the old Leon, not the present site.

PLACES TO STAY

Hotel Telika is quite a ways from the center of town; it may be easier to take a taxi to the hotel. The hotel is basic, with water but no private baths. The price is ¢15. ($3. US) per person. The single rooms are very small, but the doubles are much bigger and cheerier. The beds are made of straw mats and have clean sheets, both top and bottom. When I was there, they even offered soap.

Hotel Europe costs ¢55. ($11. US) per night. There are private baths, soft clean sheets, towels, toilet paper, a fan, a spacious clean room and friendly staff. As well, the restaurant serves excellent breakfasts and has a fruit and sandwich bar for snacks. The courtyard is lovely and has chairs and tables interspersed among the trees. This is by far the most desirable hotel in town.

Hotel America is ¢35. ($7. US) per person and is the second best. Although not as elegant as the Europe, it is very clean and cheery. It is also in the center of town. The owner is pleasant and helpful.

Hospedaje Brandon costs ¢15. ($3. US) per person and is definitely the last choice. It is basic, situated beside the railway tracks and is quite noisy. It is also the least comfortable.

RESTAURANTS

Hotel Europe has the best meals in town; as well, the fruit and sandwich bar is almost always open. The restaurant serves excellent meals, but they are not the cheapest.

THINGS TO DO

The Cathedral on the square is the largest in Central America. Originally, it was to be built in Lima, Peru, but the plans got mixed up. Peru got a modest church and Leon got the grand, baroque style cathedral. The construction of the cathedral was started in 1746.

The Cathedral holds the tomb of Rubin Dario, the famous Nicaraguan poet (1867-1916). His real name was Felix Ruben Garcia Sarmiento. His tomb may be found below one of the twelve statues of the apostles. It is guarded by a stone lion. Dario's second and most famous works was "Prosas Profanas" (Profane Prose), written in 1896, and later translated into English.

The Cathedral has a beautiful ivory statue of Christ . The most interesting artifact is the sacred, topaz studded object brought from India. There is also a silver hammered altar in one of the chapels. If you want to appreciate all the treasures kept at the cathedral, plan to spend a leisurely afternoon.

Ruben Dario Museum is just around the corner from the Cathedral, on the corner, opposite the La Salle College. This is a must when in Leon. Although he spent most of his life abroad, this was Ruben Darios home when he was a child. The museum is interesting and well organized displaying the different aspects of Ruben's life. Some of his manuscripts are on display.

Subtiava Church, built in 1530 and an old haunt of Bartholome de las Casas, is the oldest church in Leon. It is located in the Barrio of Subtiava. Inside, there are some very old carvings. The Indians are said to worship the carving of the sun. The figure of Christ carrying a staff is considered quite old (what is old?).

Adiact Museum is in the Subtiava barrio of Leon. It is a small archaeological museum which should be visited if in the area.

There are nice, clean beaches close to Leon. See under "Poneloya" for details.

LOS MANOS

This is the border town you pass after leaving Ocotal. You can get drinks or snacks at the various comedors but you wouldn't want to stay here. In the event of a problem at the border, there is a pension in Los Manos. The crossing here is easy. The Hondurans love to see the exhausted, dirty traveller happily leaving Nicaragua. The crossing costs seven limp per person.

MANAGUA

Managua is a sprawling city bordering the mercury polluted lake of Managua. Managua became the capital of Nicaragua in 1858, but was destroyed by earthquake and fire in 1931. It was restored but again destroyed by earthquake in 1972. The revolution of 1978-79 caused even more damage in the center of town. Today, remnants of ruined buildings are interspersed with new government buildings and monuments. It is not uncommon to see cows, pigs and chickens roaming in empty lots in the center of town. On the outskirts of the city are glorious mansions and cardboard shacks, comedors and a few expensive restaurants.

Very few street signs can be found; finding directions is usually through reference to landmarks. The Intercontinental Hotel is a huge, white plaster building in the center of the city; it is the best landmark. Another visible building is a tall white government building which is about four blocks towards the lake from the Intercontinental. This government building is not open to tourists. **The Casa Benjamin Linder** is a traveller's information center. It offers information about places to stay. There is a bulletin board where you may leave notes for other travellers, and it is a good drop in center.

PLACES TO STAY

There are many places to stay in Managua; some cheap, some middle class and many expensive. I have only listed a few which are downtown and not too hard to find. I have excluded those that require buses to access. The best are the guest houses. If the tourist office is open when you arrive in town, you can check there for information. It is found across from the Intercontinental, to the south, and 50 meters to the west.

Hotel Dorado is a clean hospedaje in Managua, down from the Cine Dorado. It is a favorite with travellers. The cost is ¢15. ($3. US) per person and they will accept US currency. The showers are communal but very clean. You may use their phone (for a price). You may leave your pack while you travel (for a price). You may have a key to the hotel and room (for a price). They will return the key deposit when you return the key.

Hospedaje Norma will cost about ¢10. ($2. US) per person and is basic and clean. This is another favorite for the travellers.

There are no private bathrooms. Tables and hammocks are in the courtyard where people gather and enjoy each other's company. The hotel is one block south and half block to the east of the Cine Dorado.

Hospedaje Santos   very close to the Cine Dorado charges ¢15. ($3. US) per person   for a basic room without bath. The communal bath is clean; the large, pleasant courtyard is the drawing card. They have a small snack bar in the yard. This is a popular place with chickenbusers.

Hotel Colibre costs ¢40. ($8. US) per person and includes a private bath. It is a lovely little place, which is clean and comfortable. You will find it one block to the south and then half block to the west of the Cine Dorado.

Casa Fiedler is another guest house like the Colibre and is found one block to the north and one and a half blocks to the west of the Cine Dorado. This is a delightful place that costs ¢50. ($10. US) per room.

The Carlos is a guest house close to the Tica bus terminal. The hotel is two blocks to the east and one and a half blocks to the south of the Cine Dorado. It is another place that costs ¢50. ($10. US) it is more than acceptable.

The Gladys Guest House has been highly recommended by an old friend. It is one block to the east and half a block to the north of the Cine Dorado. The place is very secure, with a locked outside gate. The rooms are, larger than many and the owners are very pleasant. The cost is ¢40. ($8. US) per night per room. This is a place where the older travellers seem to hang out.

RESTAURANTS

Los Antojitos on Ave. Bolivar is across from the Intercontinental Hotel. This is an excellent place to eat supper, to meet a friend or just to have a cool relaxing drink. Many brigade workers meet there because of the relaxed atmosphere, excellent service and good food. The shish kebab is recommended. It is excellent.

Hotel Intercontinental has a smorgasbord for breakfast which is quite good but costly. They serve both continental and typical food; there is no limit to the amount you eat. However, the price is $7.00 US per person. If you are hungry, this is an excellent deal; food all over Nicaragua is expensive. The hotel also has other places for eating and drinking. The Piano Bar is delightful in the evenings.

Pizza Maria is close to the market area; if looking for a good lunch, this is the place. It is one block up from the Cine Jardin on the same side as the government market. The pizzas are large, the fillings are super size and the selection is great. Besides, the price is reasonable.

Juices are best purchased from the tienda just past the Cine Dorado at the first Fanta sign. Maria Terica is the young lady who lives there and she loves to converse in English. The typical meals served at the tienda are the best I have tasted. I truly recommend this comedor. Also, the prices are excellent.

China Palace Restaurant is in front of the Plaza del Sol on the highway to Masaya. This is an excellent place for a good meal if you are in need of spending some money. The piano bar section is open until 1:00AM, but they play an organ instead of a piano. The restaurant serves meals, which are excellent from noon until 10:00PM.

Coffee Garden in the Camino Real is a pleasant treat if you want a quiet place to read and write. You can take a bus to the hotel which is nine and a half kilometers on the highway going north, between the center of town and the airport. The prices are not cheap.

Reggae House discotheque is about five kilometers out the highway going toward the airport. It is a popular spot for some and close enough to town to walk.

Amatl restaurant is two blocks south of Los Antojitos; it offers free coffee all day.

THINGS TO DO

The Tourist Bureau is one block from the Intercontinental Hotel. You may purchase a city map or try and rent a room they recommend. The map will cost a couple of dollars. Other information is pretty sparce; they have no print-outs with tourist information. A better place to go is Casa Benjamin Linder which provides accurate information. However, the government is trying to improve resources and services for the tourist.

The Cathedral is on the east side of the main square; it is another landmark in Managua. It was destroyed during the last earthquake, and restoration has not occurred. Entering these ruins is parallel to entering the Acropolis in Greece. The cathedral is hauntingly beautiful and magnificent. Inside the building, there is grass growing between tiles. The front altar still has ceramic tile murals. The roof is missing, but most of the side walls are intact. This is an imaginative photographer's dream.

The Central Park is towards the lake from the Intercontinental Hotel. It is a beautiful park. An eternal flame burns for the glory of the revolution. The park is shaded and provides a nice rest stop while walking around Managua. The park also contained the tomb of Carlos Fonseca, the founder of the Sandinistas. Carlos was killed in the Zinica region on November 7, 1976. At that time rumors spread that the National Guards who killed him had cut off his head and that only his body was buried in the area. The Guards claimed he was burried by a local peasant. Later, when the body was moved to the park, it was totally intact. However, when I was in the north of Nicaragua, I read that some right-wing enthusiasts had blown up the grave of Carlos Fonseca; I do not know how much damage was done to the body or the grave.

The National Palace is across from the Cathedral in the square. The building is now being reconstructed into government offices. There are some huge murals in the entrance way which the Nicaraguan guards encourage you to photograph. They are proud of their accomplishments.

Rubin Dario Theatre is a beautiful new theatre where cultural events occur. It is only one block past the National Palace. For information, you must go to the tourist office. The local ballet, Tepenahautle, for example, will cost $7.00 or $8.00 US per person for a very good seat. The theatre is an architectural beauty.

Baseball is as popular in Nicaragua as it is in the USA. You will often see young children, barefooted, playing in the streets on the roughest of diamonds. So, if you are a baseball fan, you will be happy to know there are games every Sunday, Tuesday and Wednesday at the stadium. The Sunday game is a doubleheader starting at noon. On other days, the games start at 2:00PM. These games are wonderful and full of spirit.

The Revolutionary Museum is across from the Escuardo Conferas bus station. The museum has many pictures of local heros and covers the revolutions of the last one-hundred years. There are a few artifacts and guns, many old documents, and some instruments of torture used by the Samoza regime. The museum is not cluttered nor junky and worth taking the time to visit, especially if you are interested in modern history.

Huellas de Acahualinca is found between the lake and the railway tracks. Turn left down Calle el Triunfo when facing the lake, walk until you reach the Santa Ana barrio and then turn towards the lake. It is not far. Continue until you come to the Acahualinca barrio. This archaeological site has footprints of humans and animals dating back 5,000 years. It is believed these prints were left as people tried to escape a volcanic eruption. Some prints are deeper than others indicating the owner was probably carrying some of his possessions. This museum is worth the time to visit.

Artesanias Salvadoreñas is a little shop one street down from the Hospedaje Dorado, between the tree in the middle of the street and the Dorado. The goods produced here are made by Salvadorian refugees in Nicaragua; by supporting the shop, you in turn support their cause. There are some great crafts in this shop.

National Museum is at the Cultural Center of Leonel Rugama on Antigual Colonial Dambach. It is a museum which displays some archaeological specimens. Renovations are underway to make the museum more attractive. It also has a natural section.

The Art Museum of the Americas has some delightful contemporary paintings and sculptures. This is a peaceful and pleasant place to visit. It is found in front of the Communications center.

The Alfabetizacion Museum was a pride and joy of the Sandinistas. It is half a block north of the Park of the Palmas. You can walk there. The museum displays the country's history of the struggle for literacy. It was built in 1980, during the literacy campaign led by the leftists. When Sandinistas were training the peasants how to shoot, Carlos Fonseca told his men that when those lessons were over, the soldiers were to teach the peasants how to read.

English Books can be acquired at the Intercontinental Hotel but they are expensive. Remember that if you are going into Salvador, Costa Rica or Honduras, you will not be allowed to carry revolutionary material. At best it will be confiscated and at worst you could be detained. However, some English pocket books not revolutionary by our standards, may appear to be so by others. When crossing into Costa Rica, I had a book called "Kaffir Boy" about a South African tennis player; the border guards confiscated it. Be careful.

Lago de Managua is a polluted lake and swimming is certainly not advisable. The volcano, Momotombo, can be seen from the lake shore in Managua. During the heat of the day, this is often a pleasant place to visit. You get a few refreshing breezes from the lake.

Election campaign

Artesans Market at Mercado Huembes specializes in local pottery. It has quite a nice selection. This market should not be missed, even if just going to watch the people. It is always crowded and busy; photographic possibilities are great.

Xiloa is 18 kilometers west of the city center. There is a lovely little volcanic lake by the same name. This spot is a tourist center which has a picnic area, a restaurant (expensive), a bar (of course) and a few souvenir kiosks.

Trapiche is another tourist center 17 kilometers to the east of the capital on the old highway to Tipitapa. There are a number of places where the water flows from the rocks and forms fountains which are caught in lovely pools. The entire area is surrounded by beautiful gardens. Many different priced restaurants are available. Trapiche is easily reached from Managua by bus.

MASAYA

This is a pleasant little town above the Laguna de Masaya. The market is well known here for its beautiful hammocks. They are the large cotton type and are the best in all of Central America. The town has solved gasoline shortage problems by changing the motorized taxis for the horse and cart version. This town a delightful little place and much more pleasant than Managua.

PLACES TO STAY

There are a few places to stay around the park, but nothing is exceptional. It is better to stay in Managua and commute to Masaya.

Hotel Rex is beside the church and is reported to be fairly good. I have not been in this hotel, so I have no first hand information. It is a basic hotel.

Hotel Regis is another acceptable hotel. It is half a block north of the Cine Gonzalez. I would suggest this be the first choice if staying in Masaya.

RESTAURANTS

You are on your own. The cafeteria at the park is okay, but expensive for the quality.

THINGS TO DO

The Cultural Center sells first quality crafts from all over Nicaragua. There is a large wall map showing where each item is made. If you want quality, this is the place to shop. The prices are much higher than in the markets.

Volcano Masaya National Park is the main reason for visiting Masaya. To get there, take the bus to Granada/Masaya; the driver will let you off at kilometer 23. You must then walk the seven kilometers along a paved road, to the top of the volcano. It is sometimes possible to hitch a ride. As tourism increases in Nicaragua, the government will see the need to put a regular bus on this route. Also, there will be more cars which will make hitch-hiking easier.

The park is open every day from 9:00AM to 5:00PM, except Mondays. They have special events during festival days.

The park has an area of 54 square kilometers with 15 kilometers of footpaths developed. These paths go around the craters and to the Laguna. There is a Visitor's Center which has a natural history display, restaurant (expensive) and a cafeteria. There is also a picnic area, drinking water and washroom facilities. Guided tours are available, but they must be booked in advance.

When walking along the paths, you will see many wild flowers including the black lily, white sacuanjoches and many species of orchids. Some trees have grown quite large. There are also coyotes and other carnivorous animals living on the mountain.

Originally, natives of Nicaragua made human sacrifices to the volcano. When the Spaniards arrived, they named the volcano the "Mouth of the Inferno", and built a cross on its borders in order to "rid the volcano of the devil". The volcano is called Santiago and the one crater is called Nindiri.

In 1529, Gonzalo Fernandez de Oviedo, a famous monk, wrote to the King of Spain concerning the volcano's special legend. In 1538, another man, Blas del Castillo, decided to investigate the volcano. He climbed into the crater believing the lava was melted gold. He carried a bucket to fill with gold. When he dipped the bucket into the lava, the bucket melted. He ended with neither the bucket nor the gold.

In 1670, the Nindiri crater erupted, and the lava flowed down the north slope of the hill. In March 1772, the volcano erupted again, down the north-east section of the hill. This lava flow is visible across the main highway and along the road going into the park. In 1852, the Santiago crater started making noises. The area sank; gases, ash and lava activity were seen. This is the crater beside the washrooms and parking area. Santiago erupted again in 1902 and 1927 spreading ash as far as the mountains near Managua. Since then, there have been minor eruptions in 1946, 1959, and 1965. The gases from Santiago form water, hydrochloric acid and sulphur gas.

Nindiri's crater is 400 meters around. San Fernando has beautiful vegetation in its crater. San Pedro is no longer active.

MATAGALPA

This northern little town, nuzzled into the mountains is both friendly and pretty. Many brigade workers stationed out of Matagalpa come into town for rest, recuperation and a good meal. Matagalpa is rapidly repairing itself after the war. Very few bullet holes remain in the buildings, and the airplane propeller is no longer sitting on the street.

If taking a taxi to the center of town, you will pay ¢2. (.40¢ US) during the day and ¢3. (.40¢ US) after dark. You can walk during the day as it is only about six blocks. Go along the road beside the river where it turns to the right. The left goes over a small foot bridge. Continue walking uphill for about four blocks. You will come to the square.

Carlos Fonseca, hero of the Sandinistas, was born in the El Laborio neighborhood of Matagalpa on June 23, 1936, to a peasant woman, Justina Fonseca, and his father, Fausto F. Amador. During the revolution, Matagalpa was a stronghold for the Sandinistas.

PLACES TO STAY

Hospedaje Plaza will cost ¢16. ($3.25 US) per person and this includes a private bath. It is clean and quiet. You may sit in their living room and watch television. The hotel is on the square.

Hospedaje Colonial is also on the square and costs ¢16. ($3.25 US) per person; it is often full. This is the most popular hotel for travellers. It is clean and friendly.

The Maria Rivera is around the corner from the Plaza and costs ¢15. ($3. US) for one. It is basic and not exceptional.

Pension under the "Andrews Farmacia" sign on the square is difficult to find as there is no sign advertising the hotel. Enter the door next to the farmacia. The rooms are very quiet and fairly clean. The very small rooms cost ¢15. ($3. US) each and the larger rooms cost ¢20. ($4. US) each without private bathrooms. The bigger rooms are acceptable, but the little rooms are claustrophobic.

The Bermuda is the best hotel in town. Go up the street on the lefthand side of the cathedral. Walk for two blocks; the hotel is on the far corner. The cost is ¢25. ($5. US) for one and ¢35. ($7. US) for two. The rooms are very clean, bright and have private bathrooms. There is a small courtyard and the staff are friendly and helpful.

RESTAURANTS

La Cabaña is two blocks up from the square on the side of the Colonial Hotel. You can get an excellent meal, and the salads are recommended. This is also one of the few places that has mineral water. A complete chicken dinner runs about ¢20. ($4. US).

Pizza File is next door to the Burmuda Hotel. It is quite expensive, but it is a treat to have something other than chicken, or beans and rice. Although not the best pizza in Central America, it is fairly good. You may even get a couple of olives in a cocktail glass as an appetizer. If they have run out of olives, your appetizer will be a surprise.

THINGS TO DO

The Cathedral has been totally repaired and looks quite nice. There are many old paintings behind the altar. On the square, near the Cathedral, Carlos Fonseca, leader and hero of the Sandinistas, sold newspapers and candy to help his mother between 1945 and 1950.

Ciudad Dario is on the highway before the turn off to Matagalpa when coming from Managua. This is not a place to stay overnight but is interesting to visit during the day. This is the home town of the famous poet, Rubin Dario, who lived here in his youth. There is a small house with a few of his possessions on display. Rubin Dario's real name was Felix Ruben Garcia Sarmiento, and he lived from 1867 to 1916. He is a famous poet from the Period of Consolidation. His best piece of work was Prosas Profanas (1896) which was translated into English during that period. The house is only two blocks off the highway and is a small, humble dwelling.

Artisans Market is right on the highway when coming into town. It specializes in black ceramics and carved marble figurines.

MONTELIMAR

Montelimar is a beach along the Pacific, just up from Pochomil. The richer Nicaraguans visit here but it is also interesting for us chickenbusers. There are beautiful gardens to walk through, a small forest to visit, a nice long beach on which to suntan. The big hotel has the largest swimming pool in all of Central America. You can visit the pool for a small admission fee, which is small in comparison to staying for the entire night. There are restaurants, bars, a discoteque and other cheaper places to eat. The seafood along the beach is highly recommended.

MOYOGALPA - ISLA OMETEPE

This island has the relaxed atmosphere of the Caribbean, the hospitality of the Nicaraguans, the peacefulness of a Cathedral, and a variety of activities. I highly recommend a visit to this little paradise. To get there, you must take a ferry from Rivas-San Jorge. At present the ferry goes every day at 8:00AM, 11:00AM and 4:00PM. It is very crowded and sitting down would be real luck. The ferry lands in Moyogalpa, and you must take a bus or truck to the other town of Alta Gracia. During the night, Moyogalpa has the usual orchestra of dogs and roosters, but Alta Gracia is very quiet. Both towns are delightful, but I liked Alta Gracia best. You must bring US cash with you as the bank in Moyogalpa does not change traveller's cheques and there is no bank at Alta Gracia.

The buses leave for Alta Gracia when the ferry arrives; the last bus returns from Alta Gracia at 5:00PM

There are two island legends. One says that if you eat the fish from the volcanic lake, you will never leave the island. The other says that if you curse the island, then the island monster will get you. I don't know what he will do after he gets you but I was warned to beware.

PLACES TO STAY

Pension Moyogalpa is a clean, very friendly, three generation, family run establishment. It is the first pension along the strip from the ferry. They have soft beds and good meals. The owners are honest and will provide information about island happenings.

Hospedaje Aby is further up the strip. It has a beautiful garden in the center, but the beds have straw mattresses.

Hospedaje Ramon Castillo is the only place to stay in Alta Gracia. It is very clean and quiet, but the beds are very hard. The cost is ¢12. ($2.50 US) per person. Ramon will tell you anything you want to know about the island. He also has some knowledge of local herbal medicines but he speaks very fast Spanish. He also serves meals.

RESTAURANTS

Pension Moyogalpa has a nice little dining room in the back of the pension; the owner cooks a great fish dinner with the fresh fish from the lake. Her prices are not too high; however, her coffee is fake and to be avoided.

Ramon Castillo serves excellent meals, less expensive than in Moyogalpa, and they are a good size. His chicken (not again) is delightful and could easily put some of the franchise chicken shops out of business. You can make a day trip to Alta Gracia and eat at Ramon's.

As tourism increases, so will the services.

THINGS TO DO

The Natural Barrier just out of Moyogalpa is a small barrier which keeps the waves from going into shore. It is a wonderful two hour walk through primitive settlements close to the beach. The beaches are all black sand on this side of the island. The barrier can be seen from the docks in the town.

OCOTAL

This is a grubby, little town and the last one of any size when coming or going to Honduras. If you are late in the day, there are places to stay. Although the town is not pretty, the surrounding area is appealing and especially pretty when the trees are in bloom.

PLACES TO STAY

Pension Centroamerica is about the best place to stay. It is cleaner than some of the others. No private baths and the rooms cost ¢16. ($3.20 US); this is expensive for what you get.

OMETEPE ISLAND

This is a delightful island which should be visited. There are lava beds to explore, original petroglyphs to see in the mountains in their original homes and two beautiful volcanoes to climb. For all information on the island, see Moyogalpa and Alta Gracia.

PIÑAS BLANCAS

This is the border town between Costa Rica and Nicaragua. It is a small village with a very basic hospedaje; one can stay here if travelling late in the day or if the border guards delay you longer than anticipated. However, taxi to Rivas costs ₡15. ($3. US) per person; it is recommended going to Rivas.

POCHOMIL

Ah - the beach at last. And this is a beautiful Pacific Ocean beach just outside Managua. Many Managuans visit this area. The beach is about two miles long and is very clean. The ride into Pochomil is also spectacular. The road winds down a mountain road through lush green farmland. There are a few rather expensive hotels in Pochomil; it is better to commute from Managua. The last bus for Managua leaves at 6:00PM. The mountain road is not used by many so do not try and hitch a ride late in the day.

PLACES TO STAY

Hotel Bajamar has 28 units complete with private baths. There is a restaurant at the hotel which specializes in seafoods. I do not have a price for the hotel but it is not one of the cheapies. I obviously did not stay here.

Centro Turisticos has an area where you can sit under palm huts during the heat of the day.

RESTAURANTS

There are many very good seafood restaurants on the beach; it is your choice. The lobster is delicious but not very cheap.

PONELOYA

Poneloya is my preferred. This beautiful, unpolluted white sandy beach is free of crowds and the people are very friendly. They often offer the visitor a place to stay. However, being only about 35 minutes from Leon, you can commute or just stay at the beach. The last bus returns to Leon at about 4:00PM.

PLACES TO STAY

Hotel La Cayo is near the center of town and is a lovely old building. If you ask for a room with a view, you will get a large spacious room complete with balcony and private bath. The cost is ₡25. ($5. US) per person. There is a restaurant at the hotel.

If you go all the way through town, down to the end of the beach, you may find a room. People will approach you and ask if you would like accommodations. The prices are less expensive than the hotels, and the big bonus is that you will live with a Nicaraguan family. This enables the interested visitor to see life as it really is in Nicaragua. I highly recommend this.

RESTAURANTS

Hotel Cayo has a restaurant with excellent fresh seafood. The prices are reasonable, but they occasionally run out of items.

THINGS TO DO

Other than relaxing on the beach, you may get some of the fishermen to take you fishing. Again, go down to the end of the beach and ask around. When the boats return from fishing during the day, one never sees a boat empty of fish. This is an uncrowded, delightful area.

RAMA

This is only a stopping off place on the way to Bluefields. It is a grubby little town, but much friendlier than Juigalpa or San Carlos. You may take a bus from the Ivan Montenegro bus station in Managua. The first bus at 2:30AM is the express bus; it meets the slow boat going down the river Escondido to Bluefields. Other buses and trucks go all day. It is better to take a later bus from Managua, spend a night in Rama, and then go on in the morning.

A number of robberies have occurred on the early buses from Managua; it is often safer to take a later bus or truck even if they are not express. Listen for the latest gossip as these conditions may change. The Rama road has always been a bit dangerous to travel because of its isolation.

The slow boat takes five to nine hours and costs ₡20. ($4. US); the fast boats cost ₡100. ($20. US) and take two to four hours, depending on the sobriety of your captain.

The first hill on your left, going out of Rama is where a large boat landed during the 1988 hurricane. Quite a wind. The river is wide and pleasant. You see the shores dotted with shacks, some of which belong to the Mosquitia Indians.

PLACES TO STAY

Emma's Hotel by the docks is the best place to stay, but it fills early in the day. There is a bar downstairs; the potential for too much noise very great. The cost is ₡15. ($3. US) per person. If Emma's is full, walk one more block up the street and try the next hotel. The conditions and costs are about the same.

The third hotel in town is two blocks farther up from the second one and one block to the right. It has 38 rooms and is very noisy. The bar downstairs plays Spanish Country and Western music accompanied by drunk singers. Imagine amor barrato (cheap love) in Spanish until midnight. The rooms are small and very clean. However, people start leaving at 3:30AM and the paper thin walls muffle nothing.

RESTAURANTS

The market area is the best place to eat in Rama. It is fairly clean and the prices are good.

THINGS TO DO

Uriel Rivera Park is in the center of the town. There is a distinct, but not particularly interesting, church on the square. Other than this and the market, there is not much else to do in Rama.

RIVAS - SAN JORGE

This is a delightful little town with two churches, two banks, a market and a central park. It is the hub for many places such as the Island of Ometepe, San Juan del Sur and the Costa Rican border. In this area, buses may charge extra for your backpack. The cost of a taxi to the border is ¢15. ($3. US) per person and they run all day.

San Jorge is only four kilometers down the road toward the lake. This is where you catch a ferry and STD if you stay in the rooms along the beach.

PLACES TO STAY

Hospedaje Primavera is on the corner of the road going to San Jorge and the main highway. The rooms are ¢20. ($4. US) per person; the rooms are larger than those in the other two hospedajes. There are no private baths; but it is the best along this strip.

Hospedaje International is small and clean enough with excellent one tap showers, especially on a hot day. The rooms are very basic and small. It is on the right side of the highway, not in the town center. The cost is ¢25. ($5. US) per person.

Hospedaje Coco is just up the road from the International and would be my second choice. The cost is ¢20. ($4. US) per person with no private baths, but it is clean.

Pension Lidia costs ¢25. ($5. US) per person. The hotel is clean with large rooms. No private baths nor two tap showers but there is a sitting area in the court room. The owner also offers good meals at a decent price but there is no menu; you get what she has.

Hotel Nicarao is almost in San Jorge. You go half a block down Calle Maria Luisa which is off the main street leading to the docks. When facing the lake, turn left to the hotel. The cost is ¢50. ($10. US) for a very basic room without sheets. If you want a room with sheets and a fan, the cost doubles. The place is quite nice, but the owner would not come down in price. The rooms did have small bathrooms.

Rooms along the beach rent by the hour. The cost depends on whether you want one with a girl.

RESTAURANTS

Restaurant Chop Suey is on the main square and is a great place to eat. The prices are excellent, the food is good and the quantity is sufficient to fill almost any appetite.

Juices are best found along the highway on the road to the border. There are many little stalls and all are fairly safe to drink from. The juices made by Nicaraguan women are really something to experience.

Comedor Lucy serves vegetarian food. The cafe is clean and prices are inexpensive, and the food is excellent. If there is fresh bread in town, you will find it here. Reading the hand drawn nutritional posters on the walls are worth the visit. They also have real coffee, a difficult commodity to find in Nicaragua.

THINGS TO DO

The Cathedral on the square in Rivas has some beautiful paintings on the ceilings. It is one of the nicer Cathedrals in Nicaragua. There is an excellent sculptured silver altar in the church, and the side altars are in the process of restoration. Many of the buildings are currently being restored; even the bullet holes are being patched in the Cathedral.

The Square is great. There are pleasant places to sit. Some interesting paintings are on the walls across from the square. You can purchase refreshments, meals and booze from small tiendas on the square.

San Jorge has a beach on the lake, but it is not a real drawing card. However, it is very hot in this area and the lake always has a nice breeze coming off it.

Island of Ometepe - see Alta Garcia and Moyogalpa for details. Visiting this island is highly recommended.

SAN CARLOS

If you are planning on taking the boat from Granada across the lake, this would be your ultimate destination . The lake itself boasts of being the only fresh water lake in the world with sharks. They come up the San Juan River from the Caribbean and play around the lake before returning. The archipelago along the lake is very beautiful; the trip can be quite pleasant.

To get there, you can go by road along the north shore of the lake or you can take the ferry. The ferry leaves Granada in the afternoon and gets to Alta Garcia on the island of Ometepe between 6:00PM and 8:00PM. The boat is always less crowded than the buses. Take a plastic sheet to lay on and a plastic bag to cover your pack. It is comfortable out on the back deck as the air is fresher than inside. Find yourself a spot where you will be out of the wind. The trip takes at least seven hours and you will get to San Carlos around 3:00AM. You can remain on the boat and sleep on an inside bench until daylight. Do not try to get a place in town at that time of night as you will not succeed.

San Carlos is a small place and not that pleasant. This is a stopover place if going to San Juan del Norte or Solentiname.

PLACES TO STAY

There are the **Rio San Juan or the San Carlos** Hotels. Both are basic and grubby. The cost is ¢20. ($4. US) per person without private bathrooms. The Rio San Juan also has a restaurant where you may purchase meals.

THINGS TO DO

The river trip down the Rio San Juan is again possible. However, it is expensive once you are out of Nicaragua. Castillo Viejo is the border town; with tourism being as popular as it is in Costa Rica, the cost from Castillo Viejo into Costa Rica is anywhere from $200.00 US to $700.00 US. This route can take you down the River Colorado and to the Caribbean or down the natural canals to Limon in Costa Rica. That is a spectacular trip, but it will be expensive if coming all the way from Castillo Viejo.

Another option after leaving Castillo Viejo is to get a boat to Rio San Carlos and then land at Boca Tapada, Costa Rica. That will leave you at a road where you can get a bus. This is also a delightful but costly trip.

The last option is to go all the way to San Juan del Norte and then get a freighter going either north or south along the Caribbean. I have no information about San Juan del Norte as this area has been closed until recently. When I was enquiring about this trip, the information was scanty and varied. However, it appears to be a long and delightful trip through the jungle; at one time the most popular river trip in Nicaragua.

Regardless of which trip you decide, you must go to the police station in San Carlos and get permission to travel along the rivers. They will issue you a permit. You may also check with the Park Service in San Carlos to see if you can get a ride with them up the river. They often take visitors when they go. Otherwise, you will have to negotiate a trip with one of the boatmen at the docks.

Solentiname is a delightful little island inhabited by artists. The island is highly recommended - see under Solentiname.

SAN JUAN DEL SUR

This is a very popular resort area for brigade workers after their stint in the fields. The village is pleasant, the beach is excellent, and the water in the bay is freezing cold! The village is surrounded by gentle rolling hills and the area is very clean. The visitor may walk for miles along either shore and enjoy pebbly little coves or rocky nooks for reading, resting and suntanning. Watch the tides, however, as you could be stuck away from the village and unable to get back to the next cove. There is good fishing in this area, and many men are willing to take you out for the day.

PLACES TO STAY

Hotel Estrella is on the beach street at the far end of town. It is a large rambling building with lovely rooms. The cost is ¢25. ($5. US) per person. This hotel was once a favorite resting place of the National Guard in the Samosa days.

The Hospedaje across from the Estrella has no name, but the restaurant area is the hotel entrance. The rooms are basic but there is a nice balcony with hammocks. The rooms cost ¢20. ($4. US) per person.

Hospedaje Casa 28 is one block from the beach and half a block closer to the main road. This is really the place to stay. The rooms are very basic, the beds are only wooden army cots but the owners are like Mom and Dad. The lady will cook your dinner at the time you want and will generally look after your well-being. If you are in need of some basic home style loving, I would recommend this place as the best no frills hotel in town.

RESTAURANTS

If you don't want to eat at the Casa 28, then go to the corner where the other hospedaje is located. The meals are great; I recommend the shrimp dinners. Some of the little places along the beach are okay for a drink but are not the best for food.

THINGS TO DO

Beach it, fish it or drink it.

SOLENTINAME

This is the Arts Center of Nicaragua. The little island is a paradise inhabited only by the friendliest of artists. To get there, take a boat from San Carlos. This little boat meets the big boat and takes everyone across. You may hire a private boat at different times of the day if you wish to go across in the daytime. There is only one pension on the island, and it is fairly expensive. However, it is very easy to meet people; they are always happy to have you come and stay with them. There are many artists trying to make a living on the island, but since the war, money has been scarce and selling pictures or crafts has been difficult. With tourism increasing, this will soon change. Get there before the rush!!

TIPITAPA

This delightful little town is on Lake Managua between Managua and Granada. The prison in Tipitapa held Tomas Borge prisoner at the time of Carlos Fonseca's death in the Zinica region on November 7, 1976. Fonseca was the hero of the Sandinistas and Borge became the Minister of the Interior after the Sandinistas came to power.

Tipitapa has hot springs with water hot enough to cook eggs. But who wants hot water in the heat of the Managua area? However, the springs are said to be excellent for healing arthritic pain.

Tipitapa is also known for its fish dinners. The fish is said to be a boneless fish which comes from the lake. However, with the present pollution, I would hesitate to make a special trip just for the fish. You could end up with more chicken.

CHICKENBUS TALES

SLOW BOAT
first printed in the Prince George Citizen in 1992.

I wanted to go up the River Escondido, to the Mosquito Coast in Nicaragua. After enquiring at the docks in Rama, I found that I had a choice of taking an expensive fast boat that would take only two hours or the cheaper slow boat that would take six hours.

I decided to take the fast boat and I talked to the captain. He agreed to take me. I climbed in between ten other passengers, all their luggage plus piles of beer cans. Because this was the expensive boat, there were no animals.

We were soon off, speeding down the river, everyone laughing and drinking beer. Every so often the boat would slow down so one of the men could get rid of some processed beer. I had to abstain as my female method of getting rid of beer is much more difficult.

After about an hour, the motor died on the boat. Ten minutes and another beer later, they found dirt in the gas line. The captain fixed the gas line and we went for about twenty minutes before there was another stop. The spark plug was wet. The next stop was to pick up some sugar cane at one of the farms. Of course this meant another chat and another beer. Further along the river we dropped off some nails and after more beer and chatting were off again.

After four hours on the fast boat, I wondered if the slow boat would pass us. When the captain and his mates finished the beer they realized that the gasoline tank was almost as empty as their beer tins. They tried to bum some gas from other boats on the river. Nobody would kick up a gallon. Soon we were paddling down the river with heavy oars. My two hour expensive fast boat took six hours in all.

A few days later, on the way back up river, my experience with the fast boat was still fresh in my mind. I decided to take the slow boat.

I climbed aboard the slow boat, sat on a sack of coconuts and watched the men load bananas and empty pop bottles, more coconuts and fresh fish, crates of unknowns and a very loudly protesting pig. The dock workers gently helped any ladies that wanted to board the boat. They passed babies onto the boat after the moms were settled and they helped a blind man get settled on a sack of beans.

At 11:00 AM sharp, the scheduled departure time, the motor started and the gang plank was lifted. We were on our way. Slowly.

I settled in to read for a few hours but the horrible drone of Spanish country and western music broke my concentration. When I heard "Amor barrato" (cheap love) being wailed away in Spanish, at top volume, I knew I would never complain about Willy Nelson again.

After about six hours of slow sailing, the motor stopped. The crew started scurrying around trying to rectify the problem. Things got very warm on board. The music got louder and the pig complained more frequently.

One man said they had run out of gas. Another said the motor was broken. When I enquired what would happen to the passengers, one lady informed me that if help didn't pass by, we would just sleep where we were. Between the pig and the music, I really wanted to get on my way.

We had drifted along the river for about two hours, the crew frantically trying to fix the problem when a tug boat pulling a flat bed full of tandem trucks came along. He would give us a tow.

After everything was hitched, the tug towed us up the river for a few hundred feet. Then, surprisingly, our motor started. We cut loose from the tug and were on our way again.

Three hours later, I arrived in Rama, after dark, tired, dirty, hungry and a confirmed land lover.

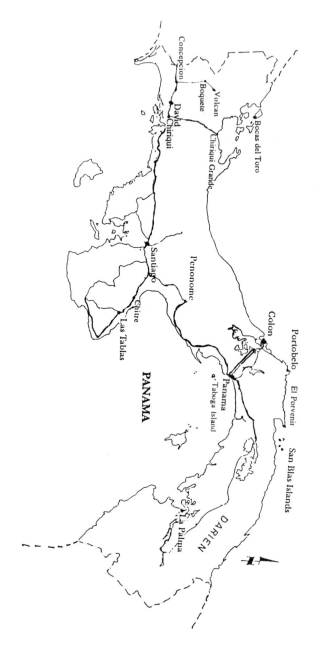

PANAMA

Since the last edition of Chickenbus in 1988, things have changed drastically in Panama. In the past I wrote of the dangers in the country and to check with your consulate before going there. Since the apprehension and incarceration of "Mr. Pineapple Face", Noriega, attitudes among the Panamanian people have changed dramatically. I admired the man for having the guts to double-cross the United States; otherwise, he was bad news for Panama.

Today, Panamanians have changed their attitudes toward gringos. This movement has started taking over the canal and the people can see that the Americans were not ALL bad. Today, the people spend hours discussing the outcome of the canal take over, Noriega's ultimate future, the next election and the future of their beloved country. They are also pleased to speak to visiting gringos about the same things.

When I was in Panama doing the research for this edition, I was constantly surprised by the warm and helpful welcomes I received. People often stopped me on the street to say something pleasant and when I was in the mountains, ladies stopped to give me flowers. When asking directions I was taken to where I wanted to go rather than just being given directions. Every time I had an encounter with a Panamanian, it was enjoyable.

There is the draw of the cheap shopping in Panama for things like crystal, linen, perfumes and jewelry in the many duty free shops that were once owned by Noriega. Panama City is the best for this but if you are in Boco del Toro in the north along the Caribbean, there is also duty free shopping in Changuinola.

When I was in Panama City, I was warned about the rough section of town because it was dangerous. I find there is that type of section in any big city and if you are looking for trouble, it is a good place to visit. I never visit this type of area in any city, including my own. That way, I am around to write another book.

So, in the final analysis, I would suggest that you make your Costa Rican visit shorter and spend some time in Panama. It has everything Costa Rica has except the droves of tourists. There are high mountains and beautiful beaches. One beach I went to had an open air restaurant hanging over a cliff that overlooked the beautiful Pacific Ocean. It was a romantic scene from a 1940's Bogart & Becall movie. The prices in Panama are no more than Costa Rica and often cheaper. Transportation is clean and organized, and Panama has some of the friendliest people in Central America. I would suggest that you go before it is re-discovered.

HISTORY

At one time there were over 60 different tribes of aboriginal Indians in Panama. Today, the main groups left after Spanish annihi-

407

lation, include the Choco, the Cuna and the Guaymi. The **Cuna** fought long and hard against Spanish rule. They eventually withdrew from the mainland of Panama to the San Blas archipelago where they continue to try and live as they have for centuries.

The **Choco** are forest people and live along the rivers of the Darian Gap. This area is virtually impenetrable, particularly without the help of the native people.

The **Guaymi** are the easiest people to come in contact with because they live in the central highlands and along the Caribbean in the Chiriqui area. Their lives today are different than they were 500 years ago and they practice fewer traditions than the Cuna and Choco.

The first Spaniard to see Panama was **Rodrigo de Bastidas** who touched ground at Portobelo just above Colon in 1501. This discovery was followed by **Christopher Columbus** the following year, but it was not until 1513 when **Vasca de Balboa** discovered the Pacific that the area became important. Until that time, the King of Spain had assigned **Diego de Nicuesa** to manage Panama.

Once the Spanish realized how short the distance was between the two oceans, treasures from Peru were sent up the Pacific coast to Panama City, transported by mule and Indian to Portobelo and then transferred to ships heading for Spain. It was a heyday for the pirates **Sir Francis Drake** and **Sir Henry Morgan** who constantly tried stealing the goods by hiding in the many coves and bays, killing the sailors, befriending the natives and raising general havoc with the Spaniards. These actions were much to the delight of the English monarchy. The looting and robbing continued for a number of years with the Spanish building forts at important ports in order to try and keep the buccaneers out. In 1670, Morgan was so skillful as a pirate that he was able to cross the trails laden with treasure carriers and march through the jungles to Panama City. There, he burned the city to the ground. The English caused so much trouble that the Spanish were unable to use Panama as a trading route for many years while taking the treasures out of Peru and Bolivia. They had to go around the southern tip of America. Poor robbers.

The King of Spain appointed **Pedrarias** as the governor of Panama in 1519. Pedrarias quickly beheaded the amiable Balboa, gathered armies and went north as far as Honduras, slaughtering and pillaging the natives in his path. Spanish rule was harsh and difficult for the people of that area.

In 1718, Panama became part of the **viceroyalty of New Granada**. This area included Panama, Ecuador and Venezuela. However, lack of economic progress, harsh Spanish rule and the revolutionary movements of Europe brought dissention among the people, and they fought for independence from Spain, finally succeeding in 1821. Panama became a part of Columbia at that time. However, life under Columbian rule was not pleasant either and

Panama revolted through the 1830's and 1840's until it finally become independent in 1840. This lasted only two years and Columbia took control again.

The **California gold rush** of 1849 caused a new onslaught of humans to pass across the jungles of Panama. Americans received permission from Columbia to build a railway across the isthmus in order to speed up transportation. Permission was granted and the railway was completed between Colon and Panama City in 1855. That same year, Panama obtained self rule from Columbia and in 1863, Colombia's new constitution gave all the provinces, including Panama, independence. Independence was lost in 1886 when corrupt officials took control again. Panamanians were dissatisfied with negotiations for a canal across the country and more revolts took place.

The story of the building of the canal is long and interesting. Originally, a Frenchman, **Lucien Wyse**, obtained a concession to build a canal along the railroad route. Although the railroad actually followed the old treasure trail, it was not the best route for the crossing.

However, Wyse sold the concession to build the canal to **De Lesseps**, the same man that built the Suez Canal. Between disease, scandal and corruption, the French company went broke before the canal was completed. It was recognized that the Americans were the only people who had the resources and desire to finish the project.

In 1902, the US bought out the French company, but because Panama still belonged to Columbia, the Americans were only able to secure administrative right over the canal. Columbia maintained all sovereignty rights because the Columbians could easily guess the value of the project.

However, a group of Panamanian businessmen declared themselves independent from Columbia and the US marines moved in to support the rebellion.

A new treaty was drawn up and one of the businessmen, **Bunau-Varilla**, made certain this treaty was in favor of the Americans. He illegally signed the treaty before the rest of the representatives of the new government arrived in Washington to complete the negotiations.

Banau-Varilla then convinced the new government that the deal was okay. The new government didn't realize the full implication of the treaty which gave the US both administrative and sovereignty rights. By 1914 the canal was in operation.

The canal's treaty resulted in a new master to be resented. Although the US decreased military intervention in Panama, nationalists continued to resent their presence and revolts continued until 1931 when **Harmodio Arias** took control. Arias became president and things improved. The US devalued its dollar and tried to pay Panama with the lower currency but again the Panamanians fought against this act and won. Not only did they get more payment but they also revised the 1903 treaty in favor of Panama. The US could use military power to protect the canal but it could not interfere with any of Panama's internal strife.

During both the World Wars, Panama became an ally even though one leader disagreed during World War ll. The leader was quickly ousted and the country joined the US side. In 1948, after the war, all US military bases that were sprinkled around the country were ousted and the US could only control the canal area.

However, Panamanians were still discontent with foreign rule in their land and re-negotiated payments for the use of the canal zone. All through the 50's, 60's and 70's, there were nationalist groups wanting to oust the US and take control of the canal. Many leaders have been defeated or removed in the effort of taking control of the canal.

In 1968, President Arias was kicked out of office after eleven days and a provisional government was set up to take the place of the National Assembly. This consisted of a two-man Junta and a civilian cabinet. In 1969, the Junta was replaced by civilians.

A new Constitution was adopted in 1972 and amended in 1978. This provided for an Assembly of 505 elected municipal representatives who were elected on a community rather than a party basis. In 1979, parties were again made legal but under strict governmental control. Panamanians still wanted control of the canal and finally negotiated a contract whereby they will have full control by 1999.

The first step in this process was the taking over of the railway in 1990. Today it is no longer running. The canal has been partially taken over by the Panamanians. The garbage and disrepair of the area makes it easy to distinguish which sections belong to Panama and which are run by the US. Now, the Panamanians are talking about re-negotiating the canal with more help from the US than what the last treaty declared. Some people realize that the organizational skills of the Americans are a bit superior to the Panamanians. Future outcomes will be interesting.

GENERAL INFORMATION

Panama's **constitution** was adopted in 1972 and it gave the people freedom of speech, the right to vote at age 18 and freedom of religion. It also states that a President should be elected by free election for a period of five years.

The **centralized government** is broken down into three branches; the executive, the legislative and the judicial with the elected president at the head. In the president's absence, there is a vice-president who has presidential powers. The president's cabinet is made up of eight members.

The **legislature** or national assembly has forty-two elected deputies which serve four year terms. The provinces are divided into municipal districts and are administered by a governor who is appointed by the president. Mayors and council persons are elected for a term of four years.

The judicial system (which is Napoleonic Law) has a supreme court, a circuit court and a municipal court. There is a social security fund which offers medical and hospital services, old age and disability pensions and welfare to TB victims. There is no state charity for the poor.

The law states that children must go to **school** between the ages of seven and fifteen or they must complete grade six. However, because of widespread poverty, most children of poor families go to work before finishing sixth grade.

The National Guard is the power house of Panama and includes the military, the police and para-military forces.

Panama sits in the **geographical** center of the American continent with the Caribbean Ocean on the north, the Pacific on the south, Costa Rica to the west and Columbia to the east. The longest portion of Panama is 775 kilometers (480 miles) and the width varies from 60 kilometers (37 miles) to 175 kilometers (110 miles). Panama has 685 kilometers (426 miles) of coastline along the Caribbean and 1250 kilometers (770 miles) along the Pacific Ocean. The total land area is 77,082 square kilometers (28,575 sq. miles). The population is approximately 2,315,000.

Panama has two **mountain** ranges; the vast Costa Rican and the smaller Darien mountains. The highest mountain in Panama is the Chiriqui which stands at 3500 meters (11,410 feet). The two mountain ranges protect a central fertile valley. The largest **river** is the Tuira which flows into the bay of San Miguel on the Pacific coast. The second largest river is the Chagres which is dammed at Gatun forming an artificial lake which is important in the functioning of the canal.

The climate of Panama is tropical with an average of 21 - 32ºC (70ºF - 90ºF), except for the higher elevations which have an average temperature of 18ºC (65ºF). The average rainfall on the Caribbean is 300 cm. (120 in) per year and 160 cm. (63 in.) on the Pacific side of the mountains.

The people speak Spanish in Panama and most belong to the Catholic religion. **The flag** of Panama is divided into four squares. On one side there is a white square with a blue star above the blue square. The blue star represents purity and honesty. The reverse side of the flag is a red square above a white square which has a red star in the center. This represents law and order.

INDIGENOUS GROUPS

Before the Spanish arrived there were over 60 different Indian groups, but today there is only three distinct groups left. They are the Cuna, the Chocò and the Guaymi. The Cuna is the group that is the most visible to the visitor in Panama. This is because these Indians are easily accessed.

In pre-Spanish times **the Cuna** occupied most of the isthmus; after fierce battling they were finally pushed as far as the San Blas Islands on the Caribbean Ocean.

The Cuna are culturally a South American Indian and speak a dialect of the Chibchan language. The Chibcha lived on the upper Magdalena River near Bogota, Columbia and resembled the Inca in their methods of agriculture complete with irrigation, the weaving of cotton, and the skill displayed in goldsmithing. Next to the Inca, the Chibcha had the largest, most politically centralized society in the area when the white man arrived. The Cuna have had albino births and thus their legends include stories about the arrival of the white Indian.

The Cuna call themselves the "Gold People" and gold plays an important part in their lives. The women wear gold nose-rings, gold bracelets, necklaces and finger-rings. The amount of gold a woman wears indicates the amount of wealth her husband has. When the husband dies, this gold is used to cover his body and journey with him to heaven.

Today, men of the San Blas wear North American style clothes but they wear animal tooth necklaces which are the last trace of their traditional ways. The women, on the other hand, still wear their gold jewelry complete with nose rings and their famous "mola" blouses. These are beautifully sewn pieces of material which form pictures of objects important to the Cuna woman's life by a reverse applique method. These designs are usually of fish, animals or birds, but the modern hi-tech lady has advanced to designs such as Bugs Bunny. The women also wear wrist and ankle beads that have been perfectly calculated in order to form a design when wrapped around the arm or leg. These beads are put on at a young age and the leg or arm does not grow where the beads restrict growth. It is reminiscent of the foot binding era in China.

The Choco Indians are much more difficult to see. They travel in cayucos or dugout canoes and live in tambos or conically shaped, thatched roofed houses along the jungle protected rivers of the Darien Gap. Their houses are built on stilts and have almost no walls so that the air conditioning works at an optimum. The entrance is a notched tree trunk which can be pulled up behind the user to prevent unwanted company. The men still wear loincloths and the women wear long, brightly colored skirts which are tucked in at the waist. A few of the younger women appear with painted chests that are otherwise unclad. During festivities, the women wear bead or animal tooth necklaces. Children generally go unclad.

The roles of the people are rigid with the men hunting and fishing and the women cooking and sewing. Women look after the gardens, weave baskets from palm leaves and raise the domestic animals. However, women have equal rights in property and inheritance.

The Choco have a shaman that will cast spells, perform exorcism rites or cure the sick with herbs, chants and carved sticks which are said to hold celestial powers. During puberty rites, young boys go to a special hut where they fast, take hallucinogenics and receive visions from their ancestors. When these boys are ready for marriage, they take only one wife but may re-marry if she dies.

The Guaymi Indians are seen in the northern mountains of Panama and around the Boco del Toro area on the Caribbean coast. They have maintained the least of their traditional habits. Their bead-work and feather usage is similar to the North American Indian. Their beaded collars that are sold in the stores in Panama are from this group. They are beautiful when worn on a blouse. These collars are called Chaquiras.

Panamanian women wear a beautiful traditional costume called "La Pollera" which is a hand made dress adorned with jewelry. These may be seen during national holidays. Some dresses may cost as much as $20,000.00US each.

LAWS

Panama has Napoleonic Law which means that you are guilty until proven innocent. This could mean a long time in the slammer if you are under suspicion for anything. Keep out of trouble in this country. Fortunately, there is no death penalty. Unfortunately, it is not guaranteed that you will survive incarceration. Panama has signed a treaty of mutual legal assistance with neighboring countries regarding criminal matters as an instrument in the fight against drug trafficking. My usual rules apply to this matter. If you want to play with this dangerous social killer, do it at home where you stand a better chance of survival.

Other than the usual rules of travel, I know of no other special laws that could give you problems.

MONEY

The American green back dollar is the money of the land but it is called the balboa. The coins are the same size as American coins but are in fact balboa coins, not US coins. Both silver currencies are interchangeable in Panama as the exchange value is equal. American currency travellers cheques are cashed anywhere in Panama.

The banking system in Panama is quite extensive and banks from everywhere in the world are represented here. However, there is no central statutory bank of Panama and government accounts are handled through the Banco National de Panama. If you have modern banking methods in your country of origin, it would not be difficult to get help if you should need immediate funds. Some of the leading international banks represented in Panama are: Citibank, Bank of London, Bank of South America, Chase Manhattan of New

York, Bank of America, and the leading banks of Canada, Columbia, Switzerland, Germany, France, Spain, Holland, Taiwan, Japan and Brazil.

VISAS

Upon entry to Panama, you will need a valid passport, a visa, or tourist card which can be obtained at the airport upon arrival. The tourist card is valid for 30 days and may be renewed for an additional 60 days. You must also have a ticket to leave Panama and proof of economic solvency. Of course these rules change often. The last time I entered Panama, I needed a visa even though I was flying in.

A tourist card will be given to citizens of independent countries of the western hemisphere, excluding only citizens of Cuba. In addition, it will be given to citizens of European countries, except citizens of Yugoslavia, and Europeans who previously were citizens of non-democratic countries (a bit communist-phobic). Every tourist should carry a valid passport except citizens of the United States who only need proof of citizenship to obtain a tourist card.

Visas are needed by everyone except citizens of Costa Rica, Honduras, Spain, Germany, Great Britain, Austria, Switzerland, Denmark, Finland, Norway, and Sweden. Some countries that have a special agreement with Panama may obtain a visa free of charge. The rest of us must pay the $10.00 US visa fees. However, we can get a visa when we are abroad from the Panamanian consulate if there is one in that particular country.

Citizens from the following countries can only obtain a visa by applying to the Immigration Department in Panama: China, Cuba, India, North Korea, Nicaragua, El Salvador, Russia, Iran, Iraq, Philippines, Poland, Hungary, Bulgaria,Czechoslovakia, Yugoslavia, Afghanistan, South Africa, Vietnam, and Cambodia.

Those who stay in Panama longer than 30 days must obtain a Paz y Salvo from the Finance Ministry (Ministerio de Hacienda y Tesoro) and an Exit Permit (permiso de salida) from Immigration before departure. A 60 day extension may also be obtained from the Immigration Department.

I find that trying to get all this at the government offices takes hours of valuable time and I prefer to move on to an adjoining country, stay there a couple of days, and return to Panama. It is easier.

Anyone entering Panama as a visitor must have an exit ticket to another country. This is not always checked but if you are checked and do not have one, expect to be sent back from where you came.

GETTING THERE

If you fly into Panama City there is little hassle as there are not many tourists and the Panamanians are friendly. Once there, you can cash traveller's cheques at any of the counters as long as the currency is the American dollar. The airport is half an hour from the city and the cost of a shared taxi is $8.00 US per person or $20.00 US if you want one to yourself. If arriving after dark, I would suggest you use this method. There are buses but you must walk down to the main road and then wait. This is not very safe. Use the taxi system as the prices are fixed and thus everyone pays the same.

If you are coming overland from Costa Rica, down the Pan American Highway, TICA bus goes through Paso Cañoas and there is little hassle. You may also chickenbus it down to the border but the border is closed from noon until 2:00PM for lunch and from 6:00 to 7:00PM for supper. You must have an onward ticket and American money. You may be asked to show some.

If crossing at Sixaola, Costa Rica to Guabito, you will have to walk across the bridge on your own as buses do not cross this border. The lady at this crossing can be persuaded to supply a visa if you need one under special conditions. However, you must be certain that no official is around. I would suggest that you get a visa in San Josè before crossing just in case the time is not good for negotiations.

If coming or going from Colombia, you must cross the Darien. You may do this by walking, flying or sailing. There are no roads through this swampy jungle area. See the section on the Darien if you are interested in walking. People coming from South America into Panama will be scrutinized a bit more than if coming from Costa Rica, because of the drug trafficking opportunities down in those countries. Just be patient with the Panamanians. If you have no dope on you, things will be okay. And, for heaven's sake, don't have any dope on you. Remember, they do not have the death penalty in Panama but they do not guarantee to keep you alive either.

CONSULATES

Canadian Consulate, Cl. Manuel Ma Icaza, Ph. 64-7014
Guatemalan Consulate, Cl 55 & Erick del Valle, El Cangreje, Ph. 69-3475
Costa Rican Consulate, Cl. Gerardo Ortega, Ph. 64-2937
El Salvadorian Consulate, Edificio Citibank, 4th floor, Via España, 124, Ph. 23-3020
American Embassy, Ave. Balboa, Zone 5, Ph. 27-1777
Honduran Embassy, Cl. 31 & Jto. A Rosemena, 3-80, Ph. 25-8200
Nicaraguan Embassy, Ave. Federico Boyd & Cl 50, Ph. 69-6721

There is an embassy for almost every country in the world in Panama City except Belize. If your country is not listed here it is because I have only listed Central and North American countries. If your Spanish is not such that you can find your consulate in the phone book, ask for help at your hotel. The patrons will be only too glad to give you a hand.

PUBLIC HOLIDAYS

January 1	New Year's Day
January 9	Day of the Martyrs of 1964
March 3	Carnival
April	Good Friday and Easter
May 1	Labor Day
August 15	Foundation of Old Panama Day
September 27	World Tourism Day
October 11	Celebration of the 1968 Revolution
October 12	Columbus Day
November 2	Remembrance Day
November 3	Independence from Columbia
November 4	Flag Day
November 28	Independence from Spain Day (1821)
December 8	Mother's Day
December 25	Christmas
December 31	New Year's Eve

TRANSPORTATION

Bus travel in Panama is not difficult nor is it expensive. Although not as frequent nor convenient as Guatemala's system, it is certainly as colorful. The Panamanians paint the outside of the buses in brilliant colors and decorate the insides with every type of colored bobble, bangle and decal they can get their hands on. They also include many types of passengers, some of which oink.

You may also get the first class international TICA bus which takes you to the Costa Rican border or beyond. This station is at the Hotel Ideal on Calle 22B. You must book in advance for any TICA bus and Panama is no exception. Buses leave every day at 11:00AM for San Josè, Costa Rica. To chickenbus up to the border will take twice as long as riding the TICA buses but it is also twice as interesting.

Travelling on the regular chickenbuses between towns will cost you about one dollar an hour, but if you get on the smaller mini buses which do not allow anyone to stand, are not overly crowded, and travel at a good speed, you will pay about $2.00 per hour.

Buses in Panama City are safe and easy to take. They go in all directions during the day and most of the night. The cost is 15¢ for most inter-city travel. If you want to get off you must shout "parada!" quite loudly because most drivers are busy talking or thinking about more important things than where you want to get off.

The railway to Colon is no longer in operation. When the Panamanians took it over, it started running later and later as the weeks progressed, and within a short time was taking twice as long to get to Colon as the buses. Now the train is not running at all. This may change in the future. Buses to Colon go every half hour in the mornings and then every hour from 11:00AM on.

SAN CARLOS

San Carlos is along the Pacific coast, below Chame in La Chorrera province. The Pacific coastline is gorgeous from Alaska to the tip of Chili so picking a beautiful beach along the coast is usually a successful venture. San Carlos is no exception. There is only **one hotel** in San Carlos and it costs $16.00 for a double with private bath and air con. It is near a 24-hour disco that blares music for miles. If you go down the beach to Angelos you can pitch a tent or a hammock for $8.00 per night and this includes the use of the shower room. Angelos is a spectacular spot with white sandy beaches, nice soft surf, thatched roof huts for shade during the day, a restaurant, flower gardens and a hospitable host. The hotel is about one kilometer from the highway.

If you are in San Carlos you must go up to **El Valle de Anton** which is one of the most beautiful areas in Panama. It is also where the square trees and rare golden frogs can be seen. There are places to stay in El Valle.

TABOGA ISLAND

This delightful little island is off the coast of Panama City on the Pacific Ocean. It is locally called the island of flowers. It is not certain how the island got its name but some believe that the chief of the island was called Haboga and the name eventually became Taboga. Others believe that Taboga is an Indian name for fish while others believe it means "mountain of water".

The island was first inhabited by Don Hernando de Luque, the first Bishop of Panama who helped Francisco Pizarro. Pizarro stayed there before conquering Peru. The island is where Errol Flynn pirate movies were filmed. It is a great background for this type of entertainment. Taboga is where the steamship trade of the Pacific West Coast was once based.

The island has a small, clean, community of houses with narrow, cobbled streets and lots of garden space for flowers. There are no cars on the island but there is daily boat service. It is a quiet town in which to rest.

To get to Taboga, go to Balboa pier in Panama City. The ferry leaves daily at 8:30AM and returns at 5:30PM. There is a 10:00AM boat on week-ends. The cost of the ferry is $2.50 each way. The trip takes one hour, passes under the Bridge of the Americas and past the large ships anchored in deep water waiting to enter the canal. The boat trip is worth the two dollars it costs.

PLACES TO STAY

There are two hotels on the island; an expensive one and a cheaper one. The cheaper one is the most popular with chickenbusers.

Hotel Chu is towards the town. Turn left when leaving the pier. The hotel is a classic old wooden building sitting right on the beach. Rooms cost $22.00 for a double with private bath and $15.00 for a double without private bath. It is an excellent place to stay.

Hotel Taboga is to the right when coming from the pier. It is a beautiful, modern hotel that charges $1. per day for use of the beach, $5.00 per day for a little cabina and $50. a day for a room. The rooms are excellent with private bath and all the luxuries Panama has to offer.

RESTAURANTS

Other than a couple of little juice stands on the street, there is nowhere to eat in Taboga except the two hotels. The Hotel Taboga serves good meals at a reasonable price. The hotel Chu offers meals that are comparable to the Taboga Hotel but the restaurant sits on a porch overlooking the ocean. The view is gorgeous. The entire atmosphere of the island is one of relaxation.

THINGS TO DO

You can go to Restinga Beach near the Taboga Hotel. The entrance fee is $1.00 per day and if you want one of the thatched huts for the day it will cost $5.00. You may go snorkeling in the calm bay waters or you may walk out to the island of Morro during low tide. You will see remains of the administration building from the Pacific Steam Navigation Co. and the Pacific Mail Steamship Co. You will see some of its fleet rusting on the rocky shores of the island. This is a delightful place to spend a few hours but watch that the tide does not rise while you are there or you may have to swim back to shore.

The tiny town square has a tiny church that is claimed to be the second oldest in Panama. The island was first discovered by the Spanish in 1515, and it is believed that the church was built around that time.

Taboga is an excellent place to spend a few relaxing days.

VOLCAN

This is a pleasant little town tucked in the mountains and away from the sweltering heat of the beaches. The police station is the town center. If you can not find a room in Volcan, catch the bus by the police station and go to Nuevo California where there are cheaper rooms at La Luna. It takes one hour to get to Volcan from Concepcion.

PLACES TO STAY

Pension Volcan is at the edge of town. Get off the bus before reaching the town center. It is very basic for $6.00 a double. The rooms are mouldy but the lady is pleasant. There are no private baths and only one tap showers. This can be a problem when it is cold in the mountains.

Hotel **Riena** is reached by following the signs down the road for half a kilometer. When you reach the end of the road, turn right and follow the pavement. You will see cream colored cabins behind a wire fence. Go to the house directly across. It is also cream colored. The cost is $20.00 for a double but if he is not busy, he will rent the rooms for $15.00 The cabins have a kitchen, clean beds, TV, hot water and the yard is decorated with flowers to make it homey. It is also away from the main road so it is quite quiet. This is the best buy in town.

Motel California costs $16.50 for a double with hot water, TV, and a bar. The owner speaks English and will answer many questions about fishing in the area. The cabins are a bit rustic.

RESTAURANTS

Restaurant Oasis is excellent. The pizzas are large and the prices are low. The owner, Kayo, will not boost prices for gringos because he wants them to return. He will spend time giving directions to interesting sites. You can also hire a guide here if you need one to go over to Boquete. The restaurant has mineral water. This is often difficult to purchase in Panama.

Restaurant Yugo Burguesas is on the main road and offers beer at two for one during happy hour. It is sparkling clean and the food is good.

The restaurant beside the pension Volcan offers good food but the service is slow. The owners make excellent french fries and you can purchase real coffee early in the morning.

THINGS TO DO

Balneario Las Fuentes is a natural spring pool which is often frequented by lovers. It is a fifteen minute walk from town. The water goes into the swimming pool from the large rock at one end of the pool. This is known as the "Ojo de Agua". The water is extremely cold but refreshing. The officials block one end of the pool if they want to raise the water level. To get there, walk past the police station and turn left at the bank. Follow the paved road for about three minutes, to the end. Continue straight ahead, along the gravel, over the hill and down again. You will walk beside the creek before coming to the pool and park.

Three Lakes are a popular fishing spot for locals and they claim to have big fish. The walk is a nice 45 minute to one hour walk. The legend of the lakes is that there is a ghost who lives in the lakes and when anyone swims there, the ghost pulls the swimmer under and steals his soul. It takes a few days for the ghost to release the body. Personally, I think the arms of the ghost are long, green and weedy. These are not swimming lakes.

To get there, walk past the police station and turn left at the sign for Antojitos Cabañas. After five to ten minutes, veer to the right. Stay on the pavement for about half an hour to 45 minutes. You will come to one of Noriega's private air strips. Cross the air strip and go along the gravel road that is directly ahead. You will be walking in a south-west direction. Continue for about fifteen minutes and take the left hand fork to the lakes. There are three lakes in all. If you walk this way early in the morning, you will see wild parrots.

November 27 & 28th are the days given to the Independence from Spain celebrations and the locals celebrate it by getting rid of all their secrets from the past year. They build a huge door and then they tell everyone present about affairs, scandals and other gossip. When all the tales of the year are told, the door is burned and a new year starts. There is a tremendous amount of merry making and the more liquid humor they drink, the more secrets are revealed. If you can be at this celebration, you should not pass it up. In Volcan, any stranger would be welcome for this fun event.

There is a **hike to Boquete** which goes from Cerro Punta. See under Cerro Punta. The hike is one of the highlights of the country.

CHICKENBUS TALES

THE CUNA INDIANS
first printed in the Prince George Citizen in 1992.

The indigenous Cuna Indians have lived on the archipelago of San Blas for centuries, trading in coconuts and living a simple life. Of the 365 islands situated in the Caribbean Sea, off the southeastern coast of Panama, the Cuna inhabit about half.

In the past, the Cuna fought fiercely and successfully with poison dart guns against the Spanish and Panamanians in order to keep their autonomy and traditional way of life.

The Cuna are a small, brown-skinned people who flash beautiful teeth through their smiles and cover their shortly cropped hair with bright red shawls. The women wear gold nose rings and dark wrap-around skirts that reach to just below the knee. Their calves and ankles are adorned with tightly layered strands of colored beads. The beads are put on a puberty in order to keep the leg and calf thin, a sign of sexuality among the Cuna. The custom is similar to the foot-binding practice used in China in the past.

The final touch of beauty for the women is a long, black stripe from the forehead to the nose.

For centuries, the Cuna ladies have made a special, religiously symbolic blouse. These blouses, called molas, are intricately designed in a reverse appliqued manner and sewn together with tiny, perfect stitches. The molas are both colorful and beautiful. In the past, it could take a lady three months, working fourteen hours a day, to make a complicated mola.

But today, things have changed. Instead of trading in coconuts, the Cuna trade in dollars, and often drive a hard bargain. The men now wear western-style shorts and T-shirts.

The molas offered for trade are made with designs the tourists understand. For example, we saw molas with turtles, fish and tucans worked into them. We even saw one with Bugs Bunny. The Cuna also design T-shirts in the appliqued style but with "San Blas" printed on them.

The molas aren't the only things that have changed. There are schools on some of the more densely populated islands, and girls (who previously were kept out of school) are now allowed to attend classes until grade three.

The hotel we stayed in had the traditional, thatched-roof, bamboo huts, but the doors had padlocks on them and the beds had foam mattresses.

The public shower was "manual." It had two tubs of water and a gourd for throwing the water on yourself. The western-style outhouse was complete with a seat. It was built at the end of a pier and swayed with the gentle rhythm of the waves. I found it very relaxing.

Where there was once only moonlight at night, today there are coal-oil lamps. A group of young boys had a ghetto-blaster which they paraded around town after dark, sharing their reggae music with everyone.

The hotel restaurant, also a bamboo hut, offered fresh buns in the morning and beer and pop all day.

The small cayucas, or dugout canoes, are no longer paddled by hand but are propelled by outboard motors.

There are rumors of a bigger hotel, with running water and electricity, being built soon.

So it seems that "progress" has come to the Cuna after all, and in a fairly peaceful fashion. However, as we waited for our small plane back to the mainland we wondered if this peaceful progress would have the same devastating effect it has had in other parts of the world. How long would it take all that pop to rot the teeth behind all those friendly smiles? Our one consolation was that the Cuna Indians are a fiercely independent and resourceful people.

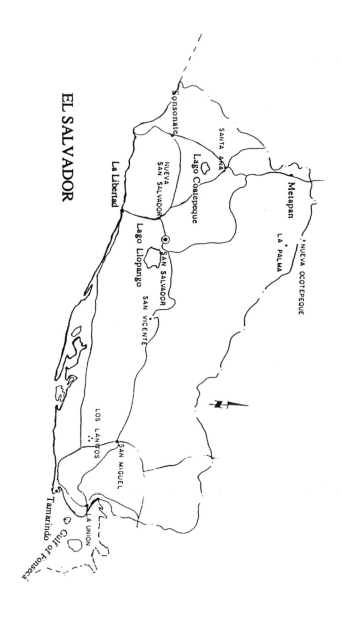

EL SALVADOR

EL SALVADOR

Upon entering El Salvador, one is immediately struck by the richness and beauty of the land. The volcanoes are covered with lush jungle foliage, the lakes sparkle like the crystal clear waters of northern Canada, and the black and gold sandy beaches of the Pacific lure the visitors with their soft surf and sunny days. One can actually hear the coffee growing in the fields and see the bananas ripening on the trees.

The war has ended in El Salvador, and the people are ready for an onslaught of tourists. Because Costa Rica has now been discovered, prices there are increasing as rapidly as the numbers of tourists. People want an undiscovered place; El Salvador is it. Also, Guatemala has few beaches and El Salvador meets the need of the sun and sand traveller. The people of El Salvador are friendly and pleasant. The country offers one of the nicest climates in the world; the sun shines every day and the average temperature is 28ºC (82ºF.). In El Salvador, you can climb a cool mountain in the morning, sun yourself at the beach in the afternoon and spend the evening eating and drinking beer in a classy disco in the capital city of San Salvador. This is truly a delightful little country.

Although the military is still very visible, this presence will soon decline. The people are tired of war and death squads; they are ready to get on with life. The tourist is made to feel more than welcome. I cannot predict how long peace will last but when I was there, I felt hope for continued peace was certainly high. The country is ready to give peace a chance.

El Salvador has great mountain hiking which is recommended for day trips. There are also gorgeous lakes which are not terribly polluted. El Salvador has a few Maya archaeological sites that are interesting and some of the museums are well worth visiting. The colonial town of Santa Ana is so delightful that I was ready to look for a retirement spot when I was there. San Salvador has the most modern conveniences of any capital city in Latin America and it is easy to travel by public transportation.

Because of the decline in tourism during the war, almost no English is spoken in the country. By the time the ink on this page is dry, that will change.

Bus travel in El Salvador is easy and fairly organized. Frequent buses go to all corners of the country at almost any time of day. Often the buses are crowded but they are never in extremely poor condition. Most buses stop running by eight o'clock at night and start up again by five in the morning. I never got on a bus in El Salvador where the people did not try to talk to me. It was a mixture of curiosity and friendliness. I was often invited into someone's home and I was always treated with the greatest of respect. The conductors will always help you with your bags. Places where buses don't go are accessible by public trucks. This is a bit more difficult but certainly satisfactory.

Hotels were generally clean and cheap, and hot water was common. However, I could often tell that the price of the hotel automatically went up when they saw a gringo. I would just say that I was not interested in paying that price, or that I could get cheaper accomodation down the road, and the price would fall. Restaurants all had set prices and food was generally very good. In some places, the food was exceptional.

HISTORY

The aboriginal Indians of El Salvador called the country "Cuscutlàn" which means "land of precious things". These Indians are believed to have been influenced by the Mexican Indians, the Olmecs. As well, it is believed that the local Indians were influenced by the Maya Indians from Guatemala in the south of El Salvador and the Lencas from Honduras in the north of the country. These tribes have left traces of existence that go back to 1500BC.

The Indian tribes came and went in El Salvador until the Pipiles finally settled in the western and central zones around the 11th century. These were the Indians that inhabited the country when the Spaniards finally arrived.

It was May 31st, 1522, that Andres Niño arrived on the island of Meanguera in the Gulf of Fonseca. He was the first Spaniard to set foot on Salvadorian land. However, because there was no gold or silver in the area, the Spanish had no interest and they moved on.

It was not until June of 1524 that Pedro de Alvarado began a war against the native tribes of this little country. They fought bitterly for 30 days, killing many men on both sides. In these battles, the Indian leader Atonal was killed and Alvarado received a wound in his left thigh which left him with a limp. Alvarado retreated to Guatemala after being wounded. It was not until 1528 that Alvarado's cousin, Diego, returned and established a little village at La Bermuda, close to the town of Suchitoto.

Life continued in El Salvador much as elsewhere in Latin America. The Indians worked for the Spaniards under slavery conditions and against the proclamations of the Spanish kings. El Salvador was then part of the captaincy-general of Guatemala. On November 5th, 1811, knowing that the time was ripe, Father Matias Delgado rang the bells of La Merced Church calling the people to revolt. This act is termed the "first cry of independence". This they did, but it was not until September 15, 1821, that the "Act of Independence of Central America" was signed. They were now free from Spain, but the people of El Salvador were not free from the slavery imposed upon them by the rich Spanish landowners.

El Salvador was then ruled under the Mexican empire and dictated by Agustin de Iturbide. That union was dissolved in 1823 and El Salvador became one of the states in the Federation of Central America. This federation also broke up and El Salvador was considered a republic in 1859. There was some discontent and turbulence in the country for the next 80 years, but the economy grew and a few families got richer and richer by exporting coffee. A railway system was developed, and the port at La Union became a bustling metropolis. However, the general population became poorer and poorer. Because they wanted land and social reforms, another revolution occurred.

In 1931, General Maximiliano Hernandez Martinez seized power, squelched the revolution and ruled as a dictator until 1944. His rule was brought to an end by a student revolt. Small reforms were then made and another revolt occurred. This pattern has continued until today. Any time the peasants appear to upitty, they are quickly put down by the military. In this country, irregardless of the alleged ruler, the military is in absolute control.

In 1962, a new constitution appeared and an elected president sat in office. However, peace and land reform did not come to the people, and civil war continued.

The US has given financial and military aid to the dictators of El Salvador all during the 1980's. Publicly the US states that land reforms should occur and human rights increase. This has not happened. There are fourteen families in El Salvador that own almost all the land and most of the wealth. They also control the military. The peasants are numerous and poor. If reform does not come, these people will catch their breath after the last twelve years of war and start again. I do not know how the people maintain their cheerfulness through this.

GENERAL INFORMATION

El Salvador claims to have a democratic government with an elected president. The president is elected once every five years and is eligible for office only once in a lifetime. The country has **14 departments** with a total of **261 townships**, elected for a period of three years. But, the governor of each township is appointed by the president. The **Legislative Assembly has a total of 84 representatives.** There are also the executive and judicial branches of the government which are greatly influenced by the president.

Military service is compulsory for two years after the age of 18. However, this is not what has happened in El Salvador. Because the country was broke and a civil war was in progress, the army was often unpaid. The military would then capture boys as young as 13 years of age and put them in the local jail. If the parents could not afford to pay a "fine" for the release of the children, they were then put into the military. Hopefully, this practice will change.

457

The area of El Salvador is **21,000 square km. (8000 sq. miles)** with **306 km (190 miles) of Pacific coastline.** The coast consists mainly of flat sandy beaches except near the Bay of Fonseca where it is dotted with cliff edges, rocky ridges, and tiny isolated bays and coves. El Salvador is the only Central American country that does not have a Caribbean coast line.

El Salvador has more than **25 extinct volcanoes,** many with large craters which show petrified lava flows. The three main volcanoes, San Miguel, Santa Ana and Izalco last erupted in 1957. These three volcanoes do show intermittent activity by spewing the odd puff of smoke. San Salvador volcano last erupted in 1917; the fertility of the land is attributed to this last eruption. Although there are some small parks on these mountains, the coffee, cotton, sugar cane and other agricultural fields cover most of the area. There is almost no wilderness in El Salvador. However, El Salvador is the only grower in Central America of **Balsam of Peru,** a plant used for medicines and cosmetics.

The main rivers in El Salvador are the **Lempa, Goascoran, Rio Grande of San Miguel, Torola, La Paz and the Jiboa.** The most important volcanic lakes are Llopango and Coatepeque. Guija is the largest natural lake in El Salvador. It is only 44 square kilometers (17 sq. mi).

El Salvador has **5.5 million people;** it is the most densely populated country in Central America with **249 people per square kilometer** (750 per square mile). Only 10% of the population has pure Spanish blood and 10% of the population has pure Indian blood. The rest are Mestizo or a mixture of the two. This integration gives the people of El Salvador a feeling of being truly El Salvadorian.

For most of the year, El Salvador has a hot and pleasant climate with an average temperature of **28°C (82°F)**. The rainy season is from May to October; it rains about 1 - 2 hours per day. The dry season is from November to April; it seldom rains. The coast line of El Salvador is much warmer than the mountains. Although hot, a cool Pacific breeze makes it pleasant. If walking around at a higher elevation, you may need a sweater at night. However, the volcanoes do not exceed 2500 meters (8000 ft) so real cold is not a factor. El Salvador's **flag** has two blue horizontal stripes between one white one. The flag stands for God, unity and peace.

The **post office** is open from Monday to Friday, 7:30 AM to 5:30 PM and 9:00 - 12:00 on Saturdays. The main post office in San Salvador is on Ave. 13 North, at the Government Center. The Antel Office and the Immigration Office are also on the same square block.

The **tourist office** is at Calle Ruben Dario #619 in San Salvador. It is open Monday to Friday, 8:00AM to 4:00PM. The tourist office at the airport is open every day from 8:00AM to 4:30PM. The tourist offices at Amatillo (Hond.) and Las Chinamas (Guat.) are open Monday to Friday, 8:00 to 12:00 and 2:00PM to 6:00PM. I found the tourist office in the capital very friendly and helpful. However, I went to many sites they recommended and found that the places no longer existed.

The law states that children between seven and twelve must go to school; due to a lack of facilities and teachers, this law is not strongly enforced. Depending on the sources, the illiteracy rate is believed to be between 50% and 60%. The minimum wage is about ten colones per day (one US dollar) which is an indication of the poverty. Working conditions are very coercive; for example, if an employee has to do a delivery as part of his job, he is expected to do it on his own time and he must pay for the gasoline. If the man argues, the employer will just hire another man. There are now protection laws for the workers, but how well they are enforced is your guess.

VOLCANOES IN EL SALVADOR

A volcano is the upheaval of igneous matter over the earth's surface which comes from the center of the earth. Volcanos accumulate one or more chimneys, or vents, during eruptions and these reach all different sizes. A volcano is usually cone shaped with a depression on the top which may be a crater or a caldron.

A **crater** is a steep walled cavity from which volcanic materials are expelled. The diameter very seldom exceeds 300 meters (1000 ft), and the depth may go a few hundred meters. The crater may be located on the summit or on the flank of the mountain.

A **caldron** is bigger than a crater and is a basin-like depression on the top of the volcano. A caldron is usually more than 1.5 kilometers wide and has a depth of several hundred meters.

When a volcanic eruption occurs, the pressure of the gases and steam looks for an outlet. The outlet is the weakest part of the mountain which is usually in a relatively flat area. When an eruption occurs, pyroclastic materials and gases are ejected from the earth's center.

A volcano remains **active** due to materials coming from a large and deep deposit of molten rock within the mountain. When this molten rock remains inside, it is called "magma". When it spews forth and pours out over the surface, it becomes "lava". Between successive eruptions, the volcanic channel may become clogged with solidified rock from the magma of previous eruptions. Sometimes gases escape through cracks or fissures in the plug and reach the surface. This has occurred recently in the Izalco, Santa Ana and San Miguel volcanoes.

Magma is a blend of minerals and volatile components which form rocks. These sometimes reach very high temperatures producing extreme pressures. Magma also plays an important role in the igneous activity in the ground.

Water is the main and most important volatile component in an eruption. When magma gets near the surface, water and gases tend to separate from the other components and are the first to be expelled. If the volcanic chimney is clogged, these gases accumulate and the pressure rises. When it can not be held back, the steam forces an **explosion**.

If the temperature is 980°C or higher when the steam escapes, the steam increases its expansive power, shattering the rock that was obstructing the chimney and hurling the magma through the air. After the explosion, the magma becomes less volatile but still fluid enough to flow. It moves slowly toward the surface and clogs the chimney again. The remaining water and other volatile substances keep moving and accumulating, forming another eruption. These eruptions can be relatively quiet, forming small lava flows like on Mt. Izalco, or quite violent like that experienced at Mt. St. Helen in 1980.

Proclastic substances are the fragments of explosives pushed from the volcano and eventually deposited on the ground. Volcanic **dust** is the tiniest matter, made of small particles no larger than 1/4000 cm. in diameter. When hurled into the atmosphere, this dust may remain there for months or years and travel large distances. Volcanic **ash** are particles that are smaller than 4 mm. in diameter. Volcanic **blocks** are cone fragments or shattered angular masses detached from the rock which clogs the chimney. **Scorias** are small solidified magma fragments that are 5 - 25 mm. in diameter. **Pumice stone** are small magma pieces a few centimeters large that have caught steam bubbles or other gases when they were hurled from the mountain. When they solidified, they formed honey combed holes corresponding to the place where bubbles were formed. This makes these rocks lighter and buoyant. **A burning cloud** is an avalanche of incandescent ashes mixed with steam or other gases which may reach temperatures of 850°C. Since this substance is heavier than air, it runs down the slopes and may cover areas of up to 130 kilometers square with layers 30 meters thick.

Volcanoes are classified according to the matter which accumulates around the chimney. **A lava volcano** will be formed entirely by lava. When the ejected matter is fluid, it flows from a central chimney or through fissures forming more layers and a wider and higher volcano. These volcanos seldom have slopes that exceed 10° on the top and 2° on the bottom. **Compound volcanoes** are formed when the proclastic substances and lava flows form around the chimney. It is characterized by a 30° slope on the top and no more than a 5° slope at the base. A volcano may develop a shield during part of its history and later become compound such as Mt. Etna in Sicily. **Cinder volcanoes** are made mainly of proclastic substances, particularly ashes. Their slopes may reach from 30° to 40° and are very seldom over 500 meters tall. **Gaseous volcanoes** are produced by violent and explosive eruptions which throw or hurl gases. These are often called pit craters.

LAWS

A valid driver's licence from your own country, or an international licence, is needed when taking a car into the country or when renting a car.

Any Communist literature is highly illegal and could net you some trouble. However, the last time I crossed the border the guards spent more time looking at my legs than they did looking into my bags. They were not interested in subversive communist materials.

Taking artifacts out of the country is illegal.

El Salvador has about the same tolerance level for drugs as the United States. The big guy can do it but the little guy (you and me) can't. Don't leave yourself open for question. Because the country is so poor, if you are suspected of drug abuse, the police could make money at your expence.

For women, wearing shorts in public puts them in the category of a prostitute as prostitutes wear shorts to advertise their business. The ladies of the street would give you a bad time for infringing on their turf, so please wear only skirts or long baggy shorts.

MONEY

The colon is the currency of the country and one colon has 100 centavos. Presently, the exchange rate is eight colones for one US dollar and the easiest way to change money is with US cash dollars. This can be done almost anywhere in the country. The borders will exchange Honduran limeras and Guatemalan quetzales; Nicaraguan cordobas can be changed at La Union.

If you wish to exchange traveller's cheques, the process is more complicated. You may go to either a casa de cambio or a bank; the casas pay a bit more. However, you must have your cheque and passport plus the receipt that proves that you are the person who purchased the traveller's cheques. This receipt is not required by the banks. I have never before experienced this procedure before.

If changing money in the banks, not all banks change cheques. Ask before standing in line. All banks are guarded by military men flaunting large machine guns.

I found the exchange of American cash dollars to be the easiest method in El Salvador. If you are in either Guatemala or Honduras, change your cheques into the local currency and then exchange that currency for colones in El Salvador.

Money changers within the country change only cash dollars; however, the rate hardly makes it worthwhile. Black market currency exchange gives money to illegal causes so it is advised to ignore this practice.

VISAS

Visas are required by everyone at the present time, and it is difficult to get one. If applying for a visa from Guatemala City or Tegucigalpa, you will need to have two pictures of yourself, plus $25.US so the consulate can run you through a police check. This takes two weeks. When you finally do get your visa, it will be good only for thirty days. If you want more time, you would then need to apply for an extension while in San Salvador.

If you try to get your visa at the border, you have to wait for the man at the consulate office; often he is not there. You must have the same documents as in Teguc or Guat City, but it should only take a couple of days at the most. However, the amount of time can depend on the terms of the negotiations. In Nuevo Ocotepeque, Honduras, the visa would have cost me an extra day, the $25. US, plus the Swiss made watch hanging on my back pack. I declined the terms and returned to Teguc.

You may also apply for a multiple entry or permanent visa which is available from the Salvadorian consulate. This costs ¢300 ($40. US) but is good for the life of your passport. It takes about a month to obtain. You may come and go as often as you please at no extra cost. This is popular with business men. The main immigration office in the capital is at the Government Center and is open weekdays from 8:00 AM to 4:00 PM.

Once at the border, the guards barely acknowledged me. In fact, when I was leaving, it was hard to get them to notice me enough to get my exit stamp so border conditions have changed drastically since the peace settlement. The guards never looked in my bags, only at my legs.

GETTING THERE

You may cross the borders into El Salvador from Guatemala, Honduras and again across the Bay of Fonseca from Nicaragua.

There are a number of crossings from **Guatemala** but the best is a direct bus from Guatemala City to San Salvador along the Pan American Highway. This crossing is quick and easy. The other crossing goes through Sonsonate, follows the coast along a hot, dusty, gravel road to Hachadura and then you get a bus to Escuintla. This is a slow and difficult route taking about eight hours to get from Sonsonate to Guatemala City.

If coming or going from **Honduras**, you may cross from Nuevo Ocotepeque to El Poy; there are a number of buses every day. There are also many money changers at the borders. This route will give you a quick trip along a fairly good road to the capital. You can also come from Esquipulas to the border and then to Metapan. This is a nice way to get to Santa Ana. There is a place to stay in Metapan and the town is pleasant. Further south, you may enter El Salvador from El Amatillo, Honduras and then continue to San Miguel, a pleasant town. It is also close to the Pacific beaches. If you are going the opposite way, there is no problem getting a visa for Honduras at the borders.

There is a border crossing at La Union for those getting on the ferry going to **Nicaragua**. The safety of the boat is suspect so I would be hesitant to cross if the water is rough. Nicaragua offers visas at the border, but it is easier if you have your visa beforehand.

Entry to El Salvador costs about ten colones. A number of stops require minimal amounts of money. Usually, you must walk the entire length of the border building. Then you find the first wicket and pay five colones. I think they should pay you for figuring out the process. Then you continue and pay another four colones at the next wicket. However, payments must be made in the correct order. If you go to the four colon wicket first, you will be refused until you figure out the location of the five colon wicket. You should have your bags checked, but the guards were not interested in mine at either border crossing. These overland crossings are easy.

There are some **flights** into El Salvador that offer a "one day" special, but you must have your visa before entering, or you will not be allowed to leave the airport area. You can not get a visa to enter the country at the airport. There are presently 23 airlines flying into El Salvador including Japan Air, KLM, Iberia, Varig and Lufthansa plus most of the Latin American airlines. Most of these make connections in the US or Mexico. Airport tax is about $9. US per person. The cost of a taxi from the airport is $20. US per person and is not negotiable.

CONSULATES

American Consulate, 25 Ave. Norte, 1230, San Salvador
British Embassy, 70 Calle Poniente, #320, Centro de Gobierno, San Salvador.
Canadian Consulate, 111 Ave. Las Palmas, Colonia San Bonito, San Salvador.
Guatemalan Embassy, 15 Ave. Norte & Calle Poniente, San Salvador. This is just up from Roosevelt.
Nicaraguan Embassy on Ave. Maracaibo and Colonia Miramonte, San Salvador.

PUBLIC HOLIDAYS

January 1	New Year's Day
January 13-24	Sonsonate Festival in Sonsonate
March/April	Easter
April/May	El Salvador beauty pageant in capital
May 1 - 7	Palm Festival - in Pachimalco
May 1	Labor Day
May 3	Holy Cross Day

May 10	Mother's Day
July 17-26	Festivities in Santa Ana
Aug. 1-6	Festivities in San Salvador
September 15	Independence Day
October 12	Columbus Day
November 2	All Soul's Day
November 5-22	International Fair - San Salvador
November 20 & 21	San Miguel Carnival - San Miguel
December 24-25	Christmas

TRANSPORTATION

There are two main bus terminals in San Salvador. The **Terminal de Occidente** has buses departing and arriving from the west; to get to this bus station, you should take city bus # 4, 27 or 34. **Terminal de Oriente** has buses coming and going from the east; to get to this station, take city bus # 7, 33 or 29.

To access other cities or sites, you may have to first get to a closer city and then change buses. For example, if you wish to go to Tamarindo Beach, you will have to go to San Miguel or La Union and then catch a bus going to Tamarindo. I will list the smaller towns in alphabetical order and then say which terminal is required.

The terminals are crowded and busy but buses run regularly from 5:00AM to 8:00PM. You should leave no later than 7:00PM on a bus that is going anywhere out of the city center. Most interstate buses depart every half hour. In the city, bus fare starts at 40 centavos and increases depending on your destination. Out of town buses cost about three colones per hour and buses travel about 50 kilometers per hour.

There are a few bus stops in the center of El Salvador where you will catch buses for closer and more popular areas.

Destination	Bus No.	Bus Terminal	Cost
Acajutla Port	207	West Terminal	3.50
Ahuachapan	202	West Terminal	3.70
Amatillo, Honduras	346	East Terminal Leaves at 12:30PM	10.50
	330	San Miguel Terminal	3.90
	353	La Union Terminal	2.15
Anguiatu	201	West Terminal	2.40
	235	Santa Ana	3.70

I have some addresses of transport companies in Panama but no schedules. You will have to telephone the companies (or get your hotel to), in order to find times.

Transport to Colon is at side of the theater Polo on Calidonia at Calle P. Telephone 62-9293
Transporte Transchiri is at the end of Ave. Balboa, Telephone 62-9436, 75-8444 or 75-0268
Expreso Inazum is on Ave. "B" #98, Telephone 62-6795
Expreso Veraguense is on Calle 15 west #3, telephone 62-2208 or 62-5333
CPTT de Azuero is on Ave. 3, Telephone 62-9971
Transporte Ferguson on Via Fernandez de Cordoba

Buses in David and most other smaller towns are all at the same station and there are signs saying when the buses leave. Panama City has buses leaving from different areas at all times.
The ferry to Taboga leaves the Balboa dock at 8:30AM and 4:00PM and returns to Panama at 10:00AM or 5:30PM during the weekdays. An extra sailing on weekends at 11:30AM returns to Panama at 3:00PM. The cost is $2.50 per person each way.
Taxis cost $8.00 from the International Airport to the center of the city unless you want a private one which will cost $20.00. It is a half hour drive from the airport along the Via del Muerte (way of the dead). Not a very encouraging entrance to a city.
You can also take a **taxi** to Colon in which case it will cost you $60.00 and the driver will take up to four people. You may be able to negotiate a return rate. In town the prices are negotiable but the drivers have a fixed rate and must charge according to the number of zones. Ask to see his zone map and this will give you the correct rate. Large cars cost more than the smaller taxis so if you want to be a big shot you are going to have to pay.
Domestic flights in Panama leave from the Paitilla Airport in the center (almost) of town. You should take a taxi to the airport. There are domestic flights between Panama City and Colon, Contadora, David, Bocas del Toro, Changuinola, San Blas Islands and San Miguel. The cost is about five times the overland route but about 16 times faster.

CAR RENTALS
Because Panama is traditionally a place for the rich, there are many car rental companies in the country. My advice is still to travel by bus. The cost of gas is high, the fumes are ecologically damaging and the rental cost is expensive. I would rather spend the extra money at one of the nicer hotels along the deserted beaches eating copious amounts of sea food, drinking beer and enjoying the local people.

TELEPHONE

The telephones in Panama are excellent. The lines are clear and service is easy to obtain. Often there are phones in the hotel rooms and almost every hotel has its own phone line which can be used for international calling. If you need an English speaking international operator, dial 106. Phone charges are fairly inexpensive from Panama. I paid $1.42 per minute from Panama City and $1.88 for one minute both from Costa Rica and Guatemala. Panama also allows you to have station to station collect calls whereas other countries in Central America will only allow person to person collect calls.

LOTTERY

There are tickets being sold all over Central America and it is amazing how many people like to play on a chance to win a million. Panama is no different than any other country and there are tickets being sold from little wooden stands all over town. The draws are twice weekly, on Wednesday and Sunday. The four digit tickets cost $1.00 and the first prize number pays $2000.00, the second prize pays $600.00 and the third prize pays $300.00. There are a number of other prizes such as $1.00 for the last digit of the first prize or if you have up to nine numbers up or nine numbers down from any of the three winning numbers.

Two digit tickets (chances) cost 25¢ each and apply to the last two numbers of the three winning numbers. First prize pays $14.00, second prize pays $3.00 and third prize is $2.00.

AGUA DULCE

I thought this was such a beautiful name (sweet water) but the town is anything but sweet water. There are a couple of restaurants, and only a couple of fairly decent hotels. **The Interamericano**, the more expensive one, charges $20.00 for a double with private bath, air con and television. They tell you they have color TV and then can never understand why you are not impressed with this "new" invention.

The other hotel is the **Sarita** and it charges $14.00 for a double with a private bath and a television but no air conditioning.

Both places have a bar, and the Interamericano has a restaurant. But, there is nothing else to do in Agua Dulce except eat and sleep.

Agua Dulce (sweet water) may have gotten its name from the sugar plant in the area but there is also a salt plant that supplies most of the country with salt. The salt beds are situated close by.

ALMARANDE

This is a little Caribbe town in the Bocas del Toro province where English is spoken as much as Spanish and the people are friendly. This is where the narrow gage train begins and goes to

Costa Rica. However, that trip is only recommended for real train lovers. It is similar to the narrow gage in India. It is hot, crowded, rough and slow.

PLACES TO STAY

Pension San Francisco is basic but better than a park bench if you must stay in Almarande because of bad timing. There are no private bathrooms and the wood floors creak all night long with guests coming and going.

RESTAURANTS

Almarande offers very little in the way of upper class restaurants and the market is one of the better places to shop. There are a few restaurants but they only serve meals at certain times and they often don't like gringos.

THINGS TO DO

The train ride is the narrow gage and goes through gorgeous country up to the Costa Rican border. The cost is minimal and the train runs every day. This is for train lovers. It is also replacing the jungle train that used to go from San Josè to Limon in Costa Rica. So, if you did not do that one and you have the time, this one may be to your liking.

Boca del Toro is a 30 minute boat ride from Almarande and there are often boats going. These boats may be full to the maximum and a scary ride across the waters, but once you are in Boca you can really relax. However, do not go during the rainy season as the waters are rough, there is little to do on the island, and the rains are so heavy you will grow webbed feet.

ANTON

This is just up the road from Corono Beach which is reputed as being the most beautiful in Panama but is way too expensive. If you want to play at Corono, then staying at Anton is not a bad idea. The **Hotel Rivera** charges $16.00 for a nice double room that is clean and sufficient. There is a tolerable restaurant and bar at the hotel so when you come in wiped from the beach, you don't have to stagger too far before you are fed and watered. However, I do not know how noisy the bar is at night.

BOCAS DEL TORO

To get to the island of Bocas del Toro, you must take the bus to Chiriqui Grande which takes about three hours. From there, you must take a boat to Almarande (which is an uninteresting little town), and then another boat to Bocas del Toro. It is an all day excursion to the island from David but you can take it in stages if you wish to overnight in Chiriqui Grande or Almarande. If you want to catch the ferry, you must get the first bus from David which is supposed to leave at 6:30AM. In order to get on, you must be there by 5:30AM at the latest. The bus will leave as soon as it is loaded, which is usually by 6:00AM. So, if this is your desire, get to the bus early.

The ride from David to the Caribbean is about three hours over a horrendous, unpaved road that is a nightmare during rainy season. It goes over steep hills and past deep drop-offs. It goes quite high and the trip is cold (especially the first one in the morning). Keep a sweater out for comfort.

The island of Bocas del Toro itself has great fishing, coral reefs around which to snorkel and scuba dive, beautiful jungles and white sandy beaches. However, you must make it there during the dry season. I was there during rainy season when nothing is a pleasure except maybe a wet T-shirt contest in the mud.

PLACES TO STAY

Hotel Bahia has basic rooms that cost $15.00 a double without private bathroom. The rooms are clean for this area and the porch is a good place to rest in the evening.

Hotel Botel Thomas costs $15.00 for a double without bath and $20.00 for a double with. There are telephones that work sometimes and televisions that bring in fuzzy Spanish programs, but the place is clean and the people that own the hotel will make you feel welcome. This is often rare in this area.

RESTAURANTS

Hotel Botel Thomas has the best restaurant and bar on the island. The prices are high but that is because everything has to be imported from the mainland.

Hotel Bahia has a restaurant but you may want to eat at the other hotel and drink at this one.

There are other places in town but you must pick and choose. There are many favorites depending on whose recommendations you decide to follow.

THINGS TO DO

Visiting the jungle in Bocas del Toro is the main reason you would come here. There is a canal that boats can go up and down and the scenery is spectacular. This is what the Darian would be like only it is a bit more civilized. While going along the canals you will see some signs of primitive native habitation. These are the Teribes and Bokotas Indians which inhabit this region plus the jungles on the mainland. They are said to be direct descendents of the Mayans. This is one of the three regions of the country that have natives living their traditional ways.

Other things that can be done while here are the usual beach activities like reading, writing, swimming, eating, drinking beer, talking to locals, fishing, snorkeling and beach combing. Resting sounds too active.

CERRO PUNTA

This town is just half an hour up the road from Volcan. It is small and because it is so high in the mountains, it is a tad chilly. There are two hotels in town but if you want to walk to Boquete, you must start here early in the morning.

PLACES TO STAY

Hotel Cerro Punta is right in town where the bus stops and is gorgeous for $27.50 a double and $20.00 a single. This includes clean rooms complete with lots of hot water which you will need if it is not a sunny day.

Pension Prima Vera is on the road to the International Friendship Park. Walk down the hill for about half kilometer. The pension is a large old building with basic rooms but delightful owners. The old wooden building creaks with history and is interesting to explore.

THINGS TO DO

Hike to Bouquete is a long but not too difficult hike. It should be started in Cerro Punta early in the morning. The path is clear and you will not get lost. You will have to take a taxi or hitch a ride to Finca Respingo. The trail starts there and goes up and around the mountain. At present, this is a very safe walk and a real pleasure. You will come across people living in the hills who are quite interested in your adventure. The hike is easy because you walk down to Boquete.

Be certain that you have good shoes and warm clothes. As you will go over 10,000 feet, rain gear is essential and you must carry water. I would say to start with two liters at least. You will also need food to last you the entire day. Once you pass over the 10,000 foot level, you will start to descend and the rest of the walk is easy.

CHITRE

About ten minutes before Chitre there is a bakery called Jairo Isaac. It is at "la arena". The bus will stop for you while you run in and purchase the best pastry in all of Herrera province.
Chitre is a clean and friendly little town that is excellent to make as a home base while doing day trips. The central park has a huge flower pot, the biggest I have seen even though India claims to have the biggest in the world.

PLACES TO STAY

Pension Columbia is on the main street, halfway into town and next door to the Herrera Museum. The cost is $10.00 for a double with a bath and a fan. The place is friendly and clean and certainly chickenbus price, which is sometimes difficult to find in Panama.

Hotel Hawaii is on a side road. Turn left after Manolo's Pizza and follow the signs. It is close to the entrance of the town and five blocks from the square. The cost is $16.50 for a double with TV, phone, air con, private bath, peeling wallpaper, and friendly, helpful owners.

Hotel Santa Rita is up a block from the Columbia and is only $13.20 for a double. It has a fan in the room and is secure. I like the place.

El Prado is half a block from the church. You must turn right off the main road. This is a no smoking building and one of the first in Latin America I am certain. The rooms cost $17.60 for a double with air con and $13.20 without air con. All rooms have either a private bath or bancito. These are partially walled off rooms that are not totally separate from the bedroom.

Pension Central is the best buy in town at $10.00 a double with air con. It is very clean but the owner was quite unfriendly. I hope it was just a bad day for him.

Hotel Rex is on the square and costs $24.20 for a double with everything. This is a very nice place. Food is a bit more expensive here but the portions are large and the food is good. The service is very friendly.

RESTAURANTS

Even though Chitre is a large place, there are not many places to eat right in town. The hotel El Prado has a restaurant on a balcony overlooking the street and they serve good food. It is a no smoking building so only non-smokers would go there.

Manolo's Pizza at the one end of town offers more than just pizza. They make lasagna and spaghetti, fresh buns and fairly good pies. It is a large chain in Panama but not badly run. I ate there more than once.

THINGS TO DO

The old **colonial church** on the square is exceptional in its design. Built in 1767, it has a beautiful dark wood altar, inlaid with paintings of saints and trimmed with gold. The first bell from this church is in the local museum and has the date clearly stamped on it. The church is really a place to stop.

Herrera Museum is on the corner of the main street and close to the center of town. It is a well organized museum, with a continuously changing local art show. There are some reconstructed gold pieces including, a tomb with gold believed to be dated from around 1100 AD. Ceremonial metates (used to grind corn) are there plus some ordinary, everyday ones. One area has beautiful Spanish laces and traditional dresses called polleras. Panamanian women still wear these dresses and some highly decorated ones can cost up to $20,000.00!! That is expensive!!

The Chitre area is known for its **bullfights** during festival times. The spectators make so much noise beating upon boxes and blowing whistles that the bull really gets angry. This makes for more noise and whistling. If you do not like the sport, this is not a place for you as they kill the bull in Panama.

Los Santos has a colonial church that was built in 1773. There are wooden beams and wooden ceilings made from local wood. The altar is very ornate with many gold niches holding statues of saints. Some of the crowns are studded with real gem stones. The font at the back of the church is of carved stone. Panamanians are very proud of Los Santos. The bus from Chitre to Los Santos is 20¢ but there is no place to stay.

The Museum of Los Santos is closed at the present because they can't get enough money to pay a worker to run it. The outside of the building is still being nicely kept by an on-site gardener.

Monagrillo has a doctor doing research on pre-Columbian Indians in the area. He has done some interesting archaeological research and if you are interested, he certainly loves to sit and answer all your questions in English.

To get there take the bus to Monagrillo for 20¢ and then walk on the main road going towards your right when you get off the bus at the square. Continue for 30-45 minutes until you come to the Rancho El Reten sign. Turn right here and at the next two forks take the left side. When you reach a large open field that is decorated around the edges with animal bones, you can go across if it is not rainy season. Go to the group of houses you can see across the field and ask for the doctor.

There are some interesting artifacts to see but the doctor is the most interesting. The site has been worked since 1975 and the doctor has found stone age implements including an interesting circular stamp and some ceramics with designs similar to mola designs. On returning to town, go past the village and school and then down to the beach. Hitchhiking is easy and safe in this area.

Cañas is the beach along the bottom end of Los Santos province where the large turtles lay their eggs in October. There is a research station there so the turtles are somewhat protected. To see the turtles, you must be there between 2:00AM and 3:00AM. This requires staying on the beach overnight with a sleeping bag or blanket. You would not be allowed to make a fire as this would be disturbing to the turtles. You MUST sit quietly and patiently waiting for this spectacular event to occur. It is well worth a night without sleep.

COLON

Even during the good days in Panama, Colon was a dangerous town because the robberies were so ingenious and numerous. Today, it is still the same. One of the reasons for its danger and intrigue is because it is one of Latin America's busiest ports. These ships are usually on their way to or from the canal and carry skillful thieves along with valuable cargo. Over two million tons of cargo are handled yearly from over 15,000 ships which fly under some 60 different flags.

Colon has ten-thousand tales. Not from Arabian Nights, but from seafarers that love to spin a story while drinking rum in the local bar. They especially like wide-eyed innocent chickenbus travellers listening. The stories begin with tales of Colon during the 1849 gold rush to California and continue up to date.

The railway is no longer operating but buses leave from Panama City every half hour until 11:00AM and then every hour for the rest of the day.

Be certain that you do not have much money on you nor any valuables that could be stolen. Women should not travel alone to this city and men should stay sober and clean. It is a wild and rough city but a delight to visit.

PLACES TO STAY

Hotel Washington is the most famous hotel in all of Central America. It once housed the famous writer Ernest Hemingway. That alone would be a reason for staying in the great old mansion. Built in 1913, with ornate ceilings and plush furniture, this building overlooks the Atlantic canal entrance. The price for a clean, double room complete with private bath, television, towels, soap, restaurant, bar and casino is a mere $43.00 That is not bad considering what you get. If you can't manage a night in the hotel at least go for a drink or a few hours of gambling.

Pension Andros annexo is a cheap but safe place to stay. It is clean even though it has been a favorite for a long time. The cost is $23.00 for a double and $20.00 for a single complete with bath, air con and a television to brush up on your Spanish with.

Hotel Atlantico is the cheapest I could find for a mere $7.20 a single and $10.80 for a double. There are 43 rooms in all but for this price, no private bath. In Colon, I would not stay at the cheapest places.

Hotel Garcia is another cheapie at $9.00 for a double and no singles. Guess why. They do have a very helpful information desk that will share a lot of information for nothing.

RESTAURANTS

Many hotels have restaurants and they are recommended for nothing special. You may want to visit some of the seedier but more interesting places along the water. You must go over the tracks to the Cristobol area of the town.

THINGS TO DO

The Colon Free Zone is 240 hectares of duty free shops that does a booming $4 billion business yearly. It is not really for us chickenbusers but it is intersting to have a look. The area is heavily guarded and you must show your passport before you will be allowed entry. They may also want to see your airline ticket before they allow you to shop there. Once inside the gates, you will be hounded by guides who make a living from the tips people give them when they get good deals. The only hitch is that you cannot take your goods with you. You can only pick them up once you have passed customs at the airport.

Established in 1948, the Duty Free Zone is mainly for international purchasing agents. This results in many dollars being exchanged and large quantities of goods being purchased. There are over 1400 companies that store, assemble, repackage and re-export goods from all over the world to all over the world. This includes electronic devices of all kinds, pharmaceutical products, liquors, cigarettes, furniture, furs, shoes, jewels, toys, perfumes and high-fashion clothing. Some of the goods are displayed in windows with eye-catching skill. This area is a true consumer's delight.

In order to assist real buyers, Colon has conveniently placed over 20 international banks close to the major distributors. This is just in case someone is short of a few bucks. The country makes its money from this area by the rent charged to the distributors, transportation fees, and wages paid to the local workers. This is a busy place to say the least.

Fort Lorenzo is in the opposite direction to Portobelo and sits at the entrance to the Chagres River. In 1671, dear old Henry Morgan demolished the fort, went along the river to Venta de Cruces then overland to Panama City, and made a huge haul of treasures. He also burned a large amount of Panama City at the same time. This was the biggest pirate raid in history. The fort was rebuilt, used first as a military post and then as a prison. Today it is a pleasant tourist attraction. The grounds are well kept with beautiful trees and flowers everywhere. It is a pleasant place to spend a day. The trip to the fort is spectacular as it passes over the Gatun Lock Gates. This is worth the visit.

CONCEPCION

Although there is little to do around Concepcion, it is a delightful little town with extremely pleasant people. I was looking for a hotel and many people stopped me just to chat. They were curious about me and were especially anxious to help. It is also much better than staying at one of the border towns.

PLACES TO STAY

Pension Ledezma is considered the best place to stay and as far as the locals are concerned the only place if you are on a budget but want something clean and pleasant. To get there, walk southeast two or three blocks past the square. The pension is just before the bridge on your left. It does not have private bathrooms and the walls are a bit thin (you will hear snoring and may hear breathing), but the place is very clean and the owners are friendly. The rooms are a decent size and there is a fan, all for only $8.00 a double.

Hotel Rocio is on the highway and costs $15.00 for a double. Of course there are private baths, TV and air con plus there is a restaurant on site. It is also more expensive than the restaurant in town. But the place is nice for the dollar.

RESTAURANTS

Gold Star Restaurant is two blocks from the square and is cheap and good. The french fries and barbequed chicken are excellent and recommended. The owners will go out of their way to give you good service and make you feel wanted.

THINGS TO DO

Hang out here rather than near the border regardless of which direction you are going. It is much cheaper than some of the more popular places like the beach resorts.

CONTADORA

Contadora is the most frequently visited island of the Archipelego of the Pearls, more commonly known as the Pearl Islands. It is a beautiful spot which has a ferry leaving Balboa Pier every day. However, this is not for the chickenbus budget. You would be better off on Taboga.

Contadora is 35 miles from the mainland and takes two and a half hours to reach by boat. It is close to other less developed islands such as Pachequilla, Pacheca, San Bartolome, Chapera, Chitre and Saboga.

Saboga has a little village and excellent beaches. These islands can be reached by hiring a boat at Contadora. Contadora itself is only 119 hectares in size and is surrounded by shallow waters that are excellent for snorkeling. Contadora is the fifth largest of the more than 220 Pearl Islands.

Being only about two kilometers long, Contadora is not difficult to explore. There are actually 13 beaches around the island, some more sheltered than others. All are beautiful.

PLACES TO STAY

Hotel Caesar Park only charges $100.00 per night for a well equipped room. There is everything at this hotel except a taxi service and a travel agent. But for $100.00, I would want gold laced sheets and a mate to go in between them. This delightful place was actually built by Canadians and I was surprised. However, it was a rich Canadian, one of very few. Some of the more prominent guests to have visited this area are the Shah of Iran, novelist Graham Green, movie star John Wayne, fighter Jo DiMagio, and singer Julio Iglesias. The hotel offers a restaurant, bar, cafeteria, alternate bar in the middle of the pool, disco, casino, tennis courts, kiddy corner, first aid (rare in CA) and a golf course. The gardens are delightful with birds, flowers and well maintained tropical plants.

THINGS TO DO

The island is reputed to have the oldest rocks on the isthmus, especially the green ones that are found along the beaches and close to the cliffs that come down to the beach. They are not jade. This is a beautiful place to spend a few hours while on the island. Along the north shore of the island, you will be able to see where early native people did some rock carving. There is a head of a person carved in the rock and the rock is worth the trip over to see it.

The natives have been diving for pearls for many years and the most famous one found was the Peregrina which belonged to the Queen of Spain and then Mary Tutor of England. The pearl divers retrieved pearls that decorated the Presidential Palace and the Palacio de las Garzas. Because of this, pearl fisheries were developed and black slaves were brought over to work as divers. These fisheries were still in operation at the turn of the 19th century.

The island was originally called the Counter because it belonged to a high ranking officer of the royal house. It was later changed to Contadora. The name is reminiscent of the days when the pearls and treasures were counted by traders and pirates.

Today, descendents of the old divers no longer search for pearls but you may see them working on their fish nets. They still fish with the same methods they have used for centuries. Sport fishing is popular, and the islands harbor tuna, jewfish, blackfish, snook, snapper and more.

CORONO BEACH

This beautiful Pacific beach is reputed to be the nicest beach in all of Panama. However, it is not chickenbus price. There are permanent condominium homes and all other necessary amenities that go with a wealthier lifestyle. The hotel rooms start at $60.00 per night and day use of the beach will cost $6.00 per person. I don't think so! However, rooms and meals in Anton are much cheaper. One of the neat things about Panama is it is the only Central American country where the sun rises on the Pacific and sets on the Caribbean.

THE DARIEN GAP

The Darien is the dense jungle area of Panama that is below the Canal zone and goes all the way to Colombia. It is possible to hike part of this gap. However, not only is it difficult, but you can only do it a few months of the year because the swamp becomes wet and impassable during the rainy season.

Before leaving, you must have good jungle equipment. This may be brought with you but the better things like boots may be purchased in Panama City. Maps may be purchased in Panama but I understand that the University in San Josè, Costa Rica, has the best maps available.

The trip should be done during the dry season; January to March. It takes a full two weeks to hike the trail. You may arrive at the trail head either by banana boat or plane. If you try to hike the trail during the rainy season it may take you up to six unpleasant weeks. Depending on your preference, you may start in Panama or start in Columbia. If you start in Panama, you start at Pucuro, a little village past the end of the unpaved section of the Panamerican Highway. After hiking for two weeks, you will arrive at the Atrato River travel to Turbo, Columbia, and then catch a plane to civilization.

Some of the difficulties of the trip are the number of ticks that enjoy gringo meat, mosquitoes, relatives to the ticks, and hungry pirana fish which nibble at your toes (or other parts) when you want to cool off in the rivers.

The wonderful aspects of this trip are that you will encounter Choco and Cuna Indians still living in traditional ways, untouched by modern technology. These people are friendly and hospitable. The abundant wild life in the Darien is probably better than anywhere else in America. The Panamerican Highway can not be completed in this section of the country because the swamp in the jungle is like northern muskeg. If contractors try to fill the swamp to make it solid, the land fill sinks into oblivian. The numerous rivers would require many bridges at a high cost. The jungle can be heard growing if you stand still; keeping it under control would be difficult. Before hiking this trail, consider the difficulties. If you are a highly experienced hiker, enjoy hardships and bugs, and are looking for one of the last hiking challenges on this continent, this may be the hike for you. I have not hiked this trail as I prefer mountains to swamp.

Hilary Brandt has limited information on this trip in his book <u>Backpacking in Mexico and Central America</u>. (See book section in the introduction.)

DAVID

This inland city is the first town of any size before or after crossing the Costa Rican border. Built during colonial times, it is a pleasant but hot town. You must pass here if going into the delightful highlands of the Chiriqui province. The area is rich in timber, coffee, cocoa, sugar, rice, bananas and cattle.

PLACES TO STAY

Moderna Pension is just one block from the bus station. It is the best buy in town. It is clean, quiet and cheap. The cost is $8.00 for a double with bath and fan. The hotel is small; there are only six rooms scattered around the family's living area but it is quiet and I liked the family atmosphere.

Mi Casita is across from the Nacional and is the second best place in David. The rooms are large, with fans but no private bath. The carpet was dirty. The cost was $5.00 for a single and $8.00 for a double. You can sleep at Mi Casita and eat at the Nacional.

Volcancita is down the road from the bus station in the opposite direction from going into the center of town. The room costs $7.50 for a double with a shower but no toilet. It is sufficient for one night if the Moderna is full.

Hotel Iris was $7.00 a night five years ago and is now $17.70 for a double. It is on the square which is convenient. The rooms have private bath and air con.

Hotel Savol costs $19.90 for a double without air con, with dirty rugs, a crooked floor and an empty pool. There are large rooms with a bath. This is a last choice.

Occidental Hotel is on the square and is expensive at $29.00 for a double. The tourist office says that the cost is only $20.00 for a double so I think they have one rate for gringos and one rate for Panamanians. A $10.00 discrepency is high. They have private bath, air con, bar and restaurant.

RESTAURANTS

Natural fruit shops are great and plentiful in this town. The Panamanians are very civilized when it comes to natural foods. The ice-cream is safe and delicious to eat. Highly recommended.

Churrascos is past the square but before the National Hotel. It sells jugs of beer for $2.00 and the food they serve is excellent. The meats are barbequed on an open grill and cooked to perfection. The spaghetti sauce is also   delicious.

The Nacional Hotel has a good restaurant where you can get a decent meal at a decent price. Breakfast is especially good here. They offer the non-ending cup of coffee.

THINGS TO DO

Church of San José is an old colonial church majestically sitting on the square waiting for the faithful to come and worship. It was in the process of restoration when I was there so I did not see the interior.

Playa Las Lajas at the Port of Pedregal is a tourist resort beach. If you do not have the time to go further south to the older and more romantic places in Panama then this is a good stop.

Museum of the History and Art of Jose de Obaldia is on Calle Octava in the town's center. I know nothing about the artist or the museum.

EL VALLE DE ANTON

This is one of the most fascinating areas of Panama. Since the road was built in the 1930s, Panamanians have made this a tourist attraction. Many Panamanians enjoy the hot thermal baths and delightful forests of the area. If you are on a strict budget, stay in Anton or Chame and commute as El Valle is expensive. It is about one hour from Chame or Anton to El Valle. Be certain to ask the bus driver let you off at the turn-off for El Valle because there is no direct bus for the village.

PLACES TO STAY

Hotel Campestre is expensive and costs $40.00 for a double. The hotel is clean and pleasant. It has private bath with two tap showers. Because it gets cold up in the mountains, especially during rainy season, a hot shower is often the only way to warm up.

Cabañas Potosi has a few small cabinas that cost $22.00 for a double. They are large, pleasant, clean little cabins. For the price you may want to stay here.

RESTAURANTS

Hotel Greco has a nice restaurant with good food. Hotel Campestre is also reported to be good but more expensive than Greco.

THINGS TO DO

El Valle was originally the crater of a huge volcano. The valley became a lake, then a swampland, and now a lush valley. Because of volcanic activity, you will find thermal springs which are claimed to cure arthritis and other ailments. Walking through the area, the mountains take on strange formations. When you are on your way up to or down from the valley you will pass over the top of a hill; look for the formation of **"La India Dormida"** (The Sleeping Indian). Needless to say, there is a legend attached to the sleeping woman. You should ask the locals about this. There are other configurations that look like frogs or lions.

This is where you will see the **square trees** and it is the only place on earth that has them. They are not really perfectly square but they are far from round. They produce square pieces of wood. This is also where the famous golden toad lives. When and if you see one, it looks like it is radiating sunshine off of its skin. It is very strange to see.

There are also spectacular **waterfalls** in these mountains. Take any of the trails leading into the mountains and you will be pleasantly surprised. Along the walk to the waterfall, you may see a **golden frog**. The square trees grow in an area that resembles a rain forest with its huge mossy trees. There are also **petroglyphs** that can be seen in the area. These were left by the Indians who lived here before the the white man came.

To get to any of these you must ask at your hotel for directions. It is not difficult but the walks into the hills are a bit steep. You will need good runners for this.

The market in El Valle is another popular place to purchase goods that are locally made. The best market day is Sunday.

ISLA GRANDE

Isla Grande, known as the Atlantic Diamond, can be reached by going to Guaira from Colon by bus and then renting a local boat to go to the island. It is not far from the shore and a dollar each way is a fair price.

The island has a gorgeous beach, five kilometers wide and with only 100 houses used by permanent residents. Most of the inhabitants are black and claim to be direct descendents from Africa. The beautiful empty beaches become a cesspool of human flesh on week-ends when the Panamanians arrive, so if you can be there during the week, you may enjoy it much more.

There are two places to stay on the island; both are fairly expensive. **The Isla Grande** is $72.00 for a double and the other hotel charges $60.00 for a double. Both places have a restaurant.

Because coconut palms are so abundant on the island, many restaurant dishes are made with coconut milk. The most traditional food is called **"Fufu"** and is made with seafood and coconut milk. Be certain to try some. There is also a great selection of sea food on the island such as ceviche and octopus.

One interesting attraction is the **lighthouse called "El Faro"**. It stands 30 meters high and was built by the French in 1893. Another interesting feature on the island is the architecture of the houses. Long ago, the houses on the island were made of palm roofs with bamboo walls, papered with a starch and water plaster. Later, they were built with wooden walls and zinc roofs. Today they are made of cement blocks with zinc roofs. All houses are abundantly decorated with flowers.

Popular entertainment on the island is the **congo dance**. Local women wear polleras and decorate their heads with lace and flowers. The men wear frayed jeans fastened with ropes. The dance includes songs and mime with some fantasy mixed in.

You may hire fishing boats from the locals at a reasonable price if you are interested in going fishing. **Snorkeling** is popular around the island and equipment is available. There is also an image of Christ carved in a coral reef which can be seen. Below the image of Christ is a pelican with extended wings. This represents man's sacrifice for children. The images were carved by an islander.

LAS PALMAS

Las Palmas is a beautiful beach about two hours by public bus from Panama City. It is just a few kilometers past San Carlos. The hotel charges $27.00 for a double. It is a clean, new and spotless cabin. The beach is private and also clean. The restaurant beside the cabins has friendly operators. Las Palmas is a delightful place to stay. I would prefer this to Rio Mar just a few more kilometers up the road even though Rio Mar has a more romantic restaurant setting.

BOQUETE

Boquete is a beautiful little town nestled in a valley and surrounded by high, lush mountains. This village is the Antigua of Panama. The days are warm and the nights are cool. The people are friendly and there is not a dope problem in the area, so dopers, please stay away. The beautiful sunken square is decorated with many different types of flowers and if you sit there without a flower in your hand, a local is certain to give you one. Flowers are everywhere.

PLACES TO STAY

Pension Virginia is on the square at the same place as the Virginia Restaurant. Rooms cost $8.50 for a single, $14.50 for a double and $16.50 for a double with private bath. This is a popular place for backpackers.

Pension Marilos is two blocks before the square when coming into town. Turn right when walking from the square for one block. This pension is very clean and comfortable and the best buy in town. The rooms cost $15.40 for a double with private bath. The owner speaks English.

Hotel Rebequet is across from Marilos and is beautiful. The cost is $20.00 for a large, clean, double room with a sitting area and private bathroom. There is a lovely center garden, pool table in the games room and a restaurant on the premises.

Hotel Central is past the square going away from the town entrance. This is a new hotel and was not quite ready when I was there.

RESTAURANTS

There are a few places in town. The Virginia is popular and so is the Chinese restaurant just off the square. As tourism increases, so will the restaurants.

LAS TABLAS

Las Tablas is a pretty little town that has one ornate church and a small museum. There is not much to do in town but hang around.

PLACES TO STAY

Hotel Piamonte is an interesting place. They told me they charge $29.00 for a double with air con but the government brochure says they charge $22.00. The room has private bath and air con. A room without air con is $17.00 for a double and $13.00 for a single. Gringos, however, are charged more.

Pension Mariela is across the street from the Piamonte and charges $4.00 per person per night for a very basic room. There are clean rooms with fans but no private bathrooms. You could stay at the Mariela and eat at the Piamonte (if you check the prices before you order). I liked the friendly atmosphere of the Mariela.

RESTAURANTS

You are on your own. Do not eat at the beach Agallito (see below).

THINGS TO DO

The Cathedral is a very ornate building which has a lot of decorative gold on the altar. It was built in 1789 and kept up ever since.

Museum Balisario Parras is on the square and easy to find. It is open from 9:00AM to noon and 2:00PM to 5:00PM daily and only in the mornings on Sundays. It is a little museum with a nice organized display.

Playa Uberito is the nicest beach in the area but there are no buses to the beach. A taxi costs $4.00 each way. Once at the beach, there are restaurants and snack shops. This beach is clean. Panama is the only Central American country where one can see the sun set in the Caribbean and rise on the Pacific.

Playa Agallito is easy to get to. Take a bus at the National lottery, one of the local green buses. The charge is 35¢. This dirty beach is a public recreation site with playgrounds for children and a large, noisy, unpleasant bar for adults. The restaurant owners charge gringos double the advertised price. Arguing will not change their minds. In my opinion, you would need to be desperate to go there.

LOS SANTOS

See under Chitre

PANAMA CITY

Like the rest of Panama, the city has changed dramatically. When I researched Panama City for the second edition of <u>Chickenbus,</u> I had kids throwing stones at the taxi I was in and I was not encouraged to walk around the city alone. I returned this year and I was delightfully surprised at the changes. Most of the hostility towards the gringo is gone. In the hotel and business section of town, Panama is clean and safe. Walking along the water, the city was buzzing with inexpensive shops. There are slums in Panama and they appear worse than in any other part of Central America; you must be careful if near them. Regardless of this, plan on spending a few days exploring this delightful city.

PLACES TO STAY

It is not recommended to stay in the San Filipe area of Panama City but rather stay in the Caledonia section.

Hotel Caribe is a popular hotel and highly recommended by both the tourist office and other Panamanians. If arriving late, you will be able to share a taxi with someone to get to this hotel. The cost is $30.00 for a double with a private bath, hot water, bellboys, casino (with slot machines only), restaurant, air con, TV and phone. It was quiet and the service was excellent.

Hotel Rio de Janiero on Calle 27E and Ave. 1AS, half a block from the Caribe. The cost is $19.80 for a double with a private bath, hot water, TV and clean rooms. It is secure and quiet. They will keep your bags if you go travelling and come back later.

Pension Tablas is next door to the Caribbe and not as secure as the Rio de Janiero but clean and pleasant. The rooms have fans, private bath, towels and TP for $14.00 a double. Not bad for the capital city.

Pension Los Torres is on Ave. 1AS and Calle 36. The entrance is on Calle 36. The building was built in 1931 and has a lovely tiled entrance. All of the rooms have gorgeous high ceilings and private bathrooms. A large double room with air con costs $25.00 but is not worth it. A smaller room with air con is $16.00 for two and a room with a fan and private bath will cost between $14. & $12.00 The owner has a dorm that he charges $35.00 for. It will hold six people. This is on the third floor and also clean. The owner will not let undesirables in. If he thinks you are scruffy, he will say he is full.

Turistico el Dorado on Calle 37 between Ave. 2-3 costs $16.00 for a double. This includes air con, TV, hot water and a private bath. If you pay $12.00 you get a room with an abonico which is a bathroom without a shower. The drawback to this hotel is that I found the workers quite rude.

Hotel Centro Americano will cost $22.00 for one night but only $20 if you stay longer. The large rooms have private bath, color TV, air con, telephone, restaurant, bar and security. This was a popular place with travellers when I was in the city.

Hotel America is across the street from the Centro Americano and charges $11.00 for a double without a bath or air con. The rooms are quite small. A regular size room is $15.00 for a double with a fan. The hotel is on Calle 35 (Equador) and Ave. 1AS (Peru). The more expensive Hotel Roma is next door.

Hotel California has pleasant rooms for $25.00 a double. There are private baths, television and telephones in the rooms. The restaurant/bar has average meals and the service is good. The hotel has a safe for your valuables and it is recommended by the owner to use it. The manager likes to "father" his guests. The hotel is on the highway and away from the center of town.

Hotel Colonial is on Calle 4 in San Filipe. It is a beautiful old building with a gorgeous tiled entrance and a blue tiled sitting room. The cost is $12.10 for a double with a fan and a sink in the room. This is a rundown area and is not suggested that you stay here but certainly take a look at the hotel during the day.

Hotel Central is on the square in San Felipe beside the Post Office. It was built in 1919 and has high ceilings around a central court. It has seen much better days and better clients. The rooms run from $7.00 - $17.00 for a double depending on what you get. There is no air con in the building.

Hotel Foyo is just off of the square past the post office. It is fairly decent for a lower range hotel. The only drawback is the miles of stairs you must climb in the heat. Rooms cost $11.00, $7.00, or $6.00 for a double. The $6.00 room is quite small but comes with a fan. The owner is pleasant and helpful. There is a nice balcony on the first floor where you can watch TV or the kids playing baseball down on the street. This is not a bad deal.

Pension Balboa is across from the Burger King on Ave. Central. It is secure and clean but noisy. The rooms cost $14.00 for a double with a private bathroom.

RESTAURANTS

Panama City is a hub for both day and nightlife. There are many restaurants, bars, night clubs and cafes. You do not have to look far in order to get something pleasant. The usual McDonalds, Dairy Queen, Burger King, Pizza Hut and Dunkin Donuts are available. These are always the "known" food outlets. You can get anything from good sea food to the Peruvian delicacy, cuy, in Panama. However, be careful. If they do not have a menu, ask for prices before ordering. I went into one place and had a mineral water without asking the price. The owner was a delightful conversationalist but, she also knew we would pay a high price for our water because we did not check before hand. Two glasses of mineral water cost us $6.00! It was an expensive lesson. If the prices seem to be gringo prices, walk out. Even if they change their minds when they see your hand on the door, keep walking. Giving them a second chance just sets up the next unsuspecting traveller. However, there are many Panamanians who will not rip you off.

Some typical Panamanian foods are:

Carimañola is a roll made from ground and boiled yuccas filled with chopped meat and boiled eggs. The roll is fried after it has been stuffed.

Empanadas are something like a Cornish pastry. Some are made from flour and others from corn pastry. They can be filled with meat, chicken or cheese and are great any time of day or night.

Tamales are popular delicacy throughout Central America. They are made from boiled ground corn with spices, chicken and pork in the center. The tamale is wrapped in a banana leaf and boiled before serving.

Patacones are green fried plantain, cut crossways, pressed with salt and fried.

Platanomaduro is a ripe plantain cut in slices and baked with cinnamon.

Aculpoco Restaurant is cheap, clean and they serve large portions of food. This is in a hotel and is just around the corner from the Caribe.

Vera Cruz Restaurant is in another hotel across from the Caribe. The food is expensive and the restaurant is noisy. This restaurant is often open when others are not.

Caribe has good prices and fast service. The meals are substantial but not special.

Club Alasaka is on Via España and Calle 52E and offers Karaoke singing. You are allowed to sing in English, Spanish, Japanese or German. There is a dance floor, Japanese foods and a high price.

La Tasca in the Hotel Granada serves typical Spanish seafood, and other dishes. There is live music and Spanish dancing if you would like a bit of culture. Open from Tuesday to Saturday at 5:00PM.

El Charro Tapatio on Ave. Miguel Brostella and El Dorado Blvd. is a great Mexican restaurant. Decorated in Mexican style, it has a happy atmosphere. The service is good and the prices are not too heavy. The meals are a decent size.

Vegetarian Mireya is just down the road from the Hotel Continental. The owner, Mireya Alfaro is a vegetarian chef who offers ravioli, pepper steak made with wheat and he even offers vegetarian tripe. This is culinary imagination at its best. The restaurant is open from 6:00AM to 10:00PM daily except Sundays.

Le Palace is the restaurant for those interested in an old fashioned girlie show. This nightclub is two blocks from the Hilton at Calle 52, across from the Ejecutivo. There is no cover charge but the show is covered by the cost of the drinks. I did not visit this restaurant because they did not offer naked men.

THINGS TO DO

The Panama Canal is the first and most important tourist attraction in Panama City. You must plan on one complete day to visit this engineering wonder of the world. On the canal at Miraflores, there is an observation deck, commonly called the "chicken coop" and there is an English/Spanish speaking person giving information about the canal and the ships going through at the time. This service is offered seven days a week from 9:00AM to 5:00PM. You may take a taxi, a tour bus or a public bus to the canal. The public buses leave from the station behind the Legislative Palace on the 5th of May Plaza. Ask the bus driver to let you off by the Howard Air Force Base turnoff. Tell him you want to visit the Miraflores viewing site.

You may also join a tour through part of the canal. This tour goes through the Miraflores and Pedro Miguel Locks, and the famous Gaillard Cut. This trip is dependent on a minimum number of passengers before it will proceed. The cost of the trip is $12.00 to $40.00 depending on the services and the number of people going. The two tour companies that offer this tour are Latinsel, phone 60-9235 or Argo Tours, phone 64-3549.

Charles the First of Spain, in 1534, proposed a canal route through Panama but it wasn't until 1903 that the US and Panama agreed to build the canal. The French held the right to build the canal and the US paid them $40 million for these rights. The area belonged to Columbia and the French had administrative authority at that time.

A group of Panamanian businessmen declared themselves independent from Columbia and the US marines moved in to support the resulting rebellion. A new treaty was drawn up and one of the businessmen, Bunau-Varilla made certain this treaty was in favor of the Americans. He illegally signed the treaty before the rest of the representatives of the new government arrived in Washington to complete the negotiations. Banau-Varilla then convinced the new government the deal was okay. The new government didn't realize the full implication of the treaty which gave the US both administrative and sovereignty rights.

It took ten years and $387 million to complete the building of the waterway. The Canal is 50 miles long and 312 feet above sea level at the Continental Divide. The Pacific side of the canal is situated 27 miles east and 33 miles south of the Atlantic side. It is 43 miles across as the crow flies.

There are three sets of locks, Gatun Lake and the famous Gaillard Cut, named after the engineer, Col. David DuBose Gaillard who engineered the cut along the entire canal.

Coming along the Atlantic, the entrance is a mangrove swamp six and a half miles long and 500 feet wide. To diffuse the ferocity of the gales that blow in from the Caribbean during certain times of the year, there was a three mile set of breakwaters built at the entrance. The three steps of the locks are 110 feet wide and 1000 feet long and the water may be raised or lowered by 85 feet. The length of the three locks is one and a half miles.

A vessel's trip throughout the canal must be accompanied by a skilled pilot. Unlike other world sea ports where a pilot advises the captain how to navigate his ship through a difficult area, these pilots actually take control of the ship and steer them through the narrow waterway. The pilots, after a few years of schooling, start their practicum by steering small vessels through the canal. They gradually move to larger vessels taking eight to ten years to be fully qualified to take all vessels through.

The Gatun Locks are used to raise and lower the vessels to or from Gatun Lake, a height of 85 feet. All Panama Canal locks have two parallel sets of chambers which allow ships to pass in either direction at the same time. An interesting feature of the canal are the electric lock locomotives or the "mules" which operate along the lock walls. They position vessels within the lock chambers. Some people believe that they tow the vessels but this is not true. Vessels pass under their own steam but the mules may be used to stop or slow a vessel down. Otherwise they are used only for positioning.

Each mule weights 55 tons and has two winches which can exert 35,000 pounds of pulling strength. They also have a special part which can give additional traction when needed. Small vessels require four mules to get through the canal while larger vessels may need up to six or eight mules.

When the ship is raised through Gatun Locks, it is in the fresh water of Gatun Lake. This lake was formed by the construction of an earth and rock dam, one and a half miles long and one mile thick at the bottom. The dam is across the Chagres River. At the time of building, the lake was the world's largest man-made body of water. The riverbed now lies beneath the lake and after years of improvement, the route has been widened and straightened thus ridding the lake of the original riverbed. The islands seen on the lake are the tops of hills which existed before the lake was formed.

The Madden hydro-electric plant provides the canal and some of Panama with its power. Before the dam was built in 1930, the wild Chagres River could rise up to 40 feet in a single day causing millions of cubic feet of water to be spilled and wasted. This would bring the canal to a halt. Today, the dam's reservoir holds excess water during the rainy season in order to be used during the dry season.

The bottom of the lake is constantly being dredged in order to keep its depth at an optimum, especially during dry season. The Christensen, one of the world's largest dredgers, works year around removing obstructions and silt deposits. Each ship passage requires 52 million gallons of water. If the lake was full of silt or other debris, more water would be needed. Extra water is not available during dry season.

The Gaillard Cut is next on the journey through the canal. It is nine miles of ditch. This is where the most lives were lost during the construction. Engineers had their greatest challenge at this spot. The ditch had to be dug and the remaining land reinforced. The highest point is at the Gold Hill which is 662 feet above sea level. The other side of this hill was originally 410 feet high but was reduced to 370 feet in order to stabilize the hill. Originally the cut was only 300 feet wide but it has been increased to 500 feet. One of the great challenges of the cut was the disposal of the 200 million cubic yards of dirt they removed. John F. Stevens, an engineer oversaw the removal of the dirt. He used 200 trains daily to ship the debris to other areas of the country where landfill was needed.

After the Gaillard Cut, the ships go through the Pedro Miguel locks and are lowered 31 feet into Miraflores Lake. This is the largest change in elevation on the canal. The chambers are filled and emptied by gravity, not pumps and can be filled within 10 minutes. Each chamber requires 333,000 cubic feet of water for each change.

The final lowering is at the two-stepped Miraflores Locks and Miraflores Lake. This lake was formed by the damming of the Rio Grande and the Rio Cocle. From the Miraflores Lake, the ships enter the Pacific Ocean.

The canal's locks, dams and other installations required four million cubic yards of cement to build. The lock gates range from 47 to 82 feet high, 65 feet wide and seven feet thick. They weigh from 400 to 700 tons and each set of gates can be opened or closed in two minutes.

The first ship to go through the canal was the S.S. Ancon on August 15, 1914. The highest number of ships going through the canal in one year, before the Second World War was 7,479 which occurred in 1939. In 1987, there were 13,444 ships that passed through the canal. The longest ship to go through the canal was the San Juan Prospector, an oil tanker 973 feet long. The Queen Elizabeth ll is 963 feet long and is the longest passenger ship to ever go through. This is also the ship that paid the highest toll for a passenger ship. On December 15, 1981, the Arco Texas carried 65,299 tons of oil, thus containing the largest amount of cargo to go through the canal. The average number of ships going throughout the canal daily is 34 and a record number of 68 passed through the waters in one day in 1970.

The toll fees of the canal are $1.83 per ton for laden ships and $1.46 per ton for empty ships. The largest toll paid was $99,865.10, paid by the Marina Ace in 1987 and the lowest toll paid was 36¢ by Richard Halliburton when he swam the canal in 1928. The average time it takes a ship to pass through the canal is eight to ten hours but the hydrofoil Pegasus passed through in a record two hours and 41 minutes.

At the **Miraflores Locks** there is a topo model of the canal and a sight and sound show which is enjoyed by the 300,000 people who visit the pavilion each year. In order to increase the working time of the canal, there has been a battalion of lights added to the waterway, making night passage a possibility. The lights make a beautiful spectacle of the entire area.

The **Administration** building sits on Anton Hill in Balboa overlooking a monument to George W. Goethals, one of the original administrators. It is the administrative center of the Panama Canal Commission. Goethals served as chief engineer from 1907-1914 when the canal was completed, and then as Governor of the Canal Zone from 1914-1917. The monument is a fountain with a shaft 56 feet high and made of marble. It represents the Continental Divide. The water spills into three pools symbolizing the three sets of locks.

The high domed ceiling and the marble floor and columns make the rotunda at the Administration Buildings just beyond the fountain one of the main attractions to the area. The oil paintings in the building depict the building of the Gatun Dam, the Miraflores locks, the cutting of the Gaillard ditch at Gold Hill, and the erection of a lock gate. These paintings were commissioned to W.B. Van Ingen by George Goethals. There are also statues of Ferdinand de Lesseps and F. D. Roosevelt. This is a worthwhile visit.

As specified by the Panama Canal Treaty of 1977, the commission is an agency of the US government which will operate the Canal until December 31, 1999. The commission employs and trains Panamanians at all levels of operation as agreed to in the Treaty. Today it employs about 8000 people, 82% of which are Panamanian. I bet that there are more Panamanians on the cleaning and maintenance end than administration but I hope that this will change. At present, the Canal operates on a break-even policy with neither profit or loss being shown on the books.

Stevens Circle is not far from Balboa pier and has the Balboa Theater and post office around it. There are many vendors selling goods at an inflated price. The center monument honors John F. Stevens who was the engineer that preceded Goethals from 1905-1907. Stevens is given credit for bringing order to the operations, mobilizing the railway, and establishing organizational and logistical structure to the operation thus ensuring the successful completion of the canal.

The **Bridge of the Americas** crosses the Canal at Balboa and links North and South America together. It stands 384 feet above the ocean and is 5,425 feet from one end to the other. The bridge is basically of cantilever, tied-arch or suspended span construction and was started from both sides of the canal in December 1958. It was joined with a 70 foot, 98 ton steel beam in May 1962 and finally inaugurated October 12th, Columbus Day in 1962. The total cost of building the bridge was $20 million, which was paid for by the US.

Although the bridge symbolically indicates the entrance to the canal, the channel is dredged another five miles out to sea and deep water. Under this bridge pass the ships of every nation in the world as long as they follow the safety guidelines of the canal.

Railway between Panama City and Colon was the favorite way for tourists to see the canal in days gone by, but the one and one half hour trip increased to four hours and now seldom runs at all. It would be a stroke of luck if you got there on an operating day. If you do, put all your valuables in your hotel before you go.

The railway was built along the trail the natives used to transport gold and silver from the ships coming from Peru. The treasures were taken to the Atlantic and loaded onto ships headed for Spain. This trail was not the best route for a railway but on January 28, 1855, the first train ever to cross the Americas landed in Panama City. The railroad was built through tropical jungles and was the only means of powered transportation across the Isthmus for almost 60 years until the canal was opened in 1914. The railway's primary purpose was to carry gold miners across the continent quickly. The railway is reputed to have the heaviest traffic per mile of all railroads in the world. Could this be part of the reason it is not operating any longer?

Summit Gardens are on the hill at the Continental Divide. Buses going to Colon that will let you off at the gardens. The gardens are just past the Pedro Miguel and Miraflores Locks but before Gamboa. There are signs posted along the highway before you get there. Yell "parada" when you want off. The highway passes through the larger preserve called the Soberania National Park in which the Summit Gardens are only a small portion.

The gardens are over 300 acres in size with 15,000 varieties of plant life. There is a picnic area and a small zoo that may also be visited. The National Park Headquarters are found at the gardens. The Summit Gardens were established in 1923 and the park was established in 1980. The Gardens were originally administered by the Americans; however, in 1979, the area was turned over to the Panamanians.

Soberania Park covers an area of 22,000 hectares and is on the eastern banks of the Canal between Colon and Panama. The area has over 1200 species of trees, 2000 species of plants and 300 species of birds. Some of the forests are secondary growth which are 60-70 years old. This is a long growth time for a rapidly growing jungle. Hidden among the lush jungle plants are many types of animals including monkeys, deer, salamanders, crocodiles and birds which can be spotted early in the morning.

The zoo contains some endangered species such as the jaguar, puma, the white faced money, the Galinazos vulture and some alligators.

There are places to purchase food and drink and some camping facilities. There is drinking water, washrooms and barbecue area. This is a delightful place to visit.

Old Panama is the ruins of the original city before the devastating fire Henry Morgan caused. The grounds of the ruins are beautifully kept and the ruins themselves are different from the rest found in Central America. Old Panama was built in 1519 in order to store the gold going to Spain from Peru. The pirate, Henry Morgan, upon learning that the wealth from around the world was gathered annually in Portobelo to await transportation to Spain, decided to rob the well-protected city. He sailed up the coast, walked back to the town and took the city. Although he took an entire year's treasures this only enhanced his appetite. In 1671, armed with 37 galleons and over 2000 men, Morgan marched to Panama City and destroyed it. Today at Old Panama, there is the cathedral, which has a huge tower still in good shape. The building has excellent stone work. There are some walls left of the old government buildings and the King's Bridge still stands. This was where the road across the isthmus started.

The remains of the Church of San José are close to the ocean. This church had a beautiful golden altar that the priests painted black in order to save it from Morgan. The altar is now in Panama City.

You can take a city bus to Old Panama.

Anthropological Museum is on the Plaza 5 de Mayo which is just past the hotel section of town, going towards the older area of San Filipe. The museum is open daily from 10:00AM to 3:30PM except Sundays when it is open from 3:30 - 5:50PM. It is closed Mondays and holidays. There is a 25¢ admission fee.

The museum has five rooms starting with the pre-Columbian section. This has a lava rock carving of a man on the shoulders of another man. This carving dates back to 1000BC. The second salon has an ever changing art display. In the third salon, I found a beautifully sculpted funeral jug that has a monkey embossed on it. It is different from any others found in Panama. For some reason, the Indians buried their dead face down in this area.

The gold room is a must to see. There is no air con and it is very hot, especially after visiting the other air con rooms. Just passing the heavily vaulted door makes the visit worthwhile. Inside there are many sculptured gold objects including jewellery, plain arm and breast plates and small intricately designed sculptures.

The last two salons are cultural displays of indigenous peoples. Again, these rooms are carefully displayed and have helpful guards willing to answer questions.

Historical Museum is on the square in the old Presidential Palace in San Filipe. The post office is next to the museum. The museum is open Tuesday to Saturday from 10:00AM to 3:30PM, Sundays from 3:00-5:30PM and closed Mondays. The entrance fee is 25¢.

The building was built in 1910 in neoclassical design by Florencio Harmodio Arosemena and Genaro Rugieri. On December 14, 1977, the building was inaugurated as the Historical Museum. The building houses the museum administration and the Historical Library of Panama, besides the historical display of the museum.

The museum has pictures, maps and flags from the days of the pirates and early Spanish settlement. The museum has some artifacts from Portobelo and Old Panama including rifles and an old cannon.

Another room has a collection of pictures, manuscripts and artifacts from the separatist movements of 1830, 1831 and 1841 celebrating Josè Vallarino Jimenez as one of the heros.

One room shows the principle requirements of a lawyer's studio during the early 20th century in Panama. I thought this was a bit odd but I have not seen many lawyer's rooms in museums.

All in all this will give the visitor a basic introduction to the modern history of Panama. It has always been a proud nation, willing to fight for culture and rights.

National Bank of Panama Museum is on calle 34 and Ave. Cuba in the center of Panama City. The museum is open during the regular museum hours and has a small entry fee. The museum has a fairly large and valuable coin and stamp collection.

Museum of Contemporary Art is on Ave. de los Martires and Calle San Blas in the suburb of Ancon. It is open from 9:00AM - 12:30PM and 2:30 to 6:00PM, Monday to Friday and 9:00AM to noon on Saturdays. There is no admission. This museum has a permanent collection of both Panamanian artists and Latin American artists.

The Museum of Religious Art is on Ave. A and Calle 3a in San Filipe. The museum is housed in an 18th century chapel next to the Church of Santo Domingo and the ruins of the convent of Casco Viejo. The museum if full of spectacular paintings, religious carvings of both silver and wood, and other religious paraphernalia that have been used by the Spanish priests from the time of the conquest.

The Museum of Natural Science is on Calle 30 and Ave. Cuba and is open daily from 10:00 - 3:30PM, Monday to Friday and 3:00 - 5:30PM on Saturdays. There is a 25¢ admission fee.

Cockfights are still popular and legal in Panama. You may see this gruesome sport on Saturday, Sunday or Monday at the Club Gallistico on Via España just past the junction with Via Cincuentenario. To confirm a fight, telephone 21-5652. It would be a pity to go all the way out there and then have no show.

Shopping in Panama is delightful and recommended. Unique items made in Panama are the modern huacas or gold ornaments that are replicas of orchids. These are expensive but different. The goldsmiths use an ancient Indian method of dipping the original flower to be reproduced into wax similar to dental wax. This produces a mold which has preserved the delicate petals and stamens of the original flower. The mold is then filled with gold and the huaca is produced. To date, there are 35 different orchid huacas. This souvenir would be quite expensive but a real treasure. The Reprosa store is on Samuel Lewis Ave. has other items for sale besides the huacas. Originally, huacas were the gold ornaments worn by the native people. They can be seen in the gold room of the Anthropological Museum.

PENONOME

Penonome is a friendly little town. You will not be able to sit anywhere without someone talking to you. And, it is not intrusive - just plain old country friendly. Penonome is the capital of Cocle province and is noted for having some of the best festivals in the country.

During one carnival, the people have an "up street" and a "down street" which compete with each other. They perform songs and dances with each group trying to outdo each other. Costumes play an important part in these competitions and the creations are ingenious.

One ceremony, held at the year's end carnival, is actually a mock funeral. They take a sardine and bury it while the people weep and wail under brightly colored lights. This symbolizes all of the previous year's angers and hostilities being buried so the people can start again. Maybe this custom has influenced the Panamanians so that they have forgiven the gringos and allowed them to travel freely again in their country.

During the aquatic festival, the carnival princess is placed on a gaily decorated raft in Mendoza's Bath. This is a beach on the Zarati River. The locals sing and dance as the princess goes into the bath and down the river.

The most famous tradition during a festival is the throwing of water onto everyone in the street. A person, whether he or she wants to participate or not can not go anywhere in public without being drenched under a spray of water. It is all done in good fun and luckily, Panama is hot enough so that no one a catches cold.

PLACES TO STAY

The one hotel in town is called the **Dos Continentes,** but there is no sign to identify it. The hotel is close to the bus station, at the fork in the road is. Penonome is not a big town so it won't be difficult to find. The cost of a clean room with a private bath and air con is $24.00 a double. If you want a room without air con, you can pay as little as $17.00 for two. This is a nice hotel with a decent restaurant, bar, swimming pool and tennis courts. It is affordable for most people.

THINGS TO DO

Santa Clara Beach only 35 minutes by bus from Penonome is where many Americans have taken permanent residence. It is a beautiful beach. There are expensive hotels in Santa Clara but it is much cheaper to stay in Penonome and commute.

El Caño de Nata is an archaeological site about 15 minutes past Penonome going towards Las Tablas. Nata is one of the oldest colonial cities in Panama and has the oldest church on the American continent. The church can be entered.

There is an authentic native tomb and a large stone ceremonial altar on the site. The museum was constructed by using antique engravings. There is the reproduction of a native dwelling complete with household objects that Indians used to use in their everyday lives.

The museum is not large but has some interesting artifacts from Panama's indigenous people. This site is worth visiting and you will find Panamanians proud of this area. There are also picnic tables and a small cafeteria-style restaurant where you can get needed refreshments after walking in the heat for a while.

PORTOBELO

Portobelo, known for its five Spanish forts, is a town up the coast from Colon. Until 1821, it was Spain's richest treasure port where gold and silver was stored after being stolen from Peru. It was a small fishing village, only accessible by water but it had a rich Custom House. This House, built in 1611 is still there today. Some restoration to the house has been done. Skeletons of the forts with their cannons in the yards can still be seen today.

PLACES TO STAY

Cabañas Jackson is a nice little hotel with 12 rooms. The rooms have private baths, one tap showers and a television. This costs $22.00 for a double. There is a restaurant at this hotel but prices are in the same category as the rooms.

THINGS TO DO

Sir Francis Drake died near Portobelo and was buried in a lead casket and set out to sea. This area is now called Drake's Cove.

Henry Morgan attacked this impenetrable town by coming ashore further up the coast and attacking the forts from the rear. The town was finally destroyed by Admiral Vernon in 1739.

During the building of the canal, US builders carried away the outside walls of the fort to use as fill for the Gatun Locks.

Portobelo Cathedral has a life size Black Christ made of cocobolo wood. The statue was found on the shores of Panama in 1658. It is not known where the statue came from but the Panamanians consider it a miracle since this kind of wood should sink. The celebration for the Black Christ is held every October 21st and is the biggest festival held in town all year.

Maria Chiquita is a black sand beach on the way to Portobelo. There are change rooms and a few small tiendas where you can get things to eat and drink. Maria Chiquita beach is a turicentros run by the government's tourist department.

RIO MAR

This little resort area is along the Pacific Coast about one and a half hours from Panama City by public bus. ($3.00) You must walk one kilometer from the bus stop to the resort. On a hot day, walking can be difficult. The resort is about five kilometers from San Carlos. The hotel is expensive; $32.00 for a double. The rooms are in a cabin with a shared bath. The cabins are large, clean and sleep four. There is only a one tap shower in the room. The open balcony beach restaurant sits on a cliff overlooking the Pacific Ocean and catching the gentle breezes. The restaurant is similar to a movie scene from the 1940's; I almost lit up a cigarette while sitting there. It is beautiful. The white sandy beach below is made private by the surrounding cliffs.

SAN BLAS ISLANDS

These undeveloped paradise islands in the Caribbean are a must if you are in Panama. They are an archipelago of about 300 white sand covered islands that are inhabited and owned by the Cuna Indians. You will need a few days to visit the islands and a day or so leeway in the event that the plane or boat is unable to pick you up when you expected. This can happen because of bad weather or when a plane is not full. In that case, the pilots wait until they have enough cargo to justify the flight. They take you back on their return flight.

To get to the San Blas Islands, you can take a small plane to the island of Porvenir where a local will meet you in a cayuco and take you to a hotel on a different island. ANSA charges $50.00 to get you to the island and back. We did not have reservations when we got to Paitilla Airport in the center of the city, (taxi cost us $2.00) at 5:30AM, and the ANSA flight was fully booked. The mail plane gave us a ride. If you do not have a reservation, take a chance by showing up. You may be lucky. The price of the flight is the same no matter which plane you use. The return trip left us a bit uncomfortable because we were the only people (including natives) left on the island. The other travellers were picked up early but we sat and read our books for about four hours. Finally, a tiny mail plane from Columbia landed. This created problems with immigration when we arrived in Panama City but when the officials understood that we were from the San Blas instead of Columbia, they let us into the country we never officially left.

You may take a supply boat from Colon to the San Blas for $10.00 each way. The trip takes eight hours and goes twice a week. The days are different every week so a schedule is not available.

There are two hotels on the San Blas. **Hotel San Blas** costs $25.00 per person and includes everything but your alcohol and souvenirs. The bamboo stick huts have palm leaf thatching on the roof and some of the huts do not have a cement floor. The beds are basic and there is no electricity. The shower room is fully manual. You will get a five gallon drum with water that can be poured over yourself with a half coconut shell. The outhouses are comfortable little spots over the ocean that rock with the waves. The spectacular meals are served in a central bamboo hut. We had fresh baked buns and lobster on the first day. I thought I was in heaven. The rest of the meals were as good and the quantities were plentiful. The hotels will supply a man with a cayuco to take you to one of the other islands if you want to sun tan or purchase some molas made by the women. You may also go to an uninhabited island overnight and sleep in a hammock under the stars. This is safe (there are no snakes) and recommended.

The second hotel on the San Blas near Porvenir costs $40.00 per person per day with everything included except the beer and souvenirs. This hotel, the Posada Anai which means "friend", has private rooms with walls, real floors and ceilings. They have running water, private baths and a swimming pool full of crabs and lobster. If you want North American comfort, you will find it here. Both hotels offer the same services in regard to visiting other island.

When visiting the islands you will find the Cuna women wearing their beautiful molas, gold rings, long skirts, bright red and yellow head dresses and lots of beads around their necks, arms and ankles. These ladies are hospitable and friendly. You may take their pictures but you must pay 25¢ a picture.

The lives of the Cuna are simple. They live on tiny, palm fringed islands which are free from insects, animals or snakes. They have a perfect breeze-cooled temperature and clean, white sandy beaches.

Some women go to the mainland to wash clothes in the fresh water river. Men may go to the mainland to cultivate corn, yucca and coconuts or fish and trade with other islanders.

Many of the islands are uninhabited except for a caretaker who guards the coconut trees and their precious crops. No land is owned by the Indians but the coconut trees are. In this autonomous region, any disputes are settled within the village and each village has its congress hall where people make decisions. On the San Blas, the women have many rights including the right to own trees. They protect their rights passionately.

The Cuna women sell molas to the tourists and have incorporated modern designs into their work. I saw one mola that had

Mickey Mouse worked into the pattern. Molas are pieces of cloth that have been cut into designs and a reverse applique style is used to sew one piece of cloth onto the main piece. The molas sell for about $5.00 each. They make delightful cushion covers or pictures when you get home. Some people make them into placematts for their tables but I would hate to spill soup onto these beautiful pieces of art. Some ladies have designed T-shirts with molas and sell them to the tourist. The T-shirts are a bit more expensive.

Cuna Indian lady

Balboa Park	12	Ave. 29 de Agusto & 12 Calle Poniente at the Central Market	0.40
Barra de Santiago	285	Ahuachapan Terminal	5.00
Cerro Verde	248	Santa Ana Terminal	3.20
Cihuatan Ruins	125	East Terminal Get off 1 km. after Aguilares	2.90
Coatepeque Lake	220	Santa Ana Terminal	1.20
Cojutepeque	113	East Terminal	1.20
Costa del Sol Beach	495	West Terminal	2.50
Cuco Beach	320	San Miguel Terminal	3.30
Devil's Doorway	12	Ave.29 de Agosto & 12 Calle Poniente at the Central Market	0.65
El Poy	119	East Terminal	5.20
Garita Palmera	288 & 290	Ahuachapan Terminal	5.75
Guatemala Border	406 & 202	West Terminal	4.85
Izalco	205	West Terminal	2.60
La Hachadura	200 285 & 259	West Terminal Ahuachapan Terminal	4.70 7.50
La Libertad	287	Sonsonate Terminal Or Ave. 17 & Calle Ferrocarril in San. Sal.	4.30
La Palma	119	East Terminal	5.20
Las Chinamas	201 263	West Terminal Ahuachapan Terminal	2.40 3.95

465

La Union	304	East Terminal	9.00
	324	San Miguel Terminal	2.40
Llobasco	111	East Terminal	2.40
Llopango Lake	15	2 Ave Norte at the Plaza Morazan in front of the Salvadorian Bank	0.90
Los Chorros	79	13 Ave. Sur & Calle Ruben Dario	1.10
Los Cobanos Beach	257	Sonsonate Terminal	1.20
Metalio Beach	259	Sonsonate Terminal	2.50
Metrocentro	30	Calle Arce, between Ave. 11 & 13 North	0.40
Nahuizalco Handicraft Market	253	Sonsonate Terminal	1.80
National Handicraft Market	34	4 Calle Pte. beside Bolivar Park	0.40
Panchimalco	17	12 Calle Pte. at the Central Market (can go from Devil's doorway)	1.20
Paseo General Escalon	52	Alameda Juan Pablo, in front of the Parque Infantile	0.40
Playitas	418	La Union Terminal	1.20
Puerto La Libertad	102	4 Calle Potient beside Bolivar Park	1.80
Quelepa Ruins	326	San Miguel Terminal	3.30
San Andres Ruins	201 or 202	West Terminal	2.40
San Cristobal	236	Santa Ana Terminal	1.45
San Miguel	301	East Terminal	7.00

Santa Ana	201	West Terminal	2.40
Sonsonate	205	West Terminal	2.60
Tamarindo Beach	383	La Union Terminal	2.20
Tazumal Ruins	218	Santa Ana Terminal	0.70

FERRY

There is a small cargo boat crossing the Bay of Fonseca to Nicaragua on Mondays and Wednesdays and returning on Tuesdays and Thursdays. It leaves between 5:00 and 6:00 AM and will carry about 30 people, depending on its cargo.

CAR RENTALS

I do not recommend travelling by car in any Central American country. Travelling by bus provides more money to the local people, and it allows closer contact with the majority of the people. Buses are also a more environmentally efficient way to travel. If you really want to be noble, walk.

TAXI

Taxis are very expensive in El Salvador. To go from the center of town to Metrocentro, which is only 40 centavos on the bus, will cost ten to twenty colones by taxi. Going to or from the airport is automatically $20.US per person. That is very expensive and it is not negotiable.

TELEPHONE

The telephone office in El Salvador if Antel. You must go to an Antel office if you wish to phone anywhere other than Latin America or the US. Even then, depending on the mood of the hotel owner, you may have to go to the office to make a long distance call. You can not call collect station to station in El Salvador. For information, call 114. For the correct time, call 117. For wake up service, call 23-7777. For international telephone service, call 120 or 190.

AHUACHAPAN

Ahuachapan is a town of 83,000 people and is close to the Guatemalan border. The area is tucked in amongst many beautiful volcanos and one can really appreciate the richness of El Salvador from visiting this area. Because of the geothermal activity in these mountains, there is lots to see and do.

There are two **places to stay**; both are quite basic and cheap. The only decent restaurant is near the main highway. The possibility of mountain exploration brings the traveller to this area. Otherwise, it can be an excellent day trip from Santa Ana.

THINGS TO DO

A number of volcanos are in the area; **Los Naranjos** is one of the most famous. It sits at 1961 meters (6500 ft) and has a very well formed cone. It is currently dormant and is totally covered with coffee plantations.

Los Ranas Volcano is a bit larger than Naranjos by 50 meters. This volcano has a large crater with a lake. At present, you can not climb around these mountains. This will change in the near future as the memories of war dissappear and peace becomes a fact.

Los Ausoles Geothermal Plant can be reached by catching a truck from the truck stop past the market and across from the lottery stall. I think the lottery stall is actually a bingo parlor. The trucks leave when full but if it is mid-day, the trucks will be full. If you wish to visit the geothermal plant, you will have to get a permit from the S.E.L. Office in San Salvador; you may visit the area without a permit. The geothermal activity is above ground and the Salvadorians have harnessed this activity and transformed it into power. El Salvador is the only country in Central America which produces its own electricity.

Once at the site, you will have to show your passport, and then the guards will take you around the mountain. This will take about one hour. You will see hot springs too hot to stick your hand into. You will also see small geysers and geothermal activity. It is interesting and the military men are pleasant.

River Cauta Waterfall is about 20 kilometers from the townsite. Take a bus to Jujutla and get off three kilometers after the turn off for Apaneca. Take the road to the right towards the Finca Las Canoas and then, two turns before the entrance to the finca, follow that road. The waterfall cascades down the Mountain El Arco for forty meters into the rocky shores of the river Cauta. This is a very beautiful spot.

Tehuasilla Falls are reached by taking bus #293 from Ahuachapan to Canton los Toles which is nine kilometers west of the town. From Canton los Toles, walk one kilometer south towards the River El Molino, where you will see the falls. Walk over the suspension bridge which crosses the gorge of Tehuasilla and passes by a good place to photograph the 60 meter falls plunging into the rocky river bed. Because gringos are such a novelty, you may get a ride if you wish to hitch hike.

CONCHAGUA

This is a little village on the way to Cuco Beach. There is a bus stop here so you can get off, look around, spend an hour or so, and then catch the next bus to the beach. The church in Conchagua is unique in that it is small, old and one of the first churches ever built in this country.

As in most larger towns, there is a large and active military base here. At present, the men can be seen standing guard in the hills.

On the way into Conchagua, you cross high over the hills. The view of San Miguel Volcano gives you an idea of the enormity of the mountain. I could not find any guides to take me up the volcano. **Conchagua volcano** is 8.5 kilometers southeast of the town center and is 1243 meters (4100 ft) above sea level. It is another major extinct volcano in El Salvador. Centuries ago, the lava flow from this volcano solidified and formed part of the seacoast.

There are no places to stay in and no real restaurants in Conchagua but basic foods are available from the street vendors.

San Salvador

COSTA DEL SOL

This is a beach area which caters to the wealthy visitors. Take bus #495 from the western terminal in San Salvador. There is a government operated turicentro at Costa del Sol which has swimming pools, lovely clean beaches, snack bars, restaurants and souvenir shops. You can get rooms for the night here for about ¢35 ($4.US) per night. If you want to mix with the mucky mucks but stay within your price range, you may want to sleep here.

Izalco Cabañas are the cheapest rooms at ¢275 ($25. US) for a single; you must book in town at the Izalco travel bureau. Hotel Tesoro (the Hyatt) costs ¢920 ($115. US) per night (you may not like the rooms in this one) and then there is the cheaper Pacific Paradise for ¢200 ($25. US) per night. The beach is lovely but these prices are not for a chickenbuser.

EL CUCO BEACH

This is a long, six mile strip of beautiful, sandy, beach with calm waters and a few isolated, sandy, coves. If you want the sandy coves, walk north from the center of town, past the rocky outcrop. However, I can not say that you will find isolation anywhere in El Salvador. The village of Cuco is a little fishing town with quite a few comedors or eating spots in the center of town. The people of the village boast of having an Antel office, a pharmacy and a doctor. The people are poor and very friendly.

When choosing a place to stay, look for webbed mattresses rather than cotton or straw. Scorpions are abundant here and they seem to prefer cotton or straw mattresses. Be careful in the morning when putting on shoes and clothes; shake everything well. I saw more than one scorpion during my stay here.

PLACES TO STAY

Hotel Los Leones Marinos costs ¢50 ($6.25 US) per person. The rooms are adequate and have bathrooms but no fan, making the rooms somewhat stuffy at night. These rooms have the webbed beds. The owners are great and the hotel is extremely quiet at night. You can sit in the large treed yard and have a drink. You can also rent these rooms for the day at a much cheaper rate.

San Miguel Hospadaje Anexo Model is at the highway out of the center. Not bad if you want to be near the highway, but I prefer to be near the center where the restaurants are nearby.

Motel Palmera is next door to Los Leones and costs ¢70 ($8.75 US) with a private bath and oldfashioned cement urinals along one wall. This place is not quite as clean as Leones, but it is nice enough. However, the price is high for what you get. There are water taps in the yard; the locals spend hours playing here rather than swimming in the sea.

Cucolinda is one kilometer from the town center which is a long walk after supper, in the dark. There are no street lights in this town. There is no comedor at the hotel. The rooms are basic with very lumpy beds, but there is a wonderful wooden balcony where one can feel the ocean breeze. The lady wanted ¢40 ($5. US) per person, but she will barter. If the town is crowded, you will have to pay her price.

Tropico Club is down the beach about three kilometers and the cost is ¢150 - ¢200 per night ($20. - $25. US). Of course you get more amenities here than in town. If you are walking the beach visit the Tropico, enjoy a cool beer and then head back into town. I don't recommend the restaurant at the Tropico because of the high prices.

RESTAURANTS

There are numerous comedors around the center of town where you can eat. The food and the prices are good. The cost is ¢12 - 15 ($1.50 - $2. US) for a chicken or fish dinner. The portions are not exceptionally big but the service is good and the people are really friendly. In this village, I spent more time talking to local women about women's issues than anywhere else in El Salvador. The women are interested and outspoken on current social issues.

LA LIBERTAD

This is a lovely little resort town and port. It has the best sea food I have ever tasted anywhere in the world. It also has quiet little hotels, great black sandy beaches and super surf. It is friendly and safe. The movie "Salvador" was set at this beach but filmed in Guatemala.

If you want to visit some of the other beaches close to La Libertad, take bus #187 eastbound to San Diego or walk the five kilometers. Beaches to the west are El Obispo, La Paz, Conchalio, El Zunzal and El Zonte; these are known for their great surfing conditions. Take bus # 287 to get to the westbound beaches of Mizata and Sihuapilapa. The first few beaches to the west are only about five or six kilometers apart and you may walk along the shore which is more pleasant than taking a bus.

La Libertad Turicentro was built in 1977 has everything from swimming pools to restaurants to kiosks to souvenir shops. This is truly a tourist center.

PLACES TO STAY

Pension San Miguel is one of the cheaper places in town and is very basic. It is just off the main street. There are no showers.

Riche is also just off the main street but closer to the town center. It is fairly clean and, although not really cheap, it has a pleasant atmosphere.

La Posada de Don Lito costs ¢160 ($20. US) per night. There is a restaurant on premises.

El Malecon de Don Lito is at Playa La Paz and costs ¢75 ($8.80 US) per night for one and ¢90 ($11. US) for two. This is a good buy as you get private bath; plus, it is clean and quiet.

Hotel Conchalio at Conchalio beach costs ¢80 ($10. US) per person. It has 22 rooms in all. The other hotel in Conchalio is the Los Arcos which costs about $20 per night for a room. That is a bit high, but you are getting the pleasure (?) of a resort.

San Diego beach has both medium range and cheaper hotels and is a nice place to stay. It has been recommended by many.

RESTAURANTS

The Mariscos is a wonderful and popular restaurant right on the beach at the west end of town. This is where I enjoyed the most spectacular shrimp dinner in my whole life. If you go to El Salvador for no other reason than to have this dinner, you will not be sorry. I would suggest you eat all your food here but that may only help promote your gout!!

There are many small tiendas in town and sea food is the specialty.

THINGS TO DO

Other than relaxing on the closest beach, you could walk to so other beaches close by. The shore can be a bit rocky and in some places there are cliffs, so watch the tide. Otherwise veg-out and have a good rest.

Falls and Cave of the Mangos is close to La Libertad. Take the road towards Motel Siboney near kilometer 29, turn left and walk for 2 kilometers until you come to the River San Antonio. Walk down river to the 50 meter water fall which has a cave beside it. Eventually this river will flow into the Pacific Ocean close to San Diego beach. You can make a circle route by returning along the shore. To do the circle takes a whole day.

LA PALMA

This is a little village you will pass through if coming from Nuevo Ocotepeque, Honduras and El Poy. The people in this village are noted for their wood carvings. They produce carvings of people, trees, houses and animals of microscopic size, all hand carved and hand painted. The carvings are truly a delicate work of art. There is a basic hospedaje which offers overnight accommodations.

LA UNION

This is a lovely little town on the Bay of Fonseca. The people are friendly, the sites are interesting things and there is a great hotel. What more could you want? If you are commuting to Tamarindo (which is preferable to staying there) this makes a delightful home base.

There is a military base in La Union and a lot of military presence. At the time of writing, the military has not bothered travellers.

There is a small **cargo boat that goes to Nicaragua** on Mondays and Wednesdays and returns Tuesdays and Thursdays. Depending on the amount of cargo, the boat can usually take about 30 people. It leaves between 5:00AM and 6:00AM. Be there early.

PLACES TO STAY

Casa de Huespedes has large, fairly clean rooms, with fan, desk and mirror but no bath for ¢30 (3.75 US) per room. It is quiet and friendly. It is owned by Hondurans and is recommended. You will feel welcome, and they will give you any information you may wish.

RESTAURANTS

El Asador is just a couple of blocks from Casa de Huespedes in the direction of the docks. It is an excellent place to eat and always offers lobster, shrimp or fish cooked to your specifications. The most expensive meal on the menu is lobster served with salad, rice and cheese pupusas for ¢40 ($5. US).

THINGS TO DO

Playa Tamarindo is about one hour from La Union on bus number 383. This is a delightful beach where you can enjoy eating seafood, talking to the locals and walking. There is a nice hike along the rocky coves, over a few cliff edges and across beautiful sandy beaches to Las Tunas near the highway. You will pass many small settlements where you can visit and eat, purchase pop but not mineral water. This walk which is about five miles should take about two to three hours depending on how often you stop to swim and play. I loved the walk and spent most of a day.

Meanguera Island is situated off the coast. This is where Andres Niño and Gil Gonzalez Davila first landed in 1519, being the first Spaniards to arrive on Salvadorian soil. Five years passed before Alvarado actually came to El Salvador and caused some trouble.

There is one **place to stay** in Tamarindo but it is sub-basic. with no lights, lots of spaces in the walls for bugs to enter the room, no windows, no paint and all for only ¢10 ($1.20 US). I never even bothered checking out the bathroom.

However, there are comedors with good food and lots of friendly kids who will try to convince you that your size 10 runners will fit their size three feet.

Las Playitas is another little beach just out of La Union but there is no place to stay. Wait until the next time you come to El

Salvador to visit this beach. If you really must go there, take bus 418
from La Union.

METAPAN

This is a pleasant little town close to the border of
Guatemala and Honduras. The town itself is somewhat grubby and
dusty, but the people are a real treat after Honduras. Metapan is only
one and a half hours from Santa Ana, and if it is before 6:30PM when
you arrive, you may still be able to get to Santa Ana. However, if not,
you will not be disappointed with this little town.

PLACES TO STAY

Hospadaje Central is the only place in town to stay and the
cost is ¢30 ($3.75 US) per person per night without bath. Basic but
clean enough. As for places to eat, I would suggest just looking
around. There is nothing outstanding in this little town. I only saw
one restaurant; you may prefer a comedor.

THINGS TO DO

The Colonial Church in the city is called La Parroquia; construction started in 1700 but was not completed until 1743. This church
is unique because most colonial churches are built low to the ground to
outlive numerous earthquakes. But this spectacular church is tall and
almost daring the gods to destroy it. Inside the church are nine altars,
some with statues of the Virgin of Guatelupe, San Sebastian and Joseph.
The main altar is covered in silver from the local mines.

Iglesia del Carvallo is the other church in town; it is the
Indian church. It has a Black Christ inside. This statue is very similar
to the one in Esquipulas, Guatemala.

Montecristo Cloud Forest and Park is the main reason you
would visit this area. Once you reach the forest, you will have to take
a guide with you to visit the park. Take a bus from the bus stop in
Metapan for the park which is 14 kilometers from Metapan, in the
direction of Honduras and Guatemala. The point where the three
countries meet is called "el Trifinio". This point, which is in the park
is at the peak of the Montecristo mountain which stands 2100 meters
(6900 ft) above sea level.

The park was established in 1971 and covers 1972 hectares.
The park was established to harness the Rio San Josè which was constantly flooding the town of Metapan. The huge tree plantations help
prevent erosion.

Not only is Montecristo mountain in the park but so are El
Brujo and Miramundo. The park has 2000 mm of rain every year
which causes a tremendous amount of humidity. There is a constant
cloud cover at night. The average temperature is between 10º and
15ºC. This cooler temperature is a relief from the heat of the low-
land and coast.

The forest is mostly pine, oak and ceder trees; the underbrush is composed of orchids, ferns, mushrooms and moss which grow abundantly. Some of the ferns grow as high as eight meters (25 ft).

Several small animals live in the park; the deer is the most dangerous. Monkeys are numberous. Of the rarer birds, the Elliot hummingbird and the Quetzal are said to be here.

Lake Guija is just south of Metapan. If you are interested in the petroglyphs around the lake, you must take a bus for Igualtepec. This is the little peninsula on the lake. There are many petroglyphs all around this peninsula. You just walk and look. The island of Azacualpa Teotipa, on the lake, has a few ruins from the Indians who lived there before the Spanish.

The lake itself was formed when an eruption of San Diego volcano blocked off the river. This volcano is at the south east corner of the lake and is covered with vegetation. The lake is fairly large; 44 square kilometers with a depth of 20 meters.

SAN MIGUEL

This is a bustling town of 184,000 people. It is quite clean once you move away from the main market area. The people are friendly but not as friendly as in other areas of El Salvador. Because this area was the scene of much fighting before the peace settlement, tourist attractions have not been developed.

The climate here is quite hot so you don't need hot water showers.

The area between the church on the square and the market is the red light district with many "by the hour" places to stay.

Volcano San Miguel makes a wonderful backdrop to the city. This is a photographer's delight.

PLACES TO STAY

Hotel San Rafael is on 6 Calle Oriente #614 and is one block past the market and bus terminal. There are large, clean rooms with bathrooms and one-tap showers. The cost is ₡40 ($5. US) per room. The hotel is quiet with a private parking lot. There is a sitting room with a TV for those wanting to improve Spanish through listening to a television. There is also a small comedor at the hotel which sells simple meals from 6:00AM to 8:00PM.

Hotel Santa Rosa is on a side street before the bus terminal; it is a delightful family-run place. The owner only has 6 rooms and will only give you a room if he likes your looks. He speaks perfect English and can give you tourist information. The rooms run at ₡35 ($4.25 US) for a room without bath and ₡40 with a bath ($5. US). This would definitely be my first choice if I was to stay in San Miguel.

El Molita is on a side street across from the bus terminal. This is an enclosed building and is a bit grubbier than the other two. The rooms cost ₡35 ($4.25 US) per person, but it is small and quiet.

Hotel China House is on the highway just a block from the main road going to the center of San Miguel. It is a nice place with a restaurant on the premises. The cost is ¢60 ($7.50 US) per person with bathroom. It is okay but you must get a room off the highway because the trucks start roaring early in the morning.

RESTAURANTS

There are no outstanding restaurants in San Miguel. I stayed a few days and was glad to get to the beach where the food was better. The fresh fruit juice stands that are popular throughout Central America are abundant in San Miguel.

THINGS TO DO

Central Park in San Miguel is not exceptional. Places to change money, the telephone office and of course the usual church are here. The church is quite basic but again, this has been a stronghold for the guerrillas and the art treasures may be hidden for safekeeping. The name of the church, Nuestra Señora de la Paz, is in honor of the patron saint of San Miguel.

Playa El Cuco is popular because it is one of the nicest beaches in El Salvador. The beach is clean, but the town is a bit grubby. The El Cuco women are very interested in women's issues such as birth control, abortion, child support and education. Learn to recognize some of these words in Spanish, and you will hear some great stories from these women as they wash their clothes and entertain the gringo. See "El Cuco" for more information.

Quelepa are the ruins found on the mountain of San Miguel. The site is less than half an hour by bus from the town of San Miguel. The remains of a Pre-Columbian city are in a six kilometer area on the north slope of the mountain. At the time of writing, there are no guides to take you to Quelepa and then up the mountain to the crater. I would not suggest going up alone. With the peace settlements, conditions will change rapidly and guides may be available in the future. If you enquire at the ruins, you may be able to find someone to take you up the mountain.

San Miguel Volcano or Chaparrastique volcano When I was in San Miguel looking for a guide to go up the mountain, the people told me to talk to the people in El Cuco. But when I was in El Cuco, the people told me to talk to those in San Miguel. The best place to get information is at Quelepa. The mountain itself still has some bare volcanic slopes where vegetation is not growing. This is difficult walking unless you have heavy hiking boots. Runners get cut on the sharp rock edges. I did not climb this volcano. However, if you take the bus along the Panamerican highway, you will pass some of the lava flows coming off this mountain.

San Miguel is a compound volcano with one of the most impressive cones in all of Central America. The volcano stands away from the Chinameca range and dominates a flat valley which emphasizes its majesty. The mountain is 2130 meters (7000 ft) high with a crater that is 900 meters (300 ft) wide and 344 meters (100 ft) deep. The chimney has vertical walls surrounding the crater. From time to time, there are puffs of smoke and clouds of dust from the still active crater. On the southwest flank are some lava flows which were formed during the 1819 and 1835 eruptions. The recorded eruptions were in 1699, 1762, 1798, 1811, 1819, 1835, 1844, 1868, 1919, 1920, 1924, 1930, 1931, 1939, 1954, and 1965. If these dates are accurate, the volcano seems to be increasing its activity.

Morazan Caves are about two hours from San Miguel; I am uncertain whether you can visit them. You must take a bus from San Miguel to San Francisco Gotera and then another bus to Corinto. Once in Corinto, you must take the road heading north for one kilometer. The actual caves are situated on a large flat plain. The two caves lead into the Espiritu Santo or the "Saint's spirit" and Cabeza de Duende or "head of the goblin" hills. The "saint's spirit" is 36 meters long, 16 meters high and 7 meters wide. Inside the caves are wall paintings which are supposedly about 10,000 years old. Be certain to have a flash light. I did not actually visit these caves.

Lake Olamega turnoff is about halfway between La Union and San Miguel. The walk to the lake is about seven or eight kilometers. The lake is the fifth largest in El Salvador and is noted for its good fishing. There are no places to eat or to stay overnight. Take food or a picnic lunch. This is an area recommended for bird watching. This is a great place to escape crowds.

San Miguel Carnival takes place on the 20th and 21st of November and is a must if you are in the area. Known as the "Eastern Sultan", San Miguel entertains with rich Arabic flare. During the carnival, there are traditional dances, modern balls, singing, fireworks, go-cart and motorcycles races, street carnival games and lots and lots of food. The Salvadorians truly know how to celebrate. The festivities are in honor of the Virgin of Peace.

Altos de la Cueva can be walked to from San Miguel. It is a turicenter run by the Salvadorian government. If riding, take city bus number 60 in San Miguel. Once at the turicenter, there are swimming pools for both children and adults. This is a treat given the heat of the area. There are nicely kept gardens, restaurants and many small stalls from which to purchase food and drinks. Rooms cost ¢10 ($1.25US) for day use but they are not for overnight accomodations. There is a small entrance fee. This is really a nice place to relax for a few hours.

SANTA ROSA DE LIMA

This is your counterpart to Nacaome on the other side of the border in Honduras; a grubby, hot little border town. I did not find anything really attractive here. If you are late and need a place to stay, then stay at the **Hotel Florida** for ¢40 ($5. US). There are a few other places in town but ... It is only another hour to San Miguel, so if it is before 7:00PM then by all means make the effort to get to San Miguel.

SAN SALVADOR

The capital of El Salvador has changed in the last few years. The war is over, buildings are being repaired, and people want to get on with living, not with hating. There are wonderful restaurants, nice places to stay that are close to town and many tourist attractions for the visitor. The night life surpasses that of any other city in Central America.

When you arrive, your bus will stop at either the east or west terminal, depending where you are coming from. A taxi will cost about ¢15 ($2. US) to the center of town, a small pick up truck will cost about half of that and a local bus will cost 40 centavos. To catch a local bus, go out onto the main street. Buses 3, 7 and 9 all go to the center.

When in the center, the places below Hula Hula square are very rough; I do not advise staying in that section. The lower section is the red light district and has many pickpockets and daytime robbers. At night this area would be pretty rough. Even the locals avoid this section. Go up the hill (east) from the square.

One hotel in the poorer section of town which had rooms for ¢10 per person was so bad that I did not think the hotel would remain standing long enough for me to leave it. I checked out many other places in town, but they charged by the hour and I have not listed them here either. My first choice is the Family Guest House, then the American or the San Carlos. I have given phone numbers so you can make reservation. When in a big city, I always suggest spending a few more cents on accommodations. Hotels listed below which do not have special comments are those I did not stay in or did not check them very thoroughly.

PLACES TO STAY

Family Guest House on 1 Calle Poniente #925 (around the corner from the American) is excellent. It is much brighter and cleaner than the American and has a large, pleasant sitting room in the center. Meals can be included. The price is ¢50 ($6.25 US) for a single without bath, ¢80 ($10. US) for a single with bath. There is a laundry service. This is really a large, old house with rooms situated all around the building. I had one room in the back behind the kitchen, and except for the buzzer used to call the boys, there was very little noise. The owner speaks excellent English. Phone 22-1902

American Guest House Anexo on 17 Ave. Norte #116 costs
¢100 ($12.50 US) for two with private bath and ¢85 ($10.50 US) for a
single. This price includes some meals, but not the main meal of the
day. The rooms are fairly large and pleasant. There is also a restaurant at the house. Phone 71-5613

San Carlos on Calle Concepcion #121 is still in business and
now costs about ¢40 ($5. US) per person; this includes hot water and
a private bathroom. The owner speaks English and his wife knows
everything going on in town. They make a great combination for the
traveller needing information. Definitely a goodie if you can't get a
room in the Family Guest House. Phone 22-4808

Florida Guest House is on Los Almendros and Los Heroes
#115 and the rooms cost ¢60 ($7.50 US) per person or ¢100 ($12.50
US) for two. There are 11 rooms but this great house is a bit away
from the center. However, bus service is very good in San Salvador.
Phone 26-1858

Hospadaje Izalco on Calle Concepcion #66 on the other
side of the street from the San Carlos; it costs ¢42 ($5.25 US) with
bath. This is a large building with small rooms. Phone 22-2613

Hotel Imperial on Calle Concepcion #659 costs ¢25 ($3.
US) per person without bath. There are 26 rooms. Phone 22-4920

Hotel Leon is a hotel the locals will often recommend. It is
not too bad and is on Calle Delgado #621. The cost is ¢30 ($3.75 US)
without a bathroom. Phone 22-0951

Hotel Ritz Continental is upper class, costing $22 US per
single room and $28 for a double. There is a private bath, excellent
room service, friendly staff, toilet paper, clean towels, and soap that
lathers. It is close to the center on 7 Ave. Sur #219. There is also a
restaurant with good meals and it opens at 6:00AM. Phone 22-0033

Hotel Panamericano is also close to the center on 8 Ave. Sur,
#113 and costs only ¢35 ($4.25 US) per person. This is not too bad,
but I have no phone number.

RESTAURANTS

Camino Real on the Boulevar Los Heroes is not a place to
stay as the rooms run around $100. US dollars for a single nor is the
atmosphere such that you would want to have a meal there. However,
the hotel does serve as a landmark for some of the best restaurants in
town which are on the street behind the Camino Real. The journalists hang out in these restaurants so if you need news information,
then try these places out. The prices are expensive but the atmosphere is excellent.

Metro Centro can be reached by taking bus number 29 or
30. This will put you across the street from the Camino Real. The
Metro Centro has an open air restaurant with many small food stalls
serving anything from excellent French pastry to Chinese food but
unfortunately, the food is served in styrofoam dishes (the only draw-

back). The food is not expensive. The restaurant is a great place to sit and read or write.

Zona Rosa is a delightful area which is a must to visit. To get there, take bus #34 to the David Guzman Museum. Walk up Ave. La Revolucion, past the museum and up the hill. When you come to the first street going to the right, follow it until you find a restaurant that suits your fancy. Because there are so many places along this strip, you can't go wrong.

Pollo Campero is a franchise which is actually quite good. It certainly has run some "Kentucky Fried Chicken" restaurants out of business. The food and service are good, and the place is always packed. These restaurants can be found all over town.

MacDonalds is here because the Americans invested here even prior to the war. If you are desperate.... They do serve good coffee, which is difficult to get in Latin America.

Actoteatro on 1 Calle Poniente has a wonderful patio in which to sit and listen to local music. This is the restaurant that is noted for its pupusas and other typical Salvadorian foods. Pupusas are the national dish which consists of a wheat tortilla stuffed with cheese or spiced meats. They are excellent tasting.

Hotel Ritz Continental on 7 Ave. South, #219 is a great place for breakfast. I like these old, British-style quiet restaurants for my coffee in the morning. The pancakes are great too.

Family Guest House has a restaurant section, but I do not recommend it as the prices are high and the portions are low. I had a chicken dinner that cost ¢20 ($2.50 US) and it only included one small piece of chicken. I ordered one more small piece of chicken and the second piece cost an additional ¢12 ($1.50 US) and I was still hungry when I left the table. This is much too expensive.

THINGS TO DO

Because El Salvador is so small, it is almost possible to do a day trip to anywhere in the country. So, if you like the capital, you may use it as a base. However, I also like staying in Santa Ana and La Union. It is easier to tour those areas if staying in those cities.

The city of San Salvador is built in the shape of a cross; the National Palace is the center. Ave. España runs north, Ave. Cuscutlàn runs south, Calle Arce runs west and Calle Delgado goes east. After orienting yourself to the cross, all calles going north are odd numbered, and all calles going south are even numbered. The avenues going east are odd numbered and the avenues going west are even numbered. Easy eh?

August Festivities take place in San Salvador from August 1st to August 6th with the 5th being the most solemn day. The celebration is in honor of the patron saint "The Savior of the World". This is a time when the people are reminded of the resurrection of Christ.

During the festivities, there are dances, balls, fireworks and parades complete with beauty-queen contests.

National Palace is on the main square and is a beautiful building which houses the government office. At present, repairs are in process and entrance is restricted.

The Cathedral is next to the Palace and is another huge, beautiful building which was under construction when I was there. This is the building where more than 20 people were shot down by armed government police during the 1979 anti-government demonstrations. They were fleeing from the police and looking for shelter in the church, but many never quite made it to safety.

The National Theatre is a spectacular building which has more than one theatre room. The largest will hold 700 people. On the walls are beautiful murals painted by Salvadorian Carlos Canas. The woodwork, the crystal chandeliers and the marble floors are wonderful. This theatre is as beautiful as that in San Josè, Costa Rica and I believe it also has more gold leaf than the theatre in San Josè. If you have the opportunity to attend a concert, do!

Plaza Libertad is a great square with the church of El Rosario on one side. This modern church has stained glass windows which angle in to modern wood altars. The altars act as the separating line between the windows and the floor. The tomb of Father Delgado, the leader of independence for Central America, is in this church. On the south side of the square is a monument built to the memory of Father Delgado and others who helped in the 1811 rebellion for independence.

La Merced Church is on Ave. 10 and Calle Modelo. The church houses the bell which Father Delgado rang. In August, 1810, a group of men met and organized so that they could liberate the area from Spanish rule. Father Josè Matìas Delgado was the leader of the group. On November 5th, 1811, just before dawn, a tremendous sound came from La Merced Church. Father Delgado was clanging the bells. He proclaimed the "first cry for independence" with this ringing. The original revolt was stifled by a Spaniard called Josè Maria Peinado. The fight for independence continued until September 15, 1821, when the Act of Independence was signed in the National Palace in Guatemala City.

The Mercado Cuartel is found along Calle Delgado, a few blocks east of the Cathedral. This is the handicraft and non-food market. It is a delight to visit. Everything from anywhere in El Salvador is here. The colors used in the handicrafts are exquisite. This is a must for souvenirs. Bartering is a custom and is expected. The colors of this market are reminiscent of Guatemala's markets.

The Central Market is a different story from the Mercado Cuartel. It is noisy, crowded, dirty and a bustle of humanity. However, you can get almost anything that you need in the way of food. I love visiting markets for the opportunity of talking with the women and watching the activities of the people. However, be careful of pick-pockets in this market.

Tourist Office is on 8 Calle and Ave. 9-11. The people in the office are very helpful. Many speak English. There are some rather inadequate maps available for free. Unfortunately, their information about the country is outdated. Many places that they recommend are closed or blown up. Some of the natural sites of beauty are so full of garbage, I would not recommend it to my worst enemy. More information if available through reading this book.

Libreria & Revistos El Quijote on Calle Arce #708 has some English books. The owner is willing to buy or trade books. This store has more English books than anywhere else in San Salvador but that is not really saying much.

El Centro Textiles on 2 Calle Poniente and Ave. Morazan #130 has the best prices I could find for towels. Other than the hand-painted wooden objects, the typical Salvadorian towels are about the best product to take back to your country. This store will give you quite a deal if you purchase a dozen or more towels. This would be a good idea if you got a couple of people together and bought. For example, if you buy one large beach towel you will pay ¢102 ($11.50 US) but if you buy a dozen you only pay ¢80 ($10. US) each. The quality of Salvadorian towels is exceptional and they are much cheaper than in Guatemala. The only thing is you must pack them.

El Salvador del Mundo is on Alamedo Roosevelt. It is the famous statue associated with El Salvador. This huge statue features Christ on top of the world; it sits in a small square in the center of the street. You can take bus #7 to get to this statue. Christ is the patron saint of the city.

David Guzman Museum is on Ave. La Revolucion and you can take bus #34 at the south end of the main square in town. Except Monday, the museum is open every day from 9:00AM to 12:00 and 2:00PM to 5:00PM. Although the museum is not large, it is well planned. You walk through time, beginning with the first native migrations until you reach the coming of the Spanish and modern day. Because of how it is laid out, you don't have to run back and forth across a room so you won't miss anything. Only very large, distinct pieces are placed in the center of the room. Some of the Pre-Columbian pieces date back to 1500BC. There are sculptures from many parts of Salvador. The most famous are the stelae of Tazumal, the Chac-mool of Chalchuapa and the solar disc from Ahuachapan. These can be photographed.

The museum was built in 1885 by President Rafael Zaldivar and was dedicated to David Guzman, the first director of the museum. He died in 1927.

The Fair Grounds and the Artisans Market are below the David Guzman Museum. The fair grounds are not open often, but they do have a fair once every two years for all the Central American countries. The Artisans Market is not large, but you can view and buy quality art work by Salvadorian artists. The wood carvings, used for things like alphabet letters for children's rooms, key hangers, napkin holders, and salt and pepper shakers, are delightfully decorated with tiny, colorful figures depicting Salvadorian life. There are also many tiny, tiny statuettes that show life in this little country. These miniature figurines are exquisitely made in fine detail with eyes and eye lashes visible on some. They stand no bigger than an inch high and the platform is never bigger than two inches. Even if you don't want to purchase, be certain to stop and look. You may be able to buy some of these carvings for a lower price in town but the quality may not be as good.

There is a busy cafeteria on the grounds, but I recommend going past the museum to some of the nicer restaurants in the Zona Rosa area.

The Zoo is on Calle Modelo. You can walk the two kilometers from the town square, or you can take bus #2 on Cuscatlan Ave. on the west side of the cathedral. The zoo can also be visited on your way back from Panchimalco. It is open every day except Monday and Tuesday from 9:00AM to 5:00PM. It was built in 1953 on 17 acres of land which now houses 650 animals. Although I believe this does not give the animals much space, Salvadorians will argue this point. However, they have tried to create environments similar to the animal's own natural habitat. There is a small entrance fee.

Saburo Hirao Park and Museum of Natural History is on Calle Viveros and Colonial Nicaragua. The museum is open from 9:30 AM to 4:30PM and is closed on Monday and Tuesday. You can take bus #2 on 4 Ave. South to get there. Get off at Colonia Minerva, one stop before the bridge, and then walk the one kilometer through the park to the museum. It is a pleasant walk. The park was built in memory of Mr. Saburo Hirao, a Japanese philanthropist who left the grounds for a park for the youth of El Salvador. There are 19 acres of botanical gardens, children's park and playground facilities.

The museum is at the south end of the park and was built in 1976. It has ten sections which feature rocks, animals, flowers and fossils. This makes a nice trip.

San Jacinto Cable Car and amusement park was blown up by the guerillas in 1989. Perhaps it will be repaired in the near future. The amusement park was a beautiful place for concerts, festivals or quiet meals. Today, the cables and the buildings are still standing. The hill itself is 1100 meters high; the Indian name for it is Amatepec.

La Laguna Botanical Gardens can be reached by taking bus #101 on 11 Ave. south and Calle Ruben Dario. Get off at the stop after the Basilica of Guadalupe. The gardens are open Tuesday to Friday from 10:00AM to 5:00PM, and there is an entrance fee.

These gardens are located in the crater of an extinct volcano. For more than a century, three generations of people have devoted themselves to making these gardens. They have planted thousands of local and foreign trees which serve as windbreakers and allow the formation of underground water deposits.

For hundreds of years, a small lagoon existed in the crater, 800 meters (2600 feet) above sea level. During the 18th century, a small eruption changed the lake into a swamp making it possible for plants to grow. There are pieces of lava scattered around the gardens.

Balboa Park is a must if you are in the capital for more than a day. This trip can include the park, Los Planes lookout point, the Devil's Doorway and Panchimalco. To get to the park, take bus #12 which has "mil Cumbres" on it. This bus is on the east side of the Market on Ave. 29 de Agosto and 12 Calle. Wear good shoes for this trip as you will be doing some rock hopping and climbing.

The park is in Los Planes de Renderos which is 12 kilometers from the city. You start at 972 meters (3200 feet) above sea level and hike up. The park is the first turicentro built by the government and is on 70 acres of land. It is a delightful area which is kept clean and quiet. There are tiendas and small restaurants where you can buy food and drink. You can sit on the stone benches and listen to the birds or look for the sloth that is supposed to be here. Sculptures of ancient gods and local heros are scattered throughout the park.

The Los Planes lookout point is on the road going towards Panchimalco. There is a wonderful panoramic view of San Salvador and the San Jacinto Mountain. In the other direction is beautiful Llopango Lake.

Continuing along up the road, look for the **Pupuseria Los Nebinas** which has excellent food, good prices and friendly folks. If you want to stay in the area for more than a month, they may be able to find you a room. This is an excellent place to rest.

The Devil's Doorway is actually two huge rocks located on the edge of a precipice which cuts the mountain and looks like a huge doorway to the valley below. At one time, these rocks were joined into one, but an earthquake probably shook them apart, forming the Devil's Doorway. It is located on the summit of Chulo Hill and sits 1000 meters (3300 ft.) above sea level. To get to the top of the doorway, you can go up the stone steps to 1131 meters (3700 ft). From there you can see Llopango Lake, San Vicente Volcano which is extremely photogenic from this side, and then the Pacific Ocean.

If you walk the other way, down the stone steps from the road, you will come to the acoustic rock. This would be a great place to have a rock concert. The entire valley could be entertained for a few volts of electricity. Listen to your voice while under the rock.

Panchimalco is a little Indian village below the Devil's Doorway. To get there you can take bus #17P from the park entrance or from the center of San Salvador. It is a nice trip into the valley. The Colonial church is over 400 years old, and the great cieba tree in the courtyard is believed to have been planted at the same time as the church was built. Panchimalco is a quiet little town with cobblestone streets and red tiled adobe houses. The ladies in this area weave panuelas (fancy head scarves) which are popular with the tourists. These people are direct descendents of the original Nahua speaking Pipil Indians who, years ago met Alvarado.

The **Palm Festival** occurs in Panchimalco from May 1st to the 7th. It is a celebration dating from the Pre-Columbian times. This festival is celebrated with a colorful exhibition dance called the "Dance of the Flowers" where Indian girls offer flowers to the Blessed Virgin Mary. This dance is accompanied by traditional Indian pipe music. This is a must to see if in the area at that time.

The people are very friendly. There are a few places to eat and buses come and go every hour. Be certain to visit.

Lake Llopango can be reached by taking bus #15 on 2 Ave. Norte by the Banco de Salvadoreño. This volcanic lake is believed to have been formed in the 2nd century. At the time of the eruptions, white dust like particles were hurled into the air and fell to the ground in layers up to 50 meters thick in places. This caused the people of the area to move away, some as far as Guatemala and Mexico. This lake is similar in origin to Lake Coatepeque. The last eruptions in the lake were between January and May, 1880, when small volcanic islands were formed. They are called Cerros Quemados which means "burnt hills". There are also two older islands on the lake called Los Patos and Portillon.

At the lake is a turicentro which makes it very attractive and worthwhile to stay overnight. The lake itself is larger than Atitlan in Guatemala, being 72 kilometers square with a width of 11 kilometers. The depth does not exceed 250 meters. You can rent boats to explore the lake.

Hotel Familiar can be reached by walking through the town or by going to the turicentro and then walking back along the beach. The rooms are ¢25 ($3. US) per person; they are clean but without private bathrooms. The **rooms at the turicentro** are the same price, but not nearly as nice.

There are many places to eat and the hotel has a restaurant. The turicentro has nice restaurants which serve excellent food. Never the less, I like eating from the little stalls owned by the local people.

Los Chorros can be reached by taking bus # 79 on 13 Ave. South and Calle Ruben Dario. Los Chorros is a delightful turicentro. Some of you may not like turicentros but I do because they are clean. This center is located 18 kilometers from the capital and was built in 1952. A series of waterfalls cascade from the side of the mountain and pour down into four man-made pools. The first one is for kids and is to be avoided while the other three are for "real" people. You can stroll along some lovely trails which head off towards the hills. The gardens are also nicely kept. Overall, it is refreshing to be in this area. There are also many food stands and a few government-run restaurants.

Joya de Ceren is an archaeological site discovered in 1967. It is eight kilometers outside the village of San Juan Opico. The village was buried under volcanic ash; the findings are comparable to Pompeii in Italy. Before you can go to the site, you must get a pass from the Cultural Patrimony at the government offices in San Salvador. This ruin is very important as it shows how the common man (you and me) lived many years ago. We always get a picture of the elite, but seldom of the rest.

It is believed that when the Llopango volcano erupted in 260AD, it formed the lake and covered a vast area with ash. Part of this area was this village at Joya de Ceren. But that eruption only left about 6 feet of ash on the ground. It took about 400 years for the area to be resettled. Then just after the resettlement occurred the Laguna Caldera volcano erupted and buried the area again. This time about 16 feet of hot ash covered the area. Because of the intense heat, the living matter in the area was instantly carbonized and preserved. When all had settled, the village was buried under about 20 feet of volcanic matter.

A bulldozer was digging ground in the area for the purpose of constructing silos. It uncovered an ancient Maya farmhouse. Inside the farmhouse were bodies and pottery vessels. The find was reported and excavation was proposed. However, the first excavations did not occur until 1976 and the bodies had disappeared. The excavations were under the direction of Dr. Payton Sheets from the University of Colorado.

In the pantry of the farmhouse, Dr. Sheets found vessels which contained beans. He also found a stone maul, pottery smoothers and paint. Some of these vessels were from as far away as Copan.

Away from the main house was another outbuilding with a fired clay platform and a palm thatched roof. Because of the number of obsidian pieces it is believed this is where stone tools were made and sold.

After more excavations in 1989, experts concluded the style of living of those times probably surpasses that of the peasants in the same area today. The excavation of the surrounding cornfields made Shields believe the volcanic eruption occured in June as the growth of the corn indicated it was near harvesting. Due to well constructed houses, the people were dry during rainy season and the houses were not crowded as they are today. The people had flowers, cooking pots, digging sticks, pestles and mortars, metates and grinding stones, and sharp knives. As well, a book was found tucked away in a small cubby-hole. This book was found in a peasant's home. Usually, any sophisticated writing found is in a wealthy person's tomb.

This is one of the most important finds in Mesoamerica and if at all possible, it should be visited.

San Salvador or Quezaltepec Volcano can not be visited but it is so visible that it arouses curiosity. It is to old that it is classified in another geological era. At that time, it was the only mountain in the area, and when it blew, the explosion left a crater one and a half kilometers wide and 543 meters deep. The original mountain was called El Picacho and was 1960 meters high. When the volcano erupted, it decreased the size of El Picacho to 1893 meters, a loss of 67 meters.

The last eruption on this volcano occurred in 1917 and caused a lava flow six and a half kilometers long with a width of up to three kilometers. When this happened it covered part of a railway track. The eruption dried up a lagoon that lay on the bottom of the crater and left a cone with a small crater on its top, 45 meters high. At the time of the eruption, an earthquake shook San Salvador and destroyed most of the city. This active volcano has had many small eruptions; the most significant in recent years were in 1575, 1770, 1876, plus of course the 1917 one.

Quezaltepeque is a small town, 25 kilometers north of San Salvador. Take bus #109 from the eastern terminal to get there. Make this a day trip from the capital. Toma de Quezaltepeque is near the town of Quezaltepeque, and you can get a bus there. This area has natural springs; the locals believe these springs have restorative powers. There are swimming pools and many types of sports facilities such as baseball diamonds. There are cabins available but they are basic. There are many places to visit where you can eat, drink and enjoy the day.

Laguna Verde is a pleasant day trip. You take bus # 206-A from the west terminal to the town of Apaneca. From the town, you walk towards the area of Palo Verde and then to the hamlet of Hoyo de Cuajuste. This walk is all up hill, I might add. At the end of the street in Hoyo, you will see the lake at a distance of about one kilometer. The lake itself sits in an old volcanic crater which is about one and a half kilometers wide. Huge trees which are hundreds of years old are interspersed amongst the rocks. The spot is about 1600 meters (5250 ft) above sea level. This is a delightful place to visit and is a relatively unknown tourist spot.

San Andres Ruins are about one hour from San Salvador in the Zapotitan Valley on the way to Santa Ana. This is an important settlement; it has about 60 mounds near the center between the two rivers. Other structures may be found in about a two kilometer radius. These ruins rank third in importance after Joya de Ceren and Tazumal.

SANTA ANA

This is a beautiful, friendly Colonial town of 250,000 people. It has two squares with a central market between. I spent a lot of time in this area because it was so refreshing after being in the capital. The people are extremely friendly and the hustle and bustle of the big city is absent in Santa Ana. I would recommend planning at least a week here. All in all, this is my favorite town in El Salvador.

PLACES TO STAY

Many places in Santa Ana rent by the hour and they won't even talk to you if you inquire about overnight accommodations. However, women, please be careful in your dress as you would certainly get lots of offers if your attire is correct for the job and remember, they don't pay union wages in El Salvador.

Hospadaje Livingston cost ₡30 ($3.75 US) per person with bath and ₡20 ($2.50 US) without bath. It is dreary but friendly. Okay if the budget is tight. It is on 10 Ave. 7-9.

Hotel Roosevelt is very quiet, clean and recommended. They have caged monkeys to entertain the guests. The cost is ₡40 ($5. US) per person. The hotel is between the two parks.

Hotel 2-X is a small place that is clean, quiet and very safe. They require a ₡5 key deposit and the rooms cost ₡40 ($5. US) with a private bath. It is a small hotel and very good. If the Roosevelt is full, try this one. They also do laundry for a very reasonable price. Bus #55 goes past this hotel. The only drawback is the 15 minute walk from Libertad Square.

Hotel Libertad is close to Libertad Square on 4 Calle. They have beautiful clean rooms with private bath for ₡70 ($9.75 US) per room. The rooms are large with high ceilings and this is the best place to stay. It is close to the square, quiet, clean and friendly. The only drawback is the price.

The Colonial on Ave. 2, just off the square, has rooms for ₡40 ($5. US) per person, but it is bare and a bit grubby. For the price, go to the Hotel 2-X. The Colonial does not have private baths.

RESTAURANTS

Chinese restaurant across from Banco Comercial and one block up from Libertad Square is excellent. This is recommended by the locals. The food is good, the service is good, and the prices are reasonable. It is very clean.

Hamburger joint next door to the Chinese restaurant is also very good. Because it is so clean, it is recommended by the locals. I tried the food here and it was okay, but not exceptional.

Totos Pizza is popular. The owners go out of their way to try and please you. The prices are high and I found the crusts somewhat soggy. I would rather patronize a small place owned by a local than patronize one of the franchises.

Popeyes Chicken is another popular place and the price is okay. There is a Popeyes Chicken close to the Livingston Hotel. However, they saturate their food with grease.

Restaurant Regis on 9 Calle 6 Ave. is a clean restaurant and the food is very good. Since this place is locally owned, try it out and keep the money in the country.

Tienda Frutolin is on the corner of Josè Mariana Mendez and Au Fray Felipe Jesus Moragua Sur across from the Hotel 2-X and is excellent for both local foods and fruit juices. Once the gals get to know you, they will give you a little extra fruit juice and the price never goes up. This is an excellent place to eat.

THINGS TO DO

Libertad Square is the center of town and has a beautiful park where you can often watch a band playing. On the square is the National Palace, National Theatre and the Cathedral. All three buildings are colonial in style and in excellent repair. Be certain to visit them. The taxi drivers hang out around here also and their fares are reasonable. I had a lot of fun with the drivers. Like many people in Central America, these people like to talk to strangers and once they feel comfortable, they like to tease.

Metapan Square is the other square in town; it is fairly close to the Hotel 2-X. This is a bit grubbier and you will find a lot of drunks sleeping around this area. This is also closer to the market area and the red-light district. The square has many benches and trees but does not have the important buildings found in Libertad.

July Festivities begin on July 22nd in honor of "Our Lady Saint Ann". The original name of Santa Ana was "Cihuatehuacan" which means the "site of the sacred women". The festival includes a religious celebration, dances, fireworks, parades and a general atmosphere of fiesta.

Tazumal Ruins are probably the nicest in El Salvador and certainly the most important. They are found in the town of Chalchuapa. To get there, take a bus to Chalchuapa from the bus terminal in Santa Ana and when the bus driver lets you off, you walk only one city block to the ruins. The area is closed on Monday. Tazumal was inhabited from about 300 - 1200AD, but the reconstruction of the area has incorporated styles from all the different eras. This gives the visitor an opportunity to see changes in the society without visiting a number of different areas.

Structure One was built during the Early Classic period and is believed to have been inhabited for 700 years. During this time it underwent 14 different changes. There have been 27 tombs discovered in the area. Pottery shards were discovered which are similar to those found in Copan, Kaminaljuyu, Guatemala and Teotihuacan in Mexico. These people travelled!

The ruins are not huge, but there are some nice carvings. Some of the pyramids have been covered over with cement. They do not take more than an hour or two to visit, unless you wish to just sit and enjoy the lack of people. In about a four mile radius, are the other ceremonial sites called Pampe, El Trapiche, Casa Blanca and Las Victorias where the Olmec head was found.

You can visit the museum which displays some of the people and artifacts found in the tombs. The museum is small, but really tells the story of these ruins. There is a slight entrance fee to the ruins.

Hotel Gloria is in town; it is basic and quiet. Since the town has not catered to tourists for a long time, it may be more comfortable to make this a day trip.

Ahuachapan is the location of the geothermal plant; it can be visited in a day. However, if you wish to explore that beautiful area, it is advisable to stay in the village of Ahuachapan. There are not the same luxuries in Ahuachapan as there are in Santa Ana. See Ahuachapan for further information.

Lake Coatepeque is a beautiful crater lake. There is no other lake that is so obviously crater-formed. This lake is large and pleasant. To get there, take bus #220 from the Santa Ana terminal. You may go to Cerro Verde first, and then visit Coatepeque or make two different day trips. If doing both, you should take bus #248 first. This takes you to Cerro Verde and on your return, you may have enough time to visit the lake. Seeing the lake from above is breathtaking.

There are two expensive hotels charging ¢100 per person ($12.50 US) around the lake. I did not see any cheapies. There are numerous upper middle class summer homes around the lake which have boat houses full of expensive boats and driveways full of expensive cars used to pull the boats.

The lake is located on the eastern slope of the Santa Ana volcano. It is six kilometers wide, 120 meters deep and 740 meters above sea level. A number of cones around and inside the lake were formed after the original, large eruption which formed the crater where the lake is. These cones surround the entire lake, and give the mountains above the lake an undulating appearance. The name of the volcano at the southern end is called Cerro Alto; it looks like an upside down saucer. The two similar hills at the northeast end of the lake are called San Marcelino and Cerro Chino. The lake itself is considered thousands of years old; this is determined by the erosion of the pumice rock and ash on the walls of the cone.

Santa Ana Volcano is the highest in the Pacific Volcanic chain and sits 2365 meters (7800 ft) above sea level. This mountain is also the largest in volume. There are four super-imposed craters inside the original one which is 289 meters deep. The volcano's active belt runs along the mountains going towards Chalchuapa and includes Cerro Verde and Cerro El Astillero.

Santa Ana was most active during the 16th century; it has also erupted in 1621, 1874, 1904, 1920 and 1937. The last three of these eruptions occurred at the same time as Izalco's eruptions.

Cerro Verde is reached by staying on the same bus that goes to Coatepeque, #248 from the Santa Ana terminal. The ride up is two and one half hours and the return is only one and one half hours. The last bus going down the mountain goes at 6:00PM. This will not get you back to Santa Ana before nightfall as it only goes to the junction of the main highway. Then you will have to catch another bus or hitch a ride. There are no places to stay in the area. The first bus going to Cerro Verde is at 10:30AM. If you see lots of cars at the top of the mountain, then by all means stay and play as long as you wish. There will be a very good chance that someone would give you a ride back.

Looking down into **Mt. Izalco's** double crater from the top of Cerro Verde is spectacular. Hiking Mt. Izalco would have to be done from the town of Izalco which is reached from the bus station in Sonsonate. However, this would be a difficult hike and you would have to carry all your water as the place is as dry as the surface of the moon. There is a turicentro on the top of the mountain where you can sit in the hotel and enjoy a beer or a meal. You could stay at the hotel for ₡200 per person per night ($25. US). I wouldn't. There is a nice park-like area for you to walk around and enjoy the spectacular scenery. You may also picnic here. This trip is truly a must.

Cerro Verde is about 250 thousand years old; it eventually became covered with vegetation. It has two craters on the northeast side. The volcano is 2030 meters (6700 ft) high and has a natural passage through it which links it to the Santa Ana volcano. This passage is called the "Meseta de San Blas".

Izalco Volcano is considered one of the youngest volcanos in the world and is still active. It had its last eruption in 1966. This compound volcano stands 1870 meters (6150 ft) above sea level. The Indians of the area called this mountain the "infiernillos de los españoles" or the "hells of the Spaniards" because, while it was forming, it continuously bellowed black sulfur-smelling smoke. Finally, in February1770, a cone was formed and was visible from a great distance.

Over the years, the mountain has erupted periodically. In 1958, it had a major eruption and then stopped all activity until 1968 when a small eruption occurred forming a blow hole on the southeast slope.

The Indians living near Izalco have attached a legend to the mountain. If a child is born during the eclipse of a full moon, and in the shadow of the mountain, the child will be born with a hair lip and called an "Janiche". In these areas, a misfortune like this often goes untreated and leaves the child an outcast for life.

The hotel on the top of Cerro Verde was built was so people could watch Izalco perform its beautiful activity. However, the hotel just opened when Izalco decided to sleep.

Sihuatehuacan is another turicentro that is in the town of Santa Ana. It is on the highway and has the usual swimming pools and baseball field. It also has a roller staking rink and an open air theatre. You can stay in the small cabins but I prefer to stay in the city center.

SAN VICENTE

This town of 75,000 people is only 60 kilometers from the capital. I did not stay there. The main attraction to the city is the magnificent twin peak Volcano of San Vicente. It is seven and one half kilometers southeast of the city and has a flat summit of 2105 meters (7000 ft) on one cone and 2181 meters (7200 ft) on the other. The depression in the center of the two cones was once a crater but is now filled in with vegetation. The volcano has no known activity, but there are hot springs and geysers at the bottom so it is not considered dead.

Turicentro Amapulapa is close to San Vicente. You take bus #172 from the terminal in San Vicente. The center has restaurants, swimming pools, sports facilities and tiendas operated by locals. There are places you can rent for ₡10 per day. This is not for overnight staying.

Tehuacan ruins are eight kilometers south of the town and on the same road as the turicentro. There are small traces of a Pre-Columbian city at this site.

SONSONATE

This is not a nice town. There is nothing special about it. The once beautiful river flowing through is thick with garbage. The market area is busy and dirty and the town is hot and unpleasant. It is also fairly spread out, so you must walk a long way from the bus station to the center.

Sonsonate is not the place to do your shopping. If you want anything, go to Santa Ana or the capital as Sonsonate is quite expensive and the people are not willing to bargain.

Do not take the bus from Sonsonate to Hachadura if you are going to Guatemala. The road is a gravel road, does not travel along the coast, and is four hours to the border. It is much better to return to the capital and then take a direct bus to Guat City. Plus, the border guard is not accustomed to gringos going that way and does not know what to do if you already have a visa. He only knows to send you back if you don't have one.

PLACES TO STAY

Hotel Orbe is on 4 Calle Oeste and charges ₡35 ($4.25 US) per person without a private bath. This is a difficult building to locate.

Hotel New York is a groovy little place for ₡40 ($5. US) per person with bath. There are two rooms with bath and the rest are cheaper and without bath. The rooms have all sorts of funky furniture in them to try and make them look classy. However, I think some of the smaller rooms may go by the hour.

Pension Castro is on the street on the south side of the square and two blocks past. They charge ¢30 ($4.75 US) per person with private bath. It is really clean but you may have to wait ten minutes for the water to finally work its way along and out your shower. Otherwise the owners are quite friendly.

RESTAURANTS

I only found one place to eat on the west side of the square. There are a few nicer places closer to the bus station but that is a long way to walk if staying in the center.

THINGS TO DO

The Sonsonate Festival is known as the "Verbena de Sonsonate" and occurs January 13th to 24th. It is a street celebration organized by the Red Cross of Sonsonate.

Easter Week is celebrated throughout the country; Sonsonate does the best job. Like Antigua in Guatemala, the religious processions are the most elaborate in the country and occur from Monday to Friday of Easter week. Saturday and Sunday are not quite as spectacular. If in El Salvador for this period, be certain to visit Sonsonate.

San Antonio del Monte is a church on the outskirts of town and is given credit for housing Saint Anthony who has performed miracles. This is a famous church.

Nahuizalco is a little village close to Sonsonate which is noted for it handicrafts. You may be able to make better purchases in this village than in the capital. Take bus number 253 from the terminal.

Beaches close to Sonsonate are near the port town of Acajutla which also has a beach. North of Acajutla is the beach of **Metalio** and south is **Los Cobanos**. For Metalio, take bus #259; to get to Los Cobanos, take bus #257. This coast is known as "La Costa del Balsalmo" or the Balsam Coast because the trees produce the medicinal product called Balsam of Peru. This is the only place in the world where these trees are found. The natives cut the trees with a machete and then soak up the sap in a rag. The rags are then boiled to produce Balsam of Peru. This medicine is used for chest ailments, such as asthma, as an antiseptic, as a base for soap or perfumes, and the old sea captains used it to heal sword wounds. The name "Balsam of Peru" is obviously a mistake. In the early trading days, the medicine was shipped with gold from Peru, to Spain via Panama. The Spaniards who received the goods believed that the gold and the medicine actually came from Peru. Hence the name Balsam of Peru.

This coast is rocky and rugged with high cliffs and secluded coves. It is truly beautiful. You can stay at Acajutla, but I do not know the quality of the accommodations. You may be better returning to Sonsonate for the night.

In Los Cobanos, **Hotel Solimar** has rooms for ¢60 ($7.50 US) per person and they also have cabañas for less, but you must bring your own hammock. There is also the **Hotel Mar de Plata** with basic rooms for ¢25 ($3. US) per person. This is quite a popular place.

Victoria Falls is a nice place to visit. You take bus #432 from the Sonsonate bus terminal going to the village of Caluco. Get off the bus half a kilometer after the turnoff for the turicentro Atecozol, and take the street going to the left. Walk towards the River Chiquihuat for two kilometers until you pass the farm with houses. You will then cross the railway tracks. Continue along until you come to the river. The falls are not very large, falling only about six meters (20 feet) into a small pool. The erosion has formed a deep hole. There are caves above the waterfall that deserve exploration. There is a lot of garbage in the area which you will have to ignore.

If you wish to go to the **hot springs,** you go only one kilometer south of the town of Caluco. You will see two streams of hot water joining the river Shuteca. The spot is called "Los Enquentros". If you continue up the river for five kilometers, you will see the La Chapina farm and then a lovely natural swimming hole.

Back in the village of Caluco, there is a striking colonial church built in 1780. Ruins of a church built by the Dominican order prior to the one still standing are also visible. This was destroyed by the 1773 Santa Marta earthquake.

You may also go to the turicentro of **Atecozol** and enjoy a hot spring bath as well as all the other pleasures of a turicentro such as a beer and food.

Quebrada Waterfalls can be reached by walking from the town, past the church on the square and straight out in a westerly direction. I went part way and was appalled by the garbage. However, if you follow the river for at least three or four kilometers from town, you will see two sets of waterfalls. The first one falls about 70 meters (225 ft) and the other falls about 90 meters (300 feet). Near the second falls are where native Indians, particularly the women, still dress in their traditional skirts and come to the river to wash. They sell hand-made baskets and flower pots that are indigenous to this area.

Ruin at Old Panama